WITHDRAWN

HELL ON THE RANGE

RECENT TITLES

Furs and Frontiers in the Far North: The Contest among Native and Foreign Nations for the Bering Strait Fur Trade, by John R. Bockstoce

War of a Thousand Deserts: Indian Raids and the U.S.–Mexican War, by Brian DeLay

Defying the Odds: The Tule River Tribe's Struggle for Sovereignty in Three Centuries, by Gelya Frank and Carole Goldberg

The Bourgeois Frontier: French Towns, French Traders, and American Expansion, by Jay Gitlin

"Liberty to the Downtrodden": Thomas L. Kane, Romantic Reformer, by Matthew J. Grow

The Comanche Empire, by Pekka Hämäläinen

Oceans of Wine: Madeira and the Emergence of American Trade and Taste, by David Hancock

Frontiers: A Short History of the American West, by Robert V. Hine and John Mack Faragher

Bordertown: The Odyssey of an American Place, by Benjamin Heber Johnson and Jeffrey Gusky

William Clark's World: Describing America in an Age of Unknowns, by Peter Kastor

Emerald City: An Environmental History of Seattle, by Matthew Klingle

Making Indian Law: The Hualapai Land Case and the Birth of Ethnohistory, by Christian W. McMillen

The American Far West in the Twentieth Century, by Earl Pomeroy

Borderlines in Borderlands: James Madison and the Spanish-American Frontier, 1776–1821, by J. C. A. Stagg

Fugitive Landscapes: The Forgotten History of the U.S.–Mexico Borderlands, by Samuel Truett

Bárbaros: Spaniards and Their Savages in the Age of Enlightenment, by David J. Weber

The Spanish Frontier in North America: The Brief Edition, by David J. Weber

FORTHCOMING TITLES

The Shapes of Power: Frontiers, Borderlands, Middle Grounds, and Empires of North America, by Pekka Hämäläinen

The Jeffersons at Shadwell, by Susan Kern

Bold Spirits, by Monica Rico

Chosen Land: The Legal Creation of White Manhood on the Eighteenth-Century Kentucky Frontier, by Honor Sachs

Making Los Angeles: Race, Space, and Municipal Power, by David Torres-Rouff

HELL ON THE RANGE

A Story of Honor, Conscience, and the American West

Daniel Justin Herman

PUBLISHED IN ASSOCIATION WITH
THE WILLIAM P. CLEMENTS CENTER FOR SOUTHWEST STUDIES,
SOUTHERN METHODIST UNIVERSITY

Yale

UNIVERSITY

PRESS

New Haven & London

Published with assistance from the Mary Cady Tew Memorial Fund.

Set in Electra type by Tseng Information Systems, Inc., Durham, North Carolina.
Printed in the United States of America.

Library of Congress Cataloging-in-Publication Data

Herman, Daniel Justin.
Hell on the range : a story of honor, conscience, and the American West /
Daniel Justin Herman.
p. cm. — (The Lamar series in western history)
Includes bibliographical references and index.
ISBN 978-0-300-13736-1 (clothbound : alk. paper)
1. Payson Region (Ariz.)—History—19th century. 2. Frontier and pioneer life—Arizona—
Payson Region. 3. Rangelands—Arizona—Payson Region—History—19th century.
4. Mormons—Arizona—Payson Region—History—19th century. 5. Ranchers—
Arizona—Payson Region—History—19th century. I. Title.
F819.P39H47 2010
979.1'5504—dc22
2010015132

A catalogue record for this book is available from the British Library.

This paper meets the requirements of ANSI/NISO Z39.48–1992 (Permanence of Paper).

10 9 8 7 6 5 4 3 2 1

"As has been well said, 'the cow has always been
the advance agent of civilization.'"
— Will C. Barnes, The Story of the Range (1926)

"For the Lord worketh not in secret combinations,
neither doth he will that man should shed blood, but in all
things hath forbidden it, from the beginning of man."
— Book of Mormon (Ether, 8:19)

CONTENTS

Map of Arizona's Rim Country and
Surrounding Geography, 1887   viii

Introduction   xi

Acknowledgments   xxv

Part 1 BEGINNINGS

1. Home on the Range   3

2. The Saints March In   22

3. The Honor of Ruin   50

Part 2 WAR

4. The Trials of the Saints   69

5. Cowboys and Criminals   89

6. Hell on the Range   121

7. The Honor of Vengeance   138

8. Killing Conscience   167

9. Understanding   197

Part 3 LEGACY

10. Water on the Fires   217

11. Courting Conscience   229

12. Honor Anew   255

Conclusion   282

List of Abbreviations   293

Notes   295

Index   343

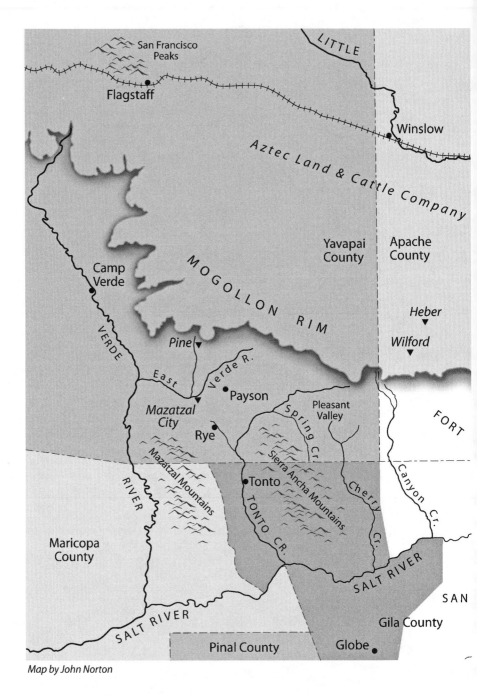

Map by John Norton

Arizona's Rim Country and surrounding geography in 1887

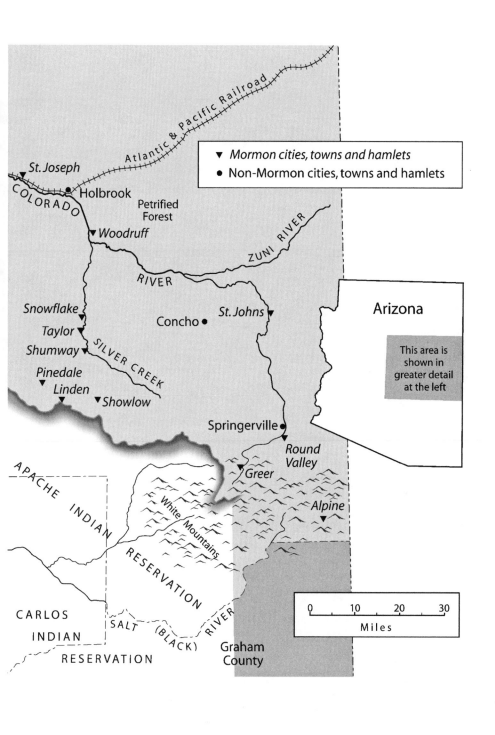

▼ *Mormon cities, towns and hamlets*
● Non-Mormon cities, towns and hamlets

Atlantic & Pacific Railroad

St. Joseph ▼

COLORADO

● Holbrook

Petrified
Forest

▼ Woodruff

ZUNI RIVER

RIVER

Snowflake ▼

Taylor ▼

Shumway ▼

SILVER CREEK

Concho ●

St. Johns ▼

Pinedale ▼

Linden ▼

▼ Showlow

Springerville ●

▼

Round
Valley

Arizona

This area is
shown in
greater detail
at the left

APACHE

INDIAN

White Mountains

RESERVATION

▼ Greer

Alpine ▼

CARLOS

INDIAN

SALT

(BLACK)

RIVER

RESERVATION

Graham
County

0   10   20   30
Miles

INTRODUCTION

Just after seven in the morning on August 2, 1892, two horsemen rode through the streets of Tempe, Arizona, bearing down on a man driving a wagon loaded with barley. As they closed in, each drew a rifle. Glancing back in time to see them aim, the man in the wagon instantly dove forward, dodging one of the bullets. A second bullet drove into the base of his neck, knocking him unconscious and leaving him paralyzed, his feet dangling over the side of his buckboard.[1]

As they rode away, the assassins made half-hearted attempts to escape detection. A teenaged girl driving a buggy recalled that one of the men, finding the road narrowed by debris, was forced to ride so close that she could have touched him. The man pulled his hat down low on his face to hide his features. As soon as he had passed, his horse broke into a gallop. Other witnesses saw the same man—a thick-chested, dark-skinned man—on the road that morning. He wore a straw or cloth "sombrero" with a wide red band around the crown and rode a handsome bay horse with a black mane and tail. Still more witnesses recalled seeing him at a bar a few hours before the shooting. A twenty-two-year-old bootblack reported that the man had paid him fifty cents to shine his boots at four o'clock in the morning. After that, the man had stepped into a hotel bar, where he snatched a freshly poured drink from a cattleman named W. J. White. Taken aback, White told the offender that he was in a hurry and could not wait for another drink. The man replied that he, too, was in a hurry.[2]

At eight o'clock in the morning in the nearby Mormon settlement of Mesa, a deputy sheriff received a telegram reporting the shooting. As he saddled up to pursue the perpetrators, he saw a rider approaching at a trot. Supposing that the man was too dark complected to be a suspect—the telegram had described a white man with a heavy chin beard—he watched him pass. Only later did the deputy discover that he had let a killer go by.

Meanwhile the victim of the shooting, Thomas Graham, though mortally wounded, managed to whisper the names of his murderers: Ed Tewksbury and John Rhodes. It was Rhodes's ball, he thought, that had struck him. Graham, hoping to put his enemies in his past, had recently married, become a father, and settled in Tempe, where he took up the quiet vocation of farming. His enemies came looking for him anyway.[3]

After the shooting, the assassins followed separate avenues of escape. How Rhodes managed to disappear is unclear. Tewksbury's route, however, is known. Riding briskly eastward for a hundred miles, he crossed first the Mazatzal range and then the Sierra Ancha before arriving at his home in Pleasant Valley. Trading tired horses for strong ones at a series of relay stations, Tewksbury made the return trip from Tempe in a day, the same length of time it had taken him to ride to Tempe two days earlier. He was sure that no number of witnesses would be enough to convict a man who had been seen by other witnesses, far from the crime, both a day before and a day after the murder.

Tewksbury's alibi did not keep him from being arrested. Nor did Rhodes avoid detection. He, no less than Tewksbury, was a striking man, described as "tall" and "swarthy" with "a trace of Cherokee blood in his veins." He had black hair "tinged with gray," a thick mustache that hung down over "a rather hard mouth," and sharp features "accentuated by a prominent Roman nose." Witnesses nonetheless found it difficult to identify him, especially in the face of an alibi offered by his employer. Fearing that Rhodes would gain release, Tom Graham's wife, Annie, took matters into her own hands. During the preliminary hearing, she dug into her satchel to retrieve the six-gun that had belonged to her husband. When she pressed the trigger, the hammer somehow came down against a piece of fabric, failing to ignite the bullet. Onlookers pinioned her before she could fire. Talk of lynching Rhodes spilled across the avenues of Tempe. Just as quickly, it evaporated.[4] Rhodes went free.

Tewksbury's case seemed easier to prosecute. He was a bigger, more powerful man than Rhodes, broad-shouldered and "keg chested," and with a darker complexion (Tewksbury was half-Indian). He was impossible to forget if one saw him up close. One after another, witnesses identified Tewksbury as Graham's killer. The court sentenced him to life imprisonment, but his legal team—the best in Arizona—got the decision overturned on a technicality. Somehow Tewksbury had never been allowed to enter an official plea.[5] At a second trial, fewer witnesses appeared and more doubt was cast, resulting in a hung jury. In 1895, after

Tewksbury had spent three years in jail, the territory decided to forego a third trial. He, like Rhodes, went free.

How Ed Tewksbury and John Rhodes managed to kill Tom Graham and escape justice was one of the mysteries that Arizonans pondered as they sought to "civilize" the territory and gain statehood. The mystery of the murder and the escape, however, pales in comparison to the mystery of how hatred had reached such a pitch. Graham, indeed, was the third of three brothers to die in a feud that had begun almost a decade earlier. Tewksbury's three brothers also died during the war, one from an ambush and two from illness. The war, as novelist Zane Grey later remembered it, was "to the last man."

To speak of a fight "to the last man" brings us to the story of another feud, a feud involving fictional families in Mark Twain's *Adventures of Huckleberry Finn*. In the course of Huck's voyage down the Mississippi with Jim, the runaway slave, Huck finds shelter with the Grangerfords. Colonel Grangerford, the patriarch of the family, "was a gentleman all over, and so was his family." He is "very tall and very slim," reports Huck, with a "darkish-paly complexion" and "clean-shaved every morning." He has thin lips, thin nostrils, a high nose, heavy brows, "and the blackest kind of eyes." His forehead is high; his hair "black and straight" and hanging to his shoulders; and "every day of his life" he puts on "a clean shirt and a full suit from head to foot made out of white linen so white it hurt your eyes to look at it." "There warn't no frivolishness about him, not a bit," continues Huck, "and he warn't ever loud." "The old gentleman," concludes Huck, "owned a lot of farms, and over a hundred niggers."[6]

But there is one more thing that defines Colonel Grangerford and his sons, all "tall, beautiful men with very broad shoulders and brown faces, and long black hair and black eyes." They are at war with the Shepherdsons, a family equally genteel, equally handsome, equally brave.

The trouble between the two families began with a court battle. The man who lost—no one remembers who it was, or to which family he belonged—"up and shot the man that won the suit," exclaims Buck Grangerford, "which he would naturally do, of course. Anybody would." If the trouble began in the fog of family memory, however, it ends with an event etched into Huck's mind: the Grangerfords' attack on the Shepherdsons after Miss Sophia—Miss Sophia Grangerford—elopes with Harney Shepherdson. In the melee that follows, Buck Grangerford is killed, along with several of his kinsman. Only Huck escapes; he and Jim resume their journey down the Mississippi.

The Grangerfords and Shepherdsons were involved in a classic American feud.

When Huck asks what "a feud" is, Buck Grangerford replies with astonishment. "Why, where was you raised?" he asks, "don't you know what a feud is? . . . A feud is this way. A man has a quarrel with another man, and kills him; then that other man's brother kills *him*; then the other brothers, on both sides, goes for one another; then the *cousins* chip in—and by-and-by, everybody's killed off, and there ain't no more feud. But it's kind of slow, and takes a long time." A feud, suggests Buck, is something fundamentally American, something everyone must understand.

When I began investigating the conflict between the Grahams and the Tewksburys—the struggle that Arizonans call the Pleasant Valley War—I conceived of it as a just that: an archetypal American feud. I conceived of it, moreover, as a quarrel of honor, a quarrel between families—albeit rustic and simple rather than genteel—rather than a war between factions. As I investigated further, however, I saw not only connections between the Pleasant Valley conflict and the feud between Grangerfords and Shepherdsons but, more important, an Arizona manifestation of a battle between honor and conscience.

To comprehend honor and conscience demands explanation. It is critical to point out, first of all, that ours is not the honor of Grangerfords and Shepherdsons, or even of Grahams and Tewksburys. Americans today associate honor with self-sacrifice. Honor means remaining loyal to one's word, one's friends, one's principles, even if one must suffer to do that. The vocations we associate with honor are those involving peril: soldiering, enforcing the law, fighting fires. The honor of nineteenth-century feudists, by contrast, is an honor apart; it is an honor involving a broad set of mores that shaped European cultures over the centuries but that, with the Enlightenment, became moderated, controlled, and reshaped into the narrower honor that prevails today.

In several seminal books on the Old South, Bertram Wyatt-Brown describes a nineteenth-century culture of honor epitomized by physical courage, loyalty to kin, fierce defense of family and personal reputation, conspicuous display of wealth, eager hospitality, gambling, drinking, ritualized braggadocio, and communal shaming. Though honor is commonly associated with Southern gentlemen—men like the Grangerfords and Shepherdsons—Wyatt-Brown and others argue that it shaped plebeian culture, too. If the duel with its strict rites was a forum for honor among gentlemen of the early nineteenth century, the "rough-and-tumble" fight was the forum for honor among the plebeian. If the horse race was a place for gentlemen to affirm honor by making staggering wagers, so too was it a place for lesser men to make smaller bets of their own. If drinking fine bourbon was the prerogative of men of standing, drinking

still-burned whiskey was the prerogative of yeoman farmers. Both elites and ple-
beians, finally, agreed that whiteness meant honor and blackness meant shame.[7]

Honor's antagonist was "conscience," a worldview that placed moral courage
above physical courage; individual piety above family reputation; frugality and
work above displays of wealth and luxury; sobriety and rectitude above drinking
and gambling; exhortation and rehabilitation above punishment and shaming.
As a code of behavior, conscience emerged from evangelical Protestantism, the
Enlightenment, and the nineteenth-century market revolution. In its behavioral mode—the form of conscience that forged the Mormon community—
conscience emphasized moderation, modesty, and restraint, which often equaled
the refusal to sin by drinking, smoking, gambling, or seeking sex out of wedlock.
In its humanitarian incarnation—epitomized not in Mormons but in Arizona's
first elected governor, George W. P. Hunt—conscience took the form of legislative reform. Hunt campaigned against gambling, drinking, boxing, and capital
punishment and for women's rights, penal reform, and humane treatment for
prisoners and the mentally ill. Before the Civil War, conscience also took the
form of abolition. Each of those reforms was meant to replace vengeance and
shaming with sympathy and persuasion. Though many of them made headway
in the South even before the Civil War, they exerted their greatest influence in
the North and Upper Midwest.

The contest between honor and conscience helped steer the nation toward
civil war but did not end there. It also played out in the West, especially in places
settled by immigrants from the South and Lower Midwest. One of those places
was Arizona.

At its outset, to be sure, the Pleasant Valley conflict was not—or not wholly—
driven by honor. Ranchers with small herds and little money contested the range
with a man who had bigger herds and more money. Racial animus, too, pushed
men toward violence. James Tewksbury's four sons were "half-breeds," to use
the racialized parlance of the time, who had come from California. Like other
mixed-race Americans, they faced deep prejudice. Far from being a separate
issue from honor, racism lay at honor's core. American racism was premised on
the distinction between the honor of whites and the shame of "blacks," be they
African-American, Mexican, or Indian.

Honor, however, was more than a paradigm of race. Though some Pleasant Valley settlers were emigrants from Europe, many, like the cowboys of Apache
County, came from Texas and the Lower Midwest. They had grown up in the
climes of honor. They—like the Grangerfords and the Shepherdsons—believed
in self-assertion. They addressed problems with hard words and sometimes with

guns. Aggressive self-assertion came with settlers. It was part of their cultural baggage, but it did not have to thrive in Arizona. Often it remained inchoate, subtle. It became manifest in times of stress. When the economic catastrophe of 1886–87 made the struggle for the range more intense, assertion gave way to fanatical killing. In Pleasant Valley, home on the range became hell. Honor—or at least the resolution of problems through grim assertion—triumphed.

If honor precipitated a death struggle between Grahams and Tewksburys, however, it is critical to note that they were not alone as combatants. In 1887, five years before Tom Graham's murder, settlers had drawn up sides and killed one another with abandon. Between nineteen and fifty men died in the so-called Pleasant Valley War, making it perhaps the bloodiest feud in American history. The central mystery of that feud was never how John Rhodes and Ed Tewksbury killed Tom Graham and escaped justice. Nor was it how two families—the Grahams and the Tewksburys—had come to blows. The central mystery was—and is—how dozens of men, perhaps hundreds, brought terror to Arizona, and what that terror tells us about Western social relations, Western culture, and American history.

Historians have not shied from chronicling the Pleasant Valley War. Like participants in the war, however, they have suffered from nearsightedness. They understand the minutiae of events and motives but offer little in the way of context or meaning. They take gleaming nuggets from the surface but leave buried the lode underground.[8] How, then, do we resolve the mystery of the Pleasant Valley War? How do we recover its meaning?

We might start by giving the war a new name. It was a complex phenomenon in Pleasant Valley, but it becomes even more complex when we realize that it encompassed three counties and a wide swath of humanity. The war involved Protestants, Catholics, Jews, and Mormons; Southerners, Northerners, New Mexicans, and European immigrants; prosperous men, middling men, and men near destitution. What has been called the Pleasant Valley War was part of a broader set of conflicts that played themselves out along the vast east-west arc of the Mogollon (or "Tonto") Rim, the thousand-foot wall that separates the Colorado Plateau from the Sonoran Desert. The war stretched from Tonto Basin below the Rim to the White Mountains at the Rim's eastern extremity. The Pleasant Valley War, then, was only part of the Rim Country War.

To understand that war one must understand its complexity. Casus belli were multiple. Motives shifted. So did alliances. The war was many things. As I argue in chapters 1 and 3, the war was in part a Western "tragedy of the commons," a battle to control grazing and water rights on "free range," federal land that was open to all comers. The battle started in Pleasant Valley in 1883, when cattle prices were high, but got far worse in 1886–87, when the cattle market collapsed. Economic competition, however, was only one piece of the puzzle. Alongside it was a religious quarrel.

To understand the religious aspect of conflict we must look north and east of Pleasant Valley to the Little Colorado River Valley. In the late 1870s, Brigham Young—viewing east-central Arizona as a waste that would serve as a refuge from worldly sin—sent Mormon colonists southward. Far from finding refuge, they found competitors.

From 1878 to 1887, Mormons engaged in a tug-of-war with New Mexican sheepherders and their Jewish patrons, the Barth brothers, for land and resources. Non-Mormon ranchers and townspeople—"gentiles" in Mormon parlance—added their own anger to the flame, siding largely with New Mexicans against Mormons. In 1884, the battle widened when the Aztec Land and Cattle Company bought a million acres of range and hired a small army of Texas cowboys to run its cattle.

Ally to neither New Mexicans nor Mormons, the Aztec pushed both off its range. Sometimes it relied on the courts and sometimes on the violence of cowboys. Conflict yielded to cruelty. Alliances shifted. Aztec cowboys—deeply imbued with honor—went far beyond their employees' directives, launching a war of persecution. As I show in chapters 4 and 5, some Mormons sought to fight the Aztec by allying with New Mexicans and the Barths. Others—fearing collapse of their colonies—appealed to Aztec managers, asking them to rein in their cowboys. The success of their appeal transformed the conflict.

In 1886, a new alliance linked Mormons in western Apache County with gentile ranchers and Aztec managers. All three sought to tame the Texas cowboys in their midst. In some ways, theirs was an alliance of conscience, an alliance among men who sought to curb the excesses of honor—the drinking, the gambling, and especially the gunplay and violence that prevailed among cowboys. In another sense, the new alliance bespoke honor. It was an agreement to use the gun and the rope to destroy enemies. Mormons and their allies sought the victory of behavioral conscience over cowboy honor, but in doing so, they came to accept cowboy rites of assertion and shaming.

Just as Mormons succeeded in defining their enemies as criminals, so too did the Tewksbury faction of Pleasant Valley. Their enemies, the Graham faction, had the misfortune of seeking alliance with the Texas cowboys whom Mormons had come to despise. Rather than being mere feudists—rather than being honorable men like the Grangerfords and Shepherdsons—the Grahams and their cowboy allies became known as rustlers, horse thieves, persecutors, cutthroats.

Suddenly two wars—one pitting Mormons and ranchers against Texas cowboys and another pitting Tewksbury sheepherders against Graham cattlemen—merged into a single struggle pitting "law" against "crime." The Pleasant Valley War became the Rim Country War.

In November 1886, a new Mormon-Democrat alliance in Apache County elected a sheriff whose job was to destroy its enemies. Both Mormon settlers and non-Mormon ranchers meanwhile entered into a vigilante network that linked the law-and-order campaign in Apache County with the Tewksbury war against the Grahams. As I show in chapters 7 and 8, what resulted was horror and irony. The persecuted became persecutors; nonviolence became bloodlust; good men died at the hands of men who were convinced that they were accomplishing good. What many participants remembered about their ordeal, however, was not its complexity. What they remembered was a story of upstanding men defeating scoundrels by resorting to the gun and the rope. What they remembered was the righteousness of at least one form of honor, an honor that celebrated violence and shaming above conciliation and dignity. It was that aspect of honor that became a rallying point for Western identity.[9]

Western identity, however, is a complex thing. It changed over time. It not only changed, it boomeranged. Amid the quest to civilize the West—a quest particularly visible as politicians strove to make territories into states—Arizona steered away from honor. Among the legacies of the Rim Country War, as I show in chapters 10 and 11, was a move toward humanitarian conscience.

Among those who made the range amenable to conscience were the first two chiefs of grazing of the U.S. Forest Service, Albert Potter and Will Barnes. Both had been Rim Country ranchers. Both had experienced the Rim Country War. Both sought to end rampant overstocking and the rampant hostility that came with it. Both, in turn, made the Forest Service itself the target of animus, uniting ranchers in opposition to a common enemy: the federal government. Conscience, however, meant more than social unity, more than a common enemy, more than peace. Conscience was a way of understanding the world.

Even as the Forest Service poured water on the fires, it did little to change minds. It took a charismatic newcomer to do that, a sometime prospector and dishwasher named George W. P. Hunt, who arrived in Globe—de facto capital of the southern part of the Rim Country—in the early 1880s. There he embarked on a business career and began courting Helen Duett Ellison, whose father had led the vigilantes in Pleasant Valley in 1887–88. For fourteen years they exchanged books, gifts, and letters about the boundaries of duty, politics, and love.

Separated by seventy miles of mountainous terrain as well as by Ellison's dedication to her family and father, the two struggled through an ordeal of hope and disappointment. Not until 1904 did they marry. Unlike the hero of a Western novel, Hunt won Ellison's heart not by using guns and fists against "bad guys" but by appealing to her conscience. It was in their fourteen-year dialogue that Hunt and Ellison imagined a world of humanitarian conscience, a world antithetical to the honor of the range.

The courtship of George Hunt and Duett Ellison is among the forgotten stories of Western history, a story lost in the tide of violence and honor that begot a Western mythology. In many ways, however, it was another chapter in the Rim Country War. With Duett at his side, George W. P. Hunt ascended the ladder of Arizona politics, all the while using his powerful voice to decry drinking, gambling, prize fighting, and capital punishment, to promote rehabilitation for convicts, and to advocate new rights for workers and women. If the Rim Country War spawned Western honor, Governor George Hunt, with Duett Ellison to sustain him, countered with Western conscience, linking the West with humanitarian currents that had begun centuries before. Behind the curtain of conscience, however, old ideals persisted, allowing novelists and entertainers to burnish and showcase honor anew in the 1920s. Arizona's move toward conscience ended not with triumph but with a pendulum swing. That, too, was a legacy of the war.

Beyond the Rim Country War or even Western identity, there is a bigger story to tell, a story not just about Arizona but about American history. That story begins, in a sense, at Appomattox, Virginia, when the North and the South began their struggle toward reconciliation. By century's end, Americans had turned their backs on both Southern honor and Northern conscience. The former, it seemed, had produced the evils of slavery, whereas the latter had produced the evils of Reconstruction. Fanaticism had led the nation astray. The search for cultural identity, then, took a new turn. Americans looked west for redemption. "The scars left by the sectional strife" of the Civil War "healed in Cattleland long before they did in other parts of the country," observed Will Barnes. In the West, he averred, "the men who had fought against one another in the Civil War and those who had inherited the animosities born of slavery and its consequences were brought together on an equal footing. They learned to understand each the viewpoint of the other, and with understanding came respect. The hatreds of the war were forgotten."[10]

Barnes was partly correct. The nation did look to the West as a place of cultural rebirth, a place unsullied by sectional animus. As Barnes well knew, however, the West was not an environment of toleration. It created new frictions. Those frictions, however, had a peculiar effect. Rather than defining the West as barbaric, they made it heroic. Just as Rim Country settlers had come to believe that they were a peculiarly honorable people, a people who had lived through an epic period of lawlessness and who had survived by resorting to the gun and the rope, so too did Americans elsewhere come to associate Westerners with honor.

The man who, more than anyone else, celebrated that honor was Zane Grey, a novelist who spent his career touring the West's expanses and writing about its scenery, its people, and its history. Grey was particularly attracted to Arizona's Rim Country, a place he discovered during a hunting trip in 1915. Four years later, Grey, probably the most widely read novelist in the world in the 1910s and 1920s, built a hunting cabin under the Rim and began to interview settlers about their 1880s conflict.[11] Armed with what he considered to be historical understanding, Grey produced his own fictive account of the war, *To the Last Man* (1922), as well as several other novels based loosely on the Rim Country past. In those novels and in the films they spawned, Grey presented Americans with tales of honorable men fighting scoundrels rather than stories of economic, religious, and ethnic conflict.

Grey's novels did more than transform a complex story into a simple one. By interviewing settlers who had experienced the war, he validated their version of its meaning. He sold that meaning to readers who thirsted for authentic stories of honor. Grey, as I show in the last chapter of this book, was a conduit between settlers' ideas about who they were and readers' ideas about who Westerners should be. As Grey admitted, he was a romantic rather than a realist, but it was romanticism that both settlers and readers longed to celebrate. Grey helped create a tourist movement—a mass migration toward a partly real and partly imagined Western honor—that trumped George Hunt's conscience reforms. More than that, Grey helped create a movement that trumped the humanitarian conscience of the Progressive Era.

What I argue, then, is that we cannot understand the Rim Country War—or any conflict in the West—without understanding its place in popular culture. Via novels and films about Rim Country conflict—as well as in numerous other dramas about the West—Zane Grey and those who followed him redefined honor, conscience, and history for an America transformed by women's suffrage, consumerism, and Progressive reform. In his Rim Country novels, Grey pitted the "code of the West" against the "immorality" of the larger society. Subtly, ironically, perhaps strangely, meanwhile, he endorsed the immorality that he attacked. His novels validated—even taught—new mores of consumerism, leisure, and sex. He succeeded, however, not by overtly celebrating the new. He gave readers a raft to the future that was anchored to the past. Grey tied new mores to seemingly old ones. He tied Americans to the honor of the West.

Honor and conscience are cornerstones of this book. But I also seek to tell a story. I have shied from presenting honor and conscience as abstractions. I have sought to write as a historian rather than a social scientist. To understand history, we sometimes need to follow it inch by inch, or, in this case, blow by blow. I have used the power of narrative to make honor and conscience into concrete forces, forces that shaped Arizona and the nation. I suspect that even if this book lacked overt references to honor and conscience, readers would find them in the events it chronicles. In some ways, honor and conscience are concepts that we under-stand implicitly. We do not, however, understand the degree to which they were pitted against each other in the past.

I should also mention here that, though I did not plan to write a book on vio-lence per se, my subject made it impossible not to do so. Readers may note affini-ties between this book and others that take a more direct approach to the theme of violence, especially those by Richard Slotkin and Richard Maxwell Brown. I do not so much challenge their ideas as give them depth and dimension. Rather than tracking—à la Slotkin—a "frontier myth" in literary works stretching back to the 1600s, I seek to understand honor and conscience, and thus violence, in a discrete historical setting: Arizona's Rim Country in the 1880s. Only after ex-amining violence in that setting do I seek to understand its interpretation in lit-erature. Rather than seeking to explain—à la Brown—the origins of American violence, moreover, I seek to understand cultural contradictions that produced both violence and peace.[12]

If I add depth and dimension to Slotkin and Brown, meanwhile, I challenge other historians who, in the words of John Mack Faragher, "tend to see [Western violence] as a straightforward and uncomplicated phenomenon." Violence is so-cialized. I also dispute those who have argued—with limited evidence—that the West was not peculiarly violent, or at least no more violent than longer settled re-gions. Though I have not figured homicide statistics, I have tracked several dozen killings. Those killings alone would make decadal homicide rates per hundred thousand residents for Apache, Gila, and Yavapai counties astronomical. The kill-ings related to the war, however, represent only part of frontier Arizona's rich his-tory of homicides and self-defense killings. The West—or at least the strata of the West I examine—was not "a far more civilized, more peaceful and safer place than American society is today."[13]

I challenge, too, those who suggest that we change the subject. Historians, writes Susan Lee Johnson, must cease to view "the 'American West' as a masculine preserve." They must steer away from "Big Myths and True Heroes." They must "yield up guns and colors."[14] They must cease, in other words, to focus on the male realm of violence and war and instead focus on women, on nonwhites, on the gendered and racialized logic that made them marginal. Scholars, moreover, should focus on the way that marginalized peoples have exerted agency—controlled their own destinies—in spite of oppression.

Those tasks are necessary and good. To study violence, however, does not require us to ignore everything else. Indeed one cannot (in the twenty-first century) write about violence without writing about gender and race. What one can do, however, is sidestep methodologies that narrow our thinking. Too often historians portray social reality as a product of words, of discourse, of ideas that people wield to marginalize others or to empower themselves. There is truth in those observations, but there is also danger. The danger is that we see potential for historical change—contestation—wherever we look. Though contestation exists—readers will find it here—social patterns often persist over decades, even centuries. Poststructural theory—because it posits a social order, an imagined reality, that is never secure—does not do well at explaining persistence. Nor does it do well at explaining long-term change.

Honor and conscience, I would argue, though defined partly through discourse, cannot be reduced to words and ideas. Behind words stood emotion, impulse, half-conscious strategies for action and being. Such strategies precede consciousness. They shape it. They transcend it. Honor trended toward assertion, strength, fierceness, combat. Conscience trended toward restraint, modesty, sympathy. Each of them could be—and were—expressed in words and ideas, but at their core they consisted of feeling (or, more suggestively, what sociologist Pierre Bourdieu calls "habitus"). The fact that they were rooted in feeling gave them persistence. They replicated themselves not just via rhetoric, ideas, and speech but via child-rearing, familial relations, participatory games, and the simultaneously structured and unstructured pursuit of cultural rewards.[15] They did not, however, replicate themselves perfectly. They gave issue to ideas, to challenges, to quarrels, to alliances, and finally to change.

I wrote this book, finally, not merely to critique scholars. I wrote it to critique myself. I was born in Arizona and raised on its romance. Like early twentieth-century tourists, my understanding of the state's history and scenic beauty came via promotional literature, movies, and television Westerns. As I saw it, Arizonans—especially cowboys—were made of sterner, stronger stuff than people who grew up elsewhere.

I, to be sure, was no cowboy, nor were my relatives. My forebears were middle-class people who came from Arkansas in the late 1920s. Like millions of boys, however, I donned cowboy hats and boots and played "cowboys and Indians." Later, I vexed my bookish father until he promised to drive me to the Mazatzal Mountains or the Mogollon Rim to fish, hike, catch snakes, ride horses, and hunt for arrowheads. I vividly remember him sitting on a streamside boulder, novel in hand, watching me slosh away through Sycamore Creek. I remember, too, when he and my grandparents took me to Zane Grey's cabin under the Rim, where I admired the bearskin rug and dreamed of living in just such a place.

Still other currents swept me toward this topic. From age eleven to thirteen, I was a member of Troop 269 of the Boy Scouts of America, a troop sponsored by the Church of Jesus Christ of Latter-Day Saints (LDS). Though I was not Mormon, my friends were, and they invited me into their activities. With my fellow scouts, I spent a week at Camp Geronimo on the Mogollon Rim, where I waded in a frigid creek, fished in a fishless pond, and listened to chilling tales around the campfire. What I did not realize was that some of my fellow scouts were descendants of Mormons who had settled the Rim Country.

Thirty years later, I decided to return to the Rim Country. I had gotten my doctorate and finished my first book, a cultural study of hunting, and I was in search of a new project. At first I wanted to write an environmental history of Arizona's Salt River—the lifeblood of Phoenix and its satellites—but that project proved to be enormous and ill defined. In my preliminary research, however, I reconnected with an old acquaintance: Zane Grey.

I had read little of Zane Grey, though he had played a silent role in my family history. For the last two decades of my grandfather's life, one of Grey's Rim Country novels, *Nevada*, sat on the end table next to his easy chair. The book was an old favorite, one that Granddad loved to revisit. Granddad, commented my father, though visible to us, lived among cowboys and outlaws. In truth, all three of us spent part of our lives among cowboys and outlaws, Granddad with Zane Grey, me with my cap guns, and my father as weekend novelist. In the early 1970s, a small publisher asked him to revise and resubmit a manuscript Western titled "The Guns of Redemption." Before he could do so, the publisher folded, and the manuscript disappeared into a trunk.

In 2002, thirteen years after my grandfather's death, I at last picked up Zane Grey's *Nevada* and gave it a read, finding historical meanings that I never imagined it could have. I also returned to another fixture in my grandfather's den: a leather-bound set of *Arizona Highways*. Because the magazine was published by the Arizona Highway Department (now the Arizona Department of Transportation), my grandfather—who had been blacksmith, shop foreman, and state highway director—had every copy all the way back to 1940. In my youth, I had spent countless hours poring over those magazines, learning the lore and history of the state and imagining myself into its most remote, most sublime corners.

From Zane Grey and *Arizona Highways*, I became interested in the Pleasant Valley War. Grey had written a novel about the war—*To the Last Man*—that appeared in 1922. *Arizona Highways*, too, had spiced its pages with anecdotes and photos of the places where the war had occurred. During the summer after my graduation from college I became more familiar with the war when I signed on as an intern for *Arizona Highways* and its gifted editor, Don Dedera. Dedera was writing a book about the war—*A Little War of Our Own: The Pleasant Valley Feud Revisited*—which came out in 1988. In 1983, when I did my internship, Dedera asked me to write a short piece about the assassination of Tom Graham, the last victim of the war. I, however, rushed off to Washington, D.C., without finishing the project.

After a long hiatus, I have returned to write that story. It has become bigger than I intended. I had planned to devote a hundred pages to the Pleasant Valley conflict in a book that would cover a wide swath of Rim Country history, including relations between settlers and Indians. As the pages added up, however, I realized that I was writing two books, one on the Rim Country War and its legacy and another on the conquest, exile, and return of the Yavapai and Dilzhe'e ("Tonto Apache") to their Rim Country homeland. That book, unlike this one, will explore the darker side of conscience, the conscience that begot new divisions between "reformed" settlers and "unreformed" Indians.

ACKNOWLEDGMENTS

To thank those who have helped with this project is to go on an adventure. There are a lot of people to thank, and each reminds me of a new place and a new bit of information—or sometimes a new mountain of information. Thanks go especially to the staff at Arizona State University's Luhrs Reading Room, University of Arizona Special Collections, Arizona Historical Society, Arizona State Library Division of Records and Archives, the Harold D. Lee Library at Brigham Young University, Special Collections at the University of Utah's J. Willard Marriott Library, the LDS Family History Library, and the North Gila County Historical Society. At my home library at Central Washington University, I had the constant and speedy help of Becky Smith at the Interlibrary Loan office.

After all the assistance on the research, I got more on the writing. Those who commented on the manuscript were historians Jackie Moore, Elliott West, Ben Johnson, Thom Bahde, and my colleagues at Central Washington University, Roxanne Easley and Dean Marji Morgan. Bertram-Wyatt Brown and an anonymous reviewer were kind enough to serve as referees for Yale University Press. I am in their debt for suggestions on tightening prose and strengthening argumentation. The self-confessed "snarkiest" former president of the Western Literary Association, Robert Murray Davis, likewise helped with the Zane Grey chapter. Chris Rogers, my editor at Yale, meanwhile gave me alternate shots of encouragement and suggestion. I am grateful both to him and to Laura Davulis, associate editor, for their infinite patience in answering petty queries. Laura Jones Dooley, finally—Yale's manuscript editor—combed out the snarls in my prose.

A number of people recommended my project for funding. Special thanks go to Louis Warren, Bill Deverell, Karen Blair, and Tom Wellock. I also wish to thank Stan Brown, who opened his personal archive to me, and to Rita

Ackerman, whose book, whose comments, and whose box of photocopied newspaper articles gave me a jump start on the research. Roann Monson at ASU's Luhrs Reading Room gave me another jump start when she told me about the correspondence between George W. P. Hunt and his fiancée, Duett Ellison. In the later stages of the project, Jill McCleary of the Arizona Historical Society tirelessly helped me locate photographs. Lisa Long of the Ohio Historical Society and Carrol McClain of the Apache County Historical Society did likewise. Still more help came from Wendi Goen at the Arizona State Library and Jeremy Rowe of Jeremy Rowe Vintage Photography. Meanwhile Angie Hill, the Department of History's administrative assistant, juggled emails, orders, and invoices in order to convert proposed illustrations into digital images. I also wish to thank Nancy Lowell and her staff at the Oasis Cafe in Dallas, where hot coffee and tasty *migas* empowered me to edit on summer mornings in 2008.

In addition to the individuals who helped, there were institutions. In 2002, Central Washington University gave me a seed grant. The next year, the university gave me a one-quarter research leave. More support came in 2005, when the National Endowment for the Humanities awarded me a summer stipend. In 2008, the William Clements Center for Southwestern Studies at Southern Methodist University gave me a six-month fellowship to write the book. Six additional months came via sabbatical leave. Finally, the Graduate Studies office at Central Washington University stepped in to provide money for illustrations.

Beyond all that, I received the Justin Herman fellowship five times, which allowed me to live in my father's house for free while rambling around Arizona's archives. My father got me started on this book more than forty years ago when he regaled me with stories of Commodore Perry Owens, Governor George W. P. Hunt, and old Arizona. I hope it won't embarrass Dad to tell readers that he is ancient enough to have met Governor Hunt in 1934, when Lena Ellison escorted my grandparents, six-year old Justin in tow, to the upstairs bedroom where her brother-in-law lay stricken with heart failure. Hunt told Little Justin to tell his father, Big Justin, to run for the legislature. Hunt died that year and Big Justin never did run for office.

Above all, thanks go to my amazing wife, Margareta, who read the manuscript and suggested wise changes, put up with research trips and night writing, and fields bad jokes with good humor. She knows it already, but she makes life fun.

Part One

BEGINNINGS

Home on the Range

With the discovery of placer gold in the Bradshaw Mountains of central Arizona in the 1860s came hardened men who panned and sluiced and split rock. They came with pickaxes in one hand and rifles in the other and almost immediately became embroiled in wars of extermination against the Yavapai and the Dilzhe'e (or "Tonto Apache"). Pushed from their hunting and gathering lands, the Indians had little choice but to work for the newcomers or to attack. They did both.

In a climate of fear, even Indians who preferred working to fighting became targets. Atrocity by one side met with atrocity by the other, though settlers killed many more Indians than Indians killed settlers. Amid calls by editors and politicians for the extermination of the "red" foe, the U.S. Army sent one of its most gifted Indian fighters, General George Crook, to Arizona. Using the tactic of search-and-destroy, Crook sent small parties of soldiers and Indian scouts—many of them recruited from among defeated Yavapai and Apache bands—into the Tonto Basin, ordering them to cover the field like columns of ants, dodging this way and that, crossing and recrossing one another's paths. Continuously harassed, unable to hunt or to gather or to farm, driven to the extremities of the mountains, the Indians gave way.

In chasing the Yavapai and Apache through the canyons and mountains of the Rim Country, Crook's troops accomplished more than victory. They also reconnoitered some of the richest and most spectacular country in the territory. Far from finding more of the Great American Desert, they found the largest continuous stand of ponderosa pine in the world, stretching across the Mogollon Rim from the San Francisco Peaks in the west to the White Mountains on the New Mexico line. Just below the Rim, on a high bench connecting the Rim

with the Sierra Ancha ("Wide Mountains") to its south, they found a landscape
even more to their liking. Here they rode through grasses that grew above their
stirrups and watered their horses in perennial streams. They called the place
Pleasant Valley and imagined it as a rancher's paradise.[1]

When the Yavapai and Dilzhe'e surrendered in 1872–73, settlers were at last
free to avail themselves of the Rim Country's forests and pastures. There was
little incentive to relocate east of the army post in the Verde Valley, however,
given the lack of any market for surplus other than the territorial capital at Prescott. Prospectors soon changed that state of affairs by locating rich lodes of
silver in the vicinity of Pinal Creek, just south of the Salt River. Though the new
mining district lacked a railroad, it rapidly drew investors, miners, and merchants
who constructed the boomtown of Globe. Named for a "globe of almost pure
silver" found by a prospector, Globe by 1878 could boast a newspaper, the Arizona *Silver Belt*, which in turn could boast of seventy-four "good and substantial
houses" in the growing town.[2] With its multiplying population of miners, Globe
offered an excellent market for beef, butter, and produce.

Among the first ranchers to enter Pleasant Valley was James D. Tewksbury.
Tewksbury was a Maine man who had traveled to California in the 1850s, where
he joined a Masonic lodge and probably searched for gold in Humboldt County.
He may have come with a brother, John, who appears on the rolls of George
Crook's staff in the 1850s as a civilian scout. Between 1855 and 1864, James
Tewksbury raised livestock in northern California's Eel River District and lived
with a Hupa woman—an Athabascan speaker—who bore him four sons and a
daughter.[3]

Thus in the 1850s and 1860s, Tewksbury participated in what historians call
a "middle ground," a place where whites and Indians traded, negotiated, and
sometimes intermarried. Gold rush California, in fact, had perhaps the highest
rate of intermarriage between whites and Indians in the United States. Tewksbury, like more than half the white men in California who fathered children by
Indian women, gave his name to his offspring, indicating that he saw his relationship as something more than convenience.[4] The history of gold rush California,
however, is far from a tale of harmony.

In Humboldt County, settlers arrived a few years after the original gold rush
of 1849. Most came in the 1850s after prospectors discovered gold in waters that
drained the Trinity Mountains. As in Arizona a decade later, settlers killed off
game, poisoned streams, transformed hunting and gathering lands into farms
and ranches, and failed to distinguish between hostile and peaceful Indians.
A mineral strike like the one in Humboldt County, explains Elliott West, resembled "an artillery shell lobbed into the outback. Its concussion spread out-

View from Mogollon Rim looking into Tonto Basin. Courtesy of Northern Arizona University, Cline Library, Special Collections and Archives, Josef Muench Collection.

ward and rolled over native peoples who would never see a sluice or a mine, and as the expanding waves rippled into one another every part of the interior West felt the force of change."[5]

Indians in Humboldt County retaliated against that "artillery shell" by attacking settlers, including those who had done them no immediate wrong. In

Pleasant Valley. Courtesy of Northern Arizona University, Cline Library,
Special Collections and Archives, Josef Muench Collection.

turn settlers called for the annihilation of Indians. When the U.S. Army arrived, soldiers found themselves building a fort to protect Indians rather than to protect whites. Even after the construction of that fort, bloodshed continued. The well-known writer Brett Hart, who lived in Eureka in the 1860s, documented a single attack in which settlers killed as many as two hundred peaceful Wiyots.

How James Tewksbury negotiated the straits between cultural understanding and genocidal hatred, we do not know. What we do know is that sometime before 1870, he became a widower. In 1871, he moved his children to Battle Mountain, Nevada (near Virginia City), where he raised horses and joined the Knights of Pythias, a fraternal order founded to bring rapprochement between North and South. Like many other pioneers, Tewksbury soon moved again. Sometime around 1877, he entered Arizona, probably hoping to prospect in the Bradshaw Mountains. As early as 1878, he and his sons reconnoitered Pleasant Valley, where they built a dogtrot cabin, corrals, a bunkhouse, and a blacksmith shop amid a large meadow at the confluence of Cherry and Rock creeks. Shortly thereafter

Tewksbury married a widow with three children, Lydia Ann Shultes, and moved his large family to his new ranch.[6]

When the Tewksburys arrived in Pleasant Valley, they, like the soldiers before them, found grass that grew "belly deep." They also found a small number of fellow settlers, including a mysterious man named Emmett Gentry who had married an Apache woman. Other Rim Country settlers had also wed Apache women, including Corydon Cooley, a scout for General Crook who took two Apache wives. Had there been some chance for a biracial society to develop, however, it disappeared quickly with the conquest of the Dilzhe'e and the influx of whites.[7]

Among the newcomers in 1882 were the Graham brothers. John, the elder of the two, spoke with a brogue, having been raised in Northern Ireland. Thomas, the younger, lacked his brother's accent. He had been born in Ohio and, with his family, had moved to Iowa as a boy. The Graham brothers tried their hand at prospecting in the Globe region but decided that ranching offered better prospects. According to one account, they had won a few cattle in games of chance and needed to locate a range. Ed Tewksbury, James's eldest son, suggested they try Pleasant Valley, telling the handsome Tom Graham that he could become a cattle king. By the end of 1882, the Grahams had taken up residence not far north of the Tewksbury ranch, where they constructed the "Graham stronghold," a place suited to withstand attacks by Indians—or other settlers. By 1885, the Grahams held preemption claims to three quarter-sections—480 acres—and possessed 120 cows. The Tewksburys, similarly, held three quarter-sections along the Cherry Creek drainage, along with some 50 cows.[8]

A third early arrival in Pleasant Valley, a "jolly Irishman of doubtful morals," as Mormon settlers remembered him, was James Stinson, who had migrated from Maine to Colorado in 1855, then to Texas, New Mexico, and finally to the Rim Country in 1873. Stinson, with two partners, claimed twenty square miles of land on the Rio de la Plata (Silver Creek) drainage above the Rim and east of Pleasant Valley. Here he employed laborers from New Mexico to help construct "several flat, Mexican-style houses and farm buildings," dig irrigation lines, and cultivate three hundred acres with barley and vegetables.

With his big sombrero adorned with silver birds, his sealskin chaps, and his silver spurs, Stinson was the image of panache and confidence. Panache and confidence, however, brought little money. Despite his contract with the army to supply beef to Indian reservations, Stinson's ranching business suffered. In 1878, he sold his Silver Creek holdings to a Mormon colonizer and moved to Pleasant Valley, bringing half of his twelve hundred head of cattle. Stinson moved the other half to Chino Valley, near Prescott, some one hundred miles west of Pleasant Valley.[9]

Pleasant Valley was not the first American frontier to fill quickly with eager pioneers. It differed, however, from older frontiers in several respects. In the first half of the nineteenth century, pioneers tended to move into frontier areas first as market hunters then as farmers. Once settled, those pioneers participated in a barter economy. In Sangamon County, Illinois, to cite one example, settlers harvested and traded maple sap, roots and herbs, and wild game before they established mills to grind grain into meal. Only gradually did settlers in the Old Northwest, the Midwest, and the Upper South enter the world of market capitalism.[10] Indeed market capitalism could flourish only with improvements in transportation—turnpikes, canals, steamboats, and railroads—that offered farmers cost-effective ways to send crops to market and to obtain goods from industrial regions. For much of the nineteenth century, settlers understood that to take up land on the frontier was to separate themselves from economic and social progress, at least for a time.

In Pleasant Valley, by contrast, prosperity seemed imminent. Everywhere they looked, settlers saw the potential for profit despite the broken geography of mountain and canyon. As early as September 1879, the Phoenix *Herald* reported "big bonanzas" of gold ore in the Tonto Basin, giving "every indication of hilarious prosperity in the near future." A few months later, the *Herald* reported that "professional mining men" had pronounced the basin "one of the best mineral sections in the Territory." With investors now turning their attention to the region, "we expect to see plenty of money in circulation and bright and lively times on the sweet 'poco tiempo.'"[11]

Agriculture promised similar riches. With "luxurian" grass that "waves like a field of growing grain," the Tonto region was a "paradise for stock," announced the Phoenix *Herald* in April 1880. "Arizona cattlemen have struck a boom which promises to be lasting," added the Arizona *Gazette*, explaining that San Francisco had turned its eyes to Arizona for its beef supply. Even without the San Francisco market, ranchers could expect good business from the many Indian reservations and army posts in Arizona, all of which demanded beef, mutton, hay, grain, and horses. With Arizona's mild winters, moreover, cattle could fatten on grass and browse throughout the year. There was no need to ship cows to winter pastures or to store hay for winter feed. And of all the prime ranch country in the territory, none was better than the central part of the state. With its abundant grama, buffalo, mesquite, and alfilaria grasses, Tonto Basin was producing "some of the fattest beeves we have ever seen," announced the *Silver Belt* in 1884. "Every man, young or old, having money to invest in the ranch business," advised the editor, "will do well to lend a listening ear to some of things said about this section. Reliable men, with capital, are coming every day, and one by one the choice places are taken up. Let everyone come, and come now, and prove to all inquirers that what has been said about Arizona is true."[12]

Recalling the cattle boom of the early 1880s from the perspective of the Great Depression, former Rim Country settler Will Barnes and his coauthor, William MacLeod Raine, noted that Americans had "speculated in cows as they did during the 1929 boom in stocks." The prosperity of the late 1870s and early 1880s raised the demand for steaks and soup bones, especially in Eastern and Midwestern cities where thousands upon thousands of immigrants crowded together. Packing houses meanwhile improved technologies in canning and dressing beef as well as refrigerating it during shipment. With wealthy Americans and not a few Europeans promoting a limitless cattle boom, prices jumped to twenty dollars a head in the early 1880s, then to thirty dollars. "Feeders"—cows sent to Midwestern pastures for fattening prior to slaughter—went as high as fifty dollars. Such high prices pushed the cattle industry into Montana and the Pacific Northwest in the late 1870s and led to feverish speculation in Colorado, New Mexico, Texas, and Arizona. In the early 1880s, recalled Barnes and Raine, "the bonanza cattle days were at hand all over the West. Anyone could make a fortune in cows. No gold mine could be as profitable. . . . Money rolled in by a law of natural growth."[13]

The cattle boom, together with the rapid expansion of Globe, drew the Tewksburys, the Grahams, and Stinson to Pleasant Valley. They came not to escape industrial society but to feed it. They were as much entrepreneurs as pioneers, men who embraced the times and hoped to flourish with them. Surely they would have approved the Socorro *Bulletin*'s characterization of the stockman as "a practical man of business."[14]

With opportunity came traffic. By spring 1881, the old Fort Reno road that connected Phoenix with the Tonto Basin was streaming with settlers. Soldiers simultaneously worked to complete a road connecting Globe with Prescott. By 1885, a stage from Globe made stops in Wild Rye below the Rim as well as Green Valley and Pine above the Rim, encouraging rapid settlement on the entire line. The *Silver Belt* reported that some three to four thousand settlers in the Tonto Basin had now entered the stock business. Cattlemen did not raise only cows; they also grew vegetables and grain and produced butter that commanded a dollar a pound in Globe. These men were of the "well-to-do class" of settlers, explained the *Silver Belt*, "all having more or less personal property to add to the county's wealth."[15]

More promising than new roads was the proposed Arizona Mineral Belt Railroad, which would take on the seemingly impossible task of snaking across the Rim in order to connect the Atlantic and Pacific line at Flagstaff to the Tonto Basin. The track would then run south to connect Globe with the Southern Pacific Railroad and the silver district of Tombstone. Construction would include a 3,100-foot tunnel connecting the base of the Rim with the top. The railroad's promoter, James Eddy, had grand ambitions. In addition to the tunnel, he proposed to harness the water power of the Salt and Gila rivers to mill ores. His railroad would transport ore from the mines to the mills, then transport bullion from the mills to smelters and mints. "Nowhere else," intoned the *Silver Belt*, "is there so grand an opening for capitalists as the one here proposed."

By 1883 Eddy had begun blasting out his tunnel, but he got no further than seventy feet before he ran out of capital. In 1884, the press was still assuring readers that "the building of the A.M.B.R.R. is a fixed fact." Work did not resume, however, until 1887, when laborers completed thirty-five miles of track before Eddy again ran out of money. In 1888, he was forced to sell his road to satisfy labor liens and county taxes.[16]

Despite its failure, the Mineral Belt Railroad had inspired new heights of boosterism. The railroad, with its proposed stops at Pine, Green Valley, and Wild Rye, would offer good shipment points for both cattle and sheep. It also promised to bring a boom in land prices. "This picture of our coming prosperity" drawn by backers of the railroad, promised the *Silver Belt* as late as 1887, "is in nowise overdrawn."[17]

Pleasant Valley itself was somewhat removed from both the new wagon roads and from the proposed rail line. Riding a horse, noted one Arizona politician in 1891, was the only way to access "that lost corner of the Earth." Even on horseback, the valley could be entered by way of only three "very rough trails." The "upper trail" ran east from Flagstaff via Strawberry, then down the Rim at the northern end of the valley. The Hellgate Trail ran eastward from Green Valley (modern Payson) toward the massive gorge known as Hell's Gate, ascended the Sierra Ancha, then dropped into Pleasant Valley. Finally the Jerked Beef Butte or Houdon Trail came north from the Salt River, crossing a six-thousand-foot-high pass in the Sierra Ancha and emptying into the valley's southwest corner.[18]

Getting in and out of Pleasant Valley was a difficult proposition, especially when driving a herd of cattle. The richness of the country and the promise of a rail stop close by, however, lured a steady trickle of settlers. By the end of 1882, Pleasant Valley had been peopled by men—and a few women—born in such diverse places as California, Iowa, Kentucky, Maine, Michigan, Missouri, New York, and Texas, as well as Canada, England, Germany, Ireland, Mexico, and Sweden.

Given the diversity of Pleasant Valley's settlers and their competition for range, conflict was likely. Not only were settlers far from law enforcement—the nearest courts and sheriffs were a hundred miles west in Prescott—but they also lacked a cultural center of gravity. Unlike settlers in the Old Northwest, the Midwest, the South, and in Oregon, those in Pleasant Valley tended to come as young, single men rather than as families. The Tewksburys, to be sure, arrived as a family, but among the eight children were only two females, one of whom married and left Pleasant Valley in 1880. The Grahams came without mothers, sisters, daughters, or wives.

What bound settlers in the absence of intermarriage was the fear of Apaches. In 1881 and again in 1882, Indians fled the White Mountain Reservation and attacked settlers in Pleasant Valley, killing several. In those actions, the Grahams and the Tewksburys, along with every other settler, joined in self-defense. Whatever solidarity the Apache threat created, however, was temporary. After the raids were over, frictions returned.

What might also have tied settlers together were the shards of gossip, storytelling, and conversation shared at social events. Rim Country settlers mixed at Fourth of July celebrations, barbecues, fiddle dances, horse races, and shooting matches. In the mid-1880s, moreover, they invented the "cowboy tournament," later known as rodeo. In the 1890s, settlers—or at least those in Globe—also formed teams and played baseball.[19] Despite occasional gatherings, however, isolation was the norm. Settlers remained cleaved by ethnic, regional, and religious divisions. Individualism prevailed over community.

Economic relations nonetheless yielded social relations. The Grahams, for instance, helped the Tewksburys construct a cabin in 1883. To return the favor, at least one of the Tewksburys helped the Grahams build a corral. Even as they amassed cattle herds, moreover, settlers scoured the countryside for minerals, often filing joint claims on promising ground. Though the Tewksburys never teamed up with the Grahams in prospecting ventures, they did team up with two others, Christian Jurgensen and William Jacobs, both of whom would later become partners with the Tewksburys in sheepherding.[20]

What also tied together settlers was hospitality. Settlers made it a point of pride to feed and shelter passersby, whether they were acquaintances or strangers. Rim Country cowboys, wrote Will Barnes, "would share their last meal with a total stranger." Barnes's observation is born out in the annals of the Ellison family, who came to the Rim Country in 1885. Its patriarch, a Texan known as "Colonel" Jesse Ellison, kept an "open house" even though "it nearly ate him out of pocket." Ellison was by no means a rarity. A letter to the St. Johns *Herald* from "Puncher, On the Range," explained in 1887 that "there is not a good man" in the entire region who would be "unwilling to entertain a traveling stranger—to the contrary, they are glad to see them, and to treat them well."[21]

Western conventions regarding hospitality arrived with settlers from the South. "Southern hospitality," in turn, came from Scots, Scots-Irish, and Irish immigrants of the seventeenth and eighteenth centuries. The Celtic peoples of the British Isles, argued historian Grady McWhiney, exhibited both gregarious displays of hospitality and friendship along with keen sensitivity to insult and a readiness to fight. McWhiney may have exaggerated his thesis, yet it is certainly true that nineteenth-century travelers to the South described displays of hospitality that bordered on the prodigal—or even crossed the border. A similar emphasis on hospitality appeared in the West. As late as 1930 Will Barnes noted that Westerners remained "more careless and casual, more spontaneous in quick friendships, gayer in temperament, more prodigal of hospitality to strangers" than other Americans.[22]

Hospitality, however, was not solely an invention of Southern immigrants. The Tewksburys, who had no Southern roots, gave lavish barbecues for their neighbors, at least until hostilities made such events impossible. Despite their leaders' warnings about the danger of associating with "gentiles" (non-Mormons), Mormon settlers, too, sometimes opened their doors to strangers. William Flake of Snowflake, a Mormon settlement above the Rim, refused to turn away any traveler who came to his door. Similarly the Shelley family of Heber, another Mormon settlement of the Rim Country, was "hospitable to a fault," offering food and shelter even to those they suspected to be killers and thieves.[23]

Hospitality formed a kind of security policy. As they faced droughts, floods, crop failures, Indian wars, and long journeys over broken country, settlers were forced to rely on one another for comfort and aid. To provide comfort and aid was to create solidarity. To refuse hospitality, on the other hand, might be construed as an act of hostility. It was important to keep one's door open.

If hospitality created bonds of community, however, it also weakened them. Those who appeared to be too friendly to shady sorts might be judged shady themselves. "Under the guise of hospitality," wrote "Puncher" in the St. Johns *Herald* of March 3, 1887, "food, shelter, and rest are supplied to desperadoes, gamblers and thieves." When confronted with the fact that their guests were evildoers, insisted Puncher, such hosts gave fierce replies. "Them G-d—n s—s of b————s, that beats hell. We always believed 'em to be straight men. When we last seen 'em, they were hard workin' fellers. The next time they come along, we'll shoot out the s—s of b————s."[24] Far from shooting them out, wrote Puncher, the hosts divided the loot with their criminal companions.

The flipside of hospitality and bonhomie was suspicion and fear in part because ranchers and cowboys were continuously taking one another's cattle. In the Rim Country and, indeed, throughout the West, accusations of rustling were ubiquitous. Accusations became all the more frequent as ranchers increasingly defined branding mistakes and "mavericking"—the practice of branding the calf of another man's cow—as "rustling," an act punishable by prison or even, when adjudicated by vigilantes, by death.

The beginning of the Pleasant Valley trouble occurred when the Tewksburys branded some of James Stinson's cows in 1882. When Stinson discovered the theft—or mistake—the Tewksburys offered to "vent" the cows, meaning they would cross out their brand and give them back to Stinson. Stinson refused the offer. He wanted to prosecute. Years later, he claimed that he had heard bad reports about the Tewksburys from their neighbors, George Church and the Rose brothers, Al and Ed, who had encouraged Stinson to come to Pleasant Valley to "freezer" the Tewksburys. By prosecuting the Tewksburys for rustling, he had his chance to do so. For their part, the Tewksburys later admitted to having pilfered Stinson's cattle. They had tried to get along with the "old man," according to a cowboy who had worked with the Tewksburys, but Stinson proved to be cantankerous and vindictive, so they began to steal his cows to spite him.[25] Hospitality was valued in cattle country, but petty theft—usually without consequences to the thief—was a common way to retaliate against enemies.

By December 1882, Stinson had changed his mind about prosecuting. What caused his change of heart is unclear. He made no overt demonstration of goodwill, but he did allow the Tewksburys to vent the cows. Having become an absentee owner—Stinson had moved to Phoenix so that his stepson could attend school—he directed his foreman, John Gilliland, to convey his decision to the Tewksburys.[26]

Gilliland may or may not have been following orders when he, with his sixteen-year-old nephew, Elisha Gilliland, and another Stinson hand, Epitacio "Potash" Ruiz, made their way to James Tewksbury's ranch on New Year's Day, 1883. They arrived at ten in the morning on horseback, wearing sidearms and ammunition belts. Young Elisha, hoping to bag some turkeys that day, also carried a .22 rifle.[27]

According to a newspaper account, Gilliland had come to deliver a message: "Go ahead and vent the cows." Perhaps, too, Gilliland carried a warning: "Go ahead and vent the cows, but don't steal any more." Or "Go ahead and vent the cows and then clear out." Ed Tewksbury, in his subsequent court testimony, claimed that a man named "Shell"—either Robert Shell, who lived in Tonto Basin, or Samuel Shull, who lived atop the Rim—had told him that Stinson was trying to get up a mob to drive out or kill the Tewksburys. Evidence also suggests that Stinson sought to buy out the Tewksburys, as well as the Grahams. When the Tewksburys refused him, Stinson seems to have withdrawn his offer to the Grahams.[28]

When the Gilliland party arrived, the Tewksburys were building a cabin. John Graham pounded lead into rivets. Ed and Jim Tewksbury worked alongside him at the forge, pumping a bellows and monitoring coffee. Tom Graham stood inside the unchinked walls of the new building, splitting wood to make a cupboard. As the horsemen approached, Ed Tewksbury walked out to meet them, carrying a small pistol in his hip pocket. Words passed between him and John Gilliland. Gilliland and his companions testified that Ed had asked whether they were looking for someone, to which Gilliland replied no. Ed then said, "Well I am," simultaneously pulling his gun and firing. The Tewksbury witnesses remembered things differently. They recalled Ed walking out to meet the party and asking, "Who are you looking for?" to which Gilliland replied, "For you, you son-of-a-bitch," as he pulled his gun.[29] Neither version sounds authentic. Something is missing, some provocation, spoken or unspoken.

In all, some dozen shots were exchanged. None of Gilliland's took effect, though one whizzed through John Graham's hat and nearly hit Jim Tewksbury (time and again, men on horseback failed to hit their targets; their mounts were too unsteady). No one else in the Gilliland party fired a shot. Ruiz may or may not have reached for his gun. Either his horse wheeled on its own, preventing him from pulling the gun, or, as he told the story, he wheeled the horse purposely to flee. Elisha Gilliland fled, too, but a shot from Tewksbury's pistol caught him in the back. He traveled a short distance before falling from his horse. Another Tewksbury bullet hit John Gilliland in the shoulder. Gilliland fired one last errant round before galloping away.[30]

Believing Elisha had been killed, his uncle, William McDonald of Wild Rye, brought charges of murder against the Tewksburys as well as against John Graham. Elisha's wound, however, turned out to be minor. John Graham and Ed Tewksbury also brought charges of attempted murder against the Gilliland party. Depositions and trials followed, but conflicting testimony led authorities to drop charges.[31]

For legal purposes, who said what and who fired first mattered. For purposes of history, who said what and who fired first matters little. What does matter is that animus had come to the boiling point, a fact of which Gilliland was surely aware. He could not have expected a cordial reception. What is also clear is that settlers coveted Pleasant Valley despite its remoteness from roads and trains. Here was where Stinson hoped to prosper after several years of losing money. Here, too, was where the Tewksburys and the inexperienced Grahams hoped to establish

Ed Tewksbury, circa 1890. Courtesy of Arizona
State Library, Archives and Public Records,
History and Archives Division, Phoenix,
no. 97-8493.

their ranches, though they could not expect to profit the way Stinson could, with
his herd of six hundred.

The struggle to control grass and water, then, provoked a quarrel. But to say
that is not enough. The two men who fired on each other that day, Ed Tewksbury and John Gilliland, seem to have absorbed the cultural currents of honor.
Who said what and who shot first hardly matter assuming that both men sought
to resolve their differences through violence. They participated in a culture that
taught men to gauge one another's character via acts of bravado and aggression.
It was not a culture that valued the diplomacy of soft words. If competition for
resources led to the fight, honor stoked its fires.

We can add to the story a bit of hearsay reported over the years. More than one
old-timer insisted that both the Tewksburys and the Grahams were stealing Stinson's cattle. According to some accounts, Stinson had hired Ed Tewksbury and
the Graham brothers to work his Chino Valley operation.[32] They used their wages
to start their own ranch and pilfered Stinson's cows to stock it. It seems unlikely,

however, that Stinson would have hired any Tewksbury to run his cattle if he had come to Pleasant Valley to "freezer" them.

Another rumor purports that Charlie Duchet, who would become a hardened Graham partisan, was employed by the Tewksburys and Grahams to watch over the Chino Valley operation, along with the cows they had stolen from Stinson. Duchet, in his reminiscences, dictated in a rambling, dreamlike fashion while he lay near death as an old man, claimed that the Tewksburys had stolen more than 600 of Stinson's cattle and 4,000 altogether. Those figures are utterly implausible. Stinson had only 1,200 animals on his two ranches. The county assessor taxed him in 1884 for 560 cattle in Pleasant Valley, meaning a loss of some 40 head, perhaps as a result of predation, disease, Apache hunters (who were often reported in the area), or simply an inaccurate tally by the assessor. Ranchers were notorious for showing assessors only part of their cattle.[33]

In all probability, however, the Tewksburys were rustling a few of Stinson's cattle, perhaps with help from the Grahams. Stinson longed to retaliate and did so by following the dictum of divide and conquer. Quietly he negotiated with the Grahams. He offered to help them build a herd by giving them cattle — fifty head — if they would supply evidence leading to the prosecution of those stealing his animals. The parties seem to have reached a tentative agreement in November 1883, though not until March 28, 1884, did they put the agreement into writing. A day later, the Grahams charged the Tewksburys with rustling sixty-two of Stinson's cattle. The Grahamses' accusations did not stop there; they also implicated William Richards, H. H. Bishop, and George Blaine.[34]

In the trials that followed, old friends became enemies and truth became farce. Judge Summer Howard, widely known for his prosecution of the Mountain Meadows Massacre case in the 1870s, heard the case in his Prescott court. The Grahams, however, made poor witnesses and found themselves snared by their own testimony. By the end of the trials, Stinson was testifying in favor of the defendants. Juries found them not guilty. In what the Arizona *Champion* called a "scathing address," Howard accused the Grahams of perjuring themselves and directed the district attorney to issue warrants for their arrest. The perjury case was tried in St. Johns, Apache County, but the court rendered no verdict.[35]

The trials of 1884 reveal how profound the divide in Pleasant Valley had become. This was not merely a feud between the Tewksburys and Grahams. The Grahams implicated other small operators, too. Rustling — whether in the form of "mavericking," mistaken branding, or deliberate theft — was endemic on free range. One accusation led to another.

What we might reiterate here is that free range encouraged small operators — especially those like the Tewksburys, who were among the earliest settlers in

Tom Graham, circa 1882. Courtesy of Arizona Historical Society/Tucson, no. 4886.

Pleasant Valley—to hope to become independent and prosperous. "Free range" had the same resonance in Arizona as "freehold" had in the Midwest. Small ranchers hoped to gain self-sufficiency and respect by harvesting the fruits of the land. The problem was that a man like Stinson, who owned a large herd, might dominate the range before small operators could gain stability. To achieve parity, small operators often took cows from their nemeses.

What we might also note is that prosperity was more elusive than settlers believed in part because of competition for range. Powerful men, newcomers with more money, more animals, and better connections than the first settlers, continuously searched for good land. To get that land, they came into conflict with small operators. There was, however, an alternative. Powerful men might also forge alliances with settlers who knew the land and the cattle business. Small operators needed capital for horses, clothing, weapons, building and fencing materials, and such necessities as flour, bacon, and garden seeds. In a remote place like Pleasant Valley, it might be years before a ranch turned a profit, even if men expected money to flow sooner. By allying themselves with investors, men like the Tewksburys could get much-needed capital to tide them over. Small operators could fight against powerful newcomers, or they could help them.

The most important revelation at the 1884 trials was the nature of the relationship between small operators and bigger men. Stinson was the biggest operator in Pleasant Valley, and he teamed up with the Grahams. His attempt to buy out the Tewksburys (as well as the Grahams), however, shows that he had initially eschewed any "deal."

J. J. Vosburgh and George Newton did not make the same mistake. They sought to work with settlers from the outset. Vosburgh and Newton, like Stinson, were prosperous men with big ambitions. Unlike Stinson, they directed their affairs from Globe, which demanded that they cast their lot with the Tewksburys. Vosburgh and Newton could not succeed without allies on the range.

Vosburgh, an Iowa native, was probably the wealthier of the two. In addition to serving as secretary of the Central Arizona Live Stock and Ranchmen's Association, he was the Globe agent for Wells Fargo, operated his own stage and freight line between Globe and Ft. Thomas, and invested in ranching and mines. In 1885, the *Silver Belt* reported that he and his wife, while traveling in the East, had bought a luxurious buggy of a kind not seen in Globe and had it shipped home. The paper also reported that Mrs. Vosburgh summered in Saratoga and Chittenango, New York, and White Sulphur Springs, West Virginia. She was no impoverished settler's wife.[36]

Newton, who came from Massachusetts by way of Virginia City, Nevada, operated a jewelry store in Globe, sold and repaired watches, sewing machines, and pistols, and invested in mines and ranches. Like Vosburgh, he sported about Globe in a "stylish cart" that he had ordered from California in 1885. More important, he was Vosburgh's partner in the Flying V ranch on Cherry Creek, the ranch originally owned by the Middleton family, who had been driven out by Apaches. Thanks to Vosburgh and Newton's capital, the Flying V held the largest herd in Pleasant Valley next to Stinson's. Its foreman was Ed Tewksbury. Not surprisingly, Newton testified against the Grahams at their trial for perjury in 1884. Vosburgh had already testified for the Tewksburys in Prescott.[37]

Still another revelation of the 1884 trials was the relationship between the

Tewksburys and the Daggs brothers of Flagstaff, who possessed something on the order of fifty thousand sheep. The Daggs brothers ran their flocks on free range in central and east-central Arizona, north of the Rim. In 1884, they found themselves reckoning with an obstacle to continued success: the Aztec Land and Cattle Company, new claimant to a million acres between Flagstaff and New Mexico. The Aztec refused to allow the Daggses' herders to cross its lands, even though it lacked a warranty deed (the Aztec bought the land from the Atlantic and Pacific Railroad, which could not finalize a warranty deed until the lands were surveyed). The Daggses' herders continued to trespass despite threats from the Aztec's gun-wielding cowboys. Far preferable, however, was to move sheep underneath Aztec lands and into Tonto Basin. To do that, the Daggs brothers needed help from parties in Pleasant Valley. The Tewksburys fit the bill.

The Daggs brothers not only appeared at the Tewksbury trials but also helped the Tewksburys pay their bills. Peru Daggs bought Jim Tewksbury's ranch for thirty-five hundred dollars, an astronomical price for property that was probably worth a few hundred dollars, but enough to pay Tewksbury's legal expenses. Tewksbury ally George Blaine also sold his ranch to Peru Daggs; he received thirty-two hundred dollars.[38] Both Tewksbury and Blaine desperately needed the money. In 1885, they were scheduled to stand trial for having robbed a Mormon store in Woodruff, a settlement above the Rim. For the Daggs brothers, the robbery was fortuitous. Without access to Tonto Basin, their profits would plummet; now they had access. Not surprisingly, the Tewksburys and several of their neighbors also agreed to help the Daggs brothers bring sheep into Pleasant Valley.

By the beginning of 1884 Stinson must have realized that his battle to dominate Pleasant Valley was more than a fight against a few rustlers. He was fighting Vosburgh, Newton, the Daggs brothers, the Tewksburys, and other small operators simultaneously. In its earliest stage, then, the Pleasant Valley conflict was not solely a case of small operators fighting big operators, though that was part of the problem. The small operators, in their attempt to defend their stake in the valley, had made allies among big operators — or at least men who hoped to become big operators.

Stinson could have lived with the threat posed by Newton and Vosburgh. Their herds might preclude him from becoming a cattle baron, but they would not depose him from the valley. He apparently could not live, however, with the threat posed by the Daggses' sheep. According to the Mormon historian Joseph Fish, who lived in the Rim Country at the time, Stinson offered five hundred dollars for the "head of any man who should drive sheep into the valley, or across a designated line."[39] Stinson denied that he had offered such a reward, but he could not have been neutral. Cattlemen far and wide despised sheep for eating the grass down to the roots. Some insisted that cattle could not bear the smell of sheep and would refuse to eat anywhere they had grazed. The fact that sheepherders tended to be New Mexican, Indian, or Basque added to cattlemen's disgust.[40] Conflict between sheepmen and cattlemen was ubiquitous. Pleasant Valley was no exception. Stinson, however, would not lead the fight against sheep. The Grahams and their allies—cowboys from Texas—would do that.

Realizing what he was up against, Stinson surrendered even before the Tewksbury trials. In May 1884, he sold his Pleasant Valley ranch and cattle. Before he could leave, however, violence erupted again. Not long after they had arrived home from the Prescott trials, John Tewksbury, George Blaine, and Ed Rose visited the Stinson ranch to confer about the "rodeo," or roundup, that Stinson would conduct to find and separate his cattle from those of others. Rose came as a sheriff's deputy, having been appointed by Judge Howard to keep the peace. Blaine came as a Tewksbury friend and Stinson enemy. Several of Stinson's cowboys loitered at the ranch house when the three arrived. F. M. McCann, Stinson's new foreman, ordered Tewksbury and Blaine to leave. Tewksbury and Blaine then began to curse him, saying he'd "bulldozed that part of the country long enough." Blaine challenged McCann to step away from the ranch house and have it out. When McCann obliged, Blaine, still on horseback, fired on him, missing. McCann responded in kind, hitting Blaine in the jaw. The bullet came out through Blaine's neck just below the skull. Tewksbury, also on horseback, returned McCann's fire without effect. McCann shot back, and Tewksbury slumped on his horse as he rode away.[41]

Violence trumped diplomacy. The competition of the free range spawned honor. Likely those who participated in the gunfight were already imbued with honor when they arrived in Pleasant Valley. Blaine, who was born in New York, had apprenticed as a cowboy in Texas, where he surely absorbed the norms of his comrades. New York's laboring class, moreover, had its own ethic of manly self-assertion, an ethic that may have shaped Blaine long before he emigrated. In all probability, McCann, who was born in Arkansas, had also learned the cowboy trade in Texas or the Southwest.[42] What is certain is that the small battles that took place in Pleasant Valley—indeed, the small battles that occurred throughout cattle country—were not solely the result of competition for resources. The behaviors of honor and the competition for range acted symbiotically; one exacerbated the other.

On August 23, 1884, the *Silver Belt* reported that George Newton and Ed Tewksbury anticipated no further trouble after the shooting. Stinson, added the *Silver Belt*, "has turned his cattle over to Murray & Reed and nearly all of them have been driven away." Tewksbury's wound turned out to be minor. Blaine, however, lay near death. He had survived the initial shot and the subsequent attempt by a surgeon to remove splinters of bone and lead from his head. He recovered—at least to all appearances—though he subsequently lost his sanity, perhaps owing to the wound.[43]

When 1884 came to a close, no lives had been lost. The Tewksburys and their allies had prevailed—or so it seemed. Stinson had left, though his erstwhile allies, the Grahams, remained. The optimism of arrival had given way to contest. Within two years, economic catastrophe would add to the bitterness. A devastating collapse in beef prices turned anger into hate. The Pleasant Valley conflict, however, would involve more than competition for range. Both racial division and religious animus would add to its fires. Honor, too, would continue to insinuate itself into the war, offering settlers both a prescription for conflict and a way to understand it in later years.

THE SAINTS MARCH IN

Fifteen-year-old Lucy White struggled to contain her excitement. Day after day, her family had sat down to meals of "mush and milk," or, as her father called it, "lumpy dick."[1] Today, however, a young man, a stranger, would be coming to Lucy's Utah home, and the White women busily prepared a meal in his honor. Mashed potatoes, chicken and noodles, pickled beets, and custard pie would grace the table, dishes Lucy seldom tasted.

The stranger whom Lucy would soon meet—William Jordan Flake—was a tall eighteen-year-old with blue-gray eyes, reddish hair, and the patina of manners and chivalry. Her people, unlike his, were Yankee converts to the Church of Jesus Christ of Latter-day Saints, but today they prepared cornbread to make their guest feel at home. Whatever acrimony existed between North and South in 1857, few Mormons shared it. The Flakes, like Lucy's own family, had gathered among the faithful at Nauvoo, Illinois, more than a decade earlier. Despite their regional origins, the two families shared the belief that a prophet had come to earth to resurrect Christianity, and they shared the persecution that came with that belief. After the assassination of Joseph Smith, both the Flakes and the Whites had embarked on the great exodus to Utah, where they hoped to live quiet, prosperous, godly lives.

Quiet and prosperity, however, were far from view in 1857, as the Whites, along with William Flake and thousands of their fellow Mormons, prepared to fight the force sent by President James Buchanan to impose federal rule on Utah Territory. Young Flake was to be a soldier in the war that seemed certain to break out. For that purpose church authorities had called him back from San Bernardino, California, where his family had been sent in 1851. Rather than extending the reach of mighty Deseret—the "empire" of the Mormons—to the Pacific Ocean, Flake would defend its innermost bastions.

For the time being, the Whites put the threat of war out of their minds and thought instead of their daughter's happiness. For several days, Lucy's father had been telling her about the gentleman from California with his Southern manners and his tall good looks. When in the company of Flake, meanwhile, Lucy's father spoke of his pretty fifteen-year-old daughter. As Lucy recalled in later years, she was blessed with allure. She had delicate hands and feet, a round face, a small nose and lips, and straight, white teeth. Like other Mormon girls, Lucy showed the effects of hard labor. Her skin had become deeply tanned, though she managed to keep her face rosy through daily applications of sour cream and buttermilk. Her rosy face was framed by auburn hair, which she parted in the middle and braided in two strands "crossed . . . back and forth on the back like an oval shaped rug."[2]

Beauty did not make Lucy faultless. As her father might have told young Flake, at times she gave way to tremors of laughter on the most solemn occasions—at church, even at funerals. In such emergencies she had the good sense to cover her face so that others would mistake her laughter for "paroxysms" of grief.[3] Despite her outbursts, Lucy's father could assure young Flake that there was nothing amiss about his daughter's reputation.

Piety, indeed, was the anchor and compass of Lucy's life, and she took to heart the patriarchal blessing bestowed on her in adolescence. She was a "daughter of Abraham, the loins of Joseph and blood of Ephram," the patriarch assured her, "a royal heir to all their blessings, privileges and powers which pertain to the Holy Priesthood according to thy sex." "Thou shalt be connected with a man of God," the patriarch continued, "thru whom thou shalt receive the priesthood, exaltation and power and eternal glory and become a mother in Israel." Lucy then received an even greater prophecy: she would witness the Redeemer's return. She would live to see her posterity born in the millennium, when she would "be anointed a queen and priestess unto the most high God, receive thy crown, dominion, power, and eternal increase."[4] The blessing was heady brew for an adolescent. Lucy might be giddy at inappropriate times, but she was one of God's chosen.

The two youths awaited their meeting with hope and anxiety. When they were at last introduced, Lucy found that she had "under estimated his looks." She blushed and looked down, not knowing what to say. Despite his chagrin, William stretched out a hand in greeting. They would be married within the year.

In many ways the romance was typical. Frontier youths had short courtships and married young. Though marriages in Utah were seldom arranged by church authorities or by parents—except when older men took "plural" wives—the choice of mate was usually someone from nearby, someone known and approved by parents. If the pairing was typical, however, William's Southern background was not. Most converts had come from New England. A second wave had come from the laboring classes of England and Scandinavia. Relatively few came from the American South.

William Flake was born in Anson County, North Carolina, on a "large plantation" on July 3, 1839. According to family tradition, some of his forebears were English Cavaliers who came to Virginia in the seventeenth century. William's Cavalier ancestors subsequently mixed with Scots-Irish settlers who populated the piedmont areas of the South. Though the Scots-Irish were poor, frontier people, William's grandfather was well-to-do. In 1771, indeed, George III granted him land in North Carolina, though it is unclear why the king so favored him.[5]

Like other Southern planters, William's progenitors succumbed to the waves of evangelism that came with the Great Awakening. Some of his forebears were Quakers, whereas others became Baptists and Methodists, denominations that grew rapidly in the 1760s and 1770s even as they opposed Anglican orthodoxy. Above all, Baptists and Methodists preached spiritual equality, which led them to attack the Southern gentry for its pretensions to social authority and its tepid piety. At times, they attacked slavery itself. If the Flakes had ever opposed the gentry or its institutions, however, they were themselves plantation owners and slaveholders by the time William was born. They were also ardent Democrats who, in the 1830s, supported territorial expansion, Indian removal, and what one historians calls "herrenvolk"—or white only—democracy. Like many other members of the planter elite, moreover, William's father, James Madison Flake, kept a pack of trained dogs for hunting.[6] He was gentleman, master, and sportsman.

Following the trajectory of thousands of sons of landed men, James Madison Flake saw his future not on his father's land but on the frontier. In 1842, when William was three, James loaded a prairie schooner and moved his family and slaves to Mississippi. What they could not have known was that this move would be the first in a chain of peregrinations that would end in Arizona.

Two years after the Flakes arrived in Mississippi, something unexpected, something strange and exciting, occurred. James and Agnes Flake were approached by a missionary who told them of a "new heaven and a new earth." The missionary not only bore witness to the prophet—Joseph Smith—but also gave the Flakes a sacred document, *The Book of Mormon*, that Smith claimed to have translated from golden tablets long buried in New York's black loam. James and Agnes read it carefully and came to the same conclusion: it was true.[7] Christianity—full-throated Christianity—had disappeared long ago and was now to be rekindled among the few who followed Joseph Smith.

Having converted to Mormonism, the Flakes became outcasts. The only solution was to sell everything and leave for Nauvoo, Illinois, where Joseph Smith was gathering the faithful. Having once removed to Mississippi, the Flakes—like innumerable pioneer families—would move again.[8]

The move posed problems. Would the Flakes' slaves remain slaves in the free state of Illinois? Would other Mormons accept blacks into their community? Would they accept slavery itself? Behind those questions loomed another: Would Mormons—a people dedicated to conscience—make accommodations for the habiliments of honor brought by Southern converts?[9] The Southern culture of honor, indeed, hinged on the nobility of one race and the shame of another, a distinction that Mormons at times resisted.

In the 1830s and 1840s, Mormons were in the midst of a controversy about race. Even though the Book of Mormon equated dark skin with God's curse, Joseph Smith and many of his converts disliked slavery and preached universalism. Black and white, slave and free were all to be welcomed into the fold. In the church's early years, Smith initiated a few blacks into the priesthood. In Missouri, however, the church found itself pilloried for its supposed opposition to slavery. For their own safety—and for the sake of unity—Mormons began to speak out not against slavery but against abolitionism, going so far as to accept the myth that blacks were the cursed descendants of Canaan, destined only to servitude. Mormons, like Baptists and Methodist before them, made peace with slavery even as they retained a commitment to conscience. Thus the Flakes— slaves and all—found acceptance in Nauvoo.[10]

Young William Flake, just five when his family left for Nauvoo, had few memories of the trip, but he had many of Nauvoo itself, perhaps the grandest of which was when "Negro Green" took him to the top of the temple. From there, they could look out over a vast expanse of woods and farms that were now in Mormon hands. It was the most impressive view the boy had ever seen. The kingdom had come, it seemed, and the Flakes were bound to prosper. The boy might also have recalled that, shortly after they had arrived, his father had received a patriarchal blessing from no less a figure than Hyrum Smith, brother of Joseph. In that blessing, Hyrum Smith would have foretold to James the powers of "revelating" and "prophesying" that would allow him to triumph over adversity. Hyrum Smith would have also told Flake that a guardian angel stood over him. He would have prophesied, finally, that Flake would witness the return of Christ. According to Mormon folklorist Austin Fife, the bestower of the patriarchal blessing "intones a ritual that is so poetic, so prophetic, so rhythmical, so inspired that the young man is made to feel that he is shortly to become, like Peter of old, a custodian of the keys of the Kingdom of Heaven."[11]

But the kingdom in Nauvoo could not last, and young William's memories would soon include his own attempts to hide while gentiles attacked and looted the followers of Joseph Smith.[12] On June 27, 1844, just fifteen days after Hyrum Smith imparted a patriarchal blessing to James Madison Flake, Hyrum was dead. He, with his prophet brother, fell victim to a mob that gathered at the Carthage, Illinois, jail, where Hyrum and Joseph had been imprisoned for having ordered the destruction of an anti-Mormon printing press.

By February 1846, the Flakes found themselves again on the move. This time they followed a new prophet, Brigham Young, into the recesses of the West, where, they hoped, persecution would be at an end. James Madison Flake contributed generously to funding the journey, even providing his finest carriage and mules, along with the services of Green, to Brigham Young. Flake himself became captain of an emigrant company consisting of 502 whites and 24 blacks, presumably slaves. Young William was assigned to assist Liz, a slave girl, with driving the cattle that trailed the wagons.[13]

For four years—1847 to 1851—the Flakes remained in Utah, advancing the cause of Zion. Then Brigham Young, impressed with James Madison Flake's zeal and ability, asked him to help colonize California. Young sought to open a trading corridor to the Pacific while at the same time fulfilling Joseph Smith's prophecy that Mormons would populate the whole of the western hemisphere.[14]

Again young William Flake experienced the ordeal of emigration. This time he went through even greater trials. On one occasion, he became lost and nearly died of thirst; another time he was trailed by wolves but was saved by a heroic mule that drove them away; and on yet another occasion, Indians killed his oxen and nearly struck him with an arrow. He was lucky, or blessed, or both; but tragedy found him nonetheless. In 1851, James Madison Flake was thrown from his mule, breaking his neck. His last words are said to have been, "brethren, administer to me."[15] William was twelve.

Hearing of the tragedy, Agnes Flake's brother journeyed to California to entreat his sister to come home. She refused. She was a Mormon, and she intended to continue to be one. She was weary and thin, however, and in 1855 she followed her husband to the grave. William, now sixteen, became head of his family. Unable to survive without charity, the Flake children were instructed to live with a family who had accompanied them to San Bernardino. The Flakes' "maid," Liz, however, did not go with them. According to one account, Agnes Flake while on her deathbed granted Liz freedom.[16]

When William returned to Utah to fight U.S. troops, he brought no slaves, but he did bring a heritage that included Southern ideas about race. Like many slaveholders, William believed that his family's slaves had loved their masters. Family tradition tells us, for example, that Liz said she "would have died before I would have let [Agnes Flake] work," adding that her mistress had "never as much as washed a pocket handkerchief." When Agnes died, Liz is said to have cried out with grief. When asked by a neighbor whether she wasn't glad that she would no longer be beaten, Liz tried to drive the neighbor out of the house. "She never hit me when I didn't deserve it," cried Liz; her mistress had been the "best woman whatever lived."[17]

Green, too, was said to have been heroically devoted to his master. "Like the old slaves," wrote William Flake's son in telling the story of Green going ahead of the family to prepare for their arrival in Utah, he "carried out his instructions." For all his loyalty, Green remained two-dimensional to the Flakes. During the journey to Utah, for example, a coyote supposedly entered the camp at night and made straight for Green. While others slept, Green jumped out of his pallet, yelling, "You rascal would you bit a Nigger?"[18] How the Flakes knew this story—given that they were not with Green during most of the journey—is unclear. Nonetheless it reveals much about the Flakes' concept of race: slaves were child-like, comical figures. They could be devoted to their masters; they could be diligent and even noble in servitude; yet they were a people without honor. An antidote to shame was the dignity of pioneering, but even that polish never rubbed the blackness from their skins.

It should come as no surprise that James Madison and Agnes Flake, along with their children, imbibed the honor culture of the Old South, a culture premised on the idea of white honor and black shame. What is more interesting is that they entered a religious culture tied so closely with honor's contrary: conscience. Mormons participated in a religious movement—really a trajectory—that had begun centuries earlier. Mormons—even more than their Puritan forebears—decried drinking, gambling, and individual combat, behaviors that defined the honor culture of Southern men. Mormons were not the first to challenge those behaviors. Baptists, Methodists, and Quakers had already pushed Southerners in new directions, undermining and altering old concepts of honor. Mormons, however, made conscience more central than did other Protestants. Joseph Smith, at the direction of the Lord, or so he claimed, consecrated his people to the "Word of Wisdom," meaning abstinence from liquor, tea, coffee, and tobacco. Only by living a "clean" life could one achieve the godhood that was the purpose of existence. As Austin Fife observed, Mormonism partook strongly of the currents of nineteenth-century self-improvement. To be a Mormon was to engage in a process of learning, of acquiring perfection, until one achieved godhood.[19] Mormons were paragons of behavioral conscience.

The idea that one could become as God bespoke a perfectionism that no Baptist or Methodist would admit. Baptists and Methodists repented sins, strove to live as Christ, attended church regularly, and avoided profanity and drink. Wesleyan Methodists even broached their own concept of Christian perfection, though it meant little more than the idea that faith could steer one from sin. For most mainstream evangelicals, sin was the human condition. The idea of achieving godhood struck them as heresy.

The evangelical background of the Flakes thus prepared them for Mormonism but by no means made conversion easy. Nor did the honor culture of the South pave the way. Throughout the nineteenth century and into the twentieth, Mormon missionaries met bitterness in the South, where they were sometimes hounded, tarred and feathered, even murdered. The Flakes' own son Charles was tarred while on his mission in Mississippi in 1883.[20] Mormons met with the peculiar rituals of shaming inflicted on those who did not conform.

Persecution, however, strengthened the Saints' antipathy to honor. Not only did they reject gambling, drinking, fighting, and dueling; they also worked together to glorify the church rather than working individually to glorify themselves or their families. Whereas Southern honor measured the status of individuals and families, Mormon conscience measured one's devotion to a cause.

In 1857, when William Flake met Lucy White, he was not strictly Southern or Mormon or Western; he was all those things. He was also a happy man, destined to be wed. What never appears in the Flake manuscripts, however, is another event in 1857 that surely made him profoundly unhappy, an event so grim that it became unspeakable. In that year a wagon train with some 150 emigrants from Arkansas passed through Utah en route to California. It was called the Fancher-Baker train, named for the families who organized it and who comprised most of its members.

As the Fancher-Baker train wound its way to Salt Lake, Mormons were preparing for war. By September 1857, a sizeable force—one-third of the U.S. Army—had crossed South Pass in Wyoming en route to Utah to install a governor appointed by Congress. To forestall his overthrow, Brigham Young sent his militia—the Nauvoo Legion—to guard the passes through the Wasatch Range that led to the Salt Lake Valley. Should the troops draw closer, warned Young, buzzards would pick their bones.[21]

No war occurred, though Mormons burned the army's supply trains and took a few prisoners. Failing to find a way around Utah's defenses in fall 1857, the soldiers were forced to wait until spring to try again. By then, President Buchanan had communicated to Brigham Young that he wished to avoid bloodshed. The troops entered Salt Lake peacefully in 1858, installing the new governor and stationing themselves uneasily at Camp Floyd. Before the agreement that ended the conflict, meanwhile, Brigham Young had readied his people for evacuation, planning to burn Salt Lake behind him. Late in 1857, hundreds of Mormons had fled their homes to take refuge in the south.

Precisely when William Flake arrived in southern Utah is unclear. It is likely, however, that he was there in September when the Fancher-Baker train rolled through, making its way to Mountain Meadows. There, the emigrants had been told, they would find abundant grass for their cattle and horses.

Reports of grass proved accurate, but what the party could not foresee was a Mormon attack. For four days they held out, forcing the attackers at last to negotiate. The attackers—the local militia, many dressed to look like Indians, along with some Paiute allies—convinced the emigrants to lay down their weapons in return for safe escort to Cedar City. No quarter, however, was given. After surrendering, male and female emigrants were separated. As the men were marched away, their guards turned and slew them. Then the women were slain, many falling as they pled for their lives. Only children under age eight were saved. They, according to Mormon belief, were too young to have been marred by sin.[22]

Whether Flake was among the fifty to sixty Mormon men who carried out the massacre, we do not know.[23] It seems quite possible that he was, however, given that he was a soldier, and given that Mountain Meadows was only a few miles from Cedar City, where he was stationed when he met Lucy and where militia leaders had planned the attack.

Flake would have also been aware of—perhaps a participant in—the revival that had stirred his people to action. It began in 1856 in Kaysville, a northern settlement, with fiery calls for repentance. By 1857, some of the church's highest officers were rededicating themselves to live without sin. In the midst of the revival came talk of "blood atonement," the doctrine that some sinners had so offended God that only execution could earn them mercy.[24]

Blood atonement added its yeast to the brew of violence. The more proximate cause, however, was the threat of invasion and the rumor that members of the Fancher-Baker party had murdered Mormon apostle Parley Pratt in Arkansas earlier in the year. Other rumors spread, too. Some of the emigrants, claimed Mormons, bragged of having taken part in the Haun's Mill Massacre of 1838, when a Missouri militia had attacked the Saints. The emigrants, moreover, supposedly reviled Mormons they met on the trail, calling their women whores because they practiced polygamy. Deed followed word, averred Mormons, when emigrants poisoned a well and killed a cow. Some of the rumors may have been partly true. Others, it seems, sprang from anger. Bitter rumors found credulous ears.[25]

Even given the hysteria—and even given the doctrine of blood atonement—one wonders how a people of conscience could massacre innocents. Do the killings suggest that Mormons were as much part of an honor culture as those they repudiated? What, indeed, distinguishes the violence of honor from any other act of violence? These are difficult questions.

They are, however, amenable to answers. On the surface the answers suggest that the killings were acts of honor. To condemn the women as whores, it seems, a few of the killers made females strip and dance before executing them. Shaming—perhaps the most profound trait of cultures shaped by honor—comes readily to humans in times of war. Authorities did not intend the massacre, however, to be a ritual of shaming. The treachery of the killings resulted from the desire to conduct them efficiently. Having attacked the wagon train, Mormons reasoned that they could let none survive to tell the tale. If survivors did tell the tale, Mormons would suffer retribution. Gentiles, they believed, would return to kill their women and children. What began as a strike against sin, then, ended in massacre.[26]

We might describe the Mountain Meadows Massacre, finally, as the violence of conscience. It was meant as vengeance against the Lord's enemies, enemies who had murdered Joseph Smith and Parley Pratt. Violence confirmed allegiance to God. Mormons carried out the attack as a group of believers, acting on instructions from superiors. Unlike duelists or gunfighters or lynchers, theirs was not a personal violence, a violence intended to uphold the honor of an individual, a lineage, or a race. The violence that transpired in Arizona in the 1880s was a different affair.

Knowing whether the massacre was motivated by honor or conscience or by human depravity tells us nothing of how it affected the Flakes. Nor do family archives offer insight. Far from suggesting the anguish that must have followed the massacre, the family histories focus on the happiness of marriage. William and Lucy were poor, to be sure, but not desperate. Immediately after marrying, they moved to Beaver, just north of Cedar City, where William began farming and ranching. Lucy recalled that, when they moved into their new house, their possessions consisted of one skillet, two pewter bowls, two spoons (one whittled from wood), two knives, two forks, a silver ladle, and a mattress. William, however, was an able provider. Like other Mormons, he engaged in multiple sorts of work. He farmed, herded sheep, raised oxen, and, in 1861, he rode for the Pony Express. Lucy meanwhile followed the example of her forebears, shearing sheep, spinning wool, and making clothing for her offspring, who arrived with regularity over the next decade.[27]

William also retained his role in protecting Utah. Not only did he serve as bodyguard to Brigham Young when Young made trips to southern Utah, but he also served as a Minute Man, a member of a militia whose purpose was to ward off Indian attack and to deal with disruptive gentiles. For that purpose, William was expected to keep a gun and a horse at the ready. He likely found need for both during the Black Hawk War of 1865–67, when Utes, Paiutes, and Navajos raided Mormon settlements. According to family tradition, however, he armed himself merely with rocks, preferring them to bullets when subduing drunken miners and deserting soldiers.[28] Far from being a vigilante bent on blood atonement, he was a man of peace and gentleness. Judging from family accounts, he was a paragon of conscience.

William in his devoutness was indeed favored by God. On one occasion, he searched to the point of exhaustion for lost oxen. Just as he was on the verge of giving up, an old man, a stranger, told him to look over the hill. There William found his animals. Later he realized he had been visited by one of the Nephi prophets spoken of in the Book of Mormon. Yet tragedy struck, too. Lucy bore two boys who died in infancy. A third child, a girl, was horribly burned when, at age two, she fell into a cauldron of boiling soap. Other babies fared better. James, Lucy's firstborn, proved healthy, as did Charles, born in 1862, and Osmer, born in 1868. All three would play important roles in the family's Arizona ordeal two decades later.[29]

William's reputation for piety and business, meanwhile, led the couple to a new challenge: plural marriage. In 1868, church leaders counseled William to take a second wife. When he told Lucy, she burst into tears. Neither of them "spoke again," she recalled, "but I could tell by his tears that dropped on my bowed head that he was suffering." For days, a battle raged within her. "Never had my husband been so precious to me, our home so dear." She knew, however, that plural marriage was God's will. She had "seen the sick healed instantly, the deaf made to hear, the blind to see." If faith was that powerful, then surely the command to plural marriage must be obeyed.[30]

Like Lucy, many Mormons shied from polygamy. Some left the church over it. Gentiles, moreover, attacked Mormons repeatedly over polygamy. In return, Mormons argued that even those outside the church practiced polygamy of a sort, by which they meant prostitution and extramarital affairs. Mormon husbands, by contrast, did not "cast the woman out into the mire" after finding sexual gratification. In theory, they remained loyal to plural wives throughout their lives. Mormon polygamy, moreover, "fills our school houses and Church buildings," argued Apostle Erastus Snow. "There [is] no better 'stock' on earth," reasoned Lucy Flake as she struggled to accept polygamy, "than the people of my faith who believed and practiced abstinence from all vices. None who could bring forth sturdier or more intelligent offspring." Plural marriage, finally, gave godly women priestly powers. Once married, a woman could preside over child-births, offering anointments and blessings. Perhaps most important, she received admission into the highest realm of the afterlife. Only by being bound to a pious man could she achieve godhood. Some Mormons even argued that the women who had watched over Jesus' tomb were his plural wives.[31]

After long reflection and bouts of tears, Lucy consented to her husband's second marriage. One night, after the children were in bed, she invited him to accompany her on a stroll. Under the glow of the moon, she turned and asked, "Who are we going to marry?" Taken by surprise, he asked for reassurance that she was willing. She gave it. At last he described the eighteen-year-old girl he in-tended to take as his second wife. She was the "picture of health and vitality," a girl whom he had watched admiringly as she had grown to womanhood. She had dark hair, expressive eyes, and "delicately moulded features." She also had energy. She liked to dance, sing, and whistle. Her name was Prudence Kartchner.[32]

For the next eight years, William continued to freight, farm, ranch, and do his duty as a Minute Man. For months at a stretch, Lucy and Prudence—separated from William while he labored far away—raised their children in isolation. Yet they lived with the assurance that they had a faithful and industrious husband. Even in plural marriage, life was rich. Then, in 1876, William came to Lucy with tears in his eyes. "Lucy," he told her, "we must leave this beautiful home forever." The family had been called on a "mission" to settle Arizona. They would be re-quired to sell everything in order to provision themselves for the trip.[33]

"Arizona!" thought Lucy, "the very name made me shudder." The word called to mind fierce Apaches and arid desolation. Again she found comfort in faith. "We believed in the Bible," she recalled, "where it said that in the last days would the Lord raise up a Prophet to guide his people." That prophet was Joseph Smith. When he was killed, she had seen a new prophet rise up. Christ was coming. If the church needed her and her family to "build up waste places" in preparation for the millennium, "we would go, even to the last Frontier."[34]

William Flake was no stranger to Arizona. He had traveled there in 1873 after being tapped by the church to explore the territory. The church, indeed, had spent decades collecting information on northern Arizona. By exploring and colonizing the territory to the south of Utah, Brigham Young sought to fulfill Joseph Smith's prophecy that Zion would extend to the whole of the Americas. His more immediate concerns, however, were making room for a growing population and opening a corridor to Mexico, much as he had opened a corridor to the Pacific in earlier years.[35]

Though Flake's exploration party had found deep snow and little grass, church leaders continued to plan for settlement. More explorers penetrated Arizona in 1876, finding several sites for colonization in the valley of the Little Colorado. Optimistic that colonization would succeed, the church drafted recruits for the "Arizona mission," asking each to be rebaptized in order to wash away old sins before embarking. For six months the Flakes prepared for the move. The women produced quantities of cheese, butter, dried fruits and vegetables, and new clothes, though Lucy was slowed by pregnancy. She bore her tenth child, a daughter, on August 19, 1877, ten days before Brigham Young died. The Kartchner family, too—Prudence's people—assisted. They, with five hired men, joined the Flakes for the brutal three-month journey.[36]

The expedition began in fall, after the crops had been harvested and the property sold. The fall departure made sense for a number of reasons. Grass and fodder could still be found along the trail. The waters of the Colorado River, moreover, would be lower than in spring, when snowmelt raised its banks, or in summer, when violent thunderstorms flooded its tributaries. Most important, a fall departure allowed colonists to arrive in time to clear fields and plant crops.[37]

On the trail, the women took turns cooking, washing dishes, watching the young, and serving meals. To keep warm, the emigrants placed skillets heaped with hot coals inside the wagons. Those who drove rested their feet on hot rocks wrapped in old sacks. The men even poured pepper into their boots hoping to stave off the cold.[38]

The path south from Beaver was the easiest part of the journey. After crossing into the Arizona Strip, however—the section of Arizona north of the Grand Canyon—the party found itself following roads that "were only blazed trails." The men went ahead to prepare the way with pick and shovel. On one occasion, they came upon the motionless wagon of another emigrant family. Beside it, a man paced fitfully back and forth. Inside a young mother cried inconsolably. Her child, a year old, had died. Lucy washed the baby and prepared it for burial, placing it in a small wooden box. Now Lucy's daughters, too, became ill with diphtheria, the disease that had killed the baby.[39]

Further on, the Flakes found another wagon sitting motionless. This one was occupied by a lone man who had been abandoned by his party after a quarrel. He had no animals with which to pull the wagon; they had been taken by the others. The Flake party gave him aid and moved on.[40]

Soon the party entered House Rock Valley, a broad swath of desert rimmed by forbidding cliffs of vermilion and containing a spring.[41] After watering the horses, the adventurers continued to Marble Canyon—the upper reach of the Grand Canyon—where they met new travails. At the bottom of the canyon, at Lee's Ferry, the party made its crossing of the Colorado River, following the path that Flake had taken in 1873. Until a few months earlier, John D. Lee had manned the ferry. Excommunicated yet loyal to his faith, he had lived in utter poverty in the shadowy chasm. In March 1877 a firing squad executed him for his role in the Mountain Meadows Massacre.

It was Lee's large flatboat that carried across teams and wagons. For the Flake party, the ferrying went smoothly. For others, it did not. Crossing the river sounded straightforward but could be complicated by weather. At times the river became so high, or so clogged with driftwood or even ice, that emigrants were forced to wait days to cross. If they lacked feed for their animals, they might be forced to unload the wagons, dismantle them, and float everything piecemeal across the river. The process could be so slow that draft animals were required to swim, causing some to drown.[42]

Equally daunting was the climb on the other side. The only way to move wagons up the canyon was via Lee's Backbone, a diagonal bench that juts from the canyon's south wall. The backbone extends toward the river (parallel to it) like an enormous ramp of solid rock. Here the party used multiple teams to haul up one wagon at a time. While the women and children walked ahead—it was too dangerous to walk behind, and the path was too narrow to walk alongside— the teams would strain for a short distance, then be brought to rest. As the animals panted the men deftly chocked the wagon wheels to prevent any backward motion. "The same process," wrote Evans Coleman, recalling his family's trip up the backbone, "had to be repeated again with more or less excitement, exasperation and discouragement, until camp was made for the night."[43]

Arriving at the summit did not mean that the work was over. The teams had to be sent back down to fetch water. After camp had been set up, the women went to work preparing a meal. By the time it was ready, the wind began to blow, causing wagon covers and tarps to swish and flap. Cattle lowed and horses pawed at the ground while coyotes yipped and howled. The men arranged bedrolls on the ground while women and children slept in the wagons. The best word that Evans Coleman could find to describe the scene was "desolation."[44]

The next day came the trip down the far side of the backbone. From its apex, it sloped southward toward desert mountains. Here, the men chained ponderosa logs to the wagons to serve as anchors. If gravity became too great during descent, the wagons might roll into the animals that pulled them, even with the brakes engaged. The use of logs to create drag, however, enabled the men to control their forward motion.[45]

As they moved steadily south, each wagon traveled far apart to avoid competing for scarce water and feed. On a good day, the emigrants made twenty miles. In the evenings, they sang to keep up their spirits. After a mid-December storm so fierce that the animals refused to go farther, the travelers broke into a familiar refrain:

> Come, come ye saints
> No toil nor labor fear,
> But with joy, wend your way,
> Though hard to you this journey may appear
> Grace shall be as your day,
> Gird up your loins
> Fresh courage take,
> Our God will never us forsake,
> And soon we'll have this tale to tell,
> All is Well![46]

All was not well, however. When the party reached the Little Colorado, they found ice eight inches thick. Even where it was not frozen, the water was so saturated with alkali that it made the horses sick.[47]

At a place called Black Falls the party found another emigrant couple with a dead child. The young couple was forced to set out again for the nearest settlement, eight days away, carrying a tiny, frozen corpse in their baggage. Though Lucy's sick daughters were recovering, the cattle were too thin to continue. The Flakes' fifteen-year-old son Charles was left to care for the animals while the others went ahead.[48]

In January Lucy gave out. Exhausted, she hung close to death. At last, on January 15, 1878, the party arrived at Ballinger's Camp, a beachhead about two-and-a-half miles from modern Winslow. Lucy might have agreed with Evans Coleman, who would make the same journey two years later. "When Job scans the pages of Mormon pioneer history," he commented, "he'll wish he hadn't given that little individual boil episode of his so much publicity."[49]

What Coleman might have added was that the ordeal of emigration became another glue that bound the faithful. Few American emigrants experienced an overland trail with so many hazards and so much hardship. The way across the Colorado Plateau—including passage across the Grand Canyon—was among

the most harrowing routes of the nineteenth century. It gave the Arizona colo-
nists the sense of being special, the sense of being soldiers to the cause of faith.
The solidarity that came with the common trials and communal success of the
Arizona mission added to the solidarity that came with the earlier migration to
Utah. Pioneering in some sense gave all Westerners, perhaps all Americans, a
sense of solidarity, but it created even more powerful bonds among the Saints.
More hardships, however, awaited.

The initial wave of colonists to the Little Colorado River basin consisted of
four groups, each with fifty people, whose objective was to spread out and found
towns. Obed, Sunset, Brigham City, and St. Joseph were the first. As Lucy recovered, William Flake, with W. D. Kartchner and his sons, moved up the Little
Colorado some twenty miles where they located another new town called Taylor,
named for a Mormon apostle.[50]

The Little Colorado River Valley comprises what one Mormon historian describes as a "huge bowl" with a diameter of some two hundred miles. The lowest
point in the bowl lies 5,000 feet above sea level; its perimeter rises to 7,000 feet.
To the east, just across the line in New Mexico, is the Continental Divide, which
separates waters that flow into the Gulf of Mexico from those that flow into the
Gulf of California. At the southern perimeter of the bowl rise the gentle, rounded
cinder cones of the White Mountains. From a distance, they look like mere hills,
yet they rise to 11,590 feet. Within their forested peaks, it was said, lived the *gaan*,
the mountain spirits of Apache lore. At the western edge of the valley stands a
more compact, more precipitous range, the San Francisco Peaks, dominated by
12,670-foot Mt. Humphreys, home to the spirit beings of Hopis and Navajos.
Along the southwestern fringe of the bowl stretches the Mogollon Rim, with
its great cliffs, jumbled rocks, and gnarled canyons. Roughly speaking, two vol-
canic fields—those of the White Mountains and the San Francisco Peaks—
comprise bookends for the Rim. Waters flowing southward enter the Salt River,
which winds west and south through Tonto Basin toward the Salt River Valley
(modern Phoenix) before joining the Gila. Waters flowing northward enter the
Little Colorado, which flows north and west toward its junction with its mighty
namesake. It was here that Mormon settlers would build their home.[51]

It proved to be an inauspicious setting. True, Indians were few. Most of the
Western Apaches lived to the south, in the White Mountain country and below
the Rim. The Navajos, meanwhile, kept to the north and east, nearer the Rio
Puerco and San Juan rivers. One settler insisted that the Navajos and the Apaches
recognized the Little Colorado as the boundary between them.[52] There may or

may not have been such an understanding, but in point of fact, the region was something of a no-man's-land.

Whatever its advantages, the valley was a "hard looking country," as one pioneer put it. Strong winds blew with more or less consistency, bringing great clouds of sand, cracking settlers' lips and hurling dirt into their faces. "The spring winds," recalled Lucy Flake, "filled the air with that fine sand until one couldn't see two rods away," all the while causing wagon covers to "flop and pop." "We were nearly buried in sand every morning after a night of hard wind," she added.[53]

The watershed, moreover, was fickle. The Little Colorado ran feebly in summer but swelled after downpours in the mountains. Time and again, floods washed away dams and ditches. Even when streams permitted irrigation, the water was sometimes so full of sediment that it choked the crops. One pioneer reported filling a seven-gallon kettle with water from the Little Colorado. After allowing the sediment to settle for a day, he found an inch of water at the top.[54]

After the agonies of the journey, settlers found more agonies. Profoundly demoralized, they whispered bitter complaints. Fully three-quarters of the first settlers in Allen's Camp (later St. Joseph) left Arizona before 1876 had ended. Some called the exodus a "stampede." Others simply turned around and went home after gauging the situation.[55]

Before he died in 1877, Brigham Young thundered an answer to his summer soldiers. "Those whose mouths are full of murmuring and whose hearts incline to apostasy . . . should not remain lest they poison the camps with their ill feelings." After that, remarked one colonist, nary a complaint was heard. Far from finding fault with their situation, settlers embraced it. Faith and piety would ameliorate what was worst in the new country. "The waters of the Little Colorado River," insisted John Young, "are wholesome [and] if we would keep the Word of Wisdom they would be palatable to us."[56]

The Saints told themselves over and over that the Lord had appointed his people to inhabit mountains and wastes. There they would grow strong. "Like the eagle that selects the highest tree in which to build her nest," Apostle Erastus Snow told Arizona settlers, "so have the Saints come to the highest mountains in which to make their homes."[57] Within that refuge, the Saints would build conscience.

In 1877, the settlers of Obed, Taylor, Sunset, Brigham City, and Woodruff sought to accomplish that goal by entering the United Order of Enoch. The United Order represented an attempt to reestablish Zion, the ancient community of the faithful gathered by Enoch of the Old Testament. Taking cues from Mormon sacred texts that describe Enoch's life and deeds, United Order members worked together, ate together, prayed together, dressed and lived simply, and avoided vanity and contention. There would be no dishonesty, no deception, no profit-seeking, no poor. Members gave their property to the collective. If they refused, they could partake in neither the redemption of Zion nor the glory of the hereafter. "If ever we get into the Celestial Kingdom," averred Apostle Wilford Woodruff in 1880, "we will find the United Order stricter there than we ever lived it here."[58]

The United Order of Enoch was not a new undertaking. At Brigham Young's direction, Utah Mormons had established more than a hundred United Order "companies" in the early 1870s. Many colonists had enrolled before leaving Utah. Church leaders envisioned the order, indeed, as the future of Deseret. Yet the order revealed as much pessimism as hope. As economic development and individualism undermined communitarian spirit, leaders groped for the past. The more prosperous they became, the less willing were rank-and-file Mormons to restrict themselves to barter relations and communal equality.[59] The result, feared church leaders, would be greed, self-infatuation, and the death of corporatism. Satan would wound the church from within.

In Arizona, the United Order received the powerful—too powerful—leadership of Lot Smith, hero of the 1857 Utah War and leonine president of the administrative unit known as the Little Colorado Stake of Zion. Smith committed himself absolutely to the order's success. "Unless we [have] a desire for the whole people's rights," he maintained, "the Lord [will] be displeased. . . . We should love our neighbors as ourselves." Offering himself as a model, Smith presided over each evening meal at Sunset, seating his family at one end of a table that accommodated several dozen diners.[60]

Disputes broke out nonetheless. Those who worked hard to sustain the enterprise accused others of laziness. Those who had artisanal skills resented the socialistic system of pay that rewarded everyone equally. Quarrels also erupted over polygamy. When a Sunset man was counseled to take a second wife, his first wife threatened to fire the village's grain. Smith had her bound and sent back to Utah. The greatest frustration, however, was nature. Year after painful year, dams of brush, rocks, and clay washed out and had to be rebuilt. The settlement of St. Joseph suffered worst. It averaged a dam per year until 1894, when residents at last built a structure that held. During several years, there simply was no harvest.[61]

To guard against Indian attack, meanwhile, settlers built forts of timber and stone. For living quarters, they turned over their wagon boxes and lived underneath them until they could construct dugouts, cabins, and brush houses. The houses were no great improvement. Often they consisted of a single room into which an entire family would squeeze. When rains rotted the timbers that supported dirt ceilings, the ceilings caved in. More permanent log homes might consist of a front room and two tiny bedrooms, separated by a cloth partition. A crude rock chimney drew smoke from the hearth, which was used for both heating and cooking. On the floor, settlers lay carpets stitched from rags that had been cut into strips, then braided or woven on a loom. Furniture was fashioned from wooden crates. The walls received whitewash concocted from chalk dug in the mountains. For decoration, settlers pinned up illustrations from stray magazines. A single bucket served for washing. Sanitation, according to Evans Coleman, was not so much lacking as absent.[62]

Communal spirit lightened the poverty. Despite occasional bickering, women worked together in quilting, wool carding, crop picking, and "rag bees," in which they sewed rags into carpet and clothing. During such times, recalled Lucy Flake, they would "talk about the absent ones, cooking recipes, and remedies." For their part, men would go hunting together, with varying success. Game — particularly mule deer and pronghorn — was plentiful. Mormons, however, had little money to spend on ammunition, requiring them to cast their own bullets. Amid the work of building settlements, moreover, time for hunting was scarce. Some families found themselves able to subsist on wild turkey in the fall, though they might be reduced to eating a single beef during the rest of the year.[63]

From the outset the Flakes were unhappy. The snow was heavy; the river flooded; crops failed; food was scant. Worse, they found their fellows at Sunset to be "queer unsociable folks." Despite her devotion to the mission, Lucy despised her new life. The last straw came when William traded a cow from the communal herd to an impoverished emigrant family. The "board" that oversaw the herd complained that he had acted without its consent. He replied that the trade was an act of charity. When the board refused to vindicate him, he searched for another place to settle.[64]

Flake had another reason for leaving. In 1876, thirty-eight families — converts from Georgia, Alabama, and Arkansas — headed west with a missionary. They were desperately poor; they came with only a few oxen and light wagons. For thirteen months they plodded toward Zion. When they reached New Mexico, they were beset with smallpox, causing several deaths. They straggled on to the Little Colorado settlements, where they took refuge. Lucy recalled that the Flakes "divided everything we had with them, even cut up our wagon covers and seamless sacks to make them clothing." Like the Flakes, however, the converts chafed "under the restraint, the new conditions, new ways." "Bound down with restrictions," they looked to William Flake for leadership. He would deliver them from their ordeal.[65]

In July 1878, as Flake and a brother-in-law, A. Z. Palmer, scoured the country-side for a site for a new colony, they came to a small valley that stretched eight miles alongside Silver Creek, a perennial stream that flows north from the Rim. Later that month, Flake brought his family to see the place, driving them to the brow of a hill overlooking the valley. Lucy was speechless. "As far as the eyes could see," she recalled, "the rolling hills were covered with waving grass. One large house and a line of small adobes nestled in a little brown patch among tussled corn and ripening barley in the center of the valley below. A few cotton-wood trees and willows fringed the banks of the silvery stream that gave it its name." "If Heaven is any better than this," she declared, "I am glad I saw this first, so as to kinda get used to such beauty."[66]

Away from the riparian environment of the creek, the land consisted of rolling hills dotted with juniper, piñon, and oak, with occasional outcroppings of white or red sandstone. At six thousand feet, the place received substantial snowfall, but the weather was no worse than at Sunset. Altogether, the valley held two thousand irrigable acres. Just as important, it was situated only eighteen miles from the Rim's heavy stands of pine. Here, too, however, sandstorms erupted with fury.[67]

The man who owned the valley, James Stinson—who would soon be em-broiled in the Pleasant Valley conflict—wanted twelve thousand dollars for the sale. Flake turned him down, discouraged by the price and by the fear of leaving Sunset. When he asked Lucy for her advice, she gave a determined answer: "Go buy the place, I will do his washing, sewing, anything to help pay the bill, but I can't stay here."[68]

The departure was painful. Those in the United Order of Enoch "turned the cold shoulder" on the Flakes, claiming that the death of their infant, George, was God's judgment. Sunset's leaders called Flake an apostate. Then came a dream in which Brigham Young, dead for a year, appeared to Flake with his hand in his pocket. "How much money do you want?" he asked Flake.[69]

Flake took heart. On his way to Utah to sell a load of wool, he met with Apostle Snow. Recounting his dream, Flake explained that he had told Brigham Young that he wanted no money; he sought only blessings. Snow regarded the dream as a revelation. "That was all the council you need," he replied.[70]

After Flake returned from Utah in September, he and Snow traveled to Stin-son's ranch to close the deal. Stinson agreed to sell possessory rights for eleven thousand dollars, if Flake would agree to harvest his crops. Though Flake lacked capital, Stinson agreed to take five hundred dollars down and three yearly pay-ments of 150 good, sturdy Utah cattle. The deal also required Flake to give Stinson his best saddle mule as token collateral. Three years later, Stinson lived

Monument depicting Snowflake's founders. William Flake talks with Apostle Erastus
Snow. Lucy Flake, with infant, stands next to her husband. Future stake president Jesse
Smith looks on, while behind him appears Ira Hinckley. Photograph by author.

up to the contract, grudgingly returning the mule. Flake promptly gave it back,
telling Stinson that he was "one of the squarest men I ever met."[71]

The Mormons, indeed, could thank Stinson not only for the success of Snowflake but also for their first taste of political power. When the legislature created Apache County in 1879, Stinson, who had the ear of his fellow Republican,
Governor John C. Frémont, got Snowflake designated as the county seat. He
also convinced Frémont to appoint Mormons to county office. Flake became
a county supervisor. Nat Greer, a Mormon from Texas who would soon enter
combat with New Mexican sheepherders, became county treasurer. Other Mormons were appointed justice of the peace and county recorder.[72]

After Flake had finalized the deal, Snow chose the site for a town, calling it
"Snowflake" as a tribute to himself and to Flake. He also created a new ward, or
congregation, with John Hunt, a friend of Flake, as bishop. Flake and his in-law
John Kartchner would be Hunt's "counselors."[73]

Having made the down payment, the Flakes took control of Stinson's adobe
ranch house, with its granary, tack room, machine room, horse stable, and bunk-

house. At Flake's request, Stinson replaced his half-dozen Mexican workers with impoverished converts from Sunset, paying them a dollar an acre to pick crops. He also replaced his Mexican common-law wife with a Mormon woman, Melissa Bagley, a mother of three who had left a polygamous marriage. Stinson kept only his "personal servant," Epitacio Ruiz, who would soon be involved in the fighting in Pleasant Valley.[74]

Work on building the town now commenced. Flake called in a surveyor to plat a site that conformed to the layout of Salt Lake City, with its emphasis on millennial harmony and order. Snowflake, like the mother city of Deseret, would be a city of God. The surveyor laid off twenty blocks of four lots each, with each lot comprising twelve square rods. Streets ran north-south and east-west on a precise grid. Each male head of household received one city lot in exchange for thirty dollars, or two lots for sixty dollars if he had two wives. For an additional sixty dollars, the men received twenty acres of "second class" land for farming or pasture. If a man had no money, he could pay in labor.[75]

There would be no United Order in Snowflake, but neither was the town a product of individualism. From the outset, Flake instituted the "Mormon village system," which meant that individuals owned animals privately but appointed community herders to graze them. Snowflake's residents also continued to isolate themselves. "There is less gentile element and influence" in Snowflake, noted a Mormon settler in 1884, "than in any other [town] in the Stake." Adding to Snowflake's corporatist thrust was the spirit of cooperation. Men worked together to build homes, hauling logs from the Rim and hefting stones from Indian ruins. The center of the town served as a public square.[76]

To feed themselves, the men ate Stinson's corn and scoured the hills for wild longhorns, remnants of herds brought by Spaniards. Meanwhile new settlements sprang up, many of them on land purchased by Flake. "He bought ranches; he made them towns," Flake's obituary would read. The Stinson purchase alone made room for Snowflake, Shumway, and Taylor (the second Taylor; the first was abandoned). In subsequent years, Flake would buy, or help buy, lands farther afield that permitted Mormon settlement at Concho, Eagar, Nutrioso, and Showlow. In the same year that Snowflake was settled, another group of Saints, fifteen families strong, settled a few miles north at a place they called Woodruff (this, too, was the second such town, the first having been abandoned). South of Snowflake, close to the Fort Apache Reservation or even on it, appeared Linden, Pinedale, and Forestdale. To the west, along Chevelon Creek appeared the outposts of Wilford and Heber, prime sites for growing potatoes. Farther west along the Rim, near the nascent gentile community of Green Valley (soon to be called

Payson), a hardy few settled at a place called Pine. To the south, below the Rim, finally, Mormons occupied a hamlet on the East Verde River.[77]

In all those settlements together, some two thousand souls eked out a livelihood in the early 1880s. While Flake's communities prospered, meanwhile, the United Order of Enoch deteriorated. The last settler abandoned Sunset in 1885, causing the church to divide United Order holdings among individual families.[78]

Though the United Order fell victim to discord, Mormon isolation did not. Mormons still sought to become "independent of Babylon." As Jesse Smith, president of the Eastern Arizona Stake, asserted during a quarterly conference, Mormons were "pioneers in the moral world as much as in the settling of the country." The Saints, he insisted, must never "encourage the wicked to dwell with you. . . . Learn to discern the difference between the sheep and the goats. . . . Be careful about those who never did belong to the Church."[79]

Repeatedly, church leaders exhorted the flock to avoid contamination. They were told to avoid business contacts with non-Mormons and to forbid their sons and daughters from socializing with them. "If a sister marries an outsider," said Smith, "she brings sorrow upon herself and her family and deprives herself of husband and children for eternity." Nor would Smith "consent to have our daughters led away [to work for] the wicked." Even too much friendliness toward gentiles posed problems. "It is not safe to have wicked men in your houses," warned Smith, "even though you may be there to preside."[80]

When Mormons sold their land, they were to sell only to fellow members. When they had disputes, they were expected to seek arbitration by a bishop or a ward teacher or, in serious cases, an ecclesiastical court. Elders (members of the Melchizedek priesthood) and bishops, meanwhile, were "watchmen to keep off the wolves." They were asked to make sure that "unclean" people gained no foothold in the lives of members.[81]

The departure of Flake and others from the United Order represented a compromise with individualism but not a surrender. Mormons remained a people of conscience. They continued to repudiate sin in all its manifestations. They also repudiated physical confrontation. They carried no guns. Nor did they seek gain in transactions with fellow Mormons. Barter and fair trade remained watchwords. Even the "apostate" Flake eschewed profit. He bought land not to assure the success of his sons but to advance the frontiers of his church.

Like the Puritans before them, Mormon settlers sought to create well-ordered towns and cooperative commonwealths. They did not entirely repudiate capitalism; they sought profit in dealings with outsiders. Among themselves, however, they followed the dictates of Christian love, paid tithings, and engaged in

ACMI canceled check from 1898. Author's collection.

corporatism. They geared their small farms more to subsistence than profit. Even as they rejected the United Order, moreover, they formed the Arizona Cooperative Mercantile Institution (ACMI), whose purpose was to offer cheap goods—especially seed and farm equipment—to settlers. Though its capital came from prosperous individuals who were entitled to collect dividends and withdraw funds, the operation was communitarian and socialistic. "The kingdom," insisted Jesse Smith, "cannot be built upon the credit system."[82]

In other ways, too, Mormons promoted corporatism. Each ward sent "teachers" once a month to visit members and ensure that they were praying regularly, keeping the Word of Wisdom, paying tithing, and harboring no ill feelings toward Mormon neighbors. To read any Mormon diary of the era, moreover, is to see the perpetual renewal of community. Settlers continuously visited one another, bartering, sharing labor, ministering to the sick, and socializing. Time-keeping itself reminded settlers of their corporate identity. Members of at least one community set their watches by the steady ring of the church bell at 9:30 each Sunday morning.[83]

Yet another glue that bound the faithful was the Mormon "re-enchantment" of the world at a time when both scientists and theologians were rendering it inert. Most Christians believed that God had acted through prophecies, revelations, and visitations only in ancient times. Mormons thought otherwise. Among early Utah settlers, stories about visitations from Nephite prophets—powerful figures from the Book of Mormon—abounded; William Flake himself had received such a visit. Visitations were more likely to come, however, from deceased ancestors or church leaders who brought "messages or consolation or testimonies to the necessity for the execution of various temple rites." Failing visitation from spirits, earnest prayer could work miracles. It could bring rain, end hunger, deter death. Prayer itself did not cause miracles, to be sure, but it triggered God's action.[84] Belief in prayer's efficacy bound Mormons as a community.

Miracles wrought by prayer came particularly in sickness. Those who gathered to pray over a sick person might find themselves blessed with the "gift of tongues." They might also heal by anointing the sick with consecrated oil followed by the laying on of hands.[85] When in 1885 a Wilford couple, the Whitings, became desperately ill, the brethren came to their side but departed without working a cure. Then, as John Bushman recorded in his diary, Charles Whiting

asked his wife to pray & she prayed & he prayed & they prayed, sang & he prayed again with great power then they sang God Moves & c. . . . We Thank Thee O God & c., when they heard Heavenly Voices until their voices were drowned, & a most glorious light appeared in the room & Bro. Whitings face shone, also Sister Amys face burned. She did not look up. They both testify that the most glorious feeling they experienced after this glorious experience. Bro. Whiting dressed & him & his wife came to meeting . . . to the joy of all present. Bro. Whiting testified to the truth of the Gospel & that he had been healed by the prayer of faith.[86]

If prayers failed, there were folk remedies. When Alson Hamblin became sick, someone "caught a frog, split it open alive, and applied it to the throat as a poultice." Poultices came in numerous forms: "the bread and milk poultice, carrot poultice, sugar and fat bacon poultice, manure poltice, stick gum poultice," and others. Nor were poultices the only folk cures available. When one stepped on a nail or received a cut, the solution was to "get the offending missile, grease it, wrap it up and keep it warm," which was thought to prevent infection. For cramps, the antidote was to "turn a shoe upside down under the bed, even in the cramps of childbirth." To relieve pain following childbirth, the mother swallowed "a few drops of blood from the infant's cord" or placed the afterbirth "under the bed," or she might "plant potatoes in the dark of the moon."[87]

Even ward teachers—those charged with teaching the faith to the young— were "not . . . far removed from superstitions, witches and ghosts," recalled Evans Coleman. Mormons, indeed, differed little from their seventeenth-century New England ancestors, who likewise engaged in occult practices, believed in witches and ghosts, and practiced the occasional exorcism. Like New England colonists, Mormons saw God's hand in their fates, as when gulls came en masse to devour teeming crickets in 1848, or when clouds concealed missionaries who were forced to pass near U.S. troops while on the way home to Utah in 1857.[88]

None of this is meant to portray Mormons as backwards. In their emphasis on folk wisdom, Mormons differed little from the Texans and New Mexicans whom they met in Arizona. Miracles, however—tongues, visitations, answers to prayers—gave Mormons a sense of themselves as a chosen people. Miracles were not individual triumphs; they were religious and community triumphs. They taught individuals to see themselves in relation to the group. Miracles, moreover, reinforced conscience. Miracles came through right living, through the Word of Wisdom, through Christian brotherhood, and through faith.

For William Flake, meanwhile, the task at hand was to bring income to his impoverished community. Almost all Mormon settlers were poor, but Flake's group was particularly so. There was but one span of horses among the first four families who settled at Snowflake. None of them brought food, and only one could boast of owning a change of clothes. As late as 1880, the Snowflake settlement and others in its vicinity verged on starvation.[89]

To create a viable economy, Flake contracted with the U.S. Army to freight supplies to Fort Apache. With several partners he also bought a sawmill and moved it to the Rim Country, thus putting to work some of his Southern men in cutting trees, hauling logs, and splitting shingles. He also managed to find eight thousand dollars to buy a sheep herd, which he ran on shares with other Mormons. Whenever Flake or his sons caught maverick cattle or wild horses, meanwhile, they paid the value of the animal into a public fund. That fund helped pay for a school and a teacher.[90]

Though Flake was no farmer—he favored stock raising—others dug irrigation ditches and planted fruit trees and crops, including corn, sorghum, potatoes, cane, wheat, barley, oats, and melons. Despite Flake's preference for herding, Mormons were people of the plow. Ranching and herding—as opposed to raising a few cattle and sheep to produce milk, butter, cheese, and meat—remained suspect occupations. Ranching and herding were the enterprises of New Mexicans and Texas cowboys. Far preferable to working for such men—or employing them—was to engage in farming near to home.[91]

The agricultural tenor of Mormon life was manifest in threshing time, the biggest social occasion of the year. In Snowflake, men from throughout the region gathered in August and remained for several days, visiting friends and relatives and accepting hospitality. Though married women dreaded spending days at the hearth, they looked forward to showing off their culinary skill and clean homes. By keeping the house dark until evening, women sought to avoid attracting swarms of flies, yet they were forced to wield newspapers as the men ate. "If someone got switched across the face," recalled Lucy Flake, "it furnished a laugh." Unmarried women used the occasion to evaluate potential mates.[92]

During the day, the men maneuvered teams of horses that pulled threshers in big circles, sometimes betting a pound of candy or peanuts on how much grain they would have at the end of the day. The occasion was celebratory. The driver cracked his whip and yelled "hup-hup-hup," while children ran gleefully behind. "Huskin' bees" also became festive occasions. Villagers competed to see who could shuck fastest. The winner might get to trade every tenth ear that he'd shucked for a bit of candy or a pair of shoes.[93]

Other festive occasions included the Fourth of July and Pioneer Day on July 24, which commemorated the 1847 arrival of settlers in Salt Lake Valley. On Pioneer Day, settlers reenacted the migration to Utah. Bands played, men made speeches, couples danced. Similar doings marked the Fourth of July. Mormons followed the lead of Joseph Smith in patriotic celebration. "The Book of Mormon," explained Jesse Smith, "tells us that this is a land worth gathering to, choice above all other lands, a land of liberty kept and preserved for a wise purpose, where kings should not hold dominion." The Lord, added Apostle Erastus Snow, "has commanded us to uphold the constitution of the United States," and in particular the First Amendment guarantee of religious freedom. At times, George Washington and the signers of the Declaration of Independence were said to have visited the temples in Salt Lake City and St. George to "bear witness to the divinity of temple work on their behalf," and by implication to link Mormonism with the country's republican heritage.[94]

Caught up in the church's patriotism, Arizona Mormons celebrated the Fourth by playing fifes and beating drums, raising homemade flags, reading the Declaration of Independence, and giving patriotic orations. Celebrants also simulated cannon shots by igniting gunpowder sandwiched between anvils, causing babies to cry and girls to cover their ears. Wrestling, jumping, and rowing contests would follow, along with footraces, horse races, and dancing.[95]

Gentiles did not miss the irony in the Mormon celebration of the Fourth of July. At the same time that they testified to their patriotism, Mormon leaders damned Americans. One Arizonan recalled that church president Heber Kimball—for whom Heber, Arizona, was named—had in 1863 described the Civil War as fratricide in which the unjust struck down the unjust. The righteous few, said Kimball, had fled "to the Mountains to the Latter Day Saints for Safety." Apostle Snow made similar comments in 1884, finding that "peace has departed forever from this land" and that "most of the officers and men of [the Civil War] have abandoned themselves to the lowest acts and walks of life." Soldiers, he said, had become tramps, thieves, and murderers. "Those that were begotten during the war have this disposition born in them and they delight in blood."[96]

Snow did not realize that his own contempt, his own tendency to see sin in the world outside, spawned hostility. Far from escaping bloodshed and war, the Mormon emphasis on their own perfection—and the corresponding wickedness of gentiles—brought them into conflict. Mormon love for America counted for little in the face of Mormon contempt for Americans.

Apostle and future church president Wilford Woodruff added his voice to the Mormon chorus. He had read the history of the world, he told settlers, and he calculated that three years in four had "been occupied in war." Now another war was coming, a war in which "Zion will rise and Babylon will fall. . . . The Lord will sweep the wicked from the face of the earth. There is not a crime that could be named but what this nation is guilty of." By 1890, prophesied Woodruff, the U.S. would go just as the Jaredites of *The Book of Mormon* had gone: in civil war, in fire and blood.[97]

Mormon patriotism, then, was ambiguous. Mormons loved their country yet condemned its iniquity. If calamity was in the offing, however, Woodruff implied that Mormons would remain out of harm's way. Woodruff pointed to a passage in the Book of Mormon where God curses the Jaredites by hiding their property, thus making them suspicious of one another and leading them to an apocalyptic civil war. Those who practiced charity, by implication, would have no occasion to quarrel.[98]

What is interesting is not so much Woodruff's emphasis on God's punishment as the implication that Mormons would not be involved in meting it out. At Mountain Meadows, they had involved themselves profoundly in punishment, slaying "the wicked" with an Old Testament ruthlessness. By prophesying that the righteous would take refuge in the mountains, far from battle, however, Woodruff suggested a different tilt to Mormonism. Though the church did not formally repudiate the doctrine of blood atonement until 1889, God's favorites would live in meekness and peace in their refuge. They would be people of conscience. The unrighteous, by contrast, would writhe in hatred. They would destroy one another much as they had done in the Civil War. In comparing Americans to Jaredites, Woodruff described a cataclysmic explosion produced by individualism. The antidote to individualism was faith, peace, corporatism, conscience.

Mormons were very different from those who came to Pleasant Valley. Whereas Pleasant Valley settlers were individualists in search of profit, Mormons were corporatists in search of community. Whereas Pleasant Valley settlers were overwhelmingly male and invariably monogamous, Mormons were almost equally male and female and often polygamous. Whereas Pleasant Valley settlers drank, smoked, and cursed, Mormons repudiated drinking, smoking, and cursing. Whereas Pleasant Valley settlers embraced honor as a way to resolve disputes — physical assertion, that is, over soft-spoken conciliation — Mormons preached restraint. They conceived of themselves as people of conscience.

What Woodruff might have noted, had he been a careful student of the sociology around him, was that latter-day Jaredites lived next door. Jaredites lived in Pleasant Valley. Like the Jaredites of the Book of Mormon, they entered "secret combinations" to defeat one another. They writhed in a hatred born of mistrust. They kept weapons at their sides. They became addicted to vengeance. They refused to repent.[99]

If Pleasant Valley settlers resembled Jaredites, however, they came to discord by a different route. They were not descended from an ancient people transported to the New World by God. Pleasant Valley settlers, indeed, lacked common origins. They lacked the community that came with common origins. They lacked, too, churches and ministers. They lacked even lay leaders who might hold prayer meetings. They also lacked a belief in perfectionism: the idea that one could live without sin and the ideal that one should make the attempt to do so. They lacked common purpose.

What Pleasant Valley settlers had in common was the centrifugal commitment to profit. The pursuit of money pushed them not together but apart. What they also had in common was a dedication to honor, a belief that only hard words backed by violent actions brought respect. The fact of their competition and difference made honor more powerful. They had no church authorities to help resolve disputes, nor even did they have legal authorities close at hand. In contrast to the honor culture of Old South, moreover, they lacked an accepted elite — a class of wealthy planters — to resolve disputes. They had only their resolve and their weapons.

Mormons, to be sure, drifted at times toward violence. Despite their righteous fury at Mountain Meadows, however, they were people of peace, order, and stability. Or at least they were people who valued peace, order, and stability. Like the Puritans before them, they sought to be an example to the world, a city on a hill, a people of industry, order, and harmony, a people of conscience. It was that very ambition that enmeshed them in conflict.

3

THE HONOR OF RUIN

In the Arizona *Silver Belt* of October 9, 1886, there appeared a "communication" from someone—presumably a man—identified only as "C." His letter concerned the death of John Monk, a gentile rancher who had settled in the Mazatzal range at the southwestern edge of Tonto Basin. While digging a well with the help of one other man, the earth around Monk came crashing down. Only his head remained unburied, allowing him to suck in just enough air to stay alive—temporarily. His hired man immediately ran to the ranch of a neighbor, A. A. Ward, where he recruited four men to help: Houston Ward, Ross Gruell, a man named Schafer or Schater, and Tom Graham. Why Graham was there is a mystery, though Ward had paid his bond, along with that of his brother, John, when the two were arraigned for rustling in 1885. Monk begged the men to dig him out, "telling them that if they would only save him from such a horrible death, they should want for nothing while he lived." Fearing another cave-in, they refused. They watched as Monk slowly strangled. His end came after forty hours of suffering.[1]

"C" thought it suspicious that five men could not dig Monk out in forty hours. The reason they failed to act, he speculated, was not so much fear of a cave-in as ill will. "It seems," he reported, "that [Monk] had had some difficulty about the ranch with some of the parties who were present at his death, they claiming the ranch." He followed that statement with a telling observation. Ranchers, he wrote, "are a peculiar class of individuals." "When one rancher meets his neighbor coming in his direction, in place of going up to him and saying, 'I am delighted to see you my friend this morning. How are your stock and mine getting along on the range?' In place of him greeting his neighbor in the above style, he thinks it more becoming to take a roundabout course so as to keep a pistol-shot away from him, and from this long-ranged distance, they eye each other askance, till their forms vanish behind the rolling hills."[2]

Ranchers, in other words, saw one another not as brethren but as enemies. Monk's story, then, was every bit as much a "tragedy of the commons"—or rather a "tragedy of the free range"—as was the feud between Stinson and the Tewksburys. Men battled one another for resources. They claimed one another's homesteads. They took one another's cattle. And they let one another die—or they killed one another. The same phenomenon—though not always with the same bloody results—occurred throughout the rural West.

Even in flush times, hostilities could erupt. In hard times, however, hostilities could become wars, and it was hard times that descended on cattle country as early as 1885. By 1886, it was becoming clear that the excited boosterism in the first years of the decade was a snare. Prosperity was not around the corner. It was somewhere else entirely, and would not soon return. In the midst of recession, hopes for fortunes dimmed and anger burned hot. Quarrels and distrust turned to bitterness and paranoia. Before those quarrels broke out into full-scale war, settlers endured two trying years that confirmed their fears of manipulation and defeat at the hands of beef trusts, banks, and, not least, one another. Rather than looking ahead to high profits, cattlemen turned their attention to keeping their ranches afloat and chasing away rivals.

As early as February 1884, Tonto Basin stock growers posted a notice in the *Silver Belt* warning newcomers with cattle to steer clear; the range was full. A similar notice appeared in 1885. The cattle industry of Tonto Basin, noted the *Silver Belt* in May 1885, had become "almost of equal importance with mining" and "no business when intelligently conducted will give larger returns than cattle breeding"; but ranges were overcrowded and all water had been allocated.[3]

The problem was that ranges had become overcrowded elsewhere, too. The Arizona *Champion* noted in 1886 that "thousands of head of Texas cattle" had been driven to Arizona due to "the cutting off of ranges" by men stringing barbed wire across private lands. New laws that restricted the importation of cattle from Texas compounded the problem. Fear of a "fever tick" along with fears of overstocked ranges led several states and territories to require inspections and quarantines before admitting Texas cattle.[4] Quarantine or no, Texas cattlemen had to find range. The glut of cattle in Texas, as well as in Colorado, New Mexico, and Wyoming, was "rendering it necessary for owners of large or even medium-sized herds to push on," according to the San Juan *Prospector* of August 6, 1885, "but where?"

One answer was Arizona. In part because it had a weak inspection law and no mandatory quarantine, Arizona saw an enormous influx of cattlemen and herds—almost an invasion—from Texas in 1885 and 1886. New settlers in the Rim Country in 1886 included Sam Haught from Dallas with his five hundred head. Other members of the Haught family would follow. Jesse Ellison migrated from Shackelford County, Texas, to Arizona in the same year, bringing eight children, ten hired men, and eighteen hundred cattle. Ed Rogers and nine hired men brought four thousand head of Aztec cattle from Texas, situating them just south of the Mormon town of Snowflake.[5] Soon the Aztec would bring in twenty-eight thousand more. Arizona men, too, relocated cattle to the Rim Country. Dan Ming, with two partners, brought a thousand head to Pleasant Valley in late 1886.[6]

"The increase in live stock" in Arizona over the previous five years, bragged the *Champion* in April 1886, "is said to be as great as in any country ever known." What had been a "wilderness" in 1880 "is now occupied by stockmen, whose cattle range everywhere." Cattlemen, noted the editor, were suddenly talking of overstocked ranges, but their talk was premature. Good range and good water could still be found. Others were pessimistic. Summer range remained, warned the *Silver Belt*, but no winter range, which demanded access to scarce water on the Verde, Salt, and Little Colorado watersheds. *Hoof and Horn*, a cattleman's newspaper published in Prescott, assured readers that the influx from Texas would "cause prices to decline and ranges to be overstocked," meaning "heavy losses in the future, through lack of feed and water." "If these Texas cattle are taken in starving condition from their ranges," warned the St. Johns *Herald*, "and driven over a long parched and barren trail to the already taxed pastures of Arizona, we do not see how they will go through the coming winter without great mortality, and at the same time cutting off the supply of sustenance for our resident herds."[7]

So alarmed were Tonto Basin cattlemen that, on one occasion at least, they commandeered an alien herd and drove it to Globe, requiring the owner to make new arrangements for his stock. A better solution was simply to ban cattle from entering the territory. Because, however, it was federal land—free range—that lured newcomers, private individuals had no legal power to stop the onslaught. Only the federal or territorial government could stop it. Neither showed any inclination to act in part because cattlemen failed to lobby for change. Arizona cattlemen displayed "an apathy . . . that is inexplicable," lamented the *Silver Belt* in 1886.[8]

In April 1887 the legislature finally created a livestock commission with the power to quarantine. That act was too little and too late. According to its assessor, Apache County, which included much of the Rim Country, held just 38,461 cattle in 1886 not counting animals on Indian reservations. Likely, however, there were double or triple that number. Gila County officially held 25,000 cattle in the same year, though that figure, too, was far lower than the actual number. The assessor's figures, moreover, did not include sheep, goats, or horses, each of which numbered in the tens of thousands.[9]

Alarmed, the *Herald* on October 7, 1886, reprinted an article from the *National Stockman* calling for a new consciousness among cattlemen. "Nothing but hard experience," announced the *Stockman*, would "open the eyes of a ranchman to the greatest danger attending their industry—the danger of overstocking the range, and thus killing the goose [that] laid such a magnificent golden egg." The *Silver Belt* agreed, arguing that cattlemen must cull rather than increase their herds. Instead of breeding more animals, cattlemen must make efforts to breed hardier and heavier animals. Ventures that in the past had been conducted in "a haphazard way" would have to be conducted "on business principles."[10] If cattlemen made such changes, however, they did not do so quickly. Even a year before the Great Die-Up of 1886–87, hundreds of ranchers, in Arizona and elsewhere, found themselves bankrupt amid oversupply, drought, and falling prices.

The Great Die-Up—when Western cattle died by the thousands after a prolonged drought followed by the fierce winter of 1886–87—was only one episode in a series of catastrophes that ended the "cowboy era." Cattle prices peaked in 1883, then sagged for the rest of the decade. The *Herald* reprinted a bulletin from the *Stock Grower* in 1886 expressing certainty that the market had reached its low, but prices continued to fall for three more years. From at least 1886, it was all but impossible to find deep-pocket investors in the cattle business.[11] Cattlemen had found themselves tremendously popular among moneyed men in the early 1880s. Now they found themselves alone as they struggled to stay afloat.

What had happened to the cattle industry was typical of investment bubbles. So long as prices remained high, cattlemen sold few cows capable of bearing calves. By keeping the cows, they hoped to enlarge their herds, which in turn created artificial scarcity. Despite the appearance of scarcity, supply was rapidly increasing. When beef prices dipped in 1885, the dam that had kept cattle pooled on ranches rather than flowing into slaughterhouses began to leak. Like Midwestern and Southern farmers, cattlemen's inclination was to sell more "product" in the hope of treading water. When prices fell further, the response was the same: sell cattle. Prices continued to fall. Catastrophe lurked. Suddenly "ranchmen from Texas to Montana commenced to ship cows, heifers, two-year olds and calves to market. They had bought in at the top and when the turn came were crazy to get out at any sacrifice."[12]

The situation would soon reverse itself, promised the *Herald* in 1890. Whereas once cattlemen had created scarcity by holding on to cows and calves, now they were creating abundance by selling them. When herds had diminished, predicted the *Herald*, selling would slow and prices would rise.[13]

Not everyone could wait out the crisis. In 1888, Charlie Meadows, a Rim Country rancher, sought a new line of work. Eight years earlier, his father, a Confederate veteran and a breeder of horses, had moved his family from northern California to Tonto Basin, only to be killed in an Apache uprising. With their father gone, the Meadows boys sold their holdings and moved to another corner of the basin. There, Charlie, still an adolescent, planned to build a herd of five or six hundred head. In 1884, when cattle sold for twenty-five dollars a head, his prospects looked good. By the end of the decade, however, cattle were selling for eight dollars a head, and the Rim Country was overstocked.

"Every little valley was taken up" by Texans, recalled Meadows. Because the Texans "had come short-handed, very little money was circulated and times were dull." Most of the "live boys" (young men with energy) moved on, some to Washington state, others to South America. Still others got married, moved to towns, and got elected to office. As a consequence, wrote Meadows, "the country was dead" and "I began looking for a loophole where I could get out." Selling his ranch was impossible; there were no buyers. "All the money in the Tonto Basin," he wrote, "was not enough loose change to take me out of the country." Meadows tried his hand at prospecting, but the tiny gold vein he discovered was soon "pinched out." His salvation was Wirth's Circus, which he joined in 1890 as a trick rider and "head cowboy." Soon Meadows would become "Arizona Charlie," star of a Wild West show that toured Australia, New Zealand, and the Far East.[14]

Few men shared Meadows's opportunities. Wild West shows might absorb a talented cowboy here and there, but they could not improve the economic straits of most ranchers. Nor could immigration to towns or to other states and territories help. Other parts of the West, like Arizona, suffered from depressed cattle prices. Men who knew the cattle business but little else were hard-pressed to find lucrative work. Towns, too, suffered, insofar as their economies depended on the cattle industry rather than mining or farming. Low cattle prices meant little spending and little construction.

To compensate for their woes, cattlemen cried loudly and often for lower assessment rates on their livestock. The two largest property holders in Apache County—the Atlantic and Pacific Railroad (A&P) and the Aztec Land and Cattle Company—meanwhile balked at paying property taxes, arguing that they owed no taxes until the government had surveyed and deeded their lands.[15] Their lack of warranty deeds, on the other hand, did not deter either company from

Charles Meadows image from *National Police Gazette*, 1889. Meadows escaped the Rim Country by joining Wirth's Circus. Courtesy of General Research Division, The New York Public Library, Astor, Lenox and Tilden Foundations.

evicting settlers and driving away herders from their claims, thus infuriating the entire population of Apache County. Anger against monopolies near to home and against monopolies far away created a boomerang effect. Invective hurled at a local target could morph into invective hurled against a distant target, and vice versa.

If meatpacking houses in Chicago ranked first on cattlemen's list of tyrannical monopolies, railroads were a close second. Arizona cattlemen found that their shipments to Kansas City met disaster repeatedly because railroads—especially the A&P—charged too much, ran too slow, and left cattle in poor condition when they reached consignors. Rim Country cattlemen were among those who suffered most. They were simply too far from railroads to make shipments profitable. Animals were compromised first by the long drives to the A&P loading yards in Winslow, Holbrook, or Flagstaff and then by the long trip to Missouri or to California.[16]

When in December 1886 the *Herald* urged cattlemen to fight back against the "oppressive warfare waged upon them by railroad pools and autocratic syndicates," it was not alone. Stock growers' newspapers throughout the country urged cattlemen to take "active, persistent, and . . . aggressive measures" against the railroads and the beef trust, measures that could be taken only by organizing and lobbying on a national scale.[17]

In many ways, the cattlemen of the West attacked the same economic oligarchy that Midwestern and Southern farmers attacked. All were injured by overproduction, falling prices, and high shipping costs. Political action proved possible—though not necessarily effective—for Midwestern and Southern farmers who joined the Populist movement. Populism appeared in the West, too, where miners and ranchers supported "free silver," meaning the unlimited coinage of silver with a sixteen-to-one value ratio to gold. More coin, reasoned Populists, would create more demand for their produce.

Though they helped win the occasional Western election, cattlemen were never a critical Populist constituency. Most remained Democrats. Not a few were Republicans. If cattlemen were going to organize, then, they would do so not via any new political party but instead via state, territorial and national stock growers associations that would lobby government for favorable legislation. Even that sort of organization proved difficult, however, for men whose ranches were dispersed in the hinterlands and who felt no love for one another.

The long-term solution for Rim Country ranchers was not so much political as economic. By the 1890s, they had learned to ship animals to the Salt River Valley—the Phoenix region—where they could fatten on alfalfa in irrigated feeding yards until they were loaded on trains. Cattle prices, meanwhile, rose in the 1890s, ensuring modest prosperity. In 1886 and 1887, however, no solution seemed possible. What existed instead among cattlemen was animus toward fellow cattlemen, especially those deemed to be rustlers or, at the other end of the social scale, "bull-ionaires."[18]

If the country saw the rising power of trusts and the plutocrats who ran them, cattlemen witnessed the same trend in the West. Cattle barons seemed to be taking over the range. The evidence was everywhere. In Texas, "cattle kings, who number their cattle by tens of thousands," were crowding out their smaller neighbors. In New Mexico, a single operation, the American Valley Cattle Company, owned by W. B. Slaughter, Thomas H. Catron, and Henry M. Atkinson, boasted fifteen thousand head valued at $367,500. In southern Arizona, a single ranch sold in 1886 for $110,000. The Arizona Cattle Company organized by John W. Young, a Mormon entrepreneur, meanwhile controlled 132,000 acres above Flagstaff and west of the Little Colorado.[19] Rim Country ranchers had an example of gigantism closer to home: the Aztec Land and Cattle Company, with its million acres and its thirty-two thousand head.

By the standards of those ranches, James Stinson was a dwarf. Even some of the "small operators" migrating to New Mexico and Arizona from Texas came with eighteen hundred head, three times the number that Stinson ran in Pleasant Valley. Witnessing the trend toward bigness, *Hoof and Horn* opined that "the day of the small stockman, the man possessing a thousand head of cattle and under, is of the past."[20]

Others took issue with that assessment. Despite the example of a few large companies, insisted the *Silver Belt*, "we should not fall into the error of supposing that the gobbling up of all the little fellows, happy in the possession of their bunch of two or three hundred head, will follow." The *Silver Belt* pointed out that Arizona's rangelands were broken and mountainous, unsuited to large operations that needed vast contiguous acreage. Water, moreover, was scarce and scattered. A wide, flat, grassy country like the Aztec range might work for a large operation, but ranges in most of the Rim Country, as well as in the rest of the territory, could not hold large herds, nor could they be easily administered by one outfit. "As yet," concluded the *Silver Belt*, "the large holdings of cattle in Arizona are an experiment, the success of which is extremely doubtful. Therefore, to the stockmen of small possessions we say, there is no occasion for alarm. They may rest secure that Arizona is their El Dorado."[21]

Other newspapers added to the chorus. The Prescott *Courier* declared that "Arizona is a good poor man's country" and that big operations must be discouraged. In order to gain statehood, it explained, "the valleys, mountains, etc., will have to be filled by families, not by employees of great corporations." The Tombstone *Record-Epitaph*, speaking for the southern part of the territory, affirmed its support for small ranchers who had decided to bar big newcomers from Texas. "We have no particular use for 'cattle barons' or 'bull-ionaires,'" testified the *Record-Epitaph*, "but if all the springs and waterholes in the territory were occupied by settlers with small bands of cattle, our ultimate prosperity would be assured."[22]

To some extent the newspapers were right. Arizona, if not an El Dorado for small operators, was nonetheless dominated by them. In Gila County, whose county seat was Globe, the vast majority of cattlemen held between two hundred and five hundred, meaning an average assessed worth per ranch of between three hundred and a thousand dollars. Yavapai County herds, including those in Pleasant Valley, were similarly small. As in Gila County, most cattlemen held only a few hundred.[23] The *Silver Belt* knew its geography. Arizona's broken terrain made big operations problematic. That same terrain, however, divided small operators into a thousand tiny fiefdoms, each at odds with its neighbors.

To fight railroads and the beef trust, small operators would have to give up individualism and create a territorial stockmen's association, wrote *Hoof and Horn*.

In doing so, they would have to send delegates from each of the county stock-men's associations—dominated by small operators—to make sure that the terri-torial association would not be "composed of the rich, and for the rich, and that the small fry had no show or share in the results of its deliberations." The various cattle associations—both territorial and county-level—would then have to regu-late the industry within their areas, making sure that the number of cattle run by any one operation would be commensurate with its land and water claims. That way, big operators could not commandeer a quarter-section or two and run enormous herds on free range. If small operators, meanwhile, organized coopera-tive drives to the railroads, argued the *Silver Belt*—drives that would save labor costs—they would see profit.[24]

Such proposals fell on deaf ears. The *Silver Belt* had predicted as much, recog-nizing that cattlemen were too suspicious of one another to change. "The want of harmony, and in many instances open hostility towards each other, among our cattlemen," the newspaper lamented, "is doing more injury to the cattle industry of Gila County than all other causes combined." Though the Gila County Live Stock Association already boasted a large membership, "we are, nevertheless, unable to recall any material benefit whatever from that organization."[25] Rather than organize and lobby in large associations, cattlemen often found it more ex-pedient to organize in smaller, localistic groups—factions—to prosecute wars against one another and to lynch those deemed to be rustlers.

In a sense, making war on rustlers was a way to make war on individualism. Rustlers—men who made too many "branding mistakes"—were the ultimate lone wolves. They refused to make common cause with their neighbors. They were more likely, however, to take cattle from big operators than small ones. In their book *Cattle*, published in 1930, Will Barnes and William McLeod Raine recalled that most small operators smiled at their fellows who stole cattle from big operators in the 1880s. "Never before or since has there been as much cattle thieving as in the days of the big companies," they observed. Because jurors tended to be drawn from the ranks of small operators who might themselves be accused of rustling—and who in any event disliked big operators or feared being thought sympathetic to them—they repeatedly refused to convict accused rustlers.[26]

Rustling, however, sometimes pitted small operators against other small opera-tors. Forty-four years before the publication of *Cattle*, Barnes had suggested as much. As secretary of the Apache County Stock Growers Association, he found that the small operators of the Rim Country "mistakenly" branded one an-other's animals with regularity. He proposed that, when they discovered a mistaken brand on an animal, ranchers should rebrand the animal with an "M," for mistake, and give it back to its rightful owner. Alternately a rancher might give the rightful owner another animal.[27] In 1886, Barnes seemed to recognize how fine the line was between mistakes and rustling, and seemed willing to give the benefit of the doubt to his fellows. Within a year, he had lost his will to forgive.

To improve the situation, the legislature set forth rules governing "rodeos" (from the Spanish *rodear*, "to surround"), which initially meant simply a joint roundup by stockmen in a given area. Those participating chose a delegate to serve as "judge of the Plains" whose job was to arbitrate disputes over ownership. Cattlemen's associations, meanwhile, along with the legislature, tried to combat the rustling problem by requiring ranchers to register marks and brands. As early as 1884, the Mogollon Live Stock Association published the brands and ear-marks of each member "in both pamphlet and card form." It also required each member to supply other members with "a copy of his brand burned in leather, accompanied by a description of the ear marks used." No man could plead ignorance of the brands or marks used by his neighbors. Those directives, however, failed to stop the problem. Two years later, the Globe Stock Growers Association advertised a $250 reward for information leading to the arrest and conviction of men who altered brands. Signatories included J. J. Vosburgh.[28]

The offer of a $250 reward indicates that, in the midst of their economic troubles, cattlemen agreed that the real villain—the villain whom they could attack directly, without the headache of political organization—was not the railroad or the beef trust or the newcomers from Texas. Cattlemen railed against those forces, but apart from the Texas newcomers, they were impersonal and distant. What cattlemen agreed on as their common problem was the rustler, who was a liar, a thief, a man without dignity. Problems on the range were the result not of economic relationships or legal codes but of character.

Rustlers, to be sure, did exist. The poor man's temptation to steal a few cows to build his herd—or to get even with enemies—made rustling ubiquitous. Rustling was part of the fabric of life and often received little more than a wink and a nod. In the Rim Country and, indeed, throughout the West, cowboys were said to carry running irons with which to alter brands whenever they got a chance. The running iron looked like a pot hook, about eighteen inches long, with a hooked or ringed end. Rustlers used running irons as painters use brushes, heating them up, then stroking the hindquarters of a calf or cow to transform its brand into a new shape.

Small operators were also said to practice mavericking—taking unbranded calves from their mothers—and sleepering—giving calves the earmarks but not the brand of their owner's herd. Other cowboys, on seeing the earmarks, as-

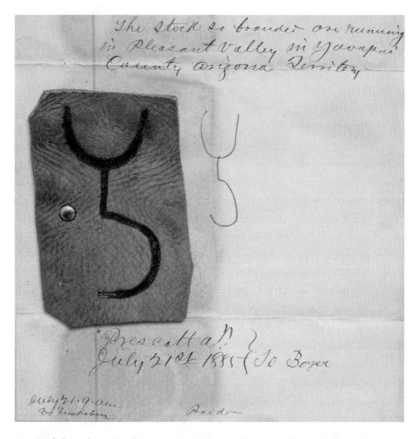

Tewksbury brand on leather. Counties, and later the Territory, kept brand registrations on file in order to prevent rustling. Collection of Jeremy Rowe Vintage Photography (vintagephoto.com).

sumed that "sleepered" calves had been properly branded and investigated no further. When the calves got old enough to leave their mothers, the thief would alter their earmarks and give them his own brand. Clarence Durham, one of the hands who worked for the Aztec, recalled hearing rumors of such tricks in 1888, shortly after the company had hired him. "None of the little outfits" in the vicinity of the Aztec, he recalled, were immune to innuendo.[29] Similar innuendo echoed throughout the West.

Part of the problem was the weakness of law enforcement. Low tax revenues—a perennial problem in Arizona, particularly during the cattle recession—made enforcement and prosecution difficult. The fact that courts failed to diffuse tension, however, does not mean that they ignored it. Even in the 1880s—three decades before Arizona was granted statehood—court dockets brimmed with cases involving cattle theft. When court was in session, noted the *Silver Belt*, "nearly the entire male population [of Tonto Basin] would repair" to Globe "to indulge in charges against each other for calf or horse stealing, which almost invariably resulted in acquittal."[30] Few cases were clear-cut. "Hardly a term of court passes in any county of this Territory," lamented the *Silver Belt*, "but what two or three cases of alleged cattle stealing by men previously bearing good reputations, are tried, the only result being to demonstrate the existence of a dispute between neighbors over the possession of a cow or calf, which could have been more easily and satisfactorily settled in a justice court, without involving the expenditure of several hundred dollars by the county."[31]

The situation became so frustrating that, in July 1885, Justice Summer Howard of the Territorial Circuit Court directed a grand jury to ignore rustling charges when there was doubt of criminal intent. The *Silver Belt* commended his action. The appropriate remedy, insisted Howard, was to file civil suits to reclaim ("replevin") animals in the possession of others.[32]

Courts could not resolve tensions on the range for good reason. Evidence was scanty. Witnesses were rare. Testimony conflicted. Frequently a case resulted from a mistake. The problem was beyond the courts' capacity to resolve. The problem was atomization. Individuals—many of them Southerners and Midwesterners who had been trained from birth to think of themselves as noble individualists, jealous of their rights and ready to fight for them—were not amenable to the piecemeal solutions offered by courts.

By fall 1887 tensions seemed to have improved. "The Salt and Tonto contingent was very small" in the court session that year, remarked the *Silver Belt*. Cattlemen, it reasoned, had "gained wisdom with years" and now devoted "themselves singly to pastoral and agricultural pursuits."[33] In fact, the Salt and Tonto contingent had gained wisdom of a different sort. They had witnessed the devastation in Pleasant Valley in August and September when more than a dozen men met bloody ends in ambushes and gun battles. If cattlemen had become hesitant to sue one another, perhaps it was because they feared that the result would be extralegal retaliation. Or perhaps they had learned that legal battles solved nothing and that "rustling" had to be prosecuted in the field. Meanwhile, a new enemy compounded cattlemen's problems: drought.

The drought began in 1885, when cattlemen noticed that the grass was failing to come up on schedule. By 1886, cattle had begun to die. No one in Apache County could remember a drier year. The lack of summer rains, along with overstocking, caused Tonto Basin cattle to "suffer severely." Drought continued into

1887. In February, the *Silver Belt* noted that Tonto Creek had become "almost entirely denuded of grass for several miles out," and cattle had become thin and sickly. In the *Herald*, "Rangeman" complained that the "winter has been too nice." "We want snow," he continued, "and we want it badly." From Silver Creek to Clear Creek, all along the Rim, almost no snow had fallen. "No snow in winter, no grass and water in summer." The dry winter had forced cattle to remain along "rivers and permanent waters, until all the grass is eaten and tramped out for ten or fifteen miles back." By May, the *Silver Belt* could proclaim that "the present season is the most unfavorable for grazing that Arizona has ever experienced."[34]

As often happens in Arizona's high country, fortunes changed quickly. In June, the *Herald* reported that Rim Country cattlemen "are exultant over the fine appearance and excellent condition of their beef." The winter precipitation pattern, a pattern consisting of storms generated in the Pacific that sweep eastward over California to dump snow on Arizona highlands—had failed. The summer pattern, however—consisting of warm, moist air sweeping up from the Gulf of Mexico to create thunderstorms—had succeeded. Though little rain fell near Globe, the "Tonto area" to the north of Globe, including Pleasant Valley, had received plenty, leaving stockmen "jubilant." By September, stockholders could report that cattle were in "magnificent condition."[35] Rain, however, did not bring harmony.

In Pleasant Valley, animus had begun in the early 1880s, when cattle prices were high and times were good. Men competed for the range and for prosperity. They rustled one another's cows; they threatened one another; they shot at one another; they informed on one another; and they battled one another in court. After James Stinson moved out of Pleasant Valley in 1884, the animus seemed to subside. The Grahams were tried for perjury in summer 1884, but the county dropped charges. After that, court cases and gun battles temporarily ceased. All was quiet. Pressure grew, however, not only because of the internal dynamics of Pleasant Valley but also because of conditions in the cattle industry. Supply rose. Prices fell. The big packing houses in Chicago conspired with one another, seemingly, to pay low prices and make high profits. Railroads charged exorbitant rates for shipping. Big cattlemen from Texas, driven out of their home state by drought and fences, crowded into Arizona. Then came drought.

Cattlemen joined together to lobby the federal government to combat the beef trust and the railroads. They combined to lobby the territorial government to stop the incessant importation of cattle. And they banded together to stop the endemic problem of mistakenly claimed cattle, or "rustling," as the problem was increasingly known. Relations were tense and conflict was almost inevitable, not just in Pleasant Valley, but throughout the free range country of the West. Even as they came together in stock associations to fight for their futures, cattlemen remained at odds.

Will Barnes knew the situation. In 1885, Barnes, who ran a small operation above the Rim called the Esperanza, could boast that his nearest neighbor was twenty-five miles away. Then came a pair of Texas cowmen, "squeezed out . . . by nesters," with a thousand heifers. Even though the two operations were twenty miles apart, Barnes and his men "felt much aggrieved at the nerve of the newcomer to crowd in on us." When Barnes repeatedly found cattle from the new operation mixed with his own, he became enraged. He rode to the headquarters of his nemeses, demanding that they keep their animals off his range. The newcomers, however, knew their rights. The land was free range, they told Barnes, and he had no right to claim it.[36]

"This was the beginning of the end of our delightful isolation," recalled Barnes, "and we lived to see stockmen's cabins at every water hole and available location all over the country. Where we had felt crowded by 2000 cattle, 50,000 were hunting grass and water on the same range a few years later. And our case was typical of what was happening all over the range country." By 1887, cattle "swarmed" over free range "like maggots on a carcass." With his few cattle now mixed with tens of thousands of others, "it was a case of 'ride to 'em, Cowboy or lose all you have.'"[37]

Ride to 'em was not always enough. In some cases—even before the invasion by Texas cattle—newcomers might take your land and make you leave, or kill you. Or so, at least, went the story told by L. J. Horton, who arrived in the Rim Country in 1883. Horton claimed a small piece of land and ran cattle not far from Pleasant Valley. Thinking to grow his own produce, Horton planted watermelons. One day, as he visited his watermelon patch with a shotgun to drive away rabbits, he found a newcomer. The man picked a watermelon, presented it to Horton, and told him that the next time he wanted one he would have to pay. The newcomer—who bragged that he was a rustler and a crack shot—had jumped Horton's claim. Horton, still clutching his shotgun, feigned a hasty retreat then turned and rushed the man, causing him to tremble so badly "that he could not hold [his] gun up." The man fired several shots into the dirt around Horton, then ducked behind his wife for cover, who obligingly "held up her petticoats to shield him." Horton intended to kill his adversary, but the man's wife and young son begged him not to shoot. Horton finally disarmed the interloper and told him not to return. The man and his family were gone within two days.[38]

How Horton's "rustler" would have related the story is anyone's guess. It seems unlikely, at any rate, that a self-respecting rustler would brag to an enemy—or even to a friend—of his trade. In all probability, Horton and his enemy simply claimed the same land. Boundaries were uncertain. Claims were based on preemption and guesswork. Both men may have been in the right or in the wrong. It matters little because the story constructed by Horton was, it seems, more myth than truth. In Horton's telling, he was a man of honor. He defended himself and his claim heroically, risking life and limb. His opponent was a man without honor, a rustler and a coward who took refuge behind a woman's petticoat. Throughout the West cattlemen told similar tales, tales that portrayed their enemies as rustlers, cowards, and villains. Through those tales they constructed the very image of the Wild West with its idealized heroes and vicious desperadoes.

The Rim Country produced many such stories. Consider the case of Charlie Meadows, who acted out stories of honor in his daredevil performances in Wirth's Circus but who also told more personal tales of fighting bad men. In March 1887, Meadows and his partner, Frank Pedthero, were forced to drive out men employed by a "Mr. Hoy" who laid claim to the Meadows ranch. The next day, Meadows met Hoy on the road, took him prisoner at gunpoint, and marched him to Payson.[39] No record exists of what happened in Payson, but the lesson was evident: to survive in the Rim Country, or anywhere in the West, a man had to be made of strong stuff.

That was not the only scrape involving good-natured Charlie Meadows. On another occasion, the Graham brothers accused him of killing a calf belonging to the Waters Cattle Company. The Waters men, recalled Meadows, sought revenge. Somehow Meadows avoided any penalty though he never explained how. Perhaps his exit from the Rim Country was in part an escape from men gunning for him. Though Meadows played no role in the Pleasant Valley conflict, his experience soured him on the Grahams, whom he labeled "a band of organized rustlers." The trouble with the Waters Company, however, was not the last time that the Meadows boys would see trouble. One of Charlie's brothers was prosecuted for rustling in 1888.[40] Amid the confusion and paranoia on the free range, even respectable men could seem like desperadoes.

Hate, fury, and retaliation would soon come to a head. War was in the offing. There were, however, other ways to respond, not the least effective of which was humor. In the late 1880s, Dan Ming explained the situation in a "prayer for rain" befitting of Mark Twain:

> You know, oh Lord, that I never asked you for anything before, but . . . at the earnest request of my fellow cow punchers, I beseech you in a most supplicating manner to give us a sure enough rain. . . . The impression is abroad that we have been such terrible sinners that you have purposely overlooked our

range; and now, heavenly father, you know that ain't a square deal; and even if we have sinned a little we'll promise not to do it any more if you will just give us a good rain. Our cattle are rolling their tails for the mountains and dying of thirst and hunger; our calf crop will be light, and the mavericks which have been our main stand-by will vamoos to the ranges of some other slick puncher, who is just as handy with his string and branding iron. . . . Now, oh God, we don't think that's right when all we ask is a little rain and a square cut. But if you do not grant our prayer, for Christ's sake stop it from raining on Joe Hampson's range, for all our cattle are going over there. Hampson, oh Lord, is a powerful sinner, and undeserving of such goodness from you, and he will build to our mavericks if he is allowed to cut them on us.[41]

Perhaps Ming had help in writing his "prayer." Surely it was not the spontaneous product of cowboy wit. It was carefully constructed satire. Satire or no, Ming's prayer exhibits the sociology of the range. He and his men have sinned "a little," he admits, implying that they have engaged in mavericking. If it does not rain on his range, he fears, the mavericks will migrate to the range of some other "slick puncher"—meaning rustler—"who is just as handy with his string and branding iron." Even if the Lord does not see fit to make it rain on his range, Ming begs him to stop the rain from falling on the range of his neighbor, a "powerful sinner" who, like Ming, builds his herd with mavericks. There is no love of thy neighbor here, but neither is there any hard-and-fast distinction between honorable men and scoundrels. Unlike Horton or Meadows, Ming maintained a wry, almost anthropological perspective on the culture of the free range. In Ming's telling, every cowboy was a sinner and scoundrel.

Had others viewed their situation with Ming's sense of the absurd, they might have avoided the war. Few, however, maintained detached bemusement in the face of economic crisis, drought, and interlopers. When they had arrived in Arizona, moreover, many of them brought along a lively sense of honor defined by strict loyalty to kin and comrades, boisterous friendship, an equally boisterous sense of pride, and readiness to personally avenge an insult or a wrong. The older culture of honor from the South and Lower Midwest, however, did not have to flourish in the West. It did so because environmental, economic, and legal conditions promoted it.

Quarrels between small operator and big operator and, equally important, between small operator and small operator, would reach epic proportions. The irony of those quarrels is that, far from casting doubt on the efficacy of honor, they perpetuated it. The solution to quarrels that seemed to be about honor—or, rather, quarrels that seemed to represent a struggle between honor and ignominy—was more honor. In the end, Westerners would remember their past not as an allegory of the evils of free range but as a great tableau of honor, where good men came together to drive out bad ones.

Pleasant Valley—like much of the cattle country of the West—befit the Mormon description of the wars of the Jaredites. The ranchers and cowboys of Pleasant Valley saw one another not as friends but as enemies. They were competitors for the fruits of the earth. They suspected one another of stealing stock. They hated one another for "stealing" range. And in 1887 they fell into civil war.

Part Two

———————◆———————

WAR

The Trials of the Saints

Amid the teeming social and spiritual life of Arizona's Mormon frontier lurked demons. The trouble began in the hamlet of St. Johns at the far eastern edge of the Mormon frontier, near the New Mexico line. To accommodate newcomers from Utah, the church instructed Nathan Tenney to purchase more land on the Little Colorado River. Tenney carried out his instructions, buying the area in and around the hamlet of San Juan, or St. Johns (probably named for the popular Mexican fiesta day), from a Jewish trader named Solomon Barth in 1879. In the deal, Tenney was to pay Barth 770 head of Utah cattle worth seventeen thousand dollars in exchange for twelve hundred acres and all rights to the waters of the Little Colorado.[1]

In Barth, Mormons found a man who, like them, was every bit the bold adventurer but, unlike them, lacked devotion to conscience. At the time Tenney met him, Barth was "a sturdy little man" of thirty-seven, "with a long brown beard, a very bright eye, pleasing face, and nerves of iron." Born in Prussia, Barth came to the United States in 1855. According to an account of his life written by a Mormon settler, he was brought to America by an uncle, a merchant who had converted to Mormonism. When they reached the East Coast, the uncle continued to California by ship while making his nephew proceed overland. Young Barth, now fifteen, joined a Mormon "handcart company" and pushed his meager belongings from Council Bluffs, Iowa, all the way to Salt Lake City.[2]

From Salt Lake, Barth made his way to San Bernardino but failed to report to the uncle, for whom he bore an intense dislike. Instead of working for the uncle, he ventured to Arizona to work for merchant Michael Goldwater. First Barth went to Tucson, then to the goldfields of La Paz, Rich Hill, and Wickenberg. Discovering that he could make a profit by freighting from New Mexico to Ari-

Sol Barth with his wife, Refugio Landavazo y Sanchez Barth, and family, circa 1890s.
Barth was a Jewish merchant, patrón, and—in the 1880s—an enemy to Mormons.
Courtesy of Apache County Historical Society.

zona by mule, Barth traveled back and forth between those territories routinely,
hauling salt and carrying mail. Once, it is said, Apaches captured him, made him
strip, and sent him on his way to the Zuni villages, a hundred miles distant.[3]

At some point in the 1860s or early 1870s, Barth's brothers, Nathan and Morris,
joined him. The three hauled supplies from Kansas to Fort Apache under government contract. The year 1874 was good to Barth. He married Refugio Landavazo y Sánchez of Cubero, New Mexico, who brought a dowry of four thousand
sheep; he began selling goods at Zuni; he opened a store at Fort Apache; and he
made a home in San Juan, where he could run his sheep. Supposedly he had won
squatting rights to the area around San Juan, plus sheep and cash, in a card game
in 1873, suggesting how closely he was tied to the Western culture of honor.[4] His
future seemed assured . . . until the Mormons came.

After purchasing the land from Barth, Tenney located the new Mormon
settlement, called Salem, about a mile northeast of San Juan. Hoping to head off

petty speculators who might file homestead claims in order to sell them to Mormons, Apostle Wilford Woodruff directed Tenney to bring settlers before word of the sale leaked out. Settlers hearkened to Tenney's call but quickly discovered that Salem sat on swampland; hence Tenney arranged to survey land nearer to San Juan.[5] Seeing the surveyors—and seeing fresh Mormon recruits—the New Mexican population took alarm. Mormons, it seemed, had come to drive them out.

The New Mexicans were not far wrong. The Mormons indeed intended to take control of the area, though not with guns. "We would rather buy out the place," Woodruff instructed Tenney, "so as to make a Mormon town of it, and not be mixed with Jews, Mexicans and Gentiles." "Take all the desireable places as fast as the brethren come," he added. "I do not intend to let daylight, dark night or grass grow under my feet to stop me trying to do my duty of helping to settle Arizona or New Mexico or bringing the House of Israel into the Kingdom of God."[6] The bitterness that followed burned through the 1880s.

The demons that Mormon colonists faced as they sought to bring "the House of Israel into the Kingdom of God" were not merely New Mexicans. The demons were within the Mormons themselves. Mormons were not Jaredites. They would not succumb to civil war. They had common faith, common purpose. They were people of conscience. But conscience could be aggressive. Self-righteousness no less than honor could yield assertion, even aggrandizement. As Apostle Woodruff suggested, the Mormons—in keeping with Joseph Smith's prophecy— formulated their own special version of Manifest Destiny. Conscience shaped Mormon views in other ways, too. Mormons saw gentiles—whether New Mexicans or Americans—only in contradistinction to themselves. Gentiles were sinners, polluters, criminals. Mormons seldom viewed their competitors as both good and bad, virtuous and flawed. The very fact that Mormons were not Jaredites—the fact that they were people of conscience—led them into conflict.

On October 26, 1880, thirty New Mexican residents of St. Johns presented a petition to the bishop of the St. Johns ward, David Udall, claiming that the Mormon survey was conducted with "the intention of surrounding and oppressing us." Mormons, they argued, intended to choke off the town by occupying its periphery. The Little Colorado blocked the town on the east; desert hills blocked it to the south; now Mormons would block it on the north and east. Arguing that their "Catholic town" held rights to those lands "by antiquity," the petitioners relegated Mormon claims to pretense. They directed the petition specifically to Udall because "all the world knows that the members of the Mormon sect live under blind obedience to their leaders."[7]

The claim to ownership "by antiquity" reflected a regional truism. Spanish colonists under the authority of king and pope had settled New Mexico as early as 1598, which included what later became Arizona. Under Spanish law, townships received rights to surrounding pastures. New Mexican settlers did not venture beyond Mt. Taylor, however, until the mid-1860s, when the United States subjugated the Navajo. During the brief Navajo exile to eastern New Mexico, sheepherders began moving west with their flocks, penetrating the highlands of west-central New Mexico and east-central Arizona and founding several small villages. In that sense, antiquity was a decade.[8]

Like all emigrants, New Mexicans brought cultural baggage. In particular, they brought an emphasis on family. "Compared to the Anglo-American," explains anthropologist Munro Edmonson, "the person of Hispanic-American kinship is placed in a more populous universe and extends his immediate (incest) solidarity to more people. He is less individual but more personal toward his distant relatives." New Mexicans identified themselves as members of an extended family first and as individuals second. Thus New Mexican parents gave infants not a single surname but all four of their great-grandfathers' surnames.[9] New Mexicans extended kinship even further by appointing godparents—*compadrazgo*—for each child. To some degree, the New Mexican emphasis on kinship corresponded to cultural patterns in the American South. In the South, however, constant migration tended to loosen old ties.

If New Mexicans and Southerners shared an emphasis on extended family, they also shared an orientation toward honor. New Mexican men took pride in their personal and familial reputations for courage. As a mark of honor, men glorified and defended the fidelity of mothers, sisters, and wives, even as they considered it a mark of pride to seduce the mothers, sisters, and wives of other men. Into the early nineteenth century, too, honorable men defined themselves in opposition to Indian slaves, who were often subjected to rituals of shame, especially whippings. New Mexican men and women both, meanwhile, showed their honor via fine clothing ("only outward appearances impress them," wrote an eighteenth-century observer of New Mexico life). As in the South, finally, honor included the male prerogatives of gambling and drinking.[10] New Mexicans did not share the Mormon dedication to conscience.

New Mexican society, too, was in some ways more hierarchical than that of Mormons. Mormons, to be sure, had their own hierarchy. The president of the church stood at its apex, with subordinate leaders descending down the scale all the way to ward bishops, elders, and deacons. With a spiritual hierarchy that orbited around a chief revelator and prophet, the Mormon church bore a resemblance to Catholicism with its pope. Among the Saints, however, "farm land, water rights, grazing land, stock, and agricultural machinery" were used both individually and cooperatively. Mormons—at least in theory—identified one another as spiritual and social equals.

New Mexicans, by contrast, practiced the *partido* system, in which a wealthy man, a *patrón*, leased sheep to poorer men for a period of years. The lessee contracted to provide the patrón a specific number of sheep, or a specific amount of wool, each year. The lessee, in turn, might be a *caporal*—or corporal—who took possession of three to four bands, assigning a herder to each one, plus a man to take care of camp and several burros to carry supplies. The caporal served as pathfinder, moving ahead of his flocks to scout good pasture. The herders meanwhile tended the flocks—an especially taxing duty during lambing season, when predators lurked—while their partners set up camp. At the end of the contractual period—usually five years—the lessee gave back the precise number of sheep that he had received at the outset.[11]

When Solomon Barth married Refugio Landavazo y Sánchez in 1874, he moved almost seamlessly into the role of patrón. After relocating his family and his sheep to San Juan (soon to be called St. Johns), Barth contracted out his flocks. In addition, he operated a hotel and a store. By buying supplies from Santa Fe and Albuquerque, Barth became "the banker, the provider, the broker for the whole country." Nobody—including Indians and poor Hispanics—"was refused credit" by Barth, who, claimed one editor, "has probably given away more merchandise in his time than smaller merchants have sold."[12]

Barth and the Mormons, however, found themselves at odds. As early as 1878, Barth is said to have pulled a revolver on William Flake after a dispute involving the sale of a mare. Barth supposedly told Flake that "colts make all men equal," to which Flake replied, "I was not born in the woods to be scared of a coyote." Barth—who had already killed a man in a quarrel near Fort Apache—had acquired the habits of honor. He sought to resolve a dispute via bluster and violence. Neither fisticuffs nor gunplay ensued, in part because Nathan Barth told his brother to back down and in part because Flake, a man of conscience, did not respond in kind.[13] Tensions nonetheless escalated, not only between Barth and the Mormons but, more important, between New Mexicans and Mormons.

After the New Mexican protest against Mormon incursions, Bishop Udall offered to hold a public meeting to explain the purpose of the survey and to adjudicate water rights. Privately, Udall assailed Barth for failing to tell the New Mexicans that the Mormons had bought the land. Given Apostle Woodruff's commitment to secrecy, however, Tenney may well have asked Barth to keep the deal quiet. Apostle Snow, meanwhile, fumed at Tenney, who had failed to evaluate Barth's offer before making the deal. "Ammon," Snow reportedly asked, "what did you buy? The air? There is nothing here. What did you buy?"[14]

Barth was not blameless. He had a bona fide claim to only a fraction of the land—a quarter-section, or 160 acres—and one-sixth of the flow of the Little Colorado, though he had sold every drop of its water. Even the land that Barth possessed legally was "so lacking in fertility one couldn't have raised a disturbance on it with a barrel of whiskey, ten Apache warriors and seventeen Texas cowboys," complained Evans Coleman. After arbitration by Udall and New Mexican leaders and adjudication in the courts, Mormons received only Barth's 160 acres, though they somehow obtained three-fifths of the river's flow.[15]

The St. Johns purchase was the beginning of conflict. To build their town, Mormons were forced to buy additional lands from those who claimed possessory rights. Mormons believed they were being cheated. New Mexicans claimed lands that they had never settled, complained Mormons, whereas the few white gentiles in the area required payments for "improvements" where none existed. Even when Mormons lay claim to lands via preemption, others—usually but not always New Mexicans—would jump the claim.[16]

The taste of hate rose in all throats. Racial and religious taunts echoed in the streets. The "blood of Cain," worried Jesse Smith, "was more predominant in those Mexicans than that of Israel." Joseph Fish, the Mormon diarist, explained that the New Mexicans of St. Johns were "renegade[s]" who had fled their native country after committing crimes. The "few whites" who lived among them "were no better," he added. When New Mexicans refused to leave the area, Mormons called in more settlers.[17]

Smith's reference to "Cain" refers to the Cain of Genesis who kills Abel and is cursed by Yahweh to wander for the rest of his life. Though Cain's descendants were said to have died in the great flood, Mormons believed that one of them survived: Egyptus, who became wife to Noah's son Ham and progenitor of Egypt. Thus Mormons linked "the mark of Cain"—which they took to be dark skin—to another curse: that of Canaan, Ham's son. Noah cursed Ham, according to the Bible, for failing to cover him when he lay drunk and undressed. Noah's curse was to pronounce Ham's son, Canaan, a servant unto his brothers. Slaveholders translated that curse into a justification for slavery. Supposedly, Canaan's mark of servitude was his dark skin, though the Bible says nothing of the sort. Neither does the Bible explain what sort of mark God put on Cain. Like other Americans, Mormons adapted the myth of the curse to their own purposes, using it to explain the darkness and "inferiority" of New Mexicans.[18]

If Smith's comments showed that Mormon racism paralleled an older American racism that marked out one race for honor and another for shame, Joseph Fish's comments gave a different picture. St. Johns New Mexicans, said Fish, were "criminals" and "renegades." He did not portray all New Mexicans as equally bad, only those who seemed to lack conscience. The white gentiles who lived among the New Mexicans, stressed Fish, were no better. Fish's "othering" was not racial but cultural. It was premised not on skin color but on a distinction between those who eschewed sin and observed the law and those who did not, or at least seemingly did not.

Mormon teachings about race were ambiguous. In part they were premised on the concept of an honorable race and a shamed one. That concept, however, was often subordinate to teachings about individual virtue, teachings premised on conscience. Either way, tensions would soon erupt into actions. Mormons, angered by incursions of sheepherders who crossed vast swaths of land to graze their animals, drove New Mexican herds from their ranges.[19] New Mexicans did likewise to Mormon cattle. Both sides prepared for war.

In 1877, the Greer family, Mormon converts from Texas, carved out ranches in the Little Colorado country. One branch of the family was headed by Thomas Lacy, a Mexican War veteran who converted in the 1850s, became a merchant in Salt Lake, then moved his family back to Texas in 1856 as part of a colonization plan, where he turned to ranching and grew prosperous. Still eager for adventure, Greer joined the Arizona "mission" in 1877 and located a ranch near Springerville, a few miles south of St. Johns.[20]

The other branch was headed by Americus Vespucius Greer, who followed much the same path as his relative. After living in Utah in the 1850s, he returned to Texas and homesteaded 160 acres. In 1877, he followed Thomas Lacy to Arizona, bringing his wife, children, and cattle to Concho, a hamlet situated a few miles west of St. Johns and just twenty-five miles from Juan Candelaria's ranch with its 750 sheep. Candelaria would die in 1930 as the richest man in Apache County.[21] In 1877, however, he was about to begin a prolonged struggle with Mormons.

Americus Vespucius, nicknamed "H" for the Confederate unit in which he had been captain, was an impressive man with a full, white beard, deep-set eyes, and white hair that stood at attention on his head. Within three years of settling in Arizona, he was also a widower with six children to feed. Given their needs, their proximity, and their Southern emphasis on family, the Greer brothers worked together. Despite church directives against socializing with gentiles, they also extended "Southern hospitality" to everyone except their New Mexican neighbors.[22]

By the early 1880s, meanwhile, Candelaria had added thousands more sheep—ninety thousand by one report—requiring him to use more range. Most of the sheep belonged to his three brothers, who left New Mexico to join him. To make room, the Candelarias directed their herders to drive away any Mormon cattle they found, including those of Americus Greer. Greer claimed to have lost half his stock. In response, Thomas Lacy's son, Nat Greer, a lukewarm Mormon in his midtwenties, along with his teenaged brothers, Richard and Harris, and the family's hired hands, "raided every sheep camp that he found and threatened to shoot the Mexican herders." On one occasion, Nat Greer is said to have found a New Mexican man riding a Greer horse. Greer lassoed the man and jerked him off the horse, giving him the choice of death or mutilation. The man chose the latter, and Greer used his pocketknife to slice an "underslope"—a cattle mark—into each of his ears before releasing him. This was a classic example of shaming.[23]

Nat Greer's actions show that Mormons, too, were attracted to the behaviors of honor. They, too, sometimes preferred resolution through violence rather than words. The Greers' propensity to honor, however, grew from their Texan roots rather than from their Mormon religion.

Events took another foul turn on San Juan Day, June 24, 1882, the festive occasion that commemorates the birth of John the Baptist. The New Mexicans of St. Johns on that day held a carnival that included musicians, acrobats, and a bullfight. Supposedly interested in the proceedings, the Greer boys—three brothers and five hired hands—attended in force, entering town with six-guns on their belts. Few Mormons carried guns, much less got into gunfights. The Greers were exceptions. On this occasion, at least, they put on another display of honor, a display likely intended to intimidate their New Mexican enemies.[24]

Reports of what happened next differ. Either the Greer party wanted to see the bullfight or they were planning to buy supplies. Some accounts claim that the sheriff, Ebenezer Stover, asked the Greer men to give up their guns, a request they refused. Almost immediately, they noticed a knot of New Mexican men near Barth's hotel who appeared "rowdy and excitable." The Greer men ducked into an eatery. When they emerged, they found themselves under fire. Four of the Greer party scrambled to take cover in a vacant house while the others mounted and rode away.[25]

All four of the men in the house—or maybe two, depending on which account one trusts—were hit. James Vaughn died within minutes. Harris Greer received a bullet through the hand. Jeff Tribit, aka "Nigger Jeff," a former Greer slave and now a cowboy, and Hyrum Hatch, a young and pious Mormon, were also hit. Both would recover, though Hatch's family shipped him to Idaho to escape revenge. On the other side, at least one—Francisco Tafolla—was wounded, though the Greer fighters claimed to have killed eight and wounded four.[26]

Hearing gunfire, "Father" Nathan Tenney, Ammon's father, rushed to the scene to act as peacemaker. "For God's sake," he yelled as he waved his hands and took a position between the two sides, "quit firing!" When the shots slowed, he made his way into the house to confer. He stood looking out the window when his noble appeal to nonviolence—and conscience—ended abruptly. A bullet struck him in the head, killing him instantly. Meanwhile Sheriff Stover had entered the house and disarmed the Greer men, who may have realized that the alternative was doom. "It was very exciting to me," wrote James Warren LeSueur, a Mormon who, as a boy, had witnessed the fight, "like seeing a war in action."[27]

Mormons convened at the town jail to guard the Greer men from lynching, though no lynching party gathered. The aftermath of the battle was a trial in far-away Prescott, where the Greer men were given light sentences for carrying guns into town. Despite such lenient treatment, both Mormons and "cowboys"—including the Greers, whom the Mormons put into the "cowboy" category even though the Greers were themselves Mormons—believed they were persecuted. Almost all the local offices, recalled LeSueur, were in the hands of New Mexicans, including sheriff, deputy, assessor, tax collector, and probate judge. "When a Mexican was brought up for trial," he reported, "he was freed at the least sign of a defense. If a cowboy should be tried for the least offense, he was sure to get the limit." LeSueur, indeed, had witnessed the lynching of three cowboys in Sol Barth's barn, an act that demonstrated that New Mexicans, no less than Texans, could partake in rituals of honor and shame. Though John Hunt—county supervisor, Mormon bishop of Snowflake, and a resolute man of conscience—stood "like a stone wall" against lynching, it did not cease.[28]

For the time being, gun battles stopped. Bitterness did not. After the killing of Tenney—apparently from a shot fired from Barth's hotel—Joseph Fish expressed certainty that "J. L. Hubbell and Sol Barth were . . . at the bottom of this cold-blooded murder." Mormons also charged Barth with creating a "ring" whose purpose was to drive them out. The ring would do "everything to hinder [Mormons'] progress and to work against them," wrote Fish. "The law was used on every possible occasion to retard the work of the new settlers." Those most active in the ring, reported Fish, were not only Hubbell and Barth but also St. George Creaghe, Charles Kinnear, Luther Martin, Antonio Gonzales, Henry Huning, and Tomas Perez, several of whom held county office. "Jackals, vultures, and vampires," cursed Fish.[29]

Once the ring had formed, county politics became the arena of contest. Apache County—geographically among the biggest counties in the United States—was carved from Yavapai County in 1879, with a temporary seat in Snowflake. In June, voters chose St. Johns over Springerville as the county's permanent seat, a decision that served the Barth brothers insofar as they stood to gain business. By throwing out the vote from several Mormon precincts, the Barth faction won all important county offices. To make sure that the count would go their way, the Barth faction supposedly told "their" county supervisors, St. George Creaghe and Tomas Perez, to count the ballots for probate judge first, then have the new probate judge—a member of the ring—count the votes for county seat. The new probate judge was expected to throw out suspect votes—Mormon votes—against St. Johns. The Barth faction supposedly took the added precaution of hiding a gunman behind a curtain while the counting was done. If the old probate judge, stake president Jesse Smith, made trouble, the gunman was told to assassinate him. In his journal, Smith, ignorant of any assassination plot but furious nonetheless, reported being "bulldozed" by Creaghe and Perez as they nullified Mormon votes.[30]

Yet peace remained possible. In 1880, Ammon Tenney worked with Lorenzo Hubbell to fashion a compromise ticket that would include both Mormons and members of the Barth faction. Tenney proposed to meet with Hubbell in St. Johns, after which he would travel to Snowflake with the names of prospective candidates. Delegates to a nominating convention in Snowflake would then choose the men on Tenney's list. Tenney stayed in St. Johns too long, however, and the Snowflake convention was forced to make nominations without his input. With Apostle Woodruff urging Mormons to use their majority to put their men into office, the Snowflake delegates nominated only Mormons. Once word got back to Hubbell and Barth, they cried treason.[31]

Realizing their mistake, the Mormons tried again to compromise. Two weeks before the election, Jesse Smith and L. H. Hatch, with Apostles Brigham Young, Jr., and John W. Young, traveled to St. Johns to meet with Barth, Hubbell, and Ebenezer Stover. The Mormons proposed mutual concessions, though just what is a mystery. The Barth faction, however, rejected "all offers for peace and reconciliation," preferring to settle things on election day.[32] In November, the Mormon candidates lost.

With the Barth faction at the helm of county government, frictions mounted. The schools became a particular bone of contention. In St. Johns, the Barth faction chose non-Mormon teachers yet required Mormons to pay taxes to support the schools. Unable to create their own school district, Mormons were forced to "associate their children with those of low filthy habits in the school room," meaning New Mexicans. Once again, the Mormon preoccupation with conscience—with good, clean habits rather than "low filthy" ones—led them to prejudice. The Mormons' opponents countered by refusing to certify Mormons to teach in the public schools, failing them for minor mistakes on their exams. Even when Mormons managed to gain certification, the county refused to hire them on the grounds that they taught religious classes before or after school.[33]

The height of the Mormon versus gentile conflict came in 1883–84. In those years, the county supervisors "laid out a road," reported Joseph Fish, "through the center of three or four city lots" that belonged to Mormons. Meanwhile one of Sol Barth's clerks "started the jumping of streets" in Mormon neighborhoods "and erected a cabin in the center of one of them." Vacant city lots, added Fish, "were jumped and held by force of arms." "To all human appearances," he recalled, "it would be a death struggle, yet by the blessing of God, it was averted." In at least one case, however, it was not averted. In 1883, a man called "Dutchy" attempted to jump a claim held by Mormons James E. and D. J. Porter. The Porters drove him off. When Dutchy returned—drunk, according to Mormons—he came with a gun. Dutchy fired on one of the Porters as he sat on his porch. Both Porters fired back and Dutchy fell, mortally wounded.[34]

Tales of claim jumping abounded in the West. Where land was free for the taking, people took it. Often they took it from Indians. Sometimes they took it from other settlers. Possessory rights were difficult to prove and open to contest. Evans Coleman, explaining his own experiences as a Mormon pioneer in the White Mountains, explained that "if a man wanted to settle" in a "desirable spot," he simply cut four logs "as if he were going to build a house, lay those logs as if they were the foundation for a house, cut a hole at one end of the enclosure for a door, and his claim stood." Sometimes not even that was necessary. One Mormon pioneer in 1879 simply "put up a notice reading: 'We claim this valley for dairy purposes.'"[35] If another settler was using the claim for pasturing livestock or gathering wood, conflict ensued.

Disputes over land claims, however, do not in themselves explain the bitterness of the conflict. Beyond those disputes lay self-righteousness at one extreme and honor on the other. Mormons defined their enemies as sinners, criminals, defilers. Gentiles defined Mormons as fanatics, a people so imbued with conscience, or at least their own version of conscience, that they refused to see their own wrongs. Gentiles, too—even those with no roots in the Lower Midwest and South—practiced the aggressive assertion born of honor.

The claim issue grew more heated as Mormons brought in two thousand additional settlers in 1884, thus doubling their numbers. "If we do not settle these places," inveighed Jesse Smith, "someone else will. If you move away from this place someone else will occupy it. The Mexicans will come in here and get fat without the blessings of God."[36] If Mormons did not occupy the land, conscience would suffer. Conscience, it seemed, gave Mormons the right to expand, whereas sinfulness denied their enemies the right to resist. Amid the struggle, the

Little Colorado basin somehow ceased to be waste and desert, appointed by God as a refuge. It became prime real estate.

Rumblings of war continued to shake the county. The "outlaws" who opposed the Mormons, wrote Ida Hunt Udall, one of Bishop David Udall's wives, "were backed by the whole, jew, gentile, and Mexican town. . . . The spirit of bloodshed seemed to be in the very air." Among gentiles, meanwhile, circulated a rumor that Mormons were recruiting Indians to drive out their enemies, just as they had done at Mountain Meadows. Mormons vigorously denied any role in the 1857 massacre, despite John D. Lee's conviction in 1876. They could not shake the charge of fomenting Indian violence, however, in part because Mormons had spoken of Indians as the "battle ax of the Lord." Jesse Smith used precisely those words in 1883 while urging the Saints to redouble their missionary efforts among the "Lamanites" (the Book of Mormon's term for Indians), implying that the apocalypse in Apache County might come sooner than expected. By May 1884, Smith was proclaiming a fast day in order that the Saints could "plead their cause before the Lord in relation to our enemies in this land."[37]

To make matters worse, Barth and Hubbell brought in a newspaper editor in 1883 whose mission was to rid the county of Mormons. The editor, a U.S. court commissioner named John McCarter, founded the *Apache Chief*, the weekly newspaper of St. Johns. In his "Official County Paper," McCarter began a drum-beat of anti-Mormon polemic. "How did Missouri and Illinois get rid of the Mormons?" wrote McCarter in the May 30, 1884, issue of his paper.

> By the use of the shot gun and rope. Apache county can rid herself of them also. In a year from now the Mormons will have the power here and Gentiles had better leave. . . . The Mormon disease is a desperate one and the rope and shot gun is the only cure. . . . Take the needed steps while it is yet time. . . . No Mormon should be allowed to cast a vote. He has no rights and should be allowed none. Down with them. Grind out their very existence.[38]

McCarter did not merely suggest vigilante action; he singled out specific individuals for lynching. Stake president Jesse Smith, Snowflake bishop John Hunt, and St. Johns bishop David Udall made the list. Meanwhile, when two Mormon apostles—Brigham Young, Jr., and Francis M. Lyman—journeyed to Apache County in spring 1884, McCarter and two others proposed to castrate them. Rituals of shaming promised to resolve bitter conflicts. The dictates of honor, it seemed, would crush the mandate of conscience. The plan fizzled, however, when Hubbell refused to participate.[39]

Even as they stopped short of vigilantism, McCarter and his allies sought victory through politics. In St. Johns in August 1884, they held an "Anti-Mormon" convention that was charged with nominating a list of anti-Mormon candidates. Those present included New Mexicans and gentile cattlemen who had little previous involvement in politics. The rancher contingent included Ike Clanton, who was widely known for his leadership of the "Cow-boys" in southern Arizona and his escape from the wrath of Wyatt Earp. Clanton's brother-in-law, Ebin Stanley, one of General Crook's most trusted scouts in the Tonto Basin campaign of the early 1870s, also attended. Per the makeup of the convention, the ticket they presented included stalwart Barth allies. For the critical office of sheriff, they put up Lorenzo Hubbell, who, wrote McCarter, was "a staunch anti-Mormon, an old tried citizen, and a heavy taxpayer and property owner."[40]

Though consisting in part of Democrats who signed on to fight Mormons, the anti-Mormon ticket leaned Republican. Republicans had opposed Mormonism—and especially polygamy—since their entry into national politics in 1856. Their opposition continued after the Civil War. In Apache County, the anti-Mormon ticket benefited from Republican success in disqualifying Mormons voters via a "test oath." Arizona's Republican governor, Frederick Tritle, signed the test oath into law in 1882, thus enabling local officials to enforce the federal government's Edmunds Act of the same year. At the polls, voters were asked whether they supported the laws of the United States, including—by implication—those banning polygamy. Only if they answered affirmatively could they vote.[41]

At best the test oath was porous. When Joseph Fish went to the polls, James Houck, a Republican legislator who would become an active fighter in Pleasant Valley, challenged his right to vote. Because the oath did not specifically mention polygamy, Fish took it in good faith and proceeded to cast his ballot.[42] Hundreds of others did the same.

By appointing election judges, however, the ring was able to disqualify enough Mormons to ensure victory. The ring did not stop there, complained Mormons. Barth's men also stuffed ballot boxes, which by 1884 seemed a timeworn tradition. Worse, charged Fish, the ring's candidate for sheriff, Lorenzo Hubbell, had "entered into a compact with the leading horse and cattle thieves of the county pledging to shield them in their freebooting business for their support at the election."[43]

"They have stuffed the ballot boxes," cried Fish,

> they have thrown out our votes without counting them, they have deprived our people of holding office when elected and of voting at the polls. They have raised our taxes higher than assessed without our knowledge, they have squandered the public funds, they have instigated the Indians and Mexicans to prey

upon our stock. They have called our most respected sisters prostitutes, and our children bastards. They advocated lynch law and the use of the rope and shot gun upon our best and most worthy citizens for no other reason than that they were Mormons.[44]

Fish recognized that his enemies were calling on honor—rituals of shaming—to defeat his people.

Mormon conscience, however, could be as intransigent as gentile honor. As far as their eyes could see, Mormons found evil. Their corporatism, their insularity, their repudiation of sin—their conscience—made it impossible for them to comprehend their role in stirring discord. They saw "jackals, vultures, and vampires." To the Mormons, neither New Mexicans nor white gentiles had any legitimate reason to vie for supremacy.[45] The Saints brought the kingdom of conscience. They brooked no opposition. The solution to their problems was not conciliation but virtue.

Stake president Jesse Smith, remarked one settler in September 1884, had asked "the Bishop to root out evil from the Saints and set your faces like flint against unrighteousness." Smith further "reproved those who allow their daughters to work for outsiders." Bishop Udall and his high counselors, meanwhile, called "upon the Lord to remember our Enemies that their power may be broken and confusion come upon them and they reap that which they desire to bring upon the Saints."[46]

Apostle Snow took a more prophetic tone. "Perhaps no county more than yours has felt the hand of the oppressor," he told his fellows shortly before the 1884 election. Snow then mentioned the murder of two missionaries in Tennessee, blaming the murders not on Southerners but on the anti-Mormon platform of the Republican Party. "The time is coming," he prophesied, "when God will call" the persecutors "to account for it, but not until all [persecutors] have had a chance to stain their garments with the blood of innocence." "It is better to die," he concluded, while "enjoying liberty than live to be enslaved. The Saints have something to live for and something to die for. . . . If you are forced into it, fight like angels, and not like devils. Keep your powder dry, and if you have no gun, sell your coat and buy one."[47]

Snow's warning reveals a paradox. Repeatedly Mormons countenanced restraint. Few of them—with occasional exceptions such as the Greers—attached pride to physical assertion. Few of them engaged in fisticuffs, duels, or gunfights. The temptation to do violence, however, was constant. In general, church leaders kept that temptation under control, though Mormons were not pacifists. When

Mormons did take up arms, as Snow suggested, they tended to do so not as individuals defending their honor but as a group defending its righteousness.

In early 1885, McCarter departed and Henry Reed took over the *Apache Chief*, renaming it the St. Johns *Herald*. Mormons briefly took hope that the new man would be better than the old one. By July 1885, however, Reed was advertising his paper as "the only exclusively anti-Mormon paper in Arizona." Reed lost no time in administering harangues. He wrote that Mormon men—polygamists—made slaves of their wives, thus breeching middle-class views of women as weaker vessels who merited protection. When a Mormon was accused of killing a New Mexican man, Reed damned other Mormons for helping the fugitive escape. Reed gave vent to rhetorical apoplexy at the idea put forth by a short-lived Mormon newspaper, the *Orion Era*, that Apache County's vaunted sheriff had simply failed to detain the accused man. "Don't let the recollections of the Mountain Meadows Massacre befuddle the ideas in your liquidized brain," he told the *Era*'s new editor, Juan Milner. To those who worried over the increasing presence of guns on the streets of St. Johns, Reed cried, "Look out for the peace of your own homes and assist us to crush out the giant crime of the day, the horror of a civilized people—polygamy." At the bottom of page 1 of the *Herald*, Reed placed a single declaration: "The polygamists must go."[48]

The gentile campaign against polygamy itself suggests conscience. The issue was religious and cultural. Polygamy violated the Christian dedication to monogamy. It seemed tantamount to lust, adultery, exploitation. Yet polygamy equally violated the codes of honor. Men imbued with honor—in the Old South and outside it—saw themselves as chivalrous defenders of white women. Pure, chaste, and good, women symbolized the sanctity of a lineage. To "defile" a woman—whether through rape or polygamy—was to defile her family. The campaign against polygamy, then, partook of both conscience and honor. The means that gentiles proposed to use in abolishing polygamy, however, were profoundly those of honor. McCarter and his allies sought not merely to attack polygamists via the law but to attack their manhood itself.

Threats of castration and lynching, however, were more bluster than action. The campaign against polygamy in the end prevailed not through rope, gun, or knife but through appeals to the courts. First convicted was St. Johns bishop David Udall, who was sentenced to three years in a federal penitentiary for falsely signing his name as witness to a homestead claim by Miles Romney, editor of the *Orion Era*. Romney escaped conviction by fleeing to Mexico, where he helped build a new Mormon colony.[49] Those prosecutions were but ripples in a mighty wake of legal condemnation.

Wholesale convictions began two years after Congress passed the 1882 Edmunds Act, which stiffened penalties for polygamy and barred polygamists from voting and from holding office. Initially church leaders welcomed a court battle, certain that the statute of limitations had run its course, since the marriages in question had occurred years earlier. Church leaders also believed that Arizona courts could not try men for breaking the laws of Utah, where the marriages had taken place. On those arguments rested the success of the Arizona mission. One scholar has estimated that fully 85 percent of Mormon families in Arizona were polygamous, many having come from Utah specifically to escape prosecution there.[50] That figure is surely too high—much too high—but certainly polygamists made up the cream of the leadership. If they fell, so might their brethren.

The man presiding over the polygamy cases was that old Mormon foe, Summer Howard, he of the Mountain Meadows case that had led to the conviction of John D. Lee. Mormon arguments failed to persuade him. In the first trials, five Mormons—all church leaders—were found guilty. Fish recorded that no fewer than forty members of the St. Johns "ring" testified against them. Judge Howard sentenced three men—Ammon Tenney, Peter Christopherson, and Christopher Kempe—to three-and-a-half-year terms and five-hundred-dollar fines. Two others—William Flake and James Skousen—got six months in the Yuma penitentiary, popularly known as the "Hell Hole." Fearing that they, too, would be convicted, some 10 percent of adult Mormon men in Arizona fled to Mexico, where they joined the mission in Chihuahua. Others went into hiding.[51]

The crisis was not just in Arizona. In Utah, Congress forbade polygamists from voting or holding office. Idaho went further; it forbade any Mormon from voting or holding office after 1884. When the Edmunds Act proved weak, moreover, Congress got tougher. In 1887, it passed the Edmunds-Tucker Act, which enacted a stronger test oath, placed Utah's schools under federal authority, abolished suffrage for Utah women, and dissolved the LDS Church as a corporation. With the Edmunds-Tucker Act in force, a new round of antipolygamy prosecutions shook Deseret.[52]

The blows failed to weaken Mormons' faith, but they devastated their economy. Of the Arizona colonies, Snowflake suffered worst. By early 1885, nearly all of its "leading men" had either been convicted or had fled to Mexico, including stake president Jesse Smith, Snowflake bishop John Hunt, and Hunt's right-hand man and pillar of the community, William Flake. Because polygamous men tended to be prosperous and powerful, their crisis wrought havoc. When all of the officers of the Arizona Cooperative Mercantile Institution were forced to defend themselves in court or flee to Mexico, they were also forced to shut down the co-op. "Hell," wrote Joseph Fish, "appeared on every corner."[53]

In the Eastern Arizona Stake, figured Fish, twelve men faced prosecution and forty-eight fled, many taking their families with them. The effect among the faithful was distress and fury. John Henry Standifird, a Mormon resident of Taylor, scrawled sanguine predictions into his journal in March 1885. "We may expect," he wrote, "our own nation before long will be broken to pieces because of their unjust dealings with the saints. Ere long the red man will sorely vex the United States. There is also a desolating sickness to cover the land and we are commanded to stand in Holy places while the indignation of the Lord passes over the wicked."[54]

Standifird exempted the Saints from the violence that would beset their enemies. The Saints would stand apart, at peace, protected, while the Lord killed millions. The threat of retaliation came not from Mormons—a people of conscience—but from God. Not all church leaders, however, blew the same trumpet.

Standifird noted in his journal that Apostle John Smith had told Mormons that persecution would continue until it had touched every Mormon, forcing them to repent.[55] The call for repentance was a call to revitalize the Word of Wisdom and to return to right living. To Smith's way of thinking, God was punishing not the persecutors but the Saints themselves. It was they who had done wrong. Smith affirmed Mormon conscience.

Smith's call to repentance, moreover, obliquely suggested a call to moderation. Only a few years later, the church entered an era of compromise. It repudiated the doctrine of Blood Atonement in 1889 and ceased to countenance plural marriage in 1890. The year 1890 also saw new church president Wilford Woodruff urge Mormons to embrace the two-party political system rather than vote as a bloc for their own candidates. Woodruff, once a man of dire prophecies, presided over moderation and reform.

As Woodruff paved the way for the mainstreaming of Mormonism, changes were occurring at the local level, especially in Arizona. The changes did not necessarily come quickly or consciously. They came gradually, for the most part, and sometimes convulsively in response to crises. What they created was a new solidarity—a common identity—among Mormons and gentiles. That identity, as we shall see, led away from conscience and toward honor. But the changes did not proceed from Mormons alone. Gentiles, too, sought a new relationship with their old enemies, particularly to achieve political gain.

In 1885, one of the great enemies of Apache County's Mormons, Ebenezer Stover, convinced the Arizona legislature to pass a yet stricter test oath that would strip all Mormons of the right to vote. President Grover Cleveland, however, aware that Mormons favored the Democratic Party over the GOP, offered détente by pardoning David Udall. Cleveland's gubernatorial appointee for Arizona, Conrad Meyer Zulick, meanwhile convinced the legislature to repeal the test oath. The "spirit of persecution," wrote Joseph Smith, Jr., "gradually died out, and things began to settle down to a living basis with the Mormons."[56]

The spirit of persecution did not die, however, before William Flake went to prison. In 1884, a U.S. marshal came to arrest him. Flake invited the marshal to sit with his family for dinner, and the marshal accepted. After entering custody Flake was taken to Prescott to stand trial in the court of Summer Howard. "We had known Judge Howard from Utah," wrote Lucy Flake, "where he had done all he could against our people" in the Mountain Meadows trials. Publicly, Flake warned Howard of damnation. Privately, Flake predicted the judge's death. "Where is that man," he wrote in his diary, "that has taken an active part against the Saints that has lasted long[?] . . . To day they are on the bench [but] to morrow they are under the sod."[57] Nevertheless Flake pled guilty, was convicted, and received a sentence.

Despite his conviction, Flake could count on at least one friend among the gentiles. The "jolly Irishman of doubtful morals," James Stinson, made his way from Tempe to Prescott to help Flake in his hour of need. When Flake was unable to make bail, Stinson, with a Snowflake Mormon named George Bagnall, loaned him two thousand dollars. The money paid not only Flake's bail but also the bail of Miles Romney. When Romney fled to Mexico, Flake was left to pay the debt. Stinson, recalled Flake's son in later years, was William Flake's "main help all the way and . . . took [the conviction] the hardest of the two."[58]

Flake lost no dignity in prison at Yuma. When he arrived, the warden cropped his hair and beard, then stood back, uttering, "That will do." Inside, Flake found conditions to be tolerable—in part because he served during winter. His hair, beard, and skin soon became "soft and free from the effects of harsh wind and sun," and he was able to spend a great deal of time reading, resting, and ministering to other prisoners ("some of the cons think it is worse to have more than 1 wife than it is to kill," he confided in his journal). On one occasion, he led the prisoners in a protest against the rotten meat that comprised their diet. The prisoners won. When he left, they presented him with gifts they had made, including a horsehair bridle, an "elaborately carved cane," and a work box inlaid with 2,400 pieces of native wood. The warden, having taken a liking to Flake, told him that he would be missed. Flake's son went so far as to suggest that Flake had transformed the prison into "a heaven." Such testimony—all of it from Flake's family—bore witness to the triumph of conscience over persecution.[59]

William Flake in prison garb, 1885. Note the
fine hat, presumably not prison issue. Courtesy
of Yuma Territorial Prison Museum.

When he returned to Snowflake, Flake met jubilance. Church bells rang
as the townspeople escorted him to the public square, where they sang songs,
played music—including the Confederate anthem, "Dixie"—and read "sentiments" written for the occasion. At the end of the celebration, William went back
to his home and his wives. He refused to sever ties to either of them. He would
never again go to prison, but his troubles remained great. It would take him seven
years—seven hard years—to repay his debt to Stinson.[60] Those years would be
pivotal in the history of the county, the territory, and even, in a sense, the nation.

By 1886, the polygamy trials had ended, but Mormons still reeled. God's people
had proven to be vulnerable. They could not withstand another withering legal
blast like that of 1884–85. They could not fight New Mexicans, fight the Barth

faction, and fight the territory simultaneously. Even a victory against those enemies would leave another in the field. By 1886, just when the polygamy persecutions receded, a new threat appeared on the horizon, the Aztec Land and Cattle
Company and its legion of young cowboys. In desperation, Mormons grasped
for the hand of rescue. They could no longer isolate themselves. They could no
longer act as though the outside world was one great undifferentiated realm of
evil. They could no longer follow Bishop Udall's recommendation to "carefully
avoid acts of violence."[61] They would have to make common cause with some old
enemies in order to defeat others. They would have to make common cause with
honor.

5

COWBOYS AND CRIMINALS

Joseph Fish, manager of the Woodruff ACMI—the Mormon cooperative store—was posting accounts on May 29, 1884, when two masked men holding cocked pistols burst through the door. While one robber held a gun on Fish, the other retrieved the clerk, James Clark Owens, Jr., from the back room. The robbers demanded the contents of the safe. Remaining at a distance from the gunmen, Fish opened the safe and tossed them the money. The robbers took five hundred dollars in cash, then commandeered a pistol, a supply of ammunition, a pair of field glasses, a few cans of peaches, and some tobacco, stuffing them into a pair of new overalls with the bottoms tied. To slow Fish and Owens in their effort to gather a posse, the robbers marched them to the edge of town. Then the robbers rode away, the stuffed overalls strapped to one of their horses like a saddlebag.[1]

While Fish returned to the store, Owens and another man tracked the robbers toward Holbrook. A jog in the trail, however, suggested a devious turn toward Tonto Basin. Now sure of the robbers' destination, Owens and his partner went back to gather a posse. No posse could be assembled on such short notice, as it turned out, but Fish and Owens retained high hopes for justice. Earlier in the year Owens had been in Prescott, where he had seen one of the robbers. Despite the mask, Owens knew the man from his dark complexion and his Indian features. The robber, he recalled, had been a defendant in the Tewksbury larceny trial. His name was James Tewksbury.[2]

Authorities somehow learned the name of the second suspect, too. He was George Blaine, a Tewksbury ally who, before the year was out, would be shot through the jaw by the foreman of the Stinson ranch in Pleasant Valley. Both Blaine and Jim Tewksbury were charged with armed robbery. Trial was scheduled for February 1885, though neither of the accused appeared. Tewksbury told the court that he had miscalculated the time it took to ride to St. Johns, causing him to arrive two days late. Blaine was too ill to travel, his bullet wound requiring several months to heal. Neither did Fish and Owens attend. Fish had fled to Mexico to escape polygamy charges. Owens for some reason was out of town. Only one witness testified, Baily Brimhall, who may have been the man who had helped Owens track the robbers. The court dismissed the case.[3]

Mormons already believed that the Tewksburys had stolen some of their horses.[4] Now they had another grievance. What Mormons were beginning to realize was that the campaign against them had moved from legal attacks to criminal attacks. As events would soon prove, Mormons were fair game for an array of persecutions ranging from arrests for polygamy to robbery, horse theft, and beatings. The Mormon struggle for a home on the range evolved from a struggle against organized political enemies into a struggle against individuals who operated outside the law and without coordination. "During these perilous times," wrote one observer, "Mormons were being persecuted for their religious beliefs. Anyone who was so inclined felt he had a right to add to their troubles."[5]

The ACMI heist nonetheless had political implications. The ACMI anchored the Arizona mission. It served as a bank; it offered credit; it sold goods at a discount; it even paid for the legal defense of polygamists.[6] To attack the ACMI was to attack the Mormon community. In all probability, the robbers believed that no sheriff would hold them accountable. Mormons were vulnerable. Thanks to the polygamy prosecutions, they were too weak to resist. With at least two Apache County editors making no bones about their hatred for the Saints, those who attacked Mormons might even account themselves heroes.

Criminal attacks pushed Mormons further into the redoubt of conscience. Each new attack confirmed Mormons in their belief that Rim Country gentiles were "other." Gentiles were everything that Mormons defined themselves against. From the Mormon point of view, their struggle to survive became all the more a struggle for righteousness.

Mormons sought redress via the courts, but the courts, too, were against them. Jim Tewksbury may have feared prosecution enough, however, to make a deal with his accusers. He agreed to appear at court in July 1885 to testify not in his own case but against two men who had stolen cows from Snowflake Mormons. Those men were John and Thomas Graham.

The alleged theft had occurred in 1882, when the Grahams were just beginning their career as ranchers. To stock their range, they had bought two hundred head from William Flake along with a few head belonging to other Mormons. As the Grahams drove away the herd, Mormon wranglers cut out twelve to fourteen strays that were not part of the sale. When the Mormon wranglers left, the Grahams allegedly retrieved the strays and drove them with their herd to Pleasant Valley. At least two of the stolen animals belonged to William Atchison, who was alerted to the theft by Jim Stinson in December 1882. Atchison, who was "careless and indifferent as to religion, yet with a heart as big as his body," chose not to prosecute. To do so, he believed, would bring more trouble than gain.[7]

In 1885, Atchison changed his mind. Mormons now wanted to fight the steady drizzle of criminal acts against them, acts that were beginning to take a toll. To back up the testimony promised by Tewksbury, Mormons recruited an undercover detective. The detective — Robert Carr Blassingame — hired on as a cowboy in Pleasant Valley in 1885, which allowed him to locate the Atchison cows and report back to his employers.[8]

Later, Blassingame would marry into the Greer family, convert to Mormonism, and become a county commissioner. His activities as a detective, however — and perhaps his actions as a vigilante — made his life dangerous. In December 1886, not long after his service in Pleasant Valley, some eight to ten "Mexicans" (likely New Mexicans) set an ambush for him. Blassingame and his partner survived the attack but were at a loss to explain its motive. The *Herald* helpfully suggested that the attackers may have sought revenge for the killings of some sheepherders. Beyond that information, we know little about Blassingame's activities. All we know is that in 1885 he was a cowboy fresh from New Mexico who needed work and that desperate Mormons — backed by the Apache County Stock Growers Association — accommodated him.[9]

Thanks to Blassingame's detective work and Tewksbury's promised testimony, Apache County scheduled a trial for the Graham brothers for summer 1885. The court set bail at a thousand dollars for each brother, which was promptly paid by Tomas Perez, the anti-Mormon sheriff of Apache County, and A. A. Ward, the Mazatzal Mountains sheepherder and friend of the Grahams. At about the same time, the Grahams attempted to sell their ranches, perhaps to pay back their bondsmen. No one bought. The brothers triumphed, however, when in March 1886 Apache County dropped the charges and refunded the bond.[10]

A pattern was emerging. Outlaws would steal from Mormons, then rely on weak, indifferent, or overtly anti-Mormon prosecutors, judges, and jurors to escape justice. Even as the storm over polygamy began to fade, persecution continued to seethe. Criminality, it seemed, would defeat conscience.

Still another chain of events, this one beginning in December 1884, spawned new bouts of animus and persecution. In that month, five men in New York City sent a shell hurtling toward Mormons when they incorporated the Aztec Land

and Cattle Company, Limited. The five included a wealthy New Yorker turned Texas cattleman, a lawyer whose firm represented the A&P, and several "merchant princes." The inspiration for the venture probably came from a New Yorker named Edward Kinsley, who had seen prime cow country while surveying the A&P line in 1882.[11]

The Aztec was no shoestring operation, nor was it built from the ground up in the manner of some of the famous Texas ranches. It was solidly Northern, solidly Republican, solidly elite. The stockholders, like the principals, were wealthy men from New York and New England. The board of directors included a pair of former Massachusetts governors.[12] The Aztec, then, was created by men who espoused conscience. They were men drawn from the ranks not only of financiers but also of abolition. If they thought about Mormon polygamy, they likely opposed it. Polygamy squared neither with the conscience of the Yankee North nor the honor of the Old South. Yet Aztec managers and Mormons had much in common. Both sustained law and order. Both celebrated the principle of work. Neither valued the gambling, drinking, braggadocio, or aggressive assertion that came with honor. In the long run, Aztec managers and Mormons would join forces. In the short run, they competed for range.

For operating capital, Aztec managers sold ten thousand shares of stock with a par value of a hundred dollars a share, putting one million dollars into company coffers. Roughly half went to the purchase of a million acres of alternate, odd sections from the A&P. That gave the Aztec control of a strip of land fifty miles wide and ninety miles long, stretching from Snowflake (or just east of it) all the way to Flagstaff. So big was the Aztec that it took two days to ride across it from north to south and four days from east to west.[13]

To stock its range the Aztec mortgaged thirty-three thousand animals from the Continental Land and Cattle Company of Abilene, Texas. The Continental's brand depicted a "hashknife"—a "hand-forged, single-bladed" knife used to make hash—hence it was called simply the "Hashknife Outfit." The name carried over to the Aztec, whose cowboys were called "Hashknifes." The company then set up headquarters ten miles west of Holbrook (a stop on the A&P) and only a few miles from the Mormon settlement of St. Joseph. The land there is dry; average precipitation is nine inches a year. The Colorado Plateau tips upward, however, as one moves south toward the Rim, where higher rainfall spawns lusher grass. There cattle could thrive on bunch grass, antelope grass, sacatone grass, and various grammas. The nutritious Bigelow sage added variety. Even with the Rim Country lands, however, the carrying capacity for the entire range was between four and eight cattle per square mile. The range could sustainably accommodate between twelve thousand and twenty-four thousand cattle, num-

Aztec Land and Cattle Company brands posted
in the St. Johns *Herald*, August 25, 1887. Courtesy
of Arizona Historical Society/Tucson.

bers far below what the Aztec brought.[14] Making matters worse were the tens of thousands of animals already grazing the Aztec's range.

"Our cattle and horses were rolling fat," recalled Lucy Flake of the early 1880s. Even as conflict and prosecution overwhelmed them, Mormons looked hopefully to the future. The land around Snowflake was "a stockman's paradise and we were by far the largest owners," she wrote. William Flake, indeed, was prescient in his emphasis on stock raising despite the Mormon disposition toward farming. His profits helped him to buy more land for settlement. The problem was that others, too, were discovering the lush grasses of the Rim Country. Gentiles like Will Barnes arrived to carve out small ranches on free range.[15] So, too, did New Mexican sheepmen bring flocks, moving them across the high pastures, then bringing them back across the territorial line. From Flagstaff in the west, the Daggs brothers likewise brought huge herds of sheep.

In 1882, when Edward Kinsley had surveyed A&P lands, he had seen prime country grazed by few animals. The native grazing species, the pronghorn, had been reduced by hungry Indians as well as by settlers, and sheep had only begun to make their way into the vast stretches of grass. By 1885, when the Aztec published its brand in the St. Johns *Herald*, the range was heavily stocked. The Aztec moved into land that had become contested.

Into the mix the Aztec brought soldiers in the guise of Texas cowboys. As a Flagstaff newspaper would observe in 1929, cowboys "were loyal, brave and sagacious, mostly southerners, whose blood carried traces of that of cavalier ancestors, bent on adventure, quick to hate, and love and fight." Mormons of the 1880s thought of them differently. To Mormons, Aztec cowboys were "Texas rustlers" who "made their living by stealing cattle, holding up stage coaches, [and] gambling," and who were likely to have "at least one murder to account for." Joseph Fish cited Major Ben Truman on the cowboy: "ostensibly a herder of stock . . . but in reality a stealer of horses and cattle, a guzzler of adulterated spirits, and a shooter of men, he fears neither God, man, nor devil."[16]

As the *Sun* suggested, cowboys became romantic figures in part because they embodied key aspects of honor. They were not exponents of a timeless, pristine sort of honor that came with cavaliers, but they were exponents of an honor that spoke to a new century, as we shall see. What matters here, however, is not whether cowboys were heroic or villainous but that, either way, they were more than creatures of myth. They brought their peculiar baggage to the West.

Equally important is the oppositional relationship that cowboys established with Mormons. Cowboys were capable of temperance, diplomacy, gentleness, sympathy, and faith. They were capable of conscience. Their behavioral trajectory, however, veered often in the other direction. To Mormons, they seemed the very souls of iniquity. To an even greater degree than cowboys merited, Mormons identified them with vice and criminality—with honor—with behaviors that contradicted goodness, justice, fairness. Among Mormons, cowboys surpassed New Mexicans as symbols of sin.

Part of the reason that Mormons saw cowboys as "other" was their flamboyance. Will Barnes recalled that the Texas men who flocked to Arizona in the 1880s sported "broad-brimmed beaver hats" adorned by long leather hat strings with complex knots that took hours to plait and to tie. The favorite hats, which ran about ten dollars apiece, were those made by John Stetson of Texas. On their feet the Texans wore not the cheap footwear of farmers but handmade boots with intricately stitched uppers and images of half-moons and stars dyed blue or red. The best boots, said to come from John Cubine of Coffeyville, Kansas, included stars, crescents, horseshoes, "bleeding hearts," and fancy stitching. "Next to our saddles," wrote Barnes, "a pair of Coffeyville boots was the choicest thing in this life, something every rider coveted and bought if it took his last cent." A good pair cost as much as twenty dollars, more than half a month's wages.[17]

Strapped to those boots were silver-mounted spurs that cost twice as much as the boots themselves. In their hands cowboys held quirts, reins, and ropes that they had plaited or woven over days, weeks, even months. Like their hat strings, their quirts and reins, as well as their halters and saddles, displayed "wonderful knots, fancy buttons and tassels." Covering the cowboy's torso was a "fancy" shirt and vest, while on his legs appeared leather chaps, sometimes with long rows of "conchos," rounded plates flattened by hammering out silver coins. The cowboy completed his costume with a carbine in his saddle holster and a six-gun, frequently with a pearl or ivory handle, strapped to his waist.[18]

The most important accoutrement was the saddle, which was often hand tooled and finished with silver mountings. The best saddles cost a thousand dollars. It is hard to imagine how Arizona cowboys, who in the 1880s made a dollar a day, could afford such expensive equipment. Like modern ranchers who spend thousands on new pickups, however, they invested earnings in equipment that symbolized individual power. To an Arizona cowboy, the worst insult was to say that he "would sell his saddle," which meant that he had no pride, no virtue, no honor.[19]

A Mormon historian of the Rim Country estimated that the cost of the average outfit of an Arizona cowboy in the 1880s, including an average saddle and horse, ran to $190, about what a cowboy could expect to make in six months. If he bought a good horse and saddle, he could expect to pay far more. Wages, then, went to one's personal outfit, as well as to gambling, drinking, and prostitution. The point here is not to invoke the clichéd image of the "colorful cowboy" but to understand the cowboy as a creature of honor. Like Californio and Tejano vaqueros—like Southern planters, for that matter—cowboys spent earnings on costume, on show, on what we might call personal performance.

Seldom did they put away money for investment, not even for buying a ranch, given that they could claim land via preemption and homesteading. To populate that land with livestock, cowboys needed only to buy a few animals and breed them or, perhaps, rope a few mavericks. Cowboys did not reject the idea of getting ahead; they simply saw no reason to save wages to arrive there. To a cowboy, the most important component of the good life was to earn the respect of one's fellows via performance, via physical courage, via shooting if need be, but failing that, by riding broncs and tackling steers, as well as by gambling, drinking, brawling, and womanizing. Cowboys, then, were capitalist and precapitalist, entrepreneurial and proletarian, imbued with honor and bordering on criminal.

In addition to bringing the mores of honor, Texas cowboys brought new technologies: double-cinch saddles, grass ropes "tied hard and fast to the nub," and
"little old potmaker spurs." The Texas men called old-time Arizona wranglers like
Barnes "Chaps, Taps, and Latigo Straps," making fun of their California outfits.
"We watched them for a while," reported Barnes, "and then, realizing the unwel-
come fact that they knew more cow stuff in a week than we did in a year," the
Arizona men put away their high-horn California saddles, their long ropes, and
their "flapping tapaderos," or hooded stirrups, and adopted the gear and the techniques of the newcomers.[20]

If Texas cowboys altered the physical culture of Apache County, they also
altered its moral culture. For a time in the mid-1880s, after the Aztec's arrival,
cowboys routinely got drunk and shot up towns. Springerville did not quiet down
until the law-and-order campaign of 1887. Cowboys also invaded Winslow and
Holbrook, the two major stops on the A&P. On one occasion, a few Hashknife
men "on a cowboy hilarity" shouted and yelped in the streets of Winslow while
firing over five hundred shots into the air. At other times, cowboys commanded
unarmed Mormons to dance while firing at the ground in front of their feet,
bringing to mind a stereotypical scene from 1950s Westerns. After one such performance, the victim removed his boots "and dump[ed] the urine out." Just
across the border in Luna, New Mexico, similarly, cowboys would gather "on
gala days" from forty and fifty miles around, "to drink, gamble, run horses, shoot
up the town and fight." "Monkey ye not," intoned the *Herald*, "with the festive
cow boys, or your days will be short and full of trouble."[21]

In St. Johns and Holbrook, meanwhile, opportunists catered to cowboys by
"set[ting] up gambling dens and bawdy houses." With cowboys also came horse
racing with its attendant boozing and bragging. Springerville saw regular horse
races, including some famous ones in which the notorious Clanton family put
forward their best animals. One of the biggest races occurred each Christmas,
when entrants put up ten dollars to run their horses. No one brought blooded
horses. Only cow ponies ran, carrying the smallest, lightest cowboys on their
backs. The course extended for three hundred yards. Horses and riders would
train for up to three weeks in advance. As the racers gathered, they and the
crowd engaged in banter and bragging. Afterward, winners, losers, and onlookers
gathered to eat, dance, and gulp whiskey.[22]

In addition to betting at horse races, Texas cowboys bet at cards, a pastime that
often led to quarreling. In December 1886, Joe P. "Kid" Thomas shot and killed
Frank Ward after a dispute over cards. The killing occurred in an Aztec camp,
though the two men were no longer Aztec employees. Kid Thomas was said
to be a braggart and a swaggerer who habitually shot up Holbrook after getting

Hashknife foreman Ed Rogers playing cards with two cowboys. Note six-shooters
stacked in foreground. Gambling and guns were key components of honor.
Courtesy of Arizona Historical Society/Tucson, no. 2016.

drunk. He reportedly fled to Pleasant Valley. That was far from the only shooting
scrape involving Aztec cowboys. On one occasion, a drunken cowboy, aiming at
a swinging lamp on a railroad, managed instead to shoot the conductor. Another
cowboy held up a dance in Winslow, receiving a shotgun blast in the face for
his pains. At a Mexican *baile* (dance) in Holbrook in 1887, several Aztec men
got into a shooting match with Mexicans who resented the cowboys' monopoly
on the women in attendance. One Mexican was killed; one Aztec man limped
for the rest of his life, a bullet having found his foot. The favorite hangout of the
Aztec cowboys, indeed, was a Holbrook saloon called the Bucket of Blood, ostensibly to commemorate the gore that covered its floor when an Aztec cowboy
killed two Mexicans after a gambling dispute. Cowboy honor begot cowboy violence.[23]

None of those affrays resemble the "walkdown" gunfight, endlessly re-created
in fiction and film, wherein two or more men face each other on the street, each
ready to draw. Gunfights were nonetheless common in part because American
law permitted accused murderers to escape prosecution by claiming self-defense.

In England, a man who failed to make every attempt to escape an attacker before slaying him could be tried for homicide. American law, however, upheld gunplay as a legitimate forum for the resolution of disputes. In a careful study of Bodie, California, one scholar found that bravado born of drink and legal impunity led men routinely to slay "enemies" who had slighted their honor. Because of the legal doctrine of self-defense, few were prosecuted. Thus did the ritualized code duello evolve into the chaos of the gunfight.[24] The ideal of honor survived, but not the rules.

The difference between duel and gunfight, however, involved more than rules. In a duel, participants were elite men whose political disputes had become personal. We do not remember duels as "good versus evil"; we remember them as battles between equals. The gunfight, by contrast, was endlessly portrayed in twentieth-century fiction and film as a war between the righteous and the wicked. An evil gunfighter could strike down a decent, ordinary man who had no chance against him. The evil gunfighter, however, invariably fell to the six-shooter of a righteous gunfighter, the man in the white hat. As one might expect, reality was more complex. Gunplay grew out of quarreling. There were few villains and fewer heroes. That Americans came to remember gunfights as moral dramas, however, tells us much about how the West evolved and how Westerners—and Easterners—learned to think of honor.

If cowboys partook in the honor culture of the Old South, they also moved away from that culture. Consider how cowboys differed from the settlers of Sublimity, Oregon. Sublimity, like Arizona and many other parts of the West, was settled by emigrants from the South and Lower Midwest. Unlike Arizona cowboys, Sublimity's settlers arrived as families. True to their cultural heritage, Sublimity settlers placed great importance on lineage. The foremost goal for a male head of family was to locate land for his sons. Sublimity's settlers, moreover, extended the concept of "we" to a wide cluster of kin and neighbors.[25] Like New Mexicans, they saw themselves as links in a familial chain that extended backward in time and horizontally across the present.

The Texas cowboys who flooded Arizona in the 1880s showed less interest in lineage. They were largely single men, footloose, seeing little chance for upward mobility beyond ownership of a small ranch. They maintained ties with kin in Texas. Sometimes they even scouted sites for homesteads for kin. On the whole, however, they showed no interest in creating a cradle of extended family. They were individualists. In that regard, they resembled the Northern youths who broke off from their families during the market revolution of the early nineteenth century, when modern individualism emerged full-blown.

In the North, individualism begat conscience—a rejection of the "sins" of gambling, whoring, drinking, smoking, cursing, and spending recklessly. Or, at least in theory — in the minds of ministers and moralists — individualism was supposed to produce conscience. Young men would not, in theory, measure success via bravado and physical courage. They would measure success via self-control, thrift, work, and moderation. They would measure success, moreover, in their commitment to creating a moral society, a society that embraced the gospel, repudiated "demon rum," perhaps even repudiated the "barbarism" of slavery. Mormonism — a religion born in New York — epitomized Northern conscience.

Like Northern youths of the early nineteenth century, cowboys were ardent individualists, yet they held no love for "Yankee" morality. They, like their Southern ancestors, measured success via old rites of manliness, rites of courage, excess, and exuberance. Cowboys did not repudiate the ethic of work or the pursuit of profit, yet they were first and foremost creatures of honor.

Harvard University's 1950s study of the peoples of "Rimrock" — west-central New Mexico, which bordered the Little Colorado Basin and the White Mountains — may offer insight into the psychological matrix of cowboy honor. In one part of a broader study conducted in 1950–51, several members of the team compared childrearing patterns among Texans to those among Mormons and Zunis. Their findings are instructive. Texan mothers, they found, weaned children at a younger age (average nine months) than either Mormons (eleven months) or Zunis (two years). Texan mothers also toilet trained children at an earlier age than those in the other groups. Texan mothers, moreover, spent less time with their children than did Mormons or Zunis, in part because Texan women were expected to work outside the home (if only in and around the farm or ranch) even when their children were young.[26]

By age six, the researchers found, Texan children were assigned to do chores by themselves, including milking cows and gathering eggs. Mormon children of the same age, by contrast, accompanied their mothers as they accomplished those tasks; Mormons called this "helping." Zuni children at age six were expected neither to help parents nor to do chores independently. In addition to requiring children to perform chores at a young age, Texan mothers were less apt than Mormons or Zunis to intervene in quarrels. Whereas Mormons and Zunis detested conflict between children and intervened immediately, Texan mothers were likely to explain that children should "fight it out" or "settle it themselves."[27]

It is dangerous to read such studies into the past. Childrearing practices are mutable. They change from generation to generation, particularly as new sorts of advice — whether from ministers, psychologists, or moralists — become popular. We can, however, compare the Harvard study's findings with patterns that appear in historical records. In defining Texans as individualists and fighters, the

Harvard study comports with broader studies of homicide and violence rates in the South, which have been consistently higher than those of the North.[28] More important, the Harvard study comports with patterns of violence among Texas cowboys in 1880s Arizona. There are differences, of course. Apache County's cowboys, unlike the Texan youths in the Harvard study, did not imagine themselves becoming doctors and lawyers. If anything, they imagined themselves as ranchers with a patch of land to call their own, just as their ancestors had been freehold farmers in the Midwest and Old South. Universal schooling—especially high schools—had given youths new ambitions by the 1950s. Other behavioral patterns, however, seem to have remained intact.

Apache County was not the only place where Texas cowboys displayed honor. In Graham County, too, which lies south of Apache along the New Mexico border, Texans and Mormons settled simultaneously. There, too, Texans were "a fearsome presence," recalled Mormons, a "kind of outlaw people, kinda tough people." At times Texans would "swoop down on Mormon dances, shooting out the lights and causing other mischief." If a Mormon dared to attend one of the Texans' fiddle dances, on the other hand, "you'd better be prepared to fight." The Texas men, drinking heavily, "would haul off and hit you and knock you as far as against the door." If no Mormon showed up, the Texan men would fight among themselves (the same scenarios occurred routinely at Rim Country fiddle dances). By the late 1970s, however, the Texans had "tamed down."[29]

By themselves, Texan cowboys would have brought discord, but they did not come by themselves. They came with the Aztec. Worse, they came with economic ruin. In 1885, precisely when Aztec investors embarked on their cattle venture, livestock prices began to fall. They kept falling in 1886, when sure wealth turned to grim survival—or failure—for ranchers throughout the West. Drought in Texas, moreover, claimed some five thousand to six thousand Aztec head before they arrived in Arizona.[30]

Amid the economic crisis, the Aztec had another issue to deal with: sheep. By the estimate of Albert Potter, an Apache County rancher who later became chief of grazing of the U.S. Forest Service, some 150,000 sheep from outside the county trespassed on Aztec lands in the mid-1880s. Another 120,000 sheep from within the county might or might not have access to Aztec range.[31]

Like most cattlemen, Aztec managers and the cowboys they hired despised sheep. Almost anywhere in cattle country, one would hear the same indictment. A herd of sheep left "a wide swath" across a range, rendering it "as clean of vegetation as if a fire had passed over it." In addition to eating grass to the roots, sheep cut up and compacted the soil with their hard, sharp-edged hooves, rendering it sterile. Not only did sheep destroy the range; they also left a scent that "precluded cattle from grazing on the same range for years afterward."[32]

Cattlemen overstated their case. "It was a common saying," noted an early Forest Service ranger, "that sheep and cattle could get along on the same range when both belonged to the same owner." Sheep, indeed, preferred eating weeds to grass, making them a complement to cows, provided they were properly managed. Herding sheep too close together, however, caused "close cropping" and trampling. In places where sheep were bedded together over a period of years, denuding might cover a full square mile. Lambing sites, too, could become denuded when lambs ate all the new growth. Unmanaged sheep, then, could devastate the range, but so might cows. Because cattle tended to spread out more than sheep, the damage they caused was slower to appear and harder to see. On the other hand, cows often congregated around waterholes, thus denuding riparian areas. Sheepmen could damn cows every bit as much as cowmen damned sheep.[33]

Even if sheep proved harder on rangelands than cows, they were often a better proposition. The *Herald* reported in May 1886 that more than a million head of sheep grazed on Arizona ranges, with the vast majority concentrated above the Rim. An average Arizona sheep, reported the *Herald*, produced seven to ten pounds of wool, equaling between $1.19 and $2.10 per shear. Some sheep could be both sheared and slaughtered for mutton, adding to the profit. A large sheep might produce twelve pounds of wool and sixty pounds of dressed meat. Even the meat from an ordinary animal brought between $5.75 to $6.25 from the packing houses of Chicago (the highest rate for mutton since 1874). Because, moreover, sheep matured and reproduced faster than cows, men "who started in the business less than seven years ago with a few hundred head now count their sheep by the thousands."[34]

July 1886 found the market for wool still brisk and prices rising, despite President Cleveland's decision to lower the wool tariff. The good market encouraged sheepmen to expand their ranges. Expansion, in turn, spawned conflict.

The most virulent conflict was between sheepmen and the Aztec. With the railroad completed through northern Arizona, New Mexicans became particularly bold in herding sheep onto Aztec land, keen to take advantage of profits. Without the completion of a government survey, they reasoned, the Aztec could not patent its land, and without a patent, the Aztec had no authority to evict trespassers. The land remained free range, especially since the Aztec claimed only alternate sections. While Aztec managers fumed, sheepmen prospered. "Trouble is likely to occur at any time," noted the *Silver Belt* in April 1886, "as a very bitter feeling exists."[35]

That bitter feeling gave rise to war. Will Barnes recalled that sheepmen from New Mexico once sent twenty-five thousand sheep in ten bands toward the San Francisco Peaks, where they were to graze for the summer. Along the way, a dozen or more cowboys drove some one hundred wild horses into the sheep. The men had tied cowbells to the horses to frighten the sheep and keep them running. As they galloped close behind the wild horses, the cowboys fired into the air. The sheepmen managed to shoot a few horses, but the sound of their guns only added to the terror. It took the sheepmen a week to regroup their animals.[36]

On another occasion, recalled Barnes, cowboys captured a group of sheepherders and tied them to trees, then drove four thousand sheep into bogs along the Little Colorado, where hundreds became trapped and died. Afterward, the cowboys destroyed the sheepmen's camp, killing their horses and mules. Still another attack ended when cowboys whipped a captive sheepherder and cut cattle marks into his ears. Honor again shaped behavior. Rituals of shaming promised to resolve conflict. Looking back on it, mused Barnes, "one cannot help wondering what these men were thinking of." Yet he himself had taken "a lively part in this struggle, and did my full share to stop the onward march of the herds."[37]

Barnes does not tell us whether Aztec cowboys took the lead in attacking sheepherders, nor do newspaper and court records. The war went on with only occasional recourse to the law, each side bearing silent witness to its losses. That Aztec cowboys were profoundly involved, however, was borne out by Jamie Stott, a rancher who joined the Aztec men for "a little war all of itself" in early 1886. Sheepmen, reported Stott, had proposed to drive fifty thousand head across Aztec land but were stopped by a small army. "Guns and six shooters were used pretty plenty for a short time," he testified, before the sheepmen had turned back. At other times, it seems, they did not turn back. On at least one occasion, recalled Hashknife cowboy Lucien Creswell, they died fighting.[38]

The period between 1880 and the early 1910s saw conflicts between sheepmen and cattlemen throughout the West. The reasons for those conflicts were as much ethnic as environmental. Sheepherders were often New Mexican, Indian, or Basque, whereas most cowboys were native-born white Americans. Historians tell us, to be sure, that sizable numbers of blacks and Mexicans—and even the occasional Indian—became cowboys.[39] In the Rim Country, however, black cowboys are all but invisible in the records (apart from brief mentions of Jeff Tribit, the former slave of the Greer family). Hispanic cowboys in the Rim Country were almost as rare. Only a few appear in Rim Country annals, including Stinson's erstwhile cook, Epitacio Ruiz, and the Pleasant Valley wrangler Miguel Apodaca. The occasional mixed-blood cowboy—notably the four Tewksbury boys—also appears. The vast majority of cowboys, however, were white men whose concept of honor and shame revolved around the color of one's skin.

Sheepherding had a different history. New Mexicans had been running *churros*—small, bristly-haired, hardy sheep of Spanish derivation—for more than two centuries when Americans took possession of the Southwest. In the late 1860s, New Mexicans of the Rio Grande Valley, their herds barred from West Texas by cattlemen, began sending sheep into Arizona. Soon their herds were crossing the entire expanse of forest and grassland from the Little Colorado to the San Francisco Peaks.

White men—native-born Americans—also saw profit in running sheep. Like New Mexicans, they hired Hispanic, Navajo, and Ute herders, as well as whites. Navajos and Utes made especially good herders, given their peoples' long experience with sheep. Two centuries earlier, they had alternately traded with and raided New Mexicans and Pueblo Indians. In the process they acquired churros and transformed themselves into herders. When wage labor became critical for survival in the 1880s, Navajos sometimes left the reservation to work for Anglo-American sheepmen. Basques, too, left their homes in the Pyrenees to herd sheep in the American West. Some still run sheep there today.

If owners of sheep were increasingly white, native-born Americans, then, the men who handled sheep were likely to be emigrants and dark-skinned men who spoke broken English. Perhaps that was reason enough for cowboys to dislike sheepherders, but disdain had other sources as well. Whereas cowboys mounted horses and rode after cows, sheepherders walked the range with their herds or rode donkeys. Sheepherders did not (it seemed) engage in the courageous acts of breaking horses or roping and tackling cows. They did not wear six-shooters, nor did they don the fancy regalia—boots, spurs, chaps—that defined the cowboy. Sheepherders resembled the *peons* that Americans read about after the Mexican-American War of 1846–48, whereas their employers were patróns. In the eyes of cowboys, it was a contemptible relationship: meek, impoverished mixed-blood men, incapable of social improvement and unwilling to seek it, commanded by wealthy tyrants whose main concern was to perpetuate their tyranny. Cowboys, by contrast, thought of themselves as bold individualists who might be loyal to an employer but never bowed to one.[40]

Cowboys and Mormons alike, then, despised the brown-skinned men who herded sheep. They did not despise them, however, for the same reasons. Mormons were apt to say that "Mexicans"—a term that white settlers invariably used to describe New Mexicans—were "dirty" and "sinful." Mexican men manufactured, sold, and consumed spirits. They gambled and visited prostitutes. Often, it seemed, they crossed the boundaries of the law to steal cattle, stuff ballot boxes, and jump claims. The fact that the Mormon push for hegemony led Mexicans to those very behaviors—led New Mexicans, that is, to acts of resistance—never entered into Mormon thinking.

Cowboys, on the other hand, objected to none of those behaviors. What they despised about New Mexicans was their lack of honor. New Mexicans seemed contemptible not because of their vices but because of their dark skins, their lack of manly assertion, their willingness to herd sheep rather than punch cattle. That New Mexicans themselves were beholden to honor seldom occurred to cowboys, it seems, except during quarrels involving guns.

Such quarrels, however, were far from rare, even when no sheep were involved. In his brief memoir, Lorenzo Hubbell—Indian trader and Apache County sheriff in 1885–86—testified that New Mexicans and their allies had waged an intermittent battle with Texas "outlaws" for several years before the Aztec's arrival. "That war," recalled Hubbell, flared "at times like fire." Before he left office as sheriff in early 1887, he claimed, at least two dozen men had lost their lives.[41]

It could not have surprised New Mexicans, then, to see a letter in the *Herald* in spring 1886 praising the Aztec for its fight against sheepherders and urging others to come to its aid. "Sooner or later," inveighed the anonymous author, "these Arabs and their homeless hordes will meet a community tired of such trifling with law, and who have determined to take the law into their own hands. Then look out." The Aztec won its battle, however, not in the field but in the courtroom, where its high-paid attorneys held tactical supremacy. In May 1886, two months after Stott reported a "little war," the court found Santos and Policarpio Armijo guilty of trespass on Aztec lands. The same fate befell Santiago Baca. The *Herald* heartily agreed with the court's decision, complaining that sheepherders "use up the grass, yet pay no county taxes."[42]

On the Aztec's western flank, meanwhile, the Daggs brothers continued to trespass. For several years before the Aztec arrived, the brothers had run huge herds—tens of thousands—across the Little Colorado Basin. Like the New Mexicans, the Daggs brothers argued that the Aztec lacked a patent and could not bar entry.

The Daggs brothers were not new to Arizona. Two of the five had arrived in 1876, bringing fine Vermont merinos that they married to California ewes, creating a line of sheep "unexcelled in the Southwest for quality and weight of fleece" and taking first prize at a New Mexico livestock fair. Though not as hardy as churros, the Daggs's merinos were bigger and produced better wool.[43]

Initially the brothers began sheeping on Silver Creek, not far from Stinson's ranch and the future site of Snowflake. On the promise of the A&P's arrival, they saw new opportunity. They soon sold their ranch and relocated to Flagstaff, whence they employed herders to trail sheep eastward onto the Little Colorado Basin. Once the railroad arrived, they could profit both from wool and mutton. In 1886, their dreams of wealth met the cold stare of the Aztec.[44]

At its annual meeting in April 1886, the Arizona Wool Growers' Association, presided over by J. W. Daggs, fired a shot over the Aztec's bow. Decrying "certain land and cattle companies that have taken possession of a large extent of the public domain . . . under a pretended color of title," the association resolved "that we . . . do emphatically denounce the illegal acts of those corporations who have attempted to intimidate actual settlers on the public domain."[45]

The Daggs brothers, it seems, were attempting to make common cause with Mormons, many of whom herded small bands of sheep. The resolution, however, had little effect. The legislature passed a bill in the same year permitting cattle to trespass on ranges claimed by sheepmen but forbidding sheep to trespass on ranges claimed by cattlemen. The courts, meanwhile, reaffirmed the Aztec's right to drive out intruders, leaving the Daggs brothers bereft of any outlet to lands above the Rim.[46] Out of one fire and into another: the brothers would now move their sheep south, into the seething rivalries of Pleasant Valley.

The Aztec's legal victories did not end its struggles. A more intractable problem came from Mormons. Snowflake, Taylor, Shumway, and Woodruff lay within the Aztec's domain. When Mormons had settled those places, no railroad appeared in the works. They assumed that the A&P would not go through and its land claims would lapse. When the railroad did go through, Jesse Smith visited A&P officials who assured him that Mormons would have first claim to their lands, which would be sold without any added value for improvements. Smith filled out paperwork for the claims, but the A&P promptly forgot its promise.[47]

When the Aztec bought lands from the A&P, negotiations began again. Not until 1889 did the Aztec agree to sell the land for $4.50 an acre, with the LDS church making the first payment and settlers paying the rest. Mormons believed they had been "defrauded."[48] Snowflake settlers had now paid for their land twice, once to Stinson and once—for the odd sections—to the Aztec. Mormons, however, had no choice. From early 1885 until spring 1887, the Aztec had pushed and shoved Mormons off both odd sections and even, using means fair and foul, thus taking control of an additional million acres above the million it owned.

Mormon settler L. Barr Turley recalled that immediately on arriving, Aztec cowboys set to work building "a corral with a cabin" every fifteen miles from Aztec headquarters near Holbrook all the way to the Rim. The idea was to work cattle efficiently but also to "protect the cattle ranges." To accomplish that, recalled Lucien Creswell, the Aztec hired Texans. One noted gunman, he added, was moved from outpost to outpost "whenever and wherever trouble erupted." The Aztec hired only "the roughest of characters," averred Mormons, many of whom "were in trouble with the law and fleeing from justice."[49]

Whether or not the Aztec deliberately hired bad men, the cowboys knew their job. Many had come from the Continental Land and Cattle Company—the original Hashknife Outfit—whose cowboys had once hanged five alleged rustlers in Orla, Texas, at a place subsequently called Rustler Springs. Cowboys of the Millet ranch, which the Continental subsequently bought and operated, even drove out local law enforcement in order to enforce the company's will, prompting Texas Rangers to intervene. Like other big Texas operations, the Continental operated as a quasi-military organization.[50] Employers—whether in Texas or in Arizona—relied on cowboy honor to protect their interests. Individual honor metamorphosed into company honor.

"When the Hashknife Outfit came into the country," wrote one Mormon, "it looked as though their coming was to be almost the downfall for the Mormon Colonies." Among those who suffered first were the settlers of Snowflake, whose thriving cooperative herd was forced to compete with thousands upon thousands of new cattle. Almost as soon as they had arrived, the Snowflake settlers had built a "drift fence"—an open-ended barrier stretching across ten sections to the west of Silver Creek—to keep stock from wandering back toward Utah. The fence, made of brush, took months to build but only minutes to destroy. Hashknife cowboys set it afire or simply knocked it down when they came to it, claiming that it blocked Aztec cattle from Aztec range.[51]

Hardest hit by the plague of cowboys were the hamlets of Heber and Wilford, both situated west of Snowflake, close to the Rim, amid prime grazing lands. Wilford got its start in 1883 when Edmund Richardson built a cabin there and began farming half a mile away. Others escaping the difficulties of Sunset soon joined him: the Whitings, the Petersens, the Jameses, the Savages, the Nielsons, the Porters, the Mortensens, the Shelleys. By 1883, thirteen families lived in and around the hamlets of Wilford and Heber, with good prospects for subsistence. "Tall, waving" grass grew everywhere, recalled Thomas Shelley, making it good country for farming and ranching.[52]

Then came the Aztec cattle, taxing water holes and "stripping the lush grasses much like locusts attacking a wheat field." Worse, the Aztec turned its "outlaw desperadoes loose upon us." The first attacks took the form of claim jumping. George Gladden, a Texas cowboy and experienced feudist who had brought his wife, Susan, and a daughter, Oberia, took Joe James's place while James was away on business. Daniel Boone "Red" Holcomb jumped the claim of S. A.

Winsor while Winsor was away. Another cowboy took Andrew Petersen's place.[53] More industrious were the Blevins boys. They commandeered the homes of the Richardson family and the Adams brothers, not to mention the home of a Mormon widow, Edith Brookbanks.

Though Brookbanks had little recourse, the Adams brothers confronted the Blevinses and asserted their right to the claim. To defuse the situation, Andy Cooper—whose real name was Blevins—agreed to pay Will Adams and his brother, John Quincy Adams, two hundred dollars in compensation. Though Will refused the money, John Quincy agreed to take it. Cooper then forbade the Adams brothers to speak of the payment, fearing that such news would make him look weak.[54]

Edmund Richardson and his wife, Sadie—sister of the Adams brothers— also stood up for themselves. When the Blevins boys had jumped their farm in 1886, they were attending the stake conference in Snowflake. There, Edmund Richardson received news from his father-in-law, Jerome Jefferson Adams, telling him that cowboys occupied his home. Adams suggested that he and Richardson ambush the cowboys and kill them. Richardson—a conscience man—declined. Returning to his home in Wilford late on a December evening, Richardson, with his wife, Sadie, and their infant, decided to wait out the claim jumpers. Just outside their own front door, they shivered in their wagon until morning. Then Richardson demanded that the claim jumpers leave. They did so, though the Richardsons found that they had made a gaping hole in the floor to accommodate a fireplace. Later, the Blevins boys returned with a compromise: they would pay Richardson $125 for the property. To head off trouble, he accepted.[55]

Aztec records do not show whether the chief instigator of the claim jumping, Andy Cooper, was an actual employee or a hopeful settler. Mormon records, however, identify him with the company. Whether he came as an Aztec employee or as a friend to Aztec cowboys, Cooper had arrived in 1886 from Llano, Texas. With him were two brothers, Albert ("Charlie") and William Hampton ("Hamp"). Both Andy and Hamp had already been accused of horse theft. According to Lucien Creswell, Andy had fled Texas on a stolen horse to escape the vindictive family of a woman with whom he had sought to elope. Others claimed that he had escaped from Texas Rangers by jumping out of a moving train. To avoid detection, he changed his name to Cooper. Hamp meanwhile had done a year in prison before receiving a pardon. He was just sixteen.[56]

By spring 1887, Andy Cooper had convinced his clan that good land—land belonging to Mormons—could be had on Canyon Creek, just a few dozen miles from Holbrook, where springs emerge from a saddle along the Rim. The creek formed by the springs runs southward, off the Rim and into the Salt River,

From left to right: Daniel Boone "Red" Holcomb, Hampton "Hamp"
Blevins, and Albert "Charlie" Blevins. Don Dedera Papers, Arizona
Collection, Arizona State University Libraries.

forming a shallow canyon. Not only did the place boast perennial water, but it
had the added advantage of serving as a natural holding pen for stock. It was also
the only good avenue between Tonto Basin—including Pleasant Valley—and
the Little Colorado Basin.[57]

The three boys were joined by their father, Martin "Old Man" Blevins, a
Texas rancher with a taste for race horses, along with an adolescent brother,
Sam Houston, and another adult brother, John, who brought his wife, Eva. The

boys' mother, Mary, and sister, Artimesia, also came. Unlike most Texans associated with the Aztec, Andy Cooper brought his extended family. Remaining in Texas was a married sister, Delila, as well as Hamp's sweetheart, Ellen Wyckoff, to whom Hamp had sent a "kiss under the nose" via his sister because "it would be vulgar to say kiss her on the lips."[58] Belying that sweetness was something else that the Blevins boys brought: a bravado born of honor.

Yet another claim jumper was John Herbert Payne, an Aztec cowboy, a Texan, a Christian, and a family man who retained a taste for whiskey and fighting. John Oscar Reidhead and James Pearce were among the first Mormons to meet Payne's wrath. In early 1887, Payne drove Reidhead off his farm because it lay on an odd section of the "lieu" lands.[59] The lieu lands consisted of a ten-mile belt adjacent to the regular A&P grant from which the A&P, or later the Aztec, could withdraw choice sections as compensation for other sections that had been claimed before Congress's 1872 grant. In 1887, when Payne made his threats, the lieu lands had not been surveyed, meaning that the Aztec could make no selections. It could, however, warn off interlopers.

When Payne tried to drive them out, Reidhead, Pearce, and their families had been living on lieu lands for nine years. Neither Payne nor the Aztec had sympathy. Payne, reported Reidhead, "moved upon my farm, occupied my house, and took possession thereof," then threatened to kill and scalp him should he so much as harvest his potatoes. Payne made the same threat to Pearce. The two settlers testified that Payne and the Aztec had ordered all the Mormon families of Heber and Wilford to vacate within ten days. Reidhead remarked that he would rather fight the Apaches and Navajos than "the outlaws, the Texans, which the Aztec Cattle Company have imported."[60]

Joseph Fish fared little better. For a short time after he had quit as bookkeeper for the ACMI, he had taken up ranching near Pinedale, buying the property from a family who had fled to Mesa to escape persecution by cowboys. Payne, he recalled, would ride "back and forth in the lane in front of our home," taunting his family. When the Fish's dog barked at him, Payne shot it dead. One day, Payne showed up claiming falsely that he had been deputized and had come to arrest Fish for polygamy. If Fish would clear out, Payne promised to leave him alone. Fish soon departed.[61]

The trouble that had begun with claim jumping quickly escalated. After leaving their home, the Richardsons moved closer to Sadie's parents near Wilford. There the Richardsons met a party of Navajos who claimed they were on the way to Fort Apache to trade blankets for guns. Richardson quickly surmised that the Indians were in fact looking for horses stolen by the Blevins boys. While taking 103 horses from the Navajos in March 1887, it seems, the Blevins boys had killed several men, causing their relatives to seek vengeance. Two years earlier, Andy Cooper had killed a Navajo boy on the reservation, a murder that the Navajo agent pronounced "wholly uncalled for." In January 1886, Cooper had killed two more Navajos, accusing them of stealing horses. The Blevins boys apparently considered their theft of Navajo horses to be a retaliatory strike. The killings and the horse theft, however, threatened to incur an Indian war.[62]

Despite Edmund Richardson's expressions of friendship, the Navajos remained wary. Three times he approached, telling them in Spanish that he was a friend. To prove that he was a Mormon, he showed the men his underclothing, garments that only those married in the temple could wear. He then offered to take them to their stolen horses, which his brother-in-law had seen en route to Canyon Creek. A few Indians, guided by either Sadie's father or brother, were sent to retrieve the horses.[63]

While most of the Navajos remained gathered at the Richardson home, Hamp Blevins blundered onto the scene. According to Sadie Richardson's account, some of the Navajos excitedly pointed to the approaching Hamp, exclaiming that he was one of the thieves. Unfazed, Hamp continued toward the group. The Indians loaded their guns and pointed them. Richardson, refusing to allow an execution in front of his wife and children, demanded that they put down the guns. Hamp, he argued, was a beardless boy; perhaps he was innocent. White with fear, Hamp wheeled and galloped away. The Navajos waited until he had disappeared behind a hill, then dashed after him. "I shall never forget the sight!" recalled Sadie. "They lay down on their horses, guns in position and rode like mad, shooting to scare him."[64]

Hamp headed for the only refuge he knew, a dugout where Hashknife cowboys resided. As he raised himself to get off his horse and into the shelter, a ball struck his hip, leaving his left leg "dangling." Others in the dugout began to fire at the Indians, at last driving them away.[65]

In his fright after the attack, Hamp spoke incoherently. Adrenaline, it seems, triggered an epileptic seizure. Believing that Richardson had sent the Indians charging after him—and perhaps having heard the Mormon prophecy that Lamanites would become the battle-ax of the Lord—Hamp struggled to tell his companions that Richardson was responsible. The name came out garbled, however, and his companions believed he had said "Petersen." When Andy Cooper arrived, he and the others set out after Niels Petersen but found that he was away. Only later did Hamp succeed in communicating that Richardson was to blame. Realizing his danger, Richardson had taken his wife and child to Snowflake.[66]

The next morning, Cooper and his friends came again to Richardson's home, threatening now to shoot the guts out of Edmund. Cooper's "vocal holocaust of scorching threats," testified Sadie, who heard about the visit from her family, "fanned his own temper into white heat." After the men departed, Sadie's father, Jerome Jefferson Adams, rode out after them. After hiding behind a large rock, he waited for the Blevins party to come by, praying all the while for guidance. At length he returned to his wife, telling her, "The Lord doesn't want me to kill Cooper."[67]

Edmund Richardson, like many Mormons, made sure to carry a gun from then on. Indeed, he considered challenging Cooper to a gunfight until he remembered the Lord's commandment "Thou shalt not kill." He was a conscience man, and he wished to remain one. His brother-in-law, however, was not so scrupulous. On one occasion, it seems, Will Adams went so far as to challenge Cooper to a gunfight. Though unarmed, Will proposed to borrow a gun from a cowboy. Cooper declined. After still another run-in with Cooper, Adams supposedly demonstrated his skill with a gun by throwing a cork in the air and shooting it. Whether apocryphal or true, the story shows that "thou shalt not kill" was fast becoming "thou shalt not cower."[68]

Another Mormon who drifted toward honor was Zechariah ("Zach") Bruyn Decker, who had brought his family to Arizona in 1880. He, like William Flake, was a former Minute Man who chose Snowflake over the United Order colonies. In 1883, he took on seventeen hundred sheep in a fifty-fifty partnership with Flake, making him a target for Hashknife cowboys. Decker refused to be cowed. Though a small man, he would grin when threatened, ready for action. When in 1886 John Payne and his Hashknife companions threatened to drive Decker and his sheep out of the territory, Decker raised his gun. Apprised of his marksmanship, they cursed and turned around. "All those Decker boys need," the Hashknife cowboys supposedly said of Decker and his hard-nosed sons, "is a sack of flour, a book and a gun."[69]

In early 1887, Decker displayed the same grit when he faced off against the Blevins boys. Just after Decker had made a remarkable shot to bring down a squirrel, he saw Andy Cooper lurking behind a tree as if to hide. "How is it," Cooper complained after being discovered, "that you Mormons . . . lay it onto us whenever your horses come up missing?" Cooper rode near enough to grab for Decker's gun, but Decker got it first. Cooper then bragged of killing a Navajo, offering to show Decker how he'd done it, if only Decker would let him borrow the gun. Decker held the gun on Cooper until he departed.[70]

Cooper and Payne were not the only hard men who ran up against Decker. On one occasion, a Hashknife cowboy named Lucas rode to Decker's home and threatened to horsewhip him. Decker was away. When he found out about

Lucas's visit, Decker rode after him. After catching up, Decker pretended not to know him. Calmly, Decker asked whether he had seen "Lucas." His nerve failing him, Lucas said he had not. "Well if you do," replied Decker, "tell him he can find me whenever he wants to horse whip me." Lucas made no reply.[71]

One wonders how many of Decker's stories are true. Are they all true? Are any of them true? It is hard to imagine that Hashknife cowboys would have left Decker and his sheep alone. He was competing for range. On the other hand, it is hard to imagine that Decker faced down every bad man in the area. Even if stories of Mormon resistance were exaggerated, they conveyed patterns. Mormons—desperate after the polygamy trials and the arrival of the Aztec—gravitated toward the honor that they had long eschewed. The stories also show that the Blevins boys believed that Mormons were out to get them. Mormons, it seemed, would stoop so low as to send Indians to kill them. The Mormons, meanwhile, believed the Blevinses to be not only claim jumpers but also horse thieves and murderers.

Interestingly, Mormons seldom challenged the claim jumping in court, perhaps realizing that the deck would be stacked against them. One Mormon claimed in 1886 that the Aztec was "so wealthy that they control the petty courts," which refused to hear his complaint against claim jumpers. The district attorney—a member of the Barth faction—treated him with "silent contempt."[72] Mormons may have been slow to bring complaints, however, because the legality of their claims were dubious. The Aztec, by contrast, was not slow to assert its claims, nor were its cowboys, who carried out their employer's mandate with zeal. For cowboys, to show physical courage—to threaten and bluster and perhaps to fight and kill—was to prove one's worth.

The war for the range in Arizona's Rim Country tells us much about Mormons and cowboys, but more than that, it complicates our understanding of violence in the West. One of the most important authorities on that topic, Richard Maxwell Brown, argues that Western gunmen came in two forms. Some, like Wyatt Earp and Wild Bill Hickok, were "incorporation gunfighters." Often Republicans, they saw eye to eye with Eastern men of wealth who brought vast capital with which to extract the West's resources, a task that required "law and order." Earp in particular fits the mold; he mixed easily with the mining investors of Tombstone, who supported his campaign against the loosely organized confederation of immigrants from the South and Lower Midwest known as the "Cowboys." The other sort of gunman, according to Brown, was the "resister," who did not so much oppose law and order as seek to uphold the dignity of the common man, the freeholder, the man who wanted no constraints on his liberties. The resister represented the gun-toting incarnation of the Jacksonian individualist, contemptuous of the moneyed elite and their Republican politics. Brown's model resisters were the Clantons and McLaurys, whom the Earps and their allies battled in the famous OK Corral gunfight of 1881.[73]

In the case of the Aztec-Mormon conflict, that paradigm becomes muddy. Surely the Hashknife cowboys qualify as resisters. They were exquisitely individualistic. They rejected any official attempt to regulate behavior. They drank and gambled and used guns to keep townspeople in fear. Yet those same cowboys put their honor—their physical prowess and their guns—to work for Eastern capitalists. Here, resisters worked for incorporators; the two operated symbiotically to tyrannize over Mormons. That symbiosis, however, proved tenuous. In 1886 and 1887, Mormons—who might themselves be called incorporators insofar as they besought a law and order that would enable them to dominate parts of the West—appealed to the Aztec management's conscience. If Mormons could convince the Aztec that its men were criminals, the Mormons might make their enemy into an ally.

Even as Hashknife cowboys and Mormons squared off against one another, meanwhile, they sometimes engaged in acts of friendship. Despite Jesse Smith's warnings against socializing with gentiles, Margaret Shelley of Heber bragged of hosting the meanest of cowboys for supper when they passed her ranch. One of those guests, she claimed, had asked whether horses had been disappearing from Mormon barns. Yes, she replied; both her family and the Nielsons had lost their teams. The following day, the Nielson team showed up in a nearby pasture. Even more surprising, one story has the Shelleys hiding Hamp Blevins from a Navajo war party, putting him in the cellar, and covering him with potatoes.[74]

The Turley family, too, fed Hashknife bad men, including the much despised Red Holcomb, who was said to have jumped a Mormon claim near Pinedale. Sometime thereafter—likely in 1887, when Mormons entered a network of vigilantes—Holcomb found a note on his door telling him that if he did not abandon the place, he would die. He paid no attention. Four or five times a year, he would visit the Turleys, invariably telling them it was his birthday. Grace Turley, sympathetic to him, "always gave him a good dinner."[75]

Mormons also befriended Susan Gladden in her hour of need. Though Susan's husband, George, had jumped a Mormon claim, Mary Adams agreed to act as Susan's midwife. Susan was desperate. Her husband was away—killed during a train heist, according to Mormons, though more likely he had returned to Texas. Gladden, it seems, had told his hapless wife that he would support no more children, leaving her alone and fearful. It would appear that Mary Adams, by acting as midwife, was merely extending Christian charity. Yet charity worked two ways.

On another occasion, the Gladdens had searched for, and found, the Adams children after they had become lost while gathering pine nuts.[76]

Despite glimmers of humanity, the crisis took on epic proportions in spring 1887. Mormons realized that the campaign against them was not just an Aztec attempt to move them off the range. The Aztec promoted the campaign, but it quickly dissolved into the chaos of honor. The Aztec did not instruct cowboys to attack Mormons with whips and pistol butts, nor did it advise cowboys to threaten Mormons with death. But the Aztec's attempt to guard its range, coupled with anti-Mormon blasts from the newspapers, transformed cowboy honor into cowboy lawlessness. Rather than acting as knights, cowboys acted as hoodlums. They fought for the company; they fought against Mormons; they fought to prove their honor. And they fast became outlaws.

For Mormons, spring 1887 was a time to strike back. In January, John Bushman reported coming to Heber for a "big talk" on the claim jumping. Then, in early April, three horses disappeared from Snowflake and ten more from near Showlow. Bushman and five Snowflake men—including William Flake— tracked the thieves. On the road to Canyon Creek, Will Adams and two others joined the searchers. According to one report, the trackers met "so many desperate characters who threatened them" that they were forced to turn back. Will Barnes testified that they "were shot at, beaten with rope ends, set on foot and warned never again to enter. . . . Two or three never came back at all." Bushman's journal, however, mentions only that Andy Cooper and another man "abused" a Mormon tracker, probably in or around Canyon Creek. It was there that the men found some of their horses. They found more horses a few miles away.[77]

Even if he exaggerated the attacks on trackers, Barnes knew a great deal about the developing campaign against "thieves." On April 6, the trackers had spent the night at his ranch. At Canyon Creek, he recalled, they had found a way station for thieves where "brands were altered or worked over, new brands 'picked on,' tails pulled out, manes clipped and thinned and other well known tricks used to disguise the horses and cover up [their] tracks." Barnes reported that he himself once hid in a cave alongside the Canyon Creek trail, watching through binoculars—by moonlight—as three men led twenty-five stolen horses. One of them was Andy Cooper.[78] How Barnes, even with binoculars, managed to identify Cooper at night and at a great distance, not to mention identify the brands on the horses, is a mystery. Nonetheless he and his Mormon associates were confident of the Blevins boys' guilt.

Assuming that the Blevins boys really were stealing horses—which seems likely—their actions stemmed neither from their eagerness to carry out the orders of the Aztec nor from pure delinquency. They surely saw themselves as part of Apache County's feverish anti-Mormon campaign, a campaign that transcended both Aztec directives and hoodlumism. Beyond that, they had the motive of revenge. Edmund Richardson, they believed, had sent Navajo warriors after Hamp, which, in effect, meant sending warriors after the whole of the Blevins clan. One of Richardson's relatives had also led vengeful Navajos to Canyon Creek. Mormons, moreover, had spoken of Indians as the "battle ax of the Lord." The rash of horse thefts from Mormon towns began immediately after those events, in March 1887, likely as a means of revenge. Apache County at the same time issued a warrant for the arrest of Cooper on the charge of stealing horses from Navajos. The Apache County sheriff, it seems, deputized William Flake to make the arrest.[79]

Deputized or not, Flake, "afraid of no man," set off alone into Tonto Basin in mid-April 1887. After descending the Rim, he made his way to Reno Trail, which connected Tonto Basin to the Salt River Valley. After ten days, he discovered the hide and horns of one of his cows. Sure that the thieves were taking stock to the Salt River Valley, he decided to question settlers living near the trail. One young couple knew the thieves but refused to talk, fearing retaliation. At last, Flake persuaded them to help. They told him that he would find the missing horses in Phoenix.[80]

Flake's informants proved honest. At Gibson's stable in Phoenix, Flake found several stolen animals. Gibson, however, refused to hand them over. Gibson's angry neighbors threatened to mob Flake, but he had an ally with him: Jim Stinson. Stinson, who had sold his Silver Creek land to Flake and who had loaned Flake money for bail during his polygamy trial, now backed up Flake's assertions with $20,000. It is unlikely that Stinson had that much money at the ready, but the offer of collateral won the day. Flake telegraphed those who had lost horses, urging them to come to Phoenix. When they arrived, Stinson hosted them at his home and loaned them $150 to cover the expense of filing affidavits. In all, they recovered thirty animals.[81]

The way home was almost as eventful as the trip to Phoenix. Somewhere between Phoenix and Pleasant Valley, Flake ran into three men on horseback, one of whom was Louis Parker, nephew of John and Tom Graham. Parker asked Flake what he was doing, to which Flake replied, "Looking for stolen horses." "Have you found any?" queried Parker in a mocking tone. "Yes," said Flake, "you are riding on one." Parker laughed and asked Flake whether he thought he would take the horse. Flake demurred but suggested that they would meet again. He proved wrong—Flake saw neither Parker nor the horse—though his son, Osmer, did see Parker, or so he claimed, when in fall 1887 Parker fled a posse that Osmer had joined.[82]

The story of William Flake seeing Parker on a stolen horse is another tale that may or may not be true. John Bushman's diary, however, testifies to something more intriguing: on May 7, Flake's party stopped for dinner at the Graham ranch even though they suspected that the Grahams were in league with the Blevins boys. A day earlier, four other Snowflake Mormons had descended on Pleasant Valley, apparently to rendezvous with those returning from Phoenix.[83] What do we make of that? Were Mormon men employing the cover of frontier hospitality to gain intelligence? In what spirit did the Grahams greet them? Were they surly? Friendly? What conversations transpired? Did the Mormons warn the Grahams against participating in horse theft? Did the Mormons scour Pleasant Valley to recruit vigilantes? Something was afoot. To venture into Pleasant Valley—the precinct of thieves and their consorts—was no social trip.

Rather than ceasing, persecution grew worse. Perhaps Hashknife cowboys sensed new danger in the wake of Flake's trip to Phoenix and sought revenge. In May 1887, John Payne found Niels Petersen hunting horses on Aztec range. Payne rode up to Petersen, telling him that "the cowboys" intended to drive Mormons off the range and whipping him with the "butt end of his loaded black snake." Petersen, riding a half-broken horse and carrying no gun, was helpless.[84]

A few days later, Payne assaulted another Mormon settler, George Lewis. Lewis, like Petersen, was looking for stolen horses. Payne confiscated Lewis's pistol, then used it to hit him across the head and face. Payne supposedly told Lewis that he was a member of a band of horse thieves who intended to drive Mormons "out of the forest." Then Payne returned the pistol. Two other Mormons, Spence Shumway and Mark Kartchner, met the same treatment.[85]

Mormons who faced Payne's wrath did not lie down. After Payne whipped him, Petersen had ridden to a neighbor's house to fetch a gun. He then searched for Payne but could not find him. When he returned home, his wife begged him to visit the stake president, Jesse Smith, before going after Payne again.[86]

"On the way to the grist mill," wrote Jesse Smith in his journal, "met Bro. N. Petersen at Taylor." Petersen told him that Payne had threatened his life. "It seems that Payne is employed by the cattlemen," noted Smith, "and proposes to run the Mormons out of the forest." Other than that, the journal is silent. Petersen family history, however, tells us more. Petersen, it seems, sought permission to kill Payne, apparently by ambush. James Pearce asked Smith the same question, perhaps at the same time. Smith counseled the men to take no action. "If you will promise me that you will not molest your enemy," he told Petersen,

"I will promise you that he shall never molest you again, and that it will only be a short time until he will be out of the way." Another Mormon memoirist claims that Smith said that the Lord would "take care" of Payne. Still another quotes Smith as saying that the Mormons' enemies—including Payne—"would take care of everything within their own ranks, the wicked would slay the wicked." Finally we have this from an account of Wilford's history based on the journals and reminiscences of Sadie Richardson: Smith, she reported, told Petersen that "work of that sort [assassination] is not the business of our people." Conscience, it seemed, would prevail over hate.[87]

Whatever Smith said, the Petersen family remembered the incident as a turning point in Niels's life. Only after the beating and the consultation with Smith did Petersen give himself wholly to a life of piety. He rejected not just violence but also drink and tobacco.[88] He rededicated himself to conscience. The effect of his experience must have moved him profoundly, especially when Smith proved correct. A week later, Payne was dead.

We are left wondering what precisely Smith meant when he consulted with Petersen. Certainly Mormons interpreted Smith's words as affirmation of conscience. Mormons would stand aside while God struck down their enemies. Mormons would remain dedicated to peace; God would do the work of violence.

Perhaps, too, Smith steered Petersen away from taking vengeance in part because Smith remained sensitive to the legacy of Mountain Meadows. The church continued to insist that it had played no role in the massacre. Smith must have realized, however, that more vengeance risked more recrimination. Vengeance might create full-blown war with cowboys. Too, vengeance would create trouble with the law at the very moment that Mormons struggled under the weight of an antipolygamy campaign.

However one reads Smith's message, his meaning is mysterious. The most logical conclusion, however, is that Smith was privy to secret plans. Rather than delivering a prophecy, he knew that a different set of powers—not God but vigilantes, sheriffs, and Aztec management—would deal with the problem.

It is likely, moreover, that Mormons themselves had taken steps to deal with their problem. Two men—Petersen and Pearce—had asked Jesse Smith whether he would approve murder. Another—Jerome Jefferson Adams—had hidden by the roadside, planning to assassinate Andy Cooper. Despite their peacefulness—despite their conscience—Mormon men took to wearing six-guns and carrying rifles when they went abroad. At regular meetings, meanwhile, they wrestled with the crisis, some discussing "the advisability of organizing and going out to try to kill" their enemies.[89]

What, then, were Mormons doing in Pleasant Valley in early May 1887? It seems likely that plans were being laid. Traps were being set. Some men were being warned against transgressions. Others were being recruited into a net of vigilantes. Even if Mormons themselves played little role in the violence to come, they helped create the environment that made violence inevitable. They responded to terror by creating more terror.

Though cowboys may not have realized what was occurring, the ground was shifting. Tentatively, quietly, Mormons, Hashknife managers, and gentile cattlemen began to see their common interests. Their alliance had taken a step forward as early as April 1886, when a mysterious "company of cattlemen" had bought the St. Johns *Herald* from Henry Reed and put it in the hands of a lawyer from Texarkana named Barry Matthews. Matthews was to honor born. After he died in a saloon brawl in 1889, his own paper—the *Herald*—described him as a man eager to resort to knife or gun when insulted or impugned.[90]

No records tell us who paid for the *Herald* or why the buyers tapped Matthews as editor. Several parties, however, might have contributed. Gentile ranchers—including Aztec managers—might have helped buy the newspaper in order to use its pages to campaign against rustling. Mormons had even greater impetus to seek change. For two years they had suffered Reed's attacks. They, too, might have contributed to the purchase. All we can know is that powerful groups had strong motives to buy the paper and bring aboard an editor who would fight for "law and order," even if that editor was himself a creature of honor.

After the sale, Reed moved to Holbrook, where he became editor of the Apache County *Critic*. The two papers soon find themselves at odds, especially because Matthews quickly proved that he, far from despising Mormons, sought to bring them into a Mormon-Democrat political alliance. As early as May 6, 1886, Matthews displayed the *Herald*'s new editorial policy when he praised Mormons for opening a flour mill. Mormons, he wrote, showed a "progressive spirit" that greatly benefited the community.[91]

In February 1887, the editorship changed hands again when J. F. Wallace took over. Matthews remained on the staff. Editorial policy did not change. On April 7, Wallace's *Herald* called on "white men" to unite against the outlaws who had stolen Navajo horses. "It's all very well to talk about the Navajos being thieves themselves," intoned the *Herald*, but it pointed out that two wrongs did not make a right. If good citizens did not deal with the thieves, the country risked an Indian war. "Scarcely a day passes," noted the *Herald*, "that we do not hear of horses being taken from some locality or other. . . . The people have borne such things almost as long as human nature can endure it, and we would not be surprised at any time, to hear of men being found hanged—by whom, no one will know."[92]

On May 26, the *Herald* reiterated the claim that rustlers had taken over Canyon Creek and were busily ferrying stolen horses to Phoenix. "We predict," it darkly warned, "that when the people finally make up their minds they have stood it long enough, their mode of dealing with these outlaws will be as swift and terrible as they have been patient and enduring." On July 28, the *Herald* decried lax efforts by the sheriff to deal with "a reign of terror" in the western part of the county. Criminals "have driven settlers out of their houses—torn down their place of public worship—driven stolen stock along the public highways in the broad glare of the noonday sun." Perhaps, the *Herald* suggested, the criminals had even committed murder.[93] The *Herald* transformed a core of truth into a cloud of bombast. No record points to the destruction of any house of worship, though anti-Mormon hysteria could have led to such an event. True or not, the accusation testifies to an important fact: the problem in Apache County was not just hoodlumism; it was a campaign to drive out Mormons.

On August 11 came an angrier diatribe. "One can scarcely believe that a set of men could commit so many and such atrocious crimes, and carry it on for so long a time, with impunity," lamented the *Herald*. Andy Cooper, it added, "had lain in wait" for one citizen—presumably Edmund Richardson—"for two or three weeks, for no other purpose than to take his life." The Blevins boys and their confederates, screamed the *Herald*, "go openly in broad daylight, and drive off horses in sight of their owners. . . . They will steal their neighbors poor, and eventually drive them out of the country."[94] Left unsaid was the fact that those neighbors were Mormons.

The August 11 issue also marked the first time that the Graham brothers of Pleasant Valley were publicly associated with the Blevins boys. The *Herald* now reported—likely having gotten its facts from Mormons who had dined with the Grahams in May—that the Graham ranch was a "perfect arsenal," with "portholes commanding every approach" and provisioned to withstand a long siege. "The fort is never left unoccupied," explained the *Herald*, "there are always five or six men on duty." After identifying the Graham ranch as the rendezvous of thieves, the *Herald* repeated its call for action: "The people have borne it, until 'forbearance ceased to be a virtue,' and when that time arrived, have taken the law into their own hands and acted as lawyer, judge and jury; the sentence pronounced always being death. It is time, and full time, for the people to do the same in this case, and we feel safe in predicting that the best citizens of both counties [Apache and neighboring Yavapai, which included Pleasant Valley] will uphold them in any measures they may adopt."[95]

The *Herald* and its "best citizens" did not go unanswered. Reed's Apache County *Critic* reported that Cooper, though he knew of a horse theft ring, claimed to play no role in it. The *Herald* responded with fury. On September 1, it assured readers that the case against Cooper came from a neighbor of Reed's, a man who lived near Holbrook—possibly Flake—who was no alarmist. The *Herald* went on to recount the events of the previous year, including Cooper's killing of a Navajo, his theft of Mormon horses, and Flake's recovery of horses in Phoenix. The *Herald* added new accusations: one of Cooper's brothers— likely Hamp—was suspected of murdering Samuel Shull, a gentile sheepherder who had lived near Heber. Hamp was also suspected of having murdered another sheepherder—probably the man who was the first to be killed in the war in Pleasant Valley.[96]

When the *Critic* continued to give Cooper the benefit of the doubt, the *Herald* opened up its battery of sarcasm. "Mr. Cooper," it reported, "is climbing the ladder. He is Andy Cooper, Esq., now. In a few weeks more it will be Col. Cooper." What the *Herald* did not say was that, in the short term, the Mormons had lost. They would soon abandon both Heber and Wilford. Persecution, however, was not the only cause for abandonment. Both hamlets suffered from lack of water. Polygamy prosecutions also took a toll, draining leadership and capital. Because the Aztec forbade Mormons from crossing its lands, moreover, settlers were forced to take circuitous, time-consuming routes to reach the railroad station at Holbrook.[97] In the end it was easier to desert Heber and Wilford than to save them, though Mormons later returned to Heber, at least.

For Mormons, however, much had also been gained. By spring 1887, they had allied with the Aztec and with the more prosperous cattlemen of Apache County. They had convinced the Aztec to fire cowboys suspected of rustling. They had recovered stolen horses in Phoenix. In addition, they had helped organize vigilante cells all across the Rim Country. Though they made no record of it, their rendezvous in Pleasant Valley in May was likely not only a warning to the Grahams but also an effort to recruit vigilantes.

Beyond all that, Mormons like Niels Petersen had found new dedication to conscience. Jesse Smith's counsel against violence seemed to affirm that dedication. What was going on under the surface, however, suggests something different. Mormons were quietly embracing the very honor—including rituals of humiliation and shaming—that they condemned in their enemies.

The Blevins family knew that something was afoot. In summer 1887 Mart Blevins wrote Delila, his daughter in Texas, to tell her that he was trying to sell the family's ranches. Something bad had happened, though he did not say what.[98] Something far worse was on the way.

6

———————————————

HELL ON THE RANGE

Sometime around August 3, 1887, Hamp Blevins rode into a Hashknife camp at Big Dry Lake, just above the Rim and not far from his family's ranch. He came with several cowboys whom he had run into earlier that day, including John Payne, Tom Tucker, Bob Gillespie, and Robert Carrington. All four either worked for the Aztec or had done so until recently.

At Big Dry Lake, Hamp explained his mission. He was looking for his father, Mart, who had disappeared a few days earlier after going out to find lost—or stolen—horses. The horses had turned up missing while the Blevins boys were in Holbrook. Mart and one of his neighbors decided to track them. After four days, the neighbor returned to tell Mart's wife, Mary, that her husband remained on the trail. When Mart's sons returned from Holbrook, he had still not come home. Fearing the worst, the boys rode out to find him, each moving in a different direction. Hamp traveled toward the Mormon settlement of Pinedale. On his way, he ran into the Hashknife cowboys.[1]

The men whom Hamp met on the trail were at a crossroads of their own. Their trail boss, Ed Rogers, responding to Aztec management, had just lain down the law to his cowboys. Either they would help put a stop to the rustling and horse theft that Mormons complained of, or they would quit. Five did quit, including Payne, Gillespie, and Carrington. Now footloose, those three joined Hamp in his quest for his father. They may also have joined in order to help Hamp put an end to sheepherding in Pleasant Valley. Will Barnes would later claim that he had been there when Hamp and his recruits had ridden into the Hashknife camp, and that he had warned them that Pleasant Valley was a tinder box. Payne responded that the men might "start a little war of our own."[2]

Over the next few days, the five men scoured the Rim Country, stopping perhaps at the Graham stronghold to pick up recruits. At noon on August 9, the party—eight men strong and "heavily armed"—arrived at the Middleton cabin just east of Pleasant Valley, now owned by George Newton of Globe. Ed Tewksbury was Newton's foreman.[3]

The cowboys rode cautiously to the fence in front of the cabin, spying one of the Tewksburys standing at the door. They asked for food, thus calling on an old frontier tradition of hospitality. An angry reply hurtled back like a knife. "No sir. We do not keep a hotel here." That rejection itself must have put the cowboys on the defensive, assuming they were not already squaring off for a fight. On the Arizona frontier, denying hospitality was tantamount to declaring hostility. One of the cowboys then asked whether Morris Belknap—a friend of Ed Tewksbury—was inside, thinking perhaps to gauge the forces in the house. Belknap, they were told, was not there. As they turned to go, the cabin's occupants opened fire. Or, as the Tewksbury men told the story, it was Blevins and his men who opened fire.[4]

The next few minutes were fraught with panic. Hamp Blevins died immediately, a rifle bullet striking him between the eyes. Payne managed to reel off a shot at the man in the doorway before his horse crumpled underneath him, pinning his leg. As he struggled to free himself, a bullet clipped his ear, causing blood to run freely. Just as he managed to stand, a second bullet killed him. Tucker and Gillespie, wheeling to flee, became targets, too. Tucker caught a ball that pierced both lungs as it traveled across his chest. He managed to ride a short distance before his horse gave out, forcing him to walk and crawl for help. Gillespie was hit where his buttocks joined his leg, the bullet tearing away a large chunk of flesh after passing through the cantle of his saddle. Another bullet killed his horse. Carrington and the others managed to escape without wounds, abandoning the field to the men in the cabin.[5]

Separated in the din of battle, Tucker and Gillespie moved in opposite directions. Those inside the cabin, fearing that their enemies might regroup, made no attempt to see about the wounded men. In the space of three days, Tucker managed to stumble through a violent thunderstorm and fend off a bear before arriving at the ranch of a neutral. When he got there, blowflies crawled in his wound, perhaps keeping down infection by eating rotten flesh. Gillespie, after binding his wound with his underwear, walked for three days and two nights until he reached a Hashknife camp.[6] Both men survived.

The suddenness of the volley from the cabin made it appear that the Tewksbury faction was ready for a fight. In later years, however, Mary Ann Tewksbury claimed that they had been "reading and telling lies without even there [sic] guns near them" when their enemies arrived.[7] In her telling, they anticipated no attack. Neither, however, were they oblivious to that possibility. For two years, they had avoided the Grahams and their allies, keeping to the east side of the Cherry Creek boundary that divided the factions. Both sides embraced honor; both viewed violence as the only way to resolve their dispute. Both knew that fighting could erupt at any moment.

Hostilities had begun in Pleasant Valley in 1883, when the Tewksburys and the Grahams had contested the range with James Stinson. By 1884, the Tewksburys and the Grahams had turned on one another. Then came the herds of Daggs sheep, pushed south by the Aztec. Graham partisan Charlie Duchet insisted that Peru Daggs believed that if he "could get the cattlemen fighting" among themselves, "he could get the range for his sheep. His money hired a lot of killers on [the Tewksbury] side."[8] In all probability, however, the Daggs brothers did not purposely start a war; they simply took advantage of social fractures in order to further their business.

The Tewksburys, however, may well have hoped to use sheep to rid the valley of the Grahams. Robert Voris, son of a Tewksbury ally, insisted that the Tewksburys brought in sheep to run out "rustlers," meaning the Grahams. For a time, it looked as if the tactic might succeed. In 1885, the Grahams—fearing, it seems, both the arrival of sheep and the steep legal fees for their rustling trial in St. Johns—tried to sell their possessory right to 480 acres plus three hundred cattle. Their agent, however, could not sell the claims, perhaps because the Grahams lacked title and claimed more acres than were theirs. They also appear to have claimed more cattle than were theirs.[9]

After the spring roundup in 1885, the Grahams had not 300 animals but only 120. They blamed the Tewksburys for stealing cows, though a host of factors might have caused the loss. Grizzly and black bears, as well as cougars and wolves, patrolled the Rim Country. Forest fires took a toll. Apaches often left the reservation to hunt and gather, and occasionally to kill a beef, especially as the deer population declined. Beyond all that, the chaos caused by the rustling trials of 1884 had kept Pleasant Valley ranchers from holding a rodeo that year. That meant that a lot of range cattle became "wild," making them difficult to find and to herd.[10]

Whether or not the Tewksburys had stolen their cows, the Grahams faced catastrophe. Cattle prices had begun to drop. They could not sell their land. Now their enemies were running sheep. By January 1886, at least two bands of sheep had entered the valley, one of which was leased by John Tewksbury and his partner, William Jacobs. Apparently Jacobs and Tewksbury moved their sheep southward following the Cherry Creek drainage, where the Tewksbury ranches were, then down the Salt River to its confluence with Tonto Creek. Cattlemen there barred entry, forcing them back to Pleasant Valley.[11]

The number of sheep that the Daggs put into the care of Jacobs and Tewksbury is uncertain. According to 1887 tax rolls, John Tewksbury—the only true sheep-herder in the Tewksbury family—held four hundred sheep and eight hundred hogs. A Yavapai County official, however, censured the assessor for not counting "the bands of sheep he found in the charge of the Tewksburys, father and sons," implying that the Tewksburys had many more than four hundred. The report further recommended that the assessor increase his count of sheep in the posses-sion of the Daggs brothers from seventy-five hundred to twenty-three thousand. Hiding animals from assessors was not solely the sin of New Mexican herders; it was ubiquitous among American-born herders, too.[12]

Whatever their number, the sheep were not welcomed, least of all by the Gra-hams. Taking advantage of their ties with Hashknife cowboys who had partici-pated in sheep wars atop the Rim, the Grahams became point men in a fight to save the valley. They shot into flocks. They drove sheep over precipices. They burned sheepmen's cabins and corrals. In February—almost as soon as the sheep arrived—they apparently managed to steal one whole band, consisting of seven hundred valuable merinos, from "a point near Pleasant Valley." Faced with the disaster of losing so many head, the Daggs brothers, with their associates, Chris-tian Jurgensen and William Jacobs, offered fifteen hundred dollars for informa-tion on the herd's whereabouts.[13]

In the coming months, it would prove almost impossible for settlers to remain neutral, though some managed to do so for a time. Jesse Ellison, a Confederate veteran who had brought his herd to the Rim Country in 1885, recalled that most settlers despised sheep and sympathized with those who wanted to ban them. Ellison, however, stayed out of harm's way. Others were less fortunate. At an un-known date, likely in 1886, someone shot Christian Jurgensen, who had part-nered with the Tewksburys in prospecting ventures and with Daggs and Jacobs in running sheep. Though he survived, he took the cue and left the Rim Country.[14]

The antisheep campaign did not end there. At some point in 1885 or 1886, the Tewksburys and their allies received mysterious letters telling them to leave or die. The Tewksburys may have issued similar warnings. Dark clouds floated across the valley without giving way to a storm. Tom Graham boasted that his partisans routinely ambushed sheepherders, shooting not at the men but at their coffeepots or at the dirt and ash under their cooking pans. Rumors of more deadly force, however, wafted through the mountains. An Indian woman in Hol-brook reportedly overheard the Grahams boasting that they had hired gunmen to kill the sheepherders; she passed on the rumor to the Tewksburys. Cattlemen

STOLEN.
$1500. -- $1500.
REWARD.

Last February we lost Seven Hundred head of Merino Sheep, from a point near Pleasant Valley, in Tonto Basin, Arizona. Said sheep were STOLEN from the range, and supposed to have been driven toward

ST. JOHNS, ARIZONA.

They were of various marks as follows, to wit:

FIRST: An over half crop in the right ear and an over slope in the left for Ewes, and the same mark reversed for Wethers.

SECOND: A swallow-fork in the left ear and an over slope in the right for Ewes, and the same mark reversed for Wethers.

THIRD: Two splits in the right ear for Ewes.

We will give Fifteen Hundred Dollars for the arrest and conviction of the Thieves and return of the Sheep, or Five Hundred Dollars for information which will convict the thieves, and Five Hundred Dollars for information leading to the whereabouts of the sheep.

Jurgensen & Jacobs.
Daggs Bros. & Co.
Flagstaff, Arizona. 20tf

Notice of reward for information leading to arrest and conviction of sheep thieves, Apache County *Critic*, December 30, 1886. This theft, along with the burning of sheepmen's homes and corrals, led to fighting in Pleasant Valley. Courtesy of Arizona Historical Society/Tucson.

in Pleasant Valley meanwhile were said to have signed an agreement to pay Andy Cooper fifty dollars for the scalp of any Tewksbury or Tewksbury ally. Those who refused to sign were forced to leave. The Grahams supposedly even asked nearby Apaches to kill the "damn blacks," meaning the Tewksburys. Their chief replied that he would prefer to side with the blacks.[15]

What was clear was that the Grahams and their allies were determined to stop the sheepmen. The war against sheep that had begun above the Rim now spilled into Pleasant Valley. For cattlemen to give up their range was to give up their future. More important, to relinquish the range to sheepmen was to lose one's dignity, one's honor, one's superiority to the dark-skinned men who herded helpless, baaing vessels of mutton and wool. To give up to the Tewksburys—halfbreed rustlers who had bested the Grahams in the trials at Prescott—was worst of all, particularly in the social milieu of 1886–87. Though honor may or may not have been a critical element of Rim Country culture when the Tewksburys and Grahams had arrived in the early 1880s, it became so amid the normative community shaped by Texas cowboys. Whereas the Grahams and Tewksburys were friendly in the early 1880s—they had helped one another herd cows, build cabins, and rustle from Stinson—they now became enemies divided not only by economics but also by the honor and shame attached to race. In that environment, the Tewksburys would have to struggle all the harder for dignity. They could neither deny nor ignore their enemies. They would have to fight. So it seemed.

Though it received little attention in the aftermath of the quarrel, race was no minor factor. Once, in 1886, William Gladden, detested among Mormons for his claim jumping, rode with several men into Payson, a hamlet just under the Rim. They sought sheepmen, and in particular the "half-breed" Tewksburys. At the local saloon, Gladden found Ed Tewksbury. After bragging of having killed two men, Gladden offered to treat everyone to drinks, except for Tewksbury. "Here is where I draw the line," smirked Gladden. "I'll not drink with a black man." Ed, dressed in his town best, approached Gladden and slapped him on both cheeks, paused, repeated the act, and then challenged him to draw. Gladden ran into the street, crying, "Give me my rifle." Tewksbury followed, challenging Gladden to a gunfight outside. Gladden departed without a fight.[16]

In the annals of honor, to surrender to a "black" meant disgrace. Gladden's failure of nerve may explain why he left suddenly to return to Texas. He had tried—but failed—to impose the South's peculiar culture of honor and shame on the Tewksburys. Gladden elided them with slaves, with negroes, with people who could be made to shuffle and look down. Ed had honor of his own. When in town, he dressed like a dandy, as if to proclaim his worth and prowess. He might be the son of an Indian woman, but he apologized to no one. He carried a gun and he would use it, not in ambush, not in passion, not in a drunken rage, but honorably. Like a duelist he challenged his man to draw, at least in this particular instance. In later conflicts, he acted less nobly.

Race made another appearance in February 1887 when the Tewksburys received a report that one of the Daggs herders—a Ute or a Navajo, or perhaps a Basque—had been killed in Pleasant Valley, his body riddled with bullets. According to one source, the murdered man was the Basque brother-in-law of Jim Houck, who was now a deputy sheriff for Apache County. Whether or not that was the case, the herder is said to have been the first man killed in what came to be known as the Pleasant Valley War. The *Silver Belt* reported that the victim had tried to shoot back but his gun had misfired. After they killed him, the attackers severed his head, perhaps to make the murder look like an act of Apaches or perhaps simply to convey his shame.[17] The Tewksburys could not have missed the symbolism. They, too, were racial others, men easily marginalized, men whose heads might be severed without regard to their humanity.

Even if the Tewksburys and their allies did not expect an attack as they lounged in front of the Middleton cabin on August 9, 1887, they knew it could come any time. Christian Jurgensen had been shot and wounded. Both Samuel Shull and a sheepherder whose name went unrecorded had been murdered. A gang might approach to shoot the Tewksbury men, lynch them, or drive them out. Perhaps the Tewksburys and their allies had gathered that day for a barbecue, to repair a fence, or to plan a roundup. But it seems equally likely that they had gathered to make themselves safe from death squads. Whatever the reason, six men and one boy were at the old Middleton place that day. Among them were two Tewksburys, Ed and Jim, as well as Joe Boyer, Jake Lauffer, George Wagner, George Wilson, and crack rifle-shot Jim Roberts. The new bride of Jim Tewksbury, Mary Ann, may also have been there. On seeing or hearing a party of cowboys riding toward the cabin, they moved quickly inside.[18]

Perhaps the Blevins party really was looking for Old Man Blevins rather than for "a little war," or perhaps they were looking for both. From the historian's viewpoint, it hardly matters. Tensions were great. As Barnes predicted, Hamp's party was about to run into a war, or perhaps more to the point, they were about to start one, even if they backed into it by mistake and without knowing what they were doing.

What then had happened to Mart Blevins? In September 1887, the Arizona *Journal-Miner* reported that someone had found his body, stripped of flesh, near Pleasant Valley. Seven years later, a cowboy reported finding what he took to be the skull of Old Man Blevins along with a rusty rifle.[19] That is all anyone knows about Blevins's fate. Perhaps the body found in 1887 was his. One wonders whether that body included the head or whether it had been severed, only to be found in 1894. Old Man Blevins could have been killed and decapitated by the Tewksburys or their allies in retaliation for the decapitation of their sheepherder. The body might then have been stripped of flesh by hogs or coyotes. Blevins could also have been killed by a grizzly. Or he could have been killed by Apaches and decapitated, a practice they borrowed from General George Crook in the 1870s after he had ordered his scouts to decapitate renegades. Blevins may even have been struck by lightning. August is the "monsoon" season in Arizona, particularly in the high country, and fatalities from lightning are not unknown. He could have met with a snakebite or a fall. After his neighbor left him, he had no one to call for help.

In the aftermath of the Middleton cabin fight, Louis Parker, nephew of Tom and John Graham, filed murder charges against the Tewksburys and their allies. George Newton, owner of the Middleton place and employer of Ed Tewksbury, meanwhile filed a complaint against Graham allies Al Rose, Miguel Apodaca, William Bonner, and two unknowns (Richard Roe and John Doe) for burning down his cabin after the battle. Those and several other men, including John Graham, had come to bury the dead, apparently taking the opportunity to avenge themselves by setting the fire. William Voris, a member of the burial party, testified that he had seen Rose stack kindling against the corral before the fire. A short while later, Voris saw flames shooting out of the house. Jurors, it seems, did not believe Voris's story only because they were bribed, a fact admitted by the attorney for the defense in later years.[20]

Sheriff Mulvenon, meanwhile,—known as "Mel Vernon"—took six deputies into Pleasant Valley to arrest those who had killed Payne and Blevins. He failed to find any of the Tewksbury faction but did parley with the Grahams and their allies, including Andy Cooper. One of the Grahams told Mulvenon that if he did not arrest their enemies, they would exterminate them or drive them out. Mulvenon then managed to hold a secret meeting on a mountaintop with George Newton, a Tewksbury partisan. Mulvenon never revealed what was said. At some point, however, someone—a Graham or a Tewksbury or both—supposedly threatened to attack him if he made the wrong move. Amid rumors that he and his posse had been killed, Mulvenon turned back.[21]

Before leaving the valley, Mulvenon heard about another atrocity. On August 17, 1887, William "Billy" Graham, the teenaged brother of John and Tom and a recent arrival to Pleasant Valley, fell victim to an ambush. Billy was traveling alone. Like several others who were attacked during the war, he was searching for horses. Shot in the arm and the gut, he somehow managed to stay mounted, his intestines stringing out of his abdomen. Three miles down the trail, he stepped off his horse, unable to continue. He lay on the ground for a time, sure that he was going to die. Yet his conscience nagged him; he wanted his killers brought to justice. With heroic strength, he pushed his intestines into his body and rode home. He succumbed to death several days later in profound agony.[22]

Jim Houck, Apache County's deputy sheriff, took credit for the killing. While hunting John Graham, he'd seen Billy on the trail. He shouted at him to "go on," but Billy drew his gun, forcing Houck to kill him. Billy told a different story. Before dying, he identified Ed Tewksbury as the killer, or so said two men who talked to Billy in his final hours, Al Rose and Louis Gruwell. Billy had told Rose, it seems, that not only Ed Tewksbury but also seven other men had set an ambush. Though Billy could not identify all of them, Rose claimed that a certain individual—whose name he could not reveal—had told him their names. They were Ed, John, and Jim Tewksbury, plus H. H. Bishop, Joe Boyer, Jim Roberts, and a man named Edmonson, claimed Rose.[23]

The coroner's jury, with the testimony of Rose and Gruwell, concluded that Graham had been shot from two sides of the trail and that his killer was probably Ed Tewksbury. Maybe the jury was right. Robert Carlock, while researching his book on the Aztec Land and Cattle Company, came across an old note stating that John Tewksbury, rather than Ed, had claimed credit for killing Billy Graham, perhaps indicating that there was an ambush party in which both John and Ed had participated.[24] But does the note have validity? Hashknife cowboys sided with the Grahams and might well have sought to implicate John Tewksbury, even without evidence.

There is likewise reason to doubt the testimony given to the coroner's jury. Rose, the most important deponent, had taken the Graham side. He had already burned the Middleton cabin, in all probability. It served his interest to tell the coroner's jury that each member of the Tewksbury faction had participated in the ambush. That way, officials would have reason to arrest them. Louis Gruwell, though never cited as a fighter, may also have taken the Graham side. A "Ross Gruell"—likely Louis's relative—had stood alongside Tom Graham as they watched John Monk slowly strangle in his caved-in well in September 1886. Interestingly, another man who spoke with Billy shortly before his death told the coroner's jury that Billy never told him who was responsible. Also interesting is an August 1887 report in the *Silver Belt* stating that Jim Houck and "a posse of fifty" had gone to Canyon Creek to capture rustlers. The writer added that he expected soon "to hear of killing in the Blivins [sic] and Cooper neighborhood."[25]

Even if the posse of fifty was a myth, Houck was probably in the area at the

John Tewksbury, the only true sheepherder among
the Tewksburys, fell victim to a Graham faction
ambush on September 1, 1887. Courtesy of Arizona
Historical Society/Tucson, no. 4880.

time of the ambush. Though he was heartily disliked by Mormons, one of whom
claimed that he had killed a man "for his money" even before his arrival in Arizona, Houck was friends with both Commodore Perry Owens, sheriff of Apache
County, and the Tewksburys. The fact that Owens deputized him gave him a
legal excuse to operate as a Tewksbury partisan. In later years, Houck identified
himself not merely as a Tewksbury soldier but as leader of the troops. "It is worthy
of note," wrote his daughter, "that not a man on his side was killed while he led
them."[26]

The Grahams faction wasted little time before striking back. On September 1,
they set up an ambush near the Cherry Creek ranch of James D. Tewksbury,
father of the Tewksbury boys. Though some members of the Tewksbury faction
were hiding in the mountains, others were at the ranch. According to the inquest after the attack, Ed Tewksbury was there but not his father. Lydia Tewksbury (stepmother of the Tewksbury boys) was also there, along with a son and a
daughter by her former husband. Mary Ann Tewksbury, wife of John, may have

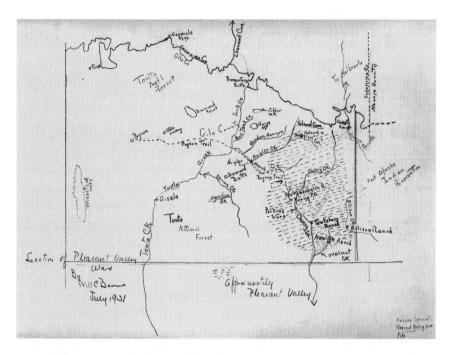

Will Barnes's map of Pleasant Valley War locations, drawn in 1931. Though not shown here, the Graham "stronghold" was situated near Cherry Creek just above Perkins's store. The valley, here identified as part of Gila County, was attached to Yavapai County until 1890. Courtesy of Arizona State Library, Archives and Public Records, Research Library, Phoenix.

been there, too. Some accounts also suggest that John Rhodes and a school-teacher — an overnight guest named Mrs. Crouch — were present.[27]

The list concludes with John Tewksbury and William Jacobs, who collaborated in herding sheep. On the night before the attack, they had camped outside in case of danger. The next morning, the two agreed to locate horses so that Mrs. Crouch could continue her journey. As they carried grain sacks and halters along the rocky bottom of Cherry Creek, assassins shot them from behind, firing as many as a hundred rounds. Jacobs appears to have died quickly, though someone crushed his head with a boulder to make sure. Tewksbury, shot in the nape of the neck, writhed and tore wads of hair from his scalp before more shots stopped any movement. The assassins then lay siege to the house for at least a day and perhaps for several days, forbidding the women from burying their dead. When one of the Tewksbury women shouted out that she wanted to bury the bodies, someone yelled back that the hogs must eat them. The Graham faction, with Andy Cooper and Charlie Duchet along, is said to have considered burning down the ranch house, only to shrink from the thought of killing women and children. Not for twelve days did the justice of the peace from Payson arrive with a coroner's jury that doubled as a burial detachment. By then, the Graham fighters were long gone. One of them, indeed, was dead.[28]

In early September, the governor of the territory, Conrad Meyer Zulick, former commander of a black unit in the Civil War and a cagey Democratic politician, decided to end the war. He called in Sheriff Mulvenon along with District Attorney John Herndon to fashion a plan. The three agreed that Mulvenon, with the sheriffs of neighboring Apache and Gila counties, must penetrate the valley and arrest anybody and everybody for whom there was a warrant. They agreed on something else, too. According to the Arizona *Journal-Miner,* the governor believed that the problem was not a feud but rather a battle against "a gang of thieves that are preying on stock men."[29] The governor viewed the matter not as a complex struggle involving race, honor, economic catastrophe, and the competition to control the range but as a struggle between good men and bad ones.

Perhaps the Apache County Stock Growers Association—as well as Apache County's Mormons—had shaped his thinking. Surely he had read the *Herald's* tirades against rustlers and criminals. Nor could he have missed the explosive story in April 1887 of William Flake finding thirty stolen horses in Phoenix. Already Zulick had committed himself to wooing Mormon voters. Now he believed that the men who attacked Mormons in western Apache County were precisely those who were attacking the Tewksburys in Pleasant Valley. He was not altogether wrong. The Graham brothers had formed ties with the Blevins family and an array of Hashknife cowboys. Years later, Jim Houck told his daughter that Zulick promised to pardon anyone on the Tewksbury side, even for murder. Sam Haught, who knew many of the participants, said the same thing.[30] Assuming that what Houck and Haught said was true, Zulick was endorsing a bloodbath.

Zulick may not have been the only man to make common cause with Mormons. Even before the Middleton cabin fight, the Tewksburys and their allies may have become part of a web of vigilantes that stretched across the Rim. In 1885, Mormons had paid Jim Tewksbury three dollars a day for gathering information on the Graham "rustlers," in effect making him into a stock detective. He worked with a second detective, Robert Carr Blassingame, whom Mormons sent to Pleasant Valley. The connection between Mormons and the Tewksburys, it seems, grew into an alliance. In May 1887, William Flake and a coterie of Mormons—fresh from retrieving stolen horses in Phoenix—had stopped in Pleasant Valley, where they had supped with the Grahams and likely warned them against mischief. They may also have conferred with the Tewksburys and their allies, perhaps drawing them into the vigilante movement that took shape that spring.

With the *Herald* in full cry for war against criminals — complete with assertions that the "best citizens" of Apache and Yavapai counties endorsed lynching — it stands to reason that the Mormons and the Tewksburys made common cause. Both sought to drive out the Grahams, the Blevinses, and their Hashknife friends. Assuming there was such an alliance, the Tewksburys had every reason to attack the cowboys who approached the Middleton cabin on August 9. The war was no longer a feud; it was a campaign against "crime."

Any tacit understanding between Mormons and the Tewksbury faction, however, did not make them friends. The Saints, recalled one Mormon, "encouraged" the "fighting in Pleasant Valley [in order] to kill all these men off," not just to kill off the Grahams. Precisely what he meant by "encouraged" is anyone's guess. With or without Mormon meddling, the storm continued.[31]

In mid-September, some of the Tewksburys traveled to Holbrook to supply themselves with ammunition, guns, and provisions. On their return, they met an ambush. In the early morning of September 17, as most of the Tewksbury men slept, Jim Roberts woke to gather horses. Almost immediately he spotted several men crawling downhill through the grass. When Roberts yelled out the Tewksbury men swung out of their bedrolls, grabbing guns and taking cover. The Graham men, too, took cover. The two sides exchanged fire from their positions, the Tewksbury men gradually moving uphill like an infantry company. The attackers got the worst of it. According to one report, three or four Graham men were killed outright, none of whose names were recorded. They were men from outside the valley who were recruited as shock troops. The two sides declared a cease-fire long enough for the Graham men to dump the dead in a crevice and cover them with rocks.[32]

The two wounded men from the Graham faction whose names were recorded were Harry Middleton and Joe Ellenwood (or possibly Ellingwood or Underwood). Middleton, a cowboy from the Aztec or perhaps from the Defiance Cattle Company, made it back to the Graham place. John Graham nursed him for several days before he died. Ellenwood, shot just below the knee, survived. Another man, identified only as "Bennett," was shot in the knee and apparently recovered. According to newspaper reports, Tom Graham and his nephew, Louie Parker, received minor wounds, as did George Newton on the Tewksbury side.[33]

Sheriff Mulvenon made his way back to the valley in late September, slowed by one of the wettest months in Arizona history. The drought had broken but not the killing. Among Mulvenon's posse were two brothers of the murdered sheepherder William Jacobs. Both surely sympathized with the Tewksburys. It seems unlikely that Mulvenon would have recruited them had he not come to view the matter as a fight against rustlers and murderers.[34]

From Apache County, meanwhile, came Deputy Sheriff Joe McKinney with another posse. Without jurisdiction in Pleasant Valley—which was then part of Yavapai County—he could only enter in hot pursuit of criminals. Now on the trail of train robbers, that was what he decided to do. During a stop in Snowflake, McKinney added a few men to his meager posse by recruiting Osmer Flake, then nineteen, and his friend, Joe Hirschey. As the posse approached the Baca ranch on the way to Canyon Creek, they ran into another of Sheriff Owens's deputies, Jim Houck. Houck claimed to hold warrants for several Pleasant Valley fighters, all of them probably on the Graham side. Knowing that Mulvenon was on the way to Pleasant Valley, Houck proposed that he and McKinney rendezvous with him.[35]

After Deputies McKinney and Houck located Mulvenon at Haigler's ranch, the three men parleyed. Mulvenon proposed to have McKinney's men ride in from the south end of Pleasant Valley in daylight, so that they would be clearly seen. Mulvenon's men, meanwhile, would descend from the north, stopping at the small rock building that served as Charley Perkins's store, where they would hide their horses and secret themselves around the building. Both factions in Pleasant Valley continued to truck with Perkins throughout the conflict. Somehow he remained neutral. Mulvenon hoped that the Graham faction, having seen McKinney, would ride to the store for a parley or, perhaps, for a mass arrest. When that tactic failed, Mulvenon ordered McKinney and his men to ride away, hoping to fool the Grahams into thinking that the posse had left.[36]

The plan worked, though far from perfectly. After McKinney and his men departed, Mulvenon spied a pair of riders four hundred yards off. The riders circled at a great distance, trying to determine whether there was a trap. Mulvenon's force of fourteen had ducked under a half-built stone wall. When the horsemen approached, Mulvenon stood up to demand their surrender. Instead they spurred their horses and reached for their guns. Mulvenon fired a shotgun blast at one of them, killing his horse. The men behind the wall then commenced shooting. When they concluded, both riders lay dying. One of them, Charlie Blevins, could not speak. The other, John Graham, managed to tell Mulvenon that he had not recognized him. Mulvenon cursed him and called him a liar. Then Mulvenon made a humane gesture, offering to bring John's brother, Tom, to sit with him in the trials of death, if only John would reveal his brother's whereabouts. Afterward, promised Mulvenon, he would let Tom go. John denied that his brother was in the valley.[37]

From atop a tree where he scanned the area with binoculars, one of the posse watched as other men—Graham men—gathered horses in order to flee. Osmer Flake offered to take a partner and head them off. Mulvenon refused him, reluctant to bring more death. According to Flake, the three who made their getaway were Tom Graham, Louie Parker, and "a man named Adams," perhaps Cap Adams, who would soon be wounded in a saloon gunfight with John Rhodes, a Tewksbury partisan. McKinney's account, however, differs. The escapees, he claimed, were Louie Parker and William Bonner. Parker appeared no more in records of the war.[38]

Mulvenon then took his men to the home of Al Rose, who, according to Flake, shouted a challenge: "If you want anything here come and get it." Rose's brother, Ed, however, raced out from behind the house, yelling, "Don't shoot," and assuring the posse that his brother intended no violence. Mulvenon arrested Al Rose before moving on to one of the Tewksbury ranches, where he took into custody Ed and Jim Tewksbury, Jim Roberts, George Newton, and Jake Lauffer, who were charged with the murders of John Payne and Hamp Blevins. There would be multiple court hearings, some at Prescott, others at Payson, before the court dropped all charges in June 1889. Defendants and witnesses, claimed the *Silver Belt*, had traveled "upwards of 1300 miles" between the valley and Prescott over the previous two years in order to testify and expressed great relief at the court's decision.[39]

Mulvenon's arrests failed to end the war. In early November, the *Silver Belt* reported the murders of Al Rose and William Bonner, proving that "the Pleasant valley war is to be one of extermination." Bonner's body was found buried in sagebrush near Tucson. Investigators determined that he had been ambushed, presumably by Tewksbury partisans. Rose also fell to an ambush. According to inquest testimony, nine masked men hid among the pines, then shot him while he was rounding up cattle. Decades later, Robert Voris testified that vigilantes had actually hanged Rose. Voris claimed that both his father, who was one of the vigilantes, and Jesse Ellison, the vigilante leader, had confirmed the lynching. They had also "mock-hanged" a German immigrant named Louis Naeglin with whom Rose was working at the time, meaning that Naeglin was lofted into the air by a noose but let down before he strangled.[40]

With Rose dead, the war ceased for the time being. In December 1887, J. J. Vosburgh, partner with George Newton in the Flying V, told the *Silver Belt* that "peace reigns in that neighborhood, and a renewal of hostilities is not looked for." The killings of John Graham and Charlie Blevins supposedly drove out the last of the "rustlers" who had allied with the Grahams. After those killings, reported L. J. Horton, "all day long, four to six at a time who had committed lesser crimes with a swinging trot, winking, and blinking, at every bush, they passed by and before the sun went down, all had skipped the country except fifteen that were shot or hung, which completely annihilated the last one."⁴¹

Assuming that the war had begun with the death of the Indian or Basque herder in February 1887, the dead added up to at least eleven by December 1, 1887. On the Tewksbury side, fatalities included John Tewksbury, William Jacobs, and the mysterious sheepherder. On the Graham side, fatalities included Hamp Blevins, John Payne, Billy Graham, Harry (or Henry) Middleton, John Graham, Charlie Blevins, William Bonner, and Al Rose. Mart "Old Man" Blevins might also fall into the Graham total, depending on how he died. The number rises again if one assumes that three to four anonymous Graham fighters—in addition to Harry Middleton—perished in the October raid on the Tewksbury faction. The number of Tewksbury fatalities might also rise if we include Samuel Shull, the sheepherder who was murdered atop the Rim in summer 1887. As a sheepman, Shull was likely sympathetic to the Tewksburys, if not an outright ally.

The fatality list grows yet again with those on Charlie Perkins's list. Perkins, the storekeeper, estimated that at least six men—parties whose names were not known—were shot while passing through the valley simply because they were suspected of being recruits for the other side. He reported, too, that he had helped bury a victim named Elliott—a Pleasant Valley settler—whose name appears nowhere else in records of the war. Perkins also noted that, in addition to John Payne and Hamp Blevins, both Robert Gillespie (or Glaspie) and another man whose name was not known had died in the hail of gunfire at the Middleton cabin. Perkins, however, was mistaken about Gillespie, who, though wounded, had survived.⁴² Perhaps the "fourth man" of whom he spoke was Tom Tucker, who also survived despite being shot through the chest.

In addition to those deaths or reputed deaths were several others. A mysterious man named John Walsh was "killed by person or persons unknown" in Pleasant Valley in May 1886. Walsh may or may not have been a victim of the war; he had told friends that he feared for his life after a scrape with a Mexican man in Bisbee. In his memoir Charlie Duchet added three more men—strangers passing through the valley whose names were not known—to those killed by the Tewksburys, perhaps some of the same anonymous dead mentioned by Perkins. Duchet also claimed to have killed three Tewksbury partisans after they wounded him in an ambush, a claim at least partly confirmed by Hashknife cowboy Lucien Creswell. Creswell testified to other killings, too. The Daggs brothers, he recalled, offered a Texan named Jim Miller five thousand dollars to assassinate Duchet and an additional five thousand to assassinate Tom Graham. Miller with two partners rode the rail to Holbrook, bragged of his assignment in a bar, then rented horses for the ride to Tonto Basin. He came back alone; his two partners had been bushwhacked.[43]

Another source added the killings of two anonymous horse herders hired by the Tewksburys. A cowboy—a neutral in the war—who was riding to Globe to retrieve medicine for a sick child may likewise have fallen victim to bush-whackers. So, perhaps, did a deputy sheriff meet death when he got in the way of a cattleman who was fleeing the conflict.[44] The likely number of deaths in 1887 alone comes to between sixteen and thirty-eight, depending on how one counts, and excluding the many killings in Apache County in the same year.

Somewhere between sixteen and thirty-eight, then, was honor's toll. The kill-ings weren't solely the product of honor. They were the product of the conflict that free range engendered. Small operators competed for resources with big operators. At times small operators and big operators, or would-be big opera-tors, forged alliances against other teams of small operators and big operators. Cattlemen competed with sheepmen. Mixed-blood men competed with whites. Old alliances broke down and new ones formed. The Grahams allied with Hash-knife cowboys. The Tewksburys allied with vigilantes, some of whom were new-comers from Texas and some of whom were Mormons. Pleasant Valley exploded.

Even if the war began as a struggle for grass and water, behind it stood the normative structures of honor. Men quickly resorted to guns. They feared being judged cowards—being shamed—more than they feared the sixth command-ment. The courts, to be sure, were the appeal of first resort. When the courts failed, contestants began killing. If they attempted any compromise—you put your sheep here, I'll put my cows there—there is no record of it. They sought to resolve conflict via honor, shaming, ambush. Both sides were culpable. Both sides engaged in savagery. It was the Grahams and their Hashknife allies, how-ever—cowboys from Texas—who initiated the fights. Again and again—from the February killing of the sheepherder to the October sneak attack—it was the Graham side that took the offensive. Unless we account the Middleton cabin battle as a Tewksbury attack—which is far from certain—the only record of the Tewksbury side initiating violence is when Houck, or the Tewksbury faction en masse, ambushed Billy Graham. In the guise of vigilantes, however, the Tewks-bury faction became the aggressors. With the execution of Al Rose, the war was given over to the grisly rituals of shaming called lynching.

THE HONOR OF VENGEANCE

On the morning of September 4, 1887, Sheriff Commodore Perry Owens rode into Holbrook, where he met briefly with his deputy, Frank Wattron, at Wattron's drugstore. Wattron told him that Andy Cooper was in town. The entire Blevins family, in fact, was there, except for Delila, who was in Texas, and Charlie, who may have been at the Graham ranch. After Mart had gone missing and Hamp had fallen in Pleasant Valley, the family had moved to Holbrook for safety.[1]

Wattron knew that a warrant existed for the arrest of Cooper for the theft of Navajo horses, but he had done nothing to carry it out. Likely Owens had not asked him to do so. Until September 4, Owens had made no attempt whatsoever to arrest Cooper. Owens may have believed the case against Cooper would not stand up in court. Most Apache County citizens considered horse theft from Indians to be a minor issue and perhaps even a positive good. No jury was likely to convict. Beyond that, Owens and Andy Cooper had been "range pals," as Will Barnes put it, when Owens had lived at Navajo Springs in 1883. According to Lucien Creswell, they had partnered in stealing Indian horses. Both, moreover, had earned reputations as Navajo killers. It is hardly surprising, then, that Owens showed no great desire to make an arrest.[2]

Only two weeks before his meeting with Wattron, Owens had spoken with Cooper. Bystanders recalled that Owens had greeted Cooper in a friendly manner and assured him there was no warrant for his arrest. Perhaps Owens simply meant that he did not intend to enforce the warrant; he surely knew it existed. Lucien Creswell testified that Cooper—a man he knew well—bragged that Owens had promised not to arrest him. Old-time Holbrook residents agreed, recalling in 1959 that Owens and Cooper had made a deal: when Owens was in town, Cooper would make sure to be away. Thus could Owens deny having had a chance to capture him.[3]

If the Mormons wanted Cooper arrested, insisted the Apache County *Critic*, they should file charges rather than rely on an old warrant. Why they did not do so is a mystery; nevertheless they did not. Thus in early September, Wattron merely spoke to Cooper about the warrant, perhaps warning him that powerful men were pressuring Owens to make an arrest. Cooper told Wattron that he would not surrender now but was willing to stand trial at the next term of court. When he did submit, he wanted no "monkey business." Almost certainly he feared he would be lynched.[4] Owens, however, could not wait.

September 4, 1887, would be a bloody day and one that marked a new chapter in Apache County history. It was on that day that a new alliance between Mormon settlers and prosperous ranchers triumphed over the honor culture of Texas cowboys. It was also a day when Mormons sacrificed the conscience that they had long espoused. No longer were they innocents fending off persecution. They had withstood too much, suffered too long. Using Owens as surrogate, they fought back. In doing so, they endorsed honor.

One chain of events that led to the new alliance between Mormons and gentile ranchers—and to the bloodshed of September 4—involved the ceaseless attacks on Mormons by Aztec cowboys. Another chain of events leading to the same result had begun in July 1885, when "parties unknown" broke into the Apache County courthouse safe. Apparently attempting to destroy evidence of embezzlement, they tore up books and papers showing transactions made by the board of supervisors and the county treasurer. In August, the clerk of the board of supervisors and the county auditor—both members of the Barth faction— were charged with forging county warrants (IOUs issued by the county that circulated as currency in lieu of cash). The men, it was said, had falsified warrants in connection with the building of "a few meager" roads as well as a bridge and a county building, for which the county had paid the inflated sum of $15,500.[5]

By April 1885, one of Sol Barth's confederates, a saloon keeper named Charlie Kinnear, had supposedly agreed to testify against Barth himself, who was said to have assisted Kinnear in destroying documents. Kinnear, however, fled before talking. A year later, a mysterious letter appeared from El Paso—perhaps a fraud—signed with Kinnear's name and claiming that Barth and others in his faction were "d——d stinkers" who had not fulfilled promises to pay hush money.[6]

The mischief did not end there. On December 27, 1885, someone kidnapped the deputy county treasurer, Francisco Baca, and forced him at gunpoint to open the county safe—or so Baca claimed. Already in August, his brother, Dionicio, the county treasurer, had lost his bond and had been dismissed from his post, though he had refused to give up his office. His opponents got the best of him in November when they elected the man who had been appointed to replace him, St. George Creaghe. Before Creaghe could assume office, Francisco—perhaps with Dionicio's help—was alleged to have opened the safe to steal eleven thousand dollars of taxpayers' money. Francisco blamed the theft on his kidnappers, whom he suspected to be the notorious Clanton "gang." Finding neither tracks nor clues, investigators charged that it was an inside job.[7]

To absolve his brother, Dionicio convinced another Baca brother, Benigno, the justice of the peace, to order a search of the homes of Ike Clanton and his brother-in-law, Ebin Stanley. When the search turned up no evidence, Clanton and Stanley charged Dionicio Baca with issuing the search warrant "feloniously, maliciously, and without probable cause."[8]

The scandals simmered for the next several years, occasionally bubbling into public view with a new accusation and a new defense. What was important, however, was not corruption itself but the political realignment that it produced. Rallying around the call of law and order, a clique of gentile cattlemen proposed to rid the county of the Barth faction and enfeeble the New Mexican electorate. By promising to go after cowboy persecutors as well as New Mexican "criminals," they brought Mormons into the fold. Both groups stood to benefit. Mormons and gentiles alike were losing stock to thieves, or at least they believed they were. The situation became especially intolerable after the bottom fell out of the cattle market in 1886–87. Cattlemen would wink no more at petty theft.

If cattlemen and Mormons joined forces behind the banner of law and order, they also rallied to the banner of honor. To deal with their enemies, they resorted to the gun and the rope. Rituals of shaming replaced appeals to forbearance. Mormons placed faith in violence—and in men willing to do violence—rather than God.

The new alliance took shape in the Peoples' Ticket of 1886, a name not meant to connote any connection to the radical People's Party that would emerge on the national stage in 1889. On the contrary, the name was likely intended to show common cause with the People's Party of the LDS church in Utah. It also called to mind the People's Party formed by San Francisco vigilantes in 1856. At the 1886 county convention in Winslow, People's Party delegates chose a "clean slate" of candidates rather than putting forth the "corrupt" incumbents associated with the Barth faction. The delegates instead presented a slate of white gentiles and Mormons. No New Mexican or Jew appeared on the ticket.[9] Not every Mormon, however, supported the reformers.

Behind the scenes, a few St. Johns Mormons had been working with New Mexicans to bring rapprochement. They came close to achieving it when in 1885 almost every county official—many of them members of the Barth faction— signed a letter to President Grover Cleveland urging the pardon of David Udall, the St. Johns bishop who had been convicted on flimsy evidence for perjury. The letter may have helped. In December 1885, Cleveland issued a pardon.[10]

Once freed, Udall went to work adjudicating water rights between New Mexicans and Mormons. By fall 1886, a contingent of Mormons and New Mexicans from the eastern part of the county was ready to field a ticket consisting of Hispanic incumbents and Mormon newcomers. Those in favor of a "clean" ticket, however, commandeered the Winslow convention and silenced opposition. Supporters of a compromise ticket were forced to hold a separate convention in St. Johns.[11]

Calling themselves the Equal Rights Party, the St. Johns group put forth a ticket that they hoped would draw votes from white gentiles, New Mexicans, and Mormons. They chose John, or "Juan," Milner, new editor of the *Orion Era*, as chairman and Alfred Ruiz, the incumbent county recorder, as secretary. After Ruiz called the convention to order, delegates elected a "committee on resolutions" that included Milner, Ruiz, the incumbent sheriff, Lorenzo Hubbell, and the alleged rustler Ebin Stanley. The committee reported back to the whole with a resolution condemning the Winslow convention for "unjustly and unfairly discriminat[ing] against" New Mexicans. "We heartily endorse every measure of true reform in the administration of Apache County affairs," resolved the committee, "but do not believe that reform means revolution, class, or race distinctions." The committee promised to recognize "American citizens of Mexican birth as the political equals and entitled to all the privileges of all other American citizens."[12]

In deeming the Winslow Convention a "revolution," the Equal Rights Party did not speak loosely. The stakes were high. If the People's Party—the "clean" party—won, its officers would empanel grand jurors consisting only of those who spoke good English—presumably white Americans. The new grand jury would then prosecute the people's "enemies," especially members of the Barth faction. The People's Party also promised to appoint only English-speaking jurors to the regular jury pool, thus excluding New Mexicans and insuring the easy conviction of Spanish-speaking defendants. People's Party candidates promised Mormons in particular that they would work to repeal the test oath that disfranchised supporters of polygamy. They also vowed to "do justice to all the school children of the county," meaning, presumably, that the county would appoint Mormon teachers or provide public funds for Mormon-only schools, thus segregating

Mormon from New Mexican children.[13] Perhaps most significant, a victory for the People's Party meant the election of Commodore Perry Owens—a much-feared gunman—as sheriff. The county would shift, then, from a place friendly to New Mexicans, most of them Republicans, to a place dominated by American-born whites, most of them Democrats.

To bring revolution, however, required more than a new party. It required a publicist. To that end—as well as to crusade against "criminals"—the mysterious "company of cattlemen" described by Henry Reed had bought the St. Johns *Herald.* The *Herald*'s new editor, Barry Matthews, promptly initiated a fierce assault on the opposition, noting that certain Equal Rights supporters "two years ago swore by all their patron saints that perdition might overtake them, if they ever voted or affiliated with a Mormon." Some Equal Rights men had even participated in jumping Mormon land claims. Above those assertions—which were exaggerated but not entirely fictitious—flew the pennant of race. Calling on decades of Democratic racial polemic, the *Herald* termed the Equal Rights ticket "mongrel," "bastard," and "mongrel black and tan." Matthews referred to Milner as "Sister Juan y Baca Milner," thus attacking him as an emasculate who served the interests of patróns like the Bacas. "If Sister Milner should lay eggs and the Equalites act as an incubator," wondered Matthews, "will some student of natural history tell us what name to give the birds. Judging from the smell of the nest we should say they would be buzzards or winged skunks."[14]

Matthews—a product of Southern honor—resorted to exercises in shaming. His attacks transcended the Mormon opposition to what they conceived of as New Mexican sin. He attacked his enemies' manliness; indeed, he attacked their humanity. They were "buzzards or winged skunks"; they were castrati; they were women. Like Southern blacks, he implied, members of the Equal Rights Party were incapable of citizenship. They merited only derogation and insult.

In addition to his rhetoric of shaming, Matthews trumpeted the corruption of the Barth faction. The Equal Rights Party, to be sure, included none of those indicted or accused of mischief—with the single exception of Hubbell—nor was it captained by the Barths. Like the People's Party, it was a new coalition, a hybrid. Matthews, however, tied the alleged criminality of the Barth faction to the sins of Aztec cowboys and New Mexican claim jumpers. "When the 'powers that be' took hold of the reins of government in this county," insisted the *Herald,* "lawlessness was rampant almost throughout her entire limits." The message: if it gained power, the Equal Rights Party would continue the reign of lawlessness. "Stock thieves," announced the *Herald,* "are calling for equal rights to follow their avocation, and they will vote for it too."[15]

To make sure that voters would take seriously their rhetoric, those promoting the People's Party convinced Commodore Perry Owens to run for sheriff. So well known had Owens become as a gunslinger that his candidacy promised to bring new voters to the polls—especially Mormons who wanted a defender.

A Tennessean by birth, Owens was named for one or perhaps both of the famous Commodore Perrys (the father, naval hero of the War of 1812, or the son, who, in the year of Owens's birth, had opened Japanese ports to American trade by threatening to bombard Tokyo). At sixteen, he had decided to escape his abusive father by running away to Indian Territory, where he worked on a ranch before moving on to Texas and New Mexico. In the early 1880s, he appeared at Navajo Springs, Arizona, where he cowboyed and served as a guard for teamsters. There he made friends with James Houck.[16]

Owens understood the West's peculiar code of honor. He looked to guns, not words or logic or sentiment, to resolve disputes. By 1886, he had gained a reputation for killing Navajos. The Indian agent at Fort Defiance wrote in 1883 that Owens and his employer, James Houck, were "men dangerous to the peace and good order of the region." The agent reported having seen two dozen Indians "who have been shot at by them during the past year or two, including an Indian woman." Dane Coolidge, who chronicled the West for a popular readership in the 1920s and 1930s, depicted Owens as a Custerian figure who, on seeing a Navajo "war party," would remove his hat and "shake out his long yellow locks" before charging, his hair streaming behind. Coolidge reckoned that Owens had killed twenty-five Navajos, including some from ambush. Owens's wife—whom he married late in life—put the number at fifty, though neither she nor Coolidge explained the basis for their counts. In conversations with his deputy, Owens admitted to having killed only one Navajo.[17]

Whatever the number of Navajos killed by Owens, he was a practiced gunman. At more than one roundup, Barnes recalled seeing Owens draw his revolvers and fire at a tomato can, keeping it "rolling and jumping" with alternate shots from each hand "until it was torn to pieces." James LeSueur similarly claimed that he had seen Owens use six-shooters to "finish driving nails in a board with bullets 50 feet away." He would shoot, according to his obituary, "not only at the drop of the hat, but before the hat was dropped." With his long, prominent nose, steel-gray eyes, and sheets of blond-red hair that draped over his shoulders, Owens resembled the Wild West performers who by the 1880s were making their mark in the popular imagination. Supposedly he "disliked being considered a 'bad man'" and grew his hair long only when he could not find a barber, but surviving photos testify to a streak of vanity. Owens was the epitome—the example par excellence—of Western honor. He was also the most superstitious man that his deputy had ever known.[18]

Commodore Perry Owens, gunfighter
and sheriff, circa 1880. Courtesy of
Arizona State Library, Archives and
Public Records, History and Archives
Division, Phoenix, no. 97–7750.

Throughout the summer and fall of 1886, the *Herald* kept up a steady drum-beat for Owens's candidacy. On October 7, the *Herald* claimed that Owens, "the man of the hour, the hope of the country," would drive "the enemies of the people . . . into their holes and hiding places, to stay 'till the day of their judgement.'" On October 21, the *Herald* continued the embroidery, claiming that "when Commodore Owens is sheriff . . . it will be a mere matter of form to brand your horses."[19]

The *Herald* targeted Mormons in particular, repeatedly calling attention to the role of Owens's opponent, Lorenzo Hubbell, in prosecuting polygamists. Hubbell, son of an American trader and his New Mexican wife, was also ac-cused of failing to serve bench warrants and subpoenas. In addition, the *Herald* accused him of absenting himself from office without hiring deputies who were capable of handling his duties. "Crime has received too much indulgence, criminals too much protection," insisted the *Herald*.[20]

"We are informed that there is scarcely a Mormon in the County," continued the *Herald*, who "has not suffered loss at the hands of thieves. . . . Are the Mormons prepared to say they want this state of affairs kept up? Do they or any other class of citizens desire to be continually plundered of their property without hope of redress?" If Owens were elected, promised the *Herald*, the jail would become a "popular and fashionable boarding house," adding that there were "a large number of guests from Concho and El Tule who have already spoken for rooms." Reacting to such statements, Hubbell told New Mexicans that Owens intended to set up a vigilance committee to lynch them.[21] Rituals of shaming, suggested Hubbell, would prevail over law.

In campaigning for Owens and the other candidates of the People's Party, the *Herald* got help from stake president Jesse Smith. In October, LDS president John Taylor directed Smith to "get the Saints in the various Arizona Stakes in line to sustain the Democratic nominee[s]." The fact that Mormon settlers favored the Democrats anyway made Smith's task easier. President Cleveland buttressed Mormon loyalty to his party by pardoning convicted polygamists. The Democratic governor of the territory simultaneously worked to repeal the test oath. Far from being criminals, Governor Zulick told Mormons in May 1887 that "they were the best citizens there was in the Territory," and that he wished fifty thousand of them had come. With Mormons representing over half the voting population of Apache County, they mattered.[22]

What was confusing was which party in Apache County represented the Democrats. Both had mixed memberships, though both claimed to be Democratic. To attract the votes of whites—and especially Mormons—Juan Milner accused the People's Party of being a stalking horse for Republicans. There was truth in his accusation. Both Will Barnes, who had served as secretary of the Winslow convention, and Robert Morrison, the People's Party candidate for county attorney, were rock-ribbed Republicans and supporters of "reform." Most People's Party candidates, however, tilted Democratic. Milner's Equal Rights Party, moreover, had its own Republican drift.[23] New Mexicans had tended to vote Republican since the Civil War, a fact of which Mormon Democrats were well aware.

Jesse Smith, then, could endorse the People's Party as an appendage of the Democracy without betraying the instructions of the church. "Went to Taylor," he reported on October 10, "and spoke on the political situation." He advised all Mormons to vote, knowing that those over whom he had authority would move en masse to the People's Party. He may, indeed, have been the "venerable

Mormon patriarch" who referred to Equal Rights supporters as "dishonorable" men who had "dug their own graves."[24]

The result was a complete victory for the People's Party. Only one of their candidates, a gentile running for the legislature, fell short. Mormons took the offices of assessor, treasurer, supervisor, and coroner. Not a single man of New Mexican or Jewish descent won office. Jesse Smith's stake—the Eastern Arizona Stake—voted overwhelmingly for People's Party candidates. Woodruff, Taylor, and Snowflake, reported the *Herald*, "are solid for the Winslow ticket to a man." Mormons throughout the county voted "without let or hindrance," noted Smith. Choosing new alliances over old enmities, Mormon opponents like Jim Houck refrained from imposing the test oath.[25]

In some ways, the election was not a victory for all Mormons in Apache County but rather a victory for Mormons of the western part of the county. The president of the Little Colorado Stake, the stake that included St. Johns, had suggested in September 1886 that Mormons "establish a confidence" with their neighbors—apparently referring to New Mexicans—and "be on good terms with them." In the spirit of rapprochement, it seems, the Equal Rights Party nominated Americus Greer for assessor despite his earlier imbroglios with New Mexican sheepherders.[26] Greer, indeed, was nominated by both parties in 1886. Rapprochement in the east, however, failed to stop the "revolution."

Perhaps because of the breach between Mormons in the western and eastern parts of the county, Commodore Perry Owens prevailed by only 91 votes out of 909 cast. His election as sheriff was nonetheless a turning point. Now his backers expected him to fulfill the promises they had made on his behalf. In particular, they expected him to go after John Payne and Andy Cooper. Helping Owens would be the new county attorney, Robert Morrison, who pledged himself to the vigorous prosecution of criminals.[27]

Elsewhere, too, the new alliance between Mormons and gentile Democrats (plus a few Republicans like Morrison and Barnes) exerted influence. As early as spring 1886, at least five Mormons showed up in the Apache County Stock Growers Association, thus making that body into another force for change. In January 1887, the association got an additional boost after the *Herald* scolded cattlemen who had still not joined, damning them for individualism. The legislature buttressed that call for action by deciding in March to require a county branding system. To stop rustling, all brands were to be registered with the county recorder, which in turn required coordination among ranchers.[28]

Prompted by Mormon complaints as well as by the new branding system, the Apache County Stock Growers Association reorganized itself in spring 1887. No one, proclaimed the association, should "remain without its pale any longer." The association had important business to address at its April meeting and promised to help cattlemen far more than they imagined it could.[29]

The first important business was to warn newcomers against bringing more cattle into the county. The members also reelected Henry Smith, a prosperous Englishman who owned the 24 Cattle Company, as president. Ben Irby of the Aztec became vice president and chairman of the executive committee. For secretary-treasurer, the members chose Will Barnes, medal of honor winner and operator of the Esperanza Cattle Company. Those who voted included Mormons James Flake, Nat Greer, W. S. Atchison, and K. V. B. Talley. Also present was Robert Morrison, Apache County's attorney, whose father had once been indicted in New Mexico for murdering squatters deemed to be rustlers.[30]

At the same time that they were welcomed into the stock association, Mormons were working to convince the General Land Office to send a special agent to investigate the Aztec's mistreatment of Mormon settlers. After the agent— Colonel S. B. Bevans—toured St. Johns, Heber, and Holbrook, he filed a report harshly critical of the Aztec. In summer 1887 he met with Aztec management, despite expressing the fear that he would be assassinated.[31]

Bevans told the Aztec that it would have to back off. Beyond that, either he or the Mormons or both told the Aztec that its cowboys were stealing Aztec cattle along with those of others. The Aztec's "cutthroats," averred Mormons, "not only made life miserable for the small outfits, but turned on the Hashknife and almost stole it out of business." One Mormon chronicler made the absurd claim that, in a single year, Aztec cowboys had stolen fifty-two thousand cows. Niels Petersen, the man whipped by John Payne, testified that the evildoers had asked even him to join their ring, supposedly telling him that they "have enough boys in these hills to wipe out anyone who dares to interfere." The Aztec policy of hiring gunslingers, insisted Mormons, "started something they couldn't stop."[32]

The year 1887 saw the Aztec face up to its first crisis. The company lost twenty-two thousand dollars that year thanks to low cattle prices and drought. Though the summer brought rain, it came too late to yield profit. The drought also saw the devaluation of the Aztec's land. The company's board of directors called for immediate changes that translated into the resignation of Henry Warren, its general manager. He was replaced by E. J. Simpson, who proved more sympathetic to Mormons. Not only did Simpson agree to sell Mormons the lands encompassing Snowflake and Taylor at what the Aztec considered to be discount rates, but he also agreed to fight the rustling. In all probability, he believed Mormon reports that Hashknife cowboys were bleeding their employer. In the desperate straits of 1887, the company could afford no losses.[33]

What Simpson also might have heard was that Mormons themselves were bleeding the Aztec. According to Lucien Creswell, "Mormons were stealing the outfit blind." They took Aztec cattle and horses, he explained, "under the pretense of getting back at the 'robber barons' for beating honest, hard-working people out of their rights." Mormon records suggest that the accusation may have had a grain of truth; not all Saints were immune to temptation.[34] From the Aztec point of view, the solution was to drive out Mormons and to fire its feckless cowboys, but to undertake both was impossible.

The company had one other option. It could fire its mischievous cowboys and ally with Mormons, who, the Aztec must have hoped, would desist from stealing stock. Mormons might even serve as a police force to guard the company's property. That strategy, as it turned out, was the one that the Aztec chose to pursue. "In justice to the Hash-knife Company," wrote one Mormon, "we must not fail to say that they did try to make amends to our folks at last, by hiring them and doing all in their power for them." In summer 1887, Simpson commanded his range bosses to inform their men that the Aztec planned to stop horse and cattle theft. If any cowboys did not wish to assist, they were free to take their pay and leave. At least five did just that, including three who participated in the Middleton cabin fight in Pleasant Valley on August 9.[35]

With Mormons, gentile ranchers, and Aztec managers now united, the stock association worked out plans for a fall rodeo so that each owner could separate and count his cattle. Though the association had organized no spring rodeo—drought and low prices made it unnecessary—it set new guidelines for the one in September. To eliminate mavericking, the association ordered that every cow be branded with the association's mark, even if the owner was not known. In previous years, the wranglers had left mavericks unbranded, which allowed the next finder to give them his brand. Until 1887, mavericking had been a tradition. The stock association, however, wanted the tradition to end.[36]

In other respects, the fall 1887 rodeo was no different than earlier ones. It required enormous organization and time. It lasted for weeks. Each rancher through whose range the wranglers passed was expected to feed the crew. Once gathered, mature cattle were sorted by brands and earmarks, after which calves received their own brands and marks. Finally the animals were driven back to the range of their owners or perhaps to market.[37]

The rodeo was traditional in another way, too. It provided no real range management, no cattle census, no systematic effort to assess ecological conditions. The executive committee agreed, however, to ban horse racing and gambling.[38] In that sense, the rodeo represented something new. With Mormons taking an active role in the stock association, "immoral" behavior was no longer tolerated.

If Mormon conscience trumped cowboy honor, the reverse was also true. With its members' consent, the association vowed to fight rustling not just via legal means but also via the rituals of honor, rituals that entailed shaming and terror. The *Herald*, under the editorship of J. F. Wallace as of February 1887, led the charge to violence with its repeated calls for vigilantism in spring and summer. "The best people" of Yavapai and Apache counties, promised the *Herald*, would "uphold" good citizens "in any measures they may adopt."[39]

In 1887 and 1888, the stock association denied the existence of a secret vigilante campaign. In his reminiscences, however, Will Barnes confirmed it. "As most of the work had to be done on the quiet," he wrote, "the president and secretary [Smith and Barnes] were given a rather free hand in . . . weeding out [the] undesirables. It was war to the bitter end. The Devil had to be fought with his own weapons." The association, continued Barnes, used an endowment of three thousand dollars to "make a good clean-up of the outlaws."[40]

Some of that money probably came from William Ellinger, whose brother, Ike, had been a member of the stock association in 1886. In November of that year Ike Ellinger had fallen victim to the six-gun of Lee Renfro, who smarted over Ellinger's threat to evict him from property in New Mexico, where Renfro and a friend had allegedly jumped Ellinger's claim. When Renfro ran into Ellinger at the Clanton ranch, Renfro shot him at point-blank range.[41]

Though mortally wounded, Ellinger remained conscious. Ike Clanton, who, according to one account, had tried to step between the two men, asked a Hashknife cowboy, T. W. "Bud" Jones, to get Ellinger's testimony while Ellinger's companion went for a doctor. As Ellinger lay dying, Renfro—allegedly on a fresh horse given him by Clanton—made his getaway.[42] Though Clanton could not have known it, the Ellinger killing would lead to the demise of his family, closing one chapter in Arizona history and opening another.

Like many Americans of their time, the Clantons had led peripatetic lives. They found themselves in Missouri in the 1840s, then successively moved to Illinois, Texas, California, and Arizona. In 1873, Newman Haynes "Old Man" Clanton built a gristmill near Camp Thomas on the Gila River and tried to lure settlers to a place he called Clantonville. When that enterprise failed, he moved his family to a ranch on the San Pedro River, where he prospered amid the silver boom that spawned Tombstone.[43]

Surrounded by wranglers who worked for their father, Newman Clanton's sons soon became involved in a loose confederation known as the "Cow-boys," a group known for rustling along the Mexican border. The rustling, one hastens to add, tended to be small-scale and ad hoc. The Cow-boys were more like a street gang than a mob family. Rustling and stage-robbing charges nonetheless led the Cow-boys into a quarrel with the Earp brothers and Doc Holliday of Tombstone, who in 1881 gunned down nineteen-year-old Billy Clanton along with Tom and Frank McLaury near the OK Corral. Ike Clanton was also in Tombstone that day. Unarmed, he avoided the fight. The OK Corral killings led to war between Cow-boys and Earp men, whom the Cow-boys accused of murder. When the courts failed to prosecute, the Clantons and their allies resorted to ambushes, managing to kill Virgil Earp and cripple his brother Morgan. Territorial governor John Gosper meanwhile organized a vigilante group that assisted Wyatt Earp in his "vendetta ride," a killing spree that left several Cow-boys dead.[44]

Perhaps to escape the vendetta, Ike and his older brother, Phineas ("Phin"), moved to Apache County, where their sister, Mary Clanton Slinkard, already lived. After her first husband died of natural causes in 1881, she had married the popular Ebin Stanley, who had won the medal of honor for his actions during General Crook's Tonto Basin Apache campaign. After their wedding, Stanley had moved his wife and family to Springerville, where he opened a saloon. Stanley also involved himself in civic affairs. In 1884 he appeared at the opening of the Springerville schoolhouse and, in August, accompanied his brother-in-law at the anti-Mormon convention. He also helped organize the Equal Rights Party in 1886.[45]

Despite their dislike for Mormons, the Clantons did not eschew interaction. One settler recalled that the Clantons sometimes attended Mormon dances, where they dramatized their honor by donning hats, spurs, and chaps. When a chaperone once asked Phin Clanton to remove his paraphernalia, he refused. The burly chaperone, it is said, threw him outside and into the arms of a surprised Commodore Perry Owens, who was approaching to make an arrest. Phin cried "law," as the story goes, and he and his companions escaped without pursuit.[46]

A more modest story comes from Leila Eagar Turley, whose family sold the Clantons dairy products. Turley recalled the Clantons as affable. One of the Clantons once tipped a Turley boy $1.50, a large sum for the time. Unfortunately the boy was made to split the money with his brother. Clanton affability, however, was not in evidence when Ike grabbed another small boy in Gustav Becker's store and locked him in a cold stove. When Clanton refused to free the boy despite his wailing, Becker punched Clanton in the face and knocked him out. Clanton's friends, it is said, dragged him outside, where he slowly came to consciousness, a wan smile on his face.[47]

Despite their imbroglios, the Clantons received favorable mentions, at least until Matthews took over the *Herald* in 1886. They were likable men. Joe

McKinney, under-sheriff to Commodore Perry Owens, said he would have never picked the Clantons for bad guys; they were too friendly. The Clantons were not, however, men of conscience. Their friendliness was emblematic of the cowboy culture of honor, with its emphasis on bonhomie and hospitality. They partook strongly of honor in their dedication to drinking, gambling, horse racing, and self-assertion. It was honor that led them into the quarrel with the Earps, and it was honor that led Ike into a shooting scrape with a Mexican man after a dispute over a card game in 1886. Both men suffered minor wounds.[48]

The Clantons probably also practiced the petty thievery—rustling—common throughout the West. In 1883, Phin Clanton and Ebin Stanley drew an indictment for cattle theft but were acquitted, much to their enemies' consternation. The Clantons themselves, meanwhile, claimed to suffer from horse theft.[49] Far more injurious, however, was the "legal" wrath to come.

Whether good or bad or some shade of gray, the Clantons became celebrated public enemies after Lee Renfro killed Ike Ellinger. Ike Ellinger's elder brother, William, immediately traveled from his home in Maryland to Washington, D.C., in his quest for justice. He then traveled to Arizona to investigate the killing. He brought money. The Ellingers' father, an immigrant from Germany, held real estate worth forty thousand dollars in 1860. It was the father's money, perhaps, that had allowed Ike to finance his New Mexico ranch. That may explain why Renfro hated him. Lee Renfro was poor and powerless; Ike Ellinger was not. Renfro, moreover, was a man of honor, whereas Ike Ellinger displayed "strict integrity, temperate habits and all the qualities that are requisite to make a good citizen."[50] Ellinger was a conscience man.

On December 15, 1886, William Ellinger cabled Governor Zulick to insist on "as large a reward" for the apprehension of Renfro "as in your best judgment will meet the requirements of the case." Ellinger promised to add to the pot, which included six hundred dollars put up by Springerville locals. In April 1887, however—the same month that Mormons recovered thirty stolen horses in Phoenix—Ellinger withdrew his offer.[51] Apparently he put his money into a more promising enterprise.

William Ellinger found Apache County at a crossroads. In January 1886, the stock association had sent a representative to the National Livestock Association convention in Denver, whose delegates decided to "form a detective service to cover the entire range country." Apache County's delegate must have found sympathetic ears when he returned with news of the proceedings. In early 1887, the "cleaning up" process began. Shortly after the district court adjourned, noted the *Critic*, newly elected county officials, "seconded by the Apache county stock association, and every citizen of the county interested in its welfare, met about hunting down . . . offenders." Over the next few months, reported a Mormon observer, "vigilante committees were organized by both Mormons and non-Mormons throughout the area," stretching from St. Johns to Pleasant Valley.[52]

When he replaced his dead brother as a member of the stock association, William Ellinger, it seems, became a vigilante. He managed to avoid the actual work of killing, however, leaving that task to another. In his memoir, Will Barnes recalled that in spring 1887 the association found "a man who said he was a range detective. He wanted a job. We gave it to him at once."[53] That man was Jonas Brighton.

After serving in the Union Army and doing a stint at Andersonville as a prisoner of war, Brighton had entered the detective business. He had taken a correspondence course, it seems, and received a badge at "nominal cost." Brighton would later brag that he had helped exterminate the James gang. If he was telling the truth, his deeds likely occurred in the late 1870s or early 1880s, when Jesse James sought to reconstitute the gang after the devastating 1876 raid on Northfield, Minnesota.[54]

What impressed Barnes and his fellows about Brighton's abilities was probably his low profile. Brighton liked publicity but was by no means flamboyant. A San Francisco *Examiner* reporter who interviewed him in the 1890s described him as "the most unsophisticated looking chap alive." He was "a man of medium height with a roly-poly shape, a twang to his voice that sounds like a down-east Yankee's, a slouchy-hands-in-his-pockets and scrape his foot-on-the-ground gait, threadbare suit of clothes, large hands, ungainly feet . . . and the most innocent-looking blue eyes."[55]

With the blessing of the stock association, Sheriff Owens made Brighton a deputy, allowing him to go straight to work pursuing his erstwhile friends the Clantons. On April 11, 1887, the grand jury, with help from Brighton, charged both Clantons with stealing a single brown-and-white-spotted cow. On May 8, the *Herald* reported that Phin had been arrested and jailed.[56]

With Phin Clanton out of the picture, the time was ripe to move on Ike. On June 1, Brighton and one of his associates, Albert Miller, located Ike at Peg Leg Wilson's ranch on the Blue River, south of Springerville. Clanton had been helping Wilson with his animal traps. Brighton claimed that the three waited in secret for Clanton to make an appearance at the ranch house. When he rode in, Clanton saw Brighton and Miller in the doorway. Clanton turned his horse to make a break while simultaneously pulling his rifle, causing Brighton to shoot him.[57]

That was how Brighton recalled events. Peg Leg Wilson told a different story many years later. He claimed that Clanton was ill that day and had stayed at the cabin while Wilson checked his traps. When Wilson returned, he found a lone man at his cabin who identified himself as a "Pinkerton." The man had shot Clanton in the back. Regardless of what had happened, the stock association rejoiced. On a transcribed article from the Phoenix *Herald* that reported the killing, Barnes wrote that he had "offered [Brighton] a good big sum for Clanton's arrest." Barnes also noted that he had purchased the horse that Clanton had ridden on the day of his death, naming it "Ike Clanton."[58] Having ridden Clanton to his death, he could now ride his namesake.

A month later, Brighton saw more action. Having been anointed a deputy U.S. marshal, Brighton could operate freely on the White Mountain Apache Reservation. There he sought rustlers with help from three men assigned to him by the commanding officer at Fort Apache. In early June, they spied a man in shirt sleeves, on foot, near Bonita Creek. Brighton had his men lure the stranger closer. The man turned out to be Lee Renfro, the murderer of Ike Ellinger. When told that he was under arrest, Renfro supposedly reached for his gun. Brighton killed him.[59]

"Now comes, on the same ghastly trail" as Ike Clanton, remarked Henry Reed in the *Critic*, "the quaking, cringing, murderous soul of Lee Renfro, all crimson with the blood of an honored citizen." Renfro's alleged partner in claim jumping, Bill Craig, had already met his reward in January after a gambling quarrel. "It is remarkable," noted the *Critic*, to see "the swift and terrible retribution which has followed every man closely connected with the jumping of the cotton woods ranch and the murder of Ike Ellinger." The stock association's "Secret Service officer," bragged Reed, "is giving the outlaw element no time to rest, but is hunting them down like wild beasts. He should receive the hearty support of all the law-abiding citizens."[60]

Next on Brighton's list was C. W. Johnson, widely known as "Kid Swingle." Johnson, a Clanton associate, was alleged to have shot and killed a Mormon man, James Hale, on Christmas Day, 1886, in Springerville. Hale and another Mormon had made the mistake of identifying rustlers—apparently Johnson's friends—to officers of the stock association. Johnson sought vengeance. One witness averred that Johnson told Hale before shooting him that he simply wanted to see whether a bullet would go through a Mormon. Johnson managed to escape the mob that gathered in the aftermath but not without being shot and taken into custody.[61]

After the county dropped charges, Johnson disappeared. In August 1887, Brighton pursued him and others only to find the tables reversed when he was arrested in an adjacent county for murdering Ike Clanton. Authorities released

him, however, after he promised that his associates, Powell and Miller, would testify that Clanton had resisted arrest. After his release, Brighton promptly located
a stolen horse that Johnson had supposedly sold at Camp Thomas on the Gila
River. Apparently he found Johnson, too, who was lynched by parties unknown.[62]

Too late came editor Reed to the rescue. Reed had recently defended Andy
Cooper against the diatribes in the Herald, but in general, he had praised the
campaign to rid the county of outlaws. On August 13, he changed his mind. On
that day, the Critic asked readers "whether they are willing to submit themselves
to be ruled over by 'the Apache county stock association,' or by the laws of the
United States and this Territory?" "Have the so-called 'association,'" queried
Reed, "the right of . . . sending out an hired assassin, to shoot down whomsoever
he may please to, without warrant of law, with simply his sweet will the arbiter as
to what lengths he may choose to carry his saturnalia of blood?"[63]

Reed's charges met indignation. The stock association hired no assassins, asserted the Herald, and "does not sanction murder." Unfortunately Brighton had
announced his affiliation while shuttling around the territory. Barnes, in his
memoir, admitted that Brighton was paid to kill. When a certain deputy marshal—presumably Brighton—ordered men "to hold up their hands," wrote
Barnes, "somehow . . . they were slow to do so." Rustlers and horse thieves "fairly
burned up the roads and tore the mountains down getting away from the unknown officer who shot first and read his warrants later over the dead bodies of
the men he was after."[64]

Though the stock association's campaign of terror suggested that legal justice
had failed, in reality the court became a critical tool in the "cleanup." As early as
March 1887, the Herald had warned malefactors to flee after the mere publication of the list of grand jurors, all men of integrity and courage. Apache County
would no longer be "a haven to criminals." The Herald urged the grand jury to indict everyone it could. For too long, claimed the Herald, criminals had escaped
justice on perjured testimony, a mockery that the new jurors would not permit.[65]

The court's "cleanup" began as soon as Owens and Morrison took office. In
January 1887, Owens arrested Sol Barth for forging warrants and destroying
records to conceal his crime. In a hasty trial Barth was convicted despite an alleged attempt by one Frederico Jiron, supposedly paid by Barth or his allies, to
assassinate a witness. The court also convicted Francisco Baca of embezzlement
and, for good measure, fined Nathan Barth, Sol's brother, five hundred dollars
for jury tampering. In spring 1887, just as he was gearing up for battle with horse
thieves, Sheriff Owens escorted Sol Barth to the Yuma Penitentiary.[66]

No sooner had the jury dispensed with Sol Barth than it took up the case
of Phin Clanton. Convicted of stealing exactly one cow, Clanton got ten years

Henry Reed, editor of the Apache County
Critic and belated opponent of Apache County
vigilantism, circa 1890. Courtesy of Arizona
State Library, Archives and Public Records,
History and Archives Division,
Phoenix, no. 96–2121.

at Yuma. The court simultaneously pursued rustling charges against Clanton's brother-in-law, Ebin Stanley. When evidence proved insufficient for conviction, the court merely required Stanley to leave the territory, a command it also gave to another accused rustler at the same time. The court left open its indictments in order to scare the men into leaving. Stanley obliged. So, too, did the three Graham brothers—not to be confused with the Graham brothers of Pleasant Valley—leave the territory after the court issued warrants for their arrest. Though not accused of rustling, they were accused of aiding rustlers by giving them "fresh mounts." After threatening revenge, the brothers purchased new clothes and crossed the New Mexico line. "May they never return," wished the *Herald*.[67]

That inventory of arrests, prosecutions, and threats conveys only the highlights of the year; a host of other men also met "justice" or left the county. The *Herald* crowed on October 20 that the jury's convictions, coupled with Judge Wright's tough sentences, "marked a new era in the judicial history of Apache county." The court had erected "a sign board on the road of progress which the rustlers might see and ride on."[68]

Two culprits, however, eluded the jury. Though Owens arrested John Payne for assault soon after taking office, he could hold Payne for only a few days. Two Holbrook merchants paid Payne's bail, giving him time to meet his end in Pleasant Valley. With Payne out of the way, Owens was expected to focus on Andy Cooper—something he was reluctant to do. By August 1887, the *Critic* was poking fun at him. "Ye sheriff," it sniffed, "having stirred-up a few license delinquents at Winslow and appointed a deputy at that place and at Holbrook, left for home Thursday." Owens meanwhile had troubles finding men to pay the bond that the county required to shield itself against indemnity. Initially a group of prosperous cattlemen—Henry Smith, Thomas Carson, and Henry Huning, all gentiles and all members of the stock association—stood behind the bond. When they backed out in August 1887—likely because Owens was slow in making arrests—Owens found others. The *Critic* smelled conspiracy among the bondsmen and demanded an investigation. Nothing came of its recommendation.[69]

By September 1887, Owens had found two Mormons to pay the bond, Richard and Ellen Greer. The stock association meanwhile lobbied the county supervisors "vigorously" to force Owens to take action, inspiring the supervisors to call him in for a scolding. Why had he not arrested Cooper, they demanded to know. If he did not do so within ten days, they threatened to relieve him of duty. Two supervisors, recalled Will Barnes, had come fully armed in case Owens grew testy. Mormons, meanwhile, floated rumors that Owens was not so much friends with Cooper as afraid of him.[70] Owens's honor was at stake.

Owens probably heard the chatter about his cowardice in late August, when he made his way to Snowflake to confer with William Flake. According to a Flake descendant, Owens was a "special friend of the Flake family and lodged with them whenever he was in the area." Another Flake descendant claims that Owens had gone to work as a sort of bounty hunter for William Flake even before his election as sheriff. Owens, he claimed, would trail stolen stock, infallibly bringing back the animals but complaining that the thieves had "got away," a not so subtle suggestion that Owens had killed them. Without corroboration, the story is hard to believe. That the Flakes considered Owens a friend, however, is certain. Owens would decline their social invitations, giving the excuse that he was unfit to be in the company of respectable women, but he conferred with the Flakes regularly.[71] In all likelihood, that friendship, along with prodding by county supervisors, prompted Owens to take action on September 4, 1887.

When Owens met Deputy Wattron in Holbrook on the morning of September 4, he declared that he was going alone to arrest Andy Cooper. Wattron offered to help, but Owens declined him. "People have talked enough," he told a man at the livery stable, "about me being afraid to arrest men." His honor, he implied, was at issue. To contradict his critics required him to act alone. He did not, however, act in secret. A small crowd of notables—including Will Barnes, who had helped push Owens into action—gathered on a platform at the rail depot to watch the action.[72]

After cleaning and loading his guns, Owens strode confidently to the Blevins house, a three-room cottage with no curtains over the windows. He carried a rifle. As he got near, someone—Eva Blevins perhaps—opened the door and peered out. Then the door closed. Owens stepped onto the porch. Looking through the window, he could see Andy Cooper and his brother, John, as well as others. Indeed eleven people were crammed into the house, including Mart's wife, Mary, her youngest son, fifteen-year-old Sam Houston, two of her daughters, Artimesia and Eva, the latter clutching an infant, and Susan Amanda Gladden with her two girls, Oberia and Grace. Also there was Mote (or perhaps Mose) Roberts, a cowboy who was writing a letter to a business associate. It is unclear just how Roberts was tied to the Blevins family. He may have been among the cowboys who had quit the Aztec rather than take part in its campaign against rustling.[73] He may also have been an innocent friend or a suitor of one of the women.

Owens called to Cooper to come out. Cooper stepped to the door—carrying a pistol, Owens claimed—and thrust his head out to talk. John Blevins simultaneously cracked open a second door that opened to the porch.

"I want you, Cooper," commanded Owens.

"What do you want with me?" Cooper asked.

"I have a warrant for you."

"What warrant?"

Owens explained that he held the warrant for the theft of Navajo horses. Cooper told Owens to wait.

"Cooper, no wait."

"I won't go," said Cooper. Owens shot him. "Oh, Commodore, don't do that," Cooper reportedly blurted as he staggered.

John Blevins—just four feet from Owens—now swung his door open and fired at Owens but instead killed Andy Cooper's horse, which stood immediately be-

Andy (Cooper) Blevins portrait circa 1880s.
Cooper—part of a de facto campaign by
Texas cowboys to drive out Mormons—
jumped the Saints' land claims and, it
seems, stole their horses. Don Dedera
Papers, Arizona Collection, Arizona
State University Libraries.

hind Owens. Owens wheeled to return fire, hitting Blevins in the shoulder. Then
Owens ran into the street, where he had visual command of the entire house.
Through the window he could see Cooper's crouching form. Owens thought he
held a gun. As Cooper moved away from the window, Owens fired through the
wall at the spot where he thought Cooper would be. Suddenly Mote Roberts
leaped through a window at the side of the house, trying to flee. Some witnesses
claimed that he held a six-shooter; others insisted he was unarmed. After taking a
few paces to get a clear view, Owens felled Roberts with a single shot, hitting him

in the back. Though mortally wounded, Roberts managed to stumble into the house through a back door. Seconds later the front door opened again, this time issuing Sam Houston Blevins, who now brandished Andy Cooper's gun. Mary Blevins came after him, grasping desperately. Her effort was in vain. Just as she managed to pull him back, Owens fired a bullet into his spine. Owens waited a few minutes, then walked away, seeing only the legs and feet of "a man"—actually a boy, Sam Houston—stretched in front of the door.[74]

Owens had expended five bullets in less than a minute, killing two men and a boy. The occupants in the house had fired one shot in return. According to Mary Blevins's testimony, her son Andy Cooper did not even have a gun when he had gone to the door.[75]

Though badly injured, John Blevins survived. Sam Houston Blevins died immediately. Andy Cooper died the next day. Mote Roberts clung to life for eleven days. Shot through the lung, his pain was terrible. Surprisingly, none of the women and children were injured, though the trauma surely stayed with them for the rest of their lives. When observers entered the house after the shooting, they recorded a hideous scene: "Dead and wounded in every room, and the blood over the floors, doors and walls. One little child, seven years of age, was literally bespattered with clots of human gore. The agonizing groans of the wounded, the death rattle of the dying, mingled with the screams of the females made a sight that no one would care to see a second time."[76]

It was a strange event even in the annals of the Wild West. In walking to the house alone and with a rifle, Owens seemed to issue a challenge. Cooper, however, might not have realized that Owens would resort to his gun, given their friendly conversation two weeks earlier. What Owens probably did not realize, moreover, was that Cooper had just come back from Pleasant Valley, where he may have been involved in the killings of John Tewksbury and William Jacobs. That Cooper himself killed them is questionable, though at least two men claimed to have overheard Cooper bragging of the murders shortly before Owens confronted him.[77] If Cooper did murder them, or if he was an accomplice, he had reason to resist arrest. One cannot help but wonder, however, whether Owens came looking for a kill.

Years later, Eva Blevins refuted the sheriff's testimony. Though at the inquest that followed the killings she had testified that she was in a back room during the fight, she now told a reporter that she, not Cooper, was the first person to come to the door, her eight-month-old son in her arms. Owens asked for Cooper, she recalled, who obediently came to the door. Saying only "I want you, Andy," Owens opened fire. Those facts had not come out at the inquest, she insisted, because no one had asked her about it.[78]

went to cleaning and oiling the weapon. While he was inside the room Johnny Blevins, Cooper's half-brother, came
to the stable, saddled Cooper's horse, led him up the
street and tied him to a cottonwood tree about twenty-five
feet from the front door of the Blevins house.

The depot platform, raised several feet above the
surrounding ground, offered a fine point from which to
see the proceedings. The word had gone round that Owens
had come in for Cooper. When I reached the depot I found
Wattron, A.F. Banta, W.H.Burbage and one or two others
waiting for the affair to open. I joined them and we
surely had reserved seats at what can well be called one
of the most exciting bits of old-time frontier life that
was ever enacted in Arizona, or anywhere else, for that matter.

D.G. Harvey, local justice of the peace, had gone
to the stable to talk to Owens. As Owens came out of the
stable, Harvey crossed the street and joined us on the railroad platform. Owens walked leisurely up the street,
his Winchester lying carelessly in the crook of his left
arm. He went boldly up to the Blevins home, which was
a small frame, "L" shaped affair with a porch across the
front about two-thirds of the way. From this porch two
doors opened. One to the south, the other to the east.

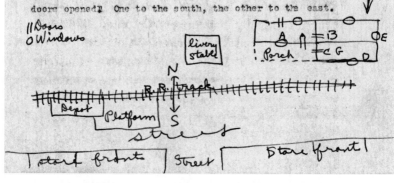

Will Barnes's manuscript account of the Owens/Blevins gunfight with handdrawn
map of the event at bottom. Barnes and others had stood on the depot platform to
watch. Courtesy of Arizona Historical Society/Tucson.

Lucien Creswell offered another interesting bit of testimony. It was Wattron, he recalled, who had roused Owens to take action that day, sending a runner across town to a small dwelling where Owens was staying with his "Mexican" girlfriend. Wattron instructed the runner to "go across the river and tell that cowardly son of a bitch sacking up with that Mexican bitch that Cooper's in town. If he don't come over here and take care of the god damned bastard I am going to do so and then I am going to take care of that yellow bellied womanish son-of-a-bitching sheriff."[79]

Perhaps Wattron so flustered Owens that he shot an unarmed Cooper, as Eva Blevins asserted. Or perhaps Owens indeed acted with "coolness," as his supporters averred. Either way, he did not act as a responsible officer. He understood, it seems, that his backers wanted Cooper killed, given the weakness of the case against him for horse theft. Owens's backers had already initiated a secret campaign to rid the county of criminals. Having deputized Brighton and his sidekicks, Powell and Miller, Owens knew of those plans. He knew, too, what he himself wanted. His honor had been impugned; he sought to reclaim it.

After hearing an account of the shootings, the *Critic* attacked Owens for his barbarity. The *Herald* shot back, calling Owens a hero and remonstrating that "this killing is simply another sign-board erected along the trail of progress by the strong hand of the law." Mormons celebrated. Their prayers had been heard, exulted Andrew Locy Rogers in his diary on New Year's Day, 1888; "the Lord said if the Saints do right He will fight our battles." Rogers went on to cite more prophecies. "It is said," he added, "that New York, Boston & other places would be destroyed in the near future."[80] What Rogers might also have said was that, with the Holbrook shooting, Rim Country Mormons had entered the culture of honor.

The Holbrook gunfight promptly took a hallowed yet blurry place in Mormon memory. Jessie Ballard Smith, daughter of a Snowflake settler, mistakenly stated that Owens had gone to arrest the Blevins boys for having stolen her father's horses. She failed to realize that Owens had no warrant for any thefts from Mormons. The thieves "refused to be taken," she wrote, "and he killed three of them," including Andy Cooper "and two men by the name of Rogers."[81] Smith betrayed ignorance, or perhaps indifference, to whom exactly Owens had killed. No one named Rogers was killed, though Mote Roberts had fallen.

Ira Wakefield, a Mormon who had lived near the Blevins family at Canyon Creek, likewise betrayed ignorance in his telling of events, or, perhaps, was willing to twist the facts. He told his wife and children that Owens had shot the gun out of the hand of "fourteen-year old Andy Cooper," merely breaking his wrist. William Flake's son, Osmer, who was in his late teens when the shooting occurred, showed more command of the facts but just as much willingness to color them. The Blevins brothers, he wrote, "intended getting the Sheriff, but he was too cool and too quick for them," ignoring the fact that Owens was the aggressor. Osmer's son, Les Flake, told his own children that Owens was "the real Lone Ranger," explaining that his father "has always believed that Commodore was guided to their area by the hand of providence."[82]

From the Mormon point of view, Owens was God's answer to prayer. "Thou shalt not kill," recalled Lucy Flake and her fellow Mormons in the midst of their crisis, "yet could we endure insult upon insult without retaliation?" As late as November 1886, Snowflake Mormons merely prayed that their enemies' hearts be softened, but something more was needed. For guidance, they wrote a letter to the apostles in Salt Lake, who prescribed a day of fasting and prayer. The Saints obliged. "God heard our prayers," said Lucy. "Our enemies 'fell into the pits they had digged for us' as the Lord promised they would." Owens, she added, "had eight or ten deaths of outlaws to his credit." James Warren LeSueur agreed. After the day of fasting and prayer, he wrote, "Commodore Perry Owens was elected sheriff. He was an unassuming man of few words but fearless." LeSueur claimed that thirty-eight outlaws met their ends during Owens's tenure, while "others were frightened out of the country. A great debt of gratitude is due Commodore Owens."[83]

From the historian's point of view, Owens was not so much an answer to prayers as a product of the collective will. He was drafted as a candidate; he was elected; he was flattered; he was cajoled; he was threatened; he was humiliated. At last he was forced into action. When he made his decision to arrest—or kill— Andy Cooper, he sought to quell any aspersion of cowardice. He would prove his honor. Perhaps, too, he expected a bounty from the stock association. Interestingly, Owens later expressed regret over the killings.[84] In 1887, however, he showed no remorse.

If God answered Mormon prayers, he answered thus: they could have revenge yet take no overt part in it. Mary Petersen, whose husband, Niels, had fallen victim to Payne's whipping, recalled that "her special request" was that "the blood of these men should not be upon the hands of the Lord's people." In spring 1887, President Smith had counseled Niels Petersen and James Pearce to avoid retribution. The bad men would meet their fates some other way, said Smith. He proved correct. Owens and his deputies, along with vigilantes and secret agents, did the Lord's dirty work. Not everyone, however, agreed that such work was providential. The Holbrook gunfight, reflected Henry Reed in the pages of the

Critic, "is simply a chapter of the Tonto Basin history, and no man as yet can fore-tell the end."[85]

In 1888, Owens's supporters jilted him. J. F. Wallace, successor to Barry Mat-thews as fire-breathing editor of the *Herald,* mysteriously changed his editorial policy in June, announcing that "our Territory has had enough of desperadoes as 'peace' officers, who parade about with abbreviated cannon strapped to their hips." Slapping Owens for his negligence in doing paperwork, the *Herald* sug-gested that the county choose a sheriff with executive ability. "The trouble with the desperado-class of officers," proclaimed the *Herald,* "is that they shoot whom they please, and are acquitted on the plea that their victim 'had it in for 'em,' and the shooting was in self-defense." Such officers belonged not in office but "be-hind good strong bars."[86]

Those sentiments must have sounded strange to readers, coming as they did from the same editor who, a year earlier, had urged citizens into acts of homi-cide. In the nominating convention, however, Owens got no reward for following the *Herald*'s 1887 dicta. The newly formed Apache County Democratic Party—successor to the People's Party—gave its nomination in 1888 to St. George Creaghe. Creaghe, an erstwhile Mormon foe who had now become a friend, de-feated the Republican nominee, Tomas Perez.[87]

"They refused me a second term because I was a killer," Owens told a friend in later years, "but a killer was what they needed then."[88] His vaunted heroism nonetheless signaled a new era in Apache County history. The Mormons' isola-tion ended with the 1886 election, when they and white gentiles—prosperous ranchers—coalesced into an anti-Barth, anti–New Mexican, anti-cowboy po-litical force. In the process, Mormons chose the honor of deadly resistance over the conscientious devotion to peace. Within two years, however, their hard work began to unravel.

In early 1889, the chief witness in the case of Phin Clanton—Brighton's as-sociate, George Powell—admitted that he had perjured himself to get Clanton convicted. Neither he nor Brighton had witnessed Clanton steal a cow. Powell went to jail for having lied under oath. When he got out, he found himself in jeopardy again when accused of larceny and jury tampering. Then in May 1889, Powell and an accomplice, Charles Rudd, son of an Apache County probate judge, allegedly stole four "fine horses" from Mormons. Five men followed the thieves and killed them, ending any possibility that Powell could further damage Brighton and the Apache County Stock Growers Association.[89]

County officials, many of them elected in 1888 to replace People's Party officials, now sent a letter to Governor Zulick asking that Phin Clanton be pardoned. Signers included Mormons J. T. LeSueur and Harris Greer as well as the editors of the St. Johns *Herald*, the Winslow *News*, and the Apache *Review*. Several men from the jury that had convicted Clanton, as well as Commodore Perry Owens, also signed. No member of the stock association followed suit.[90]

Another signer was the county recorder, Edward Nelson, a noted naturalist and ethnographer. In later years, he would conduct an epic field study of Mexico's fauna and become Chief of the U.S. Bureau of Biological Survey. In 1882, Nelson had moved to Apache County to recover from tuberculosis after his heroic survey of the Arctic. In Arizona, he gained the reputation for honesty and hard work that led to his election to county office in 1888. In that year, he became a vocal opponent of the "Mormon-Democrat" alliance that had defeated the Equal Rights Party two years before. He particularly criticized Judge James Wright, who had presided over the court during the campaign of terror. For speaking up, claimed Nelson, he earned a rebuke for "corruption." One of his political enemies convinced a grand jury to indict him and former county clerk Alfred Ruiz for having "fraudulently" secured "sixty eight dollars in County warrants worth 70 cents on the dollar, or, for the purpose of making about 24 dollars each." The charges were absurd to Nelson but not to his enemies. By the time he was charged in 1889, Nelson had moved to New Mexico, where he promised to stay so long as his nemesis, Judge Wright, continued to hold court.[91]

Others, too, seem to have been railroaded. Twenty-four years after the events of 1887, Evans Coleman, while serving his Mormon mission in Columbia, South Carolina, determined that Francisco Baca was not guilty of embezzlement. In Columbia, Coleman met a man named "Felmer" who had known all the old-timers from Apache County, including Coleman's parents. Felmer and Coleman soon became friendly and accompanied each other around town. Felmer, who was by then pressing hats for a living, confessed that he was Charlie Kinnear, the saloon keeper who had fled prosecution for forging warrants in 1885. Kinnear told Coleman that he had spent his life on the frontier; that he had always felt comfortable in the shadows between law and outlawry; and that he knew what had happened in the infamous safe robbery of December 1885. As Baca had suspected, it was the Clanton "gang" that had stolen the money, getting away on the frozen ground. The next day, the ground thawed and became muddy, leaving investigators confused when they could find no tracks.[92]

If Baca was innocent, so perhaps was Sol Barth. On February 1889, Governor Zulick pardoned him after the legislature accused prosecutors, in concert with Judge Wright, of giving him an unfair trial. Joseph Fish, who was in no way partial to Barth, expressed certainty that Kinnear had been the real culprit in the warrant forgery scandal. Barth's wife, he noted, sued the county for the value of warrants issued but never paid to her husband, finally winning the case eighteen years later.[93]

In the heat of 1887, however, few doubted that the "cleanup" was just. In addition to killing or driving out Ike and Phin Clanton, Lee Renfro, C. W. Johnson, Ebin Stanley, John Payne, the three Graham brothers, and Andy Cooper and the Blevins boys, "the people" dealt "justice" to several others. In June 1887, Charlie Thomas and his companions tracked and killed Bill Evans, aka "Jack Timberline" or "Jack of Diamonds," and his partner, Samuel Sprague, aka "Long Hair," who were accused of horse theft. Though someone spread a rumor that the vigilantes were lying about their deed, Ebin Stanley confirmed the deaths. Then in August came another killing, this time by Gila County sheriff J. H. Benbrook, who shot a man who was accused of having trafficked in stolen horses from Apache County.[94]

By the end of 1887, at least a dozen "desperadoes" had fled the county. At least eleven more had met death. Other killings probably went unreported. As late as September 8, four days after Commodore Perry Owens had decimated the Blevins family, the *Herald* reported cryptically that "the net is still being drawn, and it is almost time to land the fish. What flopping and floundering there will be when it is done." Criminals were not merely to be punished; they were to be shamed. They were to be made to "flop and flounder," a metaphor for lynching. On September 29, the *Herald* at last reported that "the net has been drawn and the fish landed," though it neglected to name fish or fishermen.[95]

The year 1887 was decisive. Conflict created factions, then alliances. Mormons, Aztec managers, and gentile ranchers joined forces in the People's Party and in the stock association. Mormons sought to put an end to persecution by the Aztec and its cowboys. The Aztec and its rancher allies sought to put an end to rustling—or at least what was now defined as rustling, despite the tradition of mavericking. Those alliances created others, pushing old enemies into one another's arms. Saloon keepers and cowboys like Ebin Stanley and the Clantons found themselves suddenly comrades to New Mexicans and St. Johns Mormons in the Equal Rights Party, only to experience defeat at the polls. Other enemies of the new powers in Apache County—cowboys who lacked political voices— moved south and west into Pleasant Valley, where several would continue the fight against sheepherders and racial others.

In a strange way, cowboy honor triumphed over Mormon conscience. Via claim jumpings, whippings, and threats—as well as drinking, gambling, shooting up towns, and consorting with prostitutes—cowboys caused Mormons both to rally around conscience and to abandon it. Throughout their trials in Arizona, Mormons struggled to remain true to the Lord by refusing to do violence. They were tempted . . . sorely tempted . . . but they left their guns holstered. In 1887, however, the very people who had professed restraint meted out death via sheriffs and vigilantes and stock detectives. They would remember their decision as a time when they—or at least their surrogates—acted heroically to stop evil. In acting thus, they deprived themselves of another sort of heroism, the kind associated with forbearance, with patience, with conscience.

From the Danite avengers of Missouri to the murderous troops at Mountain Meadows, Mormons had wrestled with the problem of violence. Never were they out-and-out pacifists. They viewed themselves, however, as a people of peace, a people who fought only in defense (despite their actions at Mountain Meadows). Their courage, like their culture, was corporatist. Unlike Texas cowboys, Mormons did not measure their fellows via the yardsticks of bluff and assertion. Their encounters in Arizona, however, changed them. One thinks of Will Adams's challenges to Andy Cooper and of Zack Decker's standoffs with Hashknife cowboys. Neither Adams nor Decker fired at their foes. To both, however, meekness came to mean shame. Other Mormons were coming to the same conclusion.

With the reign of terror in 1887, Mormons gave themselves over to the formulaic story of good defeating evil via the gun and the rope. They joined their enemies in furious triumph. Mormons, however, hired others to kill. They had prayed that no blood would be on their hands. They had spoken of taking refuge while the Lord scourged their enemies with sickness, pestilence, and civil war. They had resisted going on the attack. They were unwilling to exchange conscience for honor wholeheartedly. When honor—the will to do vengeance, the eagerness to bring shame—at last prevailed, it came with chagrin. Mormons downplayed their role in events, claiming that God had intervened. If honor prevailed, it was a dubious honor, a chastened honor, but it was an honor that shaped Western identity.

Commodore Perry Owens meanwhile faded from view. For a time he worked as a deputy marshal and as a guard for the A&P. Thanks to his Mormon supporters, he was appointed in 1895 to serve as sheriff of Navajo County after it was carved from Apache. Owens, however, lost his election bid in 1896. After that, he opened a saloon, married a "colored prostitute," and kept a pet wolf.[96]

Sinner though Owens might be, Mormons did not forget him. Shortly after his death from Bright's disease in 1919, one of his Mormon friends "went to the Temple and took endowments" for him, telling those assembled that Owens had been "providentially sent from Tennessee to assist in getting rid of the thieves."[97]

Killing Conscience

In late 1885 a young cowboy rode into Apache County, perhaps seeking work from the Aztec. He looked the part. In a photo that he sent his sister, he appeared with a gun on his hip and a sombrero on his head. He had a striking, clean-cut appearance, with a strong chin and nose and an aura of confidence. Will Barnes would later describe him as "a tall, handsome, red-headed lad, and a general favorite." Though he found no job with the Aztec Land and Cattle Company, he did locate a 160-acre claim at Aztec Springs (named for the ancient ruins nearby) some forty miles south of Holbrook. If all went well, he hoped to "prove up"—gain title—by the end of 1888.[1]

As much as he looked the part of a cowboy, Jamie Stott was a curiosity. He was a New Englander. He had grown up in North Billerica, across the street from a governor of Massachusetts, Thomas Talbot. Stott's father, like Talbot, was a prosperous man, perhaps even rich. Though he did not own one of the textile mills that begot New England's great wealth, he managed one. Despite having lost both hands in a mill accident, the elder Stott proved able and reliable to superiors. Using an artificial hand, he managed to write letters and keep on top of mill operations. He also gained the respect of Thomas Talbot, who, after his years as governor, sat on the Aztec's board of directors.[2]

Jamie Stott enjoyed a privileged upbringing. As a boy, he took riding lessons with Thomas Talbot's son. He was also enrolled in a private academy in New Hampshire, where he boarded for several years with an older sister. Though perhaps not the best student, he showed athletic promise and grew to a full six feet. Then came a time for decision. Jamie needed to choose a future. Surely that future would entail conscience. Jamie's mother was a Baptist Sunday school teacher, and the family rejected drink and profanity. His father, James Stott, Sr.,

Jamie Stott in 1883, shortly before his move
to Texas. Courtesy of Arizona Historical
Society/Tucson, no. 4879.

moreover, believed firmly in the middle-class doctrine of self-help. Jamie was expected to make his own way in the world.[3] Making one's own way meant more to Jamie, however, than plodding ahead. Like his father before him, he wanted adventure.

In the 1850s, James Stott, Sr., had joined the ranks of the argonauts who descended on gold rush California, where he became a miner and a partner in a ranching venture. Stott thus took part in one of the largest mass migrations in American history, a migration that was in some ways more an escape from Eastern society than an attempt to build communities in the West. One historian, examining the journals and letters of argonauts from New England, found that they saw in the gold rush a chance to break away from the constraints of the Yankee middle class. In the West, they explored new possibilities for behavior and expression. Though traveling companies made pacts to refrain from "immoral" behaviors, their pacts unraveled in California. Middle-class men cursed, drank, gambled, and visited prostitutes. A few, it seems, participated in lynchings. They sent photos home showing themselves in rough attire, often with a gun in their belt or hand. Then they returned to New England and New York, or to some other place, usually penniless, but rededicated to conscience.[4]

Like thousands of argonauts, Stott returned from California with rich experiences but no profit.[5] The father's stories no doubt fired the son's imagination. What also likely fired young Jamie's imagination were the welter of tales of travel and sport in the West, tales that became the hash of popular literature. We don't know what titles Jamie Stott read but, in all probability, he was exposed to the ubiquitous tales of bold hunters like Daniel Boone and Davy Crockett. Boone and his wilderness cousin, Crockett, invoked a primal honor—an honor displayed via hunting bears and fighting Indians—that served as counterweight to an ever-heavier anchor of conscience.

The hunter hero, however, was not the only proponent of honor in the nineteenth century. By the time that Stott came of age, a new hero was joining the hunter on the cultural stage. As vast Western herds of bison and elk gave way to vast herds of longhorn and Hereford, the "self-possessed" Boone of literature metamorphosed into the self-possessed cowboy, the new icon of individualism, the heroic master of savage beasts. Popularized in dime novels and Wild West shows, the cowboy symbolized the nation's ethos of democratic individualism, rough chivalry, and martial spirit.[6]

When Jamie Stott ventured west in 1883, the myth of the cowboy was in its infancy. Cowboys still figured as roughnecks and savages in the pages of such respectable journals as *Harper's*. Buffalo Bill's Wild West had only begun that year; it was yet to become the nation's foremost venue of mass entertainment. Buffalo Bill himself retained his seemingly unsavory ties to the working-class theatrical culture of Chicago and New York. He had only begun to remake himself into a hero of the middle class, a purveyor of "clean"—and uniquely American— fun.[7] Yet elite East Coast boys already showed a fascination for the cowboy, who could be unruly and rebellious yet bourgeois and self-possessed. They saw in the cowboy a man who was both Daniel Boone, the "self-possessed" individualist of the wilderness, and Davy Crockett, the drinker, braggart, and blusterer. To young men eager for adventure yet shaped by middle-class values, to be a cowboy was a kind of middle stage between rebellious adolescence and self-controlled adulthood. It could be both an avenue for adventure and—if a temporary stage in life—a school of middle-class success.

Beyond blending Boone and Crockett into a new figure of frontier individualism, the cowboy blended Northern conscience with Southern honor—or at least he did in fiction. Just as North and South sought reconciliation after the Civil War, so did Northern men identify with a new hero who mixed Northern mores with Southern. As historian Nina Silber has shown, one of the staples of popular literature in the Gilded Age was the marriage between chivalrous Southern man and pious Northern woman. Northern readers, particularly men, far from attacking former slaveholders for their "barbarity," viewed chivalrous Southerners as paragons of manhood. The noble "Southron" remained master of his wife at precisely the time when Northern women sought political rights and social freedoms in marriage.[8]

One hero of reconciliation was the protagonist of Owen Wister's novel *The Virginian: A Horseman of the Plains*, published in 1902. Wister's protagonist, "the Virginian," a Virginia emigrant to Wyoming, embodies the chivalry, grace, and honor of a Southern gentleman yet holds no animus toward Northerners. Indeed he befriends the narrator, a Northern "dude" who has come west for his health. Like a true son of honor, the Virginian refuses to shrink from the rituals of violence, whether gunfights or lynchings. Yet like a true son of conscience, he marries a Yankee schoolteacher, embarks on a career in ranching and business, and preaches that there is no luck in a man's success, only hard work and good morals.[9]

Even twenty years before *The Virginian* saw print, Yankee youths like Stott romanticized cowboys. In 1885, one of the Aztec's founders, Edward Kinsley, wrote general manager Henry Warren to tell him that he'd promised ranching jobs to several young men, presumably sons of his acquaintances. Those young men included Frank Ames, who was the nephew of Oliver Ames, governor of Massachusetts from 1887 to 1890, and grandson of Oakes Ames, who was famous for building the Union Pacific Railroad and for his role in the Credit Mobilier scandal. Frank Ames would become Jamie Stott's closest friend in Arizona and land manager for the Aztec. Another young man sent by Kinsley was George Agassiz, grandson of the great naturalist Louis Agassiz, the first director of Harvard's Lawrence Scientific School. Still another would-be cowboy in 1880s Apache County—perhaps the most pedigreed man in the territory—was the son of Senator William Evarts of New York.[10]

If those young men found adventure in Arizona, they did not necessarily find gratitude. Most worked as what we might call "interns," receiving only room and board. Even so, Texas cowboys and Aztec managers found them to be more trouble than gain. By 1886, when Stott arrived in Arizona, the company had initiated a policy of hiring only experienced cowboys.[11] Stott's benefactor, Thomas Talbot, moreover, died in October 1886, rendering Stott powerless to change the company's mind.

Unlike other privileged young men dropped on the Aztec's doorstep, however, Stott knew his trade. His first destination in 1883 had been Texas, where he apprenticed as cowboy for one of Thomas Talbot's brothers, owner of a ranch near Austin. On January 5, 1884, Stott complained to his sister that "there is nothing here to do except drink and go to dances around the country and as I never drink or dance I have not been away from the ranch yet." Stott did not fit in with the bonhomie of Texas culture. In November 1884, Stott again wrote his sister to assure her that, despite refusing to vote a straight-party ticket, he had voted mostly Republican. Though he had hoped to vote for John Pierce St. John, the Prohibitionist candidate for president, he could not determine which of the Republican electors might support St. John. Unwilling to hurt St. John's chances, Stott withheld his vote.[12]

Stott probably did not realize that St. John's candidacy was promoted by Democrats who hoped to siphon votes from James Blaine, the Republican candidate, in upstate New York. The plan worked; Blaine lost New York and narrowly lost the election to Grover Cleveland. For the Stotts, however, St. Johns's candidacy was a triumph. Yankee conscience meant more than Republican victory. For Jamie Stott, Election Day was a chance to confirm the values of the New England middle class in the barbaric precincts of Texas, where drink, gambling, and honor prevailed.

Even as Stott displayed conscience, he sought to impress friends and family with his romantic exploits. In 1883 he reported to his sister that he had sent "a yarn" about his Texas experiences to Fisherville, Massachusetts, where his father's mill was located. He hoped—probably disingenuously—that "they will not put any part into the paper." Three weeks later, he promised his sister that he would send a photo showing him in "warlike dress" so that she could "see what people dress like out here." He also bragged of his prowess in roping cattle and horses. In 1885, Jamie reported that he weighed fully 180 pounds and "am as rough looking boy as you would want to see, although not a bad case." He added that he had killed a cougar and a bobcat, promising to send home their skins along with those of other animals he had shot.[13]

What Stott found in the West was not only adventure. He found a sort of adventure prescribed by his culture and time, an adventure that involved hunting and cowboying—the same sort of adventure sought by Theodore Roosevelt when he became a rancher and cowboy in the Dakotas in the 1880s. Like Roosevelt, Stott did not enter the West to take up the plow. Both men seemed to find the farming life debasing, anachronistic, bereft of cultural power. In February 1883, Stott reported to his sister that he had ridden to several ranches looking for work without success. That was for the best, he suggested, since "I was not very well pleased with their ranches for they appeared to be about one half farmers and I do not wish to learn farming just yet." Farming, he knew, was part of life in the

West. Ranchers routinely planted barley, corn, and vegetables, as well as wheat and hay. That part of ranching, however, he wished to escape. Rather than farm, Stott proposed to move farther west, a plan that would take him to Arizona. He added a few months later that he had left his collection of hides and horns in Texas. Making a new collection, he bragged, would be easy in Arizona.[14]

His quest for a livelihood, however, proved more difficult after Talbot's death and the Aztec's refusal to hire "tenderfeet." When his situation became clear, Stott was disappointed but not demoralized. As early as August 1885, he had declared that he preferred to work for himself—if only on a hundred-acre spread—than to work "for some company on a big ranch." Jamie Stott would shift for himself. Shifting for himself, however, did not keep him from accepting a thousand dollars from his father to buy cattle and mares for his Rim Country ranch.[15]

By February 1886 Stott could proudly report that he had his own brand, the Circle Dot (a circle with a dot in the middle). He also reported on the Mormons around him. "I have just returned from the horse round up," he told his sister in May 1886, "and it was the queerest thing I about ever saw." The Mormons with whom he worked "knew about as much as some of you folks about what a round up is." He added that he would not advise his sister's fiancé to move to Arizona until there were "more gentiles in this country." Stott nonetheless hired a Mormon to help him build a house and corrals.[16]

In June 1887, Stott's sister, Hattie, and his mother, Hannah, took the train west to visit him. Presumably he ferried them by buggy from the station at Holbrook to his distant ranch, which lay just above the Rim. Entertaining family members—especially females—must have pleased him. "Women are quite a curiosity in this country," he had lamented in 1886, "except down in the towns and those are so afraid speak to anyone. I don't know when I have said six words to any woman since I came from Texas."[17] What Stott perhaps did not realize was that the women he met were Mormons, whom church leaders had counseled against socializing with outsiders.

Situated among Mormons and Hashknife cowboys, Stott found himself in a precarious situation. He had long since learned the West's code of hospitality. A man established at a ranch or a farm had to befriend those around him. He was expected to offer food and conversation to wayfarers. He was expected to share gossip and tell stories and even to offer a dram of whiskey, something Stott probably disliked. To refuse hospitality was to declare hostility and, perhaps, to be denied reciprocal favors. Yet the very men one entertained might prove to be unsavory.

"Everyone you meet up with," explained Stott to his sister in 1885, "must be accepted as a friend and companion till proved otherwise."[18] Even then—two years

Jamie Stott in cowboy garb, Flagstaff, Arizona,
1886 or 1887. The costume belied Stott's support for
conscience reforms such as temperance. Courtesy
of Arizona Historical Foundation/Tucson, no. 4875.

before the climax of the Pleasant Valley conflict—he understood the ambiguity
of Western life. One had to accept and befriend all comers, yet one could trust
no one. Competition for range set neighbor against neighbor. One man's friend
was another man's enemy. Hospitality and animosity were opposite sides of the
same strange coin of Western honor.

A few months earlier, in July 1885, Stott wrote of another frontier custom he had learned in the West. Stray saddle horses, he explained to his mother, "belong to whoever catches them," adding that he planned to try his luck at capturing a few.[19] He probably meant unbranded horses, though he did not say so. Meanwhile he set his sights not on a cattle ranch but on a horse ranch, a decision that made sense when cattle prices crashed in 1886. Catching a stray horse, or even buying a horse, however, was not as easy as Stott suggested.

In February 1887, Stott wrote his sister that he planned to travel to Tonto Basin—probably meaning Pleasant Valley—to take possession of a horse that he had bought from a man named Workman. It is unclear how Workman got the animal. Perhaps he had stolen it. Perhaps he caught it as a stray and kept it, observing the same custom that Stott cited in 1885. Perhaps ownership was disputed, something common on the frontier. However he got the horse, Workman turned it over to Stott and his companion, Tom Tucker of the Hashknife. The man who claimed to be the true owner, Jake Lauffer of Pleasant Valley, then filed a complaint with Commodore Perry Owens, who obediently arrested Stott and Tucker.[20]

If Stott or Tucker saw the inside of Owens's jail, there is no record of it. Gila County, it seems, held jurisdiction, causing Stott and Tucker to plead their case before Justice of the Peace Job Atkins in Globe in March 1887. Atkins found them not guilty, then proceeded to ridicule the plaintiff. Lauffer, averred Atkins, should have filed a civil action rather than bring a criminal complaint. Atkins found no reason to think that Stott or Tucker had stolen the horse, though he added that the seller may have done so. The *Silver Belt* complained that the proceeding cost the county $375, all to recover a horse worth $50 at most. Though a civil action would have saved the county money, "that mode of procedure carried with it no corporeal infliction."[21]

Lauffer likely sought to prosecute in part because he assumed that Stott, like Tucker, was allied to the Grahams. As early as February 1887—the same month that Stott took possession of the disputed horse—a member of the Graham faction had murdered a sheepherder, thus igniting the war. Six months later, Tucker was shot in the first battle, when Hamp Blevins led a party of cowboys to the Middleton cabin in search of his father.

The prosecution for horse theft was the first blow to Stott's reputation. Clarence Walter Durham, a Hashknife cowboy and a friend of Stott, testified in his memoir that he "never knew him to do anything wrong." Durham noted, however, that Stott was hospitable to all comers, which made some of his neighbors—Mormon neighbors—suspicious that he was harboring bad men. Stott's closest friend, Frank Ames, the Aztec's land manager, likewise noted that Stott "was compelled by circumstances to be friendly with the [cowboys] surrounding him." He had to do so, explained Ames. "He was completely in their power, as was his property." To refuse hospitality was to risk animosity. Stott nonetheless remained neutral. Though he sympathized with the Grahams, he refused to be drawn into the conflict. When forced to play host to partisans, recalled Ames, Stott "treated them the same as all cautious men did, when by circumstances brought in contact with this crowd. . . . [He] always remained perfectly neutral and associated with them only when compelled."[22]

Stott kept his family ignorant of the situation until October 1887, when he explained some of the particulars in a letter. A week earlier, he reported, the war had claimed his friend Harry (or Henry) Middleton, whom Stott's mother and sister had met at the ranch that summer. "There have been between fifteen and twenty men killed" since the trouble began, wrote Stott, adding that "the worst is over now, I think." Stott had nonetheless taken the precaution of giving Ames explicit directions on how to reach him in case "anything should happen."[23] Ames presumably would act as Stott's guardian, with the weight and authority of the Aztec behind him.

In February 1888, with the war seemingly over, Stott sent home another dour letter. "Everything" in Holbrook, he reported, "was dull . . . and is likely to remain so, for the only thing they study down there is how to beat someone out of what they have." Stott may have been referring to a specific man, Jim Houck, who was overheard bragging that he would run sheep on Stott's land. Houck likely assumed that Stott was allied with the Grahams. Some sources also testify that Stott had backed down Houck in a quarrel, telling Houck to "go and heel himself," meaning to cool his temper. Other sources maintain that it was not Stott but his friend Jim Scott who had words with Houck. Regardless of which of the two were involved, Houck had been publicly humiliated, a grave matter in the honor culture of the West.[24]

In spring 1888 came the first report of serious trouble for Stott. On May 30, the St. Johns *Herald* broadcast a report from Commodore Perry Owens that a fight in Tonto Basin had led to the killing of three men. Several others, claimed Owens, had been told to leave the territory, including Jamie Stott.[25] The fracas, assuming it occurred, came several months after the near annihilation of the Graham faction and the uneasy peace that followed.

Other dispatches explained events differently, making no reference to killings. Sometime in May, two or more men had robbed Cap Watkins's store in the lower Tonto Basin, then fled toward the Graham ranch. With a posse close behind, the thieves were forced to trade their tired horses for fresh ones. Members of the posse identified the abandoned horses as the property of Tom Graham. The thieves, it was said, also cached stolen goods near the home of Jeff Wilson, an Aztec cook, before taking refuge at Stott's ranch.[26]

The suspects were ranch hands who worked for Graham. Graham, however—who was now splitting his time between Prescott and Tempe rather than living in Pleasant Valley—insisted that the robbery was a hoax. Why would the robbers abandon horses so easily tied to him? Why would they flee toward his ranch, leaving a trail for a posse to follow? The hoax, claimed Graham, was meant to tarnish anybody who continued to support him. Graham now hoped to start a new life as a farmer alongside his bride-to-be, Annie Melton.[27] With the robbery of Watkins's store, however, controversy continued to dog him.

Stott's denial of the accusations against him appeared in the June 20, 1888, issue of the St. Johns *Herald.* He had no part in any robbery, he claimed, and no one had warned him to leave. In a postscript, however, the *Herald* warned "that Tonto Basin [is] not a healthy section for Mr. Stott to range in now-a-days." Stott, claimed the *Herald,* if not himself a thief, was at the minimum a go-between for thieves, adding that he had traveled to Holbrook to buy a saddle for one of the robbers.[28] Nowhere did the *Herald* reveal the source for its allegations, though likely they came from someone—perhaps Houck—who associated Stott with the Grahams.

Worse than allegations about Stott's association with horse thieves and robbers was a report in August that unknown parties had ambushed Jake Lauffer and Charles Livingston in Pleasant Valley. The attackers also shot at two others, George Cody and N. J. Coleman, as they were passing the old Rose ranch. No one was killed, though the attackers—apparently there were two—managed to kill Cody's horse and wound Lauffer in the shoulder, crippling him for life.[29]

At the time of the ambush, settlers were "forted up" at Perkins's rock store after an Apache chief warned them that some of his tribesman planned an attack. A pair of men who had been sent out to gain intelligence on the Indian threat managed to track the riders who had ambushed Cody and Coleman, only to find that the trail had washed away in a shower. For some reason—perhaps the tracks were those of shod horses—no one blamed Apaches. Nor did anyone blame Charlie Duchet, erstwhile sheepherder, Graham partisan, and now Tom Graham's self-appointed bodyguard. In December, Duchet would ambush Jim Houck, though he failed to get his man. Instead of suspicion falling on Duchet for the shooting of Lauffer and the killing of Cody's horse, Jamie Stott got the blame, along with two of his supposed partners, Jim Scott and Jeff Wilson. That information, reported the Arizona *Champion* of Flagstaff, came from Houck.[30]

Stott knew he was in trouble but refused to leave. To do so, he told his friend

Ames, would give his enemies more reason to find him guilty. It would mean giving up his hard-won possessory rights—rights that he hoped to convert to property by the end of the year—which was precisely what the Tewksbury faction desired. Injustice would beget greater injustice. A good man would be undone by bad ones.

With his New England upbringing and his powerful attachment to conscience, Stott believed that character would wither attacks. He was honest, honorable, aboveboard. If people judged him guilty, he told Ames, so be it. If they would not trouble themselves to determine the facts, he would not trouble himself to set them straight. Virtue would exonerate him.[31]

Meanwhile Stott boasted of his toughness. When Will Barnes warned him of danger, Stott supposedly patted his six-shooter and said, "I'd love to see the color of the man's hair who can get the drop on me."[32] Whether or not he uttered those words, Stott was sure he could defend himself. He was an athlete and a cowboy. To that extent he was as much a man of honor—a man who proved himself through physical assertion—as any of the Tewksbury faction or any of the Hashknife cowboys. He had his fists, his gun, and his integrity to parry attacks.

The culture of honor that evolved in the West, however, was never something that Jamie Stott fully understood. Honor was better comprehended by men like Jesse Ellison, who organized a vigilante squadron in Pleasant Valley, and Jim Houck, Apache County deputy sheriff and Tewksbury partisan. Though the two men had taken opposite sides in the Civil War—Ellison fought for the Confederacy and Houck for the Union—they became allies in the terror of 1887.

Jesse Ellison's family had long acquaintance with the honor culture of the South. His father, also named Jesse, had moved from Tennessee to Alabama and finally to Texas in 1836. When the Civil War broke out, Ellison the younger, then twenty, was fighting Comanches with the Texas Rangers. In September 1861 he enlisted as a scout for Texas's Sixth Volunteer Cavalry. He would see action throughout the war.[33]

Somehow Ellison survived without serious injury, but like many Southerners, he came home to ruin. In all probability, the Thirteenth Amendment cost Ellison's parents their slaves, though Ellison himself was too young to have acquired his own slaves before the war. What he had acquired instead were cows, fifty of them, which would serve as a nest egg. At war's end, only one remained. The others had strayed, died, or been stolen.[34]

Not to be discouraged, Ellison followed the example of men like Charles Goodnight, gathering stray longhorns and herding them to railheads in Kansas. Under an agreement with his partners, Ellison collected 10 percent of the profits and kept every fourth calf for his own herd. At last he saved enough to establish a ranch in Shackelford County, where he soon found himself embattled again, this time by "nesters." Nesters were small operators who lay claim to the bottom-lands, waterholes, and springs that nurtured the herds of would-be cattle kings like Ellison. When big operators — including Ellison — fenced off waterholes and range, nesters cut the fences.[35]

Ellison faced catastrophe if he remained in Shackelford County, especially after a massive sleet storm took a toll on his cattle. Drought and bovine disease, meanwhile, were cutting wide swaths through Texas herds. After hearing of prime grazing lands in Arizona's Rim Country, Ellison made his move. In 1885, he shipped eighteen hundred head on the Southern Pacific line to Bowie, Arizona, whence he drove the herd to the Rim Country. Ten men came with him, most of them as employees and a few, it seems, as friends. The only thing the men had in common was their youth and marital state. Like most Hashknife cowboys, they were single. Ellison held out hope, however, via five unmarried daughters. He also found a way to cart a grand piano, a concession to his family's genteel status and its high proportion of females.[36]

Arriving in the Tonto Basin in September 1885, Ellison met tribulation. The ranges were crowded. Stockmen had posted a warning to interlopers to keep out of their territory and refused to make exceptions. When he tried to locate his animals in the lower Tonto Basin — they numbered just four hundred after the hardships of the journey — he was told to get out. He refused. Throughout the winter of 1885–86, he managed to keep the herd near the confluence of the Tonto and the Salt. Then, in summer 1886, he moved his animals to "Apple Farm," a ranch tucked under the Rim just east of Payson. There Ellison found "grass as high as a horseman's head."[37] He also found a war in the offing in neighboring Pleasant Valley, a few scant miles east of his location.

Despite his neutrality in 1886, Ellison wanted to bring peace to Pleasant Valley even if it meant making war to do it. Criminals had forced him out of Texas; he would not move again. Indeed he could not move. He was fifteen thousand dollars in debt, an amount so great that he was forced to substitute pork — which had little market value and required no capital outlay — for precious beef on the family table. In order to save labor costs, he put his daughters to work on the range, thus ending the privileged life they had known as children. There would be no more governesses, no more convent schools, no more new dresses, only hard labor. Not until 1897 would Ellison manage to pay off his debt. One privilege that Ellison did not deny himself, however, was a pack of well-bred hunting dogs. The dogs came from Kentucky, costing Ellison between and seventy-five and a hundred dollars apiece. Even if he was in debt, Ellison retained the trap-

Jesse Ellison posing in front of the hides of grizzlies he had killed,
circa 1890s. Courtesy of Arizona Historical Society/Tucson, Jesse W. Ellison
Photograph Collection, PC 40, folder 1, no. 53899.

pings of the Old South's plantation elite, with its taste for fine dogs, fine horses, and blood sport. To that list, one might add another component of honor culture, hard liquor, for which Ellison displayed a fondness.[38]

In the Rim Country, Ellison became an instant leader, perhaps because of his Civil War experiences and the ten men who came with him to Arizona. Soon he attained the title of "Colonel," a customary designation for men of honor throughout the South. That he was a natural leader made him the anchor for the vigilantes who formed in the Pleasant Valley area in 1887. He became their commander. In all probability, he recruited them. There were never eighty-six vigilantes, as the Apache *Review* reported, but there may have been several dozen. Only eight to twelve men from the Pleasant Valley area, however, saw regular action, most of them men who had come with Ellison from Texas. Few had played any role in the war at the outset. Yet after the assault on Lauffer, Livingston, Cody, and Coleman, they came to believe that Tom Graham was gathering a bunch of "hard characters" to carry on hostilities and only "strong medacine [sic]" would "break up the band."[39]

Years later, Ellison explained that "mostly in any country, there always has got to be a cleaning up process. You could not put a horse in a barn and expect to get him the next morning. . . . They would come steal them in the night. . . . You might have a herd of cattle today and tomorrow you wouldn't have anything." He himself did not claim to have lost horses or cattle to thieves, but he knew others who had. The deed had to be done. Bad men would have to die. As in Texas, where lynching ran rampant, the culture of honor—with its emphasis on assertion, violence, and shaming—would have to be served.[40]

Jim Houck arrived at the same conclusion by a different route. Born in Ohio in 1847, Houck became a boy soldier in the Civil War, enlisting in the Thirty-first Wisconsin Infantry. After receiving an honorable discharge in 1865, he traveled to Wisconsin, only to find himself in trouble after allegedly killing a man in a gambling dispute. From Wisconsin, he moved to Iowa and then to Wyoming, where he became a miner. Like other settlers, he was restless. From Wyoming he walked all the way to New Mexico, where he finally procured a pack burro.[41]

By 1874, Houck had become a mail rider on one of the most dangerous routes in Arizona, a route that stretched from Fort Wingate in New Mexico, west into Arizona, south across the Rim, and concluding at the mining district at Fort Whipple (Prescott). Though previous riders had met their deaths on the route, General Crook made it marginally safer when his forces conquered the Dilzhe'e and Yavapai in 1872–73.[42]

Even if the route had become relatively safe, it took a brave man to ride it. At five feet, seven inches, Houck was no giant, but he had grit. Will Barnes, who knew him well, said he "was inclined to be aggressive and loved a scrap." Barnes added that Houck was a "dark haired black complexioned man," though his pension records describe him as sandy haired and blue-eyed. No doubt the Arizona sun darkened him. What one noticed about him most of all—what seemed to betray his interior self—were his small, cold eyes, eyes made fiercer by the bushy eyebrows that framed them. Houck's gaze could be frightening.[43]

After several years of service on the Wingate-Whipple mail route, Houck grew restless. His familiarity with the springs and swales of the Little Colorado country gave him the idea of becoming a rancher. Sometime around 1877, he staked a claim to lands at Navajo Springs at the south end of the Navajo Reservation, where he hired Commodore Perry Owens as a wrangler and became embroiled in feuds with Indians. In 1880, he married Beatrice Gurula—also called Beatrice McCarty—whom he claimed to have rescued after Navajos had killed her parents. When they married, she was fifteen, he was thirty-three. She would bear him seven children. He in turn sought to bring more income to his family.[44]

When the "fust railroad in the state" arrived in 1881, Houck would later tell his daughter, "I decided to build me a store an' do some trading with the Indians." Though Navajos stole his horses and threatened to tear down his building—one of them even "pulled out a fistful of ha'r and shook it in my face"—he responded

James Houck, legislative portrait, 1885. Houck
"was inclined to be aggressive and loved a scrap,"
according to Will C. Barnes. Courtesy of Arizona
State Library, Archives and Public Records, History
and Archives Division, Phoenix, no. 01-9440.

with violence. In time, he claimed, his worst Navajo enemy became his friend, even helping him locate a well. By 1882, the A&P was making regular stops at "Houck's Station," where it took on water and presumably allowed Houck to sell Indian souvenirs and foodstuffs to passengers.[45]

In the mid-1880s, Houck again shifted vocations, selling his trading post and opening a billiards parlor in Holbrook. He also carved out a sheep ranch near the Mormon town of Heber. Houck—who challenged Mormon voters at the polls but seems to have played no part in the attacks on them—meanwhile managed to get himself elected to the thirteenth territorial legislature. That legislature earned two equally damning sobriquets: the "Thieving Thirteenth" for its corrupt allocation of resources and the "Bloody Thirteenth" for its members' tendency to get into drunken fights. Houck displayed his own predilection to violence—and honor—when he pistol whipped a man after an argument about a horse trade in 1884.[46]

Although Houck shared with Stott a Republican orientation and a flair for adventure, they were otherwise opposites. Houck was crude and earthy. He chewed tobacco, drank, gambled, and ran a billiards parlor. Stott was educated and proper. He spoke well. His "language and habits," testified Will Barnes, "indicated that he had been well brought up."[47] In Texas, he had refused—if we can believe his letters home—to dance and to drink and even espoused prohibition. Likely he continued to do so in Arizona. Stott was a gentleman from New England; Houck was a rounder from the rural Midwest. Stott received remittances from his father; Houck hustled for himself. Houck, moreover, became drawn into the Pleasant Valley conflict on the Tewksbury side. Stott sympathized— from a safe distance—with the Grahams. Like Jesse Ellison, finally, Houck fit easily into the culture of honor that developed in the West. Stott did not.

In the early morning of August 11, 1888, Jim Houck, still a deputy sheriff under Commodore Perry Owens, rode into Jamie Stott's ranch, secreting himself and two companions outside Stott's cabin. Stott, fresh from a visit to his family in Massachusetts, emerged from his cabin at daylight only to find Houck holding a rifle on him. Though he had no warrant, Houck placed Stott under arrest for the shooting of Jake Lauffer. The warrant, claimed Houck, was in the pocket of a coat that he had left at camp on the previous night. With neither coat nor warrant, Houck had ridden through the breezy, cool, high country night to arrive at Stott's place before dawn.[48]

Ever the gracious host, Stott cooked breakfast for his captors. Either shortly before or shortly after that breakfast, some twenty-eight more men rode onto the scene, joking and laughing among themselves. More than half came from western Apache County. The others came from Pleasant Valley. The latter group brought a prisoner, Jim Scott, whom they had captured in Pleasant Valley, where Scott had gone to recover a horse that he had loaned out.[49]

Unarmed and surrounded, Jamie Stott had no choice but to submit. The vigilantes also took a man who was working for Stott: William "Billy," or "Jeff," Wilson. Years later, Charlie Duchet testified that Stott had hired Wilson and Scott to build a fence at his ranch. They had been working on it for a year, claimed Duchet, when the vigilantes arrived. Other records show that both Scott and Wilson had worked for the Aztec, Scott as wrangler and Wilson as cook. After quitting the Aztec, Scott went to work as a wrangler for Huning and Cooley, where he remained employed until three weeks before his capture. Neither Scott nor Wilson, according to Duchet, had ever been to Pleasant Valley before Scott went there to retrieve his horse. Neither knew their captors. Scott in particular was well known and liked in Apache County. Wilson was less well known but had a good reputation. Neither man was accused of attacking Mormons or stealing horses or cattle, nor had they taken part in the war. They were, however, friends of Jamie Stott.[50]

As the vigilantes rode off with their prisoners, two men remained behind, Alfred Ingham and Lamotte Clymer. Ingham was a consumptive whom Stott had invited to live at his ranch. There he could breathe clean mountain air and await recovery. Clymer was Ingham's attendant. The men watched, or perhaps listened from their quarters, as the vigilantes rode away with their captives. Apparently the vigilantes had not seen Ingham, though they had located Clymer in his bed. Not being a cowboy, however, Clymer could not be a rustler; they left him alone.[51]

The party traveled some ten miles, then stopped where the trail forked off to become the Old Verde Road, on the border between Yavapai and Apache counties. With their hands strapped behind them, the captives were helpless. The vigilantes looped nooses around the necks of Scott and Wilson first. Both men begged for their lives to no avail. Then the vigilantes focused on Stott, tying a silk handkerchief around his neck to keep him from getting rope burns or, more to the point, to mock him for being effete. Rather than submit to fear, Stott boiled with anger, cursing his captors, offering to fight them with gun or fists. "If they would turn him loose," wrote Will Barnes, "he would fight them all, single-handed and alone. He addressed each one by name, and called down on his head every curse and malediction his trembling lips could utter." By turns the vigilantes pulled him up, then let him down, demanding that he admit his crimes. He gave no satisfaction. With each "mock" hanging, Stott came down weaker. Still no confession came forth. Before they could finish the inquisition, Stott crossed into death.[52]

From Holbrook came a telegram to the Stott family informing them of the murder. James and Hannah Stott, elderly, distraught, and bent on justice, lost no time in boarding a train for Arizona. When they arrived at Holbrook, Will Barnes, promoter of the very terror campaign that had led to Stott's death, graciously drove them to a hotel. He advised them not to pursue justice as that would provoke more bloodshed. No grand jury would indict the killers, he promised, and no petit jury would convict. Though Barnes himself may not have known the identities of the actual killers, he knew the identities of the Apache County men who had authorized them. The hanging of Stott, Scott, and Wilson "was done by no 'mob of murderers,'" he later declared, but rather by "reputable citizens, determined to put an end to the reign of lawlessness."[53]

The Pleasant Valley lynchers—led by Colonel Ellison—did not stop at the hangings of Stott, Scott, and Wilson. William Voris, an Ellison cowboy and vigilante, told his son that "young men all over the country cleaned them [rustlers and thieves] up. Wherever they caught those guys, they hung and left them hanging for several days." Strangers unlucky enough to pass through Pleasant Valley in late 1887 and throughout 1888 met the end of a rope. William Voris himself "saw them hanging all up and down along Cherry Creek and all different places around that country," recalled his son. "You would find them hanging down there for several days and the maggots were dropping out of them! Now, that is the word you use." Joseph Fish, the Mormon historian, judged the hangings to be a great success. The vigilantes "did more to run out the cattle and horse thieves than any other," he wrote. "No amount of shooting could terrorize the cowboy element as this lynching did."[54]

Only two Mormons, Stott's hired hand and his wife—Mr. and Mrs. Day—had something positive to say about Jamie Stott. Mrs. Day told Hannah Stott that Jamie was honest and kind and that, over the years, he had given food and shelter to some of the men who killed him. "She wants to leave there now," wrote Hannah Stott to her daughters, "so far from everybody, she shall so miss Jamie." Others also wanted to leave. "Almost daily," averred the *Herald* on August 30, 1888, "parties are passing through the southern part of this county returning from the direction of Tonto Basin, which is regarded as a 'dark and bloody' ground, from which it is well to be absent."[55]

Stott's parents got no satisfaction from Barnes, but they were able to recruit D. G. Harvey, Holbrook justice of the peace, to act as executor. They hoped that Harvey would exonerate their son in the bargain, having been told—by Barnes or others—that Jamie was a thief. In his memoir, Barnes recalled that stock detectives had spied on Stott to determine his guilt. The detectives supposedly confirmed the suspicions of their employers but somehow lacked the evidence to bring charges. Powerful men resolved to step outside the law. They had ventured there before; the shadows held few terrors. With a sympathetic county attorney and a governor who might pardon them in case of prosecution, they felt secure. The vigilantes of Apache County now worked in concert with those in Yavapai County, contriving a plan to lynch their enemies on the border between the two counties, apparently thinking to cast doubt on jurisdiction should an investigation ensue.[56]

Alerted to the accusations against their son, the Stotts asked Harvey to investigate his books. Jamie had kept careful records of his transactions, in part to show his father his head for business. Harvey wrote James Stott on October 10, 1888, to report on his inspection. "I am fully convinced," he averred, "that he purchased and paid a good round price for every head of stock on his ranch." But, added Harvey, "I do think that he was imposed upon by designing parties and through his kindness he had to suffer, and I believe this opinion is concurred in by every law-abiding person in the country." Frank Ames offered a stronger indictment. "There is not an honest man in Arizona" who knew Jamie and "believed him guilty," he assured Stott. Those in Holbrook thought that the hanging was "as cowardly and brutal a murder as was ever committed. Jim's worst enemies never pretended that he ever attempted or threatened personal harm to anybody."[57]

Harvey also reported that he had convinced the authorities to subpoena witnesses to the lynching, but, he explained, they were not likely to talk. He was right. When two of the supposed killers from Pleasant Valley, William McFadden and J. W. Boyle, and another from Apache County, Hook Larson, appeared before the grand jury, they denied knowledge of the lynching. With them came "a solid phalanx" of their comrades—including Jim Houck and Ed Tewksbury—who had come to "see fair play," or at least to make their menacing presence known to jurors. When A. F. Banta became district attorney in 1889, he committed the county again to the cause of justice. In May 1889, he charged McFadden and Boyle with murder. Again a phalanx of men rode to St. Johns to stand sentinel. Without evidence and without witnesses, Banta was forced to drop charges. The two men who could have identified the vigilantes, Clymer and Ingham, had left the territory and could not be brought back.[58]

Jim Scott's mother also pled for justice. Like Stott, Scott came from a respected family. His grandfather had helped write the 1845 Texas constitution. His maternal uncle, Briggs Goodrich, served as attorney general for Arizona Territory in 1887–88. Another maternal uncle, Ben Goodrich, was a noted Arizona lawyer. Scott's mother implored Briggs Goodrich to assist in the cause of justice. She also wrote to the new governor, Lewis Wolfley, a Republican, complaining that those who had killed her son were "cattlemen who have money and with it buy up juries and witnesses, prove alibis, and control the courts." Undoubtedly she was referring to members of the Apache County Stock Growers Association. She got no help, perhaps because Briggs Goodrich, a Zulick appointee, had already agreed to forgo prosecuting the vigilantes.[59]

Ingham and Clymer, however, had told their story. It is their testimony, though never given in court, that allows us to reconstruct the events of August 11. Ingham's story entered public record on August 30, 1888, when "One Who Knows" published a letter in the *Herald*. His information, he explained, came from Ingham. Those who had hanged Stott, insisted One Who Knows, were Yavapai County men who had been whipped into hysteria by the Prescott papers. Apparently he did not know that an Apache County contingent—whipped into hysteria by the St. Johns *Herald*—accompanied them. The reason for the killing, claimed One Who Knows, was personal revenge—probably that of Houck—and "other motives" unconnected to outlawry. One Who Knows also contradicted Houck's story that forty masked men had met him on the trail and forced him to give up his prisoner. Ingham had said that twenty-eight men—joking and laughing—had accompanied Houck when he made his arrest, indicating that a rendezvous had been planned. Clymer told the story slightly differently; he claimed that the twenty-eight men arrived at the ranch just after Houck had made the arrest. The wrong could not now be righted, concluded One Who Knows, but "let the press do justice to the memory of the dead; if they cannot, do not do so much for the undeserving living."[60]

Ingham and Clymer were not the only men who cast light on the hangings. Both Joseph Fish and Will Barnes, though refusing to reveal the source of their information, later named the vigilantes whom they thought responsible. Fish listed William Voris, Glenn Reynolds, William McFadden, N. J. Coleman, Jim Tewksbury, and one of the Colcord brothers, all of Pleasant Valley, plus Jim Houck and Hook Larson of Apache County. He also added the already famous rodeo rider Tom Horn. Horn would later find his way to execution in Wyoming after being convicted of killing a teenage boy in a terror campaign similar to the one in Apache County. In 1888, when the Stott lynching occurred, he was visiting John Rhodes, with whom he was a close friend. In the memoir that Horn wrote while awaiting execution, he mentioned his role in Pleasant Valley as a "mediator." If he was ever a mediator, however, he was also a vigilante. In a letter to Will Barnes in 1931, William Colcord confirmed that Horn had "helped to clean up the Valley after Graham & Tewksbury had quit."[61]

Barnes in his memoir added another name to those cited by Fish: Pearl (or Perle) Ellison, son of Jesse Ellison. Charlie Perkins, the storekeeper, told Barnes that one of the Cline boys—who lived near Payson—was also there, as was John Rhodes. For some reason, Barnes chose not to add those names to his published list. Perhaps the most reliable list of the Pleasant Valley lynchers, however, came from Robert Voris, who agreed in 1957 to an interview with Clara Woody, the Gila County librarian. Voris had heard rumors that his father was among those who had hanged two men and a "boy." Determined to find out the truth, he visited Jesse Ellison at his home in Phoenix. The date was sometime in the late 1920s, after Ellison's wife had died. Ellison, now nearly blind, lived in a small house adjoining the home of his daughter, Duett, and her husband, who was governor of Arizona. On hearing of Voris's mission, he at first only stared and grinned. "I wouldn't worry my head about it," he told Voris. "Well, I am worried about it," replied Voris. "I want to know the truth." Ellison at last told him to come back in the evening, when they could speak privately.[62]

When Voris returned, Ellison ushered him into the house. Only one other person was there, Ellison's crippled daughter, Lena. Ellison told Voris never to repeat what he was about to say until all involved were dead. Voris agreed. Ellison then told him that he had been the leader of the Pleasant Valley vigilantes. His recruits included Voris's father, as well as John Rhodes, William Colcord, Harvey Colcord, William McFadden, Houston Kyle, and Robert "Bud" Campbell. Ellison made no mention of any Tewksbury. Nor did he mention J. W. Boyle. The men he named were his own. He also failed to mention Houck and his two associates, as well as members of the large group—perhaps twenty strong—that had come from Apache County.[63]

All those whom Ellison mentioned had accompanied him to Arizona in 1885 with the exception of Rhodes, who came from Texas at another time. Two of them, Campbell and Kyle, would later marry Ellison's daughters. All of them were products of what one scholar has called a "lynching culture." All were products of honor. They—not unlike the Texas cowboys who had attacked Mormons—celebrated physical assertion and rituals of shaming, the best example of which was the hanging of Jamie Stott. Not content with a perfunctory murder, they had taunted him by tying a handkerchief around his delicate neck. They had tortured him by hanging him repeatedly, then letting him down, demanding a confession.[64] Worse were the tortures, burnings, mutilations, and lynchings inflicted on black men in Texas and the South. The lessons of honor and shame, however—and the rituals that reified them—were profoundly similar throughout the South and the West. The business of Ellison's men was not to administer justice; it was to administer shame.

Ellison's list of vigilantes probably left out Horn because he was only a visitor to the valley. He left out Houck and Larson, meanwhile, probably because they represented a vigilante cell from Apache County. That Apache County men were involved, however, is made clear by a mysterious manuscript in the George Tanner Collection at the University of Utah. Tanner collected every record of Rim Country Mormons that he could find, using them as the basis for two honest and insightful books on his forebears. For some reason—perhaps out of loyalty to settlers—he never discussed Mormon vigilantism. He saved one document, however—unsigned but derived from the testimony of a man familiar with the events of 1887 and 1888—that sheds light on Mormon participation.

The document, in a folder labeled "miscellaneous notes," consists of a transcribed and edited interview with a settler who begins by paying tribute to "Grandfather Flake," referring to William Flake. The interviewee was apparently a friend of the Flakes, if not a family member. His references to "Grandfather Flake" show his interlocutor to be one of Flake's children or grandchildren. "Your father," added the interviewee—here referring either to William Flake or to one of his sons—was "always teaching the Gospel and living standards that were even better than his talks."[65]

"Two men from our side," explained the interviewee, were liaisons with a vigilante group from Pleasant Valley and vicinity that numbered fourteen altogether. Those two were Jim Houck and Hook Larson. Larson, a giant of a man at some three hundred pounds, today would be called a "Jack Mormon." Though baptized a Mormon, he chose not to follow the Word of Wisdom. Another settler, Clarissa Lee, described him as "a great big fat, pot-bellied man and a coward" who had shot men in the back. "No one," she added, "seemed to trust him." Larson also drank to excess and embroiled himself in fist fights. To Mormons of Snowflake and Taylor, however, he was beloved. Osmer Flake attended Larson's wedding in Heber in 1897, bringing him three quarts of whiskey as a gift from Frank Wattron of Holbrook. By the time he took his vows, Larson was "quite drunk." "We then had a dance," said Flake, "and by midnight Hook had snakes in his boots and we had a great time." Osmer Flake here bespoke his own fascination with the culture of honor and in particular with cowboys, a fascination that begot not scorn but affection. Flake also bespoke the strong ties between Larson and his Mormon neighbors. When he died in 1906, Mormons convened at his funeral, where musicians played "Our Dear Little Rose-Bud Has Left Us."[66]

The interviewee in Tanner's "miscellaneous notes" went on to explain more about the Mormons' relationship to the vigilantes. Houck and Larson were range detectives who "spent weeks watching trails to and from Pleasant Valley." After gleaning information on suspects, they would "meet with everybody," including Charles Ballard, Lehi Heward, and A. Z. Palmer, as well as other Snowflake Mormons. Undoubtedly William Flake—de facto leader of the Snowflake community and Palmer's brother-in-law—also kept in touch with Houck and Larson. The vigilantes "meant business," explained the speaker.[67]

"These good men," continued the speaker, "saw that this was their opportunity to clean up things and really fix a country that was fit to live in." To do that, they visited each "undesirable type," ordering them to cooperate or leave. "We are judged by the company we harbor," the vigilantes told their neighbors, calling to mind the strange connection between frontier hospitality and frontier suspicion. Those who refused to cooperate would find a "sign" at their ranch saying simply, "Go." The Pleasant Valley vigilantes, concluded the speaker, "are my friends. When I want to rest I go to Pleasant Valley."[68]

Osmer Flake elsewhere gave inadvertent evidence of Mormon complicity in the lynchings. In his biography of his father, Osmer wrote that William Flake had discovered the still hanging bodies of the three men while en route to

Pleasant Valley. After reaching his destination, William Flake asked his friends whether Stott had "showed the 'white feather' or died a brave man." They obliged, giving him a detailed story of the lynching.[69]

No vigilante would have spoken to Flake had he not been party to their crime. At least one later report went so far as to place a Flake at the lynching. It is equally possible that neither William nor his sons participated directly. Almost certainly, however, they were among those who authorized the deed. They were confidants and accessories, just as they had been confidants and accessories to the reign of terror in Apache County. It was via William Flake, who transmitted his information to Osmer, that we know about the silk handkerchief placed around Stott's neck, about his cursing and challenging his tormenters, and about the repeated "mock" hangings that preceded his death. J. W. Boyle, who was probably among the vigilantes, confirmed some of those details in a communication with Barnes many years later. Osmer Flake, however, admitted neither complicity nor guilt. "While we are all glad to be rid of Stott," he wrote, "we did not approve of mob law, and worse was to torture the victim."[70]

Other descendants of William Flake have presented a somewhat different story. According to Roberta Flake Clayton, her father first learned of the hangings from a Mormon settler, "Old Lady Neilson." She had gotten the news from two of Barnes's cowboys who had come across the bodies earlier in the day. "Oh, Mr. Flake!" cried Mrs. Neilson as William Flake came riding in to spend a night at her home after a weary day on the trail, "guess the good news . . . Jim Stott, Jim Scott and Bud Wilson are hanging in a tree up there." The next day, according to Clayton's account, William Flake cut down the bodies and made his way to Phoenix, where he recovered horses stolen by Stott, then wired other Mormons to come to Phoenix to do the same. Clayton confused her grandfather's recovery of stolen horses in Phoenix—an event that occurred in spring 1887—with the hanging of Stott, which occurred more than a year later.[71]

When Jamie Stott's parents came to Holbrook, added Clayton, they met silence. No one wanted to tell them of Jamie's guilt. Instead they directed the Stotts to William Flake, who "would tell them the truth." The Stotts obligingly drove a buggy to Flake's ranch, thirty miles south of Holbrook, James Stott somehow holding the reins in the crook of his one remaining elbow. They at last caught up with Flake four miles from his house, where he was engaged in a roundup. When Stott protested to Flake that his child was innocent, Flake was compelled to contradict him. Flake explained that he had tried to warn young "Jimmie" that he was keeping the wrong company "and if you don't quit 'em you may get into trouble." Far from changing his behavior, "Jimmie" had begun to accrue stolen horses. After finally convincing the Stotts that their son's murder was just, claimed Clayton, Flake escorted them to his Snowflake home and magnanimously agreed to buy Jamie's estate and take any losses for claims against it.[72]

Les Flake, a grandchild of William, built another false monument to his progenitor. In Les Flake's tale, the father of Jim Scott—not Stott—met William Flake while searching for his son in Arizona. Scott's father told Flake that he hoped to convince his son to come back home and work at the "mill." The reference to the "mill" suggests that the story is about Jamie Stott, not Jim Scott. It also suggests that the story is entirely fictitious, since Stott's father never visited Arizona before his son's murder. According to the story, Flake assured "Scott" that he would find his son and "try to talk to him." When Flake did find young Scott, he told him that he was keeping the wrong company and would be killed if he continued. Laughing and boasting that he wasn't worried, Scott asked Flake why anybody would want to kill him. Because you are stealing horses, replied Flake.[73]

Perhaps the most interesting version of events comes from a play about William Flake's life that was written and performed by his progeny. In one scene, three cowboys, Bill, Tex, and Slim, sit around a campfire and play cards while Flake watches. When Bill asks "father," meaning Flake, to join the game, he declines, explaining that "life is too short to spend in playing cards. Besides it leads to gambling, then drinking and finally ends up in shooting." One of the cowboys agrees, having seen "many a fight over a game of cards." The cowboys then ask Flake to regale them with tales of his experiences, which are "more thrilling than a dime novel and some of them as funny as a minstrel show." Flake obliges by telling of the time when Jamie Stott came riding toward him "as fast as his horse could come with his gun in his hand." Flake got off his horse and took "a good rock in each hand." When Stott got within seventy-five yards, Flake ordered him to stop. As if by magic, Stott complied, insisting that he was only chasing a coyote. Flake compelled him to admit that he was actually gunning for Flake himself, then administered a stern lecture and told him to ride off, "which he did."[74]

Flake's descendants made Stott into a generic desperado, a bully and persecutor in the mold of Andy Cooper and John Payne. Stott became an incarnation of the worst of cowboy honor, a man implicitly corrupted by gambling, drinking, and firearms. Flake himself, by contrast, became the model of Mormon conscience, a conscience made manifest not only by his refusal to drink or gamble but also by his refusal to use deadly force.

To ensure that no one might think Stott innocent, Osmer Flake offered additional testimony. When the executor, D. G. Harvey, sold Stott's estate, claimed Osmer, William Flake bought it specifically so that he could take possession of

Stott's books. When Stott's father and mother came to the Rim Country, Flake presented them with the books to confirm their son's guilt. Stott supposedly "looked them over a couple of hours" and promised never again to assert his son's innocence.[75]

As historian Leland Hanchett has noted, two problems with the story present themselves. First, it would be remarkably strange for a horse thief to record his deeds in his books. Second, the Stotts came to the Rim Country more than a month *before* Flake took possession of Jamie's estate, which included his books. Even when the Stotts did come to Arizona, it is highly unlikely that they visited Flake. A Holbrook livery operator named S. M. Brown wrote Will Barnes in 1931 that he did "not believe that Mr. Stott Sr. went out to Flake's ranch," noting that he—the only man likely to have conveyed Stott—"did not take him there." Stott may have driven himself to the Flake ranch, but that would have required exceptional skill for a man with no hands. Finally, before Flake took possession of the estate, Harvey wrote Stott to tell him that his son's books showed no evidence of malfeasance. In early October, Stott wrote to Harvey to ask about progress in bringing the murderers to justice, something he would not likely have done were he convinced of his son's guilt.[76]

What Osmer Flake left unmentioned was his father's profit from the estate. William Flake, deep in debt and desperate to shore up his community, bought all of Stott's cattle and horses other than a few sickly animals and eight horses that were awarded to other owners. Only one of those eight was replevined, meaning that legal ownership was contested. Either Stott had been boarding the other animals—a common practice—or the Flakes mistakenly rounded them up while gathering Stott's horses. In 1880s Arizona, horses were ceaselessly wandering away only to be gathered by someone other than the owner. One man recalled that he routinely returned a particularly troublesome stray to Will Barnes. Barnes rewarded him with a Stetson hat. To convey a horse back to its owner, however, could be an onerous chore. Few men were conscientious about it.[77]

Flake paid James Stott just $1,200 for Jamie's ranch and stock, though Harvey had valued them at $2,150. Flake received Jamie's possessory right to the property for free, a rare gift. Flake had managed to whittle down the price by billing James Stott for care of the stock, charging the steep fee of $7 a day, which came to $188. By comparison, Flake charged the Waters Cattle Company $2 a day for taking care of its large remuda in the early 1890s. Flake's son Charles added his own bill of $79, thus canceling an $80 debt he had owed Stott. Flake also managed to get Stott's branded horses for a bargain price because they were supposedly diseased with "disteruban."[78]

It is not clear what William Flake made from selling the horses and possessory rights to Stott's land, but it probably helped him repay the two-thousand-dollar loan that he'd received from Jim Stinson during his polygamy trial. In 1888, the year of Stott's murder, Flake was forced to resume freighting goods across Arizona in order to pay off his debt, thus requiring him to travel hundreds of miles from home. Flake was also responsible for making payments on land he had purchased for settlers.[80] If he could profit from Stott's death—if he could profit from an evil man—Flake would triumph.

Jim Houck also triumphed. According to one observer, he soon ran sheep on Stott's land. The murders, however, earned him enemies. On September 29, 1888, the Apache *Review* warned Houck that he was in danger. In January 1889, Charlie Duchet and Red McNeil—the latter already famous as the "poet robber"—allegedly tried to assassinate Houck from ambush. After they killed his mule, Houck was able to use the dead animal as cover while returning fire, finally driving away his attackers.[80]

Ed Rogers, foreman for the Aztec, came equally close to killing Houck, confronting him in a dentist's office in Holbrook. Rogers, a friend of Jim Scott, accused Houck of the murders, calling him "vile names." Houck denied the charge and damned not only Rogers but the Hashknife generally. Both men grasped their sidearms before Rogers, who at six feet tall and 180 pounds was much the bigger man, backed down. Nervous and pale, he ejected six cartridges from his gun and walked away. Rogers subsequently received a letter that read only, "Go." He did so.[81]

Will Barnes went on to enter the Forest Service, become its chief of grazing, and write extensively on his experiences. Much of our information about the Stott lynching comes from Barnes, who lionized the vigilantes' actions. Stott's cousin, Arthur Burt, corresponded with Barnes in the 1930s, asking him to explain what evidence he had of Stott's guilt. Barnes provided none. Finally Burt wrote bitterly that Barnes "never said a good word for him. On the contrary, while you do not come right out and say that he was a horse thief and can prove it, you keep publishing these stories but with never a word of proof." The letter arrived soon after Barnes had died, causing Barnes's widow to send back a scolding missive.[82]

What Burt was witnessing was not merely an injustice to his cousin. He was witnessing the deification of honor. Jamie Stott was swept along in a river of myth and memory, becoming just one of the countless "desperadoes" who populated the West. Only hard men, stern men, good men, could overcome hard men, stern men, bad men. Those good men were forced to use not the law and the courts but guns and ropes. Judges, juries, and courts refused, or at least failed, to clean up the West, according to the myth. The people had to invoke "popular sovereignty" by creating citizen courts and citizen executions. Where law was weak, lawlessness prevailed, until brave men acted. The myth of the noble vigilante appeared in popular literature from Mayne Reid to Owen Wister and Dane Coolidge, complementing a similar myth about the necessity of lynching in the South after Reconstruction. The myth of the noble vigilante, casting aside feeble law to create order, was part of the reaction against sentimentality, against conscience, against the "feminization" of American culture that arced through the Gilded Age to the First World War and beyond. It was that reaction that would build Western identity. It would bring together rural Westerners, whether they were Mormon or gentile, Catholic or Protestant, Northern- or Southern-born, into a proud whole with a bedrock of myth. They viewed themselves as descendants of heroes.

The myth grew from the grassroots. Mormon stories about Jamie Stott became ever more lurid, more fantastic, creating a folkloric past when heroes fought demons. John Addison Hunt, who recorded the standoff between Houck and Rogers, claimed that as a boy he had seen Jim Stott with his partner, Red Holcomb—a Hashknife cowboy despised by Mormons for having jumped a claim—working with two stolen mares in a hidden clearing. Blurring Stott with Andy Cooper and the Blevins gang, Hunt recalled that Stott and Holcomb began by stealing colts and ultimately "came and took fine work teams right out of the stables." "It was no wonder few tears were shed when news came that Jim Stott, Jimmie Scott and Jeff Wilson were hung." Why Scott and Wilson required killing, rather than Holcomb, got no explanation. Holcomb, indeed—despite once finding a note on his cabin saying, "Go"—lived out his life among Mormons. As late as the 1910s, he was resolutely defending his cowboy friends from old accusations.[83]

Zach Decker told a story similar to Hunt's. After Decker lost a mare, he recalled, he rode to Stott's ranch searching for her. Stott assured Decker that he did not have the mare but invited him to stay the night. Decker agreed but kept an eye open, since Stott "had bragged that he would kill him." The next morning, Stott lit out before daylight, leaving Decker to make his own breakfast. Decker secretly followed Stott, who went straight to a hidden corral that held Decker's mare. After Stott left, Decker retrieved the horse and returned to Stott's ranch. Caught in his duplicity, Stott asked Decker where he had found the horse, then invited Decker again to stay the night. Supposedly Stott's friends teased him about his failure to "get" Decker, given his threats.[84]

Decker's story recalled the Mormon motif of good men, under the eye of God, facing down their enemies. It was an old motif put to new service as Mormons became mainstream. It testified not to God's power but to Decker's. He was the good shot, the hard man who feared no one. He took responsibility for his own heroic actions, giving no credit to God. It did not matter to Decker whether that enemy was an Aztec cowboy or a New England prohibitionist. Perhaps the story speaks above all to Decker's braggadocio. Decker used Stott—and others—to gain admission into the club of Western honor.

If any of Decker's story is true, there are still multiple explanations that leave Stott innocent. Stott may have mistakenly purchased a stolen horse, or he may have been holding a horse, unknowingly, for someone who had stolen it. Or ownership of the horse may have been contested. Stott may also have found the lost horse but failed to return it promptly, then sought to hide his failure for fear that Decker would call him a thief. Decker apparently sought no answer. Nor did he file charges. One can only assume that he had no evidence, given the eagerness of Apache County to indict and convict criminals. Decker also testi-fied that a knot of vigilantes—likely from the Mormon towns on Silver Creek— had passed his encampment on their way south toward Stott's ranch. They asked Decker to join, but Decker, a moral man, refused. His morality, alas, did not ex-tend to revealing the identities of murderers.

Mormons hailed the lynchings as the beginning of a new era. The killings were "a deathblow to the bad men," proclaimed Joseph Fish, "and civilization was en-abled to take another step forward." In fact, thievery continued. Without a statis-tical study, it is difficult to gauge whether crime levels decreased in the wake of the lynchings, but certainly the newspapers continued to pour forth a stream of stories about horse theft, rustling, and murder.[85]

In December 1888, four months after the Stott hanging, Osmer Flake found himself tracking stolen horses into New Mexico. The Apache *Review* reported on December 12 that "horse stealing is again a lucrative employment in the western part of the county." On the same day, the *Review* noted that twenty horses stolen from William Flake and another Snowflake Mormon had been found near Nu-trioso, close to the New Mexico line. The thieves from the western part of the county, it speculated, finding it too dangerous to move horses south through Tonto Basin, were now moving them east. On March 15, 1889, the *Herald* re-ported that horse thieves were common around Winslow. They had stolen, claimed the *Herald*, five hundred dollars' worth of horses from the Waters Cattle Company, as well as two stallions from J. H. Breed. On April 18, 1889, Allen Frost, a Mormon settler, added that two teams of horses had been stolen from Mormon families. On May 25, 1889, the *Silver Belt* reported that a posse had killed two horse thieves, Charles Rudd and George Powell. Two years earlier, Powell had been one of the stock association's vaunted detectives. That summer, the Aztec expressed concern over a new wave of rustling. In July 1889, Hook Larson managed to capture two alleged Mexican horse thieves and kill a third one. The captives were lynched before they could be tried. The list goes on, just as rich for the 1890s as for the 1880s. In September 1893, the *Silver Belt* reported that "the juncture of Gila, Yavapai and Coconino counties seems to be a rendezvous for stock thieves, and no less than eighteen are reported to have been assembled there recently." In June 1894, the *Herald* claimed that losses from cattle theft in Apache County from the previous year amounted to twenty thousand dollars and urged cattlemen to organize themselves to stop the stealing. On May 2, 1894, Osmer Flake reported in his diary that "there is killing on every hand now days."[86]

Vigilantism did not halt crime. It did, however, give settlers comfort. They at least could take action. They could lay claim to honor. They had passed through a great ordeal and done so heroically. "I have always felt that the ends justified the means," Barnes explained in 1936 in defense of the vigilantism. The citizens of Apache and Yavapai counties had only taken the law into their own hands, he insisted, when absolutely necessary. In a book that Barnes cowrote with William MacLeod Raine, he explained the phenomenon of vigilantism in greater detail, giving it the gilding of ancestral tradition. "Even when [vigilantes] stepped outside the ordinary channels of legal procedure," averred Barnes and Raine, "there was often a sober and impersonal behavior much more like the ancient Teuton gathering of freemen in the forests of the Old World than the savage call of revolutionaries for the blood of a victim." Western vigilantes hanged men "with stern reluctance" and only after scrutinizing evidence of guilt.[87]

Cattle associations throughout the West, continued Barnes and Raine, hired stock detectives to find the guilty and dispense justice. Between 1876 and 1886— for some reason Barnes and Raine left out 1887 and 1888—"more men were killed by those working in the cattle interests than a dozen states have legally executed in fifty years." They may have been right. As one scholar observes, a "lynching belt" stretched from one end of cattle country to the other, from Texas to New Mexico and Arizona, thence northward through Colorado, Wyoming, and Montana. Between 1882 and 1903, per capita lynching within that belt surpassed that of the South.[88]

With their praise for vigilantism, Barnes and Raine repeated a myth that had gained currency as early as the 1760s, when the Regulators of the Carolinas attacked "criminal" foes. In attaching lynching to high talk of history and regicide and popular sovereignty, vigilantes gave it legitimacy. For much of the twentieth century, few cast doubt on the morality and effectiveness of vigilantism in the West or, for that matter, in the South. Vigilantism came to seem almost chivalrous, the terrible yet noble actions of white-hatted knights of Plains and mountains or, perhaps, the terrible yet noble actions of white-robed knights of the Ku Klux Klan. Tales of lynchings hearkened back to an age of honor that seemed dim by the time that Barnes and Raine wrote, an age that bespoke medieval simplicity, when good men fought bad men. Via lynching and terror, good men like Barnes brought the honor of ancients into the present.[89]

9

UNDERSTANDING

If it was not merely a tale of good men defeating bad ones, what was the Rim Country War? How do we define it? What does it teach us? Perhaps the most thoughtful of those who have written about the conflict is Don Dedera, who—informed by his experiences as a reporter in Vietnam—saw in it the "universal human condition of mixed loyalties and misguided impulses." The Pleasant Valley fight boiled up from the "limited volition and infinite disinformation" of participants. "War," he concluded, "is not intellectual design. It is subjective muddle."[1]

Despite missing the occasional detail, Dedera's *A Little War of Our Own: The Pleasant Valley War Revisited* is the most elegant and engrossing book written on the war—or at least the part of it that occurred in Pleasant Valley—yet "subjective muddle" and "universal human condition" are hardly the stuff of history. They are warnings and laments, but they are not analysis. Far from seeking patterns, Dedera concerned himself with events. Though he loosely connected Commodore Perry Owens's shootout in Holbrook with the war, his focus seldom left Pleasant Valley. In the end he saw a feud, not a war. He chronicled growing friction, court battles, and hot lead. Though he called attention to the conflict engendered by free range, he did not discuss the war as an outgrowth of recession and drought. Nor did he see the religious and political dimensions of the war. Nor did he find a struggle between honor and conscience. None of that is meant to diminish his work; it is meant to suggest how many buckets can be fetched from history's well.

If we step back from events in the valley, we see larger patterns. We see multiple causes. We see not the Pleasant Valley War but the Rim Country War. In Pleasant Valley, the war began as a struggle for the range. Small operators such as the Tewksburys came into conflict with big operators, or at least would-be big operators, such as Jim Stinson. Big operators also came into conflict with other big operators. Prosperous and ambitious men—the Daggs brothers, George Newton, J. J. Vosburgh, Jim Stinson—each took a side, or, perhaps, helped create a side to serve their interests. When Tom Graham insisted that the war was caused by "men of money [who] were trying to obtain control of ranches located, for honest purpose, by hard working and honorable boys," he was telling a profound truth.[2]

Frederick Russell Burnham, Boer War hero, friend of Theodore Roosevelt, and a father of boy scouting, confirmed Graham's supposition. Young, poor, and fresh from California, he worked briefly in the Rim Country for a struggling rancher. The rancher, recalled Burnham, was told by the Globe men who financed him that he must take their side—undoubtedly the Tewksbury side—in the war. When he refused, his creditors tried to repossess his cattle. In response, he stealthily drove his animals to a new range but was forced to kill a deputy sent to stop him. To escape prison, he found it necessary to enlist in his creditors' cause. Burnham himself became drawn in on the side of the Grahams, whom he viewed as victims of a conspiracy. "My every turn," he recalled, "was enmeshing me more completely in a network of rustlers, smugglers, and feudists. . . . A cloud hung over me. I moved warily and changed my name often."[3]

One of the *Silver Belt* editors—likely Aaron Hackney—at last talked Burnham into leaving the feud. The editor sent him to Tombstone, where he worked for a cattleman. Burnham came away from the war deeply cynical about powerful men in high places. "I sensed the growing struggle among the officials and politicians," he wrote, "as to whether Arizona should be run by a few great cattle barons or by certain wealthy sheep men backed by interests in the towns." The fighters, he recalled, "were only pawns" in the struggle for the range.[4]

If powerful men provoked war, however, so did honor. Neither Graham nor Burnham—held fast in honor's grip—appreciated their own roles in fomenting violence. Both men placed faith in arms, in assertion, in aggression. Burnham in particular practiced incessantly with pistols. "It was a harsh school of life," he recalled, "yet from this same belt of the West, [Theodore Roosevelt's] Rough Riders were largely recruited" during the Spanish-American War. "All that was really needed was a good cause and good leader to transform outlaws into heroes." The honor of feudists became the honor of patriots.

In the 1880s, however, honor produced no heroes. In the first altercation, when John Gilliland, Stinson's foreman, rode to the Tewksbury ranch and met a storm, the behaviors of honor came into play. Gilliland preferred assertion to conciliation. Or perhaps Ed Tewksbury was the first to choose assertion when he pulled a gun from his pocket. It is impossible to know who drew first. Perhaps both men chose to fight rather than negotiate. Both, it seems, were imbued with honor.

Honor indeed fueled economic competition every bit as much as economic competition fueled honor. Hostilities in turn yielded alliances. Stinson recruited the Grahams to fight the Tewksburys, whereas the Daggs brothers recruited the Tewksburys to fight Stinson. The Daggs brothers had been pushed into that arrangement by the Aztec Land and Cattle Company when it barred sheep from crossing ranges above the Rim. The conflict above the Rim spawned conflict below the Rim.

The war's causes did not end there. The Aztec brought Texas cowboys who, in addition to fighting off sheepherders, fought off Mormons. With the Aztec to back them, cowboys attacked Mormons repeatedly, jumping claims, whipping men, stealing horses, and issuing death threats. Cowboys did not require Aztec directives to take action. Most of them despised Mormons for being polygamists, for being sheepherders, for being dedicated to conscience. Cowboys drank, swore, gambled, frequented prostitutes, shot up towns, and shot one another. Though they and their forebears had been exposed to the tides of evangelism that rolled across the South even before the Civil War, few cowboys—with the intriguing exception of John Payne—were devout Christians. Holbrook, where the Aztec was headquartered, was famous not only for its saloons but also for its lack of a single church.[5] Cowboys engaged in "immoral" behaviors not merely because they were young and wild but because they were dedicated to honor.

Even if cowboys were not pious Christians, the war had a religious flavor. Mormons saw persecution not just from cowboys but also from county officials, New Mexicans, and Aztec managers. In response, Mormons withdrew into their fortress of conscience. Their leaders instructed them to interact with outsiders as little as possible. Some spoke of apocalypse. They described Indians as the battle-ax of the Lord, recalling the prophecies of Brigham Young. They predicted that their enemies—Judge Summer Howard included—would soon die. Yet the Lord was slow to bring justice. By 1886, Mormons were losing their grip on Arizona, driven to desperation by the separate forces of their enemies. They were robbed, attacked, hounded for polygamy, and defeated at the polls by a political ring. Their leaders were threatened with castration and lynching. Meanwhile their dams washed out again and again, forcing the church to pour in resources to save its outposts. Mormon settlers remained desperately impoverished, clinging to one another—to corporatism—as they bobbed up and down in a sea of animus.

The years 1886 and 1887 meanwhile saw the cattle economy come crashing down from the heights of speculative frenzy. With their irrigation, their farms, and their sheep, Mormons were only marginally hurt, but the Aztec was devastated. So were gentile ranchers situated above the Rim, near Holbrook, and below it, in Pleasant Valley. Small-scale rustling, or mavericking, which was widely practiced and seldom prosecuted, now became intolerable. New alliances formed against "criminals." Gentile ranchers and Aztec officials made common cause with Mormons to stop crime and to take over county government.

In Pleasant Valley a similar trend occurred. Each side in the war that broke out there—the Graham faction and the Tewksbury faction—vied to define the other as criminal. Both were correct. Each had likely retaliated against enemies, including one another, via rustling and horse stealing. In 1887, however, when a contingent of Aztec cowboys lined up with the Graham faction—in part because the Aztec-Mormon alliance pushed them out of Apache County—they transformed the war. The Graham side, rightly or wrongly, became associated with the "criminal" campaign to drive out Mormons. They became associated with the Blevins boys and their horse theft "ring"; with John Payne and his brutal assaults; and with Hashknife cowboys who stormed Pleasant Valley. After Stinson had repudiated them, moreover, the Grahams had lost the deep-pocket ally who could finance them and defend them in the press. The Grahams became not feudists but criminals.

Despite their effort to shape stories in the Phoenix papers, the Grahams floundered in the court of opinion. The Tewksbury faction earned better press. In addition to posting a letter attesting to his family's excellent character—signed by forty-eight citizens of Tuscarora, Nevada, where the Tewksburys had resided in the early 1870s—James D. Tewksbury responded quickly and forcefully in the papers to Tom Graham's assertions of innocence. Throughout the war, moreover, Tewksbury supporters—likely George Newton and J. J. Vosburgh—fed information to the Globe paper, the Arizona *Silver Belt*, ensuring its sympathy for the Tewksbury faction. In 1887, at least, the Tewksbury faction held the upper hand in the battle of public relations.[6]

By fall 1887, the Yavapai County sheriff and the territorial governor had come to interpret the war as a match between good men and criminals, implicitly taking the side of the Tewksburys, the moneyed men who backed them, and the Apache County men who decried the reign of hoodlums. With the sympathies of the governor, "good men" came to believe that they had license to make war. That new definition of the war emerged precisely as the governor and his Democratic Party sought Mormon voters with compliments, pardons, and a repeal of the test oath. Suddenly a war in Apache County that pitted Mormons against cowboys, Jews, and Catholic New Mexicans became a war pitting righteousness against evil, with cowboys, Jews, and New Mexicans seemingly on the side of the latter. Mormons now found it within their power to reach out to gentile ranchers, Aztec managers, and Pleasant Valley vigilantes in order to defeat the enemies of law and order. In early 1887, Mormons and their allies unleashed a campaign of terror that stopped, or at least slowed, only after the lynching of Jim Stott, Jim Scott, and Jeff Wilson.

The Rim Country War was not just a Pleasant Valley phenomenon. It extended far beyond the confines of a single valley tucked under the Rim. The war spilled across three counties—Apache, Yavapai, and Gila—each of which added fuel to the flame. To understand the war, we must identify it not as a place-bound feud but as a contagious fever that spread across east-central Arizona. In some ways it was a fever that spread across the whole of cattle country. The same sort of conflict appeared wherever settlers of diverse religious and social and backgrounds—not to mention settlers of diverse economic circumstances and ambitions—contested the range. The basic elements of the war were economic, but they were also religious, ethnic, and racial. To discern those forces, however, is to understand the war's structure, not its meaning.

One way to read the war's meaning is to view it as a "war of incorporation," to use a concept described by Richard Maxwell Brown. Following Brown's model, we might view the vigilantism that ended the war as a middle-class attempt to create order and cement hierarchy. Even those mothers of vigilante movements in the West, the San Francisco Committees of Vigilance of 1851 and 1856, saw businessmen strike out against crime and, more particularly, crime associated with young, single men and immigrant Catholics. Again and again, vigilante movements saw men of business—not necessarily wealthy men, but men who were prosperous and respected—band together to fight what they perceived as outlawry and chaos.[7]

The vigilantism that appeared in Apache and Yavapai counties in 1887 in some ways fits that definition. Prosperous ranchers joined Aztec managers and Mormons in putting down "rustlers" and "horse thieves." Common men—those whom Brown called "incorporation gunfighters" but who might also be called "incorporation lynchers"—killed "criminals" on behalf of the respectable sorts who backed them. We cannot blame the killings solely on the few who carried them out. Powerful men pushed them into action and sheltered them from prosecution. The 1887 campaign of terror was in many ways an act of hegemony by an increasingly self-conscious and assertive elite.

One might argue that Mormons were part of that elite. They, as much as the Aztec, comprised a corporation or, rather, a corporate society. Though among themselves they were socialists, their relations with outsiders were capitalist. Like any profit-driven corporation, Mormons sought to bring wealth to shareholders.

Mormons wanted social stability and control over resources. Gentile ranchers, including Aztec managers, wanted the same thing. After an initial period of conflict, those three constituencies discovered that they could work together. They held common principles. They believed in law and order and hard work. They hated rustlers and horse thieves and embezzlers. In the election of 1886, they became conscious of one another as allies in a struggle to wrest the range from the "criminal" cowboys and New Mexicans who dominated the countryside. Their victory can be interpreted as the triumph of a nascent bourgeoisie over a rural proletariat.

But to read the story thus ignores the fact that most Mormons were laborers. They were resolutely poor. Most owned only a small farm or ranch, often lacking enough water to make a profit. They suffered poverty, to be sure, in the hope of a future boon, when Christ would return or, failing that, a time when they would taste power and wealth. In the late nineteenth century, Mormons nevertheless saw themselves as working people who were forever buffeted by such powerful organizations as the Aztec, the railroad, the territorial government, and the United States government. Mormons were corporatist, yes, but they were also marginal. Their alliance with the Aztec, however, crowned their tenacious efforts to avoid destruction.

In 1889, after the Aztec sold seven sections of land in and around Snowflake and Taylor to Mormon occupants, the company and the church were at peace. "The enmity and ill feeling which existed against us . . . has disappeared," noted the Aztec's annual report for 1889. "We are looked upon as a fixture here, and treated as such." According to some Mormons, the Aztec sought to make amends for the troubles of the 1880s by hiring Mormon cowboys (including Osmer Flake). It also leased land and sold water to Mormons. The relationship was not perfect. Texas cowboys continued to plague the county, causing Mormons to resort again to prayer and fasting in the early 1890s. What resulted, according to Mormons, was the terrible drought of 1893–94, when Aztec cattle died by the thousands. By 1897, the Aztec had decided to get out of the cattle business. The drought drove out other Texans, too, leaving Mormons in possession of the range. The Aztec owned much of the land, but Mormon lessees shared the profits.[8]

Even before the Aztec's catastrophe, the company had made amends with Mormons. Like Aztec managers, Mormons wanted law and order. They opposed drinking and gambling and reckless violence. Aztec managers shared with Mormons a common set of "Yankee" values. Whereas initially the Aztec had pushed its cowboys into conflict with Mormons, in 1886 it, and the prosperous ranchers nearby, allied with Mormons against cowboys (or at least those who were troublesome). That alliance resulted in Commodore Perry Owens's shootout with the

Blevins men and Jonas Brighton's killing of Ike Clanton. It caused several Aztec cowboys—pushed out by their employer—to move south into Pleasant Valley, where they continued to engage in the dramas of honor.

In Pleasant Valley, to be sure, Aztec cowboys did not fight Mormons. They did, however, fight sheepherders. The war against New Mexican sheepherders and the Daggs brothers above the Rim became a war with Indian and "half-breed" sheepherders below the Rim. Cowboys continued to embrace an identity that revolved around honor. They gambled and drank, and most of all, they judged one another's physical courage. To be a man of honor demanded physical assertion, even gunplay. It meant inflicting on one's inferiors the rituals of shaming, whether that meant stealing their horses and cattle, forcing them to "dance" by shooting under their feet, pistol whipping them, cutting cattle marks into their ears, or killing them outright.

Among the ironies of the war was that "good men" used one ritual of shaming—lynching—to stop other rituals of shaming employed by cowboys. When Barnes and Raine described lynchings as "sober and impersonal" and compared them to "the ancient Teuton gathering of freemen," with their careful weighing of guilt and innocence, they masked a profound truth. They denied the primitive, ritualistic nature of vigilantism. Vigilantism was seldom sober and impersonal, nor did vigilantes carefully weigh guilt against innocence, good against bad. The lynching was an act of shaming. It inflicted disgrace. It denied its victims the power of arms, the power of physical assertion. Its meaning was precisely opposite that of the gunfight or the duel, which accorded participants a measure of honor. In the case of Jamie Stott—as in hundreds of lynchings in the South—it involved torture and humiliation. If Stott had any victory, it was in his unwillingness to submit to shame. He refused to confess wrongdoing. He cursed his killers and challenged them to fight. He called on them to address their grievances in a different court of honor, the court of fisticuffs and gunplay, shaming them for their cowardice. He nonetheless died at the end of a rope and remained suspended for several days in mute testimony to his powerlessness. The ritual ended with commemoration—with a warning to others that they would meet the same end—via three bodies, ghastly, dangling from a tree.[9]

The men who inflicted death on Stott, Scott, and Wilson were themselves products of honor. Jesse Ellison and his men learned the behaviors of honor from their cultural homeland of Texas and the South. Jim Houck perhaps learned it in the rough precincts of the Midwest and, subsequently, in the even rougher precincts of the Southwest. What they served, however—wittingly or not—was conscience. The murders of Stott, Scott, and Wilson were part of the campaign launched by Mormons, the Aztec, and gentile ranchers to put down the excesses of cowboy individualism and assertion. Ike and Phin Clanton, with their ethic of freedom, their refusal to submit to orderly life, fell victim to that campaign. So did the Blevins boys. So did John Payne. All were criminals, to be sure, but it is not enough to thus dismiss them. They were products of a culture of honor, a culture predicated on drinking, gambling, and aggression, a culture that taught men to value the respect—or fear—of one's peers above any injunction against killing.

Scholars have defined such behaviors as "preindustrial" and "antibourgeois." In his book on nineteenth-century prize fighting, for example, Elliott Gorn finds drinking, gambling, and physical aggression among working-class men in Northern cities. Gorn describes those behaviors as the basis for an oppositional culture, a culture that defied the middle-class ethics of propriety and achievement through moderation, politeness, and discipline. Unable to climb the social ladder, working-class men—especially Irish immigrants—created their own rules for the attainment of respect and status. Rather than valuing politeness, they valued hard fists, hale courage, and strong drink.[10]

Another scholar, David Roediger, complicates Gorn's thesis, contending that working-class men—and especially Irish immigrants—in fact did assimilate middle-class ethics, ethics he calls "industrial work discipline." Irish immigrants in the urban North, claims Roediger, shucked off preindustrial work habits—or, rather, leisure habits—by associating them with another "inferior" people, blacks. Via blackface minstrelsy—wherein white performers portrayed plantation slaves as ignorant, slothful, and clownish—working-class immigrants learned to associate their own preindustrial norms with a humiliated "other." In consequence, working-class immigrants became more disciplined, more dedicated to success, less apt to drink, gamble, or absent themselves from work. Irish Americans simultaneously acquired a worldview informed by racism, a thing they had not carried in their baggage on arrival. All the while, suggests Roediger, immigrants became ever more enamored of the leisure and freedom displayed by minstrel performers. Minstrels made money by giving audiences a "pornographic" peek into their preindustrial past, a past that members of the audience both rejected and longed for.[11]

Preindustrial norms, however, were not solely the burden of Irish Americans. Hard drinking was a national phenomenon. Until the 1830s, asserts William Rohrabaugh, the U.S. was "an alcoholic republic." In urban areas and in the countryside, Americans imbibed great quantities of ale, cider, and spirits. Middle-class reformers of the Jacksonian era, however, succeeded in cutting per capita consumption by more than half.[12] Temperance was most powerful in the industrializing North, though it entered the South even before the Civil War. As a Southern middle class emerged in the second half of the nineteenth century, its members, too, preached against drink and espoused prohibition, often with success. Texas cowboys, it seems, were not part of that middle class, though they had links to it. Rather than embrace an evangelical movement that repudiated the "sins" of cursing, gambling, drinking, and fighting, most cowboys steered clear of churches and held tight to honor.

The values associated with honor, then, were not just a cowboy phenomenon, not just a Southern phenomenon, not just a rural phenomenon. They appeared in the Northern countryside and even in Northern cities. But they did not appear there without challenge. The mores of conscience transformed the North in the first half of the nineteenth century. We might call those mores "capitalist" or "bourgeois" or "middle class." We might call them "industrial work discipline." Certainly they followed the lines of industrial development. Certainly they served the interests of capitalists, who desired an obedient and industrious workforce. Certainly they were promoted by the middle class, which was overwhelmingly evangelical and Protestant. But to identify those mores solely as by-products of class is to deny their power. The mores associated with conscience were not restricted to one class, one gender, or one race. Though they were often middle class, male, and white, they could also be working class, female, and black.

If minstrels taught Americans to identify blacks with indolence and childishness, abolitionists taught Americans that blacks, too, could be creatures of conscience. Frederick Douglass, for example, appealed to audiences by criticizing the evils of drink and praising the powers of discipline. He proved that he, no less than, say, Benjamin Franklin, could be a self-directed individual, a creature of will, a creature of restraint. Douglass embodied the ethics of conscience, ethics that had the power to cut across divisions of class, race, and gender, creating new alliances, new blocs, new orders. Honor could accomplish the same thing.

If conscience was not merely bourgeois, neither was honor merely "antibourgeois." An individual could seek both profit and honor. He could be capitalist and gunfighter, disciplined worker and heavy drinker. Honor did not preclude men from seeking financial reward, nor did honor invariably serve as antithesis to work. As James Oakes has shown, Southern planters—even those who espoused honor—were every bit as ambitious to make money as Northern entrepreneurs.[13] Nor were Texas cowboys opposed to profit. They wanted to make money. But they did not measure one another solely via the yardstick of wealth. They were not necessarily "preindustrial" or "antibourgeois" but neither did they orient their lives around industry and capital. They embraced a worldview that demeaned institutions and celebrated the individual. We might then call them "antistatist," "antihegemonic," or "radical individualists." More to the point, they were creatures of honor.

If conscience tugged at cowboys, if conscience defeated them, the same process worked in reverse. Conscience people—Mormons, established ranchers, Aztec managers—were attracted to honor. Perhaps they saw honor much as Irish immigrants saw their preindustrial past. Honor, that is, could function as "pornography," a tabooed set of behaviors that held enormous—and illicit—appeal to men held in the grip of propriety. Drinking, gambling, fighting, killing . . . all promised liberation.

To understand the force of honor, we might begin by considering the arguments of Brian Roberts vis-à-vis the California gold rush. Roberts, looking at the letters and journals of argonauts from New England, interprets the gold rush as a holiday from conscience, a carnivalesque event. To go to the gold rush was to attend a circus. Americans described both as "seeing the elephant." In the goldfields, it seems, straitlaced New England men entered a world of gambling, drinking, and whoring. The behaviors of honor transfixed them, at least temporarily, much as they transfix students at fraternities (and sororities) today. Or, as Roberts explains, much as Harley-Davidson motorcycles transfix technicians who become leather-clad bikers on weekends.[14] Honor and conscience could be, and were, opposite sides of a social divide, but they could operate in tandem, as a yin and yang of behavior. They could also mix and merge in new ways, becoming almost invisible as distinct social patterns. And they could produce irony.

The first irony of the Rim Country War was the use of honor to put down honor. Jesse Ellison, leader of the vigilantes, represented the honor culture of the West (and the South), yet so did his enemies, the Hashknife cowboys who allied with the Grahams. Ellison drew on one ritual of honor—the lynching, with its connotation of shaming—to put down other forms of honor associated with "immoral" behaviors.

If he represented honor, then, Ellison likewise represented conscience. He probably did not see himself as an opponent of gambling and drinking and braggadocio. Nor did he see himself as an opponent of physical assertion. But he did see himself as a bringer of the law and order that would create the stable economic and cultural universe necessary for conscience to flourish. He did not necessarily agree with Mormons on the particulars of good behavior (though he tried to stop drinking). Unlike Hashknife cowboys, however, he did not oppose Mormon moral hegemony. Ellison's honor—his willingness to lynch bad men—could serve the ends of Mormon conscience. That is one irony of the Rim Country War, and it complicates viewing the war as a simple battle between conscience and honor. Conscience and honor mingled in the war, becoming woven into a braid of complexity.

The war's ironies do not end there. In murdering Jamie Stott, Mormon and non-Mormon vigilantes thought they were attacking criminality. Mormons associated Stott with the culture of honor of the cowboys who jumped Mormon claims, stole Mormon stock, and assaulted Mormon men. They equated Stott with the Blevins boys, with Red Holcomb, with the Grahams. In the Mormon mind, Stott was a figure of violence, a man who tried to ride down William Flake, gun in hand, and who threatened to murder Zach Decker. Stott became blurred with John Payne and Andy Cooper.

Unknowingly, Stott promoted that idea. He came west to find adventure. He was the product of a Northern culture that wore, at times, a straitjacket of conscience. Men like Stott, or like Theodore Roosevelt, longed to escape a life they found narrow, weak, confining, and emasculating. They liberated themselves by becoming cowboys. They came to value physical assertion every bit as much, even more than, Texans. Roosevelt earned his claim to honor by brawling with those who accused him of being a tenderfoot and a weakling. He also proved his bona fides by joining a posse bent on putting down rustling and by attempting to join a party of vigilantes.[15] Stott earned his claim to honor by joining Hashknife cowboys in their war against sheepherders. Both Stott and Roosevelt claimed honor, moreover, via hunting and horsemanship. Yet both men retained middle-class attitudes toward drinking, gambling, cursing, and moral deportment. Both became hybrids of honor and conscience, creatures of a post–Civil War longing to recapture an imagined manliness from the past.

Even if he made fun of Mormons for their poor cowboying skills, then, Stott surely approved of the Mormon refusal to gamble or curse or drink. When Mormons sanctioned the lynching of Stott, they sanctioned the murder of a man who shared many of their values. They believed they were destroying a criminal; they were in fact destroying an ally. Conscience killed conscience. That, too, was one of the ironies of the war.

The Rim Country War transcends any simple dichotomy between honor and conscience. At times, honor and conscience were arrayed against each other. At other times, they mixed and mingled. The question that comes from that observation is which of them won? Which prevailed? Did Rim Country society emerge from the war with a bent toward conscience? Or, with the lynchings that ended the war, did it emerge with a bent toward honor? There is no easy answer. Both honor and conscience won the war; both honor and conscience lost the war.

After the lynchings of Stott, Scott, and Wilson, one last drama remained. On August 2, 1892, Ed Tewksbury and John Rhodes ambushed Tom Graham on the streets of Tempe. Some five years earlier, Graham had married Annie

Melton, who was more than a decade his junior. The couple had then established a farm in Tempe, where Annie gave birth to a daughter.[16] Just as he had begun to prosper, Graham's life came to an end.

Before the assassination, John Rhodes had married Mary Ann Crigler (or "Crigger") Tewksbury, the widow of John Tewksbury. Rhodes may have decided to participate in the assassination out of fear that Graham and his bodyguard, Charlie Duchet, were plotting against the Tewksbury family, which now included Rhodes himself. Rumors swirled of threatening letters finding their way to Tewksbury partisans.[17]

In the legal melee that followed the assassination, Rhodes and Tewksbury retained some of the most expensive lawyers in Arizona. Possibly Rim Country cattlemen, including Jesse Ellison—despite being deep in debt—mortgaged cattle to pay the fees. The Daggs brothers, too, may have contributed. In the 1920s Peru Daggs commented that that the "Tonto Basin War cost me ninety thousand dollars. General Sherman said 'War is hell.' He was right." The war also cost the brothers access to Pleasant Valley, which saw no sheep between 1887 and 1891. "The best laid plans o' mice and men," crowed the *Herald* after discerning the Daggs's loss, "aft gang aglae."[18]

For settlers who remained in Pleasant Valley, however, the war ended in victory. The first order of business after Tom Graham's death was to celebrate by holding a cowboy tournament (a "rodeo" in today's language). "It was a great gathering," wrote L. J. Horton, "and will long be remembered, coming as it did at the close of the five years' struggle." Horton himself had left the valley during the war, returning to find that his herd of 211 cows had shrunk to one. He blamed the Grahams for stealing 100 of his cattle, though he did not speculate on what happened to the others.[19] He participated in the festive rodeo nonetheless. With its displays of physical assertion, its wrestling matches pitting man against beast, its call for stoic endurance of pain—its absence of sympathy for man or beast—the cowboy tournament was a fitting tribute to the power of honor. As early as 1884, meanwhile, both Prescott and Payson, a hamlet just west of Pleasant Valley, were touting their own cowboy tournaments. Both claim to have hosted the first, and the oldest, annual rodeo in history.

Apache County Mormons, too, came to celebrate honor. In the late 1880s, when James Flake was on his mission in Europe, he attended a performance of Buffalo Bill's Wild West. He reported to his family that the Wild West was "one of the things that he possibly enjoyed the most," explaining that "he would have felt more at home in a pair of chaps, a Stetson hat and some high heeled boots, sitting in a saddle on one of those prancing horses, than he did in his . . . Prince Albert coat and tall silk hat." Osmer Flake displayed a similar bent. When he rode into Provo, Utah, to enroll at Brigham Young Academy, recalled Apostle Francis Lyman, Osmer tied his "half-wild" horse to a hitching post, removed his chaps, and entered the building with spurs jingling. He had forgotten, however, to remove his gun belt and had to go back outside to loop it over his saddle horn.[20]

Osmer Flake was by no means alone as a Mormon cowboy. That an apostle remembered the splash Flake made at Brigham Young Academy, however, showed how odd the accoutrements of cowboy honor appeared amid the staid piety of Provo. Even back home in Snowflake, Osmer's cowboy appearance seemed strange and threatening to old-time Mormons, causing him to lose the affection of a girl he was courting. Her father refused to let her continue to see such a "wild cowboy."[21]

Yet Osmer Flake represented the Mormon future, or at least part of it. Despite their dedication to farming, Arizona Mormons found that ranching provided a livelihood. In the 1890s, moreover, the Aztec began to hire Mormons — including Osmer Flake — as cowboys, creating a veritable genre of folkloric stories about Mormon boys showing their toughness (and their conscience) to Texas waddies. In neighboring Graham County, too — as well as in southern Utah — Mormons created economic and social alliances with Texas cowboys, including Texas idiom and dress.[22]

Perhaps the greatest testimonial to Mormon honor came via the induction of William Flake into the National Cowboy Hall of Fame in Oklahoma City in 1959. "Dozens of cattle-raising families . . . would have given most anything" to have been chosen, explained Marshall Flake in a tribute to his grandfather, but it was William Flake whom the Cattle Growers of Arizona had nominated, thanks to the recommendation of a gentile rancher who had read Osmer Flake's biography of his father. William Flake was inducted not because of his devotion to conscience but because he was a town builder, a rancher, and "a stabilizer of the Northern region of Arizona."[23] What "stabilizer" meant went unsaid.

The choice was appropriate, particularly given Flake's obsession with horses. If she asked her husband to gather eggs, recalled Lucy Flake, he would saddle his horse to do it. Flake was not unlike eighteenth-century planters who, it was said, would travel miles on foot to catch a saddle horse in order to ride a short distance to the church, the courthouse, or a horse race. In both South and West, to sit astride a horse was to be a man of honor. Lesser men walked; honorable men rode; powerful men bred horses for racing.[24]

Flake's sons shared their father's obsession. "It is doubtful if anyone ever loved horses and horse racing," testified one Flake descendant, "more than the Flake boys." Perhaps not surprisingly, the boys — along with their father — bet on horse races, a sin for which they received church censure.[25] The Flakes were Mormons, but they did not forget the forms of honor from their family's past—and from their present.

At the same time that the Flakes promoted cowboy values, Evans Coleman, who had grown up in the White Mountains, wrote humorous stories of Mormon cowboying in which he discussed his own indulgence in petty rustling and drinking sprees in St. Johns. Most Mormons eschewed alcohol, but they made allowances for Jack Mormons such as Coleman, who did not. They also made allowances for Coleman's other displays of cowboy honor, as when he and his brother, Prime, rode bucking horses into a crowd of churchgoers. After receiving a scolding, they left home, but they did not leave the church.[26] Indeed, they went on missions, during which each of them again testified to their cowboy honor.

During his mission in the South just after the turn of the century, Evans Coleman sported a cowboy hat, displayed his horsemanship by riding a bucking mule, and carried photos of cowboy life to show to potential converts. His brother, Prime, meanwhile, went on a mission to England, where he—like James Flake before him—managed to attend Buffalo Bill's Wild West. When Buffalo Bill supposedly offered a hundred dollars to any man brave enough to ride a treacherous mustang, Prime accepted. Realizing that Prime was a real cowboy, Buffalo Bill declined to let him ride but invited him to dinner. Years later, Prime reached the pinnacle of honor by getting into a gunfight. Though shot four times, he managed to inflict a mortal wound on his opponent.[27]

Evans Coleman got into no gunfights but did serve in midlife as a "home missionary." At Geronimo and Fort Thomas, he preached to "old time cowboys and freighters," some Mormon and some gentile. "I don't criticize them, nor ramp on them," he wrote. "I talk their language and know their ways of life and about what they think. . . . I talk Bible to them, and prove to them by the Bible that the Lord has always, beginning with Cain and Able [sic] favored the cattle man." "Wasn't Abraham one of the biggest, if not the biggest cattle man of his time?" he asked with a rhetorical wink. In comparison to Abraham, he conjectured, "I expect the Hash Knife outfit would be a milk-pen dogy bunch."[28]

If Coleman converted any cowboys, however, they also converted him. Before he died in 1954, Coleman insisted on being buried with his spurs on. He would need them, he said, to ride to heaven "on a paint horse with a white spot and a glass eye." On his arrival at Jake Armijo's saloon in the sky, he proposed to hitch "old paint" and go inside. No one need "guess what will happen next," he concluded.[29]

The fact that some Mormons adopted cowboy dress and cowboy mannerisms did not mean that all Mormons embraced cowboy honor. They did, however, make an accommodation with honor. Few gave way to drink, gambling, prostitutes, and violence. Some, however, gave way to toughness, bluster, and vigilantism, behaviors that gave them cachet in a twentieth-century Arizona dedicated to tourism.

Mormon accommodation to cowboy honor was part of a larger movement by Mormons into mainstream American life. Reacting to the catastrophes of the 1880s—in particular the Edmunds and Edmunds-Tucker Anti-Polygamy acts—the church repudiated polygamy, urged members to partake in the two-party system, and ceased to direct Utah's economic development. In addition—despite counseling members to take no side in the Civil War—the church renounced selective pacifism during the Spanish-American War of 1898, insisting that "loyalty to the nation [is] a necessary corollary of active church membership." The church's loyalty in the First World War, when many Arizona Mormons served overseas, further improved the church's image. By the 1930s, surveys indicated that most Americans for the first time viewed Mormonism positively.[30]

By emphasizing their cowboy heritage, Arizona Mormons emphasized their similarity with Western non-Mormons. Though they remained a corporate society—especially via the rise of women's relief societies and the reinvigoration of men's priesthood quorums—the endorsement of cowboy culture and cowboy values made the Saints more accepted in gentile communities.

If the conflict of the 1880s made some Mormons into cowboys, however, it doomed honor in other ways. The war had "one good effect," wrote James McClintock, Arizona state historian in the early twentieth century, which was in "establishing a bloody peak record that hardly could be approached." That bloody peak represented the high point of honor and, at the same time, "the conclusion of the 'rustler' history of Arizona." Though animus between cattlemen and sheepherders persisted, "the day of the professional frontier desperado had passed. It became unfashionable to try to start a herd with two work steers and a running iron, while the legislature declared against indiscriminate carrying of weapons that for years had been borne ostensibly for protection from Indians that no longer were feared."[31]

From McClintock's point of view, the aftermath of the war was the triumph of civilization. Order prevailed over chaos; conscience over criminality. The freewheeling culture of Texas cowboys died in the Rim Country War, or at least came closer to its end. So did the petty—and sometimes not so petty—acts of mavericking, rustling, and horse stealing come to a halt in subsequent decades, though not immediately after the lynchings that supposedly ended them. Such practices had been widely accepted among cowboys like the Clantons and Blevinses, as well as the Grahams and the Tewksburys. By the early twentieth century, they were accepted no more. Throughout the West, cattlemen strove in the 1880s and 1890s to put down old cultural patterns that reduced their profits and challenged their authority. The detectives and vigilantes whom they hired to accomplish those ends were a trans-Western phenomenon. They appeared everywhere in cattle country, doing service to elites who controlled stock associations and legislatures.

At the same time that stock detectives roamed the range, the Arizona legislature moved to tighten laws relating to the transportation and sale of livestock. To stop rustling, the territory's Live Stock Sanitary Commission inspectors—Will Barnes was one—were expected to certify the ownership of any cows to be shipped in or out of the territory or to be killed for sale. The legislature also prohibited the sale of any calf without a brand, adding that the wound from the brand had to be healed before a transaction could occur. The legislature then established a territory-wide brand registration system so that no two parties could register the same brand in different counties.[32]

Equally important in putting an end to the honor culture of cowboys was legislation barring the "indiscriminate carrying of weapons," in the words of McClintock. Those regulations helped stamp out the sort of ritual humiliations that cowboys had used against Mormons—pistol whippings, beatings, firing shots to make men "dance."[33] Honor and the long train of violence in its wake now receded into an "uncivilized" but romantic past, at least in theory. In practice, rustling and gun fighting continued through the 1890s, though they declined rapidly in the twentieth century.

Yet conscience, too, suffered a blow. Despite the intention of Mormons to avoid warfare and bloodshed, despite their prayers that their enemies' hearts would soften, despite their hopes that rocks would prevail over bullets, Mormons turned to violence. They did so probably with the sanction of Aztec management and certainly with the sanction of smaller but well-established cattlemen such as Will Barnes. They elected a gunslinger to be sheriff, a man who probably helped coordinate the activities of such stock detectives and killers as Jonas Brighton, Hook Larson, and Jim Houck. Conscience men put honor men in their service. Conscience bowed to honor. In the aftermath of their campaign of terror, Mormons and gentiles alike celebrated the murderous violence that supposedly ended the reign of criminals.

Honor and conscience danced a strange minuet in the Rim Country War, parting, embracing, pushing, vying to lead. What emerged was a hybrid of the two, a hybrid that Zane Grey and a stable of Western writers would present to a national readership in the twentieth century. Novelists, historians, and their broad swath of readers in cities, towns, farms, and ranches throughout the nation drew a moral lesson—a normative lesson—from the Western experience, a lesson that invoked and commented on honor and conscience and, through those prisms, revisited race, class, and gender.

Modern academics sometimes reduce history to the latter categories, as if the phenomena of the centuries can be divided among three great drawers in the files of history. If race, class, and gender are constructed forms of identity, however, they are also constructed modes of inquiry. They are not and have never been the sole ways that people define themselves. Honor and conscience have lives of their own. They—with other forces—chart social identity and social destiny, creating allegiances, choices, ways of viewing the world. They sometimes transcend class, race, and gender, shaping and ordering those discourses much as an artist draws lines on a canvas before applying paint.

To bring the discussion from the abstract to the specific, consider the groups who played a role in the Rim Country War. Mormons—men and women alike—defined themselves in relation to conscience. Texans defined themselves in relation to honor. Wives and mothers, to be sure, often opposed their menfolk's behavior. To some extent, honor defined Texan manliness, whereas conscience defined Texan womanliness. Yet even wives and mothers could subscribe to the codes of honor by teaching their sons to value physical assertion. Honor could define separate roles for men and women, but it could also transcend those roles. The codes of honor, like the codes of conscience, could even transcend race—thus Ed Tewksbury's readiness to challenge William Gladden to what appears to have been more a duel than a gunfight, complete with Tewksbury's ritualistic slaps to Gladden's face. Despite his mixed-race parentage, Tewksbury used the codes of honor to fashion his social identity.

To fashion identity from honor, however, did not bring Ed Tewksbury into the fold of a homogeneous Western society. The distinct social groups that entered Arizona in the 1870s and 1880s moved in separate orbits around honor or conscience, orbits that pulled against one another's trajectories. Conflict was almost inevitable as groups vied to define norms and customs and laws of the land. In that process, they began to merge, flowing into a single cultural orbit that might be called "Western identity." Though that identity came in part from the triumph of Mormon conscience over cowboy honor, it also flowed from the bedrock of conflict itself, when good men used guns and ropes to defeat bad ones. Groups that once fought for cultural dominion at last formed a common identity forged on the righteousness of conscience and the necessity for honor to defend it.

A few settlers meanwhile continued to sympathize with the "criminal" Grahams even after their destruction. The first man to produce a history of the Pleasant Valley conflict, Earl Forrest—a Rim Country cowboy and forest ranger whose *Arizona's Dark and Bloody Ground* appeared in 1936—depicted the Grahams as victims. The Grahams were done in, he insisted, by the mixed-blood Tewksburys and their "savage" inability to forgive a wrong. George Shute, in his brief account of the war, suggested the same thing. So, more recently, has Leland Hanchett, who theorizes that the Tewksburys' sense of shame and inferiority about their racial heritage led them toward aggression.[34]

What none of the Graham sympathizers, past or present, seem to fathom is the power of honor itself. They suggest *not* that the Grahams fell victim to their own predisposition to resolve conflict via bloodshed. They merely suggest that the Grahams and their allies were more sinned against than sinning, that they were fighting savages, that they were bested by treachery. The moral is not that the Grahams and the Tewksburys brought the war on themselves; the moral is that the wrong side prevailed.

What in fact prevailed was mutual destruction born of honor. There was nothing inevitable about the war. In countless places—even in the West—competition does not beget combat.[35] What created the Rim Country War was the willingness, even eagerness, of Rim Country men to fight. War came from honor. All sides—Tewksburys, Grahams, Mormons, New Mexicans, Texas cowboys—partook.

Part Three

LEGACY

WATER ON THE FIRES

To tell the story of a war but not its aftermath—as historians are apt to do—is to tell half a story. Tensions between sheepherders and cattlemen; between big operators and small operators; between Mormons and cowboys; between Mormons and New Mexicans; and between mixed-blood men and whites did not disappear after the war. But they softened. New men arrived. New institutions emerged. Progressive reform came to Arizona in the form of the U.S. Forest Service. The national quest to rationalize and conserve natural resources led to new regulations on the ground. Those regulations made the Rim Country a more pacific place. Change came not solely from above, however; change came from the Rim Country itself. It was Rim Country men whom the Forest Service recruited to make its new rules. Rim Country men—veterans of the war, though not fighters—shaped the Forest Service every bit as much as the Forest Service shaped Arizona. With their guidance, the Forest Service poured water on the fires.

Even before the rise of Progressive reform, Rim Country conflict had died down. In the 1890s, competition had given way to a cooperative model brought by one Hezekiah James Ramer, a man named for a Hebrew king. Ramer entered the Rim Country six days after Andy Cooper's death. With an absentee partner named Joe Nash, he had bought the Blevins ranch at Canyon Creek, supposedly having haggled with Cooper himself. Unlike Cooper, Ramer was not much of a cowboy. When once he tried to brand a bull, recalled settlers, Ramer put the mark on the wrong side of the animal, then vented it (crossed it out) and put it on the right side but in the wrong place. He vented the second brand and tried again, now putting the mark upside down. Then he turned the job over to his hired men.[1]

His cowboy skills notwithstanding, Ramer earned friends. He kept an "open house for all comers" and was "always . . . ready and willing to stake his friends to money and credit." Frontier hospitality thrived on Ramer's ranch, though bad men took advantage of his goodness. Soon after he came to Canyon Creek, according to a Mormon observer, Ramer had run-ins with Stott, Scott, and Wilson, who supposedly asked him to let them put stolen horses in his corral. On the third such occasion, he called them thieves and warned them of their fate. Indeed he did not stop there; he actively created the fate that he warned of. Like his friend Jesse Ellison, Ramer became a vigilante.[2] The story of Ramer's run-ins with Stott, Scott, and Wilson, however, is dubious. Perhaps the tale became confused with Ramer's attempt, two decades later, to drive out another group of "rustlers." The story nevertheless illustrates how important Ramer became in Rim Country lore.

Sporting a pointy Vandyke, wool trousers (never Levi's) stuffed into custom-made boots, and always wearing a tie, even when visiting roundups, Ramer became "one of the largest buyers of cattle in Arizona." On his own range he kept only eight hundred to a thousand "mostly wild" cows in the early 1890s, though the number soon grew. Shortly after George Newton's death in 1892, Ramer bought Newton's Pleasant Valley ranch for ten thousand dollars. He also bought the Pleasant Valley spreads of George Wilson and J. F. Montgomery. Ultimately Ramer claimed 768 acres as his own and grazing rights to tens of thousands more.[3]

More important than Ramer's spread were those of his neighbors. Year after year, he circulated among his fellow ranchers, buying cattle and shipping them out. Single buys entailed thousands of head.[4] Though he had not set out to control the range, Ramer became a cattle baron. Small operators, rather than competing against him, became his suppliers. In effect, they were his foremen; he was their manager. Individualism gave way to cooperation.

Perhaps because he came from Texas by way of New Mexico—where he had played a minor role in the Lincoln County War—Ramer was no stranger to honor. Long after the Rim Country storm had blown over, he continued to carry a large-caliber rifle and a Colt revolver. At home, he kept his guns conspicuously atop his desk. In 1909, when several "rustlers" asked him for work, Ramer picked up a gun and commanded them to leave. They complied. When on another occasion a bully in a Holbrook saloon taunted Ramer for his small stature, he replied that he had already killed two men and would happily kill a third. At the same time, Ramer proved to be a ready diplomat, ever willing to play the fiddle from dusk to dawn at dances.[5]

Though Duett Ellison called Ramer "the most tiresome man of business that I ever met," he gained admiration from her father, Jesse Ellison, as well as from Mormons above the Rim, who freighted goods to Ramer's ranch and to Pleasant Valley. In the person of Ramer, honor persisted in the Rim Country, but it was not the honor of Hashknife cowboys. It was an abbreviated honor, an honor attached to personal dignity and physical assertion but not to drinking, gambling, and cursing. It was the sort of honor that Mormons had come to value. According to one Mormon, Ramer "was sent . . . in answer to the Lord's prayer."[6]

Making the range peaceful, however, required more than a business model. It required government. In particular, it required Albert Potter and Will Barnes, Rim Country ranchers who, in the early twentieth century, became the Forest Service's first and second chiefs of grazing. Both realized that free range could no longer be free.

Potter, born in 1859 in Amador County, California, traveled to Apache County in 1883 to cure himself of "incipient tuberculosis." With a partner, he carved out a small ranch on Silver Creek just below Woodruff. By 1887, he was tracking supposed horse thieves, suggesting that he, like Barnes, had become part of the "cleanup." A few years later, he served as Apache County treasurer. After drought wiped out his cattle in 1894, he began herding sheep. When President William McKinley raised tariffs on wool, Potter became prosperous. His life changed again when in 1900 he guided Gifford Pinchot, the noted forester, during his survey of the Arizona range. Whereas Pinchot met Potter's standard for grit by riding without complaint, Potter met Pinchot's standard for intelligence. Their camaraderie cemented, Pinchot appointed Potter in 1901 as a grazing expert in his Division of Forestry of the Department of the Interior. In 1905, when Pinchot's Division of Forestry moved to the Department of Agriculture, Potter went with it, becoming inspector of grazing for the U.S. Forest Service.[7]

Pinchot put Potter in charge precisely because Potter knew the West. Potter "was an analyst and interpreter of western tradition, precedent and psychology," explained Paul Roberts, an early Forest Service ranger. Potter's Rim Country experiences made him ideal for the job. Competition for range, recalled Potter, had "degenerated into a struggle in which only the fittest survived, and the permanent good of the industry was sacrificed to individual greed. Class was arrayed against class—the cowman against the sheepman, the big owner against the little one—and might ruled more often than right. Deadlines stretched their threat-

Albert Potter (far right) rode with Apache County posses and served as county
treasurer before entering the U.S. Forest Service. The others shown here—Joseph
Woods, Jeff Tribit, Nat Greer, and Hyrum Hatch (left to right)—battled New Mexican
sheepherders in the 1880s. Greer and Woods were also members of the Apache County
Stock Growers Association in 1886–87 when it hired Jonas Brighton.
Courtesy of Arizona State Library, Archives and Public Records,
History and Archives Division, Phoenix, no. 97-9493.

ening lengths across the country, jealously guarded by armed men; battles were fought and lives sacrificed; untold thousands of animals were slaughtered in the fight for the range."[8]

"No class of men deplored this state of affairs more than the stockmen themselves," insisted Potter, yet he knew they would not welcome regulation. He and his fellow Forest Service officials would have to cajole, lobby, and proselytize. To succeed demanded "religious" attendance at the meetings of livestock associations, where ranchers would listen to Potter's proposals and fire back their own. Their conversations, recalled a Forest Service official, "were tinged with salt and sulphur, and the rich idiom of the Old West poured out less often in prose than in blank verse."[9] Without Forest Service oversight, however, ranchers would have no arbitrator. Overgrazing would continue to tax the range. Conflict would spill into the twentieth century. Whatever goodwill existed toward the Forest Service nevertheless diminished with each new rule.

As early as 1897—under the auspices of the old Division of Forestry—the government initiated a permit system for forest lands. Ranchers' reactions were "lurid," said Will Barnes. On January 1, 1906, came something even more detestable: grazing fees. "Wow!" wrote Barnes, "how we [ranchers] did raise our voices in loud protest!" "What irked us," he explained, "was the idea of having to pay a single penny for what we westerners felt was ours by right of conquest." If the rangers tried to collect, threatened some ranchers, they would be lynched.[10]

Ranchers took the Forest Service to court, arguing that no federal agency could make regulations and charge fees without explicit authorization from Congress. Ranchers also sued to bar the Forest Service from keeping livestock off unfenced federal range. Both cases wound their way to the Supreme Court, ending in victory for the government. In 1917, Arizona ranchers attacked the Forest Service again, demanding that Congress place federal lands under the control of state authorities. Congress refused, giving the Forest Service a decisive victory.[11]

The loss of a few battles did not mean submission. Cattlemen merely found ways to escape rules. Often they hid animals from rangers, who counted them for purposes of determining grazing fees. "The average stockman," explained a Rim Country ranger, "looked at the grazing fee exactly as he did at his taxes, that it was perfectly allowable to beat the Government out of every cent possible." Government attempts to enforce rules, moreover, caused ranchers to invoke honor.[12]

When Morton Cheney, a Tonto National Forest ranger, invited one of the offenders to a meeting, the man "came . . . pretty heavily armed." He "had quite a reputation," recalled Cheney. After the tense meeting ended, Cheney turned to his partner to ask what he would have done "if that man had pulled one of those guns." His partner assured him that he would have made a new door in the wall

Albert Potter (lower right) served in 1905 on a U.S. Forest Service commission that drew up a handbook of "use rules" for forests. Courtesy of the Forest History Society.

in his haste to run away. Running away, however, was not always possible. When another Tonto ranger, Fred Croxen, approached the home of a rancher named Quail, Quail called him a trespasser and tried to shoot him. Croxen fired back, killing Quail. A coroner's jury declared it "justifiable homicide." Apparently fearful that Quail's friends would seek vengeance, Croxen asked for a transfer.[13]

Resistance elsewhere took different forms. Mormon ranchers in the White Mountains—the far eastern edge of the Rim Country—on at least one occasion cut drift fences and destroyed gates that were intended to restrict the movements of cattle in the forest reserve. When the ranger confronted them, they bragged— inaccurately—that they had taken the range from Indians and would not be told where to run their stock. Unmoved, the ranger proceeded to drive eight hundred horses and fifteen to sixteen hundred cattle out of the restricted range before fixing the fences. He also took more violent measures, shooting some of the trespassing horses. In retaliation, someone shot his wife's saddle horse. When another ranger shot to death some two hundred range horses that were grazing illegally on reserve land near Pinedale, a group of cowboys—apparently Mormons—captured him and administered a beating.[14]

If rangers were victims of honor they were also participants in it. In Arizona, most of them carried guns. Early rangers, noted Fred Winn, were "men with the bark on." They were required to have "an intimate knowledge of the country" and had "to be able to take care of themselves and their horses, . . . stand severe physical hardships, live under any conditions, prepare their own food, talk the language of the natives, and engage in combat when the occasion arose."[15]

To staff its ranks with such men, the Forest Service recruited some of the very individuals it was attempting to regulate. Cowboys, gunmen, and lumberjacks worked alongside clerks, clergymen, and college graduates. Almost invariably, the rangers were under thirty, high-spirited, and energized by the "crusading spirit" of Gifford Pinchot.[16]

Paid between sixty and ninety dollars a month—two to three times the wages of a cowboy—rangers held high status in their communities despite grassroots resistance to the rules they enforced. Working as an assistant ranger in the Crook Forest Reserve, which encompassed the Sierra Ancha, F. Lee Kirby reported his salary to be seventy-five dollars a month. When Osmer Flake took a job as a ranger in 1908, he got a higher wage. His earnings came to eleven hundred dollars a year.[17]

Much of the work involved conservation. To ameliorate overgrazing near waterholes, rangers built stock tanks. They also rotated grazing pastures, built fences, seeded the range, classified timber lands, and—unwisely—poisoned varmints and predators. Meanwhile they proselytized on the dangers of overgrazing. "Accomplishments in improvement of range conditions," reflected Roberts, "were greater during the period 1905 to 1912 than in any similar period before that time or since."[18]

Perhaps rangers' most important undertaking was settling disputes. Even in the early twentieth century, recalled ranger Roscoe Willson, "cowboys were constantly threatening the sheep herders." As late as 1904, a cowboy turned goat herder named Zech Booth—already a convicted felon—murdered a Mormon sheepman and his Mexican herder as they moved their animals across the flank of the Sierra Ancha. Booth was convicted and hanged. To head off new wars, meanwhile, both cattlemen and sheepmen looked to the Forest Service. "When the sheepmen and cattlemen could not agree among themselves upon a division of the range," explained Albert Potter, "they left it up to the Forest Service men."[19]

To reduce frictions, rangers barred "tramp herds" of sheep from crossing government land and set limits on how many sheep could use the range. They also created "driveways," or extended routes, that sheep could pass over when moving to winter ranges in the desert or to summer ranges in the mountains. That solution gave way to another when sheepmen began moving animals in trucks. Finding that animus persisted into the 1920s, the Forest Service redrew allotments entirely so as to separate sheep from cattle.[20]

On the whole, the rangers and the Forest Service were more sympathetic to cattlemen than to sheepmen, which helps explain why cattlemen sometimes supported the service. Sheepmen complained bitterly of prejudice, especially when Forest Service officials excluded sheep and goats from grazing on the watershed of newly created Roosevelt Lake in the Tonto Basin. Despite the complaints, old battles diminished. By 1913, Will Barnes could testify that "conflicts have been avoided; depleted ranges have been restored, and it is the boast of the Forest Service that not a single hostile shot has been fired between the two interests, nor any stock maliciously killed on the National Forests, since they were established."[21]

Negotiating an end to cattle and sheep wars was only part of the Forest Service's mission. It also found itself charged with negotiating an end to conflicts between big operators and small ones. Relative to the Aztec Land and Cattle Company, Potter and Barnes had themselves been small operators. They understood how easily big operations could flood the range with animals, making it impossible for small operators to hold their own. The two men—like the president who employed them, Theodore Roosevelt—also endorsed the idea that small operators brought progress. By monopolizing the range, big operators seemed to retard the formation of towns, schools, and churches. Most Americans, indeed, identified big cattle operations as merely a stage in the West's development. They might be tolerated and even celebrated in the short-term, but they must give way to "civilization."[22]

To advance the national interest, the Forest Service directed rangers not only to promote conservation but also to protect "the settler and home builder against unfair competition." Rangers accomplished that goal by giving priority to small operators when issuing permits and by restricting the number of animals that big operators could run. Though ranchers could and did sell grazing permits, the service barred big operators—or would-be big operators—from buying enough permits to monopolize the range.[23]

Critics inveighed that the Forest Service was bringing socialism. Potter and Barnes, however, refused to relent. "Unfortunately" for range hogs, wrote Barnes, "the manner in which the National Forests are being handled has put most of them out of business." In truth, however, it was often not the big operators but rather the most marginal of forest users who suffered. While rangers pushed Mexican wood gatherers and Indian hunters off the range, big operators like Jim Ramer prospered.[24] The Forest Service's role in regulating the range was considerable nonetheless.

The Forest Service, noted Edward Wentworth in 1948, "brought civilization to the range." What he might have written was that the Forest Service made room for conscience. The rituals of honor—gunfights, lynchings, physical assertion—faded away under the watchful eye of the rangers.[25] What Wentworth might also have said was that the Forest Service brought civilization via its martyrdom. The Forest Service reduced conflict by becoming an arbitrator and a rule maker. In doing so, it made itself despised. Rather than attack one another, sheepherders and cattlemen, big operators and small operators, attacked the Forest Service. At times, to be sure, ranchers worked closely with the Forest Service and approved its decisions. Just as frequently, they lashed out at the service, viewing it as the instrument of oppression.

In her intriguing history of public lands disputes, Karen Merrill argues that the federal government created its own headaches. In trying to advance the cause of settlement, the government taught ranchers to regard grazing rights as property. When the Forest Service restricted or forbade the use of that "property," ranchers expressed outrage. The government urged them to settle, urged them to remain, and rewarded their grit by assigning permits that could be bought, sold, and passed to heirs. With each new restriction, however, the government seemed to betray the very people it had earlier nurtured. The government turned old allies into new antagonists, old heroes into new villains.[26]

For all the power of her thesis, Merrill sidesteps the puzzle of Western identity. As Merrill explains, settlers were by no means united in the decades that saw the federal government take control of the range. By the 1930s, however, rules of the range had minimized old tensions by separating sheep from cows and by protecting small operators from big ones. With rules came stability, even solidarity. Rural Westerners saw themselves as a homogenous people. No longer at war with one another, they turned their anger toward Washington. The Forest Service and the Bureau of Land Management became the "demonized" other. Grahams no longer fought Tewksburys. Mormons no longer fought cowboys. Daggs brothers no longer fought the Aztec. All those forces were subsumed in a homogeneous identity that dominated the rural West, an identity premised on a noble past

Will C. Barnes in cowboy garb, circa 1888.
Courtesy of Arizona State Library, Archives and
Public Records, History and Archives Division,
Phoenix, no. 96-2124.

when good men fought bad ones and an ignoble present when good men fought government.[27] The Forest Service promoted Western solidarity by becoming a common enemy to those it regulated.

Will Barnes's career epitomized the West's trajectory. As a soldier, he had helped police the Western Apache, winning the Medal of Honor for his bravery in protecting Fort Apache in 1882. As a rancher, he had fought in the war against sheep. In 1887, moreover, he helped organize and administer the Apache County Stock Growers Association, which paid Jonas Brighton and others to hunt down alleged rustlers and horse thieves. Barnes also served on Arizona's Livestock Sanitary Board and, in the 1890s, in the legislature. There he experienced the "fight of [his] life" when he proposed to carve Navajo County from the western half of Apache County. His bill succeeded. In 1896, he chaired the Arizona Republican Central Committee, complaining in one of his books of Arizona's damnable tendency to vote Democratic from that time on. In 1897, he married Edith Talbot,

Will C. Barnes during his tenure as U.S. Forest
Service assistant forester and chief of grazing, circa
1920s. Courtesy of Arizona State Library, Archives
and Public Records, History and Archives Division,
Phoenix, no. 97-6509.

unsuccessfully sought a job as U.S. marshal, and moved to New Mexico where
he continued to ranch.[28]

In 1905, his career path changed radically when he joined the Forest Service
at the behest of Gifford Pinchot, whom he, like Potter, had met in Arizona years
before. Barnes rose in 1907 to the office of inspector of grazing, then to assistant
forester in 1915, and finally to chief of grazing after Potter's retirement. Barnes
served as chief of grazing for another fourteen years, retiring in 1930, allowing
him to extend Potter's legacy. At the time of the Forest Service's inception, wrote
Barnes, "millions of cattle, sheep, and other domestic animals were grazing
where, when, and how they pleased." The men who owned those animals felt

that the range "was theirs to use as they wished" and "scoffed at any scheme of Government control." Despite having to face "a hostile and aggressive lot of stockmen," Potter and Barnes sought cooperation. With their tireless advocacy of range management and their willingness to consult stockmen on policy, they gave the Forest Service success. Yet success came with a price. With each passing year, the Forest Service fostered both a homogeneous identity among rural Westerners and a deep-seated anger toward Washington.[29]

In his last years, Barnes worked on the U.S. Geographical Board of Place Names—which allowed him to produce a fascinating volume on Arizona place-names—and served as associate editor of the *Arizona Historical Review*.[30] His status as historian gave his autobiographical accounts of Western life the appearance of objectivity. Objectivity, however, did not extend to his own role in Apache County's campaign of terror in 1887–88. He admitted no wrong; indeed his account smacked of bragging. He, in company with others, promoted the idea of the West as a place of honor, a place where good men entered into noble combat with evil men and vanquished them. He did not realize that he, too, had taken the side of evil.

COURTING CONSCIENCE

In 1885, a twenty-five-year-old George W. P. Hunt, future governor of Arizona, was waiting tables in Globe, the de facto capital of the southern part of the Rim Country. Seeing no clear future in business, mining, or politics, Hunt soon embarked on a ranching venture. With a partner named Walter Fisher he bought land near the hamlet of Wild Rye, a place that the *Silver Belt* called "one of the best ranges in the whole Tonto country." Hunt's role was to work in Globe in order to pay property taxes. Fisher was to run the cattle. When the mines closed temporarily in 1887, however, Hunt worked on the ranch full-time, where he found himself bored, lonely, and dependent on letters from friends.[19]

The year 1887 was inauspicious for Hunt. He and Fisher, like the investors who launched the Aztec, entered ranching just in time to see the cattle market go bust. They soon witnessed the value per head drop to just five dollars, too little to sustain the enterprise. Worse, Hunt found himself on the ranch precisely when Pleasant Valley erupted. According to one rumor, Hunt participated in the attack on James D. Tewksbury's cabin on September 1, 1887, the attack in which John Tewksbury and William Jacobs were murdered. It is highly unlikely that the rumor spoke truth. Judging from letters that Hunt exchanged with friends, he worried about the war but had no contact with participants. He did, however, leave the ranch shortly after the Tewksbury and Jacobs killings in order to "rustle up" money in California and, perhaps, to escape the conflict.[20]

While Hunt was in California he received updates from his friend Niles Berray, a miner who, like Hunt, had taken up ranching. In June 1888, Berray reported that "there is a little more trouble in P Valley don't know how much it will amount to. It is most all threats & rumors." Two months later, he reported "no later news

George W. P. Hunt, circa 1885. Courtesy of Arizona
State Library, Archives and Public Records, History
and Archives Division, Phoenix, no. 97-6970.

from Pleasant Valley. The only ones that go in there are the ones that are in the
row & don't talk much when they come out." He added that "several of the men"
from the hamlet of Tonto "are in it," including "Fellon, Conway, [Cap] Watkins,
and others." He had heard nothing, he noted, from Hunt's partner, Fisher, perhaps suggesting that he feared Fisher, too, might have taken sides. Finally in September 1888 Berray reported that Pleasant Valley "has [had] a rather quiet spell
[after] reports of the hanging of another man," referring probably to the murders
of Stott, Scott, and Wilson. "Hope it will be the means of making that a quiet
place," continued Berray, adding that he had no desire to go there. "I think I hear
you say me too!" he concluded.[21]

In 1890, Hunt returned to Globe and traded his interest in the ranch to Fisher in exchange for land on the Salt River, which Hunt rented out while he worked in town. Leaving ranching proved to be a good decision. Success came rapidly. In 1890, the Old Dominion Commercial Company—a mercantile, grocery, and hardware concern—hired Hunt as a delivery boy. He soon rose to grocery clerk, then, in 1896, to partner and secretary. By 1900 he was the firm's president. Meanwhile he served several terms in the legislature, where he gained a reputation for energy, diplomacy, and temperance. He had become a success.[22]

Hunt's success was not just economic and political. It was cultural. Rather than succumb to the Rim Country War, Hunt pushed Arizona toward conscience. He did not do so alone. His campaign for conscience emerged in part from his campaign for a bride. For fourteen years—from 1890 to 1904—George Hunt wooed Helen Duett Ellison, daughter of hard-boiled Jesse Ellison, leader of the Pleasant Valley vigilantes. For fourteen years, Hunt and Ellison engaged in a romantic correspondence and a dialogue about good. That dialogue confirmed Hunt's dedication to conscience. It also moved Arizona in a new direction.

By 1881, when George W. P. Hunt arrived in Arizona, he had already lived an adventure. Three years earlier, he had run away from an abusive father in Missouri. With a spare change of clothes, copies of Homer's *Iliad* and *Odyssey*, and a few silver dollars, he had walked and hopped trains to Colorado. There he worked for a laundry and a restaurant before shifting his focus to prospecting. For more than a year, Hunt and his partners scoured the mountains of southern Colorado and New Mexico for gold. Luckless, they decided to build a raft and float down the Rio Grande to a railroad camp, where they hoped to find work. They missed the camp, however, and drifted on the frigid river all the way to El Paso. Too poor to buy horses, they wandered on foot to Deming, Lordsburg, and finally Shakespeare, where they got work in the mines. Soon Hunt was on the move again. He and a friend decided to venture to Arizona in search of the lost Adams lode. After a fruitless three-month search, the weary pair crested a mountain and saw below them the boomtown of Globe.[1]

What the people of Globe did not know about the newcomer was that he would usher Arizona into a new era. If he carried a sidearm, he made no mention of it. He neither gambled nor drank. He was brown-eyed, nearsighted, a "great tease" and flatterer, an avid reader, and a man who, despite mixing easily among men, enjoyed the company of women. No doubt his preferences were shaped by childhood experiences that pushed him toward his mother. Those experiences, far from leaving him bereft of confidence, gave him a sense of mission. He walked and acted with a "haughty dignified manner" and never tired of standing up for what he thought to be justice.[2]

Mormons would have recognized young Hunt as a kindred spirit. Not only was he temperate and virtuous; he also opposed bluster and violence. The conscience he brought—or, more properly, the conscience he developed in Arizona—however, was not that of the Saints. His conscience was different, more ambitious. Hunt sought not merely to defend the righteous; he sought to reach out to the wicked. He sought to heal the wounds that made people angry and desperate.

Hunt likewise became a politician. From his parents and grandparents, he carried loyalty for the Democratic Party and pride in his ancestry. Among his forebears was John Marshall, fourth chief justice of the Supreme Court. Hunt's maternal grandfather, John Marshall Yates, was likewise a well-known lawyer and jurist in Missouri. Hunt had little hope, however, of following their path.

Too poor to attend college, Hunt had no avenue into law. Nor could he work steadily as a miner, one of his arms having been crippled by a boyhood accident. Instead he waited tables and became enmeshed in the bachelor culture that thrived in both mining camps and eastern cities. In his off hours, he read and studied. He found time nonetheless for frequent rounds of whist with males of his age and inclinations. Some of his friends were miners. Some also served stints as cowboys, including Hunt himself. Yet the relationship between Hunt and his friends bespoke none of the rough fraternity of boomtown miners. Nor did it reveal the boisterous displays of honor so common among Aztec cowboys. Judging from the abundant letters that Hunt exchanged with friends, their concerns were those of middle-class men. They talked about job prospects, politics, railroads. They talked about Shakespeare and Charles Dickens, the existence of God, the dullness of Globe. Often they talked about women.[3]

On at least one occasion, Hunt got roaring drunk, though for the most part he eschewed alcohol. If he visited prostitutes, he did not say so. Nor did he get into fights. On the contrary, he became a model of probity and hard work. In his journal, he concluded his entries for 1883 by noting that, over the past year, he had "worked steadily all the time and made a little over $600.00. I have also overcome some of my worst passions and I believe I am master of my self except in temper which I am daily fighting."[4]

No less noteworthy were Hunt's high spirits. With his "genial and humorous face, all aglow with mirth," observed one of his friends in 1885, Hunt was "a beacon of light" shining on his "hungry and impatient" friends.[5] Good humor, together with conscience, made Hunt a counselor to those around him.

From 1887 to 1889, one of Hunt's partners in whist, a miner named Frank Knapp who had moved to another camp, wrote a series of revealing letters to his high-minded friend. In his new environs the winsome Knapp found that he could not keep away from gaming tables and rough company. "There are no nice young fellows like there were at Globe," he complained. "The young men of town consist chiefly of well dressed good looking & of loose character Gambling men Pimps Rounders Railroad men & Saloon men," into whose company he too often gravitated. He vowed, however, to improve himself, asking only for Hunt's support. "Do not forget," he urged Hunt, "how much we once thought of one another[.] I can safely say never did more sincere Love and affection exist then [sic] did between us at one time. . . . I know that I am no fit companion for you but pray pity me and give me that much Friendship." Hunt returned Knapp's affection, sending him exhortatory letters and steering him away from gambling and drink.[6]

By June 19, 1887, Knapp could report progress, promising that he would soon "quit a life of gambling and sporting." Several months later, he wrote Hunt that "I never go into saloons & in fact have not even played a game of sociable whist." He also testified to a new caution in whom he befriended; no longer would he keep company with "rounders." In 1888, he continued to "lead a passably moral life" even though he was living in a dugout. Soon thereafter, Knapp got married, and the correspondence slowed to a trickle, though the friendship persisted throughout both men's lives.[7]

The exchange of letters between Hunt and Knapp reveal the power of conscience. They also reveal the power of male relationships in forging conscience. In the absence of mothers, sisters, fathers, and brothers, young men looked to one another for moral support. At times they became close enough to admit love, an emotion they felt free to express without being charged with femininity or homosexuality. They lived in a pre-Freudian world where words conveying emotion were not scrutinized for sexual meaning. In the sentimental world of the nineteenth-century middle class, same-sex friendships — among women and among men — could be charged without being sexual.[8]

The flip side of frontier honor, then, was empathy. Far from becoming isolate, stern, and vengeful, men and women could become friendly, social, and softhearted. Though sentimentality may not have bound cowboys, it often bound urban newcomers. High rates of geographical mobility — likely the highest rates in the world — prevailed not just in Arizona but throughout the United States. Young men were forever moving from east to west, from town to town, and from town to city. Persistence rates were remarkably low. Newcomers to towns and cities seldom stayed put for more than a few years.[9] They moved and they moved again, filling voids with sentimental attachments.

Geographical flux was not the sole reason for sentimentality. Sentimentality was a social movement. Its roots lay in the Enlightenment, when philosophers argued that "sympathy," in addition to reason, was necessary to achieve understanding. In the Romantic climate of the Jacksonian and antebellum decades, sympathy—an emotion that lay at the core of sentimentality—poured into the hearts and minds of Americans via novels, sermons, tracts, songs, and theater. The most important sentimental writer of the era was a man whom Hunt's mother, Sarah, described as the "immortal" Englishman, Charles Dickens, whose "great humanitarian works" moved both British readers and their American cousins to feel compassion for the poor and the outcast. In a letter to her son in 1888, Sarah Hunt recalled "seeing the tears roll down" her father's "ruddy face" as he had read the works of Dickens.[10] Even more powerful in the American context was a novel that Hunt's slave-owning forebears likely scorned: Harriet Beecher Stowe's *Uncle Tom's Cabin* (1852), which taught Americans to hate slavery by teaching them to love slaves.

Sympathy lay at the heart of abolitionist appeals, but it also lay at the heart of other reforms, reforms endorsed even by Southern women after the Civil War. Women, claimed reformers in both North and South, should be granted property rights in marriage so that they might break free from enslavement to husbands. Prisoners and the insane deserved sympathetic treatment so that they might rejoin society rather than languish in punitive institutions. The deaf and the blind and the mentally disabled deserved sympathy and education rather than avoidance. As Anna Sewell showed in her hugely popular novel, *Black Beauty: The Autobiography of a Horse* (1877), even beasts deserved compassion.[11]

Sympathy did not disappear after the Civil War; it simply moved on new tracks, shifting away from abolition and toward concern for immigrants, factory workers, and the impoverished. Stephen Crane's *Maggie: a Girl of the Streets* (1893), for example, told the story of a young woman forced by poverty and familial brutality into a life of prostitution. Frank Norris's *The Octopus* (1901) similarly chronicled the tragic fate of farmers who stand up to the railroad's attempt to take their land.[12] Unlike Dickens and Stowe, neither Crane nor Norris nor their cohort of "realists" and "naturalists" made protagonists sickly sweet or dwelled on noble deaths, but they remained concerned with sympathy.

George Hunt likewise concerned himself with sympathy. Sympathy would guide his career. It would lead him away from the honor endemic to the West and toward the pole of conscience. He became a reformer, a humanitarian, a model for twentieth-century progressives. His path, however, was not one that others readily followed.

During Hunt's youth, another Missourian—Jesse James—moved in the opposite direction, calling Missouri Democrats back to the fold of Southern honor. Refusing to make amends with defeat—or even with Unionist Democrats— James became the Robin Hood of the Lost Cause, taking from the rich—that is, from rich express companies owned by Yankees—and giving to the poor—mostly meaning himself and his gang. Made into a sensation by a rabble-rousing newspaper editor named John Newman Edwards, James became a living testament to Missouri's chivalrous Confederate past at a time when ex-Confederate Democrats were disfranchised and weak. By 1880, however, old divisions had healed, leaving James bereft of support.[13] If James represented the Democratic past, George Hunt—by embracing conscience—would be the Democratic future.

The spark for Hunt's conscience came from his mother. As Hunt exhorted and counseled others, his mother did the same to him. From 1880 to 1904, long letters in tiny script came regularly to "Pearle," likely a middle name that Hunt transformed into "Paul." Invariably the letters offered news from Missouri and then turned to moral themes. Sarah Hunt repeatedly praised her son's generosity. "You would divide a small competence," she told him, "as freely as [Jay] Gould would his millions." She also warned him of the perils of drink and gambling, complaining bitterly of his father's drunken rages and of the family's poverty.[14]

Sarah's letters spoke also of politics. "Get up a large democratic club," she instructed her son in 1887, "and do large work, and you might receive something lucrative." Meanwhile she touted free silver, damned Democratic "traitors," and chalked up William Jennings Bryan's loss in the 1896 election to Republican fraud. She wrote of successes, too. In Missouri, she averred, the people's finest hour came when they funded a home for aging and indigent Confederate veterans. Hunt remembered that lesson in later years when he lobbied for a home for aging and indigent miners, hoping to benefit old friends like Frank Knapp. "THE BEAST," complained Hunt—meaning corporate interests—defeated his proposal.[15]

Throughout Sarah Hunt's letters ran a powerful streak of optimism. She constantly invoked the name of Jesus, assuring Hunt that all things were ultimately for the best. Though a strong Baptist earlier in life, she migrated into Christian Science in the 1880s, convinced by the teachings of Mary Baker Eddy that the spirit held sovereignty over the body. All one needed was faith in Christ, right thinking, and prayer. "God will give you wisdom," she promised her son in 1896, "and eloquence to express your thoughts untill you will be surprized at your own flow of words and that is not all. He will remove obstacles out of your path, untill your success is sure." In other letters came more specific instructions. She wrote him of dreams in which he located a fabulous lode of gold and silver. "It may be foolish, but I can nearly see a mountain side, with great quantities of minerals, and it is always on the eastern or south side."[16]

Despite her faith in positive thinking, Sarah Hunt filled her letters with grief.

She complained incessantly of physical woes, including kidney disease and swelling in her ankles. Almost every letter decried the family's poverty and its dire impact on her youngest daughter, Jewel, who was nineteen years younger than Hunt. "I want you to remember," she admonished, "the life Jewel has had to endure all of her life. It is much worse for her than it was for the boys. She cannot get away." She feared, indeed, that her husband might kill both her and Jewel, adding that Jewel had threatened to take her own life rather than live with him another year. Though Hunt sent small remittances, he could not offer escape. What he could offer was sympathy. More important, he could make sympathy the focus of his career.[17]

"It fills a man with a strange awe," remarked Hunt, "to know that his old Mother far away in the East was sending up nightly a prayer on his behalf." The letters filled him with more than awe; they gave him direction. As early as the 1880s, Hunt secretly entertained the ambition of being governor of Arizona, a goal that his mother surely inspired. In 1894, he agreed to run for territorial council in part because his mother insisted that he do so. By then, he had already served as legislator and Gila County treasurer, but he was considering bowing out of politics in order to devote himself to business.[18] Beyond inspiring her son to run for office, Sarah Hunt inspired him to enlist in the cause of conscience. He would be the man whom she, in a sense, imagined into existence. He would defend the weak; he would fight the interests; he would hold himself to the highest standards of morality.

What compelled Hunt to move toward conscience was not only his mother; it was also his romance. At the close of 1890, he began corresponding with Helen Duett Ellison. The two probably met when she accompanied her father, Jesse Ellison, on a buying trip to Globe. She was a small, slim woman, eight years Hunt's junior, with a broad mouth and blue-gray eyes that shone like saucers when she was surprised. For much of her childhood, she had known privilege, having been educated at a convent in Waco, Texas, and raised by governesses. By 1890, however, she lived with her parents and siblings in the Rim Country, where her father ran cattle and dispensed justice with a rope. Duett Ellison's letters, not surprisingly, carry frequent references to Ed Tewksbury and his stepmother, Lydia, who occasionally visited the Ellison home. John Rhodes, too, visited, arriving sometimes with his brother, one of the handsomest men Duett Ellison had ever seen. It was Jesse Ellison's vigilantes, meanwhile—especially Bud Campbell and Houston Kyle—who carried Duett Ellison's letters to post offices in Payson and Young.[23]

Duett Ellison had come to Arizona with her father in 1885. Having suffered devastating losses to his cattle herd, Jesse Ellison asked his daughters—especially Duett—to work alongside him on the range. He could no longer pay for convent schools and governesses, nor could he pay for hired men to oversee his cows. In three successive years Duett Ellison helped drive cattle from her father's ranch to the railroad's holding pens at Winslow. Once she even disguised herself as a man to accompany her father when he confronted a group of Apaches whom he thought guilty of rustling. Throughout those years and into the 1890s, she was her father's constant companion and right-hand "man." She did not, however, love her work. She hated the way the Arizona sun darkened her skin, and she cried herself to sleep after finding that hard labor had swelled her fingers so much that she could no longer wear her rings. She detested, too, the monotony of ranch life.[24] But she was a dutiful daughter.

Soon after meeting her, George Hunt sent Duett Ellison a note on floral stationery and a copy of Dickens's *The Old Curiosity Shop* (1841). "Dickens is one of my favorite Authors," he told her, adding that "no one can read" his novels "without feeling & desiring to lead a nobler life. He has given me many hours of pleasure & after perusing one of his tales I feel like fighting a better fight; & leading a better life."[25] What Hunt did not realize was that he was entering a fight that would last fourteen years. The battle for Ellison's hand, however, was more than romance. It pitted a young man's conscience against a daughter's duty to family. Just as important, it shaped the politician that George Hunt became. It was in correspondence with Duett Ellison that he confirmed the sensibilities— conscience and sympathy—that became his political touchstones. For both Hunt and Ellison, romantic correspondence was an act of self-definition, an act of creating, sharing, and affirming ideals.

Ellison accepted Hunt's gift, telling him that "Dickens is a favorite with all of us." By the end of the year, Hunt had sent her additional surprises, including Edward Bulwer-Lytton's *The Last Days of Pompeii* (written in 1834 as a warning to moderns about cultural decadence) and the *Young Ladies Journal*. Over the next fourteen years, Hunt sent her a stream of novels, histories, magazines, and political tracts. She reciprocated with recommendations of her own.[26] Beyond finding each other to be ideal reading companions, they found each other to be companions in spirit. They were idealists.

In 1892 the correspondence fell silent—perhaps the letters were lost—but resumed in 1893. In that year the two discovered that they had something else in common: hard-drinking fathers. When Jesse Ellison appeared in Globe at Christmas, Hunt invited him to his quarters, where he was hosting an open house. When Hunt offered eggnog, Ellison refused it. After Hunt left to attend a dance, however, Ellison and his companion, a Mr. Henry, proceeded to get

Duett Ellison, circa 1890s. Courtesy of Arizona
Historical Society/Tucson, Jesse W. Ellison
Photograph Collection, PC 40, folder 1, no. 53859.

drunk. To men like Ellison, drinking—indeed getting drunk—was a male prerogative, a rite of camaraderie and a mark of one's liberty from the rule of women.
Drinking—with its connection to hospitality, bonhomie, and sometimes aggression—was a fixture of honor. If Jesse Ellison was determined to drink, however,
his daughter was determined to stop him. Hearing via the grapevine that Duett
Ellison policed her father's drinking, Hunt wrote her to apologize for having
"thrown temptations in his path." She responded that she was not angry at Hunt,
though she did bear malice toward Henry. "Countless are the days and nights,"
she lamented, that Henry had "helped me with papa when he was in an intoxi-
cated condition and I could not have managed him alone."[27]

Hunt's discovery that Ellison despised her father's drinking gave him a fresh
line of attack. The letters from 1893 might be called the "temperance letters."

Hunt, freshly elected to the territorial house of representatives, wrote her in January that he planned to set an example by refraining from drink. "It is generally supposed by the public & I . . . coinside with the popular belief, that a legislative assembly aside from their regular duties [puts] in the remainder of their time trying to quench a great thirst . . . no doubt caused by an unusual amount of brain work." Hunt implicitly criticized not only Jesse Ellison but also the "Bloody Thirteenth," the legislature that had earned a reputation for drinking, brawling, and recklessly spending the people's money. Among the lights of that legislature had been Jim Houck, who had vouchsafed its reputation through drinking and fighting of his own. Hunt, by contrast, preferred "the aprobation of a pair of honest gray eyes that live up under the Rim, than all the wine in our growing capital."[28]

"If you keep to your resolution," replied Ellison, "you will have the approval of every good true man and woman be their eyes gray or black." She, however, blamed the proprietresses of the boardinghouses where legislators stayed. "What are the women thinking of," she scolded, "and what can they expect of the young men when they tempt and encourage them by having wine on their tables." Women "should not blame the men or think them degraded when they give way to an uncontrollable weakness but should rather blame them selves."[29]

Ellison's attack comported with Victorian ideals. Women stood on a higher moral plain than men. Men were morally weak, whereas women were strong, or should be. Women were guardians of conscience. They were angelic. They were expected to guard the home from the world's evils. Ellison was accusing women who served alcohol of failing the standard of true womanhood.

Not only did immoral woman fail to protect virtue in their homes, as Ellison saw it, but by extension they failed to promote virtue in the world. In that way, too, her thoughts comported with larger trends. More and more, women made conscience into a rudder for the world outside. Women sought to restrain men from drinking; but beyond that, women sought to promote hygiene and education and to push for the building of libraries, schools, orphanages, and asylums. They pressed for humanitarian reform.[30] Though the nation's most visible reformers tended to be men, the bulk of the rank and file—and even some of the leadership—was female. Ellison was not among them. Her home was too isolated and her cares too great. In addition, she was from the South, where women came late to the cause of reform. Before the Civil War, reform was largely a Northern phenomenon, a thing disparaged by Southerners as do-goodism. Within Ellison's heart, however, stirred a crusader.

"All us poor sinners," Hunt wrote her in February 1893, "admire the virtues of the good & when one of the good & virtuous condescend to give one of us poor sinners good advice & take a little interest we begin to think the Sun is shining a little brighter." Ellison, in turn, congratulated him on setting an example for the legislature, dubbing it "the Sober Seventeenth."[31]

In early 1894 the correspondence took a different turn. The letters became both playful and jealous. She denied his assertion that she was interested in another man, and she laughed at the rumor that she had killed a turkey by scaring it to death. She had killed a turkey, she admitted, but by more traditional means. Then she invited him to come to the ranch to investigate the nearby Indian ruins, where "you can see the finger prints where they have plastered the walls." Whether he accepted is not clear. He did, however, report that he had begun riding a bicycle; that he was sending her Edward Gibbons's history of Rome; and that he had volunteered to teach Sunday school. "A talk in bible class," he wrote, "does one good & then we must not forget that the bible has [guided] the human race for several thousand years and is & will continue to exert a good influence on mankind for ages to come."[32]

With that statement Hunt pivoted from play to conscience, again appealing to Ellison's idealism. "I am glad you think as you do about duty & honor," she responded. "Not that I doubted you would do so, but like to hear you say it, for most men regard it so lightly. When really it should be their watchword."[33] Duty and honor, however, were inapposite words to describe Hunt's principles. As a Southerner, Ellison slid easily into a language that sounded almost military, a language informed by the honor culture of the South. Duty and honor might have described her father's service in the Texas Rangers or the Confederate Army.

Later that month Ellison offered more apt praise for her admirer along with a rejection of the honor culture that prevailed on the range. "I don't see what will become of this rough country," she wrote Hunt after hearing that another settler had been murdered. "It will have lots to answer for." Her "rough country" allusion did not specifically mention the war of the 1880s. She reported in the same letter, however, that her family was moving into the heart of Pleasant Valley. Jesse Ellison had bought the old Middleton place, where the first battle had occurred. The move surely provoked her to think about the nightmarish scenes of 1887 and 1888. "If more citizens were like you," she told Hunt, and "would attend Church and try & teach the younger generation kindness and humanity our country would certainly be the better for it."[34]

The affirmation of conscience took another turn in mid-summer of 1894, when Hunt reported—wrongly—that fifty people had been killed in conflicts resulting from a strike by Pullman Sleeping Car workers in Pullman, Illinois. "I hope & believe," responded Ellison, "that the people are at last aroused & will demand justice although it takes war to get it. For what are they but a set of slaves for the moneyed Kings, when they are supposed to be a free & independent people. All I regret if it should be war is I'm not a man so that I might take part in it."[35]

Now she was on the offensive, pushing Hunt toward a fuller embrace of sympathy for the weak and the marginal. Though he was a conscience man, he was still loyal to the moderate politics of the Democratic president, Grover Cleveland, who had sent troops to break the strike. Whether Cleveland's decision embittered Hunt is impossible to know, though by 1896 he expressed vexation at the antilabor direction of his party. Whatever else Hunt wrote about the strike is lost. What seems likely, nonetheless, is that the bond between Hunt and Ellison was growing stronger. The tide of preaching no longer flowed solely from him to her. Often it flowed in reverse.

Jealousy and rejection, too, ran through the letters. In June 1894, Ellison sarcastically congratulated Hunt on his engagement to another woman. He immediately and adamantly denied the rumor. Hunt, in turn, experienced disappointment when, in August, Ellison refused to accept a pin he had sent, explaining that the pin implied a commitment that she could not offer. The wound soon healed, however, and the two were again talking politics in November, with Hunt complaining that Pleasant Valley cowboys—including Jesse Ellison's vigilantes— were accusing him of being "hightoned" and "look[ing] down on country folks." The accusation was likely occasioned not only by Hunt's dedication to learning but, perhaps more important, by his refusal to swear and take a sociable drink, behaviors that came readily to Ellison's father. Hunt was "hightoned," it seems, because he rejected the honor culture of the West.[36]

"It does not make any difference to me," replied Hunt, "whether a man is clothed in rags so that he is honest and temperate." To Ellison, his words must have been affirmation and sting. "Temperate" did not always describe her father. Neither did it describe his friend E. J. Edwards, who was Hunt's colleague in the legislature. Hunt described Edwards as a "scoundrel" and a "rascal" in large measure because Edwards opposed temperance. Edwards reciprocated by advising Jesse Ellison to vote against Hunt. If you can strain your conscience," wrote Edwards, "vote against him and I am sure you will never regret it. He is ignorant and not capable in any respect to fill the office to which he aspires."[37]

Hunt's "temperance letters" appealed to Duett Ellison's conscience. They did not, however, bring her closer. On the night of December 6, 1894, Hunt dreamed about his beloved, only to find a letter from her the next day announcing that she would not, contrary to his expectation, be coming to Globe at Christmas. Disappointment provoked new declarations. For the first time, he professed love. He could not go on "playing the hypocrite" by pretending to be a friend. He asked whether he had any hope of winning her. Her answer must have encouraged him. She, however, was emotionally unsound. Her sister, Rosa, who had married one of her father's cowboys, had died suddenly of an infectious disease. Rosa's husband, Bud Campbell—an Ellison vigilante—was left alone to bring up two children. To ease his burden, her parents wanted to meet Campbell in Globe over Christmas to talk about his situation and, it seems, to take charge of the children.[38]

Despite telling Hunt that she would not visit, Ellison in the end accompanied her parents to Globe. Once there, she spent much of her time with Hunt, privately, in his apartment. "It was not right for us to go to your rooms," she wrote Hunt on December 30, adding that she had not slept. Whatever had happened, it did not bode well. On the same day that she expressed remorse over having spent time with him in private, he decided to give up hope for their marriage.[39]

In 1895 the agony continued. Ellison wrote on January 12 that marriage to him would make her "happy forever." Duty, however, prevailed over emotion. "I am accused of being proud, cold & heartless but it is so because no one knows my feelings, for my heart is as true & warm as any good loving woman's." Much to Hunt's surprise, another Ellison girl also wrote him on January 12, Duett's sister, Lena. After begging him to keep the letter secret, she explained that she was compelled to make him understand her sister's motives. "She thinks it her duty to stay with papa & mama as long as they live," she confided, especially now that Bud Campbell had agreed to leave his children with them. The entire Ellison family, it seemed, depended on Duett, and for their sake she would sacrifice her future. Lena praised her sister's selflessness but added that "she is not doing herself justice."[40]

Without Lena's letter, the romance might have ended. Despite his own dedication to conscience, Hunt could not believe in his beloved's. It seemed to him that she was using her devotion to family to shield herself from passion. Lena Ellison's letter, however, gave her sister's excuses legitimacy. Duett refused to marry George not because she did not love him but because she had dedicated herself to others. Among all the reasons that a woman might give for rejecting a man's offer of marriage, conscience was one that he might at last accept without ending the courtship.

Lena's letter—and those of Duett—also revealed something else that perhaps gave Hunt hope. Ellison stayed with her family out of principle. But she did not stay happily. Indeed, wrote Lena, she was so miserable that she had come to doubt God.[41] The one thing that could free her, it seems, was devotion to even nobler principles than loyalty to family. Though Ellison may not have fully understood her dilemma, her discourse with Hunt—her discourse about temperance, about sympathy, and about reform—was a way to rebel against her father's expectations. Jesse Ellison called her to one form of service; Hunt called her to another.

By February 1895, Ellison was having doubts about her decision to stay with her parents. "It seems as [if] every day is a week," she complained, especially since it had been raining and snowing incessantly. "At times," she lamented, "I feel so lifeless cold and heartless that I almost think I am ice." Hunt responded with fire. "Some of these days," he threatened, "I will do like Lockinvar of old and carry you off by force."[42]

His passion was too strong. In May she sought to end the correspondence. "Oh Mr. Hunt," she began, "it is like signing my death sentence when I say do you not honestly think we should give up this letter writing." "I cannot give you up," he answered. "I could no more help loving you than to breath."[43]

Hunt showed passion in another way, too. He endorsed women's suffrage. She did not. "You are mistaken," she admonished, "and will one day see that alowing women to vote would not . . . amount to much for . . . most of them would be influenced by fathers, brothers & husbands." Her opposition, however, went deeper. She saw herself as a Southern woman. Suffrage might be acceptable to Northern and Western women, but "I cant believe that our Southern ladies can so far loose their modesty & queenliness to wish for more than is rightfully given them when they are looked up to as Queens of their pleasant happy homes by fathers brothers & husbands[.] [T]hat shoud be enough to satisfy any sensible person at least that is the way I look at it."[44]

Only a few months before, Ellison had wished she were a man so that she could participate in a war against the "Moneyed kings." Now she meekly accepted her role in her father's home, where she was vassal to a man. If in one sense she conformed to the nineteenth-century ideal of womanhood, in another sense she conformed to the precepts of Southern honor. White women—especially those of middle-class and elite families—were to be protected, watched over, guarded. They could display strength in times of war, sickness, or dearth. Under duress, they could work outdoors alongside, or in lieu of, men—as did Ellison—but they were not to participate in the affairs of the world. The Civil War, it seems, forced Southern women to step outside their prescribed role, yet the old ideal survived. Women were to be homebound. To let them stray into law or politics or business was to jeopardize the family's honor.[45]

Ellison' opposition to women's suffrage was an oblique way to reject Hunt. They had built their correspondence around sympathy, social conscience, and political passion. She now seemed to reject the latter two ideals and restricted sympathy to her family. She rejected, too, another pin that Hunt had sent, hurling at him a stream of indignation: "How can you hurt me like this! It doesn't seem to me like I could ever look at this pretty pin with pleasure for it will remind me that you like all the rest believe me so mercenary that a pretty trinket now and then would buy my esteem and respect. I am no child to be bought with pretty things and if you can not think of me as a woman grown in sinse & yeares and pay me respect accordingly why I do not care for your friendship."[46]

Hope bubbled up in her letters, too. She wished Hunt to know that she defended him against criticism from cowboys. She praised a bill he had proposed to penalize officers of the law who drank on duty, and she chastised his enemy, Edwards, for opposing it. She again expressed chagrin—along with tinges of both racism and pride—at the work she was required to do, "riding after herds of cattle[,] running horses on ground that would make you shudder to look at, with face and hands taned by sun & wind untill I look like a Mexican. . . . You would certainly blush for my shame if you had to describe me as I really am." And she sent him endearments. "Oh George," she wrote on June 21, "I shall never tell you not to love me for it is too sweet a thought although I know it's wrong."[47]

Encouraged by her tenderness, Hunt ventured to Pleasant Valley in August. "For one short week," he later recalled, "I drank in the love of your eyes." During the visit, the two had ridden to a part of the Rim known as "The Diamond," where they had collected crystals. In lieu of a real diamond, Hunt presented Ellison a crystal he had found, which she subsequently attached to a gold band. She reciprocated by giving him a necklace that she had worn since she was four, promising him that "it will link our hearts together." He wore it under his shirt.[48]

Still she refused to leave her father. Deeply troubled, Hunt decided to bring to light the sacred promise that she had made to her father "some years ago." Somehow Hunt had learned that she had promised her father that she would never marry if he would stop drinking. "Why," Hunt now asked, "should wife hood and mother hood be withheld from you and the evening of your life be passed in solitude for the selfishness of a man[?] It is not right nor is it Justice."[49] Hunt's line of attack was to compare Ellison's cherished values to those of her father. She was selfless. She was giving. Her father was self-serving. He lacked sympathy—conscience—for his child.

How she responded is not clear. For two months, the correspondence ran dry. At the end of May, however, Ellison announced that she planned to go on an extended trip to San Antonio. Hunt was heartbroken. Still they continued to write, leading to a second revelation. In July, she admitted that her father believed that the correspondence had ended. She felt like a "thief" for accepting Hunt's letters. After that admission came an extended defense of her loyalty to her father. If she left him, "he would drink and spend every thing we have worked so hard to save." She stayed not only for her father, however, but also for her mother and sisters and her dead sister Rosa's babies. She enclosed a photo of herself but asked Hunt not to show it.[50]

The trip to San Antonio ended in late July when her father called her home. He needed her to sew clothes, something she did in addition to her duties as cowboy. There was a more urgent reason for her return, too. Bud Campbell had been murdered, leaving his children with neither mother nor father. Settlers blamed the murder on Apaches. It was awful, she wrote, that Campbell "should be murdered by those fiends." Later reports, however, attributed the murder to a white man.[51]

As anxiety about an Indian uprising faded over the next few weeks, the letters turned again to politics. William Jennings Bryan had just taken the stage as the Democratic Party's presidential candidate. Over the past year—perhaps the past two years, since President Cleveland had sent troops to break up the Pullman strike—Hunt had become disgusted with his party. When Bryan was nominated, however, he felt "like getting on the house top and shouting for joy for it shows the American people are at heart good and honest and want to make this in fact and reality the grandest nation on earth." "The Gallant South and West," he cheered, had at last taken their stand against "the moneyed kings of Wall Street." Taking a more cynical tone, Ellison predicted that if "the gold bugs" defeated Bryan and his crusade for the free coinage of silver—an inflationary measure intended to help debtors—"we will have war."[52]

The year 1896 was important in another way, too. Hunt had chosen to run for a seat on the council, Arizona Territory's upper house. October saw him campaigning in the Rim Country, particularly in and around Payson. "They have got the saloon element down on me because I do not patronize them," he wrote Ellison, but "I am very strong in the mine[s] and with the cow boys." In November, he won a resounding victory.[53]

Even as Bryan lost by thirteen million votes, Hunt won every precinct in Gila County but one. As he had predicted, he was strong among miners and cowboys, though not because of his opposition to drink and gambling. Hunt befriended ranchers and cowboys by supporting taxes on the "tramp herds" of sheep that crossed the county en route to the Salt River Valley. He gained a following among miners, meanwhile, by championing them in clashes with employers. Duett Ellison provided moral support. When in 1895 Hunt introduced legislation to protect the rights of workers, she wrote him that, of all his bills, it was the workers' bill that she most hoped would pass. "I am very much interested in the poor hard worked class that never seems to get their just dues," she averred.[54] Again she pushed him toward humanitarian conscience.

Had miners and cowboys known that Hunt wished to ban liquor and gambling and help women gain suffrage—in effect, he sought to abolish the culture of honor—they might not have been so quick to support him. Those issues were still peripheral and distant, although Hunt, with Ellison's encouragement, had signaled his intentions by getting the assembly (but not the council) to pass his bill to ban prizefighting. Hunt, however, simultaneously managed to shore up his credentials as a tough-minded frontiersman by demanding that the U.S. Army keep troops at San Carlos even when the threat of an outbreak seemed distant. He also convinced the legislature to put up a five-thousand-dollar reward for the apprehension of an infamous renegade called the Apache Kid. "You have made more friends than you can imagine by introducing the bill offering the reward for the Kid," Ellison told Hunt in March 1893.[55]

Despite winning over cowboys and miners, Hunt could not win his intended bride. "I wonder," he wrote shortly before Christmas 1896, "how long this is to continue[;] can there ever be a time when I can take you in my arms and call you my own wife[?]" As the year progressed the conversation became strained. In April, Hunt compared himself to a moth attracted to her light. He could fly to the light, but he was sure to be burned. Her letters, meanwhile, spoke of the tedium of life on the ranch, commenting that at times she felt that she "could not bear this life a day longer." Even the gramophone that her father had bought had become tiresome. Her loneliness was oppressive. All the men, she wrote, were talking of joining the Yukon gold rush, threatening to leave "the mountains . . . wilder than ever if that seems possible."[56]

Over the next few months the two followed familiar channels of discourse. Hunt lamented how many people spent their lives drinking and gambling while Ellison complained that "it is the money that governs [the United States] not the people." Words of affection, however, grew sparse. At the end of October, the conversation reverted to bitterness. Another of Ellison's sisters—Mattie— had gotten married to an Ellison cowboy, a "man-boy" from Texas, in Duett's words. Hunt could not fathom why Jesse Ellison would let his daughters marry cowboys but would not let Duett marry him. "Good bye my love, good bye," he concluded, promising to break off the correspondence.[57]

The letters continued through the year, but Hunt was morose. Having turned thirty-eight, he felt he had accomplished nothing. Again he suggested ending the correspondence. "You can understand and know now why I can never come to you," she replied, agreeing at last to stop the exchange. Still they continued to write until February, when she told him that her father was considering moving away, taking her with him. "I seem to be drifting away from life and hope," Hunt responded, "but after all it is best—best to drift away and perish than to live a life of torture, good bye my one and only love, good bye."[58] Then the letters stopped.

Over the next four years, they exchanged only a handful of letters. Each time Ellison initiated correspondence, Hunt reiterated his love and his hopelessness and asked her to stop. Then, in late 1903, shortly after Hunt had returned from a business trip to New England, he received a surprise. Duett Ellison was ready to marry.[59]

The two worked out a compromise not unlike that of Persephone in Greek myth. She would stay with her husband during winters and with her father during summers. "You can have the same observant care over [your family] as now," promised Hunt. On February 24, 1904, they were married in El Paso, whereupon they embarked on a honeymoon in Mexico. Once again, duty interfered when she cut short the honeymoon in response to her father's plea for help on the ranch.[60]

The struggle for Duett continued into 1905, with Hunt calling her father "a selfish pusilanimous ignom[ini]ous being." In May, Hunt vowed that he would never again allow his wife—once she returned to Globe—to go back to her father. By then, she was several months' pregnant and planned to have her child at the ranch, where her sisters and mother could help care for the baby. In June, she bore a healthy girl, who promptly became the central object of the tug-of-war, with Hunt suggesting that she be named "Helen" in honor of her mother and Jesse Ellison insisting that the girl be named "Jessie" in honor of himself. Four months later, the new mother and her baby, Helen Virginia Hunt, had still not returned to Globe. "The evil one keeps you there," complained Hunt.[61]

Hunt's star was nonetheless on the rise. "The one thing in life to make a man a man is a pure and noble woman," he had written Ellison in February 1904, promising that wedlock "would lead me on to greater achievements."[62] It seems he was right. He was returned to the territorial council that fall, where he became council president. In 1910, when Congress passed an enabling act to allow Arizona to draw up a constitution and seek statehood, Hunt was elected president of the constitutional convention. At the close of 1911, he was elected the first state governor. He took office on Valentine's Day, 1912. Hunt would be elected governor six more times, serving longer than any other governor in Arizona history. Throughout his career, he labored not only for working men and against corporate rule but also for the principles that he and his wife shared, the principles of conscience.

The first blow against honor culture came in 1907, when Hunt introduced a bill to abolish gambling. It passed, much to the consternation of saloonkeepers, miners, and cowboys and despite overwhelming opposition in Globe. Arizona had "long since outgrown" gambling, argued Hunt. All territories, he insisted, had "gone through this struggle," and all had emerged better suited for economic and moral development. On their last night of legal business—April 1, 1907—Globe's gambling halls drew throngs of people, some of whom gambled and others of whom came to watch. "He gambled, he gambled," they sang, "he gambled all around, / In and out of town, / He gambled, he gambled, / He gambled till the Hunt Bill cut him down."[63]

At the same time that Hunt succeeded in banning gambling, he prompted the legislature to raise licensing fees on saloons in order "to abolish the low, tough dives in small mining camps and in the tough parts of the larger towns." Other acts approved by the legislature—all pushed by Hunt—barred women from working in saloons and beer gardens; gave the governor the power to revoke the licenses of saloons that became "a nuisance"; and instituted fines for law enforcement officials who carried firearms while inebriated.[64]

More success followed. Hunt dubbed the constitution that he shepherded into existence in 1910 the "People's Constitution." Influenced by organized labor, it prohibited corporations and individuals from maintaining armed bodies of men; allowed the state to seize the property of corporations that violated state law; required the direct election of U.S. senators; gave voters the powers of initiative, referendum, and recall; and created a powerful commission to regulate utilities. The constitution was "so advanced," proclaimed Hunt, "that it has not failed to draw the fire of every foe of equality and progress."[65]

Hunt's "People's Constitution" reflected the concern for the poor and the marginalized that lay at the heart of humanitarian conscience. What also constituted conscience were Hunt's subsequent measures. In his first address to the legislature in March 1912, Hunt called for antiusury laws; anti–child labor laws; prison reform focusing on rehabilitation; old age pensions; and worker's compensation.[66]

Each of those causes was consistent with early twentieth-century Progressivism. Some of them appeared in the Theodore Roosevelt's platform when he ran for president that year. Hunt's reforms were equally consistent, however, with the push for conscience that animated American politics even before the Civil War. Before the war, conscience was a Whig or Republican cause. Members of those parties tended to push for temperance legislation, blue laws, women's rights, prison reform, humane treatment for the insane, and abolition. After the war, conscience guided many Democrats, too. Progressive factions in both

George Hunt presiding over the Arizona State Constitutional Convention, 1910.
Courtesy of Arizona State Library, Archives and Public Records, History and Archives
Division, Phoenix, no. 02-0656

parties conceived of city, state, and national governments as guardians of social welfare. Sympathy for the poor, the aged, the young, and the weak informed their politics, though Progressives did not necessarily extend that sympathy to blacks, Indians, or Mexicans. Mexicans in particular—most of them Republican voters—suffered at the hands of progressives, who imposed a literacy test for suffrage. Even as he brought into being compulsory education, meanwhile, Hunt voted to segregate Arizona's schools. At least one facet of honor—the notion of white dignity and black shame—still shaped his thought. The segregation initiative, however, lost by one vote, and Hunt made little mention of it again. By 1916, indeed, he was reaching out to racial others by supporting Mexican workers in a copper strike.[67]

The most important weapon in the conscience arsenal, argued Hunt, was women's suffrage. "If any thing will purify our nation," he had written Duett Ellison in 1895, "it is the influence of women." Though mocked for his support for women's suffrage in the 1890s, he spoke for it in the legislature. In the constitutional convention, he was only lukewarm, insisting that a women's suffrage provision might lead to the constitution's rejection. After statehood, however, he encouraged feminists to put a suffrage initiative on the ballot. They did, and it passed. Two years later, another of his desired reforms passed, this one banning the manufacture and sale of alcohol. As much as two-thirds of the vote in favor came from women.[68]

"The early acquirement of the equal participation of men and women in political life," argued Hunt in 1914, "will . . . give Arizona a decided impetus toward the adoption and perfection of a fundamentally progressive plan of government." Women's votes, he believed, would propel the rest of his conscience agenda. He was wrong. Women—especially Mormon women and farm women—liked prohibition, but they did not necessarily like laws that favored labor or that appeared to be soft on crime.[69]

Hunt made progress regardless. The most radical of his reforms was the abolition of capital punishment. For much of his first term, he succeeded in blocking executions, despite accusations that he was misusing his powers. In 1913, he went so far as to veto a penal code that allowed capital punishment. When legislators refused to go along, Hunt put the issue before the people. "I hope and sincerely think that the people of Arizona will relegate this barbarous custom to the dismal past," he wrote in his diary.[70]

A quarter century earlier, Jesse Ellison and his vigilantes, backed by Apache County Mormons, had lynched men without bothering to prove guilt. The Apache County Stock Growers Association, meanwhile, had conducted a campaign of assassination. Into the 1900s, Arizona continued to hold public executions, a custom dating to medieval times, when monarchs called communities together to watch convicts be tortured and killed. Now Arizona prepared to do away not only with vigilantism and public executions but with capital punishment entirely. In 1914, Hunt's initiative failed. Using the stir created by four executions, however, Hunt convinced voters in 1915 to ban capital punishment via referendum, thus joining just five other states that had already done so. Once home to honor, Arizona moved toward humanitarian conscience.[71]

Closely related to Hunt's campaign against capital punishment was his program of prison reform. Treated "like beasts," argued Hunt, prisoners lost hope and self-respect and longed to avenge themselves on society. The penal system had not kept pace with "civic and moral evolution." "The fostering of self-respect and the substitution of hope for despair," he argued, would produce better results.[72]

To accomplish those ends, Hunt encouraged wardens and jailers to hold musical concerts for convicts and to form prison baseball teams. He also promoted educational programs for convicts and offered work releases that allowed them to labor on public projects or, at times, to leave prison in order to attend

family matters. Hunt himself visited the penitentiary regularly, sleeping sometimes in a cell in order to get an idea of what prison was like.[73] Rather than
making prison into a school of degradation—a school of shaming—Hunt sought
to make it into a school of self-improvement. Hunt's sympathy—a sympathy he
had learned from his mother, from his wife, and from Dickens—begat his conscience reforms.

For his troubles he was caricatured by the "kept press," as he called newspapers
beholden to corporate interests. The Tucson *Citizen* likened the prison to "the
best hotels in the state for service and the most fashionable boarding schools for
culture and refinement." The Arizona *Gazette* heartily agreed. "Governor Hunt,"
it chortled, "has started something entirely new in the way of making penitentiary life appealing. If it is carried to its final analysis the time may come when
elections will be held to determine what portion of the population will serve the
next open terms in state prison."[74]

By supporting prison reform, the abolition of capital punishment, and prohibition, Hunt was cutting himself off from the electorate. Never again could
he expect cowboys and ranchers to vote for him en masse. Nor could he expect
to poll well among women, who were concentrated in farming areas and in the
growing metropolises of Phoenix and Tucson, areas that tended to be conserva-
tive. One of Hunt's closest advisers warned his boss that he was ruining his career.
Hunt vowed to push on. "I am striving," he wrote in his diary, "to uplift and to
encourage those that are the weak members of Society."[75]

To what degree Duett Hunt encouraged her husband is hard to know. True to
her concept of decorum, she was careful to stay out of the public eye. Assuming
that her opinions remained consistent with those she had expressed before marriage, however, we can be sure that she inspired her husband to seek reform.
"This rough country," she had written in 1894, "will have lots to answer for." With
his wife's encouragement, Hunt was creating that answer. The honor of Arizona's
past was a springboard to the conscience of its future. Hunt never mentioned the
vigilantism of the 1880s in his talks on abolishing capital punishment, but he was
fully aware of the honor culture of the free range. In repudiating that culture, he
was repudiating Jesse Ellison. We have no record of how Ellison responded to
Hunt's campaign to abolish gambling, drinking, pugilism, and capital punishment and to instill humanity into the penal system, state insane asylums, and
the state's treatment of the poor, the indigent, and the aged. We do know that,
in the 1920s, Robert Voris, son of a vigilante, asked "Old Man" Ellison about
the lynching of Stott, Scott, and Wilson. Ellison told him not to worry himself
about it. When Voris persisted, Ellison assured him that the lynchings were just.[76]
Ellison refused to abandon the premises of honor.

Hunt did not usher Arizona into utopia. Old attitudes toward punishment, drink, gambling, and the honor of combat remained powerful. "All the reactionaries," he complained in February 1913, were "making a combined assault" on his opposition to capital punishment and his prison reforms. That same year, he was forced to veto the legislature's attempt to overturn the law banning prizefighting. After the 1915 ban on capital punishment, the backlash grew stronger. In 1916, Hunt came within a few dozen votes of losing the gubernatorial election to Joseph Campbell, the Republican candidate. Both men declared themselves winner, but for a year, it was Campbell who served. Only a recount and a court decision made Hunt the victor. The near loss was largely the result of Hunt's conscience agenda. Even the miners who tended to support prison reform bridled at their champion's devotion to temperance.[77]

Hunt's reform program lost more steam during World War I. Crippled by accusations that he was friendly to antiwar radicals, Hunt was forced to allow the legislature's criminal syndicalism bill—a measure that essentially outlawed opposition to the war—to become law, albeit without his signature. Realizing that he could not defeat Campbell in 1918, he retired from politics. While serving in the legislature, meanwhile, Osmer Flake—personification Rim Country honor—labored to overturn the state's ban on capital punishment. In 1918, he succeeded. Voters passed an initiative that restored the death penalty. Never again would Arizona abolish it.[78]

For the next few years, Hunt served as ambassador to Siam (Thailand), a job offered to him by outgoing President Woodrow Wilson. When he returned to Arizona, Hunt jumped back into politics, winning gubernatorial races in 1922, 1924, 1926, and 1930 even as the Republican tide ran high. Never again, however, did he systematically pursue conscience reforms. He still visited prisoners, sought to humanize the state reformatory, and championed the causes of labor, but his primary concerns were tourism, highway building, and water allocation.[79]

That Hunt soft-pedaled conscience in his later career does not lessen his importance. In the late nineteenth and early twentieth centuries, George Hunt, Duett Ellison Hunt, and the U.S. Forest Service—enabled by populists, socialists, labor activists, and a powerful bloc of reform-minded voters—brought conscience to Arizona. Arizona, indeed, joined the Progressive chorus that dominated national politics. Progressive reform ameliorated honor. Just as it would be mistaken to suggest that Forest Service reforms came solely from Washington, D.C., however, so would it be mistaken to suggest that Hunt's political impetus came solely from elsewhere. Hunt's Progressivism was, to a great degree, homegrown. It came as a backlash against honor. It came, moreover, from the grassroots.

TOMB OF HELEN DUETT HUNT WIFE OF GOV. GEO. W. P. HUNT OF ARIZONA DIED APRIL 18, 1932

Tomb of Governor Hunt and family. Courtesy of Arizona State Library, Archives and Public Records, History and Archives Division, Phoenix, no. 97-6971.

Despite their energy and dedication, however, Hunt, Duett, and the Forest Service moved the state only grudgingly from honor. The move turned out to be temporary. By the late 1910s, a different force—tourism—was restoring Arizona to the glorious past when honor prevailed on the range. The reformers were only half successful. An even more powerful man than George Hunt—a novelist named Zane Grey—crusaded in the 1920s to restore honor to Arizona and, by extension, to millions of readers across the nation.

When George Hunt died in 1934, he was laid to rest in a small, white mausoleum built in the shape of a pyramid and placed on a barren hill at the outskirts of Phoenix. When Phoenicians today picnic at Papago Park or tour the Phoenix Zoo, they wonder about the odd little pyramid high and lonely on the bleak hill. If they ask about it, they might hear that it is the tomb of Governor Hunt. What they don't hear—because few know it—is that inside lie not just George Hunt but also his wife, Duett. Alongside them are her mother and father. Hunt never managed to shake Jesse Ellison from his life—or from his death—any more than he could shake honor from the life of the state. When the Hunts had moved to a new home in the state capital of Phoenix in 1912, the Ellisons had gone with them, buying property next door.[80] All of them remained in their Phoenix homes until they died, Duett's mother, Susan, passing first in the late 1920s. Duett Ellison Hunt died in 1932. Both George Hunt and Jesse Ellison died in 1934. One by one, they were laid to rest in the pyramid (along with Duett's sister, daughter, and son-in-law). When Arizonans see the pyramid high on a hill, gleaming and mysterious, they little realize that within lies a man who got the death penalty banned alongside a man who lynched innocents. With them lies the woman for whose loyalty—and whose conscience—they competed.

HONOR ANEW

In 1911, Theodore Roosevelt—out of office for two years and beginning to consider another run for the presidency—ventured to Arizona in order to commemorate the new dam on the Salt River that bore his name. At the time, it was the biggest dam in the world. The waters that it held back filled much of Tonto Basin, extending northwest along the channel of Tonto Creek toward the Sierra Ancha and northeast along the old course of the Salt. The lake that it backed up—Roosevelt Lake—promised to make the Salt River Valley into an agricultural paradise. Not only would the dam prevent the floods that periodically inundated the valley, but it would also channel irrigation waters into endless acres of cotton, melons, and citrus trees. The economic miracle of the dam, however, was not the only lesson that Roosevelt wished to highlight.

"Cherish these natural wonders," Roosevelt commanded. "Cherish the natural resources," he continued, but above all, "cherish" Arizona's "HISTORY and ROMANCE as a sacred heritage. . . . Do not let selfish men or greedy interests skin your country of its BEAUTY, its riches or its ROMANCE. The world and the future and your very children shall judge you according as you deal with this sacred trust."[1] Following Roosevelt's lead, Arizonans increasingly realized that they held the keys to a magical kingdom where Americans—and foreigners—could remake themselves through imagination.

Scenic wonders alone were not Arizona's treasure. Its treasure was also the freedom to interpret those wonders, the freedom to give them meanings that fulfilled the desires of the millions. "We are just beginning to learn," explained the editor of *Progressive Arizona and the Great Southwest*, a 1920s magazine devoted to automotive tourism, "that we can never in a lifetime tell the wonderful

Theodore Roosevelt dedicating Roosevelt Dam in 1911. Roosevelt celebrated not just the dam but also the "romance" of Arizona. Courtesy of Arizona State Library, Archives and Public Records, History and Archives Division, Phoenix, no. 99-0351.

story of Arizona; her fiction-like history; her age old legends; her inevitable prosperous future." Arizona's publicists, however, engaged in a monumental effort to do just that. In 1925, the state launched its own magazine—*Arizona Highways*—devoted to telling Arizona's wonderful stories as well as to publicizing the need for new roads to bring tourists. In its first year, the magazine reported that the annual number of visitors to the state was twice its permanent population. By 1931, the Arizona Automobile Association could announce that "Arizona, nationally now, is a new playground." With such a lucrative tourist trade to tap, "cattle rustling has gone out in favor of dude wrangling."[2]

As governor, George W. P. Hunt marched at the fore of the tourism movement when, in 1926, he presided over a dedicatory ceremony for the Coronado Trail, a north-south highway that connected Tucson with the White Mountains. The event included a rodeo, an Apache "devil dance," and great slabs of barbecued beef and bear. The new road was intended to lure "transcontinental motorists who wish to camp, fish, and hunt in a country so vast that it will never become overcrowded or commonplace."[3] Hunt little understood how dramatically tourism would move the state away from his conscience agenda.

By telling the state's stories—by giving meaning to its wonders—publicists gave the state, and the nation, not just a magical kingdom of deserts, canyons, and mountains but a magical kingdom of honor. Tourists came not only for scenery and climate but also to experience the Old West. They flocked to dude ranches and rodeos and they entered into a synergistic relationship with settlers. "According to the movies," inveighed Lotta Burney in 1931, "there still is a wild and wooly West and it's up to Arizona to prove it, and let me tell you she does, and in a large way!" In the past, explained Burney, Eastern dudes had been anathema to cowboys, but now dudes were welcomed. "Small boys and Bank Presidents long to go west and be cowboys," whereas "society matrons and stenographers yearn for the love of a real He Man, and Arizona is the answer to it all!"[4]

By 1930, tourists could interact with real cowboys at rodeos held across the entire stretch of the Rim Country from Sedona to the White Mountains. Among the best attended was the "August Doin's" rodeo at Payson, a town just west of Pleasant Valley. Payson began its rodeo in 1884—a well-documented date—making it perhaps the oldest continuously held rodeo in U.S. history. By the 1910s, Payson's rodeo had become a tourist event, bringing dozens of tin lizzies from distant places. While tourists watched bulldogging, calf roping, and horse races, locals made bets, got into fights, and drank moonshine. At the August Doin's, tourists saw honor full-blown.[5]

Mormons, too, entered into the spirit. As early as 1915, Snowflake Mormons integrated rodeo events into their Pioneer Day festivities on July 24 commemorating their forebears' trek to Utah. By 1926, the Pioneer Day rodeo had emerged as a full-fledged show with multiple events. By 1953—if not earlier—the rodeo had become the main attraction, overshadowing everything in the written program. Seeking to entertain both locals and tourists, other Mormon towns— even Salt Lake City, whose rodeo dates to the 1920s—followed suit. Mormons, too, had been cowboys, they told the world, ignoring the fact that in the 1880s

Tourists' cars lined up at Payson's "August Doin's" rodeo and festivities in 1918.
Collection of Jeremy Rowe Vintage Photography (vintagephoto.com).

they had been bitter enemies to Texas cowboys and the honor culture they represented. "Rodeo," according to Mormon authorities in the mid-twentieth century, "has always been an important form of entertainment for White Mountain folks."[6]

Tourists, however, did not restrict themselves to watching rodeo from afar. Via dude ranches they participated directly. At the Sundown Ranch near Taylor—operated by Virgil Flake, grandson of William Flake, and his cousins, the Turley brothers—Eastern youths experienced Western adventure firsthand. In their first summer, the youths were called "dudes" or "greenhorns." In their second summer, they became "cowboys." On Pioneer Day, "dudes" and "cowboys" rode in one body to the rodeo, where the most daring among them participated in steer riding. At the front of the parade, boldly carrying an American flag, rode John Addison Hunt, son of Snowflake's first bishop.[7] Forty years earlier, Mormons had isolated themselves from the unregenerate. Some had predicted that great cataclysms would destroy the United States. Now they welcomed gentiles into their midst and bowed to no one in patriotism. Mormon patriotism and Mormon honor, surely, were lessons that youths brought home to parents and friends.

What mattered in Arizona was not one's religion, one's wealth, or one's pedigree but one's adventurousness, one's willingness to ride a horse and camp out and kill game. In Arizona, Americans could put "standardization, mass production and ready-made entertainment" behind them and test their "ability to do and conquer." What tourists did not realize was that among their trials might be an automobile accident. Thanks to the state's "reckless motorist" problem, highway fatalities surged.[8]

The import of tourism was not simply that it lifted the highway fatality rate along with the economy. Nor was its import the rich irony of tourists escaping commercialism in the East only to beget commercialism in the West. What was important was that tourism stirred dreams. Those dreams changed Arizona. Hunt's conscience society turned proudly to its honor past: cowboys, gunfights, range wars, outlaws, and Indian wars. Those were the stories that gave meaning to the state's scenery. Suddenly settlers—real ranchers and cowboys—found themselves valued as experts not only on the geography of the state but also on what novelist Zane Grey called the "Code of the West," meaning toughness, virility, chivalry, and social conservatism. Some of those settlers—including the Colcord brothers, who had participated in the lynching of Jamie Stott—became not only exemplars of a noble past but also guides in the present. The Colcords escorted "professional people, public officials and businessmen from as far away as Boston" on hunting trips into the Rim Country. Far from being bumpkins and throwbacks, Arizona settlers became symbols of a golden age.[9]

Hezekiah James Ramer, friend to the Ellisons and the Colcords and owner of the OW ranch—the ranch that the Blevins family had once held—also hoped to avail himself of tourist dollars. In 1917, he sold his ranch to a former Aztec manager named Frank Wallace for $150,000. Ramer planned nonetheless to stay in the Rim Country, where he proposed to create a "hunting park" stocked with "all kinds of game." He died before he could realize that dream. While staying with Mormon friends after returning from a trip to New Mexico in 1918, Ramer appears to have suffered a heart attack. Yet the dream of a hunting retreat did not die with him. In the 1910s and 1920s, the Sierra Ancha, Pleasant Valley, and the Rim Country more broadly became popular destinations for hunters, anglers, and adventurous dudes. Frank Wallace meanwhile sold the OW to a Hollywood mogul who, in turn, sold it in 1937 to an aeronautics executive. His guests included Clark Gable and Carole Lombard.[10] What had been a realm of war became a realm of play for the rich, who could imagine themselves into a gun-studded past.

Even if one lacked the wealth to purchase a ranch, one could drive through the "excellent game and fish country" between Roosevelt and Payson via

Pleasant Valley, where, according to *Arizona Highways*, the "blood of the Grahams and the Tewkesburys [sic] incarnadined" the road. During the Great Depression, the Federal Writers' Project further publicized the drive through Pleasant Valley in its guide to the state. "In the early morning and evening," noted the authors, "when a purple haze softens the wild beauty of this secluded glen and of the rugged mountains that enclose it, its turbulent history seems incredible." Incredible or not, the guide gave directions to each site where warriors had killed one another, including the cabin of James Dunning Tewksbury, "bespattered with bullet holes" and boasting "a large black splotch where the wood was soaked with blood."[11]

What tourists valued about Arizona was not its prison reform, its abolition of capital punishment, or its care for the young, aged, sick, and indigent. Nor were they concerned about labor's struggle against capital. What tourists valued was honor, which, it seemed, defined a manliness that cowboys possessed and that moderns had lost. "With the passing of the cowboys . . . goes a people daringly individual, strong and masculine," lamented Ina Sires in *Progressive Arizona and the Great Southwest* in March 1929. In Arizona, she added, a few cowboys survived as examples for all to follow. Even if cowboys did pass out of existence, however, their way of life was "being perpetuated in movies, books, pageants, and rodeos," according to novelist Peter Kyne. The rites of entertainment, he continued, had become "the last outposts of masculinity. We must keep them true to the times they portray. They must not be overfeminized." The honor of men, Kyne suggested, must not succumb to the sympathy—the conscience—of women.[12]

Tourism—which Governor Hunt did much to promote—undermined conscience. It did not destroy conscience, but it shifted priorities. It attracted thousands upon thousands of home seekers, health seekers, and dream seekers. Arizona remained a progressive state through the 1940s, but never again did it move to the front of the slow march of conscience that had begun with the Enlightenment. With George W. P. Hunt, Arizona conscience reached its apogee and began to retreat.

If Hunt defined conscience in the years before World War I, another man defined a renascent honor for the 1920s: Zane Grey. Grey was a tourist. He first saw Arizona in 1906, when he and his wife—who lived in New York City—honeymooned at the Grand Canyon. A year later, he returned, this time in the company of the noted conservationist and cougar hunter Charles Jesse "Buffalo" Jones. Rather than killing cougars, Jones roped them live, an act so daring that Grey was compelled to write about Jones's exploits. Soon after that trip Grey produced a book about Jones's life. More than that, Grey sought adventures of his own.

"As a boy," recalled Grey, "I read of Boone with a throbbing heart" and "pored over the deeds of . . . Custer and Carson, those heroes of the plains." Having come "to see the wonder, the tragedy of their lives," Grey resolved to write about them. He would do more than write about them, however; he would relive their exploits. He would seek the "fulfillment of my dreams of border spirit!—to live for a while in the fast-fading wild environment which produced these great men."[13]

With experience came authority. Unlike the German novelist Karl May or James Fenimore Cooper or any of a raft of dime novel authors, Grey wanted to tell the true story of the West. He was no historian—he was a novelist—but he insisted that his writing was true to the West's "spirit," a thing that could be understood only by being there. Grey's Western adventures, promised *Field and Stream* in 1909, would allow him to rise "superior to hackneyed tricks of style or expression [by] writing as the men of the West talk, straight from the heart, forcefully, yet with an easy swing."[14]

Initially, Grey set his novels in the eighteenth-century Ohio Valley. Regaled in childhood with tales of the Indian fighter Lewis Wetzel as well as Grey's own ancestor Betty Zane, Grey made them into prototypes for his heroes and heroines. The Ohio Valley novels, however, made no money. Too much had been written about border heroes of the eighteenth century. The settings, even the characters, were stale.[15]

Grey's trips to Arizona moved his imagination in new directions. There he found latter-day Wetzels in the persons of Buffalo Jones and Jim Emmett, a broad-shouldered, bearded Mormon who served as one of Grey's guides. Though Grey made both men into heroes in his books, however, success still eluded him. Only in 1912 did he finally produce a smash hit—*Riders of the Purple Sage*—a story of a cowboy and gunfighter named Lassiter who comes to the defense of a beautiful Mormon woman, Jane Withersteen, who is beset by evil polygamists. True in a sense to Mormon history, Jane Withersteen is a creature of conscience. Noting that Jane is modeled on the heroine of nineteenth-century sentimental novels, literary scholar Jane Tompkins writes that she "encapsulates fifty years of Victorian piety and domesticity. She believes in spiritual salvation and in Christian love and forgiveness, in self-effacement, obedience to authority, and the sanctity of the family. She dresses in white, loves children, serves the poor, and fights against her own anger."[16]

As a creature of conscience, Jane urges Lassiter to renounce his guns in favor of gentleness. In the end, however, he must go back to his guns in order to defeat evil. His honor—his resort to violence to defend himself and the woman he loves—triumphs over conscience. Grey would repeat that theme in novel after novel. Conscience—embodied in a heroine—must give way to honor—embodied in a hero—for good to prevail.

When Arizona Mormons got wind of *Riders of the Purple Sage*, they reacted with anger. By 1912, the vast majority of Mormons had renounced polygamy, though Grey had seen a few tiny communities on the Kaibab Plateau where polygamy survived (and still survives). Grey claimed that he had not intended to "roast" the Mormons. Surely he pointed out that he had used Jim Emmett as the model for the hero of another of his novels, *Heritage of the Desert* (1910). In 1907, however, he had noted in his journal that he had "met Mormons and I hate them. I learned something of their women and I pity them."[17]

Mormon anger came to a head sometime after 1915, when Grey ventured to the Rim Country on a hunting trip. He found there "the wildest, most rugged, roughest, and most remarkable country" he had ever seen. He also found Mormons. In the early 1920s, Grey met Osmer Flake, who worked for the U.S. Forest Service. Acting at the behest of fellow Saints, Flake accosted Grey for his anti-Mormon novels. By then, there were two, *Riders of the Purple Sage* and its sequel, *The Rainbow Trail* (1915). Grey assured Flake that he held nothing against the Saints. His books, he insisted, were not meant to be social commentary. He simply wrote stories that would sell.[18]

Rim Country Mormons likely met Grey's explanation with explanations of their own, telling him of their 1880s ordeal. Like Jane Withersteen, they had been rescued in 1887 by a Lassiter named Commodore Perry Owens. Owens, however—who later in life had married a black woman and opened a saloon— seems to have held little appeal for Grey. He preferred heroes in keeping with the image of Boone, heroes who seemed morally consistent.

Mormon history did, however, find its way into Grey's novels, though shorn of religious context. In *Man of the Forest* (1920), for example, Grey dealt with claim jumping in the White Mountains, a very real phenomenon in the 1880s. When a "half-breed" sheepherder—a patrón born of a New Mexican mother and an American father—attempts to take another man's ranch and to abduct his niece, he meets righteous opposition from young Milt Dale. Dale, a sort of hermit who lives in the woods with a pet cougar, saves the day and wins a wife. In doing so he gets help not only from a gunfighter named Las Vegas but also from a set of Mormon brothers who "possessed long, wiry, powerful frames, lean, bronzed, still faces, and the quiet, keen eyes of men used to the open."[19] The story was simple and melodramatic, but it contained a kernel of truth. In the 1880s, pa-

Zane Grey with a bear he has killed in Arizona's Rim Country, 1919.
Courtesy of the Ohio Historical Society.

tróns had indeed disputed Mormon land claims, sometimes with guns. Contrary to Grey's plot, however, they had shrunk from abducting beautiful women.

Elsewhere, too, Grey dealt with real conflicts from the Rim Country's past. In *Nevada* (1928), Grey has his hero—a mysterious cowboy and gunfighter named Jim "Nevada" Lacy—go undercover to root out a gang of rustlers. He does so with the connivance of the most powerful man in the Rim Country, the honorable Judge Franklidge.[20] The plot sounds contrived, yet stock detectives—under the auspices of county officials, gentile ranchers, and Mormons—really had gone undercover in the 1880s. Almost certainly Grey had heard stories of Carr Blassingame and J. W. Brighton, both of whom had served as secret agents. If Grey relied on oral testimony to formulate his plot, however, he divested it of social meaning. The conflict he described pitted good men against bad men. It had no religious overtones, no tension between Mormons and cowboys, no dispute between small homesteaders and a large corporation like the Aztec. What it had nonetheless was a "truth" born of Rim Country experience: the idea that honorable men prevailed over outlaws by shedding their blood.

In *The Drift Fence* (1930), Grey returned to Rim Country history, writing of conflict between homesteaders under the Rim and a big cattle operation above it, almost precisely where the Aztec had been. The novel's hero, Jim Traft, who has come from Missouri to oversee his uncle's ranch, here proves his toughness—

Both Judge Franklidge and Tom Day were astounded at Texas Jack's amazing offer to rid the Mogollons of its rustlers single-handed. "This cowboy has got somethin' up his sleeve," declared Day. "Come heah, Texas Jack. Spring it!"

"Jack, are you going to persist in this mad plan?" demanded the judge.
"Dead or alive when it's over, all I want is my name cleared!"
"Of what?"
"Of the stealin' an' lyin' I'll have to do.

"I'm goin' through with it whether you stand by me or not," continued Jack with rising passion. "I only want your word, Judge, that you'd tell in court, if necessary, that you an' Tom Day were parties to the job I undertook."
"You have it. And here's my hand."

Then Texas Jack—Nevada—spoke with deep, forceful tones. "Gentlemen, I reckon the time's come fer me to give myself away. Tom Day, the starved cowboy you once took pity on happens to be Jim Lacy!"

Jack Abbott's 1933 cartoon rendering of Zane Grey's *Nevada* (Harper and Brothers, 1927). This scene depicts gunfighter and cowboy Jim "Nevada" Lacy informing his powerful friends of his decision to act as undercover detective. Courtesy of the Ohio Historical Society.

his honor—to his cowboy employees. After thrashing one of his cowboys with his fists, Traft takes on a rustler named Slinger Dunn. In the end Traft defeats Dunn, ends the rustling, and wins Dunn's sister, "little Molly Dunn of the Cibecue." A second novel about the romance between Jim Traft and Molly Dunn and their struggle against rustlers appeared in 1933 under the title *The Hash Knife Outfit*.[21]

Those were only a few of the stories by Grey that celebrated the Rim Country past. Indeed, the Rim Country became a magical font for Grey's imagination. Before his death in 1939, Grey gave Rim Country settings to fourteen novels and numerous short stories.[22] What most of those stories feature is the protagonist's honor defeating evil. Grey's hero never wins through cleverness, cajolery, or resort to the law; he wins with his fists or his guns, or both. Grey was less interested in regaling readers with actual history than with using history as a prop for the melodrama of honor.

Melodrama was not what Grey believed he was writing. He believed that he had a message. He believed that his novels conveyed balm to an ailing American soul. One story in particular—a story that obsessed Grey—became the vessel for that message. Though he had ventured to the Rim Country in the 1910s ostensibly to hunt bears and turkeys, recalled Grey, he had really gone to find out about the Pleasant Valley conflict. On his 1918 trip to the Rim Country, Grey spent two months camping and hunting, but much to his frustration, he learned little about the war. His guides would not talk. Still hoping to learn the story, Grey returned to the Rim Country in 1919, where he "packed a gun many hundreds of miles," riding "sometimes thirty and forty miles a day," climbing in and out of "deep canyons" and "desperately staying on the heels of one of those long-legged Texans." Still they refused to tell him about the war. This time, however, Grey believed that he had won their friendship.[23]

Part of the reason that settlers would not talk was their fear of aging vigilantes, who themselves feared exposure. Talk had repercussions. Old warriors mandated silence. Another reason that settlers would not talk may have been the company Grey kept. His entourage included, at different times, his brother, his sons, a mistress (there were several), and a Japanese-American cook, along with many others. Theresa Haley Boardman, a Payson settler, recalled in the early 1970s that she would "never forget the first time that outfit came on. Oooh. . . . There was quite a crew. There must have been, oh—there must have been twenty in the bunch."[24]

Grey was captain of a company of tourists that invaded once a year. Even so, he managed to earn the confidence of a settler named Sampson Elam Boles. Not only did Boles sell Grey his ranch; he also told him all he knew about the

Pleasant Valley conflict. Grey gained the confidence of others, too. Indeed he talked to so many people about the war that he found himself at a loss to know precisely what had happened. His "instinctive reaction to the facts and rumors," however, led him to a story that was "true" to his "conception of the war." "My long labors," he insisted, "have been devoted to making stories resemble the times they depict."[25] He would not admit that he was writing mere fiction. He was writing truth, albeit not the truth of facts and dates.

In the foreword to Grey's novel about the Rim Country War—*To the Last Man*, published in 1922—Grey went from discussing his search for truth to excoriating "realists" who found favor with critics. Likening himself to such romantic storytellers as Sir Walter Scott, Rudyard Kipling, and Robert Louis Stevenson, Grey argued that the world had seen too much realism. "For many years," he wrote, "all the events leading up to the great war [World War I] were realistic, and the war itself was horribly realistic, and the aftermath is likewise." Grey's antidote was romance. "Romance," he insisted, "is only another name for idealism, and never in the history of the world were ideals needed so terribly as now."[26] If he saw any conflict between writing truth and writing romance, he did not say so.

To create his antidote to realism Grey proposed to tell the story of the war in Pleasant Valley. "How can the truth be told about the pioneering of the West," he wondered, "if the struggle, the fight, the blood be left out? It cannot be done."[27] Even in the present, he could see the legacy of the "fighting past" in Arizona's Rim Country. To offer solace to Americans sickened by one war, Grey told the story of another.

Grey's plot begins with Jean Isbel, a buckskin-clad backwoodsman from Oregon—a Boone-like figure—receiving an urgent summons from his father, Gaston Isbel, a rancher in Arizona's Rim Country. The senior Isbel desperately needs his son's services as a warrior against men who have begun to run sheep on the open range, cutting off his cattle from grazing lands. When Jean arrives at the Rim, however—literally at the precipice—he happens upon a beautiful, moccasined woman, Ellen Jorth, who is tending a herd of sheep. The sublimity of the Rim stands in for passion and danger: "He felt a sheer force, a downward drawing of an immense abyss beneath him. As he looked afar he saw a black basin of timbered country, the darkest and wildest he had ever gazed upon, a hundred miles of blue distance across to an upflung mountain range, hazy purple against the sky. It seemed to be a stupendous gulf surrounded on three sides by bold, undulating lines and peaks, and on his side by a wall so high that he felt lifted aloft on the rim of the sky."[28]

The two admire one another, talk briefly, then Jean kisses Ellen impetuously and asks her to meet him again. She agrees before discovering that he is an Isbel, and thus the blood enemy of her family. Though Jean returns to rendezvous with Ellen, she hides in the forest. She finds him magnetic, yet she detests him. Both hero and heroine know that a war between their families must soon begin.

As in the actual war, the conflict begins with the killing of a sheepherder. The action that follows abbreviates history, but the Jorths do attack the Isbel cabin and lose a couple of men to Jean, who kills them not in daylight with a gun but at night with a knife. Jean Isbel—being, like Ed Tewksbury and like Grey himself, part Indian—sneaks up on attackers. Indeed Jean becomes so engrossed in vengeance that, before he kills one man, he tortures him for having cast aspersions on the chastity of Ellen Jorth. Jean's dedication to honor leads him to acts of shaming.

Subsequently the Isbels counterattack. When Gaston Isbel ventures to the ranch of his patriarchal opposite, Lee Jorth, to challenge him to a gunfight—in effect Isbel proposes a duel—Jorth and another kill him through treachery. Isbel honor becomes the measure of Jorth disgrace. The reader thirsts for vengeance and gets it when an Isbel ally, a professional gunfighter, enters the Jorth cabin and kills Lee Jorth and his henchmen.

With her father dead, Ellen is abducted by a Hashknife cowboy named Colter. After several plot twists, Jean, Ellen, and Colter end up together in an abandoned cabin. Jean, badly wounded, has chosen the cabin as a hiding place from his Hashknife pursuers. When Colter enters with Ellen in order to rape her, he does not know that Jean is there. In the denouement, Ellen seizes a rifle and kills Colter while Jean leaps from the rafters to kill a second cowboy. The bond between hero and heroine is sealed. Their ordeal turns out to be a struggle for love.[29]

Interestingly, Grey was not the first novelist to make the war into a vehicle for romance. A year before *To the Last Man* saw print, Dane Coolidge had published *The Man-Killers*, a potboiler that—like Grey's book—features a romance between hero and heroine on opposite sides of a feud. Coolidge's hero and heroine, however, are heirs to an old feud in Kentucky. Coolidge merely grafted them to a story about a different conflict in Arizona, a conflict between "half-breed" sheepherders and Texas cowboys. The Arizona feud carries the action. More important, Coolidge constructed the Arizona feud from historical research. Several scenes mirror the Pleasant Valley conflict, including the attack on the Middleton cabin, Sheriff Mulvenon's ambush of John Graham and Charlie Blevins, and Tom Graham's assassination. Coolidge's story also includes Mormon vigilantes and "Slashknife" cowboys.[30]

If Coolidge was more true to events, however, Grey wrote more lyrically of the landscape. He also achieved greater drama. He knew how to move swiftly

TO THE LAST MAN

ZANE GREY

A story based on one of the most desperate blood feuds in the annals of the old west.

Jacket from Zane Grey, *To the Last Man* (Harper and Brothers, 1922). In this novel, Grey used the Pleasant Valley conflict of 1887 as a vehicle for melodrama—a story of honor against ignominy—rather than explore the sociological tensions of the free range. Author's collection. Permission courtesy of HarperCollins Publishers.

from scene to scene, building tension and suspense. Grey's novel, far more than Coolidge's, drew readers. Its power, its popularity, gave it authority. So powerful was Grey's novel, indeed, that it threatened old investments in historical memory.

When Osmer Flake read *To the Last Man*, he was indignant. The war wasn't a conflict between cattlemen and sheepherders, he told Grey. It was a "showdown between thieves and those they were victimizing."[31] If the novel was not moralistic enough for Flake, however, neither was it morally nuanced. Grey did not portray the war merely as a struggle between cattlemen and sheepmen. In his telling, the Jorths are a family of rustlers. Though they were once respectable, their honor has deteriorated, eaten away by their hatred for the Isbels. When the Jorths bring sheep in order to drive out their enemies, the Isbels—especially Jean Isbel—have no choice but to fight. Killing and mayhem become rational responses to conflict. The reader cheers when Jean kills his family's attackers and again when a mysterious gunfighter shows up to dispatch Lee Jorth. Hashknife cowboys, moreover, appear strictly as bad guys with not so much as the grace of a fatal flaw to explain their villainy. The only fate they can expect is death at the hands of the hero and, in this case, the heroine.

Grey, to be sure, contradicted history by contriving a love story and by making the sheepmen—the Jorths—into villains. From the Mormon point of view, the sheepmen—the Tewksburys and their allies—were for the most part on the side of right. Few readers apart from Flake and his Mormon brethren, however, could have read the book as anything but a parable of honor and disgrace.

The honor of Grey's heroes was not that of Aztec cowboys. It was not a prescription for a way of life. The honor of Grey's heroes did not involve drinking and gambling and shooting up towns. It did, however, involve physical assertion. Men were gauged by their willingness to fight and to kill. There was no solution to a social problem short of death. Despite Osmer Flake's criticism, Mormons themselves—especially Flake—had come to the same conclusion in 1887. Grey was celebrating the moral that gave Arizona Mormons—and others—a Western identity, an identity formulated around the idea that evil tested good in its fires, that toughness was character, that restraint was cowardice. Western honor was the product that Grey sold to the nation. Certainly that honor had precedent in the Boone literature and the dime novels of earlier decades, but Grey gave it authenticity. He knew the West firsthand. He was writing truth, he claimed, even if his truth shaded into romance.

In selling Western honor to a cosmopolitan readership, Grey found success. He, more than Owen Wister, popularized the Western novel. Wister brought the old dime novel hero to respectability with his 1902 novel, *The Virginian*. The popular success of the 1903 short film, *The Great Train Robbery*, meanwhile showed the potential of Western stories to create profit. In the 1910s and 1920s, directors and actors improved the genre and made it popular. If actors like William S. Hart and Tom Mix made the cowboy hero a fixture of cinema, however, it was Zane Grey who made him a fixture of American fiction. From 1914 to 1928, Grey produced nine novels that made the bestseller lists, making him the most popular novelist in the United States and probably in the world. By 1927, he commanded $60,000 for a serialized novel. By 1928, the price had gone up to $71,000. In his journal, he estimated that he would make $350,000 in 1927 alone on books, short stories, and films. When Paramount Pictures made Grey novels into movies, it put Grey's name on its broadsides alongside the names of its leading actors. So singular was Grey's success that President Herbert Hoover invited him to the White House. Grey was a star.[32]

It was that very success that marked the repeal of Progressive reform. Sentiment, sympathy, conscience: they had gone too far by the 1910s and 1920s and had to be reeled in, at least fictively. Grey's novels—not unlike the Boone literature of earlier decades—offered an antidote to Harriet Beecher Stowe and Charles Dickens. The novels that had shaped the mind and the career of George Hunt were precisely those that Grey repudiated. Grey was not trying to bring back drinking sprees and gambling and lynching—his heroes almost always eschew those activities—but he was trying to bring back the "Code of the West," meaning chivalry toward women and the honor of mano a mano combat. He had little interest in poverty or workplace conditions or tainted beef or the ruthlessness of corporations. Nor was he interested in the realism and sympathy that shaped works by Frank Norris, Stephen Crane, and Theodore Dreiser, or for that matter O. E. Rolvaag, Hamlin Garland, and Willa Cather, who wrote of the rural West. True, he sought to portray the West as it was, going so far as to interview Westerners to make sure he was getting his stories right. But poetic license, along with a fundamentally Western theory of sociology, took control. Drawing on the memory of Westerners themselves, perhaps, Grey insisted that the frontier brought out the best in good people and the worst in bad ones. It spawned honor and disgrace. It created the conditions for melodrama.[33]

Grey was not content, moreover, to leave honor in the past. Via two novels about the 1920s Rim Country—the Rim Country world that Grey himself experienced—he made it clear that his moral lessons applied to the present. Those two novels—*Under the Tonto Rim* (1926) and *Code of the West* (1934)—were twins. In the first, *Under the Tonto Rim*, a straitlaced social worker named Lucy Watson, freshly minted from Arizona's normal school, gets a job doing "welfare work among backwoods people" in the Rim Country. "It was not exactly missionary work," the narrator explains, "as her employers belonged to a department of the state government. Her duty was to go among the poor families of the wilderness and help them to make better homes."[34] It is Lucy, however, who must learn the most important lesson.

Lucy worries that, just as the settlers are too proud to work with her, she is too proud to work with them. Tensions reach their climax when a handsome settler, Edd Denmeade, asks Lucy to a dance. She declines. He persists, and she persistently refuses. Finally he grabs her bodily and ties her to the back of a horse. Though furious, she is powerless to resist. At last she agrees that, if he'll let her off the horse, she will attend the dance. Without going into greater detail than necessary, Lucy, though angry for a time, falls in love with Denmeade. In the denouement, Edd kills a cowboy villain and Lucy gives up her career in order to live with Edd in the wilderness. "That dance you dragged me to," she tells him, "cured me of my vanity."[35]

Here again Grey tempered melodrama with fact. Lucy Watson was not solely a figment of Grey's imagination. She was based on the very real home demonstration agents authorized by the federal government's Smith-Lever Act of 1914. Their job was to improve the standard of living and the moral habits of the poor and the isolated, whether they were ranchers, miners, or farmers. They taught—preached—sanitation, hygiene, thrift, nutrition, and entertainment suitable for families and children. They were paragons of conscience. To Grey, it seems, demonstration agents were even more than that: they were paragons of the New Woman, the early twentieth-century woman who valued career, suffrage, and independence. It was the New Woman who argued that she deserved the vote not simply because women were fully as human as men but because women were devoted to conscience. As George W. P. Hunt had suggested in 1914, women were builders and protectors of civilization.[36]

In Grey's novels, conscience—almost invariably a female trait—proves weaker than the honor of males. Lucy in the end is helpless against evil. Edd must kill the villain who threatens her. In doing so, he metaphorically kills Lucy herself, or at least the part of her that longs for authority and independence. Man dominates woman rather than woman dominating man. In myriad ways, Grey reversed the tide of recent history. Settler dominates social worker. West dominates East. Rural dominates urban. Honor dominates conscience.[37]

In a companion novel, *Code of the West* (1934), we meet a very different protagonist, a flapper—the rebellious woman of the 1920s who engaged in petting, smoking, and drinking and who attained those freedoms by working, leasing an apartment, driving a car, and using newly available methods of birth control. In *Code*—a story first serialized in 1923—the flapper heroine, Georgiana Stockwell, ventures to the Rim Country to visit her sister. Georgiana soon finds, how-

UNDER THE TONTO RIM
Zane Grey

AUTHOR OF "THE CALL OF THE CANYON," Etc.

Jacket from Zane Grey, *Under the Tonto Rim* (Harper and Brothers, 1926). In this novel and in others, Grey pitted the honor of men against the conscience of women. Author's collection. Permission courtesy of HarperCollins Publishers.

Ad for Zane Grey's *Code of the West* (Harper and
Brothers, 1934), "The Great Tonto Basin Abduction."
In *Code of the West*, Grey's flapper heroine learns the
moral "code" of her captor, then marries him.
Courtesy of the Ohio Historical Society.

ever, that her short dresses, flirtatiousness, and lack of modesty sit poorly with her hosts. Her sister explains that Western men, unlike their conscience-ridden Eastern counterparts, "have a savageness in them, a strength born of this wilderness, a heritage from fierce, ruthless, natural men. And they have a code of honor that no woman can risk breaking." Western men hold firm to honor and to social convention. When Georgiana falls afoul of their code, she, like Lucy Watson, is abducted and thus cured of her pride. Like Lucy, she falls in love with the man who abducts her.[38]

Though Grey seems to celebrate heroines like Georgiana Stockwell and Lucy Watson—he gives them more than ordinary powers of reflection and courage—they must submit to the honor of settlers. Grey gave the New Woman and the flapper both life and power, but only in order to tame them. Grey's heroes became social anchors for an urban world that Grey feared was out of control, a world straitened by humanitarian conscience and do-goodism (epitomized in Lucy Watson) yet loosened by advertising, movies, automobiles, and sex (epitomized in Georgiana Stockwell). With their reliance on physical strength rather than moral suasion, Grey's settler heroes battled both conscience and frippery.

Behind Grey's lessons in honor, meanwhile, lurked something more subtle, something characteristic of the Jazz Age, something, indeed, that Grey professed to abhor: libertinism. During his childhood, recalled Grey, "I used to run off from home, hide in the woods, throw away my clothes, and make believe I was a savage. In strict truth I have been yearning to do that ever since."[39] He did more than yearn. Throughout his life, he continued to run away, leaving behind the unpleasant truths of his time.

Again and again in his journals, Grey attacked modernity, facts, and the idea that at the bottom of conscience lay Freud's id or Darwin's amoral struggle to reproduce. Those concepts, insisted Grey, were bringing ruin to the world, killing romance and idealism along with "honor" and "chastity." What he attacked most of all was the spirit of his age, by which he meant the easy morality of flappers and speakeasies and jazz clubs. "Life grows more realistic," he wrote in his diary in July 1925. "The ideal is jazz, money, pleasure, excitement, sex. . . . All over the world . . . is evil, and paganism, and greed." A few months later, he added another cry of anguish. "I am at odds with the literary world," he lamented, referring to "the realist, materialistic, pornographic literature" that held sway among publishers. He vowed to continue nonetheless, certain that he was "destined for some great work."[40]

What was not apparent to Grey was that he appealed to the very sensibility that he despised. His heroines are the reverse of the passionless ideal of nineteenth-century femininity; they lust. In Jean Isbell, Ellen Jorth finds a "new, sensorial life, elemental, primitive, a liberation of a million inherited instincts, quivering and physical." Grey's heroines long for the hero's kiss. They feel magnetic, powerful, unbearable attraction. Heroes reciprocate in kind. The landscapes themselves speak of eros. They are monumental, overwhelming, sublime. They pulsate and quiver and render protagonists almost helpless.[41] Invariably plots end with hero and heroine, usually accompanied by a pair of protagonists from a subplot, at last together, blissful. They remain chaste, however, until the reader extends them privacy by closing the book.

Grey meanwhile was living his romances in more ways than via riding horseback and hunting in the Rim Country wilds. He was as much a libertine as any Greenwich Village radical. Even as he courted his wife, he saw other women. He told her that he wanted something other than the staid life of a married man. He wanted freedom. Ultimately she came to terms with his wishes, giving him the latitude to travel without her and, equally important, to engage in affairs. Grey raged against the sex and the jazz and the realism of his age with the same passion that he pursued his liaisons. He was living the Jazz Age morality that he so despised.[42]

If Grey celebrated honor, then, so too did he celebrate narcissism. Like flappers who inhabited speakeasies and jazz clubs, he indulged in experience, in adventure, in freedom from social constraint. He wanted to live life fully and with gusto, without the tax of responsibility to wife, family, church, or community. He, in a sense, was running from the muckraking and reform of the 1910s. He was running from the problems of the cities, from immigrants, from blacks, from his father's Victorian worldview. He rebelled not by drinking and smoking and gambling; he rebelled by living a fantasy in the West and by writing about it. Though he did not think so, he was apotheosis and avatar of the Roaring Twenties.

Grey stood alongside such cinema stars as Douglas Fairbanks and Mary Pickford in teaching Americans new ideas about who they were and what kind of lives they should lead. Film, radio, and even Grey's novels taught Americans to turn away from the rectitude and caution of the nineteenth-century middle class. For millions toiling in factories and offices, the productive ethos of the nineteenth century made little sense. Tied to bureaucracies and corporate hierarchies or, perhaps, to mindless work on assembly lines, Americans saw little point in spending wisely and saving much. Vocation alone no longer defined status. Leisure became equally important. Exhorted by advertisers and inspired by actors, people defined their lives via play. They learned to consume—to buy clothing and cars and appliances—and to remake themselves via fantasy.[43] Like Grey, they remade themselves by going West, buying trinkets from Indians, and riding horses at dude ranches. They learned to be tourists, and by being tourists, they learned to be Western. They learned, finally, to escape the humanitarian conscience of Progressive America.

Those observations are suppositions. Cultural historians shy from reading meaning into fiction unless they know how readers reacted to it. In this case, we are fortunate. In addition to book reviews—which were largely unflattering—we have dozens of readers' comments, thanks to the decision by Grey's publisher, Harper's, to celebrate the twentieth anniversary of its relationship with its best-selling author in 1930. To honor him, Harper's asked readers to send cards and letters to the publisher naming their favorite titles and discussing what they most liked about Grey's work. The cards and letters were collected in a scrapbook and presented to Grey. For their reward, respondents received photographs of the author.[44]

Hundreds of readers—459 to be precise—wrote back, though most were too modest to offer comments. The sixty-seven who did comment, however, tell us a great deal. The most common reason for liking Grey's novels—cited by almost a quarter of commenters—was his power of description. A typical remark came from W. C. Applegate of Philadelphia, who credited Grey with having "described our western country and characters as no other has been able to do." Viola Palmseley of Detroit, Michigan, similarly received a "thrill out of the beauty of the wild country you [Grey] describe." Mrs. J. J. Hill of Closter, New Jersey, added that Grey's landscape descriptions appealed to her and her mother, whereas his adventurous plots appealed to the men and boys in her family.[45] Left unsaid was the degree to which Grey's landscape carried erotic charge.

The next most common reason for liking Zane Grey novels—cited by eleven commenters—was their cleanliness. Grey's books, asserted Edith Berry of Detroit "show us this isn't entirely a Synthetic Age—that it doesn't, in literature, take a lover and a boudoir to complete a picture of married life and that true courage isn't born of potency of your neighbor's gin." Lena Russell of Grand Ledge, Michigan, agreed, describing Grey's novels as "clean, wholesome and free from the extreme modernism and super sophistication" of contemporary literature. By "living near to nature," she explained, Grey's characters "are perforce at heart sincere and non superficial."[46] None of the commenters noticed any contradiction between the cleanliness of the characters and the eros of the plot and the descriptions. None seemed to realize that even "cleaner" books could be found in libraries and bookstores—books written by nineteenth-century sentimental writers. Grey's readers wanted protagonists who eschew drinking, smoking, gambling, and extramarital sex yet who subtly affirm the passion of the Jazz Age.

An equal number of commenters—eleven—viewed Grey's stories as authentic, even educational. Grey provided "vivid history," wrote Charles Pease
of Northboro, Maine. Mildred Cohen of El Paso, Texas, said she had "learned
more of history" from one of Grey's novels than from all her college work. Grey's
books, agreed Mrs. John Smith of Bedford, Pennsylvania, "have great value as
historical references in the form of fiction." William J. Tewksbury—grandson of
James D. Tewksbury and employee of an Illinois bank—added praise for Grey's
realistic descriptions of cowboys and landscapes. Such comments accord well
with those of Grey's biographer, Carlton Jackson, who wrote that "Grey's contri-
bution to an understanding and appreciation of Western history is almost inesti-
mable."[47] Jackson's statement sounds absurd by the standards of scholarly history,
but it contained truth. Grey was selling not factual history but an ethic of honor
that Americans attributed—rightly, to some degree—to the West.

Eight commenters noted that Grey's novels taught high ideals. Richard
Mitchell of Buffalo, New York, instructed his boys to read Grey's novels as soon
as they were old enough to appreciate chivalry. "Physical and moral courage," he
explained, "are as needful today as in years gone by." To Charles Thomas of India-
napolis, Indiana, editor of a newsletter for the college fraternity Sigma Nu, Grey
was "a chronicler of our western civilization" whom "we can all take for a model
in leading the young men of our present college generation." "You leave the hero
& heroine at the close a much better man & woman in character and circumstances," added John McGoufure of New York City, thus offering "a suggestion
. . . to continue to improve—always on the upward grade constantly striving for a
higher level, worthy of emulation—not pride of possession."[48]

It was another Grey biographer, G. M. Farley, who most fully elaborated the
idea that Grey taught virtue. "My concept of right and wrong, justice, decency,
womanhood and manhood, to a great extent, came from the pen of Zane Grey,"
he wrote, adding that Grey's novels, along with the example of his life, would
continue "to produce great men and women in the future."[49] We might dismiss
Farley as idiosyncratic but for the fact that Grey's readers agreed with him. Grey's
heroes, even if they did seal themselves off from civilization, even if they did
follow the path of passion and eros, were good and pure. More important, Grey's
heroes expressed honor. They understood that no amount of reason and moral
suasion could win the day.

Honor, adventure, and romance made Grey an especial favorite of younger
readers. Eight respondents identified themselves as boys of high school age or
younger; sixteen identified themselves as girls; and no fewer than five librarians
noted Grey's intense popularity among young people. Adults, however, read
Grey's books, too. The overwhelming majority of respondents seem to have come

from adults, though it is difficult to be sure since most respondents failed to note their ages. Twenty-two of those adults—all males—gave notice of their professions. Most were attorneys, physicians, business executives, or salesmen, showing a middle-class bent to Grey's readership. Overwhelmingly, respondents came from cities and towns, especially in the Northeast and Midwest. Eighty-five listed their address as New York City or Brooklyn, amounting to one-fifth of respondents. Even allowing for the fact that urban centers held disproportionate numbers of Americans, Grey's readership seems to have been decidedly citified. That finding is in keeping with best-seller lists, which showed that Grey's novels appealed most to readers in the urban Northeast.[50]

Perhaps the most interesting thing about the respondents is their sex. Two-hundred-sixteen females and 199 males responded to the Harper's ad, along with 27 whose sex cannot be identified (they signed with initials). Grey's audience, then, was remarkably balanced. Clearly women read Grey's novels in large numbers. Fifteen of his novels made their appearance in serialized form in two magazines—*McCall's* and *Ladies Home Journal*—that were aimed at a female market. The fact that men, too, devoured Grey's novels points to the power of his message. He may have been writing dime novels for adults, but they were dime novels that offered rich and erotic landscape descriptions, bold and adventurous heroines (who must nonetheless be tamed), lively and violent plot twists, and the chivalry and honor of heroes.[51]

Perhaps what Grey's books created above all else was a discourse between urbanites and Western settlers. Grey's novels, after all, were informed by very real Western attitudes toward honor. Urban readers thirsted for that honor. Their lives were drab, restrictive, staid. The music and dance and speakeasies of the Jazz Age promised release, but to millions of Americans, those forms of entertainment remained suspect. Victorian conscience steered them from sin. Grey's novels, however, allowed them to enjoy the freedom of the frontier—the freedom to play, to revel in landscape, to experience passion, to glory in guns and fists—without giving up every vestige of Victorian conscience. Grey's heroes and heroines— and the readers who loved them—pretended to be Victorian when in fact they were dedicated to leisure, to fantasy, and to the codes of Western honor.

Real Rim Country settlers did not always find themselves free to play, to revel in landscape, or to experience passion. They, like their Eastern counterparts, continued to pay homage to Victorian values. In the 1880s, however, they had experienced a time of crisis and conflict. They "prevailed"—those who survived, at any rate—via guns and nooses. They, like countless others throughout the West, remembered their trials as epic and formative. Conscience had proven ineffectual. Only honor—assertion through violence—could win the day. They had put down the honor culture of Texas cowboys, to be sure—including the cowboys' dedication to drinking, gambling, braggadocio, and violence—but they had done so only by resorting to more violence. In the process, they had become like those cowboys. Mormons and non-Mormons alike celebrated Arizona's cowboy past and sought to carry it into the future. They celebrated cowboys all the more because urbanites approved them. Even as urban and rural cultures grew more separate, settlers and urbanites became partners in a discourse about honor, about conscience, and about identity. Via dude ranches, rodeos, and apparel— cowboy boots, cowboy hats, western shirts, Levi jeans—Westerners and "dudes" alike displayed their dedication to honor. Whereas in the 1910s, Arizonans had sought to bring themselves to the forefront of conscience—to make their state "civilized"—by the 1920s Arizonans, along with Arizona tourists, were far more interested in celebrating the Wild West.

When Grey claimed in 1929 that he had done more than anyone else to pro-mote Arizona tourism, he was probably right. Time and again, Grey's readers averred that his novels had lured them to the West on vacation or that they planned such a vacation in the future. Grey himself, however, made his exit from Arizona in 1929, noting in his journal that "the lovely places [are] now tin-can resorts for motorists." He had helped create Arizona's tourist boom, and now he fled it. He was piqued, too, about the Arizona Game Commission's refusal to grant him a permit to hunt bears out of season. Settlers from Winslow, adding insult to injury, accused Grey's parties of killing elk surreptitiously, a charge that Grey angrily denied. "Game hogs," he claimed, were maligning him only to turn attention away from their own misdeeds. Worse, "the game commission and the Forest Service have gone over to the commercial interests. The glory and beauty of Arizona, its vanishing forests and game, are no longer for the people. They are being sacrificed to the lumbermen and the sheepmen, the cattle raisers." He complained that ranchers—particularly Mormons—wanted nothing more than range for stock. To get it, they lobbied the Forest Service to poison cougars, coy-otes, and rodents, which by happenstance killed turkeys, rabbits, squirrels, and dogs. Grey was furious.[52]

The relationship between Grey and Rim Country settlers had never been easy. Settlers had welcomed his money. They had even welcomed him. He gave them publicity, and they reciprocated with friendship, up to a point. They made fun of him, too, however, describing his fear of bears and his poor horsemanship.[53] They, at the end of the day, remained true to old values rather than becoming ardent conservationists. They wanted to make money off the land. If roads became crowded with tin lizzies, settlers did not mind. The more tourists, the better. If

Poster advertising the 1950 re-release of Paramount's *To the Last Man*, based on Zane Grey's novel of the same title. Film adaptations brought Grey's message of honor to the screen. Courtesy of the Ohio Historical Society.

cougars and coyotes along with turkeys and rabbits had to be eradicated to make way for sheep and cattle, meanwhile, settlers were not about to object. Nature was theirs to conquer. They rejected Grey's pantheist sentiments.

So Grey left Arizona, returning only once more to oversee the filming of the "talkie" version of *To the Last Man* in the early 1930s. He had put thirty thousand dollars into getting the story of the war, he told Arizonans, and he wanted to make the film as realistic as possible. It was not to be a B Western. It was meant strictly as a marquee feature, with Randolph Scott and Buster Crabbe playing heroes, Esther Ralston playing the heroine, and Noah Beery and Jack LaRue serving as villains. A toddler named Shirley Temple also made her first appearance in film, remaining in the action just long enough to be shot at by a villain. Though filmed on location—including scenes at the ranch of the Colcords, who had served as Jesse Ellison's vigilantes—the final product was even further removed from the actual war than the novel had been. In the film, the feud begins in Kentucky and continues in Arizona. Grey and director Henry Hathaway channeled the film into the well-worn grooves of the classic "mountain" feud rather than exploring the religious and ethnic tensions that caused conflict in Arizona or even the sociology of the free range. More than the book, the film promoted the idea that good could prevail over evil only with bullets.

Along with *To the Last Man*, dozens of Grey titles became films. The Western genre that Grey had done so much to create was transferred from paper to celluloid, rendering the theme of honor—the prescription for violence in quest of the good—all the more potent. Grey himself became a hero to millions of readers, not only in the United States but throughout the world. He was, to give him his due, a fine writer of hyperbolic description as well as a purveyor of melodrama. His stories gave meaning to Arizona's scenery. His stories, too, subtly brought Americans out of the Victorian era into the Jazz Age, into the age of leisure and imagination and paid holidays. He accomplished that by paying tribute to old values—by giving readers heroes and heroines who refused to drink, cheat, or flirt without shame.

If Grey gave Americans a way to escape Victorian values without renouncing those values, he also gave them a way to escape the conscience that had shaped the nation—and Arizona—in the Progressive Era. He gave them a way to escape the tedium of reform. With filmmakers on his flank, with fellow writers riding behind, and with the Rim Country War as his map, Grey led Americans into a world of Western honor.

CONCLUSION

The last man left standing in the Pleasant Valley conflict, according to legend, was Ed Tewksbury. Reality, however, was less tidy. Many men survived the Pleasant Valley conflict. Many more survived the larger conflict—the Rim Country War—of which the Pleasant Valley War was only a part. The real last man left standing, then, was neither Ed Tewksbury nor any other combatant. The real last man was Zane Grey. Though he did not defeat the Grahams or the Mormons or the Aztec Land and Cattle Company, Grey helped create a new equilibrium between honor and conscience, an equilibrium that he found on the Arizona range.

Before Zane Grey arrived in the Rim Country, it had seen war and rapprochement. It had seen the U.S. Forest Service step in to arbitrate disputes and take on the role of common enemy to sheepherders, cattlemen, small operators, and big operators alike. The Rim Country, too, had seen the rise of conscience politics in the era of Governor George W. P. Hunt, followed by an era of tourism, when honor came to the fore once more.

A similar course of events occurred in much of the West. Range wars flared repeatedly in the late nineteenth century, though seldom with the intensity of the Rim Country War. Throughout the rural West, moreover, the Forest Service, and later the Bureau of Land Management, stepped in to regulate the range and mitigate animus. Throughout the rural West, the Forest Service became a common enemy. Throughout the rural West, finally, appeared the politics of conscience in the late nineteenth and early twentieth centuries. Few states were as progressive as Arizona, but all acted to stop lynching and gunplay and to abolish—or at least to regulate—gambling, drinking, and prostitution.

The Rim Country War and its aftermath were not sui generis. Indeed the Rim

Country was in many ways a microcosm of the West. One might argue, in fact, that it was a microcosm for much of the United States. In the Lower Midwest and South, as in the West, feuds and vigilante movements broke out repeatedly in the nineteenth century. Only New England, the Upper Midwest, and Utah—regions imbued with conscience—were exempt.[1]

None of that is to say that the Rim Country War was identical to every other feud in America. Far from it. Consider, for example, the Rim Country War in relation to the archetypal family feud of American history, the Hatfield-McCoy feud of West Virginia. The differences are striking. The most careful student of the Hatfield-McCoy feud, Altina Waller, argues that it pitted a preindustrial "mountain culture" epitomized by the Hatfields against the forces of market capitalism epitomized by the McCoys. The Hatfield-McCoy feud began in 1882 as a dispute over resources—land and timber—but entered its most bitter phase after a dispute over the ownership of a hog. To condense the back-and-forth killing, five members of the McCoy family fell (including two children) along with one Hatfield. Three other Hatfields went to prison, though the clan's patriarch, Anderson Hatfield, escaped prosecution. The Hatfields also killed two deputies who were sent to arrest them.[2]

The Rim Country War similarly emerged from economic conflict and weak legal institutions. The feud in Pleasant Valley, however, was no struggle between preindustrial values and entrepreneurial capitalism. It was a uniquely Western "tragedy of the commons" catalyzed by opportunistic men who flocked to Arizona's Rim Country only to find themselves competing for grazing lands. Settlers might lay claim to land or water through preemption and homesteading laws. To succeed as cattlemen, however, they needed access to free range. The problem with free range was its promise. Even settlers with preemption and homestead claims found themselves crowded by newcomers with large herds as well as newcomers with no more than a few cows and a branding iron. All hoped to become independent—or even prosperous—in the cattle trade. Free range thus became an economic and social wrestling mat. What is important about the Rim Country War, then, is that it could have happened—and did happen—in other parts of the West where free range existed.

The main theater of conflict in the West was probably Texas, where feuds broke out repeatedly in the 1860s, 1870s, and 1880s. Many involved contestation for grass and water. Others were fueled by antipathies between former Confederates and Unionists.[3] Like the Rim Country War, the Texas feuds were cause and consequence of the honor culture that came from the South and reemerged—in altered form—in the West.

Range quarrels flared throughout the West, appearing in California, Colorado, Idaho, Montana, Oregon, Washington, and Wyoming. New Mexico experienced a particularly deadly quarrel in the 1880s—the famed Lincoln County War—though the fighting there was precipitated not so much by a contest for range as by the monopolistic business practices of Lawrence Murphy and James Dolan, who operated a mercantile business.[4] With its ethnic and racial diversity, its religious divisions, its economic tensions, and its weak law enforcement, the nineteenth-century West was home to recurrent episodes of violence and vigilantism.

It was the contest for grass and water, however, that led to some of the bitterest fights. Perhaps the most famous of the range wars occurred in Johnson County, Wyoming, where big operators cracked down on mavericking in the late 1880s and early 1890s. Having vested their power in a stock association, the big operators—as in Apache County—conducted a campaign of spying and assassination against those they regarded as rustlers. Events culminated in 1892 when the stock association hired paid killers—Texas mercenaries—to invade Wyoming. Despite their success in assassinating Nate Champion, the de facto leader of the small operators, the invaders were soon surrounded and under attack by a posse of two hundred. Only President Benjamin Harrison's decision to send in the Sixth Cavalry saved the invaders from massacre.[5]

The Rim Country War had much in common with its sister wars in the West. Like many of them—particularly those in Texas—it resembled a gang war more than a family feud. Though the Grahams and the Tewksburys came to see one another as the focus of evil, each had allies, sponsors, spies, and enablers. The concept of "gang war," however, fails to convey the war's complexity. In a Venn diagram, the Rim Country War would appear as a juncture of two regional theaters of war, each plagued by multiple conflicts. The first theater—eastern Yavapai County, including Pleasant Valley—saw conflicts between small ranchers and big ranchers; between big ranchers and other big ranchers; between white ranchers and mixed-bloods; and between cattlemen and sheepmen. The second theater—Apache County, east and north of Pleasant Valley—saw conflicts between the Aztec and sheepherders; between the Aztec and Mormons; between Mormons and cowboys; between Mormons and New Mexicans; and between established cattlemen and small-time "rustlers."

What made the Rim Country War different from other feuds and range wars was its confusion. The two theaters of conflict, however, became simpler in 1887, when they merged and boiled into ideological consistency. Forces that initially created chaos resolved themselves into a loose alliance that segregated "bad" men from "good" and administered punishment to the latter. To some extent, the conflict resembled the Johnson County War, though the stock association of

Apache County was a weak brother to the powerful and elite stock association that prosecuted a campaign of terror in Wyoming. Unlike the Johnson County grandees and their army of assassins, however, the Arizona vigilantes met little resistance.

In the final phase of the Rim Country War, settlers looked to stern men who were willing to mete out justice with gun and rope. By electing a violent sheriff and by forming vigilance committees, Mormons and their allies broke the shackles of conscience and embraced what Bertram Wyatt-Brown has called the culture of honor. In embracing honor, they helped create a distinctly Western identity, an identity more akin to that of the South than the North. The West, in turn, lured a train of historians, novelists, and movie-makers who imagined an America unblemished by sectional hatred. With the South defeated and discredited, the West became the refuge of an honor unmarred by slavery. Western honor defined and fulfilled the fantasies of American readers who found themselves aswim in a world of shifting gender roles, work relations, and new threats from abroad, a world in which conscience, it seemed, had become as much enemy as guide.[6] Honor, however, did not return in its earlier guise. The honor of twentieth-century Americans was neither that of antebellum planters nor that of Hashknife cowboys.

The man who presented the nation with a new equilibrium between honor and conscience was Zane Grey. One might argue that Grey's intention was not so much to present equilibrium as to push honor into the national discourse. The heroes of Grey's books, however—like the man himself—did not reject every aspect of conscience. They refrained from drinking, gambling, smoking, and swearing. They also eschewed prostitutes, though prostitutes were ubiquitous in the late nineteenth- and early twentieth-century West (and though Grey himself, even if he did not see prostitutes, entertained mistress after mistress). Grey's heroes and heroines embraced honor and behavioral conscience simultaneously.

Like Ed Tewksbury, John Graham, Andy Cooper, John Payne, Jim Houck, Commodore Perry Owens, or even like Osmer Flake, Will Adams, Prime Coleman, Hook Larson, and some of their Mormon brethren, Grey's heroes sought to resolve problems with a six-shooter or, at the least, with a hard fist. Grey's heroes displayed no interest in Progressive reforms. They weren't interested in abolishing capital punishment or prizefighting or in rehabilitating convicts. They were interested in winning their quarrels and their mates via physical assertion. They represented a new blend of honor and conscience that prescribed assertive manliness—and submissive womanliness—for the twentieth century.

Assuming that Grey's heroes prescribed a new formula for manly behavior, how much did that behavior alter history? Did it lead Americans into new rounds of feuding? Probably no, though race riots and lynchings were common in the 1920s, especially in the Midwest and South. The 1920s also saw the renascence and spread of the Ku Klux Klan to Northern and Midwestern states, including Connecticut, Indiana, and Ohio. The 1920s, finally, saw the rise of organized crime and mob feuding, though participants in such things were not likely, it seems, to read Zane Grey.

The honor of Grey's heroes led to no spate of feuding in part because literary message does not necessarily trigger social action. Real-life decision-making is a complex process. Confronted by the wash of events, individuals balance the need for pragmatic response with narratives of righteousness. The usual result is compromise. It is important to recognize in that context that the sort of honor promoted by dude ranches, rodeos, and Zane Grey's fiction was an honor that existed in the realm of romanticism and play. It was both serious and make-believe, both prescription for behavior in the here and now and emblematic of a bygone, exotic, uncivilized past. Americans, then, might smile and wink at the absurdity of Grey's heroes. In time of crisis, however, they might just as easily measure their own bravery, their own honor, their own will to action against those of Grey's protagonists.

Even if Grey's formula of honor led to no new epic of feuding, then, what about war? Did Grey's ethos inspire Americans to respond to crisis via aggression? Perhaps yes. One might argue that the cowboy hero who arrived with Owen Wister's 1902 novel, *The Virginian*, and who appeared again and again in the novels of Grey and in early twentieth-century film, prepared Americans to hearken to the call of war in 1917, when the United States entered the Great War on the side of Britain and France. Influenced by government propaganda, Americans saw themselves as chivalrous knights in a war against German brutality. Those suspected of opposing the war, or even the draft, at times received the sort of treatment that Hashknife cowboys had accorded Mormon settlers in the 1880s. Opponents of the war effort were often cursed, sometimes beaten, and occasionally lynched, especially in the West and Midwest. Opponents of the war were likewise silenced via sedition acts passed both by states and by Congress. The rituals of shaming so common in the nineteenth-century West and South returned to the fore of public consciousness. Even if Grey's novels did not lead to those results, they did not work against them.

After the war, Americans repudiated the Progressive reforms of the 1910s in favor of what President Warren Harding called "normalcy." Normalcy meant a turn away from humanitarian conscience. It meant political indifference to the problems of the poor, the weak, the outcast. It meant, too, a turn away from concern about corporate abuse and exploitation. Normalcy meant a new narcissism, a tendency to focus on one's prosperity and one's possessions and one's leisure. In the West, normalcy meant prosperous tourists riding horses, socializing with cowboys, and recapturing the honor of settlers.

What normalcy also meant was traditional gender codes, or at least gender codes that Americans perceived as traditional. Just as Americans looked to the West to resolve the tensions that had caused the Civil War, they looked to the West to resolve new tensions over gender that became acute as women gained the right to vote. Anxiety about the independence and authority of women was far from new; it had its origins in the antebellum crusades for abolition and temperance, movements that gave women a moral voice. The power that women exerted in the nineteenth century, and now in the twentieth, was the power of conscience. Women could not engage in duels, gunfights, or historic battles. They waged campaigns through moral suasion. If women gained power through conscience, however, men retained authority through honor. Men, too, at times, retained authority through honor's sometime corollary: wife abuse. In a careful study of Oregon, one scholar finds that the incidence of wife abuse declined in the late nineteenth and early twentieth century when an ethos of male self-control prevailed, then rose in the 1920s.[7] Though that same pattern may not hold for other states, it is provocative. Even if Grey's novels were not a direct cause of wife abuse, they preached male assertion. Female captives came to love male captors. Weak women needed strong men.

The conscience politics of the 1900s and 1910s, however, did not entirely fall by the wayside. They returned during the Great Depression, when Americans became concerned with the poor in both city and countryside. It was in the 1930s, interestingly, that Zane Grey fell from the best-seller lists. The year 1940, moreover, was the year that Walter Van Tilburg Clark unveiled his great novel about lynching, *The Ox-Bow Incident,* a novel that contradicted Grey's romantic stories of honor. Rumor has it that Clark based his story on the hanging of Jamie Stott, Jim Stott, and Jeff Wilson. In Clark's novel, a group of vigilantes assemble to track down and lynch three strangers who are accused of rustling. Though a minister, a judge, and a shopkeeper speak against lynching, they prove too weak to stop the deed. The vigilantes fear being seen as cowards more than they fear their consciences. Led by a steely former Confederate officer, the vigilantes give the accused men a quick "trial," then lynch them. Later, the vigilantes find that they have hanged innocent men.[8] In Clark's telling, honor becomes moral weakness, a product of bloodlust and fear of being thought soft.

If Clark's book did not light the way toward conscience, a cataclysm that came a year later did: American entry into World War II. In the aftermath of the war, Americans became eager to do away with Jim Crow laws and the caste system, a system that extended honor to one race and shame to another. Having defeated the Germans and the Japanese, Americans came to believe that they had defeated racism overseas. To lead the Free World, however—most of which was populated by nonwhites—Americans needed to do away with racism at home. In the wake of World War II came a new sort of conscience—or at least a sort of conscience not seen since Reconstruction—a conscience that recognized the humanity of people who were not white. The fact that non-whites themselves pushed resolutely for rights hastened the change.

If World War II buttressed conscience, however, it simultaneously buttressed honor. In the war's wake, the United States developed a culture of militarism that the fire-eaters of the Old South would have admired had they not sought to secede. With millions of men and women cycling through the nation's military bureaucracy, year after year and decade after decade—and urging their sons and daughters to do the same—the United States developed something of a cult of the warrior. Among the heroes of that cult was the cowboy, epitomized in film by John Wayne, star of both Westerns and war films. The cowboy, too, became the focus of all eyes during one of the favorite sporting events of the rural West and even of the rural South—rodeo—which was, and is, swathed in red, white, and blue, and begins with the national anthem.

In the twenty-first century—as in the past—the rural West and the rural South, or at least whites of the rural West and South, resemble one another more than they resemble the rest of the nation. The residents of each see eye to eye on the nobility of military service and the necessity to appear tough to one's enemies. Despite cowboys' indifference or even hostility to religion in the nineteenth century, meanwhile, rural Westerners and rural Southerners tend to embrace the behavioral conscience preached by Mormons and evangelicals. Rural Southerners and Westerners are precisely the sort of people—practitioners of both honor and behavioral conscience—whom Zane Grey idolized in his novels, even though Grey was not a member of an organized church.

Conscience and honor continue to form the yin and yang of American politics, with the Republican Party typically steering toward honor and the Democratic Party steering toward humanitarian conscience. Democrats, to be sure, have produced their own agents of honor, Lyndon Baines Johnson being a prime example, with his forceful style, his cowboying performances, and a foreign policy based more on stick than carrot. Via the Great Society, the War on Poverty, and civil rights legislation, however, Johnson was in other respects a spokesman for humanitarian conscience. Far more representative of honor were Ronald Reagan and George W. Bush, with their Western ranches, their cowboy personae, and their assertive patriotism. In keeping with honor, both men supported the death penalty. Both rejected limitations on the right of individuals to own and carry firearms. Both launched preemptive strikes against international foes. Both, Like Zane Grey's heroes, were devoted to behavioral conscience, Reagan by sponsoring the "War on Drugs" and Bush by publicizing his evangelical Christianity and his abstinence from liquor. Reagan and Bush were in many ways the creations of Zane Grey and the empire of Western novels and movies that followed him.

At the same time that honor has become a powerful force in politics, it has continued to meet critique. In the film *Unforgiven* (1992), Clint Eastwood offered Americans an unsentimental glance into the violence of the West. Even more provocative have been Cormac McCarthy's novels about boys—or men—who cling grimly to a Western code of honor only to find that it leads to bafflement, isolation, and defeat. Perhaps the best example of that theme comes in *All the Pretty Horses* (1993), with its likable boy pistoleer, Jimmy Blevins, its prison knife fight, its execution scene (carried out by Mexican men who, like their victim, are in the thrall of honor), and the quest of its hero, John Grady Cole, for justice via violence.

Grey's romances also met their match in the realism of Marguerite Noble's *Filaree: A Novel of an American Life* (1979). Noble, daughter of a Texas family who settled in Arizona at the old Charles Boquet ranch at the foot of the Sierra Ancha—site of a magical oasis planted with fruit trees—made her novel into a counterpoint to tourist sensationalism. Basing her tale on the life of her mother, Noble follows her heroine through the trials of spousal abuse, parenthood (including a run-in with a child molester), an affair, a separation, an exodus to California, a return to the Salt River Valley, and a cotton farming venture with a new husband. The novel is dedicated to "to those pioneer women who survived a life of oppression." The source of that oppression, in part, was the culture of honor. Though the heroine's first husband is a "predestinarian Baptist," he drinks, curses, and bullies his wife and children. He is neither gunman nor vigilante, but he dedicates himself to harshness. The novel tells the story of his wife's emancipation. In and out of it flits the romantic hero—the good cowboy, Ike Talbott—who becomes the heroine's lover and who must kill his cowboy nemesis in a gunfight before renouncing his gun.[9]

Whereas Grey's *Under the Tonto Rim* was a story of an urban woman finding herself in the thrall of a pioneer hero and a powerful landscape, Noble's *Filaree* is a story of a pioneer woman's attempt to escape that life. Far from celebrating her role as a settler, Noble's heroine—despite her abiding love for the country—comes to despise it. When she finds happiness as the wife of a cotton farmer, she asks her new husband to cut off the long, silken hair that has come to represent her enslavement. Like Hamlin Garland and O. E. Rolvaag before her, Noble wrote about the reality of the rural West rather than its romance. She wrote the sort of book that Frank Norris or Willa Cather might have written about the Rim Country, a book that explored emotional hardship and taught compassion.

In the first half of the nineteenth century, the South rallied around honor whereas the North rallied around conscience, thus creating (at least partly) the cyclone of civil war. In the second half of the nineteenth century, honor and its attendant racial division between noble whites and shamed blacks continued to influence the South. A new sort of honor, however—an honor seemingly divested of its racial component—emerged in the West. In the first half of the twentieth century, it was the honor of the West, not the South, that shaped national consciousness. Not only did the new honor—preached by Zane Grey— lead away from Progressive reform, it also led away from the equality of the sexes. Women who had once wielded conscience as a weapon found themselves subdued—at least figuratively—by the muscular honor of men.

None of that is to say that honor was all-powerful. Women and conscience no more disappeared in American culture than they did in Grey's novels. Even Grey's plots, after all, gave women the powers of thought, will, and action. His heroines are tamed by male honor but not silenced. Occasionally, indeed, Grey's heroines themselves resort to guns to defeat evil. Women read Grey's books in part because they identified with the heroines' strength.

Whatever its impact on gender, honor continues to play a role in the Rim Country and in the rural West more broadly. In the Sierra Ancha—not far from Pleasant Valley—a fourth-generation rancher displayed an old penchant for vigilante assertion when in 2002 he shot at the "bucket" of a Forest Service firefighting helicopter as it tried to scoop water from his stock tank.[10] Other descendants of Rim Country settlers, meanwhile, established Git-A-Rope! press to publicize the history of the region and its longstanding problems with the Forest Service, which, as old-time Rim Country people see it, caters to urban environmentalists. Though meant in part to be humorous, the name Git-A-Rope! evokes the honor of the Rim Country past. The Arizona legislature shows its own dedication to honor, meanwhile, by working tirelessly to undo gun control laws, laws that took root in the aftermath of the Rim County War.

Something else, too, haunts the Rim Country: massive fires, the result of drought, pine beetles, and decade upon decade of fire prevention. Old-timers blame radical environmentalists for protecting too many trees. Environmentalists blame the Forest Service for failing to eliminate undergrowth. Either way, the fires continue, as if bent on cleansing the land of its bitter past.

Just as Rim Country old-timers quarrel with Phoenix environmentalists, so too do other Americans—rural conservatives and urban liberals—quarrel over issues basic to their society, issues on which honor and conscience lead in opposite directions. There will likely never be definitive answers to the questions of whether it is best to execute murderers or attempt their rehabilitation; whether to make hostile nations fear and cower or to offer diplomacy; and whether to carry guns to ward off criminals or to eliminate guns from the streets. After all the research and all the argumentation, often our decisions boil down to our preference for honor or conscience. If the Rim Country dead ask anything, they ask us this: that we reflect carefully on our predicament.

ABBREVIATIONS

NEWSPAPERS

AC	Arizona *Champion* (Flagstaff)
ACC	Apache County *Critic* (Holbrook)
ACh	Apache *Chief* (St. Johns)
AG	Arizona *Gazette* (Phoenix)
AJM	Arizona *Journal-Miner* (Prescott)
AR	Arizona *Republican* (Phoenix)
ASB	Arizona *Silver Belt* (Globe)
DSB	*Daily Silver Belt* (Miami)
HH	*Hoof and Horn* (Prescott)
PH	Phoenix *Herald*
SJH	St. Johns *Herald*

MAGAZINES AND JOURNALS

AH	*Arizona Highways*
AHR	*Arizona Historical Review*
JAH	*Journal of Arizona History*
PAATGS	*Progressive Arizona and the Great Southwest*

LIBRARIES AND ARCHIVAL COLLECTIONS

ACCR	Apache County Criminal Records
AHS	Arizona Historical Society
ASLAPR	Arizona State Library, Division of Archives and Public Records
ASU	Arizona State University
ASUDAM	Arizona State University, Department of Archives and Manuscripts
CWP	Clara Woody Papers, Arizona Historical Society

DC   Delph Collection, North Gila County Historical Society
DDC   Don Dedera Collection, Arizona State University, Department of
                  Archives and Manuscripts
ECP   Evans Coleman Papers, Arizona Historical Society
GRMC   Gladwell Richardson Manuscript Collection, Northern Arizona
                  University, Special Collections
GSTC   George S. Tanner Collection, University of Utah J. Willard Marriott
                  Library, Special Collections
GWPHC   George W. P. Hunt Collection, Arizona State University, Department
                  of Archives and Manuscripts
GWPHNSASU   George W. P. Hunt Newspaper Scrapbooks, Arizona State University,
                  Department of Archives and Manuscripts
GWPHSUA   George W. P. Hunt Scrapbooks, University of Arizona Special
                  Collections
HDL   Harold D. Lee Library, Brigham Young University
JNSP   Jesse N. Smith Papers, Harold D. Lee Library, Brigham Young
                  University
JWLC   James Warren LeSueur Collection, Arizona Historical Society
LSUP   Levi Stewart Udall Papers, Arizona State University, Department of
                  Archives and Special Collections
NGCHS   North Gila County Historical Society
OFD   Osmer Flake Diaries, Harold D. Lee Library, Brigham Young
                  University
PFHH   Papers of Francis Henry Hereford, University of Arizona, Special
                  Collections
RFCC   Roberta Flake Clayton Collection, Arizona State University,
                  Department of Archives and Manuscripts
RRC   Ryder Ridgway Collection, Arizona State University, Department of
                  Archives and Special Collections
SFC   Silas L. Fish Collection, University of Utah J. Willard Marriott Library,
                  Special Collections
UASC   University of Arizona, Special Collections
WCBC   Will C. Barnes Collection, University of Arizona, Special Collections
YCCR   Yavapai County Criminal Records, Arizona State Library, Division of
                  Archives and Public Records
ZGNC   Zane Grey Newspaper Clippings, Ohio Historical Society

NOTES

INTRODUCTION

1. Territory vs. Ed. Tewksbury. Reporter's Transcript (Aug. 29, 30, 31, Sept. 1, 2, 3, 5, 6, 7, 8, 1892), UASC, 1:3–6, 17, 25, 91–92, 157.
2. Territory vs. Ed. Tewksbury. Reporter's Transcript, 1:14–16, 25, 30–41, 63–66, 184, 193, 204, 240, 258, 265, 270.
3. Territory vs. Ed. Tewksbury. Reporter's Transcript, 1:65, 241–50, 2:339, 343, 350–51, 353.
4. Harold D. Jenkerson, "Pleasant Valley Feud," typescript, 2 vols., NGCHS, 2:404; Territory vs. Ed Tewksbury. Reporter's Transcript, 2:396, 422, 429; Don Dedera, *A Little War of Our Own: The Pleasant Valley Feud Revisited* (Flagstaff, AZ: Northland, 1988), 225–50. There was also talk of lynching Tewksbury. ASB, Jan. 12, 26, 1895.
5. W. Webster Street to Frank Hereford, District Attorney, no place, Dec. 25, 1893, PFHH, box 1, folder 6; Frank Cox to Hereford, Phoenix, Dec. 26, 1893, PFHH, box 1, folder 6.
6. Mark Twain, *Adventures of Huckleberry Finn* (New York: Charles L. Webster, 1885), 143–56.
7. I draw my description of honor and conscience from Sheldon Hackney, "Southern Violence," *American Historical Review* 74 (1969): 906–25; Bertram Wyatt-Brown, *Southern Honor: Ethics and Behavior in the Old South* (New York: Oxford University Press, 1982); Bertram Wyatt-Brown, *Yankee Saints and Southern Sinners* (Baton Rouge: Louisiana State University Press, 1985); Kenneth S. Greenberg, *Honor and Slavery* (Princeton, NJ: Princeton University Press, 1996); Richard E. Nisbett and Dov Cohen, *Culture of Honor: The Psychology of Violence in the South* (Boulder, CO: Westview, 1996); Grady McWhiney, *Cracker Culture: Celtic Ways in the Old South* (Tuscaloosa: University of Alabama Press, 1988); Dick Steward, *Duels and the Roots of Violence in Missouri* (Columbia: University of Missouri Press, 2000); Rhys Isaac, *The Transformation of Virginia* (Chapel Hill: University of North Carolina Press, 1982); and Timothy H. Breen, "Horses and Gentlemen: The Cultural Significance of Gambling among the Gentry of Virginia," *William and Mary Quarterly*, 3rd ser., 34 (1977): 239–47. I draw also on Amy Greenberg, whose distinction between "martial manhood" and "restrained manhood" in the antebellum era mirrors the honor and conscience

dichotomy described by Wyatt-Brown, though Greenberg does not link either sort of manhood solely to the South or to the North. Amy S. Greenberg, *Manifest Manhood and the Antebellum American Empire* (Cambridge: Cambridge University Press, 2005). Key anthropological studies of honor include J. D. Peristiany, ed., *Honour and Shame: The Values of Mediterranean Society* (Chicago: University of Chicago Press, 1966); and John Davis, *People of the Mediterranean* (London: Routledge and Kegan Paul, 1977). Nisbett and Cohen—following the lead of anthropologists—argue that the codes of Southern (and implicitly Western) honor befit the economics of herding. Where property—sheep or cows—wandered far away, it became easy to steal. To deter theft, men became more "manly," more assertive, more ready to do violence. Though I do not discount Nisbett and Cohen, their thesis too readily becomes functionalist reductionism. One way to discourage one's neighbors from stealing cows, after all, was to establish rules and courts. Violence was neither necessary nor functional even among herders. David Hackett Fischer, meanwhile, notes that rustling was as common in the border region between England and Scotland as in the American West. Shaped by centuries of war, contends Fischer, "borderers" who emigrated to the American South and later to the Lower Midwest and Far West brought with them a warrior ethic, a devotion to kin and clan, and a tradition of feuding, vigilantism, and hard drinking. See also Fischer's thick description of the "distressed cavaliers" who migrated to Virginia in the 1600s; they, too, brought a baggage of honor. Fischer, *Albion's Seed*, 207–16, 243–44, 308–9, 311–12, 318–20, 360–64, 365–73, 626, 628–31, 663–38, 687, 689–90, 765–76. Hackney, by contrast, suggests that Southern violence—including high homicide rates that persisted into the twentieth century—came not only from the coercion requisite to slavery but also from the Civil War experience of conquest and dependency. The latter experience, argues Hackney, created among Southerners a tendency to see themselves as hostages to forces beyond their control, which caused them to direct violent impulses outward rather than inward. Hackney, "Southern Violence," 924–25.

8. The first book-length nonfiction treatment of the war, Earle Forrest's *Arizona's Dark and Bloody Ground* (Caldwell, ID: Caxton Printers, 1936), sought to vindicate the Grahams, as does a more recent work, Leland J. Hanchett's *Arizona's Graham-Tewksbury Feud* (Phoenix, AZ: Pine Rim, 1994). Dedera's 1988 book, *A Little War of Our Own*, stands out as an exemplary narrative and a model of dispassionate research. Not even Dedera, however, places the feud in the context of economic and social conflict. Regarding the number of dead, Forrest puts the figure at nineteen but thinks that one or two more might be added. Dedera puts the number between thirty and fifty. Forrest, *Dark and Bloody Ground*, 25; Dedera, *Little War*, 1. If we count the dead in what I call the Rim Country War, the figures are substantially higher.

9. On the nobility of vigilantism as a cornerstone of Western identity, see Clyde A. Milner II, "The Shared Memory of Montana's Pioneers," *Montana: The Magazine of Western History* 37, no. 1 (1987): 2–13.

10. William MacLeod Raine and Will C. Barnes, *Cattle* (Garden City, NY: Doubleday, Doran, 1930), 7–8.

11. Thomas H. Pauly, *Zane Grey: His Life, His Adventures, His Women* (Urbana: University of Illinois Press, 2005), 2.

12. Richard Slotkin, *Regeneration through Violence: The Mythology of the American Frontier, 1600–1860* (Middletown, CT: Wesleyan University Press, 1973); Slotkin, *The Fatal Environment: The Myth of the Frontier in the Age of Industrialization, 1800–1890* (New York: Atheneum, 1985); Slotkin, *Gunfighter Nation: The Myth of the Frontier in Twentieth-Century America* (New York: Atheneum, 1992); Richard Maxwell Brown, *Strain of Violence: Historical Studies of American Violence and Vigilantism* (New York: Oxford University Press, 1975); and Brown, *No Duty to Retreat: Violence and Values in American Society* (New York: Oxford University Press, 1992).

13. John Mack Faragher in "Roundtable on *Massacre at Mountain Meadows*," in *Dialogue: A Journal of Mormon Thought* 42, no. 1 (2009): 113; W. Eugene Hollon, *Frontier Violence: Another Look* (New York: Oxford University Press, 1974), x. For a sociological perspective on American violence, see David Peterson del Mar, *What Trouble I Have Seen: A History of Violence against Wives* (Cambridge, MA: Harvard University Press, 1996); Peterson del Mar, *Beaten Down: A History of Personal Violence in the West* (Seattle: University of Washington Press, 2002); and Christine Daniels and Michael V. Kennedy, *Over the Threshold: Intimate Violence in Early America* (New York: Routledge, 1999). Equally important are studies of Indian-white violence, especially those that transcend the "violence was inevitable" thesis. See in particular Ned Blackhawk, *Violence over the Land: Indians and Empires in the Early American West* (Cambridge, MA: Harvard University Press, 2006); and James Brooks, *Captives and Cousins: Slavery, Kinship, and Community in the Southwest Borderlands* (Chapel Hill: University of North Carolina Press, 2001). Brooks argues that honor—defined via almost formulaic raids to capture and enslave, or to defend, women and children—defined male status in both New Mexican and Indian communities in the seventeenth and eighteenth centuries. Those who argue that the West (excluding Indian wars and massacres) was no more violent than other parts of the United States include Hollon, *Frontier Violence*; Robert R. Dykstra, "Body Counts and Murder Rates: The Contested Statistics of Western Violence," *Reviews in American History* 31 (2003): 554–63; Dykstra, *The Cattle Towns* (New York: Alfred A. Knopf, 1968); and Frank Richard Prassel, *The Western Peace Officer: A Legacy of Law and Order* (Norman: University of Oklahoma Press, 1972).

14. Susan Lee Johnson, "'A Memory Sweet to Soldiers': The History of Gender in the 'American West,'" in Mary Ann Irwin and James F. Brooks, eds., *Women and Gender in the American West* (Albuquerque: University of New Mexico Press, 2004), 105, 108, 109.

15. Richard Jenkins, *Pierre Bourdieu* (London: Routledge, 2002), 70, 75, 78. Also see Pierre Bourdieu, *Outline of a Theory of Practice* (Cambridge: Cambridge University Press, 1977); and Bourdieu, "The Sentiment of Honor in Kabyle Society," trans. Philip Sharrard, in Peristiany, *Honour and Shame*, 192–211. Whereas poststructuralism veers toward subjectivism—what Claude Lévi-Strauss called spontaneity, or human free will—Bourdieu takes a more nuanced position. He denies neither free will nor structured constraint. His sociology thus allows for both continuity and change. Pierre Bourdieu, *In Other Words: Essays toward a Reflexive Sociology* (Stanford, CA: Stanford University Press, 1990), 61–65.

CHAPTER ONE: HOME ON THE RANGE

1. Will C. Barnes, *Arizona Place Names* (Tucson: University of Arizona Press, 1988); Fred W. Croxen, "History of Grazing on Tonto. Presented by Senior Forest Ranger Fred W. Croxen, at the Tonto Grazing Conference in Phoenix, Arizona, November 4–5, 1926," http://www.rangebiome.org/genesis/GrazingOnTonto-1926.html.

2. Edward H. Peplow, Jr., *History of Arizona*, 3 vols. (New York: Lewis Historical Publishing, 1958), 2:192; *ASB*, May 16, 1878, Apr. 6, 1899.

3. Leland J. Hanchett, Jr., *Arizona's Graham-Tewksbury Feud* (Phoenix, AZ: Pine Rim, 1994), 5–6; Brian Roberts, *American Alchemy: The California Gold Rush and Middle-Class Culture* (Chapel Hill: University of North Carolina Press, 2000), 152; Marilyn Keach Milota, comp., "A Guideline to Humboldt County Births before 1900," typescript, vol. 2 (Eureka, CA: Humboldt County Genealogical Society, 1999), 795; Harold D. Jenkerson, "Pleasant Valley Feud," typescript, 2 vols., NGCHS, 1:48–49. Page references to Jenkerson, "Pleasant Valley," refer to the typescript at NGCHS and may not correspond precisely to other copies.

4. Roberts, *American Alchemy*, 152–53.

5. Rodman Wilson Paul, *Mining Frontiers of the Far West, 1848–1880*, rev., exp. ed. by Elliott West (Albuquerque: University of New Mexico Press, 2001), 231.

6. Jenkerson, "Pleasant Valley," 1:49–51; Clara T. Woody, "Outlaw Valley," typescript, CWP, box 6, folder 10; L. J. Horton, "The Pleasant Valley War," CWP, box 8, folder 88; Hanchett, *Graham-Tewksbury Feud*, 7.

7. Horton, "Pleasant Valley War," 1; Woody, "Outlaw Valley," 4; *ASB*, Sept. 20, 1884, 3; Jenkerson, "Pleasant Valley," 1:45–46, 54, 212; Joseph Fish, "The Fish Manuscript, 1840–1926," ASLAPR, 595; U.S. Census, Yavapai County, Arizona, 1880; Phil Smith, "Ellisons Settle to Life on Q Ranch," *ASB*, Aug. 8, 1991, in DDC, box 22, folder 3.

8. Hanchett, *Graham-Tewksbury Feud*, 5, 7, 8, 17, 22, 27; Jenkerson, "Pleasant Valley," 1:52, 67; Deposition of John Graham, Feb. 12, 1883, *Territory of Arizona vs. John Gilliland, Epitasio Ruiz and Elisha Gilliland*, YCCR; Robert Vooris [Voris], interviewed by Clara Woody and Dale King, Gila Pueblo near Globe, Arizona, May 20, 1957, typescript, CWP, box 16, folder 64; Horton, "Pleasant Valley War," 2.

9. Melissa Stinson, "Melissa Bagley Flannigan Stinson," typescript, ed. Niva Strever, reproduced in Leland J. Hanchett, Jr., *They Shot Billy Today: The Families of the Pleasant Valley War* (Phoenix, AZ: Pine Rim, 2006), 177; Charles S. Peterson, *Take Up Your Mission: Mormon Colonizing along the Little Colorado River, 1870–1900* (Tucson: University of Arizona Press, 1973), 27 (quotation), 28–30; Joseph Fish, "History of Eastern Arizona Stake of Zion; Early Settlement of Apache County and Stake Clerk's Records and Journal, 1878–1912," mss., ASLAPR, 2; Fish, "Fish Manuscript," 465; Robert Carlock, *The Hashknife: The Early Days of the Aztec Land and Cattle Company, Limited* (Tucson, AZ: Westernlore, 1994), 33; *AR*, Nov. 2, 1930; Jenkerson, "Pleasant Valley," 1:56–57.

10. Several scholars contend that, though settlers did not necessarily reject market capitalism, neither did they rush to embrace it. See John Mack Faragher, *Sugar Creek: Life on the Illinois Prairie* (New Haven: Yale University Press, 1986); Don Harrison

Doyle, *The Social Order of a Frontier Community: Jacksonville, Illinois, 1825–1870* (Urbana: University of Illinois Press, 1978), 3, 15; and Harry Watson, *Jacksonian Politics and Community Conflict: The Emergence of the Second American Party System in Cumberland County, North Carolina* (Baton Rouge: Louisiana State University Press, 1981), 322. For a more pointed argument on settlers' opposition to market capitalism, see Charles Sellers, *The Market Revolution: Jacksonian America, 1815–1846* (Oxford: Oxford University Press, 1991).

11. AG, Dec. 20, 1880.

12. ASB, Jan. 19, Mar. 1, 8, Aug. 30, 1884.

13. William MacLeod Raine and Will C. Barnes, *Cattle* (Garden City, NY: Doubleday, Doran, 1930), 180, 226–32; Joseph G. McCoy, *Historic Sketches of the Cattle Trade of the West and Southwest* (Kansas City, MO: Ramsey, Millett and Hudson, 1874); James S. Brisbin, *The Beef Bonanza; or, How To Get Rich on the Plains, Being a Description of Cattle-Growing, Sheep-Farming, Horse-Raising, and Dairying in the West* (Philadelphia: J. B. Lippincott, 1881).

14. SJH, July 3, 1885 (quoting Socorro *Bulletin*).

15. Jenkerson, "Pleasant Valley," 1:61; ASB, July 10, 1880, Sept. 19, May 23, 1885, Nov. 27, 1886, Jan. 1, 1887; Horton, "Pleasant Valley War," 5, 10.

16. *Honor the Past . . . Mold the Future* (n.p.: Gila Centennials, Inc. Celebration Committee, 1976), 29–30; AG, Jan. 10, 1881; ASB, Jan. 22, 1881, Jan. 26, Mar. 22, 1884, Jan. 24, 1885, July 3, 1886, Jan. 22, June 4, 1887, Apr. 20, June 1, 1889; SJH, Aug. 2, 1888.

17. ASB, June 4, Sept. 10, 1887.

18. George W. P. Hunt to Helen Duett Ellison, July 19, 1891, GWPHC, box 5, folder 2; Horton, "Pleasant Valley War," 17.

19. SJH, July 30, 1885; ASB, June 28, 1884, June 26, July 17, Oct. 23, 1886, Feb. 12, 1887, July 6, 1889, Mar. 1, Apr. 2, 1892.

20. Jenkerson, "Pleasant Valley," 1:44, 51, 66, 67, 112, 186; Dedera, *Little War*, 42–48.

21. Will C. Barnes, *Apaches and Longhorns: The Reminiscences of Will C. Barnes* (Tucson: University of Arizona Press, 1982), 191; SJH, Mar. 31, 1887; Clara Woody, "Pleasant Valley Miscellany," CWP, box 13, folder 20, A-14, 1885, 2.

22. Grady McWhiney, *Cracker Culture: Celtic Ways in the Old South* (Tuscaloosa: University of Alabama Press, 1988); Raine and Barnes, *Cattle*, 9–10; Cynthia A. Kierner, "Hospitality, Sociability, and Gender in the Southern Colonies," *Journal of Southern History* 62 (1996): 449–80.

23. Les Flake, *Tales from Oz* (n.p., n.d.), 80; "Heber," typescript, 4, DC, box 1, folder 2; Carlock, *Hashknife*, 169.

24. SJH, Mar. 31, 1887.

25. James Stinson to Will Barnes, Kline, Colorado, May 31, [year illegible], WCBC, box 3, folder 23, 2; Vooris interview, 5. One student of the conflict claimed that it began as a quarrel over ownership of a milk cow. Dan R. Williamson to Will C. Barnes, Globe, Arizona, June 9, 1931, WCBC, box 1, folder 3.

26. Hanchett, *Graham-Tewksbury Feud*, 18.

27. Hanchett, *Graham-Tewksbury Feud*, 18–20. John Gilliland's 1916 account of events dif-

fered from his court testimony after the shooting. See Dane Coolidge, *Arizona Cowboys* (New York: E. P. Dutton, 1938), 148–52.

28. *PH*, Jan. 23, 1883; Testimony of Ed Tewksbury, Feb. 12, 1883, in *Territory of Arizona vs. John Gilliland, Epitasio Ruiz and Elisha Gilliland*, YCCR; *Territory of Arizona vs. Tewkesbury [sic], et al.*, YCCR; Fish, "Fish Manuscript," 686; Jenkerson, "Pleasant Valley," 1:80, 98, 101.

29. *PH*, Jan. 23, 1883; *AG*, Jan. 27, 1883.

30. Dedera, *Little War*, 48; *AG*, Jan. 30, 1883.

31. One historian claims that Gilliland's family and their neighbors in Wild Rye—a hamlet to the west of Pleasant Valley—had come to despise the Tewksburys even before the Gilliland shooting, perhaps because of their interaction with the Tewksburys in California. Having intermarried, the Wild Rye families would likely have seen eye to eye in matters involving relations with outsiders. Judicial records show that they deputized a posse that took into custody John, James, and Frank Tewksbury, as well as Tom Graham, after the shooting of Elisha Gilliland. Oddly, other than John Gilliland himself, only one man from Wild Rye spoke of the conflict in subsequent years, and he claimed that he had sympathized with the Tewksburys. Jenkerson, "Pleasant Valley," 1:63, 76, 79. Drusilla Hazelton, in her manuscript, reported that young Elisha had ridden home with his reins in his teeth. Neither the Tewksburys nor the Grahams, according to his relatives, had come to his succor. Perhaps the story confuses Elisha with John. In his 1916 version of events, John Gilliland testified that the Tewksburys and Grahams carried Elisha nine miles to shelter, then called in a doctor. Drusilla Hazelton, "The Hazeltons of Arizona," typescript, MS 344, AHS, 101; Coolidge, *Arizona Cowboys*, 150.

32. Robert Allison, "The Blevins Family: An Episode in the Pleasant Valley War," CWP, box 8, folder 77, 10–11; H. Henry Scheffer III and Sheryn R. Alger, *The Pleasant Valley War: Cattle and Sheep Don't Mix* (Apache Junction, AZ: Norseman, 1994), 3.

33. Charles Duchet, "Reminiscences of 'One-Shot' Charlie Dushey," DC, box 1, folder 8, 1; Hanchett, *Graham-Tewksbury Feud*, 22. Duchet's name was also spelled Duesha, Dushea, and Dushay. His birth name was English, but he went by his mother's family's name.

34. Hanchett, *Graham-Tewksbury Feud*, 21; Jenkerson, "Pleasant Valley," 1:100, 102; YCCR, Prescott, Ed, and Jim Tewksbury File, 1884.

35. *ASB*, July 19, 1884; *AC*, July 26, 1884; *Territory of Arizona vs. Thos. Graham and Jno. Graham*, 1884, YCCR; Jenkerson, "Pleasant Valley," 1:100, 133.

36. Jess G. Hayes, *Sheriff Thompson's Day: Turbulence in Arizona Territory* (Tucson: University of Arizona Press, 1968), 53; Jenkerson, "Pleasant Valley," 1:148; *ASB*, May 1, 1880, May 7, 1881, Oct. 25, 1884, Oct. 3, 1885, June 12, 1886.

37. Jenkerson, "Pleasant Valley," 1:53, 133, 148; *ASB*, Mar. 27, 1880, Feb. 16, Oct. 4, 18, Dec. 13, 1884, June 27, July 18, 1885; ACCR, John and Tom Graham file, deposition of Jim Tewksbury.

38. *AC*, July 26, 1884, 3; Jenkerson, "Pleasant Valley," 1:109, 124.

39. Fish, "Fish Manuscript," 686.

40. Bill O'Neal, *Cattlemen vs. Sheepherders: Five Decades of Violence in the West* (Austin, TX: Eakin, 1989), 5, 9, 163.

41. Jenkerson, "Pleasant Valley," 1:142; *Territory of Arizona vs. F. M. McCann*, 1884, YCCR.

42. Hanchett, *Graham-Tewksbury Feud*, 26; U.S. Census, 1880, Maricopa County, Arizona.

43. ASB, Aug. 23, 1884; Hanchett, *They Shot Billy*, 99.

CHAPTER TWO: THE SAINTS MARCH IN

1. Roberta Flake Clayton, ed., *To the Last Frontier: The Autobiography of Lucy Hannah White Flake* (reprint ed., n.p., 1976), 16.

2. Clayton, ed., *Frontier*, 14.

3. Clayton, ed., *Frontier*, 13.

4. Clayton, ed., *Frontier*, 9.

5. Osmer Flake, *William Jordan Flake: Pioneer, Colonizer* (n.p., n.d.), 2.

6. Clayton, ed., *Frontier*, 16, 17; Osmer Flake, "Biography of William Jordan Flake," mss., OFD, folder 11, 5.

7. Flake, *William Jordan Flake*, 1–3.

8. Flake, *William Jordan Flake*, 9, 23–24; Clayton, ed., *Frontier*, 17.

9. Flake, "Biography of Flake," 9.

10. Newell G. Bringhurst, *Saints, Slaves, and Blacks: The Changing Place of Black People within Mormonism* (Westport, CT: Greenwood, 1981), 18, 21–25, 37–40, 44–45.

11. Austin E. Fife, "A Mormon from Cradle to Grave," in Austin E. Fife, *Exploring Western Americana*, Alta Fife, ed. (Ann Arbor, MI: UMI Research Press, 1988), 6.

12. Flake, "Biography of Flake," 11.

13. Flake, "Biography of Flake," 6, 13, 19; Clayton, ed., *Frontier*, 18

14. On Mormon plans to create a separate nation in the West, see D. W. Meinig, "The Mormon Nation and the American Empire," in Dean L. May and Reid L. Neilson, with Richard Lyman Bushman, Jan Shipps, and Thomas G. Alexander, *The Mormon History Association's Tanner Lectures: The First Twenty Years* (Urbana: University of Illinois Press, 2006), 125–37.

15. Flake, "Biography of Flake," 30–35; Clayton, ed., *Frontier*, 18, 20.

16. Clayton, ed., *Frontier*, 19, 21, 85; Flake, *William Jordan Flake*, 24–25; Chad J. Flake, "William J. Flake—Biographical Sketch," in Roberta Flake Clayton, ed., *Pioneer Men of Arizona* (n.p., 1976), 168; Flake, "Biography of Flake," 35, 45.

17. Flake, "Biography of Flake," 38–39; Clayton, ed., *Frontier*, 19.

18. Flake, "Biography of Flake," 15, 21.

19. Austin E. Fife, "Folk Belief and Mormon Cultural Autonomy," in Fife, *Exploring Western Americana*, 32. On the origins and history of Mormon perfectionism, see John L. Brooke, *The Refiner's Fire: The Making of Mormon Cosmology, 1644-1844* (Cambridge: Cambridge University Press, 1994).

20. See Patrick Q. Mason, "'Sinners in the Hands of an Angry Mob': Violence against Reli-

gious Outsiders in the American South, 1865–1910" (PhD diss., University of Notre Dame, 2006); Clayton, ed., *Frontier*, 93, 95.

21. Brigham Young, *Diary of Brigham Young, 1857*, ed. Everett L. Cooley (Salt Lake City: University of Utah Tanner Trust Fund, 1980), 49 (July 24, 1857).

22. See Juanita Brooks, *The Mountain Meadows Massacre* (Norman: University of Oklahoma Press, 1962); and Will Bagley, *Blood of the Prophets: Brigham Young and the Massacre at Mountain Meadows* (Norman: University of Oklahoma Press, 2002). Though sensationalized, Sally Denton's *American Massacre: The Tragedy at Mountain Meadows, September 1857* (New York: Alfred A. Knopf, 2003), is also useful. For Mormon scholars' perspective on Bagley in particular, see reviews of *Blood of the Prophets* by Thomas G. Alexander, Lawrence Coates, and Paul H. Petersen in *BYU Studies Review*, available at: http://byustudies.byu.edu/reviews/pages/topreviews.aspx?zoom_highlight=bagley.

23. Ronald W. Walker, Richard E. Turley, Jr., and Glen M. Leonard, *Massacre at Mountain Meadows* (New York: Oxford University Press, 2008), 193.

24. Denton, *American Massacre*, 16, 69, 106.

25. Denton, *American Massacre*, 155–56, 162–63. The rumors may or may not have been true. For a thorough discussion of events leading up to the massacre—including Mormon testimony of taunts and insults from the emigrants—see Walker, Turley, and Leonard, *Massacre at Mountain Meadows*.

26. Denton, *American Massacre*, 138.

27. Flake, *William Jordan Flake*, 31–35, 37, 39; Clayton, ed., *Frontier*, 24, 26; Flake, "Biography of Flake," 55.

28. Flake, "Biography of Flake," 15, 65, 72, 105; Flake, *William Jordan Flake*, 70.

29. Flake, "Biography of Flake," 51; Flake, *William Jordan Flake*, 31, 39, 48; Clayton, ed., *Frontier*, 47.

30. Clayton, ed., *Frontier*, 40–41; Lucy Hannah White Flake, "Autobiography and Diary of Lucy Hannah White Flake," typescript, HDL, 69 (Nov. 21, 1895).

31. Dean L. May, *Three Frontiers: Family, Land, and Society in the American West, 1850–1900* (Cambridge: Cambridge University Press, 1994), 236; Linda King Newell, "A Gift Given, a Gift Taken: Washing, Anointing, and Blessing the Sick among Mormon Women," *Sunstone* 6 (November–December 1981): 26–27; Jesse Nathaniel Smith, "Journal," JNSP, box 1, folder 2, 309–10, 355 (Erastus Snow quotation, Sept. 25, 1884); Clayton, ed., *Frontier*, 40–41.

32. Clayton, ed., *Frontier*, 43.

33. Clayton, ed., *Frontier*, 52–53; Flake, "Biography of Flake," 87–89.

34. Charles S. Peterson, *Take Up Your Mission: Mormon Colonizing along the Little Colorado River, 1870–1900* (Tucson: University of Arizona Press, 1973), 41; Clayton, ed., *Frontier*, 53–54.

35. Peterson, *Take Up Your Mission*, 2; Smith, "Journal," 280–81 (Oct. 24, 1879); George S. Tanner and J. Morris Richards, *Colonization on the Little Colorado: The Joseph City Region* (Flagstaff, AZ: Northland, 1977), 37; Robert Howard Sayers, "Mormon Cultural Persistence in the Vicinity of Graham County, Arizona, 1879–1977" (PhD diss., University of Arizona, 1979), 43.

36. Charles S. Peterson, "'A Mighty Man Was Brother Lot': A Portrait of Lot Smith—Frontiersman," *Western Historical Quarterly* 1, no. 4 (1970): 393; Clayton, ed., *Frontier*, 54–55, 63.

37. Clayton, ed., *Frontier*, 55; Roberta Flake Clayton, "Pioneer Source Book," typescript, RFCC, box 1, folder 22, 19–22; Evans Coleman, "History of the Coleman Family," typescript, ECP, box 5, folder 50, 15.

38. Clayton, "Pioneer Source Book," 19–22; Clayton, ed., *Frontier*, 58, 60–62, 63.

39. Clayton, ed., *Frontier*, 57.

40. Clayton, ed., *Frontier*, 58.

41. Joseph Neal Heywood, "Reminiscences," mimeograph mss., RRC, box 11, folder 15, 2.

42. Clayton, "Pioneer Source Book," 19–22.

43. Clayton, "Pioneer Source Book"; Coleman, "Coleman Family," 21–22.

44. Clayton, "Pioneer Source Book," 23.

45. Clayton, "Pioneer Source Book," 19–22.

46. Clayton, ed., *Frontier*, 60–62.

47. Coleman, "Coleman Family," 24.

48. Clayton, ed., *Frontier*, 60–62.

49. Clayton, ed., *Frontier*, 63; Coleman, "Coleman Family," 48.

50. Flake, *William Jordan Flake*, 63.

51. Rulon E. Porter, "History of Mormon Settlements: Little Colorado River Valley," typescript, GSTC, box 13, folder 4, 25.

52. George S. Tanner, *Henry Martin Tanner: Joseph City Pioneer* (n.p., 1964), 24.

53. Tanner, *Henry Martin Tanner*, 19–21; Tanner and Richards, *Colonization on the Little Colorado*, 33; Clayton, ed., *Frontier*, 65.

54. Clayton, ed., *Frontier*, 64.

55. Tanner, *Henry Martin Tanner*, 23.

56. Tanner, *Henry Martin Tanner*, 19; Minutes of the Little Colorado Stake, typescript, RRC, 125 (May 30, 1880).

57. Smith, "Journal," 355 (Snow quotation, Sept. 25, 1884).

58. Tanner and Richards, *Colonization*, 51–52; Peterson, *Take Up Your Mission*, 98–99; Minutes of the Little Colorado Stake, 21 (Jan. 28, 1878), 113 (Feb. 28–29, 1880); John Henry Standifird, "Journal of John Henry Standifird," typescript, GSTC, box 9, folder 1, 1:2. For the Mormon account of Enoch's life and city, see *Pearl of Great Price*, Book of Moses.

59. Minutes of the Little Colorado Stake, 94 (May 29–30, 1879); Flake, "Biography of Flake," 81.

60. Flake, *William Jordan Flake*, 62; Peterson, "'Mighty Man,'" 400; Minutes of the Little Colorado Stake, 33 (May 26, 1878).

61. Tanner and Richards, *Colonization*, 60; Peterson, "'Mighty Man,'" 404; Clayton, ed., *Frontier*, 64; Rulon E. Porter, "Diary of Rulon E. Porter," from Holbrook *News*, Dec. 12, 1924, in GSTC, box 3, folder 8; Evans Coleman, "W. E. Platt," typescript, GSTC, box 5, folder 13, 12; Tanner, *Henry Martin Tanner*, 37.

62. Tanner, *Henry Martin Tanner*, 24; Gordon H. Flammer, *Stories of a Mormon Community: Linden, Arizona of the Little Colorado Arizona Mission, 1878–1945* (Provo, UT: Excel Graphics, 1995), 29–30; Mrs. Waldo Y. LeSueur, "James W. LeSueur," in

Clayton, ed., *Pioneer Men*, 289; Peterson, *Take Up Your Mission*, 258–59; Heywood, "Reminiscences," 35.

63. Clayton, ed., *Frontier*, 25, 36; Clayton, "Pioneer Source Book," 30; Coleman, "Coleman Family," 28; "Life Story of James Ward and Margaret Hunter Shelley," in Thomas Heber Shelley, "Personal History of Thomas Heber Shelley," typescript, GSTC, unnumbered.

64. Clayton, ed., *Frontier*, 64–65; Rulon E. Porter, "Joseph City History," typescript, GSTC, box 4, folder 4, 45; Osmer Flake, "Diaries, Autobiography, and Biography, 1887–1954," typescript, HDL, 4, 6.

65. Clayton, ed., *Frontier*, 68; Flake, "Biography of Flake," 109; Flake, *William Jordan Flake*, 72; Flake, "Autobiography and Diary," 23.

66. Flake, "Autobiography and Diary," 20; Clayton, ed., *Frontier*, 68.

67. Joseph Fish, "History of Eastern Arizona Stake of Zion; Early Settlement of Apache County, [and] Stake Clerk's Records and Journal, 1878–1912," mss., ASLAPR, 10; Albert Levine, ed., *The Life and Times of Snowflake, 1878–1978* (Snowflake, AZ: Centennial Committee, 1978), 64.

68. Flake, *William Jordan Flake*, 66, 69.

69. Flake, *William Jordan Flake*, 77; Clayton, ed., *Frontier*, 66.

70. Flake, "Autobiography and Diary," 21.

71. Albert J. Levine, *Indian Trails to Jet Trails: Snowflake's Centennial History* (Snowflake, AZ: Snowflake Historical Society, 1977), 14; Flake, "Biography of Flake," 117; Clayton, ed., *Frontier*, 68, 71; Flake, *William Jordan Flake*, 91–92.

72. Flake, *William Jordan Flake*, 83; ASB, Mar. 3, 1879; Peterson, *Take Up Your Mission*, 216; Fish, "Eastern Arizona Stake," 11, 23.

73. Fish, "Eastern Arizona Stake," 66; Smith, "Journal," 266; Flake, *William Jordan Flake*, 81; Peterson, *Take Up Your Mission*, 97–98, 243; Joseph Fish, "The Fish Manuscript, 1840–1926," ASLAPR, 734.

74. Flake, *William Jordan Flake*, 67–69; Levine, *Indian Trails*, 13; Leland J. Hanchett, Jr., *They Shot Billy Today: The Families of the Pleasant Valley War* (Phoenix, AZ: Pine Rim, 2006), 177; Clayton, ed., *Frontier*, 70.

75. Clayton, ed., *Frontier*, 86.

76. George L. Cathcart, "Religious Belief as a Cultural Value: Mormon Cattle Ranchers in Arizona's Little Colorado River Valley" (MA thesis, Arizona State University, 1995), 42; Fish, "Eastern Arizona Stake," 31; Alice Smith Kartchner, Alice Smith Kartchner Oral History Interview, conducted by Steven J. Christiansen, Mesa, Arizona, Feb. 17, 1979, typescript, HDL, 3; Clayton, ed., *Frontier*, 74.

77. Clayton, ed., *Frontier*, 70; Roberta Flake Clayton, ed., *Pioneer Women of Arizona* (n.p., n.d.), 271–73; Levine, *Indian Trails*, 3, 63; Les Flake, *Tales from Oz* (n.p., n.d.), 56; Flake, *William Jordan Flake*, 76, 120–21; Flammer, *Mormon Community*, 16; Leland J. Hanchett, Jr., *The Crooked Trail to Holbrook: An Arizona Cattle Trail* (Phoenix, AZ: Arrowhead Press, 1993), 175; Peterson, *Take Up Your Mission*, 25–26, 244; Fish, "Eastern Arizona Stake," 9, 14, 16.

78. Fish, "Eastern Arizona Stake," 7, 66; Minutes of the Little Colorado Stake, 11 (June 12, 1881).

79. Smith, "Journal," 299 (Sept. 24, 1881).

80. Peterson, *Take Up Your Mission*, 160, 249 (Smith quotation); Smith, "Journal," 337, 347, 352–53 (Dec. 8, 1883, May 17, Sept. 13–14, 1884).

81. Smith, "Journal," 329 (Aug. 13, 1883); Evans Coleman, "Teachers," typescript, ECP, box 2, folder 24, 1.

82. Smith, "Journal," 317, 353 (Sept. 14, 1884).

83. Heywood, "Reminiscences," 6, 9. See generally John Bushman, "Diary," 2 vols., typescript, GSTC, box 3, folders 2–3.

84. Fife, *Exploring Western Americana*, 34–35.

85. Jo Ann F. Hatch, *Willing Hands: A Biography of Lorenzo Hatch Hill, 1826–1910* (Pinedale, AZ: Kymera, 1996), 243; Coleman, "Teachers," 1.

86. Annie Richardson Johnson and Elva Richardson Shumway, and Enola Johnson Mangelson, collaborator, *Charles Edmund Richardson: Man of Destiny* (Tempe, AZ: Publication Services, 1982), DC, box 1, folder 8, 198; Bushman, "Diary," 1:15 (Aug. 30, 1885).

87. Heywood, "Reminiscences," 34; Levine, *Snowflake*, 69.

88. Coleman, "Teachers," 1; Fife, *Exploring Western Americana*, 34; Minutes of the Little Colorado Stake, 113 (Feb. 28–29, 1880). Two monographs explore the hermetic, alchemical, and occult context of early Mormonism: Brooke, *Refiner's Fire*, and D. Michael Quinn, *Early Mormonism and the Magic Worldview* (Salt Lake City: Signature Books, 1998). On Puritan practitioners of occult science, see Richard Godbeer, *The Devil's Dominion: Magic and Religion in Early New England* (Cambridge: Cambridge University Press, 1994).

89. Minutes of the Little Colorado Stake, 125 (May 30, 1880); Peterson, *Take Up Your Mission*, 129; Flake, *William Jordan Flake*, 73–74.

90. Flake, *William Jordan Flake*, 82, 97–98; Clayton, ed., *Frontier*, 76; S. Eugene Flake, *James Madison Flake, November 8, 1859–February 4, 1946: Pioneer, Leader, Missionary* (Bountiful, UT: Wasatch, 1970), 93.

91. Tanner, *Henry Martin Tanner*, 37; Smith, "Journal," 343 (Mar. 8, 1884).

92. Clayton, ed., *Frontier*, 133–35.

93. Clayton, ed., *Frontier*, 133–35, 139–40.

94. Smith, "Journal," 350 (June 8, 1884); Fife, *Exploring Western Americana*, 36.

95. Joseph West Smith, *Journal of Joseph West Smith: The Life Story of an Arizona Pioneer, 1859–1944* (n.p.: Children of Joseph W. Smith, n.d.), 30; Allen Frost, "Diary of Allen Frost," Part 2, vol. 5, 1886–1890, HDL, 454; Osmer Flake, "Autobiography and Diary," vol. 3, HDL, 298 (July 4, 1904); Tanner and Richards, *Colonization on the Little Colorado*, 118.

96. Standifird, "Journal," 1:243 (Nov. 29, 1884); Smith, "Journal," 35 (Snow quotation, Sept. 25, 1884).

97. Minutes of the Little Colorado Stake, 102 (Nov. 29–30, 1879); Smith, "Journal," 277, 280–81 (Jan. 22, Oct. 24, 1879); Standifird, "Journal," 1:110 (Mar. 9, 1879); Fish, "Eastern Arizona Stake," 34; Andrew L. Rogers, "Diary of Andrew L. Rogers, 1882–1902," typescript, HDL, 113. On the ambiguous patriotism of nineteenth-century Mormons, see Eugene E. Campbell, "Pioneers and Patriotism: Conflicting Loyalties," in *New Views of Mormon History: A Collection of Essays in Honor of Leonard J. Arrington,*

ed. Davis Bitton and Maureen Ursenbach Beecher (Salt Lake City: University of Utah Press, 1987), 307–22.

98. Smith, "Journal," 277 (Jan. 22, 1879).
99. Book of Mormon, Ether, 8:23.

CHAPTER THREE: THE HONOR OF RUIN

1. *ASB*, Sept. 18, Oct. 9, 1886.
2. *ASB*, Oct. 9, 1886.
3. Harold D. Jenkerson, "Pleasant Valley Feud," typescript, 2 vols., NGCHS, 1:205; *ASB*, May 2, 1885, July 3, 1886.
4. *SJH*, May 6, 1886, quoting *Live Stock Journal*; Harold C. Wayte, "A History of Holbrook and the Little Colorado Country (1540–1962)" (PhD diss., University of Arizona, 1962), 133.
5. Jenkerson, "Pleasant Valley Feud," 2:217–20.
6. *SJH*, Aug. 6, 1885 (quoting San Juan *Prospector*), May 6, June 17, 1886; *ASB*, June 26, July 24, Oct. 2, 16, 1886; Jenkerson, "Pleasant Valley," 2:220; Arizona *Champion*, Apr. 24, 1886. On immigrants to the Rim Country, see NGCHS, *Rim Country History* (Payson, AZ: Rim Country Printery, 1984); Jayne Peace, *History of Gisela, Arizona* (Payson, AZ: Git A Rope! 2003).
7. AC, Apr. 24, 1886; *ASB*, June 26, 1886 (quoting *Hoof and Horn*); *SJH*, June 17, 1886.
8. Jenkerson, "Pleasant Valley," 1:205; AG, Nov. 1, 1884; *SJH*, Dec. 2, 1886; *ASB*, July 3, 1886, Jan. 22, Apr. 2, 1887. Cattlemen in southeastern Arizona threatened to take similar actions. *SJH*, Aug. 6, 1885 (quoting Tombstone *Record-Epitaph*).
9. *ASB*, October 2, 16, 1886, Apr. 2, 1887; Robert H. Carlock, *The Hashknife: The Early Days of the Aztec Land and Cattle Company, Limited* (Tucson, AZ: Westernlore, 1994), 77.
10. *SJH*, Oct. 7, 1886 (quoting *National Stockman*), Sept. 12, 1889; *ASB*, Aug. 14, Oct. 2, 1886.
11. *SJH*, Nov. 18, 1886, June 14, 1888 (quoting *National Stockman*), Oct. 3, 1889.
12. *SJH*, Apr. 11, 1890 (quoting *Southwestern Live Stock Journal*).
13. *SJH*, Apr. 11, 1890 (quoting *Southwestern Live Stock Journal*).
14. Jean Beach King, ed., *Arizona Charlie* (Phoenix, AZ: Heritage, 1989), 48–49, 51–52, 61–63.
15. *SJH*, June 2, Aug. 4, 1887. On disputes between ranchers and assessors, see *ASB*, July 17, 1886, June 11, 1887, June 15, Sept. 7, 1889, Mar. 22, 1890, July 16, 1892; *SJH*, June 14, 1888, Jan. 24, Feb. 28, June 6, Aug. 8, Sept. 5, 12, 1889. See also Joseph Fish, "History of Eastern Arizona Stake of Zion; Early Settlement of Apache County; [and] Stake Clerk's Records and Journal, 1878–1912," mss., ASLAPR, 70.
16. *ASB*, Aug. 21, 1886, May 25, 1889.
17. *SJH*, Dec. 16, 1886, Aug. 18, 1887 (quoting other newspapers regarding the beef trust).
18. *SJH*, Aug. 6, 1885 (quoting Tombstone *Record-Epitaph*).
19. *SJH*, Aug. 6, 1885 (quoting Albuquerque *Journal*), Dec. 23, 1886 (quoting Wilcox

Stockman); *ASB*, Aug. 21, 1886; Jim Bob Tinsley, *The Hashknife Brand* (Gainesville: University of Florida Press, 1993), 130–31.

20. *SJH*, Aug. 6, 1886 (quoting Albuquerque *Journal*); *ASB*, Aug. 28, 1886 (quoting *Hoof and Horn*).

21. *ASB*, Aug. 28, 1886.

22. *SJH*, July 30, 1885 (quoting Prescott *Courier*), Aug. 6, 1885 (quoting Tombstone *Record-Epitaph*).

23. *ASB*, July 17, 1886.

24. *SJH*, Dec. 30, 1886 (quoting *Hoof and Horn*); *ASB*, Sept. 4, Oct. 2, 1886 (quoting New Mexico *Stock Grower*).

25. *ASB*, Sept. 4, 1886.

26. William McLeod Raine and Will C. Barnes, *Cattle* (Garden City, NY: Doubleday, Doran, 1930), 240–41.

27. *SJH*, Dec. 2, 1886.

28. Jenkerson, "Pleasant Valley," 1:37, 71; *ASB*, Aug. 23, 1884, Sept. 18, 1886.

29. Clarence W. Durham, *That Hashknife Kid* (n.p.: privately published, n.d.), 235, 236, 239–40.

30. *ASB*, Oct. 29, 1887.

31. *ASB*, July 4, 1885.

32. *ASB*, Oct. 29, 1887.

33. *ASB*, Oct. 29, 1887.

34. *SJH*, July 29, 1886 (quoting Apache County *Critic*), Mar. 17, 1887; *ASB*, Oct. 2, 1886, Feb. 12, May 21, 1887.

35. *SJH*, June 2, 1887; *ASB*, July 23, 1886, July 16, Sept. 17, 1887.

36. Will C. Barnes, *Apaches and Longhorns: The Reminiscences of Will C. Barnes*, ed. Frank C. Lockwood (Los Angeles: Ward C. Ritchie, 1941), 129–30.

37. Will C. Barnes, *Western Grazing Grounds and Forest Ranges* (Chicago: Breeder's Gazette, 1913), 82; Barnes, *Apaches and Longhorns*, 131.

38. L. J. Horton, "The Pleasant Valley War," typescript, CWP, box 8, folder 88, 12–13.

39. King, *Arizona Charlie*, 40; *ASB*, Mar. 19, 1887.

40. King, *Arizona Charlie*, 39, 41.

41. *SJH*, Jan. 5, 1888.

CHAPTER FOUR: THE TRIALS OF SAINTS

1. Joseph Fish, "The Fish Manuscript, 1840–1926," ASLAPR, 575. Sources differ on the price. See Evans Coleman, "St. Johns Purchase," typescript, GSTC, box 5, folder 24, unpaginated; and Charles S. Peterson, *Take Up Your Mission: Mormon Colonizing along the Little Colorado River, 1870–1900* (Tucson: University of Arizona Press, 1973), 33. For an alternate version of how St. Johns was named, see C. Leroy Wilhelm and Mabel R. Wilhelm, *A History of St. Johns Arizona Stake* (Orem, UT: Historical Publications, 1982), 21.

2. N. H. Greenwood, "Sol Barth: A Jewish Pioneer on the Arizona Frontier," *JAH* 14

(1973): 363. G. A. McCarter, "An Historic Deed Clipped from the St. Johns *Observer*, St. Johns, Arizona," Miami *Silver Belt* (n.d.), GSTC, box 5, folder 24; "Sol Barth of St. Johns" [from Miami *Silver Belt*], in Roberta Flake Clayton, ed., *Pioneer Men of Arizona* (n.p., 1974), 31–34.

3. Clayton, ed., *Pioneer Men*, 31–34; James T. LeSueur, "How St. Johns Was Settled," GSTC, box 5, folder 25, 1; Evans Coleman, "Sol Barth," typescript, ECP, box 5, folder 48, 3; Greenwood, "Barth," 364.

4. Greenwood, "Barth," 364–65; C. Leroy Wilhelm and Mabel R. Wilhelm, *A History of St. Johns Arizona Stake* (Orem, UT: Historical Publications, 1982), 20–22; "Sol Barth of St. Johns," 31–34.

5. Wilhelm and Wilhelm, *St. Johns*, 28, 30.

6. Lewis Allen [Wilford Woodruff] to A. M. Tenney, Sunset, Apache County, Arizona, Nov. 24, 1879, GSTC, box 5, folder 20.

7. Wilhelm and Wilhelm, *St. Johns*, 30–31.

8. Evon Z. Vogt, "Intercultural Relations," in Vogt and Ethel M. Albert, *People of Rimrock: A Study of Values in Five Cultures* (Cambridge, MA: Harvard University Press, 1966), 52–54.

9. Munro S. Edmonson, "Kinship Systems," in Vogt and Albert, *People of Rimrock*, 144, 157.

10. Ramon Gutierrez, *When Jesus Came, the Corn Mothers Went Away: Marriage, Sexuality, and Power in New Mexico, 1500–1846* (Stanford, CA: Stanford University Press, 1991), 176–226 (quotation on 205). Also see Ramon Gutierrez, "'Tell Me with Whom You Walk and I Will Tell You Who You Are': Honor and Virtue in Eighteenth-Century Colonial New Mexico," in *Crossing the Great Divide: Cultures of Manhood in the American West*, ed. Laura McCall, Matthew Basso, and Dee Garceau (New York: Routledge, 2001), 25–44. James Brooks, in his Bancroft Prize–winning book, *Captives and Cousins: Slavery, Kinship, and Community in the Southwest Borderlands* (Chapel Hill: University of North Carolina Press, 2002), argues that Spanish and Indian males of the seventeenth-, eighteenth-, and nineteenth-century Southwest demonstrated honor— and upheld patriarchal authority—by capturing, defending, redeeming, buying, and selling women and children.

11. Paul H. Roberts, *Hoof Prints on Forest Ranges: The Early Years of National Forest Range Administration* (San Antonio, TX: Naylor, 1963), 49, 57; Henry L. Benham interview, in Edwin A. Tucker, comp., *The Early Days: A Sourcebook of Southwestern Regional History*, Book 1. Cultural Resources Management Report No. 7 (n.p., 1989), 140–41.

12. McCarter, "Historic Deed," 2; Wilhelm and Wilhelm, *St. Johns*, 32, 140; "Barth Resolution," Arizona *Republican*, Dec. 22, 1928, GSTC, box 5, folder 11.

13. Greenwood, "Barth," 365; Osmer Flake, "Biography of William Jordan Flake," mss., OFD, folder 11, 119; Roberta Flake Clayton, ed., *To the Last Frontier: The Autobiography of Lucy Hannah White Flake* (reprint ed., n.p., 1976), 72; Osmer Flake, *William Jordan Flake: Pioneer, Colonizer* (n.p., n.d.), 78.

14. Wilhelm and Wilhelm, *St. Johns Arizona*, 30–31; Coleman, "St. Johns Purchase," unpaginated.

15. Coleman, "St. Johns Purchase"; LeSueur, "St. Johns," 3; McCarter, "Historic Deed," 3.

16. John W. Tate, "Journal of John W. Tate, Oct. 1880 to July 1881," typescript, GSTC, box 5, folder 23, 42 (Jan. 11, 1881); LeSueur, "St. Johns," 3.

17. Tate, "Journal," 37 (Dec. 20, 1880); Jesse Nathaniel Smith, "Journal," JNSP, box 1, folder 2, 347 (May 16, 1884); Joseph Fish, "History of Eastern Arizona Stake of Zion; Early Settlement of Apache County, [and] Stake Clerk's Records and Journal, 1878–1912," mss., ASLAPR, 1–2; Peterson, *Take Up Your Mission*, 34–35.

18. Newell G. Bringhurst, *Saints, Slaves, and Blacks: The Changing Place of Black People within Mormonism* (Westport, CT: Greenwood, 1981), 45. For Mormon ideas about cursed peoples and racial ancestries, see *Pearl of Great Price*, books of Abraham and Moses.

19. George S. Tanner and J. Morris Richards, *Colonization on the Little Colorado: The Joseph City Region* (Flagstaff, AZ: Northland, 1977), 86.

20. Nathaniel Hunt Greer Family Organization, The Greer Way West, http://www.wideopenwest.com/~GreersWest/bios/bio_tlg.htm, updated September 5, 2006; GreerZone, http://greerzone.net/9141.html?*session*id*key*=*session*id*val*.

21. Show Low Arizona Stake Presidency, *Firm as the Mountains: A History of the Show Low Arizona Stake* (Show Low: Show Low Arizona Stake, n.d.), 22; John Ray Hamblin, *Outlaws of Apache County* (n.p., n.d.), 2; Edward H. Peplow, Jr., *History of Arizona*, 3 vols. (New York: Lewis Historical Publishing, 1958), 2:147; Roberta Flake Clayton, ed., *Pioneer Women of Arizona* (n.p., n.d.), 111.

22. Clayton, ed., *Pioneer Women*, 111; Show Low Arizona Stake Presidency, *Firm as the Mountains*, 22; Hamblin, *Outlaws*, 2; Nathaniel Hunt Greer Family Organization, Greer Way West, http://www.wowway.com/~GreersWest/bios/bio_avg.htm (updated June 6, 2006).

23. Peplow, *Arizona*, 2:147; LeSueur, "St. Johns," 3; John H. Krenkel, ed., *The Life and Times of Joseph Fish, Mormon Pioneer* (Danville, IL: Interstate, 1970), 259; Hamblin, *Outlaws*, 2.

24. Hamblin, *Outlaws*, 2–3; Jo Ann F. Hatch, *Willing Hands: A Biography of Lorenzo Hatch Hill, 1826–1910* (Pinedale, AZ: Kymera, 1996), 165–67, 277–78; Fish, "Eastern Arizona Stake," 36; Wilhelm and Wilhelm, *St. Johns*, 45; James Warren LeSueur, "Autobiography," typescript, GSTC, box 5, folder 10, unpaginated. On the absence of guns among Apache County settlers before the arrival of Texas cowboys, see William N. Miller to Will C. Barnes, Darlington, Idaho, July 20, 1936, WCBC, box 2, folder 18.

25. Hatch, *Willing Hands*, 165–67, 277–78; Fish, "Eastern Arizona Stake," 36; Wilhelm and Wilhelm, *St. Johns*, 45; LeSueur, "Autobiography"; Hamblin, *Outlaws*, 2–3.

26. Hamblin, *Outlaws*, 2–3; Hatch, *Willing Hands*, 165–67, 277–78; Fish, "Eastern Arizona Stake," 36; Wilhelm and Wilhelm, *St. Johns*, 45; LeSueur, "Autobiography."

27. LeSueur, "Autobiography."

28. LeSueur, "Autobiography"; LeSueur, "St. Johns," 3; "The Life of John Hunt (1833–1917), in Clayton, ed., *Pioneer Men*, 238. New Mexicans seem to have learned the art of lynching from Texans. Capital punishment of any kind was rare in colonial New Mexico. Robert J. Tórrez, *The Myth of the Hanging Tree: Stories of Crime and Punishment in Colonial New Mexico* (Albuquerque: University of New Mexico Press, 2008), 3–4.

29. Fish, "Eastern Arizona Stake," 24, 36; Fish, "Fish Manuscript," 575, 631–32, 644–50.

30. Albert Levine, ed., *The Life and Times of Snowflake, 1878–1978* (Snowflake, AZ: Centennial Committee, 1978), 35–36; Smith, "Journal," 294 (undated entry from November 1880). The assassination plot came to light in 1906 when one of Jesse N. Smith's sons met a man in Denver who claimed to have been the assassin. The assassin had spared Smith only because his gun would not fire. Fearful of the "ring's" retribution, he fled to New Mexico, repented his sins, and became a man of conscience. See "Jesse Nathaniel Smith," http://bowers.pezao.us/history/JesseN.htm. The story sounds too perfect to be authentic. Assassination, however, had become common in New Mexico and in Kansas, a state that saw similar battles over county seats. See Richard Maxwell Brown, *Strain of Violence: Historical Studies of American Violence and Vigilantism* (New York: Oxford University Press, 1975), 11; Robert K. DeArment, *Ballots and Bullets: The Bloody County Seat Wars of Kansas* (Norman: University Oklahoma Press, 2006).

31. Wilford Woodruff to A. M. Tenney, Salt Lake City, May 25, 31, 1880, GSTC, box 5, folder 20; Peterson, *Take Up Your Mission*, 224; Howard E. Daniels, "Mormon Colonization in Northern Arizona" (MA thesis, University of Arizona, 1960), 124–25.

32. Smith, "Journal," 293 (Sept. 18, 19, 1880).

33. Fish, "Fish Manuscript," 630; Mark E. Miller, "St. John's Saints: Interethnic Conflict in Northeastern Arizona, 1880–85," *Journal of Modern History* 23 (1997): 79; Tanner and Richards, *Colonization on the Little Colorado*, 110; Fish, "Eastern Arizona Stake," 43.

34. Fish, "Eastern Arizona Stake," 44, 79. Fish, "Fish Manuscript," 630;

35. Evans Coleman, "Land Transactions in the Eighties," typescript, ECP, box 2, folder 23.

36. Robert Carlock, *The Hashknife: The Early Days of the Aztec Land and Cattle Company, Limited* (Tucson, AZ: Westernlore, 1994), 15; Peterson, *Take Up Your Mission*, 166; Smith, "Journal," 363 (Sept. 26, 1884).

37. Miller, "St. Johns's Saints," 82 (Ida Udall quotation); Peterson, *Take Up Your Mission*, 214; Smith, "Journal," 320, 341, 347 (Mar. 25, 1883, Jan. 18, May 17, 1884).

38. Fish, "Eastern Arizona Stake," 37 (McCarter quotation); AC, May 9, 1884.

39. Fish, "Fish Manuscript," 630–31; AC*h*, May 9, 1884.

40. Rita Ackerman, *OK Corral Postscript: The Death of Ike Clanton* (Honolulu, HI: Talei, 2006), 51.

41. Fish, "Fish Manuscript," 631–32, 635; Arizona *Sentinel*, July 3, 1886.

42. Krenkel, *Joseph Fish*, 258.

43. Fish, "Eastern Arizona Stake," 39.

44. Fish, "Eastern Arizona Stake," 39.

45. Fish, "Eastern Arizona Stake," 24.

46. John Henry Standifird, "Journal of John Henry Standifird," GSTC, 1:230, 238 (May 18, Sept. 14, 1884).

47. Smith, "Journal," 355 (Sept. 25, 1884).

48. W. J. Platt to Ammon M. Tenney, C. I. Kemp, and "Christopherson," Feb. 15, 1885, St. Johns, GSTC, box 5, folder 16; SJH, July 16, July 23, 25, 30, Aug. 6, 1885.

49. SJH, Aug. 20, 1885; Flake, *William Jordan Flake*, 101, 110–11.

50. Peterson, *Take Up Your Mission*, 232; Daniels, "Mormon Colonization," 110.

51. Fish, "Eastern Arizona Stake," 38; Fish, "Fish Manuscript," 632; George S. Tanner, *Henry Martin Tanner: Joseph City Pioneer* (n.p., 1964), 45–46; Peterson, *Take Up Your Mission*, 233.

52. Merle M. Wells, *Anti-Mormonism in Idaho, 1872–92* (Provo, UT: Brigham Young University Press, 1978), 179; Mark P. Leone, *Roots of Modern Mormonism* (Cambridge, MA: Harvard University Press, 1979), 150–51; Leonard J. Arrington, *Great Basin Kingdom: An Economic History of the Latter-day Saints, 1830–1900* (Cambridge, MA: Harvard University Press, 1958), 361.

53. Fish, "Eastern Arizona Stake," 45, 47, 56.

54. Krenkel, *Joseph Fish*, 293; Standifird, "Journal," 253, 258, 272 (Mar. 4, 29, Nov. 14, 16, 1885).

55. Standifird, "Journal," 272 (Nov. 14, 1885).

56. Peterson, *Take Up Your Mission*, 234; Fish, "Fish Manuscript," 633.

57. Lucy Hannah White Flake, "Autobiography and Diary of Lucy Hannah White Flake," typescript, HDL, 26; Clayton, ed., *Frontier*, 100; William J. Flake, "Prison Diary of William J. Flake," typescript, HDL, 7.

58. Flake, *William Jordan Flake*, 101–3.

59. Flake, "Biography of Flake," 147; Prudence McLaws Fyffe and William R. Ridgway, "Mormon Pioneer and the Yuma Prison," typescript, RRC, box 2, folder 4, 7; Flake, "Prison Diary," 13; Clayton, ed., *Frontier*, 106; Flake, *William Jordan Flake*, 109.

60. Clayton, ed., *Frontier*, 106–8; Flake, *William Jordan Flake*, 110–11; Flake, "Autobiography and Diary," 27.

61. Miller, "St. Johns's Saints," 90 (quotation).

CHAPTER FIVE: COWBOYS AND CRIMINALS

1. John H. Krenkel, ed., *The Life and Times of Joseph Fish, Mormon Pioneer* (Danville, IL: Interstate, 1970), 241–42; Joseph Fish, "History of Eastern Arizona Stake of Zion; Early Settlement of Apache County [and] Stake Clerk's Records and Journal, 1878–1912," mss., ASLAPR, 57, 68; James Warren LeSueur, "Trouble with the Hash Knife Company," typescript, JWLC, box 1, folder 10, 5.

2. Krenkel, *Joseph Fish*, 241–42; LeSueur, "Hash Knife," 5.

3. Leland J. Hanchett, Jr., *Arizona's Graham-Tewksbury Feud* (Phoenix, AZ: Pine Rim, 1994), 27; Harold D. Jenkerson, "Pleasant Valley Feud," typescript, 2 vols. NGCHS, 1:145, 181.

4. Annie Richardson and Elva Richardson Shumway, with Enola Johnson Mangelson, collaborator, *Charles Edmund Richardson: Man of Destiny* (Tempe, AZ: Publication Services, 1982), 201.

5. "Z. B. Decker," in Roberta Flake Clayton, ed., *Pioneer Men of Arizona* (n.p., 1974), 104.

6. Charles S. Peterson, *Take Up Your Mission: Mormon Colonizing along the Little Colorado River, 1870–1900* (Tucson: University of Arizona Press, 1973), 136–37, 146.

7. Osmer D. Flake, "Some Reminiscences of the Pleasant Valley War and the Causes that Led Up to It," typescript, LSUP, 2; Jenkerson, "Pleasant Valley," 1:69, 71, 74; Robert

Carlock, *The Hashknife: The Early Days of the Aztec Land and Cattle Company, Limited* (Tucson, AZ: Westernlore, 1994), 21–22, 34–36; Roberta Flake Clayton, ed., *To the Last Frontier: The Autobiography of Lucy Hannah White Flake* (reprint ed., n.p., 1976), 80.

8. Flake, "Reminiscences," 2.

9. Flake, "Reminiscences," 2; Apache *Review*, Dec. 12, 1888; *SJH*, Dec. 23, 1886, Nov. 1, 1888; *ACC*, Dec. 30, 1886.

10. *SJH*, July 23, 1885; *ASB*, Oct. 9, 1886; Hanchett, *Graham-Tewksbury Feud*, 28; Don Dedera, *A Little War of Our Own: The Pleasant Valley Feud Revisited* (Flagstaff, AZ: Northland, 1988), 76.

11. Carlock, *Hashknife*, 2–4, 14.

12. Carlock, *Hashknife*, 39, 65.

13. Carlock, *Hashknife*, 2, 43–44, 48, 73, 82; Jim Bob Tinsley, *The Hash Knife Brand* (Gainesville: University Press of Florida, 1993), 50; Peterson, *Take Up Your Mission*, 169; Fish, "Eastern Arizona Stake," 57.

14. Carlock, *Hashknife*, 28, 51, 59, 77, 217–18; Tinsley, *Hash Knife*, xiii; Clayton, ed., *Frontier*, 109.

15. Clayton, ed., *Frontier*, 109; Carlock, *Hashknife*, 65.

16. Coconino *Sun*, Feb. 22, 1929, quoted in Tinsley, *Hash Knife*, xviii; Mrs. Edward D. Tuttle, "Reminiscences of a Child of the Frontier Arizona," RRC, box 3, folder 1A, 5; Joseph Fish, "The Fish Manuscript, 1840–1926," ASLAPR, 621.

17. Tinsley, *Hash Knife*, 107; Will C. Barnes, "Wild Cattle and a Railroad Strike," *Cattleman* 21, no. 10 (1935): 23, 25, 27–30, 32–34; Roberta Flake Clayton, "Cowboy's Work, Wages and Outfit," typescript, RFCC, box 1, folder 9, 3; Ramon F. Adams, *The Cowboy and His Philosophy* (Austin, TX: Encino, 1963), 6.

18. Jack Weston, *The Real American Cowboy* (New York: Schocken, 1985), 10–12; Will C. Barnes, *Western Grazing Grounds and Forest Ranges* (Chicago: Breeder's Gazette, 1913), 116–19; Clayton, "Cowboy's Work," 3.

19. Clayton, "Cowboy's Work," 3, 6; Jenkerson, "Pleasant Valley," 1:221; *SJH*, July 23, 1885 (quoting Socorro *Bulletin*); Carlock, *Hashknife*, 125.

20. Will C. Barnes, "Cowpunching Forty Years Ago," *Weekly Market Report and News Letter*, Arizona Cattle Growers' Association, Phoenix, March 10, 1931, 1–4.

21. *SJH*, Aug. 6, 1885, Nov. 18, 1886, Mar. 17, 1887; Carlock, *Hashknife*, 121–22, 182; LeSueur, "Hash Knife"; Milo Wiltbank to Hank Rodgers, n.d., n.p., in Apache County Centennial Committee, *Lest Ye Forget* (n.p., n.d.), 13; Evans Coleman, "Nesters, Rustlers, and Outlaws," in Evans Coleman, "Reminiscences of an Arizona Cowboy," ECP, box 6, folder 61, 223. The same sorts of phenomena occurred elsewhere where Mormons encountered cowboys from Texas, including Moab, Utah. See John Henry Standifird, "Journal of John Henry Standifird," typescript, GSTC, 1: 292 (Dec. 26, 31, 1886).

22. Evans Coleman, "Horse Racing in the '80s and '90s," typescript, ECP, box 2, folder 1, 1–2.

23. *SJH*, Dec. 30, 1886, Apr. 14, 1887; Rita Ackerman, *OK Corral Postscript: The Death*

of Ike Clanton (Honolulu, HI: Talei, 2006), 99; Tinsley, *Hash Knife*, 45, 101 (citing Albert F. Potter, "How the Bucket of Blood Got Its Name," typescript, n.d., biographical file R 646 p—Roberts, Paul H., AHS; "Local and Personal," Holbrook *Argus*, May 5, 1997); Fish, "Eastern Arizona Stake," 79; Carlock, *Hashknife*, 134. Because it is not clear that the "Mexicans" at the dance were New Mexicans, I use the "Mexican" designation from the primary sources. On cowboy revelry and violence generally, see Jacqueline M. Moore, *Cow Boys and Cattle Men: Class and Masculinities on the Texas Frontier, 1865–1900* (New York: New York University Press, 2009), chaps. 4, 6.

24. McGrath cited in Richard Maxwell Brown, *No Duty to Retreat: Violence and Values in American Society* (New York: Oxford University Press, 1991), 64, 65. On the transition from duel to gunfight, see Dick Steward, *Duels and the Roots of Violence in Missouri* (Columbia: University of Missouri Press, 2000).

25. Dean L. May, *Three Frontiers: Family, Land, and Society in the American West, 1850–1900* (Cambridge: Cambridge University Press, 1994), 197.

26. John W. M. Whiting et al., "The Learning of Values," in Evon Z. Vogt and Ethel M. Albert, *People of Rimrock: A Study of Values in Five Cultures* (1966; reprint ed., New York: Atheneum, 1970) 83, 89, 91–92.

27. Whiting et al., "Learning," 87, 94, 97–99, 101, 106, 110–11. Historical studies of the relationship between family socialization and adult acts of violence among Westerners (or other Americans) are few. See, however, David Peterson del Mar, *What Trouble I Have Seen: A History of Violence against Wives* (Cambridge, MA: Harvard University Press, 1996); David Peterson del Mar, *Beaten Down: A History of Personal Violence in the West* (Seattle: University of Washington Press, 2002); and Christine Daniels and Michael V. Kennedy, *Over the Threshold: Intimate Violence in Early America* (New York: Routledge, 1999). It is worth quoting here a distinguished historian of the West: "From the perspective of socialization theory, people are prone to violence when their primary groups—their families, their mentors, and significant others—see violence as acceptable, hold beliefs in support of violence, and are themselves violent. The socialization to violence is a developmental process that usually takes place at home during childhood. It commonly includes violent subjugation by an authority figure, the witness of the violent abuse of a loved one, usually a mother or a sibling, and what amounts to the deliberate coaching in violent techniques. You have to learn to be violent." John Mack Faragher in "Roundtable on *Massacre at Mountain Meadows*," *Dialogue: A Journal of Mormon Thought* 42, no. 1 (2009): 113.

28. On historic homicide and violence rates in the South, see Sheldon Hackney, "Southern Violence," *American Historical Review* 74 (1969): 906–25; Raymond D. Gastil, *Cultural Regions of the United States* (Seattle: University of Washington Press), 1975, 92–116; Richard E. Nisbett and Dov Cohen, *Culture of Honor: The Psychology of Violence in the South* (Boulder, CO: Westview, 1996); and H. V. Redfield, *Homicide, North and South* (Philadelphia: James B. Lippincott, 1880).

29. Robert Howard Sayers, "Mormon Cultural Persistence in the Vicinity of Graham County, Arizona, 1879–1977" (PhD diss., University of Arizona, 1979), 239–42.

30. Carlock, *Hashknife*, 53.

31. Carlock, *Hashknife*, 17–18; Albert F. Potter, "A Brief History of the Cattle Business in Apache County," typescript, UASC, 1–7; Carlock, *Hashknife*, 38 (citing an Aztec report).

32. Barnes, *Grazing Grounds*, 27; William MacLeod Raine and Will C. Barnes, *Cattle* (Garden City, NY: Doubleday, Doran, 1930), 250; Hanchett, *Graham-Tewksbury Feud*, vi–vii.

33. Paul H. Roberts, *Hoof Prints on Forest Ranges: The Early Years of National Forest Range Administration* (San Antonio, TX: Naylor, 1963), 99–100, 132.

34. *SJH*, May 6, 1886 (reprinting articles from *Hamilton's Outlook* and from the *Exchange*); *AC*, Apr. 24, 1886.

35. *SJH*, Apr. 22, 1886 (reprinting article from the *ASB*).

36. Barnes, *Grazing Grounds*, 28–29.

37. Raine and Barnes, *Cattle*, 251–52; Will C. Barnes, *Apaches and Longhorns: The Reminiscences of Will C. Barnes*, ed. Frank C. Lockwood (Los Angeles: Ward Ritchie, 1941), 127–29.

38. James Stott to Hattie Stott, Taylor, Arizona, Feb. 28, 1886, in Leland J. Hanchett, Jr., ed., *Black Mesa: The Hanging of Jamie Stott* (Phoenix, AZ: Pine Rim, 1996), 94. Lucien Creswell, "Statement of Lucien Creswell," Flagstaff, Arizona, June 10, 1935, typescript, GRMC, 10-11. In New Mexico, cowboys also attacked Mexican sheepherders. See Robert J. Tórrez, *The Myth of the Hanging Tree: Stories of Crime and Punishment in Territorial New Mexico* (Albuquerque: University of New Mexico Press, 2008), 93–108.

39. Sara R. Massey, ed., *Black Cowboys of Texas* (College Station: Texas A&M Press, 2000).

40. Adams, *Cowboy*, 20; Paul H. Carlson, "Cowboys and Sheepherders," in Paul H. Carlson, ed., *The Cowboy Way: An Exploration of History and Culture* (Lubbock: Texas Tech University Press, 2006), 109–18.

41. "Interview with J. Lorenzo Hubbell, Jan. 10th, 1917," photocopy, Rita Ackerman files.

43. *SJH*, May 20, June 10, 1886; Jenkerson, "Pleasant Valley," 2:221; Carlock, *Hashknife*, 89.

43. *ASB*, Oct. 23, 1886; Edward H. Peplow, Jr., *History of Arizona*, 3 vols. (New York: Lewis Historical Publishing, 1958), 1:149, 150; Barnes, *Grazing Grounds*, 104.

44. Peplow, *Arizona*, 1:150.

45. *AC*, Apr. 26, May 1, 1886.

46. Jenkerson, "Pleasant Valley," 1:199, 2:234; Carlock, *Hashknife*, 67, 88; *AC*, July 16, 1887; Hanchett, *Graham-Tewksbury Feud*, 43.

47. Jesse Nathaniel Smith, "Journal," JNSP, box 1, folder 2, 427 (Apr. 16, 1887).

48. John Henry Standifird, "Journal of John Henry Standifird," typescript, GSTC, box 9, folder 1, 1:263 (June 18, 1885); Smith, "Journal," 427 (Apr. 16, 1887), 418 (July 6, 1887), 419 (Aug. 4, 9, 1887). See also Joseph West Smith, *Journal of Joseph West Smith: The Life Story of an Arizona Pioneer, 1859-1944* (Mesa, AZ: Children of Joseph W. Smith, n.d.), 49–50; LeSueur, "Hash Knife," 4; and Fish, "Fish Manuscript," 572.

49. "Ranching Days," L. Barr Turley oral history interview, taped January 1974, transcribed in Albert Levine, ed., *The Life and Times of Snowflake, 1878–1978* (Snowflake, AZ:

Centennial Committee, 1978), 102; Creswell, "Statement," 13–14; "Life's Story of James Edward and Margaret Hunter Shelley," GSTC, box 2, folder 9, 15–16.

50. Tinsley, *Hash Knife*, 11, 22, 29, 30, 37, 44–45.

51. Fish, "Eastern Arizona Stake," 57; Eugene S. Flake, *James Madison Flake, Nov. 8, 1959–Feb. 4, 1946: Pioneer, Leader, Missionary* (Bountiful, UT: Wasatch, 1970), 82.

52. Thomas H. Shelley, "A Pioneer Experience," typescript, GSTC, box 2, folder 9, 1.

53. Dave Johnson, "G. W. Gladden — Hard Luck Warrior," *National Association and Center for Outlaw and Lawman History Quarterly* 15, no. 3 (1991): 3–5; "Life's Story," 15–16; Carlock, *Hashknife*, 104–5; "Wilford," DC, box 1, folder 2, 1–3, 6–7; "Sketch in Regard to 'Old Brigham City' and Wilford (Arizona)," DC, box 1, folder 8, 4–5; Johnson, Shumway, and Mangelson, *Richardson*, 222. The two articles on Wilford from the Delph Collection are based on the journals and reminiscences of Sadie Richardson. A penciled note on the "Sketch in Regard to 'Old Brigham City' and Wilford (Arizona)" reads "Per Sadie Richardson 1934."

54. "'Old Brigham City' and Wilford," 2.

55. "'Old Brigham City' and Wilford," 5; "Wilford," 7; Johnson, Shumway, and Mangelson, *Richardson*, 222.

56. *SJH*, Oct. 6, 1887; Hanchett, *Crooked Trail*, 44; Carlock, *Hashknife*, 102–3; Robert Allison, "The Blevins Family: An Episode in the Pleasant Valley War," DC, box 1, folder 11, 1, 6–7; Creswell, "Statement," 2.

57. Carlock, *Hashknife*, 19; Jenkerson, "Pleasant Valley," 2:232.

58. Hanchett, *Crooked Trail*, 45, 48, 49; Allison, "Blevins Family," 9.

59. Carlock, *Hashknife*, 93–95; Sarah A. McGee Miller and Artie Mae McGee Rockwell to Don Dedera, no place, Feb. 17, 1988, DDC, box 3, folder 68.

60. James Pearce to L. W. C. Lamar, Mar. 26, 1887, and John Oscar Reidhead to Lamar, Mar. 29, 1887, U.S. House Executive Document No. 232, 50th Cong., 1st sess., 16, in Carlock, *Hashknife*, 185–86.

61. Joseph Lorenzo Petersen, "Life Sketches of Niels Petersen and Mary Mortensen Petersen," in "Biography of Joseph Lorenzo Petersen," typescript, GSTC, box 10, folder 1, 8; Joseph Fish, extracted diary entries, GSTC, box 10, folders 3–4, unnumbered leaf (May 30, 31, 1887); Krenkel, *Joseph Fish*, 317; Clayton, ed., *Pioneer Men*, 106; Silas L. Fish, Autobiography, typescript, SFC, box 1, folder 1, 17.

62. Larry D. Ball, "Commodore Perry Owens: The Man behind the Legend," *JAH* 33, no. 1 (1992): 36–37; ACC, Mar. 31, 1887; *SJH*, Apr. 7, 1887.

63. "'Old Brigham City' and Wilford," 6; Johnson, Shumway, and Mangelson, *Richardson*, 223–24.

64. Johnson, Shumway, and Mangelson, *Richardson*, 223–24.

65. Johnson, Shumway, and Mangelson, *Richardson*, 223–24.

66. Johnson, Shumway, and Mangelson, *Richardson*, 223–24.

67. Johnson, Shumway, and Mangelson, *Richardson*, 223–24.

68. Johnson, Shumway, and Mangelson, *Richardson*, 224, 227; "Wilford," 5–7, 11.

69. Clayton, ed., *Pioneer Men*, 100–102, 106; Jesse Smith Decker, *A Short History of Zechariah Bruyn Decker, Jr., with Brief Sketches of His Parents* (n.p., 1978), unnumbered;

Silas L. Fish, "Excerpts from the Life of Zecheriah B. Decker, a Man Who Could Not Be Bluffed," in Church of Jesus Christ of Latter-day Saints, *Diamond Jubilee Gems* (Snowflake, AZ: n.p., 1963), unnumbered.

70. Kenner Casteel Kartchner, *Frontier Fiddler: The Life of a Northern Arizona Pioneer*, ed. Larry V. Shumway (Tucson: University of Arizona Press, 1990), 225–26. See also Clayton, ed., *Pioneer Men*, 105; and James R. Jennings, *The Freight Rolled* (San Antonio, TX: Naylor, 1969), 49–50.

71. Clayton, ed., *Pioneer Men*, 103–7.

72. Pearce to Lamar and Reidhead to Lamar, in Carlock, *Hashknife*, 185–86.

73. Brown, *No Duty to Retreat*, 55, 85.

74. "Life's Story of James Edward and Margaret Hunter Shelley," typescript, GSTC, box 2, folder 9, 16, 18–19; Hanchett, *Crooked Trail*, 46.

75. Levine, *Snowflake*, 104.

76. Johnson, "Gladden," 5; "'Old Brigham City' and Wilford," 4; Hanchett, *Crooked Trail*, 158; "Wilford," 8; *SJH*, Feb. 3, 1887.

77. John Bushman, "Diary," 2 vols., typescript, GSTC, box 3, folders 2–3, 1:1 (Jan. 12, 1887), 4 (Apr. 4, 5, 1887), 5 (Apr. 7, 1887); LeSueur, "Hash Knife," 5; Will C. Barnes, "Commodore Perry Owens," typescript, WCBC, box 10, folder 68, 2–3; Barnes, *Apaches and Longhorns*, 145.

78. Bushman, "Diary," 1:294–96 (Apr. 6, 1887); Barnes, "Owens," 2, 3; Barnes, *Apaches and Longhorns*, 145–46.

79. *SJH*, Sept. 1, 1887.

80. Clayton, ed., *Frontier*, 109–10; Bushman, "Diary," 1:5–6 (Apr. 30, May 1, 2, 1887); Flake, *William Jordan Flake*, 114–15; Osmer Flake, "Biography of William Jordan Flake," mss., OFD, folder 11, 156, 158, 160, 162.

81. Flake, "Biography of Flake," 156, 158, 160, 162; Bushman, "Diary," 1:294–96 (Apr. 30, May 2, 7, 1887); *SJH*, May 12, 1887; ACC, May 5, 1887; Fish, "Eastern Arizona Stake," 63 (May 9, 1887). Some accounts refer to "Gilson" rather than "Gibson."

82. Flake, *William Jordan Flake*, 117.

83. Bushman, "Diary," 1:295–96 (May 6, 7, 1887).

84. Fish, "Fish Manuscript," 688; Fish, "Eastern Arizona Stake," 63; Krenkel, *Joseph Fish*, 317; Petersen, "Life Sketches," 9–10.

85. Petersen, "Life Sketches," 9–10; "Z. B. Decker," 106.

86. Petersen, "Life Sketches," 9–10.

87. Petersen, "Life Sketches," 9–10; Smith, "Journal," 416 (May 27, 1887); LeSueur, "Hash Knife," 5; Peterson, *Take Up Your Mission*, 170; George S. Tanner, *Henry Martin Tanner: Joseph City Pioneer* (n.p., 1964), 51; "Wilford," 6–7; "'Old Brigham City' and Wilford," 2.

88. Petersen, "Life Sketches," 9–10.

89. *SJH*, Aug. 20, 1885; Tanner, *Henry Martin Tanner*, 54; Peterson, *Take Up Your Mission*, 170; LeSueur, "Hash Knife," 10; Pearce to Lamar, in Carlock, *Hashknife*, 185–86; Gordon H. Flammer, *Stories of a Mormon Pioneering Community: Linden, Arizona of the Little Colorado Arizona Mission, 1878–1945* (Provo, UT: Excel Graphics, 1995);

60; "Faith and Cupgrease," in Church of Jesus Christ of Latter-Day Saints, Snowflake Stake, *Diamond Jubilee Gems* (Snowflake, AZ: n.p., 1963), HDL, unnumbered.

90. *SJH*, Apr. 15, 22, 1886, May 9, 1889; Ackerman, *OK Corral*, 206.

91. *SJH*, May 6, 1886.

92. *SJH*, Apr. 7, 14, 1887.

93. *SJH*, Apr. 7, May 26, July 28, 1887.

94. *SJH*, July 28, Aug. 11, 1887.

95. *SJH*, Aug. 11, 1887.

96. *SJH*, Sept. 8, 1887.

97. ACC, Aug. 20, 1887; *SJH*, Sept. 1, 8, 1887; Fish, "Eastern Arizona Stake," 61; "Wilford," 5; Peterson, *Take Up Your Mission*, 170; "'Old Brigham City' and Wilford," 4.

98. Hanchett, *Crooked Trail*, 52.

CHAPTER SIX: HELL ON THE RANGE

1. Robert Allison, "The Blevins Family: An Episode in the Pleasant Valley War," DC, box 1, folder 11, 16; ASB, Aug. 20, 1887; Don Dedera, *A Little War of Our Own: The Pleasant Valley Feud Revisited* (Flagstaff, AZ: Northland, 1988), 120–23.

2. *SJH*, Aug. 18, 1887; Dedera, *Little War*, 119–22; Earle R. Forrest, *Arizona's Dark and Bloody Ground* (Caldwell, ID: Caxton, 1936), 58–70.

3. Dedera, *Little War*, 120.

4. ASB, Aug. 20, 1887; *SJH*, Aug. 18, 1887.

5. ASB, Aug. 20, 1887; Dedera, *Little War*, 120–23.

6. ASB, Aug. 20, 1887; AR, Aug. 28, 1953; Will Barnes, "Pleasant Valley. Charley Perkins," typescript, WCBC, box 19, folder 98, 2–3; Dedera, *Little War*, 123.

7. Dedera, *Little War*, 120 (quotation).

8. Charlie Duchet, "Reminiscences of 'One-Shot' Charlie Dushey," typescript, DC, box 1, folder 8.

9. "Events of 1886," typescript, CWP, box 13, folder 20, unpaginated; Leland J. Hanchett, Jr., *They Shot Billy Today: The Families of the Pleasant Valley War* (Phoenix, AZ: Pine Rim, 2006), 112.

10. Robert Carlock, *The Hashknife: The Early Days of the Aztec Land and Cattle Company, Limited* (Tucson, AZ: Westernlore, 1994), 69, 75–76.

11. Robert Vooris [Voris], interviewed by Clara Woody and Dale King, May 20, 1957, Gila Pueblo near Globe, Arizona, typescript, CWP, box 16, folder 64, 1; "Events of 1886," unpaginated; James H. McClintock, "The Pleasant Valley War," typescript, WCBC, box 11, folder 70.

12. Leland J. Hanchett, Jr., *Arizona's Graham-Tewksbury Feud* (Phoenix, AZ: Pine Rim, 1994), 39. On the practice of hiding animals at assessment time, see *SJH*, Mar. 22, 1888.

13. *SJH*, Oct. 21, 1886; AG, Aug. 13, 1887 (Tewksbury letter); Harold D. Jenkerson, "Pleasant Valley Feud," typescript, 2 vols., NGCHS, 1:187.

14. James H. McClintock, *Arizona: The Youngest State* (Chicago: S. J. Clarke, 1916), 485; L. J. Horton, "The Pleasant Valley War," typescript dated 1935, CWP, box 8, folder 88, 15–16.

15. Horton, "Pleasant Valley War," 18; Dedera, *Little War*, 116; ASB, Sept. 10, 1887.

16. Horton, "Pleasant Valley War," 16–17.

17. Leslie Gregory and Earle R. Forrest, "Arizona's Haunted Walls of Silence," *AH*, October 1947, 4–7, 26–29; *SB*, February 12, 1887; *HH*, Feb. 10, 1887.

18. Dedera, *Little War*, 120. Friends of Wilson gave him an alibi so that he would not have to testify in the matter, but he later admitted that he had been present.

19. *AJM*, Sept. 8, 1887; *SJH*, Sept. 15, 1887; Allison, "Blevins Family," 32.

20. Hanchett, *Graham-Tewksbury Feud*, 95, 100; Jenkerson, "Pleasant Valley," 2:366. The photocopied court proceedings in the arson trial are in DDC, box 10, folder 33.

21. *SJH*, Sept. 8, 1887; *MJM*, Aug. 9, Sept. 3, 17, 1887; Joe T. McKinney, "Reminiscences," *AHR* 5, no. 3 (1932): 199; Vooris interview, 56.

22. Hanchett, *Graham-Tewksbury Feud*, 59–61. Hanchett reprints the coroner's report.

23. *SJH*, Sept. 29, 1887; McKinney, "Reminiscences," 143; Osmer Flake, "Some Reminiscences of the Pleasant Valley War and Causes That Led Up to It," typescript, SFC, box 2, folder 9, 11; Hanchett, *Graham-Tewksbury Feud*, 60–61.

24. Hanchett, *Graham-Tewksbury Feud*, 60–61; Carlock, *Hashknife*, 162.

25. Hanchett, *Graham-Tewksbury Feud*, 60–61; ASB, Aug. 27, 1887.

26. Martha Houck, "An Arizona Pioneer's Reminiscences: A Report on Pioneer Life in Arizona, Based on Information Given by Mr. and Mrs. J. D. Houck, including Relations with Indians, and the Pleasant Valley War," typescript dated 1916, ASUDAM, 4; Joseph Fish, "History of Eastern Arizona Stake of Zion; Early Settlement of Apache County, [and] Stake Clerk's Records and Journal, 1878–1912," mss., ASLAPR, 39; Leland J. Hanchett, Jr., *The Crooked Trail to Holbrook: An Arizona Cattle Trail* (Phoenix, AZ: Arrowhead, 1993), 136.

27. Vooris interview, 51; Dedera, *Little War*, 136; Hanchett, *They Shot Billy*, 20–22.

28. Dedera, *Little War*, 135–37; Will C. Barnes, "The Pleasant Valley War of 1887: Its Genesis, History, and Necrology," Part 2, *AHR* 4, no. 4 (January 1932): 31; McKinney, "Reminiscences," 145; Duchet, "Reminiscences," unpaginated.

29. *AJM*, Sept. 8, 1887.

30. Houck, "Pioneer's Reminiscences," 5; Hanchett, *Graham-Tewksbury Feud*, vii.

31. "Miscellaneous Notes," typescript mss., GSTC, box 12, folder 15, unnumbered.

32. Drusilla Hazelton, "The Tonto Basin's Early Settlers," typescript, AHS, folder 2, 153.

33. Dedera, *Little War*, 162–63; AG, Sept. 26, 1887; *MJM*, Oct. 1, 1887.

34. Hanchett, *They Shot Billy*, 92.

35. Flake, "Reminiscences," 11; McKinney, "Reminiscences," 198–204.

36. McKinney, "Reminiscences," 198–204.

36. McKinney, "Reminiscences," 198–204; Flake, "Reminiscences," 11.

38. Flake, "Reminiscences," 14; Jenkerson, "Pleasant Valley," 2:332; Dedera, *Little War*, 226–27; McKinney, "Reminiscences," 198–204; *SJH*, Sept. 29, 1887.

39. McKinney, "Reminiscences," 198–204; Flake, "Reminiscences," 15; ASB, June 15, 1889 (citing Prescott *Courier*); Hanchett, *Graham-Tewksbury Feud*, 99.

40. ASB, Nov. 5, 19, 1887; Vooris interview, 65, 68–69; "Conversations with Slim Ellison," typescript, DC, box 1, folder 9.

41. *ASB*, Dec. 3, 1887; Horton, "Pleasant Valley War," 15–18.

42. Barnes, "Perkins," 2–3.

43. *ASB*, May 8, 1886; Duchet, "Reminiscences," 1–6; Lucien Creswell, "Statement of Lucien Creswell," Flagstaff, Arizona, June 10, 1935, typescript, GRMC, 3, 11.

44. Hazelton, "Early Settlers," 10; Frederick Russell Burnham, *Scouting on Two Continents* (Garden City: Doubleday, Page, 1926), 23; Dedera, *Little War*, 160.

CHAPTER SEVEN: THE HONOR OF VENGEANCE

1. Robert Allison, "The Blevins Family: An Episode in the Pleasant Valley War," CWP, box 8, folder 77, 18.

2. Allison, "Blevins Family," 20; Larry D. Ball, "Commodore Perry Owens: The Man behind the Legend," *JAH* 33, no. 1 (1992): 37–38; Will C. Barnes, "Commodore Perry Owens," typescript, WCBC, box 10, folder 68, 5; Will C. Barnes, "Andy Cooper," typescript (note), WCBC, box 18, folder 95, unpaginated; Lucien Creswell, "Statement of Lucien Creswell," Flagstaff, Arizona, June 10, 1935, typescript, GRMC, 1; Rita Ackerman, *OK Corral Postscript: The Death of Ike Clanton* (Honolulu, HI: Talei, 2006), 77, 241; Leland J. Hanchett, Jr., *The Crooked Trail to Holbrook: An Arizona Cattle Trail* (Phoenix, AZ: Arrowhead, 1993), 60; Will C. Barnes, *Apaches and Longhorns: The Reminiscences of Will C. Barnes*, ed. Frank C. Lockwood (Los Angeles: Ward Ritchie, 1941), 146–47; Robert Carlock, *The Hashknife: The Early Days of the Aztec Land and Cattle Company, Limited* (Tucson, AZ: Westernlore, 1994), 142–43, 163.

3. *ACC*, Aug. 20, 1887; Creswell, "Statement," 8; Clara B. Lee and Clarence Lee, oral history interview with Harold C. Wayte, July 1959, in Harold C. Wayte, "A History of Holbrook and the Little Colorado Country (1540–1962)" (Ph.D. diss., University of Arizona, 1962), 163.

4. *ACC*, Aug. 20, 1887; Barnes, "Owens," 13.

5. *SJH*, Oct. 21, 28, 1886.

6. *SJH*, Apr. 22, 1885, Apr. 15, 1886, Jan. 13, 1887, Mar. 21, 1889; Ackerman, *OK Corral*, 59, 60. Kinnear's name was also spelled "Cannear" and "Caneer."

7. Evans Coleman, "Reminiscences of an Arizona Cowboy" (chap. 12), ECP, box 6, folder 61, 224.

8. Ackerman, *OK Corral*, 47–48; *SJH*, Aug. 12, 24, Dec. 16, 1886; *ACC*, Oct. 21, 1886, July 17, 1887.

9. *ACC*, Oct. 7, 1886; *SJH*, Oct. 14, 1886.

10. David King Udall, *Arizona Pioneer Mormon: David King Udall: His Story and His Family*, Pearl Udall Nelson, collaborator (Tucson: Arizona Silhouettes, 1959), 132–33; Charles S. Peterson, *Take Up Your Mission: Mormon Colonizing along the Little Colorado River, 1870–1900* (Tucson: University of Arizona Press, 1973), 237.

11. Joseph Fish, "History of Eastern Arizona Stake of Zion; Early Settlement of Apache County [and] Stake Clerk's Records and Journal, 1878–1912," mss., ASLAPR, 42; *SJH*, Oct. 28, 1886.

12. *SJH*, Oct. 21, 1886.

13. ACC, Dec. 23, 1886; Jesse Nathaniel Smith, "Journal," JNSP, box 1, folder 2, 407 (Oct. 9, 1886).

14. *SJH*, Oct. 21, 28, 1886.

15. *SJH*, Oct. 21, 1886, June 14, 1888.

16. Ball, "Owens," 28–29, 46; Harold D. Jenkerson, "Pleasant Valley Feud," typescript, 2 vols., NGCHS, 2:234; Allison, "Blevins Family," 8.

17. Leland J. Hanchett, Jr., *They Shot Billy Today: The Families of Arizona's Pleasant Valley War* (Phoenix, AZ: Pine Rim, 2006), 305–8; Ball, "Owens," 32 (Coolidge quotations); Wayte, "Holbrook," 155, 157–58; Carlock, *Hashknife*, 107.

18. Barnes, *Apaches and Longhorns*, 147; James Warren LeSueur, "The Trouble with the Hash Knife Company," typescript, JWLC, box 1, folder 10, 2; Ackerman, *OK Corral*, 86; Apache County Centennial Committee, *Lest Ye Forget* (n.p., n.d.), 4; Wayte, "Holbrook," 155–56, 159; Ball, "Owens," 29.

19. *SJH*, Oct. 7, 21, 1886, Mar. 24, 1887.

20. ASB, July 25, 1885; Ackerman, *OK Corral*, 54, 57; Ball, "Owens," 33; *SJH*, Aug. 20, Sept. 24, 1885, June 3, 17, 1886; ACC, Aug. 12, 1886.

21. *SJH*, Oct. 1, 21, 28, 1886.

22. Fish, "Eastern Arizona Stake," 59–60, 63; Peterson, *Take Up Your Mission*, 234–35, 238–39.

23. *SJH*, Oct. 28, 1886.

24. Smith, "Journal," 406–7 (Sept. 12, Oct. 10, 1886); ACC, Oct. 21, 1886.

25. Fish, "Eastern Arizona Stake," 59–60; *SJH*, Oct. 21, Nov. 4, 1886; Smith, "Journal," 408 (Nov. 10, 1886).

26. Minutes of the Little Colorado Stake of Zion, typescript, RRC, 209 (Sept. 4–5, 1886).

27. *SJH*, Nov. 18, 1886; Ackerman, *OK Corral*, 81.

28. HH, Mar. 27, Apr. 8, 1886; Ackerman, *OK Corral*, 203, 205; Edward H. Peplow, Jr., *History of Arizona*, 3 vols. (New York: Lewis Historical Publishing, 1958), 2:136, 138.

29. *SJH*, Mar. 17, 1887.

30. ACC, Oct. 7, 1886; *SJH*, Jan. 20, Mar. 5, 17, Apr. 21, 1887; Peplow, *Arizona*, 2:136, 138–39; Ackerman, *OK Corral*, 209.

31. *SJH*, Feb. 9, 1888; Peterson, *Take Up Your Mission*, 171; Jim Bob Tinsley, *The Hash Knife Brand* (Gainesville: University Press of Florida, 1993), 71.

32. John H. Krenkel, ed., *The Life and Times of Joseph Fish, Mormon Pioneer* (Danville, IL: Interstate, 1970), 316; LeSueur, "Hash Knife," 3; LeRoy C. Wilhelm and Mabel R. Wilhelm, *A History of the St. Johns Arizona Stake* (Orem, UT: Historical Publications, 1982), 48; Gordon H. Flammer, *Stories of a Mormon Community: Linden, Arizona of the Little Colorado Arizona Mission, 1878–1945* (Provo, UT: Excel Graphics, 1995), 61; Joseph Lorenso Petersen, "Life Sketches of Niels Petersen and Mary Mortensen Petersen," GSTC, box 10, folder 1, 8–9.

33. Carlock, *Hashknife*, 178–79.

34. Creswell, "Statement," 13–14; Carlock, *Hashknife*, 149, 178; Peterson, *Take Up Your Mission*, 173–75; Tinsley, *Hash Knife*, 71, 80; Smith, "Journal," 411 (Mar. 7, 1887); John Bushman, "Diary," GSTC, box 3, folders 2–3, 1:325 (Feb. 5, 7, 1889).

35. "Sketch in Regard to 'Old Brigham City' and Wilford (Arizona)," DC, box 1, folder 8, 2; *SJH*, Aug. 18, 1887.

36. "Life's Story of James Edward and Margaret Hunter Shelley," typescript, GSTC, box 2, folder 9, unnumbered; *SJH*, Aug. 4, 1887.

37. Peplow, *Arizona*, 2:155.

38. *SJH*, Sept. 1, 1887.

39. *SJH*, Aug. 11, 1887.

40. Barnes, *Apaches and Longhorns*, 132.

41. ACC, Nov. 11, 1886; Ackerman, *OK Corral*, 130–32, 135–37.

42. ACC, July 30, 1887; Ackerman, *OK Corral*, 132.

43. On the Clanton family, see Ben T. Traywick, *The Clantons of Tombstone* (Tombstone, AZ: Red Marie's Bookstore, 1996); and Sue C. Van Slyke and Dave Johnson, "Kin to the Clantons," *NOLA Quarterly* 14 (Summer 1990): 8, 21–23.

44. Ackerman, *OK Corral*, 8–10, 18.

45. H. B. Wharfield, Cooley: *Army Scout, Arizona Pioneer, Wayside Host* (El Cajon, CA: n.p., 1966), 47; *ACh*, Sept. 12, 1884; *SJH*, Sept. 10, 1885, Mar. 17, 1887; Ackerman, *OK Corral*, 25, 27, 35, 149.

46. Apache County Centennial Committee, *Lest Ye Forget*, 12.

47. Taped interview with Leila Eagar Turley transcribed in Apache County Centennial Committee, *Lest Ye Forget*, 15; Ackerman, *OK Corral*, 41–42.

48. Clifton *Clarion*, June 9, 1886; Joe T. McKinney, "Reminiscences," *AHR* 5, no. 3 (1932): 195–204; Ackerman, *OK Corral*, 163.

49. *SJH*, Sept. 3, 1885, July 1, 15, Aug. 24, 1886; Ackerman, *OK Corral*, 27, 34, 39–41.

50. ACC, July 30, 1887; Ackerman, *OK Corral*, 132.

51. Ackerman, *OK Corral*, 228, 230, 240–41.

52. Ackerman, *OK Corral*, 205; Denver *Tribune-Republican*, Jan. 31, 1886; ACC, June 18, 1887; George S. Tanner, *Henry Martin Tanner: Joseph City Arizona Pioneer* (n.p., 1964), 52.

53. Barnes, *Apaches and Longhorns*, 133–34.

54. San Francisco *Examiner*, Feb. 23, 1894; Ackerman, *OK Corral*, 160. On the botched attempts to destroy the James gang, see T. J. Stiles, *Jesse James: Last Rebel of the Civil War* (New York: Vintage Books, 2003).

55. San Francisco *Examiner*, Feb. 23, 1894; Richard Dillon, *The Biography of James B. Hume* (New York: Coward-McCann, 1969), 285–86; Ackerman, *OK Corral*, 163, 165.

56. Ball, "Owens," 38–39; *SJH*, Aug. 18, May 8, 1887; Ackerman, *OK Corral*, 143.

57. Ackerman, *OK Corral*, 145, 271; *PH*, June 22, 1887, typescript copy, WCBC, box 18, folder 95; Clifton *Clarion*, June 8, 1887; *SJH*, June 9, 1887.

58. Arizona *Daily Star*, Apr. 26–May 24, 1931 (Sunday editions); *PH*, June 22, 1887, typescript copy, WCBC, box 18, folder 95.

59. Ackerman, *OK Corral*, 169, 232.

60. ACC, July 30, 1887; Ackerman, *OK Corral*, 149–50.

61. *SJH*, Dec. 30, 1886; Socorro *Bulletin*, Jan. 26, 1887; Smith, "Journal," 410 (Dec. 27, 1886); Show Low Stake Presidency, *Firm as the Mountains: A History of the Show Low Arizona Stake* (Show Low, AZ: Show Low Arizona Stake, n.d.), 37. I have followed the

Herald's lead in identifying the August victim as Swingle, though Swingle and Samuel Sprague—who fell to another vigilante party in June 1887—may have been one and the same. Some reports also indicate that it was Sprague's companion, Bill Evans, who killed James Hale. See Jack A. Becker, "Commodore Perry Owens Helped Clean Up Early Years of Apache County," White Mountain *Independent*, Sept. 2, 1994.

62. *SJH*, Aug. 18, 25, 1887.

63. *ACC*, Aug. 13, 1887.

64. *ACC*, Aug. 13, 1887; *SJH*, Aug. 18, 25, 1887; Barnes, *Apaches and Longhorns*, 133–34.

65. *SJH*, Mar. 5, Apr. 7, 1887.

66. *ACC*, Oct. 21, 1886.

67. *SJH*, Sept. 29, Oct. 20, 1887; Ackerman, *OK Corral*, 170.

68. *SJH*, Feb. 17, Mar. 3, June 9, Oct. 20, 1887.

69. *SJH*, June 16, 1887; Joseph Fish, extracted entries from diary, entry for June 8, 1887, GSTC, box 10, folders 3–4, unpaginated; Krenkel, "Joseph Fish," 317; Carlock, *Hashknife*, 157; *ACC*, Aug. 6, 27, 1887; Ackerman, *OK Corral*, 77, 241.

70. *ACC*, Aug. 6, 27, 1887; Barnes, "Owens," 5; Barnes, "Andy Cooper," unpaginated; Ackerman, *OK Corral*, 77, 241; Hanchett, *Crooked Trail*, 60; Barnes, *Apaches and Longhorns*, 146–47; Carlock, *Hashknife*, 142–43, 163; S. Eugene Flake, *James Madison Flake, November 8, 1859–February 4, 1946: Pioneer, Leader, Missionary* (Bountiful, UT: Wasatch, 1970), 83.

71. *SJH*, Aug. 4, 1887; Les Flake, *Tales from Oz* (n.p., n.d.), 35; Flake, *James Madison Flake*, 83; Hanchett, *Crooked Trail*, 53, 61.

72. Wayte, "Holbrook," 164, 171; Barnes, "Owens," 8; Creswell, "Statement," 8.

73. Hanchett, *They Shot Billy*, 163–71, 222–26. Hanchett reprints transcripts of testimony in the hearings after the shooting, including that of Owens.

74. Hanchett, *They Shot Billy*, 164–66, 222–26, 308–10 (Owens's testimony); Carlock, *Hashknife*, 170–71; *ACC*, Sept. 10, 1887. For Mary Blevins's testimony, see Don Dedera, *A Little War of Our Own: The Pleasant Valley Feud Revisited* (Flagstaff, AZ: Northland, 1988), 151. See also Barnes's account in Will C. Barnes, *Gunfight in Apache County, 1887*, ed. Neil B. Carmony (Tucson, AZ: Trail to Yesterday Books, 1997).

75. Dedera, *Little War*, 151.

76. *ACC*, Sept. 10, 1887.

77. Leland Shelley, interview with Don Dedera, 1960, cited in Dedera, *Little War*, 141; Creswell, "Statement," 8.

78. Eva Blevins quoted in Dedera, *Little War*, 148–49.

79. Creswell, "Statement," 9.

80. *SJH*, Sept. 15, 1887; Andrew Locy Rogers, "Diary of Andrew Locy Rogers, 1882–1902," typescript, HDL, 81, 83, 84.

81. Jessie Ballard Smith, "Life Sketch of Charles Harvey Ballard," in Roberta Flake Clayton, ed., *Pioneer Men of Arizona* (n.p., 1974), 27.

82. Rhoda J. Perkins Wakefield, "Girlhood Reminiscences," *Hi-Lights* 2, no. 1 (1957): 66; Osmer Flake, *William Jordan Flake: Pioneer, Colonizer* (n.p., n.d.), 118; Flake, *Tales from Oz*, 35, 38, 39; Fish, "Eastern Arizona Stake," 79; Derryfield N. Smith, ed., *John*

Bushman: Utah-Arizona Pioneer, 1843–1926 (Provo, UT: John Bushman Family Association, 1975), 80; Rogers, "Diary," 84; Flake, *William Jordan Flake*, 118.

83. Roberta Flake Clayton, ed., *To the Last Frontier: The Autobiography of Lucy Hannah White Flake* (n.p., 1976), LeSueur, "Hashknife," 2; Minutes of the Little Colorado Stake, 212 (Nov. 11, 1886).

84. Carlock, *Hashknife*, 171.

85. Joseph Lorenzo Petersen, "Life Sketches of Niels Petersen and Mary Mortensen Petersen," GSTC, box 10, folder 1, 9; ACC, Sept. 10, 1887.

86. *SJH*, June 14, Oct. 18, 1888.

87. *SJH*, Oct. 25, 1888.

88. Hanchett, *They Shot Billy*, 168 (Owens quotation).

89. Ackerman, *OK Corral*, 175–76, 178–80. According to a subsequent newspaper story, Powell and Rudd made good their escape. In later years, however, Evans Coleman visited the site where, according to Mormon oral tradition, vigilantes had killed them, indicating that the escape story was a fabrication. Evans Coleman, "On the Trail Experiences," pt. 2, ECP, box 2, folder 21, 6–7.

90. Ackerman, *OK Corral*, 171.

91. E. W. Nelson to ——— Donnelly, Wallace, New Mexico, Feb. 23, 1890, photocopy, Rita Ackerman files; "Edward William Nelson—Naturalist," *The Auk: A Quarterly Journal of Ornithology* 52, no. 2 (1935): 135–48.

92. Coleman, "Reminiscences of an Arizona Cowboy," 224.

93. Joseph Fish, "The Fish Manuscript, 1840–1926," ASLAPR, 648–50.

94. *SJH*, June 23, Aug. 11, 1887.

95. *SJH*, June 23, July 14, Aug. 11, Sept. 8, 29, 1887; Becker, "Sheriff."

96. Wayte, "Holbrook," 145, 175; Ball, "Owens," 49; Flake, *Tales from Oz*, 39.

97. Preston Bushman, "Diary" (June 9, 1920), cited in Tanner, *Henry Martin Tanner*, 55; Ball, "Owens," 51.

CHAPTER EIGHT: KILLING CONSCIENCE

1. Will C. Barnes, *Apaches and Longhorns: The Reminiscences of Will C. Barnes*, ed. Frank Lockwood (Los Angeles: Ward Ritchie, 1941), 153; Jamie Stott (hereafter JS) to Hattie Stott (hereafter HS), Taylor, Arizona, Feb. 28, 1886, in Leland J. Hanchett, Jr., ed., *Black Mesa: The Hanging of Jamie Stott* (Phoenix, AZ: Pine Rim, 1996), 88, 94–95; Harold D. Jenkerson, "Pleasant Valley Feud," typescript, 2 vols., NGCHS, 2:309; Robert Carlock, *The Hashknife: The Early Days of the Aztec Land and Cattle Company, Limited* (Tucson, AZ: Westernlore, 1994), 88, 153. All Stott letters hereafter cited appear in full in Hanchett, *Black Mesa.*

2. Hanchett, *Black Mesa*, 3–6, 21.

3. Hanchett, *Black Mesa*, 9–10, 21, 49.

4. Brian Roberts, *American Alchemy: The California Gold Rush and Middle-Class Culture* (Chapel Hill: University of North Carolina Press, 2000).

5. Hanchett, *Black Mesa*, 90–91.

6. Daniel Justin Herman, *Hunting and the American Imagination* (Washington, DC: Smithsonian Institution Press, 2001), chaps. 8–9.

7. Louis Warren, *Buffalo Bill's America* (New York City: Vintage, 2006).

8. Nina Silber, *The Romance of Reunion: Northerners and the South, 1865–1900* (Chapel Hill: University of North Carolina Press, 1993).

9. Owen Wister, *The Virginian: A Horseman of the Plains* (New York: Macmillan, 1902), 106–13 (chap. 12, "Quality and Inequality"), 392.

10. Carlock, *Hashknife*, 42; ASB, Aug. 24, 1889.

11. Hanchett, *Black Mesa*, 84–85, 87.

12. JS to HS, Castroville, Texas, Nov. 4, 1884, 53–54; Hanchett, *Black Mesa*, 39, 41.

13. JS to HS, San Antonio, Texas, Feb. 23, Mar. 11, 1883, 23, 24–25; JS to HS, Castroville, Texas, Mar. 28, 1883, 27; JS to HS, Day Ranch, Coleman, Texas, Mar. 8, 1885, 62.

14. JS to HS, San Antonio, Texas, Feb. 23, 1883, 22; JS to James Stott, Sr., Day Ranch, Coleman, Texas, Feb. 15, 1885, 60; JS to HS, Holbrook, Arizona, Oct. 13, 1885, 83.

15. Hanchett, *Black Mesa*, 65–66, 97; JS to Hannah Stott, Sr., Running Water Ranch, New Mexico, Aug. 2, 1885, 77.

16. JS to HS, Taylor, Arizona, February, May 1, 1886, 89, 96; Hanchett, *Black Mesa*, 99.

17. JS to HS, Taylor, Arizona, Feb. 28, 1886, July 8, 1887, 91, 110.

18. JS to HS, Holbrook, Arizona, Oct. 13, 1885, 82.

19. JS to Hannah Stott, Sr., Running Water Ranch, New Mexico, July 13, 1885, 75.

20. JS to HS, Taylor, Arizona, Feb. 8, 1887, 101; Leland J. Hanchett, Jr., *The Crooked Trail to Holbrook: An Arizona Cattle Trail* (Phoenix, AZ: Arrowhead, 1993), 95.

21. ASB, Mar. 26, 1887.

22. Clarence W. Durham, *That Hashknife Kid* (n.p., n.d.), 261; Joe T. McKinney, "Reminiscences," *AHR* 5, no. 3 (1932): 202–3; F. A. Ames to James Stott, Sr., Holbrook, Arizona, Dec. 8, 1888, 160–61.

23. JS to HS, Holbrook, Arizona, Oct. 2, 1887, 115–17.

24. JS to HS, Aztec Spring, Arizona, Feb. 27, 1888, 122; *SJH*, Aug. 23, 1888; McKinney, "Reminiscences," 203.

25. *SJH*, May 30, 1888.

26. *SJH*, May 22, 1888.

27. *SJH*, July 7, 1892.

28. *SJH*, June 20, 1888.

29. AC, Aug. 18, 1888, typescript quotation, WCBC, box 11, folder 70.

30. ASB, Aug. 25, 1888; AC, Aug. 18, 1888, typescript quotation, WCBC, box 11, folder 70; McKinney, "Reminiscences," 202–3; Hanchett, *Black Mesa*, 128–29, 137.

31. F. A. Ames to James Stott, Sr., Holbrook, Arizona, Dec. 8, 1888, 160–64.

32. Barnes, *Apaches and Longhorns*, 153.

33. Sidney Kartus, "Helen Duett Ellison Hunt (Mrs. George W. P. Hunt)," *AHR* 4, no. 2 (1931): 39–40.

34. Duett Ellison to George W. P. Hunt, Ellison, Arizona, Nov. 2, 1897, GWPHC, box 6, folder 2; Kartus, "Helen Duett Ellison Hunt," 40.

35. Kartus, "Helen Duett Ellison Hunt," 40; Jenkerson, "Pleasant Valley," 2:217; Carlock, *Hashknife*, 72.

36. Ellison to Hunt, Ellison, Arizona, May 11, 1904, GWPHC, box 6, folder 10; Jenkerson, "Pleasant Valley," 2:217–19; Robert Vooris [Voris], interviewed by Clara Woody and Dale King, May 20, 1957, Gila Pueblo near Globe, Arizona, CWP, box 16, folder 64, 12, 14; Kartus, "Helen Duett Ellison Hunt," 40.

37. ASB, Sept. 12, 1885; Phil Smith, "Ellison's Welcome to Arizona," *ASB*, July 18, 1991; "Dateline of the Pleasant Valley War," typescript, CWP, box 13, folder 20; Kartus, "Helen Duett Ellison Hunt," 40; Jenkerson, "Pleasant Valley," 2:217; Carlock, *Hashknife*, 72; Hanchett, *Crooked Trail*, 27.

38. Hanchett, *Crooked Trail*, 32; Ellison to Hunt, Ellison, Arizona, Nov. 11, 1897, GWPHC, Box 6, folder 2.

39. George W. Shute, "The Pleasant Valley War," typescript, ASUDAM, 21–22; Fred W. Croxen to Will C. Barnes (hereafter WCB), Hereford, Arizona, May 27, 1931, WCBC, box 1, folder 5; William C. Colcord to WCB, Lakeside, Arizona, June 19, 1931, WCBC, box 1, folder 11.

40. Vooris interview, 67–68.

41. Martha Houck, "An Arizona Pioneer's Reminiscences: A Report on Pioneer Life in Arizona, Based on Information Given by Mr. and Mrs. J.D. Houck, including Relations with Indians, and the Pleasant Valley War," typescript dated 1916, ASUDAM, 1.

42. James D. Houck, Pension Record, Veterans Administration, No. XC2474609, ASUDAM; Hanchett, *Crooked Trail*, 133; Frances C. Carlson, "James D. Houck: The Sheep King of Cave Creek," *JAH* 21, no. 1 (1980): 44.

43. Will C. Barnes, "The Navajo Springs Incident," typescript fragment, WCBC, box 11, folder 70; Carlson, "Houck," 43; John A. Hunt, "A Verbal Battle," in *The Life and Times of Snowflake, 1878–1978*, ed. Albert Levine (Snowflake, AZ: Centennial Committee, n.d.), 106–8.

44. Houck, Pension Records; Houck, "Pioneer's Reminiscences"; Carlson, "Houck," 44–45.

45. Houck, "Pioneer's Reminiscences," 2; Carlson, "Houck," 44–45.

46. Carlson, "Houck," 45; Harold C. Wayte, "A History of Holbrook and the Little Colorado Country (1540–1962)" (PhD diss., University of Arizona, 1962), 109; Hanchett, *Crooked Trail*, 134–36.

47. Barnes, *Apaches and Longhorns*, 153.

48. Will C. Barnes, handwritten notes, WCBC, box 11, folder 70; *SJH*, Aug. 23, 30, 1888; AC, Aug. 18, 1888; McKinney, "Reminiscences," 202–3.

49. *SJH*, Aug. 23, 30, 1888; Leland J. Hanchett, Jr., *They Shot Billy Today: The Families of Arizona's Pleasant Valley War* (Phoenix, AZ: Pine Rim, 2006), 229–31.

50. *SJH*, Aug. 23, 30, 1888; Charlie Dushey (Charlie Duchet), "Reminiscences of 'One-Shot' Dushey," typescript dated Apr. 25, 1932, DC, box 1, folder 8, 5–6.

51. *SJH*, Aug. 23, 30, 1888; Dedera, *Little War*, 198.

52. William C. Colcord to WCB, n.p., n.d. [signed fragment], WCBC, box 11, folder 70. Barnes, *Apaches and Longhorns*, 161. Barnes got his information from two sources, Osmer Flake and J. W. Boyle. Boyle, if not Flake, was a vigilante. Osmer Flake, *William Jordan Flake: Pioneer, Colonizer* (n.p., n.d.), 124–26; Will C. Barnes, "Stott Case," typescript notes, WCBC, box 11, folder 70.

53. Barnes, *Apaches and Longhorns*, 157, 162–63.

54. Barbara Zachariae, *Pleasant Valley Days. Young, Arizona: A History of the People of Pleasant Valley* (Young, AZ: Pleasant Valley Historical Society, 1991), 27; Vooris interview, 78; Joseph Fish, "The Fish Manuscript, 1840–1926," ASLAPR, 690. Among the lynchers' victims was Emmett Gentry, who had married an Apache woman and become one of the first—if not the first—American settler in Pleasant Valley. The vigilantes accused him, too, of horse theft. See Phil Smith, "Settlers Settle to Life on Q Ranch," *ASB*, Aug. 8, 1991.

55. Hannah Stott, Sr., to Hattie, Hannah, and Josephine Stott, Holbrook, Arizona, Aug. 31, 1888, in Hanchett, *Black Mesa*, 147; *SJH*, Aug. 30, 1888.

56. Barnes, *Apaches and Longhorns*, 153.

57. D. G. Harvey to James Stott, Sr., Holbrook, Oct. 10, 1888, and F. A. Ames to James Stott, Sr., Boston, Dec. 8, 1888, both in Hanchett, *Black Mesa*, 156, 163.

58. *AR*, Sept. 26, 1888; *ASB*, May 25, 1889; Hanchett, *Black Mesa*, 169.

59. Hanchett, *Crooked Trail*, 88–90.

60. One Who Knows, "Unlawful Hanging. Further Particulars of the Hanging of Stott, Scott and Wilson," *SJH*, Aug. 30, 1888; *SJH*, Aug. 23, 1888.

61. Tom Horn, *The Life of Tom Horn*, ed. Doyce B. Nunis, Jr. (reprint ed., Chicago: R. R. Donnelley and Sons, 1987), 317; Fish, "Fish Manuscript," 690; Colcord to WCB, Lakeside, Arizona, June 19, 1931, WCBC, box 1, folder 11; Croxen to WCB, Hereford, Arizona, May 27, 1931, WCBC, box 1, folder 5.

62. Barnes's list is cited in Carlock, *Hashknife*, 199; Barnes, "Stott"; Vooris interview, 66–68.

63. Vooris interview, 66–68.

64. William D. Carrigan, *The Making of a Lynching Culture: Violence and Vigilantism in Central Texas, 1836–1916* (Urbana: University of Illinois Press, 2004); Barnes, *Apaches and Longhorns*, 159; Nimrod, letter to editor, Albuquerque *Democrat*, Aug. 15, 1888. Carrigan argues that white settlers in central Texas developed a "lynching culture"—or rather a culture that condoned lynching—via successive conflicts with Indians, Tejanos Reconstruction officials, freed slaves, and white lawbreakers. Though innovative, his study accords too little importance to the older behaviors of honor and shaming, behaviors that preceded the conflicts he studies.

65. S. Eugene Flake, *James Madison Flake, Nov. 8, 1859–Feb. 4, 1946: Pioneer, Leader, Missionary* (Bountiful, UT: Wasatch, 1970), 83, 91, 99; John Bushman, "Diary," GSTC, box 3, folders 2–3, 2:352–53 (March 1, 2, 1891); "Miscellaneous Notes," typescript, GSTC, box 12, folder 15, unnumbered.

66. Clarissa Bethena Workman Lee, Autobiography of Clarissa Bethena Workman Lee, http://www.workmanfamily.org/histories/CBWorkmanLeeAutoBio.html; Vooris interview, 81; Wilford Rogers, *Highlights in the Life Story of Wilford Rogers* (Show Low, AZ: Petersen, 1979), 25; Osmer Flake, "Autobiography and Diary," typescript, vol. 3, HDL, 88 (Nov. 15, 1897); Rogers, *Wilford Rogers*, 25.

67. "Miscellaneous Notes," unnumbered.

68. "Miscellaneous Notes," unnumbered.

69. Flake, *William Jordan Flake*, 124–26.

70. Hanchett, *Crooked Trail*, 97; Flake, *William Jordan Flake*, 124–26; Barnes, "Stott."

71. Roberta Flake Clayton, "Jim Stott of the Circle Dot," RFCC, box 1, folder 8, 3–4.

72. Clayton, "Jim Stott," 5.

73. Les Flake, *Tales from Oz* (n.p., n.d.), 28–30.

74. "Incidents in the Life of William Jordan Flake as Told by Him and Made into This Pageant," in Roberta Flake Clayton, ed., *Pioneer Men of Arizona* (n.p., n.d.), 174–83.

75. Flake, *William Jordan Flake*, 124–26.

76. S. M. Brown to WCB, Gallup, New Mexico, June 13, 1931, WCBC, box 1, folder 3; Hanchett, *Crooked Trail*, 103. In his letter to Barnes, Brown called the lynching a "dastardly crime." Hanchett has done a fine job of pointing out some of the same inconsistencies in the various Flake stories about the lynching and its aftermath. I take my lead from him.

77. William N. Miller to WCB, Darlington, Idaho, Aug. 7, 1936, WCBC, box 2, folder 18. On horses straying from their home ranges, see John Henry Standifird, "Journal of John Henry Standifird," typescript, GSTC, box 9, folder 1, 1:123, 130; Joseph West Smith, *Journal of Joseph West Smith: The Life Story of an Arizona Pioneer, 1859–1944* (Mesa, AZ: Children of Joseph W. Smith, n.d.), 60–66 (July 8, 1891); Hanchett, *Crooked Trail*, 51.

78. Roberta Flake Clayton, ed., *To the Last Frontier: The Autobiography of Lucy Hannah White Flake* (reprint ed., n.p., 1976), 116; Hanchett, *Crooked Trail*, 100–101; Hanchett, *Black Mesa*, 157; Carlock, *Hashknife*, 203.

79. Clayton, ed., *Frontier*, 115–16.

80. *ASB*, Jan. 19, 1889.

81. Jenkerson, "Pleasant Valley," 2:386; Hanchett, *Crooked Trail*, 101; *AR*, Sept. 29, 1888; Hunt, "Verbal Battle," 106–8; Roberta Flake Clayton, ed., "A True Story of Early Days. As Related by John A. Hunt of Snow Flake," typescript mss., RFCC, box 1, folder 2.

82. Arthur H. Burt to WCB, Hyde Park, Massachusetts, May 16, 1936, WCBC, box 1, folder 3.

83. Clayton, "True Story," 1–2; Kenner Casteel Kartchner, *Frontier Fiddler: The Life of a Northern Arizona Pioneer*, ed. Larry V. Shumway (Tucson: University of Arizona Press, 1990), 229.

84. Jesse Smith Decker, comp., "A Short History of Zechariah Bruyn Decker, Jr. with Brief Sketches of His Parents," typescript, HDL, unnumbered leaf. See also Kartchner, *Frontier Fiddler*, 222–26, and "Z. B. Decker," in Clayton, ed., *Pioneer Men*, 105.

85. Joseph Fish, "History of Eastern Arizona Stake of Zion; Early Settlement of Apache County [and] Stake Clerk's Records and Journal, 1878–1912," mss., ASLAPR, 68; John H. Krenkel, ed., *The Life and Times of Joseph Fish, Mormon Pioneer* (Danville, IL: Interstate, 1970), 321.

86. Osmer Flake, "Autobiography and Diary," typescript, HDL, 60 (May 2, 1894); *AR*, Dec. 12, 1888; Allen Frost, "Diary of Allen Frost," pt. 2, vol. 5, 1886–1890, typescript, HDL, 551 (Apr. 18, 1889); *SJH*, Mar. 15, July 4, 1889; Fish, "Eastern Arizona Stake," mss., 80 (July 15, 1889); *ASB*, Sept. 16, 1893, May 25, 1889, June 23, 1894; Osmer Flake, "Diary," 60 (May 2, 1894). See also *ASB*, Dec. 7, 1889, Apr. 5, 1890, Dec. 12, 19, 1891, Jan. 23, Apr. 9, 1892, Aug. 5, Dec. 30, 1893, June 23, Sept. 1, 1894, Sept. 28, 1895.

87. Barnes, *Apaches and Longhorns,* 135; William MacLeod Raine and Will C. Barnes, *Cattle* (Garden City, NY: Doubleday, Doran, 1930), 192.

88. Raine and Barnes, *Cattle,* 242–43, 245; Stephen J. Leonard, *Lynching in Colorado, 1859–1919* (Boulder: University Press of Colorado, 2002), 7. See also Howard W. Allen and Jerome M. Chubb, *Race, Class, and the Death Penalty: Capital Punishment in American History* (Albany: State University of New York Press, 2008), 130–32, 140. On lynching more broadly, see Michael J. Pfeiffer, *Rough Justice: Lynching and American Society, 1874–1947* (Urbana: University of Illinois Press, 2004). Though he acknowledges that "rough justice" had origins in the folkways of immigrants from Britain—folkways that I and others define as "honor"—Pfeiffer sees lynching primarily as a nineteenth-century phenomenon. According to Pfeiffer, lynching was a working-class and rural response to middle-class reformers' attempts to abolish the death penalty. Pfeiffer, *Rough Justice,* 3, 12, 186n5. Lynching in Arizona's Rim Country, however, was not so much a repudiation of legal reform as a product of conflicts on the free range coupled with the cultural baggage of honor.

89. Christopher Waldrep, *The Many Faces of Judge Lynch: Extralegal Violence and Punishment in America* (New York: Palgrave Macmillan, 2002), 13–25, 49–66. Waldrep traces the idea of lynching as a social good to late eighteenth-century discourse. Though abolitionists succeeded in redefining lynching—especially lynching in the South—as a social evil, argues Waldrep, settlers in the Far West promptly redefined it as a social good. Western rhetoric gave lynching new cachet in American thought in the second half of the nineteenth century and the first half of the twentieth. On the ideas that sustained lynching in both the South and the West, see also James Elbert Cutler, *Lynch-Law: An Investigation into the History of Lynching in the United States* (London: Longmans, Green, 1905), 197–98.

CHAPTER NINE: UNDERSTANDING

1. Don Dedera, *A Little War of Our Own: The Pleasant Valley Feud Revisited* (Flagstaff, AZ: Northland, 1988), 106.

2. Phoenix *Daily Arizonan,* Oct. 6, 1887.

3. Frederick Russell Burnham, *Scouting on Two Continents* (Garden City: Doubleday, Page, 1926), 27.

4. Burnham, *Scouting,* 23, 26.

5. Roberta Flake Clayton, "Jim Stott of the Circle Dot," typescript, RFCC, ASU, box 1, folder 8.

6. ASB, Feb. 14, 1885; AG, Aug. 13, 1887.

7. Richard Maxwell Brown, *Strain of Violence: Historical Studies of American Violence and Vigilantism* (New York: Oxford University Press, 1975), 134–43. On Western vigilantism, see Nathaniel Pitt Langford, *Vigilante Days and Ways: The Pioneers of the Rockies, the Makers and Making of Montana, Idaho, Oregon, Washington, and Wyoming* (New York: Merrill, 1893); Frederic Allen, *A Decent, Orderly Lynching: The Montana Vigilantes* (Norman: University of Oklahoma Press, 2004); Ken Gonzales-

Day, *Lynching in the West, 1850–1935* (Durham, NC: Duke University Press, 2006); William D. Carrigan, *The Making of a Lynching Culture: Violence and Vigilantism in Central Texas, 1836–1916* (Urbana: University of Illinois Press, 2004); and Stephen Leonard, *Lynching in Colorado, 1859–1919* (Boulder: University Press of Colorado, 2007).

8. Robert Carlock, *The Hashknife: The Early Days of the Aztec Land and Cattle Company, Ltd.* (Tucson, AZ: Westernlore, 1994), 234, 311; James Warren LeSueur, "Trouble with the Hash Knife Company," typescript, JWLC, box 1, folder 10, 3; James R. Jennings, *Arizona Was the West* (San Antonio, TX: Naylor, 1969), 118; George L. Cathcart, "Religious Belief as a Cultural Value: Mormon Cattle Ranchers in Arizona's Little Colorado River Valley" (MA thesis, Arizona State University, 1995), 31, 45; Beth Ericksen, ed., *Snowflake Stake Centennial, 1887–1987: A Story of Faith* (Snowflake, AZ: Snowflake Stake President's Office, 1987), 177.

9. In an intriguing study of legal hangings, Durwood Ball finds that condemned men (and women) received praise for facing the gallows with "coolness," meaning equanimity and heartfelt apologies for their crimes. Ball's thesis, however, shows more about what Victorian newspaper writers and legal officials found praiseworthy than what the condemned themselves admired. Editors, unlike cowboys, upheld middle-class views of behavior that included self-restraint and confession. In addition, the dynamics and meaning of the legal hanging differed from those of the lynching. Though the legal hanging was an artifact of honor, it was increasingly rationalized, privatized, and sanitized in the nineteenth and early twentieth centuries. As rituals, legal hangings could uphold codes associated with conscience (or at least give that appearance), whereas lynchings remained rituals of communal shaming. See Durwood Ball, "Cool to the End: Public Hangings and Western Manhood," in *Across the Great Divide: Cultures of Manhood in the American West*, ed. Laura McCall, Matthew Basso, and Dee Garceau (New York: Routledge, 2001), 97–108.

10. Elliott Gorn, *The Manly Art: Bare-Knuckle Prize Fighting in America* (Ithaca, NY: Cornell University Press, 1989).

11. David Roediger, *The Wages of Whiteness: Race and the Making of the American Working Class*, rev. and expanded ed. (New York: Verso, 2007).

12. William J. Rohrabaugh, *The Alcoholic Republic: An American Tradition* (Oxford: Oxford University Press, 1981), 8–9.

13. James Oakes, *The Ruling Race: A History of American Slaveholders* (New York: Alfred A. Knopf, 1982).

14. Brian Roberts, *American Alchemy: The California Gold Rush and Middle-Class Culture* (Chapel Hill: University of North Carolina Press, 2000).

15. Edmund Morris, *The Rise of Theodore Roosevelt* (New York: Ballantine Books, 1979), 302, 309, 323; Heather Cox Richardson, *West from Appomattox: The Reconstruction of America after the Civil War* (New Haven: Yale University Press, 2007), 229, 253; Brown, *Strain of Violence*, 23, 162–63.

16. Harold D. Jenkerson, "Pleasant Valley Feud," typescript, 2 vols., NGCHS, 2:307.

17. Robert Vooris [Voris], interviewed by Clara Woody and Dale King, May 20, 1957, Gila

Pueblo near Globe, Arizona, CWP, box 16, folder 64, 7; Jenkerson, "Pleasant Valley," 2:211–12.

18. Peru P. Daggs to Arizona Pioneers Historical Society, undated, typescript copy, WCBC, box 19, folder 98; *SJH*, Aug. 23, 1888; *ASB*, June 2, 1894, May 25, 1895.

19. L. J. Horton, "The Pleasant Valley War," typescript, CWP, box 8, folder 88, 19, 23–25; Carlock, *Hashknife*, xv.

20. Osmer Flake, "Autobiography and Diary," HDL, typescript, 81; Les Flake, *Tales from Oz* (n.p., n.d.), 6, 101.

21. Flake, *Tales from Oz*, 6, 101.

22. See "Ranching Days," taped interview with L. Barr Turley, January 1974, and Marshall Flake, "Lewis Decker and the Cowboy," in Albert Levine, ed., *The Life and Times of Snowflake, 1878–1978* (Snowflake, AZ: Centennial Committee, 1978), 2–3, 102–4; Flake, *Tales from Oz*, 6, 44; Roberta Flake Clayton, ed., *To the Last Frontier: The Autobiography of Lucy Hanna White Flake* (reprint ed., n.p., 1976), 112–14, 152; Rhoda J. Perkins Wakefield, "Girlhood Reminiscences," *Hi-Lights*, vol. 2, no. 1 (1957): 66; "Life's Story of James Edward and Margaret Hunter Shelley," in "Personal History of Thomas Heber Shelley," typescript, GSTC, unnumbered.

23. Clayton, ed., *Frontier*, 178–79, 193–94; Chuck Rand, Dickinson Research Center Director, National Cowboy and Western Heritage Museum, email to author, Jan. 7, 2009, citing index card in William Flake file.

24. Osmer Flake, "Biography of William Jordan Flake," mss., OFD, folder 11, 37, 59; Clayton, ed., *Frontier*, 116; Flake, *Tales from Oz*, 44, 46–48.

25. Flake, *Tales from Oz*, 44, 46–48; S. Eugene Flake, *James Madison Flake, Nov. 8, 1859–Feb. 4, 1946: Pioneer, Leader, Missionary* (Bountiful, UT: Wasatch, 1970), 83, 91, 99; John Bushman, "Diary," GSTC, box 3, folders 2–3, 2:352–53 (Mar. 1, 2, 1891).

26. Evans Coleman, "On the Trail Experiences," pt. 2, ECP, box 2, folder 21, 30; Evans Coleman, "Reminiscences and Funeral Instructions," typescript dated 1949, ECP, box 5, folder 57, 2; John Ray Hamblin, *Outlaws of Apache County* (n.p., n.d.), 18.

27. Apache County Centennial Committee, *Lest Ye Forget* (n.p., n.d.), 6; Hamblin, *Outlaws*, 19.

28. Evans Coleman, "Missionary Reminiscences," typescript, ECP, box 2, folder 18, 235–37.

29. "Evans Coleman, Early Day Cowboy, Still Wears Spurs," Arizona *Republic*, 1952, ECP, box 9, folder 82, scrapbook, item 41; Coleman, "Funeral Instructions."

30. Thomas G. Alexander, *Mormonism in Transition: A History of the Latter-Day Saints, 1890–1930* (reprint ed., Urbana: University of Illinois Press, 1996), 13, 37, 73, 75, 94, 195, 198, 201, 213, 239, 251, 256; Michael D. Quinn, "The Mormon Church and the Spanish War: An End to Selective Pacifism," *Pacific Historical Review*, 43, no. 3 (1974): 342–66.

31. James H. McClintock, "The Pleasant Valley War," *Arizona Cattleman*, Mar. 1, 1918, 4–5, typescript in WCBC, box 11, folder 70.

32. *ASB*, May 23, 1891; Will C. Barnes, "History of Live Stock Sanitary Board of Arizona," *Hoofs and Horns* (n.d.), WCBC, box 24, folder 115, 2.

33. Jenkerson, "Pleasant Valley," 1:37.

CHAPTER TEN: WATER ON THE FIRES

1. Leland J. Hanchett, Jr., *The Crooked Trail to Holbrook: An Arizona Cattle Trail* (Phoenix, AZ: Arrowhead, 1993), 65.

2. Holbrook *Argus*, Oct. 17, 1917; Norma Leonard, "OW Ranch: A Search for a Name," typescript, DC, box 1, folder 9, 11; "History of the Deeded Land at the OW Ranch Headquarters," DC, box 1, folder 5; Robert Carlock, *The Hashknife: The Early Days of the Aztec Land and Cattle Company, Limited* (Tucson, AZ: Westernlore, 1994), 277–78; "Miscellaneous Notes," GSTC, box 12, folder 15, unnumbered (leaf 3).

3. Austin Spurlock, *The Spurlock Story* (Provo, UT: J. Grant Stevenson, 1976), 32; "OW Ranch Owners. Ownership and Some History of the OW Ranch, Canyon Creek, AZ," printout from "Richard Aaron Pierce Family Home Page," DC, box 9, folder 9.

4. *ASB*, Oct. 22, 1892, Jan. 13, 20, May 12, 1894, Feb. 26, Apr. 27, May 4, 1895.

5. Ralph A. Fisher, Sr., "OW Ranch, North of Young, Settled by Mormon," Payson *Roundup*, Feb. 8, 1978, DC, box 1, folder 9, 15; Slim Ellison[?], "Old OW Ranch," DC, box 1, folder 9, 126–27; Hanchett, *Crooked Trail*, 27, 64–67.

6. Helen Duett Ellison to George W.P. Hunt, The Ranch [Pleasant Valley], Arizona, Apr. 4, 1897, GWPHC, box 6, folder 1; "Miscellaneous Notes," typescript, GSTC, box 12, folder 15, 2.

7. Char Miller, "Grazing Arizona: Public Land Management in the Southwest," *Forest History Today* (Fall 1999): 16; Paul H. Roberts, *Hoof Prints on Forest Ranges: The Early Years of National Forest Range Administration* (San Antonio, TX: Naylor, 1963), 38–41; Paul H. Roberts interview in Edward A. Tucker, comp., *The Early Days: A Sourcebook of Southwestern Region History*, Book 1, Cultural Resources Management Report No. 7 (n.p., 1989), 300; Franklin Horace Owens, "Autobiography of Franklin Horace Owens," in *James Clark Owens and Families, 1797–1943*, comp. Eva F. Winmill, http://bobcatsworld.com/family/Owens%20Nauvoo%20History.pdf.

8. Roberts, *Hoof Prints*, 40; Albert F. Potter, "The National Forests and the Livestock Industry, 1912," quoted in Roberts, *Hoof Prints*, 8.

9. Roberts, *Hoof Prints*, 8, 83; L. F. Kneipp, foreword to Roberts, *Hoof Prints*, v.

10. Roberts, *Hoof Prints*, 130; William MacLeod Raine and Will C. Barnes, *Cattle* (Garden City, NY: Doubleday, Doran, 1930), 306; Will C. Barnes, *Apaches and Longhorns: The Reminiscences of Will C. Barnes*, ed. Frank C. Lockwood (Los Angeles: Ward Ritchie, 1941), 199; Prescott *Weekly Herald*, Aug. 3, Nov. 11, 1905.

11. Roberts, *Hoof Prints*, 82–83; Arizona *Daily Star*, Mar. 3, 1917.

12. Minutes of the Apache Ranger Meeting Held at Springerville, Arizona, Sept. 8–14, 1910, in Tucker, *Early Days*, 227, 231–32; F. Lee Kirby interview in Tucker, *Early Days*, 166–67; Roscoe G. Willson interview in Tucker, *Early Days*, 133–34; Henry L. Benham interview in Tucker, *Early Days*, 139.

13. Morton M. Cheney interview in Tucker, *Early Days*, 278; Fred Croxen interview in Tucker, *Early Days*, 254–55.

14. Paul Roberts interview in Tucker, *Early Days*, 306; Jesse T. Fears interview in Tucker, *Early Days*, 73.

15. Benham interview in Tucker, *Early Days*, 137, 139; Fred Winn interview in Tucker, *Early Days*, 102; A. O. Waha, "The Waha Memorandum," in Tucker, *Early Days*, 87; Roberts, *Hoof Prints*, 67.

16. Roberts, *Hoof Prints*, 4–5; Stanley Wilson interview in Tucker, *Early Days*, 294; Roberts interview in Tucker, *Early Days*, 308.

17. Kirby interview in Tucker, *Early Days* 163; Osmer Flake, "Autobiography and Diary," vol. 3, HDL, 347, 352 (Dec. 31, 1908, Nov. 11, 1910); Roberts, *Hoof Prints*, 43; Winn interview in Tucker, *Early Days*, 102; Waha, "Waha Memorandum" in Tucker, *Early Days*, 87; Fred Winn, "The Fred Winn Papers," in Tucker, *Early Days*, 106.

18. Roberts, *Hoof Prints*, 51, 107–9, 112–13; Edward H. Peplow, Jr., *History of Arizona*, 3 vols. (New York: Lewis Historical Publishing, 1958), 2:157; Lewis Pyle interview in Tucker, *Early Days*, 154; Benham interview in Tucker, *Early Days* 139; Kirby interview in Tucker, *Early Days*, 168–69.

19. Roberts, *Hoof Prints*, 69 (Potter quotation).

20. Roberts, *Hoof Prints*, 69, 94, 124, 133–34, 300; Peplow, *Arizona*, 2:162, 167; Willson interview in Tucker, *Early Days*, 134–35; Kirby interview in Tucker, *Early Days*, 169; Jesse I. Bushnell interview in Tucker, *Early Days*, 207.

21. Kirby interview in Tucker, *Early Days*, 169; Roberts, *Hoof Prints*, 88–90, 122–23; Roberts interview in Tucker, *Early Days*, 297–98; Will C. Barnes, *Western Grazing Grounds and Forest Ranges* (Chicago: Breeder's Gazette, 1913), 30.

22. Karen R. Merrill, *Public Lands and Political Meaning: Ranchers, the Government, and the Property between Them* (Berkeley: University of California Press, 2002), 35; Roberts interview in Tucker, *Early Days*, 300; Roberts, *Hoof Prints*, 7, 44–47, 86.

23. Barnes, *Grazing Grounds*, 235. On Forest Service policies that discriminated against marginal users, see Louis Warren, *The Hunter's Game: Poachers and Conservationists in Twentieth-Century America* (New Haven: Yale University Press, 1997); and Karl Jacoby, *Crimes against Nature: Squatters, Poachers, Thieves, and the Hidden History of American Conservation* (Berkeley: University of California Press, 2001).

24. Roberts, *Hoof Prints*, 94 (Wentworth quotation); Minutes of Apache Ranger Meeting," in Tucker, *Early Days*, 224. See Edward N. Wentworth, *America's Sheep Trails: History, Personalities* (Ames: Iowa State College Press, 1948); and Charles Wayland Towne and Edward Norris Wentworth, *Cattle and Men* (Norman: University of Oklahoma Press, 1955). On the decline of tensions among big operators and small ones in Oregon, see Peter K. Simpson, *The Community of Cattlemen: A Social History of the Cattle Industry in Southeastern Oregon, 1869–1912* (Moscow: University of Idaho Press, 1982).

25. Merrill, *Public Lands*.

26. In his study of Harney County, Oregon, Peter Simpson finds a similar pattern. By 1934, when the Taylor Grazing Act regulated the public domain, cattlemen big and small had ceased to be enemies. Simpson notes that the "community of cattlemen" that had evolved in the early twentieth century tended to support the Taylor Grazing Act, in large part because it protected the status quo vis-à-vis range and water. Simpson, *Community of Cattlemen*, 116–51. When either the Forest Service or the Bureau of Land Management threatened old rights, however, cattlemen, as well as sheepmen, were quick to attack.

27. Barnes, *Apaches and Longhorns*, x–xv, 166–69; ASB, Apr. 29, 1897.

28. Will C. Barnes, "Eulogy," quoted in David A. Prevedal and Curtis M. Johnson, "Beginnings of Range Management: Albert F. Potter, First Chief of Grazing, U.S. Forest Service, and a Photographic Comparison of his 1902 Forest Reserve Survey in Utah with Conditions 100 Years Later," http://www.fs.fed.us/r4/publications/range/chapter_4 .pdf.

29. Barnes, *Apaches and Longhorns*, xvi–xx; Will C. Barnes, *Arizona Place Names*, rev. and enlarged ed. (Tucson: University of Arizona Press, 1960).

CHAPTER ELEVEN: COURTING CONSCIENCE

1. Charles Peter Boes, "The Biography of George W. P. Hunt, the First Governor of the State of Arizona (from His Birth until 1914)" (mss., Arizona State University, 1960), 2, 4–6. GWPH to DE, no place, July 10, 1904; SEH to GWPH, Missouri, Feb. 17, 1880, Nov. 4, 1885, Apr. 17, 1886, Apr. 14, 1898; George W. P. Hunt, "Autobiography," mss., GWPH, box 4, folder 1, 3–6, 6–10, 12–13; GWPH to DE, Globe, June 25, 1895; Lizzy Hanley to GWPH, no place, Feb. 29, 1880; George W. P. Hunt, "James H. Pascoe," in "A Book of Brief Notices of a Few Friends," typescript, GWPHC, box 9, folder 12. All letters cited in this chapter come from the George W. P. Hunt Collection (GWPHC) at Arizona State University. GWPH refers to Hunt; HDE refers to Helen Duett Ellison; SEH refers to Sarah E. Hunt; FMK refers to Frank M. Knapp; NSB refers to Niles S. Berray. "Darksville" refers to Darksville, Missouri. Other locations, unless otherwise noted, are in Arizona.

2. HDE to GWPH, At Home, Aug. 10, 1894; HDE to GWPH, Young, Oct. 22, 1895; GWPH to HDE, Globe, Nov. 29, 1894, June 25, 1895; HDE to GWPH, San Antonio, Texas, July 2, 1896.

3. E. S. Thornton to GWPH, Clark, Texas, Mar. 25, 1888. For a fuller discussion of bachelor culture, see Howard P. Chudacoff, *The Age of the Bachelor: Creating an American Subculture* (Princeton, NJ: Princeton University Press, 1999). Chudacoff argued that a bachelor subculture peaked in the late nineteenth and early twentieth centuries as urban amenities—and a desire for freedom—made bachelorhood a desirable lifestyle. In some ways, Hunt would have been exceptional in the bachelor subculture described by Chudacoff, who discerns in bachelors a wont to rebel against bourgeois convention.

4. Hunt, "Brief Notices," unnumbered.

5. E. S. Thornton to GWPH, Fort McDowell, Apr. 10, 1885.

6. FMK to GWPH, Silver King, May 17, 1887, Jan. 12, 1888; FMK to GWPH, Bisbee, Feb. 2, 1889; George W. P. Hunt, "Frank M. Knapp," in "Brief Notices," unnumbered.

7. FMK to GWPH, Silver King, June 19, 1887; FMK to GWPH, Bisbee, July 1, 1888; FMK to GWPH, Bisbee, no month, day 4, 1888.

8. Donald Yacovone, "Abolitionists and the Language of Fraternal Love," in *Meanings for Manhood: Constructions of Masculinity in Victorian America*, ed. Mark C. Carnes and Clyde Griffen (Chicago: University of Chicago Press, 1990), 85–95; E. Anthony Rotundo, "Romantic Friendship: Male Intimacy and Middle-Class Youth in the Northern United States, 1800–1900," *Journal of Social History* 23, no. 1 (1989): 1–25; Andrew C.

Isenberg, "The Code of the West: Sexuality, Homosociality, and Wyatt Earp," *Western Historical Quarterly* 40, no. 2 (2009): 25–46.

9. The literature on American social and geographical mobility is large. See, for example, Joseph P. Ferrie, "History Lessons: The End of American Exceptionalism? Mobility in the United States since 1850," *Journal of Economic Perspectives* 19, no. 3 (2005): 199–215.

10. SEH to GWPH, Missouri, Dec. 28, 1888, Dec. 14, 1889. On the Enlightenment concept of sympathy, see Robert S. Cox, *Body and Soul: A Sympathetic History of American Spiritualism* (Charlottesville: University of Virginia Press, 2003).

11. Literary scholars have been far more interested in sentimental culture than have historians. Seminal works include Ann Douglas, *The Feminization of American Culture* (New York: Knopf, 1977); and Jane Tompkins, *Sensational Designs: The Cultural Work of American Fiction, 1790–1860* (New York: Oxford University Press, 1985). Both find in sentimentalism a discourse of reform. On the history of sentimentality and animal welfare, see Keith Thomas, *Man and the Natural World: A History of Modern Sensibility* (New York: Pantheon Books, 1983); Jennifer Mason, *Civilized Creatures: Urban Animals, Sentimental Culture, and American Literature, 1850–1900* (Baltimore: Johns Hopkins University Press, 2005). On nineteenth-century Southern womanhood, see Drew Gilpin Faust, *Mothers of Invention: Women of the Slaveholding South in the American Civil War* (Chapel Hill: University of North Carolina Press, 1996). Faust argues that Southern women became more eager for reform—and especially for married women's property rights—after the Civil War.

12. Stephen Crane [Johnston Smith, pseud.], *Maggie, a Girl of the Streets* ([New York?]: n.p., 1893); Frank Norris, *The Octopus: A Story of California* (New York: Doubleday, Page, 1903).

13. T. J. Stiles, *Jesse James: Last Rebel of the Civil War* (New York: Knopf, 2002).

14. SEH to GWPH, Missouri, Dec. 24, 1887, June 18, 1889, July 23, 1894, Dec. 26, 1895, Apr. 7, July 7, 1896, Apr. 14, 1898, Aug. 6, 1899, June 23, 1900; Georgia E. Frye to GWPH, Moberly, Missouri, Jan. 21, 1900.

15. SEH to GWPH, Missouri, Dec. 24, 1887, Apr. 9, 1890, May 1, Aug. 6, 1891, Oct. 31, 1895, Nov. 20, 1896; Hunt, "Brief Notices."

16. SEH to GWPH, Missouri, Sept. 1, Dec. 4, 1890, Dec. 20, 1896.

17. Hunt biographical materials, GWPHC, box 4, folder 4, unnumbered leaf; SEH to GWPH, Missouri, Feb. 21, 1891; GWPH to HDE, Globe, June 12, 1904.

18. GWPH to HDE, Globe, Aug. 16, Sept. 9, 1894; Hunt, "Frank M. Knapp"; HDE to GWPH, Tank Ranch, Feb. 24, 1895.

19. John S. Goff, *George W. P. Hunt* (Cave Creek, AZ: Black Mountain Press, 1987), 2; ASB, June 4, 1887; Joe Dillon to GWPH, Jerome, May 30, 1887.

20. Leland J. Hanchett, *They Shot Billy Today: The Families of Arizona's Pleasant Valley War* (Phoenix, AZ: Pine Rim, 2006), 22; George W. P. Hunt, "Walter H. Fisher," in "Brief Notices," unnumbered; Joe Dillon to GWPH, Jerome, Sept. 13, 1887.

21. NSB to GWPH, Globe, May 7, June 10, Aug. 10, 31, Sept. 20, 1888.

22. Hunt, "Walter H. Fisher"; James Coffin to GWPH, Salt River, Sept. 3, 1897; Boes,

"Biography of George W. P. Hunt," 7–8; George W. P. Hunt, "Niles S. Berray," in "Brief Notices," unnumbered.

23. HDE to GWPH, At Home, Aug. 31, Mar. 4, Oct. 29, 1895; Sidney Kartus, "Helen Duett Ellison Hunt (Mrs. George W.P. Hunt)," *AHR* 4, no. 2 (1931): 41; HDE to GWPH, The Ranch, June 4, 1895, May 11, 26, 1897; HDE to GWPH, Young, Apr. 20, June 6, 1897; HDE to GWPH, Tanks Ranch, Apr. 10, 1895; GWPH to HDE, Globe, June 17, Aug. 9, 1896; HDE to GWPH, Ellison, Oct. 26, 1897.

24. HDE to GWPH, The Tanks, July 16, 1895; Kartus, "Helen Duett Ellison," 41.

25. GWPH to HDE, Globe, Jan. 24, 1891.

26. HDE to GWPH, Apple Farm, June 30, 1891; GWPH to HDE, Globe, July 19, 1891.

27. GWPH to HDE, Globe, Jan. 7, 1893; HDE to GWPH, At Home, Jan. 19, 1893; HDE to GWPH, The Tanks, July 16, 1895.

28. GWPH to HDE, Globe, Jan. 23, 1893.

29. HDE to GWPH, Apple Farm, Feb. 6, 1893.

30. Heather Cox Richardson, *West from Appomattox: The Reconstruction of America after the Civil War* (New Haven: Yale University Press, 2007), 258. There is an enormous literature on women and philanthropy in the nineteenth-century United States. A good place to begin is Mary Ann Irwin, "'Going About and Doing Good': The Politics of Benevolence, Welfare, and Gender in San Francisco, 1850–1880," in *Women and Gender in the American West*, ed. Mary Ann Irwin and James F. Brooks (Albuquerque: University of New Mexico Press, 2004).

31. GWPH to HDE, Phoenix, Feb. 21, 1893; HDE to GWPH, Apple Farm, Apr. 27, 1893.

32. HDE to GWPH, Apple Farm, Jan. 31, 1894, Mar. 9, 1894; GWPH to HDE, Globe, Feb. 17, 1894, Mar. 18, 1894.

33. HDE to GWPH, Apple Farm, Apr. 1, 1894.

34. HDE to GWPH, At Home, Apr. 30, 1894.

35. HDE to GWPH, Apple Farm, July 20, 1894.

36. HDE to GWPH, At Ranch Newton Place, June 22, 1894; GWPH to HDE, Globe, July 1, 1894; HDE to GWPH, "The Wilderness," Aug. 26, 1894; Don Dedera, untitled typescript, DDC, box 22, folder 17.

37. GWPH to HDE, Globe, Nov. 1, 1894; E. J. Edwards to J. W. Ellison, Globe, Sept. 1, 1898.

38. HDE to GWPH, Apple Farm, Dec. 7, 1894; GWPH to HDE, Globe, Dec. 11, 1894.

39. HDE to GWPH, no place, Dec. 30, 1894; GWPH to HDE, no place, Dec. 30, 1894.

40. HDE to GWPH, no place, Jan. 12, 1895; Lena Ellison to GWPH, Apple Farm, Jan. 12, 1895.

41. Lena Ellison to GWPH, Apple Farm, Jan. 12, 1895.

42. HDE to GWPH, Apple Farm, Feb. 1, 1895; HDE to GWPH, Tank Ranch, Feb. 24, Mar. 19, 1895; GWPH to HDE, Globe, Feb. 16, Apr. 27, 1895.

43. HDE to GWPH, no place, no date [context places it in May 1895]; GWPH to HDE, Globe, June 1, 1895; HDE to GWPH, Grasslands, June 7, 1895.

44. HDE to GWPH, Grasslands, Apr. 3, 1895. See also HDE to GWPH, Apple Farm, Mar. 13, 1893; HDE to GWPH, At Home, Mar. 4, 1895.

45. See, e.g., Drew Gilpin Faust, "Altars of Sacrifice: Confederate Women and the Narratives of War," *Journal of American History* 76, no. 4 (1990): 1200–1228; and Faust, *Mothers of Invention.*

46. HDE to GWPH, Grasslands, Apr. 3, 1895.

47. HDE to GWPH, Tank Ranch, Mar. 19, June 21, 1895; HDE to GWPH, Grasslands, June 26, 1895.

48. GWPH to HDE, Globe, July 12, 1896; GWPH to HDE, no place, Jan. 5, 1896; HDE to GWPH, Young, Oct. 15, 1895; HDE to GWPH, no place, 1896; GWPH to HDE, Globe, Mar. 15, 1896.

49. GWPH to HDE, no place, Apr. 5, 1896.

50. GWPH to HDE, Globe, May 29, 1896; HDE to GWPH, San Antonio, Texas, July 7, 1896.

51. GWPH to HDE, Telegram, July 9, 1896; GWPH to HDE, Globe, July 9, 1896; HDE to GWPH, San Antonio, Texas, July 2, 19, 1896.; Don Dedera, *A Little War of Our Own: The Pleasant Valley Feud Revisited* (Flagstaff, AZ: Northland Press, 1988), 257; ASB, Sept. 1, 1894, Dec. 28, 1895; HDE to GWPH, Grasslands, June 26, 1895; HDE to GWPH, no place, July 10, 1896.

52. GWPH to HDE, Globe, July 12, Aug. 2, 1896; HDE to GWPH, The Tanks, September 1896.

53. GWPH to HDE, Payson, Oct. 15, 1896; GWPH to HDE, Globe, Oct. 25, Nov. 8, 1896.

54. HDE to GWPH, Tank Ranch, Feb. 24, 1895.

55. ASB, Oct. 10, 1898; A. Hackney to GWPH, Globe, Mar. 23, 1893; HDE to GWPH, Apple Farm, Mar. 13, 1893. For Hunt's later attempts to help the cattle ranching industry in its fight against sheepherders, see GWPH to HDE, Globe, Oct. 9, 1904; and "Important Bill by Pres. Hunt," Phoenix *Enterprise*, Feb. 6, 1905.

56. HDE to GWPH, Young, June 8, 1897; HDE to GWPH, no place, June 29, 1897; HDE to GWPH, The Tanks, Aug. 26, 1897.

57. HDE to GWPH, Apple Farm, Apr. 4, 1893; HDE to GWPH, The Ranch, Aug. 31, Sept. 14, 1897; GWPH to HDE, Globe, Sept. 5, Oct. 31, 1897.

58. GWPH to HDE, Globe, Nov. 6, Dec. 12, 1897, Feb 6, 27, 1898; HDE to GWPH, Ellison, Jan. 11, Feb. 1, 1898.

59. GWPH to HDE, no place, Dec. 24, 1899; GWPH to HDE, Globe, Oct. 16, 1901, Sept. 20, Nov. 3, Dec. 14, 1903; HDE to GWPH, Ellison, Apr. 9, 1902.

60. GWPH to HDE, Globe, Dec. 14, 1903, May 1, June 26, Oct. 29, 1904.

61. GWPH to HDE, Globe, Oct. 29, 1904; May 28, Oct. 1, Oct. 28, 1905; HDE to GWPH, Ellison, July 22, 1905; Kartus, "Helen Duett Ellison Hunt," 42.

62. GWPH to HDE, no place, Feb. 7, 1904.

63. "Sentiment Submerges Gambling in Arizona," unnamed newspaper, Feb. 1, 1907, GWPNSASU; Arizona *Register*, Feb. 1, 1907, GWPNSASU; "End Comes Peacefully," unnamed newspaper, Apr. 2, 1907 [?], GWPNSASU, box 13, folder 18. On the social significance of gambling—and the antigambling crusade of the nineteenth century—see Ann Fabian, *Card Sharps, Dream Books, and Bucket Shops: Gambling in 19th-Century America* (Ithaca, NY: Cornell University Press, 1990); and Gunther Peck, "Manly Gambles: The Politics of Risk on the Comstock Lode," in *Across the Great*

Divide: Cultures of Manhood in the American West, ed. Laura McCall, Matthew Basso, and Dee Garceau (New York: Routledge, 2001), 73–96. Fabian views the anti-gambling movement as a phenomenon associated with bourgeois protectors of a social order predicated on "open-ended" acquisition, with a small proportion of great winners and large proportion of losers. Those who succeeded in the game of capitalist acquisition sought to differentiate the high morality of their success from the immorality of working-class gambling. Peck argues that working-class men—miners—embraced the irrational risk-taking of gambling as a way to define themselves in opposition to the rational risk-taking of middle-class managers. Neither argument helps us understand George Hunt, who was simultaneously an advocate for working-class miners and cowboys, a fierce opponent of unfettered capitalism, and an ardent opponent of gambling. It makes more sense to view Hunt's opposition to gambling as a function of conscience than of class.

64. Arizona *Register,* Feb. 1, 1907, GWPNSASU, box 13, folder 18.

65. GWPH, Inauguration Speech, GWPHC, box 9, folder 10 (Feb. 12, 1912); "Senate Refuses to Grant Statehood to Arizona," *DSB,* Mar. 5, 1911, GWPHSUA, vol. 1; Goff, *Hunt,* 11, 16; Edward H. Peplow, Jr., *History of Arizona,* 3 vols. (New York: Lewis Historical Publishing, 1958), 2:18–22; David R. Berman, *Reformers, Corporations, and the Electorate: An Analysis of Arizona's Age of Reform* (Niwot, CO: University Press of Colorado, 1992), 73–87.

66. Berman, *Reformers,* 88–98.

67. "Arizona, Race Question Splits Framers," Los Angeles *Times,* Nov. 23, 1911, GWPHSUA, vol. 1; "Arizona Fights over Color Line," El Paso *Herald,* Nov. 24, 1910, GWPHSUA, vol. 1.

68. Berman, *Reformers,* 92, 110; "Comprehensive Message by Governor Hunt" [March 1912], newspaper article, GWPHSUA, vol. 4 (1912); GWPH to HDE, no place, July 6, 1895; GWPH to HDE, Phoenix, Mar. 13, 1895; GWPH, "The Coming Citizen," address to Arizona Federation of Women's Clubs, Jan. 21, 1914, Nogales, Arizona, GWPHC, ASU, box 12, folder 1, 11–12; FMK to GWPH, no place, Mar. 19, 1893; Grady Gammage, "Arizona Temperance Movement," digitized typescript, undated, Arizona Memory Project, http://azmemory.lib.az.us.

69. Berman, *Reformers,* 115–18, 123, 125.

70. Kieling, "Diary of George Wylie Paul Hunt," 64 (June 6, 1913); Goff, *Hunt,* 17–18. On Hunt's reasons for opposing capital punishment, see GWPH, "Capital Punishment," address delivered at Christian Church, Tempe, Arizona, Dec. 14, 1914, GWPHC, box 12, folder 1.

71. Goff, *Hunt,* 18–19; Hunt, "Capital Punishment," typescript for AG, Oct. 28, 1914, GWPHC, box 12, folder 1, 7–8.

72. GWPH, "Capital Punishment," 9, 17, 25.

73. *Souvenir Program. Prison Musicale. Florence, Arizona, April 21, 1912,* GWPHSUA, vol. 6 (1912); "Inmates of the Asylum Charmed by Music," undated, unnamed newspaper [1912], GWPHSUA, vol. 4 (1912); "Hunt May Allow Convicts Vacations in Cool Pines during Summer Months," undated [likely March 1912], unnamed newspaper, GWPNSASU, box 13, folder 10, 73; "Experiments Continue with Convicts," AG,

Mar. 4, 1912, GWPNSASU, box 13, folder 10, 39; Kieling, ed., "Diary of Hunt," 67 (June 15, 1913).

74. Goff, *Hunt*, 22 ("kept press" quotation); Hunt, "Capital Punishment," 23 (Tucson *Citizen* quotation); "Experiments Continue with Convicts," AG, Mar. 4, 1912, GWPN-SASU, box 13, folder 10, 39.

75. "Experiments Continue with Convicts"; Kieling, ed., "Diary of Hunt," 46 (Apr. 19, 1913).

76. Vooris [Voris], interviewed by Clara Woody and Dale King, Gila Pueblo near Globe, May 20, 1957, typescript, CWP, box 16, folder 64, 64–78.

77. Kieling, ed., "Diary of Hunt," 26, 34, 45–46, 49–50, 52, 54, 56 (see entries from Feb. 20, 1913 [quotation], to May 15, 1913); Berman, *Reformers*, 123–50, 129, 133, 136, 156, 173; "Governor Hunt Says No. Prize Fight Is Vetoed," GWPHSUA, vol. 5 (1912).

78. Berman, *Reformers*, 148–50; Les Flake, *Tales from Oz* (n.p., n.d.), 7–8.

79. Goff, *Hunt*, 47–48.

80. Kartus, "Helen Duet Ellison Hunt," 42.

CHAPTER TWELVE: HONOR ANEW

1. Gusse Thomas Smith, "Arizona Be Yourself," *PAATGS* 5, no. 4 (1927): 21 (Roosevelt quotation).

2. Ward Shelby, "Editorial," *PAATGS* 5, no. 1 (1927): 4; "Arizona's Benefit from Tourist Travel," *AH* 1, no. 5 (1925): 1; Sam G. Bailie, "AAA—Host to the Touring Public," *PAATGS* 11, no. 3 (1931): 4–5; Writer's Program of the Works Progress Administration in the State of Arizona (WPA), *Arizona: A State Guide* (New York: Hastings House, 1940), 460; George Sargent, "The Call of the Canyon," *PAATGS* 8, no. 6 (1929): 24; "Northern Arizona Offers Wealth of Scenic Beauty and Grandeur to Vacationist," *AH* 5, no. 9 (1929): 13; Josephine Delatour Corbin, "Beaver Creek Ranch—in the Valley of the Sun," *PAATGS* 10, no. 9 (1930): 18–20; W. R. Hutchins, "Through Arizona's Wonderland with a District Engineer," *AH* 2, no. 5 (1926): 5–6; Grace M. Sparks, "Oak Creek Canyon, One of Arizona's Most Glorious Playgrounds," *AH* 4, no. 6 (1928): 16.

3. James Wynkoop, "Fiesta to Mark Dedicatory Services Clifton-Springerville Highway," *AH* 2, no. 4 (1926): 11, 17.

4. Lotta (Bunk) Burney, "Where Dudes Are Dudes," *PAATGS* 11, no. 9 (1931): 9.

5. Ross Santee, "1921 Payson Rodeo by Ross Santee," in Jinx Pyle and Jayne Peace, *Rodeo 101: History of the Payson, Arizona Rodeo, 1884–1984* (Payson, AZ: Git A Rope! 2004), 36–38. See also Pyle and Peace, *Rodeo 101*, 9, 11–12, 41–42.

6. Snowflake Diamond Anniversary Souvenir Program, July 20–25, 1953, SFC, box 2, folder 2, 9; Gordon H. Flammer, *Stories of a Mormon Community: Linden, Arizona of the Little Colorado Arizona Mission, 1878–1945* (Provo, UT: Excel Graphics, 1995), 159; Show Low Arizona Stake Presidency, *Firm as the Mountains: A History of the Show Low Arizona Stake* (Show Low: Show Low Arizona Stake, n.d.), 42, 43.

7. Albert Levine, ed., *The Life and Times of Snowflake, 1878–1978* (Snowflake, AZ: Centennial Committee, 1978), 80–82.

8. Smith, "Arizona Be Yourself," 21 (Roosevelt quotation); Harry E. Reisberg, "The Spirit

of Arizona," *PAATGS* 2, no. 1 (1926): 5; Lois Stice, "Arizona Solves the Boy Problem," *PAATGS* 2, no. 6 (1926): 12; Burney, "Where Dudes Are Dudes," 9; "Arizona Leads Fatalities Percentage," *AH* 7, no. 3 (March 1930), 17.

9. Ira Murphy, "One of a Kind—Frank Colcord," and "The Colcords," in "Stories of Payson," looseleaf binder containing Murphy's columns for *Mogollon Adviser*, NCGHS, 9–10; Theresa Haley Boardman, oral history interview with Ira Murphy, 1973–74, typescript, NCGHS, 27–28.

10. ASB, May 13, 1893; Holbrook *Argus*, Oct. 17, 1917; Leland J. Hanchett, Jr., *The Crooked Trail to Holbrook: An Arizona Cattle Trail* (Phoenix, AZ: Arrowhead Press, 1993), 66–67; History of the Deeded Land at the OW Ranch Headquarters, DC, box 1, folder 5.

11. Vincent J. Keating, "Roads of Arizona, Rich in Romance and Adventure, Built with Blood and Sweat, Toil and Travail," *AH* 4, no. 6 (1928): 11; WPA, *Arizona*, 457.

12. Ina Sires, "Songs of the Open Range," *PAATGS* 8, no. 3 (1929): 23, 31; Peter Kyne quoted in Patricia Wayland, "Peter B. Kyne Points Out a Few Outposts of Masculinity," *PAATGS* 12, no. 3 (1932): 5.

13. Zane Grey, *Last of the Plainsmen* (New York: Outing, 1908), preface.

14. Thomas H. Pauly, *Zane Grey: His Life, His Adventures, His Women* (Urbana: University of Illinois Press, 2005), 82 (quotation).

15. Pauly, *Zane Grey*, 7.

16. Jane Tompkins, *West of Everything: The Inner Life of Westerns* (Oxford: Oxford University Press, 1992), 174.

17. Pauly, *Zane Grey*, 74, 106 (Grey quotation).

18. Candace C. Kant, *Zane Grey's Arizona* (Flagstaff, AZ: Northland Press, 1984), 115; Les Flake, *Tales from Oz* (n.p., n.d.), 60.

19. Zane Grey, *Man of the Forest* (New York: Harper's, 1920), 28.

20. Zane Grey, *Nevada* (New York: Harper's, 1928).

21. Zane Grey, *The Drift Fence* (New York: Harper's, 1930); Zane Grey, *The Hash Knife Outfit* (New York: Harper's, 1933).

22. Kant, *Zane Grey's Arizona*, 115.

23. Zane Grey, foreword, *To the Last Man* (New York: Harper's, 1922), unnumbered page.

24. Barbara Zacharie, *Pleasant Valley Days: A History of the People of Pleasant Valley* (Young, AZ: Pleasant Valley Historical Society, 1991), 27; Theresa Haley Boardman, oral history interview with Ira Murphy and Margaret Taylor Murphy, 1973–74, typescript, "Rim Country History. Oral Interviews by Ira Murphy," NGCHS, 28–29; Columbus "Boy" Haught, oral history interview by Ira Murphy, typescript, "Rim Country History. Oral Interviews by Ira Murphy," NGCHS, 79.

25. Nomination by U.S. Forest Service of Zane Grey and Babe Haught Area for National Register of Historic Places, 1979, NGCHS (application and manuscript), item 8, 30; Columbus "Boy" Haught interview, 80; Grey, Foreword, *Last Man*, unnumbered page; "Zane Grey Says He Will Never Again Visit This State or Write about It," Flagstaff *Sun*, Oct. 10, 1930, ZGNC; Kant, *Zane Grey's Arizona*, 116.

26. Grey, foreword, *Last Man*, unnumbered page.

27. Grey, foreword, *Last Man*, unnumbered page.

28. Grey, *Last Man*, 13.

29. Grey, *Last Man*.

30. Dane Coolidge, *The Man-Killers* (New York: A. L. Burt, 1921). The story of a love affair had some precedent. The idea likely originated in the Tombstone *Epitaph* of Nov. 5, 1887, which claimed that "Sally" Blevins, daughter to Mart Blevins, had renewed a childhood affection for William Graham and that twenty men had died as a result. The story is improbable. William Graham was just sixteen in 1887 and, it seems, had never been to Texas, whence the Blevins family emigrated. Mart Blevins, moreover, had no daughter named Sally. In his 1916 testimony to Dane Coolidge, John Gilliland similarly suggested that the feud had its origins in a love triangle. Gilliland, however, claimed that Tom Graham had an affair with Mary Ann Crigler Tewksbury. Dane Coolidge, *Arizona Cowboys* (New York: E. P. Dutton, 1938), 148. Readers interested in fictional treatments of the war should also consult Ivan Lee Kuykendall, *Ghost Riders of the Mogollon* (San Antonio, TX: Naylor, 1954) a book made scarce by a court order barring its sale; and Amanda Bean, *The Feud* (New York: Doubleday, 1960).

31. Flake, *Tales from Oz*, 60.

32. Owen Wister, *The Virginian: A Horseman of the Plains* (New York: Macmillan, 1902); Zane Grey, "Diary, 1923–1939," OHS, 116–17, 122, 129 (Oct. 31, Dec. 24, 1927, Mar. 12, Apr. 8, 1928); G. M. Farley, *Zane Grey, a Documented Portrait: The Man, the Bibliography, the Filmography* (Tuscaloosa, AL: Portals Press, 1986), 22, 52; Tompkins, *West of Everything*, 164; Arthur G. Kimball, *Ace of Hearts: The Westerns of Zane Grey* (Fort Worth: Texas Christian University Press, 1993), 9; Pauly, *Zane Grey*, 2.

33. Kimball, *Ace of Hearts*, 173–74.

34. Zane Grey, *Under the Tonto Rim* (New York: Pocket Books, 1976), 1, 4, 25, 26, 28, 32, 51, 71, 80, 108, 124. *Under the Tonto Rim* was first published by Harper and Brothers in 1926. Grey supposedly based both novels on the experiences of the Haught family. Myrtle Haught Branstetter, *Pioneer Hunters of the Rim: A Historical Account of the Joys, Adventures and Hardships of the Early Explorers of the Mogollon (Tonto) Rim in Central Arizona* (Mesa, AZ: Norm's Publishing, 1976), 82.

35. Branstetter, *Pioneer Hunters*, 64, 8–39, 80–86, 105.

36. Heather Cox Richardson, *West from Appomattox: The Reconstruction of America after the Civil War* (New Haven: Yale University Press, 2007), 266.

37. On the growing power of urban culture in the early twentieth century and the rural resentment it generated, see Hal Barron, *Mixed Harvest: The Second Great Transformation in the Urban North, 1870–1930* (Chapel Hill: University of North Carolina Press, 1997); Robert H. Wiebe, *The Search for Order, 1877–1920* (New York: Hill and Wang, 1967); and Richard Hofstadter, *The Age of Reform: From Bryan to FDR* (New York: Knopf, 1955).

38. Zane Grey, *Code of the West* (New York: Harper and Brothers, 1934), 78.

39. Farley, *Zane Grey*, 3 (Grey quotation).

40. Grey, "Diaries, 1923–1939," 23–24, 80, 82, 95–96, 101, 104, 105 (Feb. 16, Apr. 26, May 10, Dec. 31, 1924, July 9, Oct. 31, Nov. 8, 1925).

41. Nancy F. Cott, "Passionlessness: An Interpretation of Victorian Sexual Ideology, 1790–1850," *Signs* 4, no. 2 (1978); Grey, *Last Man*, quoted in Carlton Jackson, *Zane Grey* (New York: Twayne, 1973), 75, 230; Lee Clark Mitchell, *Westerns: Making the Man in*

Fiction and Film (Chicago: University of Chicago Press, 1996), 147, 149. Grey knew "how to tickle the id of his era," notes literary scholar Arthur Kimball. Kimball, *Ace of Hearts*, 4, 39–40, 103. See also Tompkins, *West of Everything*, 171; William Bloodworth, "Zane Grey's Western Eroticism," *South Dakota Review* 23 (Fall 1985): 5–14; and John Nesbitt, "Uncertain Sex in the Sagebrush," *South Dakota Review* 23 (Fall 1985): 15–27.

42. Pauly, *Zane Grey*, 53, 119–22, 127.

43. Lary May, *Screening Out the Past: The Birth of Mass Culture and the Motion Picture Industry* (New York: Oxford University Press, 1980).

44. "The Voice of Zane Grey's Public," consisting of letters received "On the Occasion of the Celebration of the Twentieth Anniversary of his Association with Harper and Brothers, 1910–1930," OHS (microfilm), unnumbered.

45. "Voice of Zane Grey's Public."

46. "Voice of Zane Grey's Public."

47. "Voice of Zane Grey's Public"; Carlton Jackson, "On the Trail of Zane Grey," ZGNC. William J. Tewksbury may have been William J. Acton, son of Bertha Tewksbury Rhodes Acton, who was herself the daughter of John and Mary Ann Crigler Tewksbury. In writing Grey, it seems, he took the name Tewksbury.

48. "Voice of Zane Grey's Public."

49. Farley, *Zane Grey*, vi.

50. "Voice of Zane Grey's Public"; Pauly, *Zane Grey*, 113.

51. Kimball, *Ace of Hearts*, 86. On the marketing of dime novels to youths and, later, to working-class readers, see Christine Bold, "Malaeska's Revenge; or, The Dime Novel Tradition in Popular Fiction," in Richard Aquila, ed., *Wanted Dead or Alive: The American West in Popular Culture* (Urbana: University of Illinois Press, 1996), 27, 31; and Michael Denning, *Mechanic Accents: Dime Novels and Working-Class Culture in America* (London: Verso, 1987).

52. Jackson, "On the Trail of Zane Grey," ZGNC; Grey, "Diary, 1923–1939," OHS, 131 (Nov. 3, 1929); "Arizona Insulted Him, Zane Grey Says after Row," *New York American*, Oct. 16, 1930, in ZGNC; "Zane Grey Says He Will Never Again Visit This State or Write about It" (interview with Grey), Flagstaff *Sun*, Oct. 10, 1930, in ZGNC.

53. John Ray Hamblin, *Outlaws of Apache County* (n.p., n.d.); Branstetter, *Pioneer Hunters*, 70–79.

CONCLUSION

1. Richard Maxwell Brown, *Strain of Violence: Historical Studies of American Violence and Vigilantism* (New York: Oxford University Press, 1975), 9–11, 22, 100–101, 119–21. On the comparative absence of lynching and vigilantism in New England, the Upper Midwest, and Utah, see Michael Pfeiffer, *Rough Justice: Lynching and American Society, 1874–1947* (Urbana: University of Illinois Press, 2004); and Stephen J. Leonard, *Lynching in Colorado, 1859–1919* (Boulder: University Press of Colorado, 2002), 8.

2. Altina Waller, *Feud: Hatfields, McCoys, and Social Change in Appalachia, 1860–1890* (Chapel Hill: University of North Carolina Press, 1978).

3. C. L. Sonnichsen, *I'll Die before I'll Run: The Story of the Great Feuds of Texas* (New York: Devin-Adair, 1962; reprint ed., Lincoln: University of Nebraska Press, 1988).

4. Bill O'Neal, *Cattlemen vs. Sheepherders: Five Decades of Violence in the West, 1880–1920* (Austin, TX: Eakin, 1989), 2; Paul H. Carlson, *Texas Woolybacks: The Range Sheep and Goat Industry* (College Station: Texas A&M University Press, 1982); Robert M. Utley, *Billy the Kid: A Short and Violent Life* (Lincoln: University of Nebraska Press, 1989); Cecilia Rasmussen, "Castaic Range War Left Up to 21 Dead," Los Angeles *Times*, Apr. 15, 2001. See also Peter K. Simpson, *The Community of Cattlemen: A Social History of the Cattle Industry in Southeastern Oregon, 1869–1912* (Moscow: University of Idaho Press, 1987). Though Simpson does not chronicle a range war, he does chronicle frictions between big and small operators in southeastern Oregon that led to violence.

5. On the Johnson County War, see Bill O'Neal, *The Johnson County War* (Austin, TX: Eakin, 2004); and Daniel Belgrad, "'Power's Larger Meaning': The Johnson County War as Political Violence in an Environmental Context," *Western Historical Quarterly* 33, no. 2 (2002): 159–77.

6. On the connection between the Western and Cold War politics, see Richard Slotkin, *Gunfighter Nation: The Myth of the Frontier in Twentieth-Century America* (New York: Atheneum, 1992).

7. David Peterson Del Mar, *What Trouble I Have Seen: A History of Violence against Wives* (Cambridge, MA: Harvard University Press, 1996).

8. Jo Baeza, "The Lynching of Stott, Scott, and Wilson," White Mountains Online, http://www.therim.com/attract/lynching.htm; Walter Van Tilburg Clark, *The Ox-Bow Incident* (New York: Random House, 1940).

9. Marguerite Noble, *Filaree: A Novel of an American Woman* (New York: Random House, 1979), dedication page.

10. Stan Brown, "The Story of Greenback Valley," *Payson Roundup*, Aug. 26, 2006.

INDEX

Adams, Cap, 135
Adams, Jerome Jefferson, 107, 111, 117
Adams, John Quincy, 107
Adams, Mary, 113
Adams, Will, 107, 111, 114, 166, 285
Adams brothers, 107
Adams children, 114
Adams lode, 231
Agassiz, George, 170
Agassiz, Louis, 170
Allen's Camp, Ariz., 37
All the Pretty Horses (McCarthy), 289
American Valley Cattle Company, 56
Ames, Frank, 170, 174–75, 177, 185
Ames, Oakes, 170
Anti-Mormon convention, 80–81, 150
Apache Chief, 80, 83
Apache County, Ariz., 137, 138; Potter's career in, 219; anti-Mormon campaign in, 115; Aztec-Mormon alliance in, 120; Barnes's career in, 226–28; conflicts in, xvi–xvii, 55, 132, 200–201, 284; courts involved in "cleanup," 154–55; cowboy influence on, 96; drought in, 61; formation of, 41, 77; forms posse, 134; and honor, xiv, xvii; Mormon-gentile conflict in, 80, 132, 200–201; prosecutes lynchers, 185; stock census in, 52–53; Stott arrives in, 167; vigilantism in, 119–20, 149, 151, 165,
182–85, 189, 195, 201, 284; violence in, xx, 80
Apache County *Critic:* criticizes Sheriff Owens, 156, 161; criticizes vigilantism, 154; defends Cooper, 119, 139; posts reward for return of stolen sheep, 125; Reed edits, 118; supports "cleanup," 151–52, 153
Apache County Democratic Party, 163
Apache County Stock Growers Association, 58, 132, 162; accusations against, 154, 185; authorizes stock detectives, 91; and Barnes, 226; members of, 147, 220; members pay bond for Sheriff Owens, 156; reorganized in 1887, 146–47; and vigilantism, 149, 151–54, 163, 250, 285
Apache Kid, 246
Apache *Review,* 164, 179, 192, 194
Apaches, 109, 127, 245; accused of rustling, 237; attacks on settlers, 11, 18, 54, 70, 128, 176, 226; leave reservation to hunt, 123; married to whites, 7; recruited by Grahams, 126; territories of, 36; and tourism, 257
Apodaca, Miguel, 102, 128
Apple Farm, Ariz., 178
Applegate, W. C., 276
Appomattox, Va., xviii
Arizona, xvii, xxi, 24

343

Arizona Automobile Association, 256

Arizona Cattle Company, 56

Arizona *Champion*, 16, 51, 52

Arizona Cooperative Mercantile Assoc.
(ACMI), 44, 84, 89–90, 109

Arizona Department of Transportation,
xxii

Arizona *Gazette*, 8, 251

Arizona Highways, xxii, 256, 260

Arizona Historical Review, 228

Arizona *Journal-Miner*, 127, 132

Arizona Mineral Belt Railroad, 9, 10

Arizona mission (Mormon), 32–39, 75

Arizona *Silver Belt*, 4, 18, 229; criticizes
cattlemen, 58, 61, 174; editor urges
Burnham to quit feud; 198; promotes
railroad, 10; promotes Tonto Basin cattle
industry, 8–9, 51; reassures small operators, 57; reports Aztec-sheepherder
conflict, 101; reports death of Monk,
50; reports drought, 62; reports Houck's
whereabouts, 129; reports killings, 194;
reports Pleasant Valley conflict, 20, 135;
reports rustling, 195; sympathizes with
Tewksburys, 200; warns of overstocking,
52, 53

Arizona Wool Growers' Association, 105

Armijo, Jake, 210

Armijo, Policarpio, 104

Armijo, Santos, 104

Atchison, William S., 91, 147

Atkins, Job, 174

Atkinson, Henry M., 56

Atlantic and Pacific Railroad (A&P), 10,
93, 104, 181; criticized by cattlemen, 55;
and lieu lands, 109; neglects promise to
Mormons, 105; refuses to pay property
tax, 54; sells land to Aztec, 19, 92

August Doin's rodeo (Payson), 208, 257;
photo, 258

Aztec Land and Cattle Company (Hashknife Outfit), 60, 122, 192, 206, 210,
229, 282; alliance with Mormons, 113,
118, 165, 200–202, 209, 212; balks at

paying taxes, 54; battles Mormons, xiv,
88, 106–12, 120, 225, 284; battles sheepherders, xiv, 19, 100–105, 199, 284; concerned about rustling, 194; cowboys ally
with Grahams, 133; employs Scott and
Wilson, 182; forbids cowboys to steal
Mormon stock, 119, 121, 148; formation
of, 52, 91–93; hires Mormon cowboys,
209; lawlessness of cowboys, 96, 114–15;
overstocks range, 92–94; Stott and, 167;
suffers reverses, 147, 202; threat to small
operators, 56, 57, 224

Aztec Springs, Ariz., 167

Baca, Benigno, 140

Baca, Dionicio, 140

Baca, Francisco, 154, 139–40, 164

Baca, Santiago, 104

Baca ranch, 134

Bacas, 142

Bachelor culture, 232

Bagley, Melissa, 42

Bagnall, George, 86

Ballard, Charles, 188

Ballinger's Camp, 35

Banta, A. F., 185

Baptists, 24, 25, 27, 28, 235

Barbecues, 11, 12

Barbed wire, 51

Barnes, Will C., xvii, xviii, 9, 11, 12, 58–59,
63, 93, 96, 102, 114, 127, 146, 156, 157,
167, 177, 189, 191, 192, 195–96, 203, 212,
212; career of, 226–28; confirms Stott's
guilt; describes Houck, 180, 182; describes lynching of Stott, Scott, and
Wilson, 183; and Forest Service, 219, 221,
224; hand-drawn map of Pleasant Valley
conflict locales, 131; identifies vigilantes,
183, 186; involvement in People's Party
and Winslow convention, 145; manuscript and hand-drawn map of Holbrook
gunfight, 160; officer in stock association, 147; photos of, 226, 227; role in vigilantism, 149, 152, 154

Barth, Morris, 70

Barth, Nathan, 70, 73, 154

Barth, Refugio Landavazo y Sanchez, 70; photo, 73

Barth, Solomon: and conflicts with Mormons, 69–71, 73, 74, 77, 79; accused of destroying county warrants, 139; convicted, 154; pardoned, 164–65; photo, 70

Barth brothers, xiv

Barth faction, 78, 87, 112, 140, 141, 142; possible embezzlement by, 139

Basque (or Indian) herder (first victim in Pleasant Valley conflict), 127, 136

Basques, 20, 102, 103

Battle Mountain, Nev., 6

Beaver, Utah, 30, 33

Becker, Gustav, 150

Beery, Noah (actor), 281

Belknap, Morris, 122

Benbrook, J. H., 165

Bennett (Pleasant Valley victim), 133

Berray, Niles, 229

Berry, Edith, 276

Bevans, S. B., 147

Big operators, 282; ally with small operators, 19, 137, 217; conflicts with small operators, 56–58, 137; conflicts with other big operators, 198; regulated by Forest Service, 224–25

Bishop, H. H., 16, 129

Black Beauty: The Autobiography of a Horse (Sewell), 234

Blackface minstrelsy, 204

Black Falls, Ariz., 35

Black Hawk War (Utah), 31

Blacks, xvi, 25, 102, 204

Blaine, George, 16, 19, 20, 89–90

Blaine, James, 171

Blassingame, Robert Carr, 91, 132, 263

Blevins, Albert "Charlie," 107, 134, 135, 136, 138, 267; photo, 108

Blevins, Artimesia, 108, 157

Blevins, Delila, 108, 120, 138

Blevins, Eva, 108, 157, 159, 161

Blevins, Jimmy (Cormac McCarthy character), 289

Blevins, John, 108, 157, 159

Blevins, Mart "Old Man," 108, 120, 136, 138; body and skull found, 127–28; search for, 121

Blevins, Mary, 109, 120, 157, 159

Blevins, Sam Houston, 108, 157, 159

Blevins, William "Hamp" Hampton, 115, 136, 138, 174; arrives in Rim Country, 107; attacked by Navajos, 110; killed in Middleton cabin fight, 122; photo, 108; protected by Mormons, 113; searches for father, 120, 121

Blevins boys, 111; accused of horse theft, 114–15, 119; arrive in Rim Country, 107–9; and claim jumping, 107; conflict with Mormons, 107, 110–11; and honor, 109, 204; and Holbrook gunfight, 157–61; in Mormon memory, 161–62, 200, 204, 207, 211; ties to Grahams, 132, 133, 200

Blevins family, 259

Blood atonement, doctrine of, 29, 30, 48, 85

Bloody Thirteenth Legislature, 181, 239

Blue River, Ariz., 152

Boardman, Theresa Haley, 265

Bodie, California, 98

Boles, Sampson Elam, 265

Bonita Creek, Ariz., 153

Bonner, William, 128, 135, 136

Book of Mormon, 25, 31, 44, 47

Boone, Daniel, literature of, 169, 270

Booth, Zech, 223

Boquet, Charles, 289

Boston, Mass.: Mormon prophecy of destruction of, 161

Bourdieu, Pierre, xvi

Bowie, Ariz., 178

Boyer, Joe, 127, 129

Boyle, J. W., 185, 189

Bradshaw Mountains, Ariz., 3, 6

Breed, J. H., 194

Brigham City, Ariz., 36, 37

Brigham Young Academy, 209

Brighton, Jonas, 152–54, 161, 163, 203, 212, 220, 226, 263

Brookbanks, Edith, 107

Brown, Richard Maxwell, xx, 112, 201

Brown, S. M., 191

Bryan, William Jennings, 235, 245

Buchanan, James (U.S. president), 22, 29

Bucket of Blood saloon, 97

Buffalo Bill's Wild West, 169, 208, 210

Bull-ionaires, 56

Bulwer-Lytton, Edward (author), 237

Bureau of Land Management, 225

Burney, Lotta, 257

Burnham, Frederick Russell, 198

Burt, Arthur, 192

Bush, George H. W. (U.S. president), 288–89

Bushman, John, 45, 114

Cain, in Mormon dogma, 74

California, 4, 18, 23, 54, 55; range feuds in, 283

California gold rush, 168–69, 206

Campbell, Joseph, 252

Campbell, Robert "Bud," 187, 236, 242, 245

Camp Geronimo, Ariz., xxii

Camp Thomas, Ariz., 149, 154

Canaan, in Mormon dogma, 74

Candelaria, Juan, 75

Candelaria brothers, 75–76

Canyon Creek, Ariz., 115, 134; claimed by Blevinses, 110; claimed by Mormons, 107; purchased by Ramer, 217–18; rustlers' headquarters, 114, 129; sold to Hollywood mogul, 259

Capital punishment, xv, xviii, 250, 252, 260, 285

Carrington, Robert, 121, 122

Carson, Thomas, 156

Castration, threats of against Mormons, 83, 199

Cather, Willa (author), 270, 289

Catholics, xiii, 201

Catron, Thomas H., 56

Cattle boom, 9

Cattle Growers of Arizona, 209

Cattlemen, 9, 19, 20, 217, 282, 284; and Forest Service, 223–25; and hatred for sheep, 126

Cattle recession, 53–56, 60, 100, 199, 229

Cavaliers, 24

Cedar City, Utah, 29, 30

Central Arizona Live Stock and Ranchmen's Association, 18

Champion, Nate, 284

Cheney, Morton, 221

Cherry Creek, Ariz.: boundary in Pleasant Valley conflict, 123; claimed by Tewksburys, 6; site of ambush, 130–31; site of Flying V ranch, 18; site of lynchings, 184

Childrearing practices, 99–100

Chino Valley, 8, 15, 16

Christian Science, 235

Christopherson, Peter, 84

Church, George, 13

Church of Jesus Christ of Latter-Day Saints. *See* Mormons

Churros (sheep), 103

Civil War, 199, 204, 239, 243; and honor, conscience, xv, xviii, 290; Houck and, 180, 239, 243, 290; Jesse Ellison and, 177, 179; Mormon perceptions of, 47–48, 211; and reconciliation between North and South, xviii, 169

Claim jumping, 63–64, 79, 207

Clanton, Billy, 150

Clanton, Ike, 81, 140, 149–50, 152–53, 165, 203, 204

Clanton, Newman Haynes "Old Man," 149

Clanton, Phineas, 155, 165; and honor, 204; at Mormon dance, 150; perjury of witnesses against, 163; petition for pardon, 164; tried for cattle theft, 151, 152, 154

Clanton "gang," 140, 164

Clantons, 96, 113, 154, 211; family history, 149–51

Clantonville, Ariz., 149

Clark, Walter Van Tilburg (author), 287

Clayton, Roberta Flake, 189–90

Clean-up campaign (Apache County), 151–56, 165

Clear Creek, Ariz., 62

Cleveland, Grover (U.S. president), 86, 101, 171, 141, 241, 245

Cline boys, 186

Clymer, Lamotte, 183, 185–86

Coconino County, Ariz., 195

Code duello, 98

Code of the West (Grey), 270–71; advertisement for, 273

Code of the West, idea of, 259, 270

Cody, George, 176, 179

Cody, William "Buffalo Bill," 169

Cohen, Mildred, 277

Colcord brothers, 186, 259, 281

Colcord, Harvey, 187

Colcord, William, 186, 187

Cole, John Grady (Cormac McCarthy character), 289

Coleman, Evans, 39, 74, 79; and cowboy honor, 210; meets Kinnear, 164; and Mormon migration to Arizona, 34, 35

Coleman, N. J., 176, 179, 186

Coleman, Prime, 210, 285

Colorado Plateau, 35, 92

Colorado River, 33

Colter (Grey villain), 267

Compadrazgo (godparent system), 72

Cooley, Corydon, 7

Coolidge, Dane (author), 143, 193; writes novel about Rim Country War, 267

Concho, Ariz., 42, 75, 145

Conscience, xiv, xv, xvii, xx, xxi, 27, 30, 37, 49, 98–99, 169, 282; distinction between behavioral and humanitarian conscience, xv, 285, 288; and Duett Ellison, 237–45; and Forest Service, 225; and Grey, 276; in Grey novels, 261, 274; and Hunt, 235–37; ironies of, 206–7; and race, xv, 25, 27, 74–75, 78–79,

82, 205, 249, 287–88; and religion, 25, 27–28, 30, 43–44, 48–49, 74–75, 78–79, 205, 240; and social class, 205–8, 213; and sympathy, 234; in twentieth century, 285–91; and women, 239, 287

Consumerism, xix

Continental Land and Cattle Company, 92, 106

Conway (settler), 230

Cooper (Blevins), Andy, 285; accused of horse theft, 114–15, 120; ambushes Tewksburys, 131–32; conflict with Mormons, 107–11, 115, 117, 119, 166; defended by Reed, 154; killed by Sheriff Owens, 157–61; kills Navajos, 110; offered scalp bounty, 126; photo, 158; pursued by Houck, 129; pursued by Sheriff Owens, 146, 156; relationship with Sheriff Owens, 138–39; sells ranch to Ramer, 217; Stott blurred with, 190, 207

Cooper, James Fenimore (author), 261

Coronado Trail, 257

County branding system, 146

Cowboys, xxi, xxii, 19; celebration of, 169, 288; conflicts with Mormons, 106, 199, 202; costume and accoutrements of, 94–96; criminal acts of, 97; criticize Hunt, 244; as forest rangers, 223; hatred for sheepherders, 102–4, 223; and honor, 94–98, 199, 205, 207; lynched by New Mexicans, 77; Mormon celebration of, 257–58; and rustling, 13, 211; and sentimentality, 233; and tourists, 257–60, 279; vote for Hunt, 245, 246

Cow-Boys (Southern Arizona gang), 81, 112, 149–50

Cowboy tournaments (rodeos), 11; and honor, 208, 257

Crabbe, Buster (actor), 281

Crane, Stephen, 234, 270

Creaghe, St. George, 77, 78, 140, 163

Creswell, Lucien, 102, 106, 107, 136, 138, 148, 161

Criminal syndicalism bill, 252

Crockett, Davy, literature on, 169

Crook Forest Reserve, 223

Crook, General George, 3, 7, 81, 128, 150, 180

Crouch, Mrs., 131

Croxen, Fred, 222

Daggs, J. W., 105

Daggs, Peru, 19, 123, 208

Daggs brothers, 93; alliance with Tewksburys, 18–19, 123, 198–99; conflict with Aztec, 104–5, 203, 225; hide sheep from assessors, 124; losers in Pleasant Valley conflict, 208; recruit assassin, 136

Dale, Milt (Grey fictive hero), 262

Dancing, 171, 237

Danites, 166

Day, Mr. (Stott employee), 184

Day, Mrs. (Stott employee), 184

Decker boys, 111

Decker, Zechariah "Zach" Bruyn, 111–12, 166, 193–94, 207

Defiance Cattle Company, 133

Democratic Party, 24, 56, 226; and Apache County politics, 81, 86, 142, 145, 163; alliance with Mormons, 145, 200; and Hunt, 232, 235, 245, 249

Denmeade, Edd (Grey protagonist), 271

Deseret, 23, 84

The Diamond (Rim Country locale), 244

Dickens, Charles (author), 232, 237; and sympathy, 234, 251, 270

Dilze'eh ("Tonto" Apache), xxii, 3, 4, 7, 180

Dime novels, 169, 190

Dolan, James, 284

Douglass, Frederick, as exemplar of conscience, 205

Dreiser, Theodore (author), 270

The Drift Fence (Grey), 263

Drinking: as aspect of honor, xv, 171, 179, 237–38, 241; concept of "alcoholic republic," 204–5; and conscience politics, 282; and cowboy honor, 95, 96, 97, 98, 151, 165, 188, 190, 199, 203, 210;

forbade by Mormons, evangelicals, 27, 28, 210, 211; and New Mexicans, 72, 103; and new sort of honor, 219, 285; and Northern conscience, 99, 171, 202; opposed by Hunt, xviii, 231, 232–33, 235, 245–46, 251–52; as rebellion against conscience, 168, 207; and Western hospitality, 172

Drought, 61–62, 100, 147

Dry Lake, Ariz., 121

Duchet, Charlie, 16, 123, 132, 136, 176, 182, 192, 208

Dueling, 28, 203, 213

Dunn, "Little Molly" (Grey character), 265

Dunn, Slinger (Grey character), 265

Durham, Clarence Walter, 60, 174

Dutchy, 79

Eagar, Ariz., 42

Earp, Morgan, 150

Earp, Virgil, 150

Earp, Wyatt, 81, 112, 150

Earp brothers, 113, 150, 151

Eastern Arizona Stake of Zion, 85, 146

Eastern capitalists, 113

East Verde River, 43

Eastwood, Clint (director), 289

Eddy, James, 10

Eddy, Mary Baker, 235

Edmonson (Tewksbury ally), 129

Edmunds Act, 81, 84, 211

Edmunds-Tucker Act, 84, 211

Edwards, E. J., 241, 244

Edwards, John Newman, 235

Election of 1886 (Apache County), 140–46, 202

Ellenwood, Joe, 133

Ellinger, Ike, 149, 151, 153

Ellinger, William, 149, 151, 152

Elliott (Pleasant Valley victim), 136

Ellison, Helen Duett, xvii, xviii, xxiv, 186, 219, 231, 252; death of, 253; duty to family, 241–47; early life, 236–37; espouses conscience, 240, 242; marries

Hunt, 247; opposes drinking, 238–39; photo, 238; and women's roles, 243–44

Ellison, Jesse, 208, 236, 281; becomes cattleman, 177–78; defends conscience, 206; and drinking, 237–38; entombed with Duett and George W. P. Hunt, 253–54; friendship with Ramer, 219; and honor, 177, 180, 182, 203, 206, 237–38; and hospitality, 11; moves to Rim Country, 52, 178; names lynchers, 186–87; neutrality in Pleasant Valley conflict, 124; photo, 179; relationship with Duett Ellison, 237, 246; relationship with Hunt, 241–43, 251; Texas youth and Civil War, 177–80; as vigilante, 135, 179–80, 183–84

Ellison, Jesse, Sr., 177

Ellison, Lena, 187, 242, 254

Ellison, Mattie, 246

Ellison, Perle, 186

Ellison, Rosa, 242

Ellison, Susan, 253

Ellison family, 11, 253–54, 259

El Paso, Tex., 139, 231, 247

El Tule, Ariz., 145

Embezzlement (Apache County), 139

Emmett, Jim, 261, 262

Enlightenment, xv, 233, 260

Environmentalists, 290

Equal Rights Party, 141–42, 145, 146, 150, 164, 165

Esperanza Cattle Company, 63, 147

Evans, Bill ("Jack Timberline"), 165

Evarts, William, 170

Fairbanks, Douglas, 275

Fancher-Baker Train, 28, 29

Faragher, John Mack, xx

Farley, G. M., 277

Federal government, xvii

Federal Writer's Project, 260

Fellon (Tonto Basin settler), 230

Feminization of American culture, 193

Fever tick, 51

Fiddle dances, 11, 100, 219

Field and Stream, 261

Fife, Austin, 26, 28

Fighting, 27, 28

Filaree: A Novel of American Life (Noble), 289

Fish, Joseph, 19; accuses Kinnear, 164; and ACMI robbery, 89–90; condemns New Mexicans, 74; condemns St. Johns "ring," 77, 79; decries cowboys, 94; hails lynchings, 184, 194; and Mormon racial ideas, 74–75; names lynchers, 186; persecuted by Payne, 109; and polygamy prosecutions, 85; votes despite test oath, 81

Fisher, Walter, 229, 230

Fisherville, Mass., 171

Flagstaff, Ariz., 10, 18, 19, 55, 56, 92, 93, 105

Flagstaff *Sun*, 94

Flake, Agnes, 26, 27

Flake, Charles, 28, 31, 35, 191

Flake, George, 40

Flake, Green, 25, 27

Flake, James, 31, 147, 208, 210

Flake, James Madison, 24, 25, 27

Flake, Les, 162, 190

Flake, Liz, 26, 27

Flake, Lucy White, 28; and Arizona mission, 32–33, 35, 37, 39; condemns Justice Howard, 86; courtship of, 22–23; defends Mormon retaliation, 162; life in Snowflake, 47, 93; marriage of, 30–31; piety of, 23, 32; and plural marriage, 31–32; statue of (photo), 41; views Silver Creek townsite, 40

Flake, Osmer: birth, 31; as cowboy, 202, 208–9; and 1890s crime wave, 194–95; as forest ranger, 223; friendship with Larson, 188; and Grey, 262, 269, 285; as posse member, 134–35; recounts father's story of lynchings, 189, 190–91; sees Parker on stolen horse, 116; and story of Holbrook gunfight, 162; works to restore capital punishment, 252

Flake, Virgil, 258

Flake, William Jordan, 120, 162, 258; appointed county supervisor, 41; buys Stott's estate, 190–92; courtship of, 22–23; enters plural marriage, 31–32; and exploration of Arizona, 33; founds Snowflake, 40–43; founds Taylor, 36; friend to Sheriff Owens, 156; and hospitality, 12; inducted into National Cowboy Hall of Fame, 209; locates stolen horses, 115, 132; and Mountain Meadows Massacre, 29–30; photo, 87; polygamy conviction, 84, 86–87; puts colonists to work, 46; quarrel with Sol Barth, 73; role in vigilantism, 187–89; sees Young in dream, 40; sees Louis Parker on stolen horse, 115–16; as soldier, 22–23, 28–29, 111; Southern heritage, 24–25; statue of (photo), 41; and stock raising, 93; tracks thieves, 114; victim of 1890s crime wave, 194; visited by Nephi prophet, 31, 44; youth, 25–27

Flakes, 22, 39; engage in horse racing, 209–10

Flappers (in Grey novels), 271–72, 274

Flying V ranch, 18, 135

Forestdale, Ariz., 42

Forest fires, 123

Forest rangers, 221–25

Forrest, Earl, 214

Fort Apache, 70, 73, 109, 153, 226

Fort Apache Reservation, 42

Fort Reno road, 9

Fort Thomas, Ariz., 18, 210

Fort Whipple, Ariz., 180

Fort Wingate, N.Mex., 180

Fourth of July celebrations, 11, 47

Franklidge, Judge (Grey character), 263

Franklin, Benjamin, as exemplar of conscience, 205

Free range, 16, 17, 283

Free silver movement, 56, 235

Frémont, John C., 41

Frost, Allen (Mormon settler), 194

Gable, Clark (actor), 259

Gambling: banned during roundups, 148; banned in Arizona, 248; and conscience, 27, 28, 205, 282; and cowboys, 95–96, 165, 190, 199, 203–4; Hunt's opposition to, xviii, 231, 233, 245–46, 251, 252; and honor, xv, 151; Mormon opposition to, 27, 28, 190, 202, 207, 211; and New Mexican culture, 72, 103; and new sort of honor, 219, 285; photo, 97; and rebellion against conscience, 168, 204

Garland, Hamlin (author), 270, 289

General Land Office, 147

Gentry, Emmett, 7

Geronimo, Ariz., 210

Gibson's stable, 115

Gila County, Ariz., xx; cattle census of, 53; divisiveness among cattlemen, 58; Hunt prevails in, 245; and Rim Country War, 201; size of herds in, 57; stock thieves on border of, 195

Gila County Live Stock Association, 58

Gila River, 149, 154

Gillespie, Robert, 121, 122

Gilliland, Elisha, 13, 14

Gilliland, John, 13, 14, 15, 198

Gilliland party, 14

Git-A-Rope! press, 290

Gladden, George, 106, 113, 126, 213

Gladden, Grace, 157

Gladden, Oberia, 106, 157

Gladden, Susan, 106, 113, 157

Gladdens (Texan settlers), 114

Globe, Ariz., 57, 137, 236; Duett Ellison visits Hunt in, 241–42; founded as boomtown, 4; Grahams arrive in, 7; Hunt arrives in, xvii, 231; Hunt's career in, 230–32; Jesse Ellison gets drunk in, 237–38; and Mineral Belt Railroad, 10; rapid expansion of, 4, 9; rustling cases tried in, 61; supports Tewksbury faction, 198, 200; Vosburgh and Newton in, 18; cattle driven to, 52

Globe Stock Growers Association, 59

Godhood, Mormon concept of, 27–28, 32
Gold rush, 4
Goldwater, Michael, 69
Gonzalez, Antonio, 77
Goodnight, Charles, 177
Goodrich, Ben, 185
Goodrich, Briggs, 185
Gorn, Elliott, 204
Gosper, John (Ariz. governor), 150
Gould, Jay, 235
Graham, Annie Melton, xii, 176, 207–8
Graham, John, 7, 115, 128, 136; helps Tewks-
  burys build cabin, 14; accused of at-
  tempted murder, 14; implicated in cattle
  theft, 90–91; killed by posse, 134, 135,
  267; nurses Ellenwood, 133
Graham, Thomas, 7, 115, 128; accused
  of planning attacks, 179; assassina-
  tion of, xii-xiii, 207–8; becomes
  farmer in Tempe, 176, 207–8; blames
  Pleasant Valley conflict on "men of
  money," 198; boasts of scaring sheepherders, 124; helps Tewksburys build
  cabin, 14; implicated in cattle theft,
  90–91; implicated in robbery, 176;
  makes getaway, 135; photo, 17; watches
  Monk suffocate, 50; wounded by Tewksburys, 133
Graham, William "Billy," 128–29, 136, 137
Graham brothers (Apache County), 155,
  165
Graham County, Ariz., 209
Graham faction (of Pleasant Valley), xvi,
  135, 200; ambush Jacobs and Tewksbury,
  130–32
Graham ranch ("stronghold"), 119, 122
Grahams, xvii, 21, 186, 225, 282; accuse
  Meadows of rustling, 64; accused of
  stealing Stinson's cattle, 15–16; ally with
  Hashknife cowboys, 137, 206; ambush
  Tewksbury faction, 133; approve rustling,
  212; associated with Blevins boys, 119,
  132, 200; attempt to sell out, 123; and
  Burnham, 198; charged with perjury, 16,

62; charge Tewksburys with rustling, 16;
  drawn to Arizona, 9; feud with Tewksburys, 123, 284; flee Pleasant Valley,
  135; help Tewksburys build cabin, 11,
  14; historians sympathize with, 213–14;
  lead fight against sheep, 20, 124; roman-
  ticized, 260; seek Apache alliance, 126;
  sought by Deputy McKinney, 134; team
  up with Stinson, 16, 18, 199; tied to Stott,
  175, 182, 207; viewed as criminals, 200;
  visited by Mormons, 116, 120
Grand Canyon, 34, 35
Grazing fees, 221
Great Awakening, 24
Great Depression, 9, 260, 287
Great Die-Up of 1886–87, 53
The Great Train Robbery (film), 269
Green Valley, Ariz. *See* Payson (Green
  Valley), Ariz.
Greer, Americus Vespucius, 75, 76, 146
Greer, Ellen, 156
Greer, Harris, 76, 164
Greer, Nat, 41, 76, 147; photo, 220
Greer, Richard, 76, 156
Greer, Thomas Lacy, 75
Greer boys, 76–77
Greer family, 75, 102
Grey, Zane (author), xix, xxii, 212, 259;
  celebrity status of, 270; comes to Ari-
  zona, 260; and gender roles, 261–62,
  267, 270–75, 287, 290; and honor, 261,
  265, 269–74, 277, 278, 281, 285; impact
  of, 286, 288–91; and Jazz Age liber-
  tinism, 274–76; leaves Arizona, 279–81;
  and Mormons, 261–63; photo, 263;
  and Progressive reform, 270; readers'
  responses to, 276–78; readership of,
  277–78; relationship with settlers, 262,
  265, 279, 282, 286; and repudiation
  of conscience, 276, 278; writes about
  Pleasant Valley conflict, 265–68
Gruell (or Gruwell), Ross, 50, 129
Gruwell, Louis, 129
Gunfighters, 30

Gunfights, 97–98, 151, 170, 203, 210, 213, 225; involving Greer Boys and New Mexicans, 76–77; involving Owens and Blevins boys, 157–61; involving Tewksbury and Graham factions, 128–32; involving Tewksbury, Blaine, and McCann, 20; involving Tewksbury, Graham, and Gilliland, 13–15; involving Tewksburys, Blevins, Payne, and Hash-knife cowboys, 121–23, 127–28

"Habitus," xxi
Hackney, Aaron, 198
Haigler's ranch, 134
Hale, James, 153
Hamblin, Alson, 45
Hanchett, Leland, 191, 214
Harding, Warren (U.S. president), 286
Harper's (publisher), 276, 278
Harrison, Benjamin (U.S. president), 284
Hart, Brett, 6
Hart, William S. (actor), 270
Harvard University, 99
Harvey, D. G., 184–85, 190, 191
Hashknife cowboys (Aztec Land and Cattle Company employees), 149, 177; attack Mormons, 97–112, 116; attack sheepherders, 102–3, 111; battle Tewks-burys, 121–23, 133; befriend Stott, 174; blurred with Stott in Mormon memory, 193, 207; clothing and equipment of, 96; commanded by Aztec to stop rus-tling, 148; Cooper as, 107–11, 115; and drinking, 96, 203; family ties of, 98–99; and gambling, 96, 97 (photo), 203; in Grey's fiction, 265, 267, 269, 285, 286; and gunplay, 96–98, 203; and honor, 96–99, 112, 203, 206, 219, 232; side with Grahams, 124, 129, 137, 200, 206; tied to Barth faction, 142; and Western vio-lence, 112–13
Hashknife Outfit. *See* Aztec Land and Cattle Company (Hashknife Outfit)
Hatch, Hyrum, 76; photo, 220

Hatch, L. H., 78
Hatfield, Anderson, 283
Hatfield-McCoy feud, 283
Hathaway, Henry (director), 281
Haught, Sam, 52, 132
Haun's Mill Massacre, 29
Heber, Ariz., 12; abandonment of, 120; attacked by Hashknife cowboys, 106; Aztec sells to Mormons by Aztec, 147; Larson married in, 188; settled by Mor-mons, 42, 106; settlers told to abandon, 109; Shelley family and, 12, 113; site of Houck's sheep ranch, 181; site of Mormon meeting, 114
Hellgate Trail, 10
Hell's Gate, 10
Henry, Mr., 237–38
Herndon, John, 132
Heward, Levi, 188
Hickok, Wild Bill, 112
Hill, J. J., 276
Hirschey, Joe, 134
Holbrook, Ariz., 89, 107, 121, 124, 133, 156, 167, 176, 191, 200, 218; A&P Railroad sta-tion at, 92; assassin arrives at, 136; Aztec headquarters close to, 92, 105; Blevins family seeks safety at, 138; cattle loading yard at, 55; cowboy rowdyism at, 96, 97; Houck's billiards parlor at, 181; residents decry Stott lynching, 185; Stott's parents arrive at, 183; toured by land agent, 147
Holbrook gunfight, 157–61; in Mormon memory, 161–62
Holcomb, Daniel Boone "Red," 106, 113, 193, 207; photo, 108
Holliday, Doc, 150
Honor: ameliorated by Forest Service, 225; Barnes and, 228; Commodore Owens and, 143, 157, 161; and concept of "habitus," xxi; contributes to fight against sheep, 126; and cowboys, 94–99, 104, 106, 112–14, 139, 151, 207, 209; and drinking, 237–38, 241; death toll of, 137; defined, xiv–xv; Duett Ellison and,

240; and gender, 99–100, 213; in Grey novels and films, 261, 265, 269–72, 278, 280–81; and Houck, 175, 182; and Hunt, xviii, 233, 246, 251–52; and Jesse Ellison, 177, 179, 182; laws against, 212; and Mormons, 25, 27, 28, 30, 40, 120, 165–66, 188–89, 194, 202–3, 206–7, 209–11, 257–58; and national identity, xviii–xx, 281, 285–91; and New Mexicans, 72, 77; and North-South reconciliation, xviii–xx, 169; and Northern working class, 204; in Pleasant Valley, 49, 123, 137, 198–99; and race, xv, xvi, 25, 27, 74, 126–27, 205, 213; and Rim Country conflict, xvi–xvii, 15, 20, 21, 64–66, 71, 79–80, 82, 123, 137, 198–99; and rituals of shaming, 28, 80, 82, 251; and rodeos (cowboy tournaments), 208, 288; and social class, 205–8, 213; socialized, 98–100, 213; and South, xiv–xv, 169; in Texas, 171, 177, 180, 187; and tourists, 259–60, 279; in the twentieth century, 285–91; in Wister's *Virginian*, 170

Hoof and Horn (newspaper), 57

Hoover, Herbert (U.S. president), 270

Hopis, 36

Horn, Tom, 186, 187

Horse races, 11, 96; banned during roundups, 148; Flakes engage in, 209–10

Horse theft, 165; accusations of against Blevins boys, 109–10, 115–16, 118, 138, 157; accusations of against Stott, 184, 193–94, 218; from Mormons, 119–20, 200; lynching as penalty for, 190

Horton, L. J., 63, 65, 135, 208

Hospitality: as cover for gathering intelligence, 116; and cowboy honor, 151, 172–73; as destabilizing force, 12–13, 172–73, 175, 188; of Mormons, 12, 46, 75; and Ramer, 218; in Rim Country, 11–12, 172–73, 172–73, 175, 218; and Stott, 172–73, 175; Southern tradition of, 12, 75; Tewksbury rejection of, 122

Houck, Beatrice Gurula, 180

Houck, James, 193; accuses Stott, 175–76; arrests Stott, 182–83; attacked by foes, 176, 192; comparison to Stott, 182; disqualifies Mormon voters, 81, 146; friend of Commodore Owens, 143, 180; and honor, 177, 203, 285; and immunity for vigilantes, 132; joins Mulvenon's posse, 134; and killing of Graham, 129; leader of Tewksbury faction, 130; left out of Ellison's list of lynchers, 187; in legislature, 181, 239; life history of, 180–81; and Mormons, 212; named as lyncher, 186; named as stock detective, 188; photo, 181; quarrels with Navajos, 180–81; lynching story contradicted, 185–86

Houck's Station, Ariz., 181

House Rock Valley, 34

Howard, Summer, 16, 20, 61, 84, 86, 199

Hoy, Mr., 64

Hubbell, J. Lorenzo, 77, 80, 81, 104, 141, 142, 144, 145

Humanitarian conscience, xvii, xviii, xix, 239, 248–52

Humboldt County, 4, 5

Huning, Henry, 77, 156

Hunt, George W. P., xv, xvii, xviii, xix, xxiv, 282; and abolition of capital punishment, 250, 252; and abolition of gambling, 248; and bachelor culture, 232; and conscience, 231–32, 235–37; death of, 253; early career, 231; and humanitarian conscience, 248–52, 270; opposition to drinking, 238–39, 252; and penal reform, 248, 250–51, 252; and People's Constitution, 248; photos, 230, 249; and Pleasant Valley conflict, 229–31; political career, 239, 245–53; relationship with mother, 235–36; and rights of workers, 245–46; romantic correspondence, 237–47; tomb of (photo), 253; and tourism, 257, 260; and woman suffrage, 243, 249–50

Hunt, Helen Virginia, 247

Hunt, Jewel, 236

Hunt, John, 41, 77, 80, 84
Hunt, John Addison, 193, 258
Hunt, Sarah, 235–36
Hupa (tribe), 4

Incorporation gunfighters, 112–13, 201
Indians, 3, 20, 26, 29, 102, 225, 275; and Mormon prophecy, 115
Ingham, Alfred, 183, 185–86
Irby, Ben, 147
Isbel, Gaston (Grey character), 266, 267
Isbel, Jean (Grey protagonist), 266–67, 269

Jackson, Carlton, 277
Jacobs, William, 11, 123, 124, 131, 134, 136, 159, 229
James, Jesse, 152; and Southern honor, 234–35
James, Joe, 106
Jameses, 106
James gang, 152
Jaredites (*Book of Mormon*), 48–49, 66, 71
Jazz Age, 274, 275, 276, 278
Jerked Beef Trail (Houdon Trail), 10
Jews, 69–70, 146, 200
Jim Crow laws, 287
Jiron, Frederico, 154
Johnson, C. W. "Kid Swingle", 153–54, 165
Johnson County War, 284, 285
Johnson, Lyndon Baines (U.S. president), 288
Johnson, Susan Lee, xxi
Jones, Charles Jesse "Buffalo" 260–61
Jones, T. W. "Bud," 149
Jorth, Ellen (Grey heroine), 266–67; and passion, 275
Jorth, Lee (Grey villain), 267, 269
Jurgensen, Christian, 11, 124, 127

Kartchner, John, 41
Kartchner, Mark, 116
Kartchner, Prudence, 32
Kartchner, W. D., 36

Kartchner family, 33
Kempe, Christopher, 84
Kimball, Heber, 47
Kinnear, Charlie, 77, 139, 164
Kinsley, Edward, 92, 93, 170
Kipling, Rudyard B. (author), 266
Kirby, F. Lee, 223
Knapp, Frank, 232–33, 235
Knights of Pythias, 6
Ku Klux Klan, 196, 286
Kyle, Houston, 187, 236
Kyne, Peter (author), 260

Lacy, Jim "Nevada" (Grey protagonist), 263, 264
Ladies Home Journal, 278
Lamanites (Indians), 80, 110
Larson, Hook, 185, 186, 212, 285; named as stock detective and vigilante, 187–88; Mexican captives lynched, 194–95
LaRue, Jack (actor), 281
Lassiter (Grey protagonist), 261, 262
The Last Days of Pompeii (Bulwer-Lytton), 237
Las Vegas (Grey protagonist), 262
Lauffer, Jake, 127, 135, 179, 182; charges Stott with horse theft, 174; shot from ambush, 176
Lee, Clarissa, 188
Lee, John D., 34, 80, 84
Lee's Backbone, Ariz., 34
Lee's Ferry, Ariz., 34
Leisure, xix, 275–76
LeSueur, James Warren, 77, 162
LeSueur, J. T., 164
Lewis, George (Mormon settler), 116
Lieu lands, 109
Lincoln County War, 218, 284
Linden, Ariz., 42
Little Colorado River, 52, 56, 71; destroys Mormon dams, 38; geography of, 36; Mormons settle at, 69; rights to water adjudicated, 74; siltation of, 35, 37
Little Colorado Stake of Zion, 38, 146

Little Colorado River Valley, xiv, 33, 36, 80, 99, 103, 105, 108, 180
Live Stock Sanitary Board, 212, 226
Livingston, Charles, 176, 179
Lombard, Carole, 259
Lower Midwest, xvi, 65, 79, 98, 112, 283
Lucas (Hashknife cowboy), 111–12
Lyman, Francis M. (Mormon apostle), 80, 209
Lynchers, 30, 182–89
Lynching: Barnes's defense of, 195–96; in Clark's *The Ox-Bow Incident*, 287; dissipates, 225, 250, 282; feared by Cooper, 139; hailed by Mormons, 194; of Johnson, 154; Mormons threatened with, 80, 82, 83, 199; by New Mexicans, 77; opposed by Mormons, 77; in Pleasant Valley, 135, 137; and rebellion against middle-class mores, 168; St. Johns *Herald* hints at, 165; as shaming ritual, 203; of Stott, Scott, and Wilson, 182–89; threats of against Forest Rangers, 221
Lynching Belt, 195

McCall's, 278
McCann, F. M., 20
McCarter, John, 80, 81, 83
McCarthy, Cormac, 289
McClintock, James, 211
McDonald, William, 14
McFadden, William, 185, 186, 187
McGoufure, John, 277
McKinley, William (U.S. president), 219
McKinney, Joe, 134, 150–51
McLaury, Frank, 150
McLaury, Tom, 150
McLaury family, 113
McNeil, Red, "Poet Robber," 192
McWhiney, Grady, 12
Maggie: A Girl of the Streets (Crane), 234
Man of the Forest (Grey), 262
The Man-Killers (Grey), 267
Marble Canyon, 34

Market revolution, xv, 98–99
Marshall, John, 232
Martin, Luther, 77
Matthews, Barry, 118, 142, 150
Mavericking (rustling), 13, 16, 59, 65, 148, 165, 200, 212
May, Karl (author), 261
Mazatzal Mountains, Ariz., xxii, 50
Meadows, Charlie "Arizona Charlie", 54, 64; photo, 55
Meatpacking houses, 55, 62, 101
Melchizedek priesthood, 43
Merrill, Karen, 225
Mesa, Ariz., 109
Methodists, 24, 25, 27, 28
Mexican-American War, 103
Middle-class ethics, 204–5
Middle ground, 4
Middleton, Harry (or Henry), 133, 136, 175
Middleton cabin, 122, 127, 128, 129, 240, 267
Middleton cabin fight, 122–23, 127, 128, 132, 133, 136, 137, 148, 174
Middleton family, 18
Midwest, 8, 11, 17, 99, 182, 203, 278
Millennium (in Mormon thought), 26, 32
Miller, Al, 152, 153
Miller, Jim, 136–37
Millett ranch (Texas), 106
Milner, John ("Juan"), 83, 141, 142, 145
Ming, Dan, 52, 64–65
Minute Men (Utah), 31, 32, 111
Miracles (in Mormon thought), 45, 46
Mix, Tom (actor), 270
Mogollon Live Stock Association, 59
Mogollon Rim, 7, 12, 13, 200; drought on, 62; geography of, 36, 107, 121; as locale of conflict, xxii, 199; and location of Ellison's ranch, 178; and location of Snowflake, 12; and location of Stott's ranch, 172; and Mormon settlements, 42, 106; photo, 5; and proposed railroad, 10; as sheep range, 19, 101, 105, 124; site of Ponderosa forest, 3

Monk, John, 50–51, 129

Monopolies, 54–56

Monsoon season (in Ariz.), 128

Montgomery, J. F., 218

Mormon cowboys, 202

Mormon-Democrat alliance, xvii, 118, 146, 164

Mormons, xxii; ally with gentile ranchers apocalyptic prophecies of, 48, 85, 161; and Aztec management, xvi–xvii, 200, 201; become mainstream, 211; conflict with Aztec, xiv, 88, 106–12, 120, 225, 284; conflict with cowboys, 106, 199, 202; conflict with New Mexicans, xiv, 71–84, 139–46, 217; conscience of, xv, 28, 37, 71, 75, 79, 82, 85, 99, 113, 117, 190, 206, 207, 213, 232; corporatism of, 42, 43–45, 48, 199, 201–2; Daggs brothers seek alliance with, 105; endorse honor, 139, 140, 161, 163, 165–66, 209–11, 214, 219, 258, 285; as farmers, 46–47; and Grey, 262, 269; help form Equal Rights Party, 141; help form People's Party, 140–41, 145–46; hospitality of, 12; miracles and folk beliefs of, 45–46; oppose gambling, 148; patriotism of, 47–48, 258; and perfectionism, 28, 48; racism of, 74–75; rapprochement with Aztec, 202; and rodeo, 257–58; settle Arizona, 33–49, 70–71; taste political power, 41; and Utah War of 1857, 22, 29, 30; and vigilantism, 152, 187–88, 194

Morrison, Robert, 145, 146, 147, 154

Mortensens, 106

Mt. Taylor, N.Mex., 72

Mountain Meadows Massacre, 34, 48, 49; gentiles decry Mormons for, 80, 83; and Justice Howard, 16, 84, 86; and Mormon ambivalence about violence, 166; Mormon sensitivity to legacy of, 117; as violence of conscience, 30; and Flake, 29–30

Mulvenon, William, 132, 267; ambushes Graham and Blevins, 133–34; takes deputies to Pleasant Valley, 128

Murphy, Lawrence, 284

Naeglin, Louis, 135

Nash, Joe, 217

National Cowboy Hall of Fame, 209

National Livestock Association, 151

Nauvoo, Ill., 22, 25, 26

Nauvoo Legion, 28

Navajo County, Ariz., 226

Navajos, 31, 36, 72, 103, 109, 110, 111, 113, 115, 118, 127, 143, 180–81

Navajo Springs, Ariz., 138, 143, 180

Neilson, Old Lady, 189

Neilsons, 106, 113

Nelson, Edward (naturalist), 164

Nephi Prophets, 31

Nesters, 178

Nevada (Grey), 263; cartoon depiction of, 264

New England, 92, 167, 168, 169, 177, 182, 206, 282; middle class of, 168, 171

New Mexicans, 20, 46, 87; ambush Blassingame, 91; associated with criminality, 200, 202; as characters in Grey novels, 262; conflict with Hashknife cowboys, 103–4; conflict with Mormons, xiv, 71–84, 139–46, 199, 217, 284; culture of, 72–73; defeated in 1886 election, 146; and Equal Rights Party, 165; help form Equal Rights party, 141; honor of, 72, 77, 214; as sheepherders, 41, 75, 93, 102, 103, 124, 146, 203

New Mexico, 9, 19, 69, 99, 143, 147, 149, 151, 155, 164, 180, 194, 195, 227, 231, 259; feuds in, 284

Newton, George, 18, 19, 20, 122, 128, 133, 135, 198, 200, 218

New Woman (in Grey novels), 271, 274

New York City, 91, 278; Mormons prophesy destruction of, 161

Noble, Marguerite (author), 289

Norris, Frank (author), 234, 270, 289

North, 234, 285; and conscience, xviii, 169, 205, 290; and rapprochement with South, xviii, 6; and Mormon solidarity, 22; honor in, 204–5

North Billerica, Mass., 167

Northern conscience, xviii, 169, 207, 239

Nutrioso, Ariz., 42, 194

Oakes, James, 205

Obed, Ariz., 36, 37

The Octopus (Norris), 234

OK Corral, 150

The Old Curiosity Shop (Dickens), 237

Old Dominion Commercial Company, 231

Old South, xiv, xv, 27, 49, 83, 98, 99, 179, 288

Old Verde Road, 183

One Who Knows (correspondent), 185–86

Orion Era, 83, 141

Overstocked ranges, 52, 221, 223

Owens, Commodore Perry, xxiv, 150, 151; accused of cowardice, 156–57; advocates pardon for Clanton, 164; baptized after death as Mormon, 166; defeated in 1888 election, 163; escorts Barth to penitentiary, 154; friend of Cooper, 138–39; friend of Flake, 156; and Grey, 262; and Holbrook gunfight, 157–61, 165, 202–3; and honor, 156–57, 162, 285; life history, 143; in Mormon memory, 162; photo, 144; relationship with Houck, 130, 134, 180; runs for sheriff, 142, 143, 144, 146; and Stott, 174, 175

Owens, James Clark, Jr., 89–90

The Ox-Bow Incident (Clark), 287

Palmer, A. Z., 40, 188

Palmseley, Viola, 276

Paramount Pictures, 270

Parker, Louis, 115–16, 128, 133, 135

Partido system, 73

Patrón, 73

Payne, John Herbert, 111, 165; associated with Grahams, 200; attacks Mormons, 109, 116–17, 147; blurred with Jamie Stott, 190, 207; and Christianity, 109, 199; and honor, 204, 285; killed in Middle Cabin fight, 122, 136; and Sheriff Owens, 146, 156, 162; threatens to start "little war" in Pleasant Valley, 121

Payson (Green Valley), Ariz., 9, 10, 42, 43, 64, 132, 135, 178, 186, 208, 236, 245, 257, 259

Payson rodeo. *See* August Doin's rodeo (Payson)

Pearce, James, 109, 116, 117, 162

Pease, Charles, 277

Pedthero, Frank, 64

Penal reform, 248, 252, 285

"People's Constitution," 248

People's Party (Apache County), 141–42, 145, 163, 165; chooses "clean slate" of candidates, 140; victory in 1886 election, 146

Perez, Tomas, 77, 78, 91, 163

Perkins, Charlie, 134, 136, 176, 186

Perkins's store ambush, 134

Petersen, Andrew, 107

Petersen, Mary, 162

Petersen, Niels, 110, 116, 117, 147, 162

Petersens, 106

Phoenix, xxii, 115, 116, 120, 186, 189, 251, 253

Phoenix *Herald*, 8, 153

Pickford, Mary (actress), 275

Pinal Creek, 4

Pinchot, Gifford, 219, 223, 227

Pine, Ariz., 10

Pinedale, Ariz., 42, 113, 121

Pinkertons, 153

Pioneer Day (Mormon), 47, 257–58

Pleasant Valley, 57, 89, 108, 115, 132; conflicts in, xvi–xvii, 13–21, 42, 48–49, 62, 63, 66, 200, 284; Cooper and, 159; drought in, 62; entry of Hashknife cow-

Pleasant Valley (continued)
boys, 121–22, 165, 200, 203; entry of
sheep, 105; fatalities in, 136–37; honor
in, xiv, xvi-xvii, 15, 20, 126–27, 132; and
Hunt, 229, 244; Mormons encourage
fighting in, 133; Mormon rendezvous
in, 116, 117–18, 120; new troubles in,
176; posses in, 128, 134; prosperity anticipated, 8–10; Ramer buys ranches in,
218; rodeo in, 208; settlers in, 4, 6–7, 10,
48–49, 208; social ties in, 11–12; stock
detective in, 91; Tewksburys arrive in,
6–7; Tewksbury's escape to, xii; and
tourism, 259–60, vigilantism in, 152,
179, 184, 188–89; war against sheep in,
124–26, 165
Pleasant Valley conflict, xxiii, 61, 64, 120,
173; Barnes's map of, 131; beginnings of,
123, 127; contestants in, 19; in Coolidge's
fiction, 267; course of, 123–35; economic
causes of, 62–63; fatalities in, 136–37;
Governor Zulick's views on, 132; in
Grey's fiction, 266–68; and Houck, 129–
30, 182; and Hunt, 229–31; and Jaredites, 66; and Jesse Ellison, 178–80; and
honor, 21, 137, 214, 284; and Middleton
Cabin fight, 122–23, 127; and Rim
Country War, xiii-xiv; and Stott, 174–76;
and tourism, 259–60
Pleasant Valley vigilantes, 179, 188, 231,
265; lynch Stott, Scott, and Wilson,
182–83; names of, 186–87
Pleasant Valley War. *See* Pleasant Valley
conflict
Plural marriage. *See* Polygamy
Polygamy, 24, 31, 38, 92, 261, 262; and
honor, conscience, 83; laws against, 81,
84; LDS church repudiates, 85; trials for,
84, 86
Populism, 56
Porter, D. J., 79
Porter, James E., 79
Porters (Mormon settlers), 106
Poststructural theory, xxi

Potter, Albert, xvii, 100, 219–20, 222, 223,
224, 227–28; photos, 220, 222
Powell, George, 154, 163, 194
Pratt, Parley, 29, 30
Preindustrial values, 204–5
Prescott, Ariz., 4, 8, 9, 11, 16, 86, 135, 176,
180, 185, 208
Prescott *Courier*, 57
Prescott rodeo, 208
Prizefighting, xv, 246, 285
*Progressive Arizona and the Great South-
west*, 255, 260
Progressive Era, xix, 276, 281
Progressive party, 249
Progressive reform, 217, 252, 270, 285, 290
Prohibition, 171, 182, 194, 205, 250
Prostitution, 96, 103, 165, 168, 211, 233, 282,
285
Pullman Strike of 1894, 240–41, 245
Puncher, 12
Puritans, 27, 43, 45, 49

Quail (rancher), 222
Quakers, 24, 27
Quarantine (on cattle), 51–52

Race: as factor in Apache County politics,
137; as factor in Pleasant Valley conflict,
126–27, 284
Railroads, 54–56, 62
The Rainbow Trail (Grey), 262
Raine, William MacLeod, 58, 195–96, 203
Ralston, Esther (actress), 281
Ramer, Hezekiah James "Jim," 217–19,
225; and cooperative model in cattle
business, 218; envisions Rim Country
hunting retreat, 259; and honor, 218–19
Ranchers, 13, 16
Range feuds, 283–84
Reagan, Ronald (U.S. president), 288–89
Reconstruction, xviii, 193
Reed, Henry: comments on conflict, 162–
63; criticizes vigilantism, 154; defends
Cooper, 119–20; opposes Mormons, 83,

118; photo, 155; praises campaign against criminals, 153; sells St. Johns *Herald*, 118, 142

Regulators, 195

Reid, Mayne (author), 193

Reidhead, John Oscar, 109

Renfro, Lee, 149, 151, 153, 165

Reno Trail, 115

Republican Party: and anti-Mormon ticket, 81; blamed for attacks on Mormons, 82; and cattlemen, 56; and conscience politics, 248; damned by Sarah Hunt, 235; and Equal Rights Party, 145; favored by Jim Houck, 181; favored by New Mexicans, 142; favored by Will Barnes, 145, 226; and "incorporation gunfighters," 112; Mormons oppose, 86, 145; and People's Party, 145; and Stott, 171; success of, 252

Resisters, 112–13

Reynolds, Glenn, 186

Rhodes, John, 130, 135, 186, 208, 236; assassinates Tom Graham, xi–xiii; named as lyncher, 187

Rhodes, Mary Ann Crigler Tewksbury, 122, 127, 130, 208

Richards, William, 16

Richardson, Edmund, 106, 107, 109–11, 115, 119

Richardson, Sarah Adams "Sadie," 107, 109–11, 117

Richardson family, 107

Riders of the Purple Sage, 261

Rim Country, xxii–xxiii, 46, 64, 124, 178, 191, 198, 214, 236; attracts big operators, 52; chance for biracial society in, 7; Ellison becomes leader in, 179; few black cowboys in, 102; Globe as de facto capital, 229; Hunt campaigns in, 245; and patterns of honor, xiv, xvi, xix, xx; and patterns of hospitality, 12; regulated by Forest Service, 217, 221–24; rodeos in, 257; and rustling, 58; scoured by searchers, 122; as setting for Noble's

Filaree, 290; as setting for Grey novels, 262–74, 282; and sheep, cattle conflict, 19–20; suited for small operations, 57; as tourist destination, 259–60; vigilante cells organized in, 120

Rim Country settlers, xix, 11, 278, 279, 290

Rim Country War: definition of, xiii–xiv, 200–207; in Grey's fiction and film, 262–69, 280–81; and honor, xv–xvi; and Hunt, 231; ironies of, 206–7; legacies of, xvii–xix, 211–13; and Western identity, 213; and Western violence, 282–85

Rio Grande Valley, 103

Roaring Twenties, 275

Roberts, Brian, 168–69, 206

Roberts, Jim, 127, 129, 133, 135

Roberts, Mote (Mose?), 157, 158, 159, 161

Roberts, Paul, 219, 223

Rock Creek, 6

Rodeo (cowboy tournament), 208, 288

Rodeo (roundup), 20, 59, 148

Roediger, David, 204

Rogers, Andrew Locy, 161

Rogers, Ed, 52, 97 (photo), 121, 192, 193

Rohrabaugh, William, 204–5

Rolvaag, O. E. (author), 270, 289

Romney, Miles, 83, 86

Roosevelt, Ariz., 259

Roosevelt, Theodore (U.S. president), 171, 198, 207, 224, 248; photo, 256; speaks in Ariz., 255

Roosevelt Lake, Ariz., 224, 255

Rose, Al, 13, 128, 137; identifies Graham's killers, 128; lynched, 135

Rose, Ed, 13, 20

Rose brothers, 13

Rose ranch, 176

Rough Riders, 198

Rudd, Charles, 163, 194

Ruiz, Alfred, 141, 164

Ruiz, Epitacio "Potash," 13, 14, 42, 102

Running iron, 59

Russell, Lena, 276

Rustlers, 58–59, 63–64, 65, 106, 153, 155, 156, 201, 218; in Grey's fiction, 263–65, 269; lynched, 184

Rustling: big operations as targets of, 58, 60; campaign against, 165; and character, 59, 65; by Clantons, 149–50, 151; in Clark's *Ox-Bow Incident*, 287; end of era, 211–12; as form of retribution, 200; Grahams accused of, 64, 90–91, 208; laws preventing, 212; Mormons accused of, 148, 210; newspaper reports of, 194–95; techniques of, 59–62; Tewksburys accused of, 13, 15–16

St. John, John Pierce, 171

St. Johns, Ariz., 16, 83, 123, 147, 185, 210; anti-Mormon convention held at, 80–81; Barth and, 69–70; chosen as county seat, 77–78; gunfight at, 76–77; Mormon purchase near, 69, 71; site of gambling dens and "bawdy houses," 96; vigilante committee organized at, 152

St. Johns *Herald*, 184; attacks Sheriff Owens, 163; attributes attack to sheepherders, 91; calls for vigilantism, 104, 119–20, 132, 133, 149; hails "cleanup," 154–55; hails Daggs's loss, 208; hails Sheriff Owens, 161; mentions Clantons favorably, 150; praises Mormons, 118; promises return of prosperity, 53–54; promotes Commodore Owens for sheriff, 144–45; promotes vigilantism, 118–20; publishes Aztec brand, 94; publishes letter on hospitality and outlawry, 11–12; publishes Stott's assertion of innocence, 175; Reed becomes editor of, 83; reports drought, 62; reports horse thefts, 194–95; reports results of 1886 election, 146; reports wool prices, 101; sold to "company of cattlemen," 118, 142; urges cattlemen to fight monopolies, 55; urges pardon for Clanton, 164; urges prosecutions, 154; and Stott lynching, 185; warns of overstocking, 52

St. Johns purchase, 70–71, 74

St. Johns ring, 77, 81, 84

St. Joseph, Ariz., 36, 37, 38, 76

Salem, Ariz., 70

Salt Lake City, Utah, 42, 47, 69, 257

Salt River, xxii, 4, 52, 107, 124, 178, 230, 255

Salt River Valley, 56, 115, 245, 255, 289

San Carlos, Ariz., 246

San Francisco Committees of Vigilance of 1851 and 1856, 201

San Francisco *Examiner*, 152

San Francisco Peaks, 3, 36, 102, 103

San Francisco vigilantes, 140

Sangamon County, Ill., 8

San Juan Day (New Mexican Festival), 76

San Juan *Prospector*, 51

San Pedro River, 149

Savages (settler family), 106

Scots, 12

Scots-Irish, 12, 24

Scott, Jim, 176, 184, 185, 189, 190, 193, 201, 203, 207, 218, 230, 251, 287; lynched, 182–83

Scott, Randolph (actor), 281

Scott, Sir Walter (author), 266

Sedition acts, 286

Sedona, Ariz., 257

Sentimentality, 233, 270

Seventeenth Legislature (Ariz.), 240

Sewell, Anna (author), 234

Sex, xx, 274–75

Shaming, 137, 149; as aspect of honor, xv; lynching as ritual of, 165, 187, 203; of Mormon missionaries in South, 28; and Mountain Meadows Massacre, 29–30; by New Mexicans, 77; of New Mexicans, 76, 102; and prison, 251

Sheep, 19, 100, 104; arrival in Pleasant Valley, 123; prejudice against, 100–101, 126; profitability of, 101

Sheepherders, 211, 282; attacks on, 102, 120; cowboy prejudice against, 103; and Forest Service, 223, 224; in Grey's fiction, 266–67, 269; Hunt seeks to tax,

245; killed in Pleasant Valley, 127; race of, 20, 103; regulated by Forest Service, 217, 223–24; Tewksburys as, xvii; trespass on Aztec range, 101, 105

Sheep theft, 125 (reward posted for return of stolen sheep)

Shell, Robert, 13

Shelley, Margaret, 113

Shelley, Thomas, 106

Shelley family, 12

Shelleys, 106, 113

Showlow, Ariz., 42

Shull, Samuel, 13, 120, 127, 136

Shumway, Ariz., 42, 105

Shumway, Spence, 116

Shute, George, 214

Sierra Ancha, xii, 4, 10, 223, 255, 259, 289, 290

Silver Creek (Rio de la Plata), Ariz., 7, 40, 62, 104, 106, 115, 194, 219

Simpson, E. J., 147, 148

Skousen, James, 84

Slaughter, W. B., 56

Sleepering (rustling), 60

Slotkin, Richard, xx

Small operators: ally with big operators, 18–19, 137, 217; conflicts with big operators, 56–58, 137; cooperative drives proposed, 58; and free range, 17, 282; protected by Forest Service, 224–25; and rustling, 59–60

Smith, Henry, 147, 149, 156

Smith, Hyrum, 25, 26

Smith, Jesse: advises Mormons against vengeance, 116–17, 162; advises Mormons to avoid gentiles, 43, 82, 113; advises Mormons to settle quickly, 79; "bulldozed" in county seat election, 78; and 1886 election, 145–46; and Mormon patriotism, 47; and Mormon racism, 74; negotiates with railroad, 105; opposes credit system, 44; and polygamy convictions, 84; in sculpture (photo), 41; views Indians as "battle ax of the Lord," 80

Smith, Jessie Ballard, 161

Smith, John, Mrs., 277

Smith, Joseph, 22, 24, 25, 26, 27, 30, 32, 33, 47, 71

Smith, Joseph, Jr., 86

Smith, Lot, 38

Smith-Lever Act, 271

Snow, Erastus, 32, 37, 40, 41, 47, 82

Snowflake, Ariz., 12, 78, 92, 104, 107, 111, 134, 156, 161, 190; Aztec sells to Mormons, 147, 202; economy of, 46; chosen as county seat, 77; conflicts with Aztec, 106; holds rodeo, 257; horses stolen from, 114, 194; Richardson family flees to, 110; situated on Aztec land, 105; success of, 40–42, 93; suffers from polygamy prosecutions, 84; vigilantes meet in, 188

Social class, and honor, 205–7, 213

Socorro *Bulletin*, 9

South: and conscience reforms, 234, 239; and cowboys, 99; emphasis on family in the, 72, 98; and evangelical Christianity, 199; and Flake, 22, 24–25; and honor, xiv–xv, xvi, 65, 79, 126, 169, 177, 187, 203, 205, 206, 209, 283, 286, 290; hospitality in the, 12; and lynching, 193, 195; Mormons and, 22, 24–25, 28; and rapprochement with North, xviii, 6; and "resisters," 112; settlement of, 11; and temperance, 204; and West, 285, 288; women's roles in, 243

Southern chivalry, in literature, 170

Southern converts to Mormonism, 39

Southern honor, xviii, 25, 27, 28, 169–70, 177; and James, 234–35; and women's roles, 43

Southern hospitality, 75

Southern Pacific Railroad, 10, 178

Southerners, 27, 61, 95, 205

Spanish-American War, 198, 211

Sprague, Samuel "Long Hair", 165

Springerville, Ariz., 77, 96, 150, 151, 152

Standifird, John Henry, 85

Stanley, Ebin, 81, 140, 141, 150, 151, 155, 165

Stanley, Mary Clanton Slinkard, 150

Stevenson, Robert Louis (author), 266

Stinson, James, 9, 51, 56, 57, 62, 89, 91, 102, 104, 192, 198, 199, 200; arrives in Pleasant Valley, 7–8; helps Mormons recover stolen horses, 115; loans Flake money for bail, 86–87; sells ranch to Flake, 40–41; trouble with Tewksburys, 13–21

Stock associations, 58, 63

Stock detectives, 91, 151–54, 166, 184, 212

Stockwell, Georgiana (Grey heroine), 271, 274

Stott, Hannah, 172, 183, 184

Stott, Hattie, 172

Stott, James "Jamie," 102, 104, 185; arrested for horse theft, 174; attraction to cowboying, 167–70; blamed for ambush, 176; and Clark's *Ox-Bow Incident*, 287; comparison to Houck, 182; dislikes farming, 171–72; and honor, 169–70, 172–73, 177, 203; lynching of, 182–83, 187, 203, 230, 251, 259; in Mormon memory, 189–91; neutrality in Pleasant Valley conflict, 175; photos, 168, 173; refuses to drink or dance, 171; remembered as desperado, 192–93, 206–7; run-ins with Jim Ramer, 217; and Western hospitality, 172–73, 174

Stott, James Sr., 167–68, 183–84, 189–90, 191

Stotts, 171, 189–90

Stover, Ebenezer S., 76–77, 85

Stowe, Harriet Beecher (author), 234, 270

Strawberry, Ariz., 10

Sublimity, Oreg., 98

Sunset, Ariz., 36, 37, 39, 40, 43

Sympathy, as aspect of conscience, 234, 243, 270

Tafolla, Francisco, 76

Talbot, Edith, 226

Talbot, Ike (Noble character), 289

Talbot, Thomas (Mass. governor), 167, 170

Talley, K. V. B., 147

Tanner, George, 187

Taylor, Ariz., 36, 37, 105, 145, 147, 202, 258

Taylor, John, 145

Tempe, Ariz., xi, 176, 207–8

Temperance, 204–5, 243, 244, 248, 250, 252

Temple, Shirley (actress), 281

Tenney, Ammon, 69, 70, 71, 73, 78, 84

Tenney, Nathan, 76–77

Test Oath law, 81, 85–86, 141, 146, 200

Tewksbury, Ed, 130, 236; and ambush of Graham, 129; anticipates no more trouble, 20; arrested, 135; assassinates Graham, xi–xiii; challenges Gladden to gunfight, 126–27; foreman for Flying V, 18; and gunfight with Gilliland, 13–15; and honor, 15, 126–28, 198, 213; as "last man" in Pleasant Valley conflict, 282; in Middleton Cabin fight, 122; photo, 15; threatens St. Johns jury, 185

Tewksbury, James Dunning, 4, 6, 7, 13, 130, 200, 229, 260, 277

Tewksbury, James "Jim," xvi, 14, 19, 89–90, 127, 128, 132, 135, 186

Tewksbury, John, 20, 123, 124, 128, 131, 136, 159, 208, 229; photo, 130

Tewksbury, Lydia Ann Shultes, 7, 130, 236

Tewksbury, Mary Ann. *See* Rhodes, Mary Ann Tewksbury

Tewksbury, William J., 277

Tewksbury faction, xvi, xvii, 122, 128, 130, 133, 177, 200, 208

Tewksburys, 21, 212, 225, 260; accused of rustling, 15–16; alliance with big operators, 17–19; alliance with Houck, 130, 182; arrive in Pleasant Valley, 6–7, 9; and assassination of Graham, 208; conflict with Graham faction, 123–24, 126–28, 130–37, 284; conflict with Stinson, 13,

15–16, 19, 51, 198; and Daggs brothers, 19, 124; and Grey's *To the Last Man*, 269; gunfight with Gilliland, 14; and historical bias, 214; and honor, 198–99; and hospitality, 12; and Middleton Cabin fight, 122–23; and race, xvii, 102, 127; relations with fellow settlers, 11; and vigilantism, 132–33, 186

Tewksbury trials, 19

Texans, 46, 99, 109, 213, 265

Texas, 92, 98, 113, 143, 289; Blevins family and, 107–9, 138; cattle boom in, 9; cattle glut in, 51; cattle operations in, 56–57, 106; cattle recession in, 53; and Ellison family, 178, 187, 236; feuds in, 283, 284; Greer family and, 41, 75, 76; and honor culture, 171–72, 177–78, 203, 203; and lynching, 187, 195; and Ramer, 218, 289; Stott and, 170–72

Texas cowboys, 246; as Aztec employees, 94–99, 170; conflicts with Mormons, 105–18, 199, 202–3; crowd range, 63; and honor, xvi, 94, 94–99, 139, 187, 203, 214, 258, 279; and middle class, 205; influence Mormons, 209; and Pleasant Valley conflict, 20, 137

Texas Rangers, 177

Thirteenth Territorial Legislature, 181, 239

Thomas, Charles, 277

Thomas, Charlie, 165

Thomas, Joe P. "Kid," 96

Tombstone, Ariz., 10, 112, 150, 198

Tombstone *Record-Epitaph*, 57

Tonto, Ariz., 230

Tonto Basin, 13, 89, 108, 137, 163, 174; Apache campaign in, 3–4, 81; and Arizona geography, 36; creation of Roosevelt Lake in, 255; called "dark and bloody ground," 184; Daggs brothers and, 19, 208; development of, 8–10; Ellison arrives in, 178; Forest Service regulation of, 224; fracas reported in, 175; litigiousness of cattlemen in, 61;

Monk's death in, 50–51; overstocking in, 51–52; photo, 5; predictions of cattle boom in, 8; predictions of mineral boom in, 8; recession in, 54; trails to and from, 9, 108, 115

Tonto Basin Apache campaign, 150

Tonto Creek, 62, 124, 178, 255

Tonto National Forest, 221

To the Last Man (Grey), xix, 266; dust jacket photo, 268; film poster, 280; as talkie film, 281

Tourism, xix, 211, 279, 287; and honor, 255–59

Traft, Jim (Grey protagonist), 263, 265

Tribit, Jeff, 76, 102; photo, 220

Tritle, Frederick (Ariz. governor), 81

True womanhood, concept of, 239

Truman, Ben, Major, 94

Tucker, Tom, 121, 122, 136, 174

Tucson *Citizen*, 251

Turley, Grace, 113

Turley, L. Barr, 105

Turley, Leila Eagar, 150

Turley brothers, 258

Turley family, 113

Tuscarora, Nev., 200

Twain, Mark, xv

24 Cattle Company, 147

Udall, David, 71, 73, 74, 80, 82, 83, 86, 88, 141

Udall, Ida Hunt, 80

Uncle Tom's Cabin (Stowe), 234

Under the Tonto Rim (Grey), 270–71, 289; photo of dust jacket, 272

Unforgiven (film), 289

United Order of Enoch, 37–38, 40, 42, 43, 111

U.S. Forest Service, xvii, 100, 192, 217, 219–28, 252, 279, 282, 290; attacks on rangers, 221–23; challenged in court, 221; and conservation, 224–25; and conscience, 225; and grazing fees, 221

U.S. Geographical Board of Place Names, 228

Utah, 22, 24, 26, 27, 45, 47, 209, 257, 282

Utah War of 1857, 28–29, 45

Vaqueros, 95

Vaughan, James, 76

Verde River, Ariz., 52

Verde Valley, Ariz., 4

Victorian ideals, 239

Vigilantism, 13, 116, 117, 137; Barnes's defense of, 195–96; in Clark's *Ox-Bow Incident*, 287; committees created, 118; and honor, xvii, 285; identities of vigilantes, 185–89, 218; and Jesse Ellison, 179–80, 186–87, 242, 251; killing of Powell, 163; lynching of Stott, Scott, and Wilson, 182–83; Mormons and, 140, 152, 187–88, 194, 211, 285; myth of, 192–93, 195–96; newspaper calls for, 104, 118–20, 132, 133, 149; in Pleasant Valley, 179–80, 184; as ritual of shaming, 203, 206; and Roosevelt, 207; and San Francisco precedent, 201; secret campaign in Apache County, 149, 151–54; as trans-Western phenomenon, 212; and Western memory, xvii, 285

Violence, theories on, 112–13

Virginia City, Nevada, 18

The Virginian (Wister), 170, 269

Voris, Robert, 123, 135, 186–87, 251

Voris, William, 128, 184, 186

Vosburgh, J. J., 18, 19, 59, 135, 198, 200

Vosburgh, Mrs., 18

Wagner, George, 127

Wakefield, Ira, 161

Wallace, Frank, 259

Wallace, J. F., 118, 149, 163

Waller, Altina, 283

Walsh, John, 136

Ward, A. A., 50, 91

Ward, Frank, 96

Ward, Houston, 50

"War of incorporation," 201

Warren, Henry, 147, 170

Waters Cattle Company, 64, 191, 194

Watkins, Cap, 175, 230

Watson, Lucy (Grey heroine), 270–71, 274

Wattron, Frank, 138–39, 157, 161, 188

Wayne, John (actor), 288

Wentworth, Edward, 225

West, xviii, xix, xx, xxi, 5, 13, 187, 282, 283–87, 288, 290

Western honor: and braggadocio, 194; celebrated by Grey, xix–xx, 269, 278, 285–86; and gender codes, 270–74, 287; and Rim Country War, xviii, 213, 228, 285; in twentieth century, 285–91

Western identity, xvii, xviii, 166, 193, 213, 225–26

Westerns, xix

Wetzel, Lewis, 261

White, W. J., xi

White family, 22

White Mountain Apache Reservation, 11, 153

White Mountains, 3, 36, 79, 99, 222, 257–58

Whites (Utah settlers), 22, 23

Whiting, Amy, 45

Whiting, Charles, 45

Whitings, 106

Wild Rye, Ariz. (also called Rye), 9, 10, 14, 229

Wild West shows, 54, 143

Wilford, Ariz., 42, 106, 107, 109, 117, 120

Willson, Roscoe, 223

Wilson, Peg Leg, 152–53

Wilson, Jeff (or Billy), 176, 184, 189, 193, 201, 203, 207, 217, 230, 251, 287; lynched, 182–83

Wilson, George, 127, 218

Winn, Fred, 223

Winslow, Ariz., 35, 55, 96, 97, 140, 156, 194

Winslow convention, 140–41, 145

Winslow *News*, 164

Winsor, S. A., 107

Wirth's Circus, 54, 64
Wister, Owen, 170, 193, 269, 286
Withersteen, Jane (Grey heroine), 261–62
Wolfley, Lewis (Ariz. governor), 185
Women's suffrage, 243–44, 249
Woodruff, Ariz., 19, 37, 42, 89, 105, 219
Woodruff, Wilford (Mormon apostle), 38, 48, 71, 73, 85
Woods, Joseph, photo, 220
Woody, Clara, 186
Word of Wisdom, 27, 37, 44, 46, 85, 188
Working-class men, 204–5
Workman (Pleasant Valley settler), 174
World War I, 211, 252, 260, 266, 286
World War II, 287–88
Wright, James, Judge, 156, 164
Wyatt-Brown, Bertram, xiv–xv, 285
Wyckoff, Ellen, 109

Yates, John Marshall, 232
Yavapai, xxiii, 3, 4, 180
Yavapai County, Ariz., xx, 57, 77, 124, 149, 183, 184, 185, 195, 201, 284
Young, Ariz., 236
Young, Brigham, 26, 29, 33, 37, 38, 40, 199
Young, Brigham, Jr., 78, 80
Young, John, 37, 56, 78
Young Ladies Journal, 237
Yukon gold rush, 246
Yuma Penitentiary, 84, 86, 154

Zion, 33, 38, 39, 48
Zulick, Conrad Meyer (Ariz. governor), 86, 145, 151; pardons Clanton, 164; plan to end Pleasant Valley conflict, 132